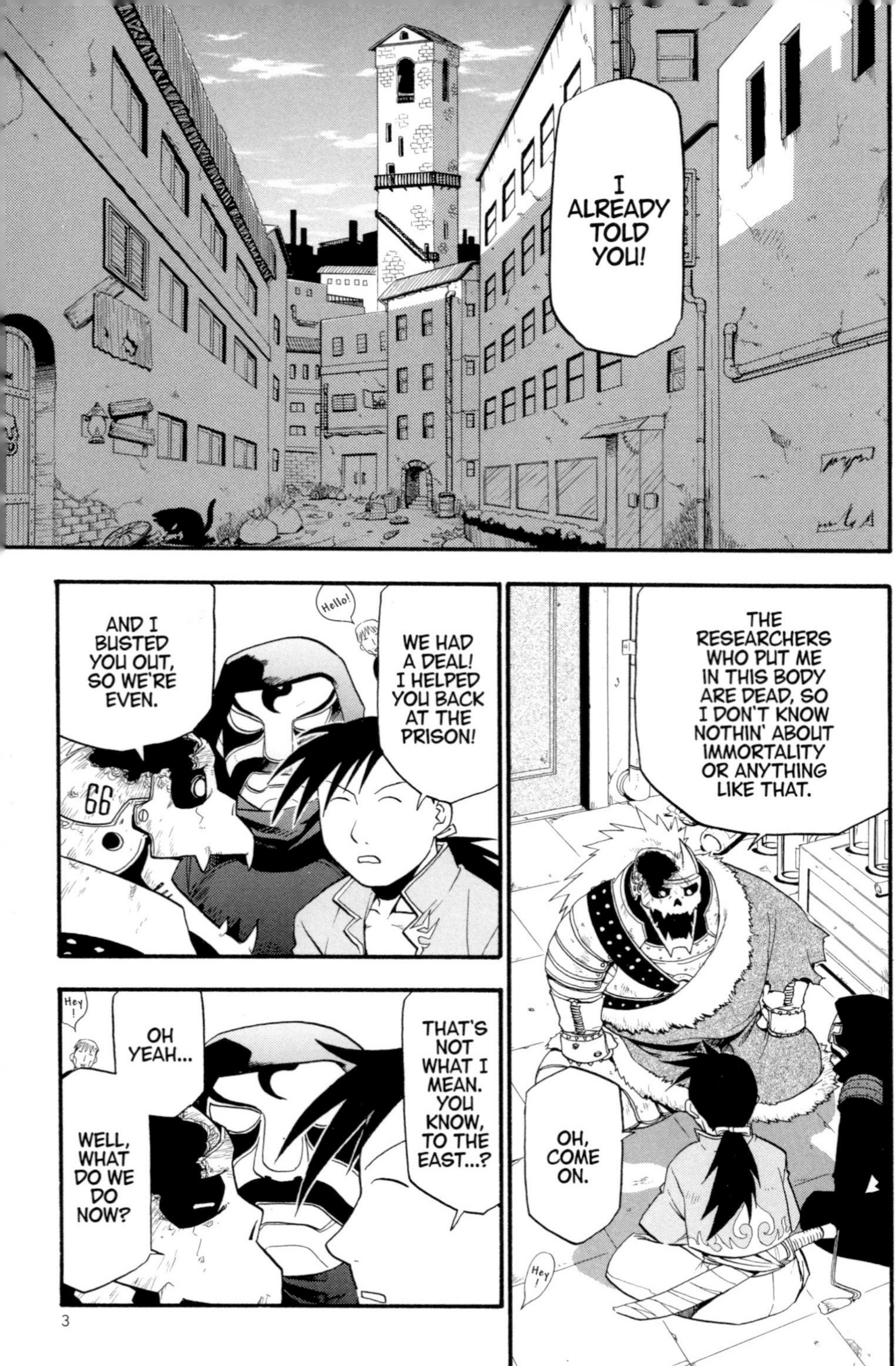
I ALREADY TOLD YOU!
THE RESEARCHERS WHO PUT ME IN THIS BODY ARE DEAD, SO I DON'T KNOW NOTHIN' ABOUT IMMORTALITY OR ANYTHING LIKE THAT.
OH, COME ON.
Hey!
WE HAD A DEAL! I HELPED YOU BACK AT THE PRISON!
Hello!
AND I BUSTED YOU OUT, SO WE'RE EVEN.
THAT'S NOT WHAT I MEAN. YOU KNOW, TO THE EAST...?
OH YEAH...
Hey!
WELL, WHAT DO WE DO NOW?

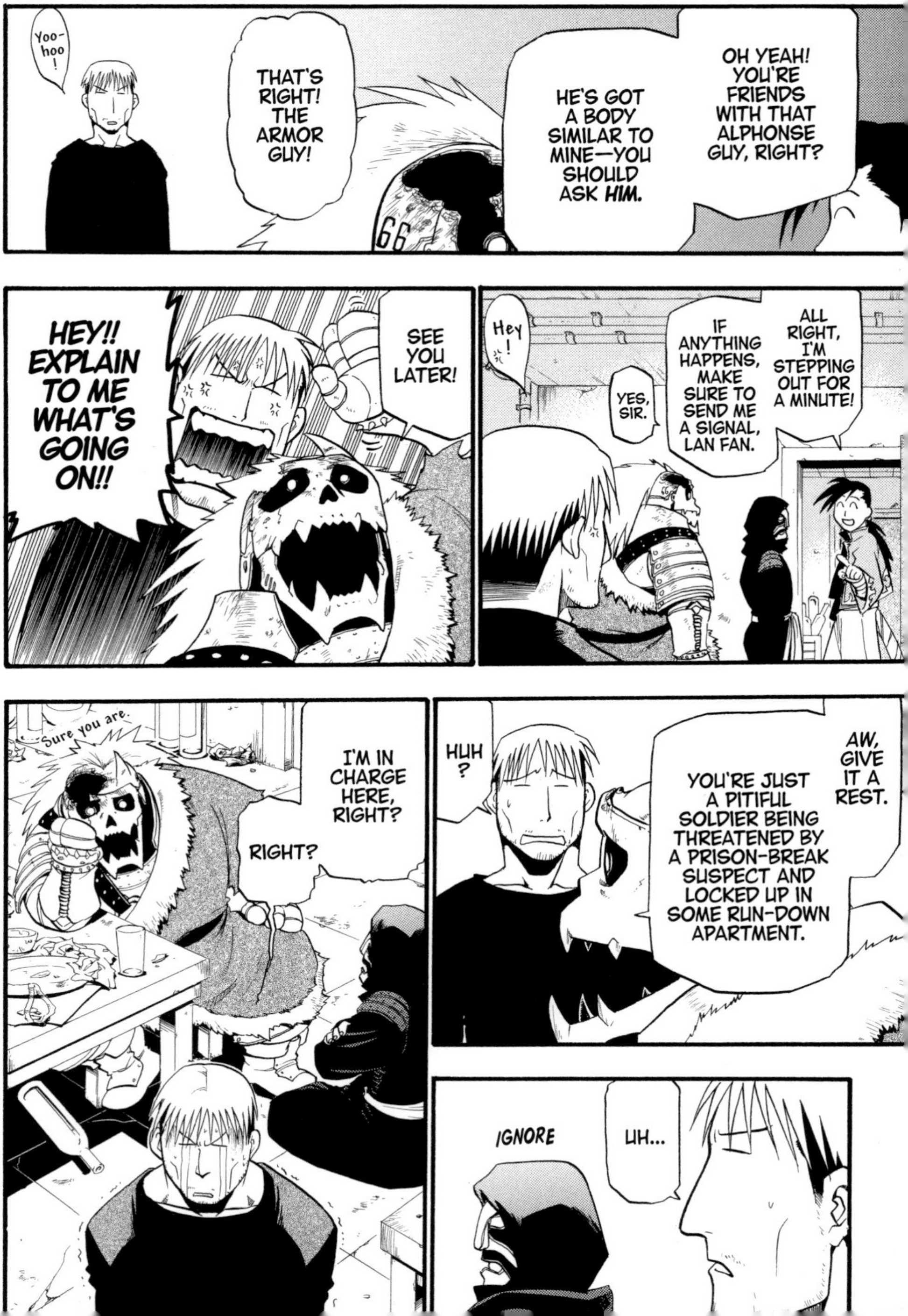
OH YEAH! YOU'RE FRIENDS WITH THAT ALPHONSE GUY, RIGHT?
HE'S GOT A BODY SIMILAR TO MINE—YOU SHOULD ASK **HIM.**
THAT'S RIGHT! THE ARMOR GUY!
Yoo-hoo!
ALL RIGHT, I'M STEPPING OUT FOR A MINUTE!
IF ANYTHING HAPPENS, MAKE SURE TO SEND ME A SIGNAL, LAN FAN.
YES, SIR.
Hey!
SEE YOU LATER!
HEY!! EXPLAIN TO ME WHAT'S GOING ON!!
AW, GIVE IT A REST.
YOU'RE JUST A PITIFUL SOLDIER BEING THREATENED BY A PRISON-BREAK SUSPECT AND LOCKED UP IN SOME RUN-DOWN APARTMENT.
HUH?
UH...
IGNORE
I'M IN CHARGE HERE, RIGHT?
RIGHT?
Sure you are.

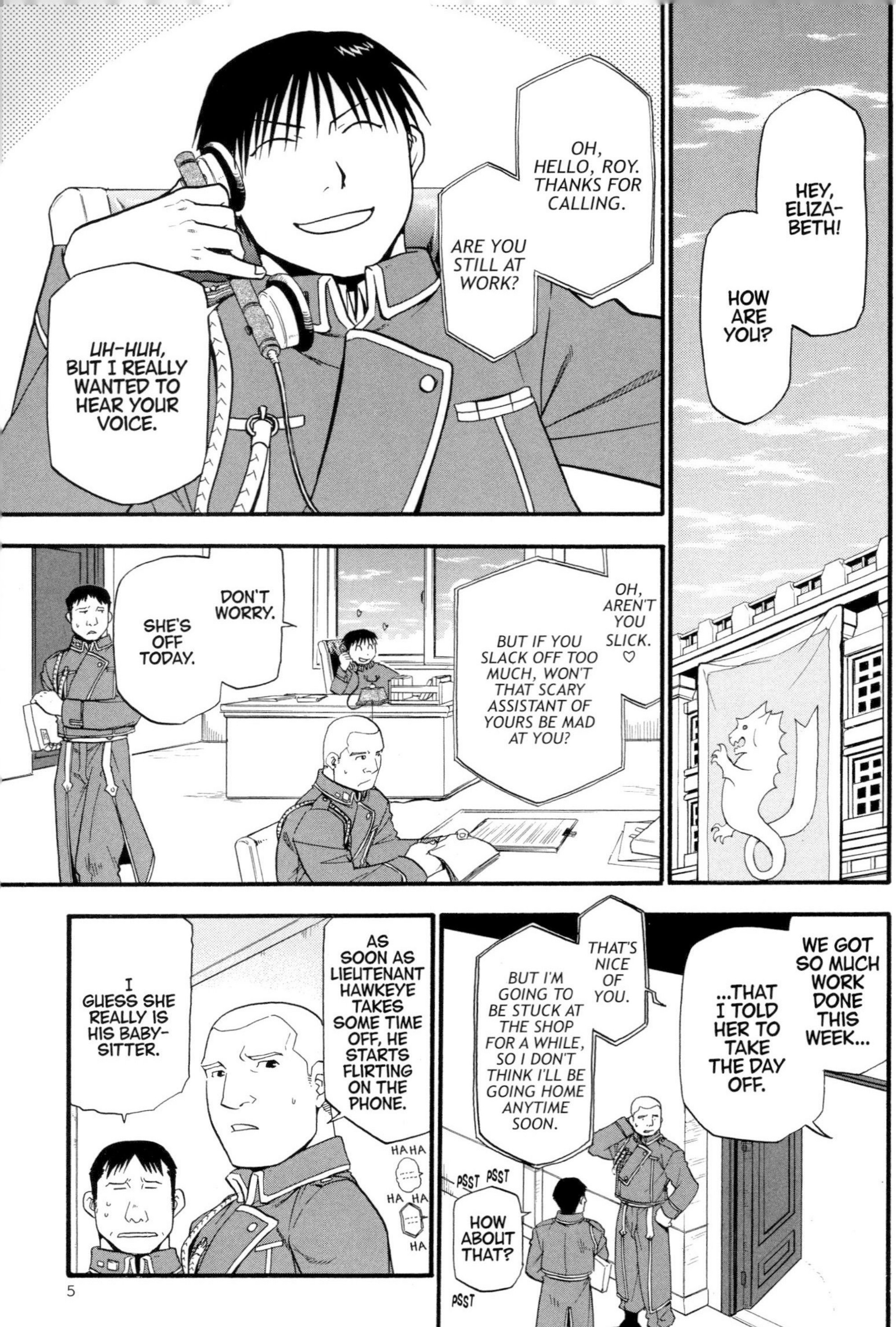
HEY, ELIZA-BETH!
HOW ARE YOU?
OH, HELLO, ROY. THANKS FOR CALLING.
ARE YOU STILL AT WORK?
UH-HUH, BUT I REALLY WANTED TO HEAR YOUR VOICE.
OH, AREN'T YOU SLICK. ♡
BUT IF YOU SLACK OFF TOO MUCH, WON'T THAT SCARY ASSISTANT OF YOURS BE MAD AT YOU?
DON'T WORRY.
SHE'S OFF TODAY.
WE GOT SO MUCH WORK DONE THIS WEEK...
...THAT I TOLD HER TO TAKE THE DAY OFF.
THAT'S NICE OF YOU.
BUT I'M GOING TO BE STUCK AT THE SHOP FOR A WHILE, SO I DON'T THINK I'LL BE GOING HOME ANYTIME SOON.
PSST PSST
HOW ABOUT THAT?
PSST
AS SOON AS LIEUTENANT HAWKEYE TAKES SOME TIME OFF, HE STARTS FLIRTING ON THE PHONE.
I GUESS SHE REALLY IS HIS BABY-SITTER.
HAHA
HA HA
HA

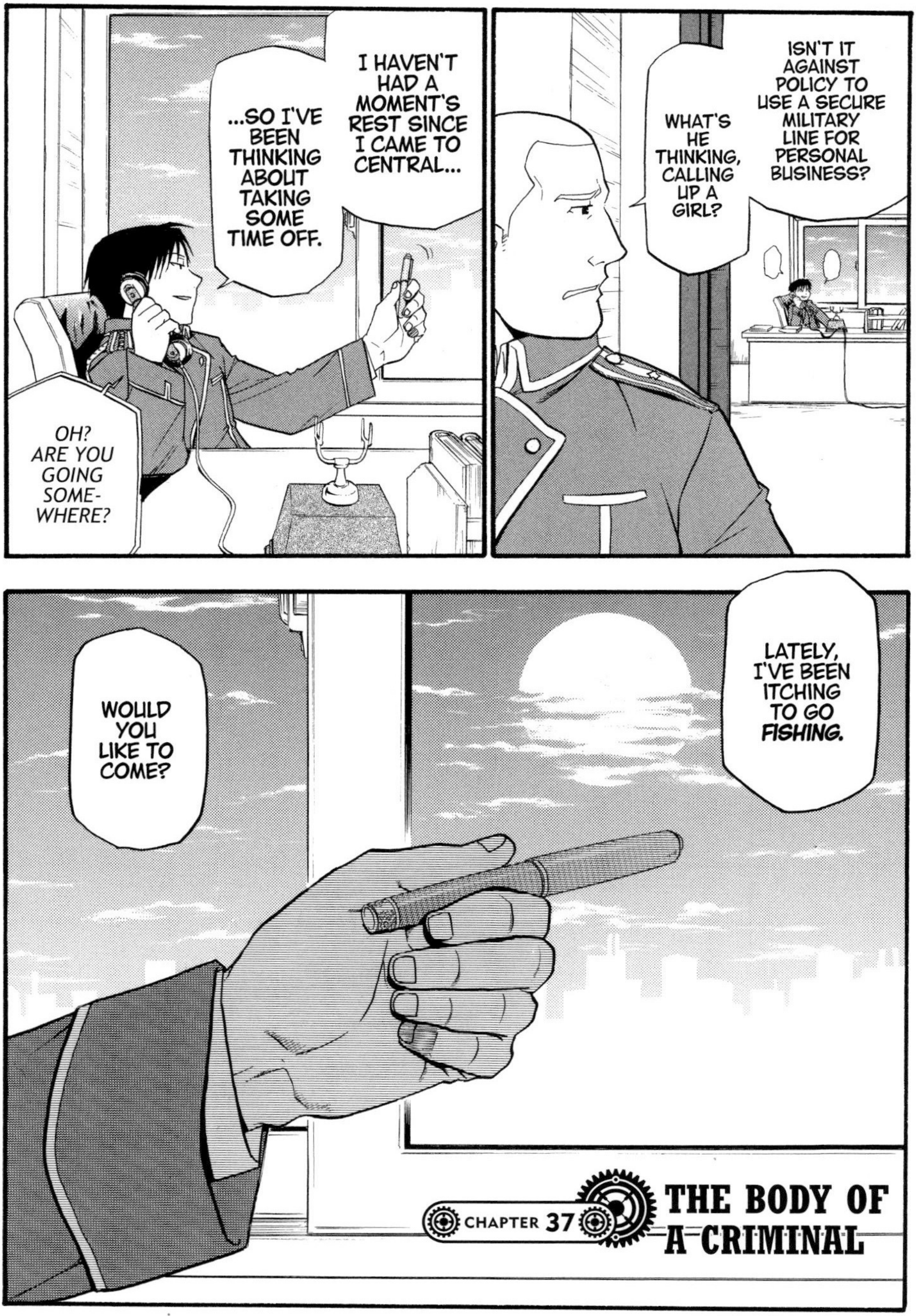
ISN'T IT AGAINST POLICY TO USE A SECURE MILITARY LINE FOR PERSONAL BUSINESS?
WHAT'S HE THINKING, CALLING UP A GIRL?
I HAVEN'T HAD A MOMENT'S REST SINCE I CAME TO CENTRAL...
...SO I'VE BEEN THINKING ABOUT TAKING SOME TIME OFF.
OH? ARE YOU GOING SOME-WHERE?
LATELY, I'VE BEEN ITCHING TO GO FISHING.
WOULD YOU LIKE TO COME?
CHAPTER 37
THE BODY OF A CRIMINAL

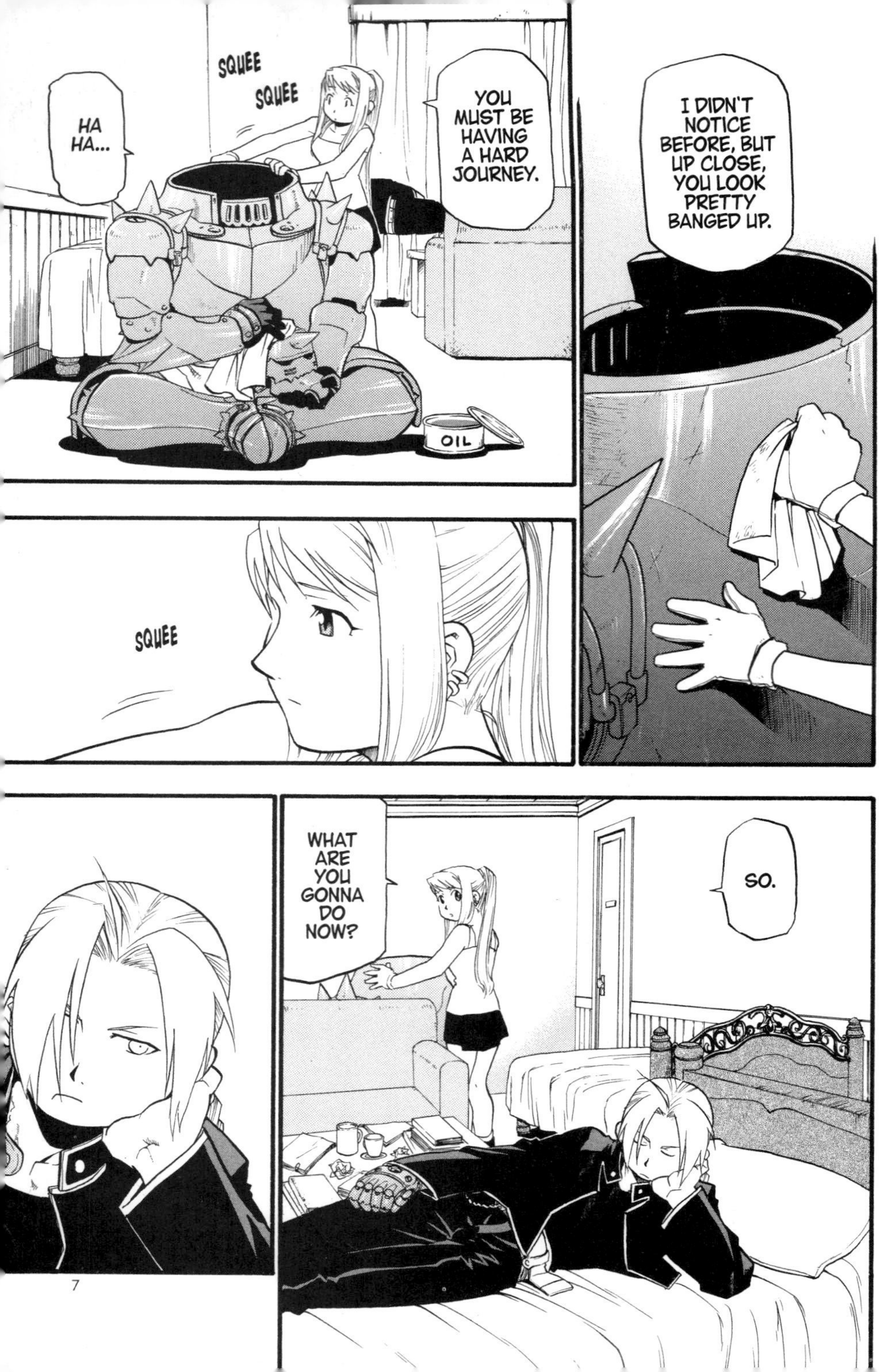

I DIDN'T NOTICE BEFORE, BUT UP CLOSE, YOU LOOK PRETTY BANGED UP.
YOU MUST BE HAVING A HARD JOURNEY.
SQUEE
SQUEE
HA HA...
SQUEE
SO.
WHAT ARE YOU GONNA DO NOW?

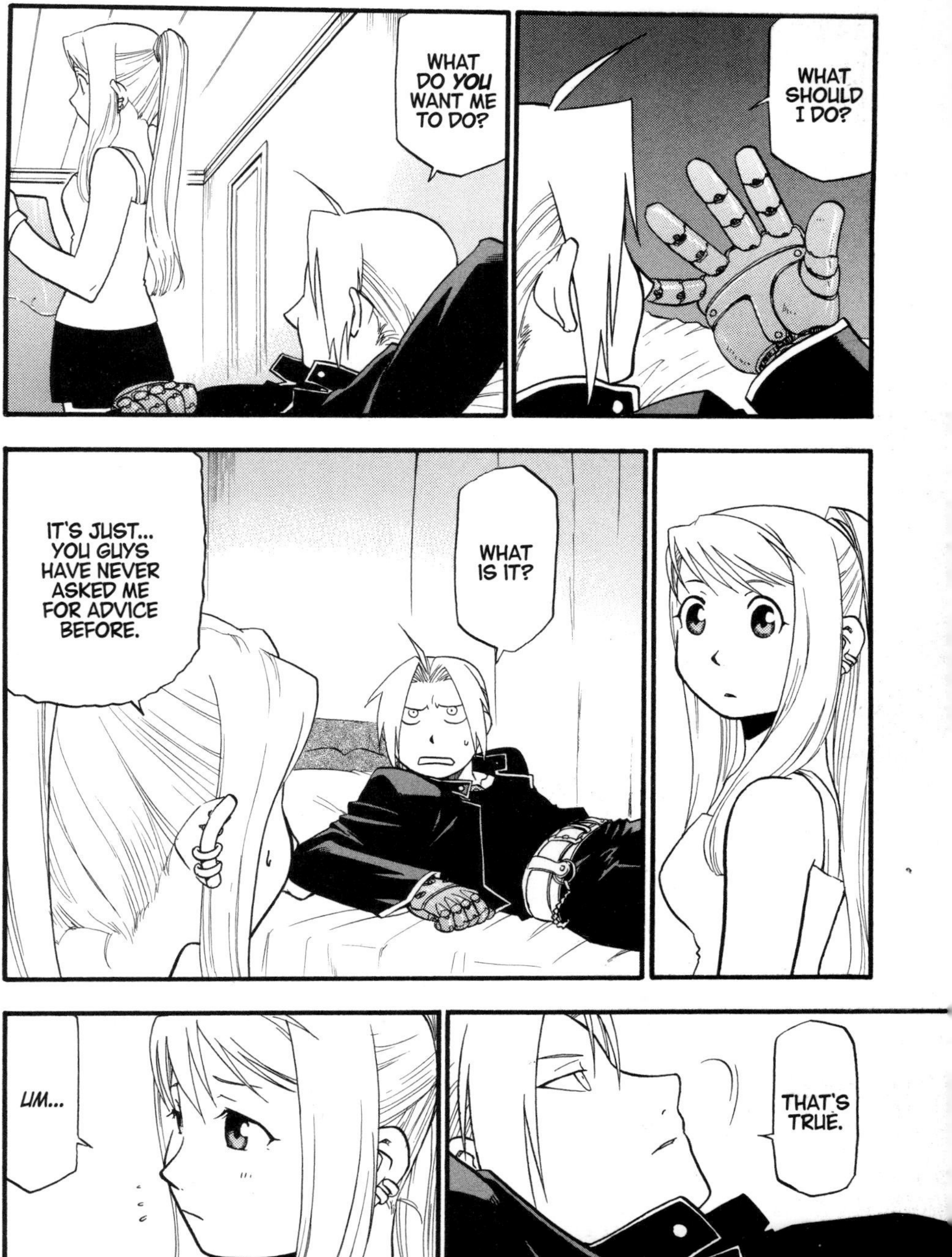
WHAT SHOULD I DO?
WHAT DO *YOU* WANT ME TO DO?
WHAT IS IT?
IT'S JUST... YOU GUYS HAVE NEVER ASKED ME FOR ADVICE BEFORE.
THAT'S TRUE.
UM...

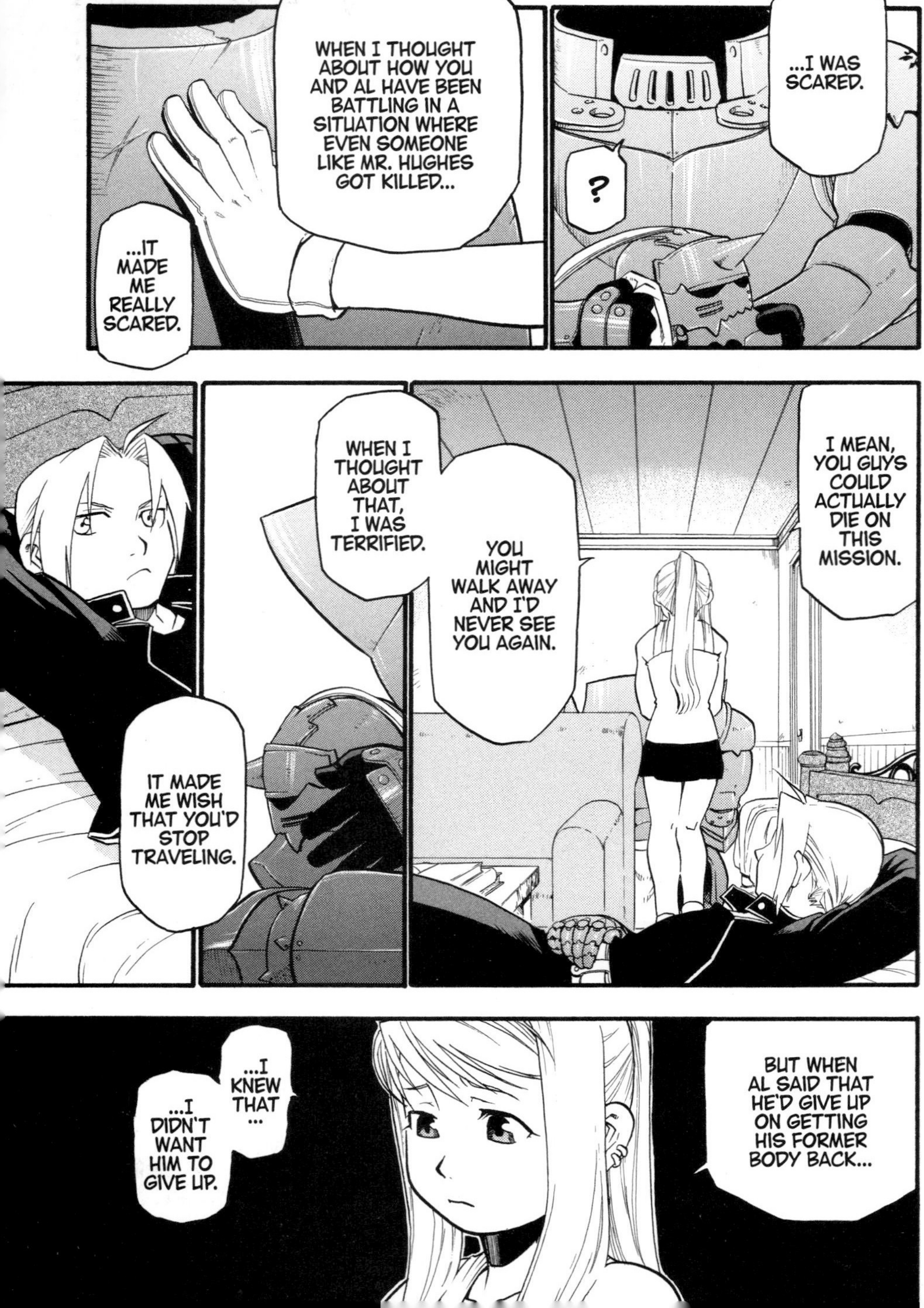
...I WAS SCARED.
?
WHEN I THOUGHT ABOUT HOW YOU AND AL HAVE BEEN BATTLING IN A SITUATION WHERE EVEN SOMEONE LIKE MR. HUGHES GOT KILLED...
...IT MADE ME REALLY SCARED.
I MEAN, YOU GUYS COULD ACTUALLY DIE ON THIS MISSION.
YOU MIGHT WALK AWAY AND I'D NEVER SEE YOU AGAIN.
WHEN I THOUGHT ABOUT THAT, I WAS TERRIFIED.
IT MADE ME WISH THAT YOU'D STOP TRAVELING.
BUT WHEN AL SAID THAT HE'D GIVE UP ON GETTING HIS FORMER BODY BACK...
...I KNEW THAT...
...I DIDN'T WANT HIM TO GIVE UP.

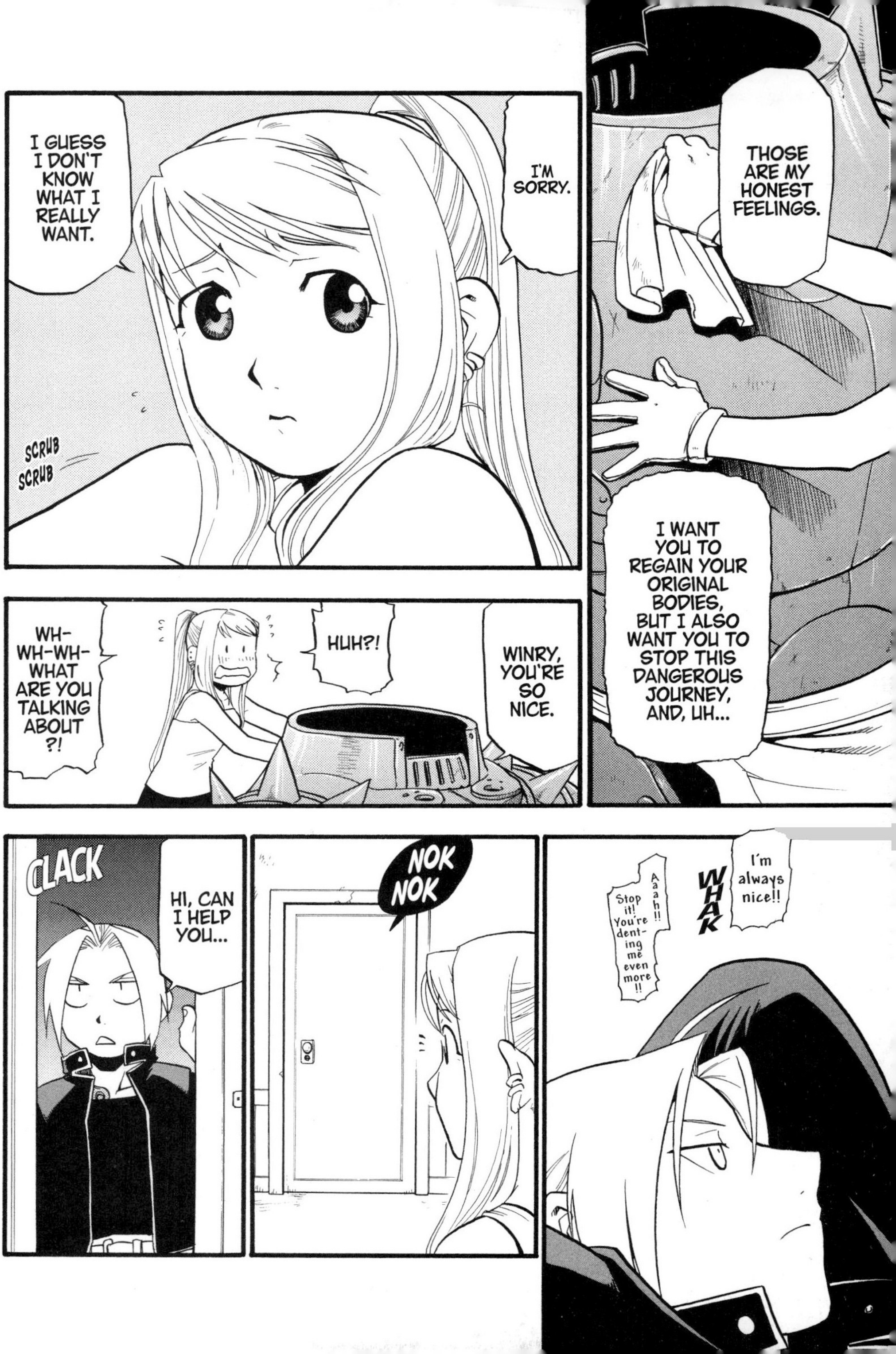
THOSE ARE MY HONEST FEELINGS.
I WANT YOU TO REGAIN YOUR ORIGINAL BODIES, BUT I ALSO WANT YOU TO STOP THIS DANGEROUS JOURNEY, AND, UH...
I'M SORRY.
I GUESS I DON'T KNOW WHAT I REALLY WANT.
SCRUB SCRUB
WINRY, YOU'RE SO NICE.
HUH?!
WH-WH-WH-WHAT ARE YOU TALKING ABOUT?!
WHAK
I'm always nice!!
Aaah!! Stop it! You're dent-ing me even more!!
NOK NOK
CLACK
HI, CAN I HELP YOU...

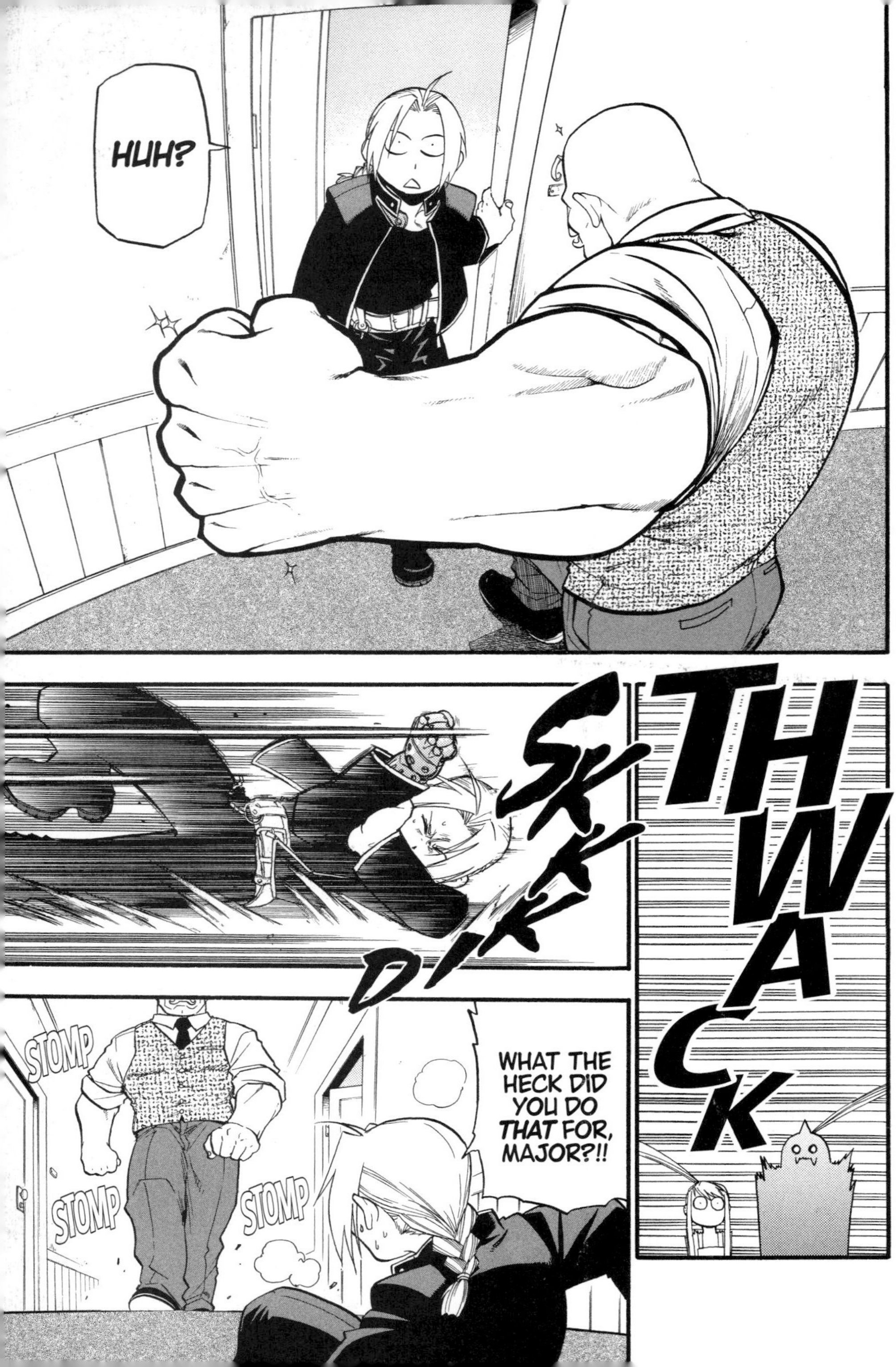
HUH?
THWACK
SKKKDIK
STOMP
STOMP
STOMP
WHAT THE HECK DID YOU DO *THAT* FOR, MAJOR?!!

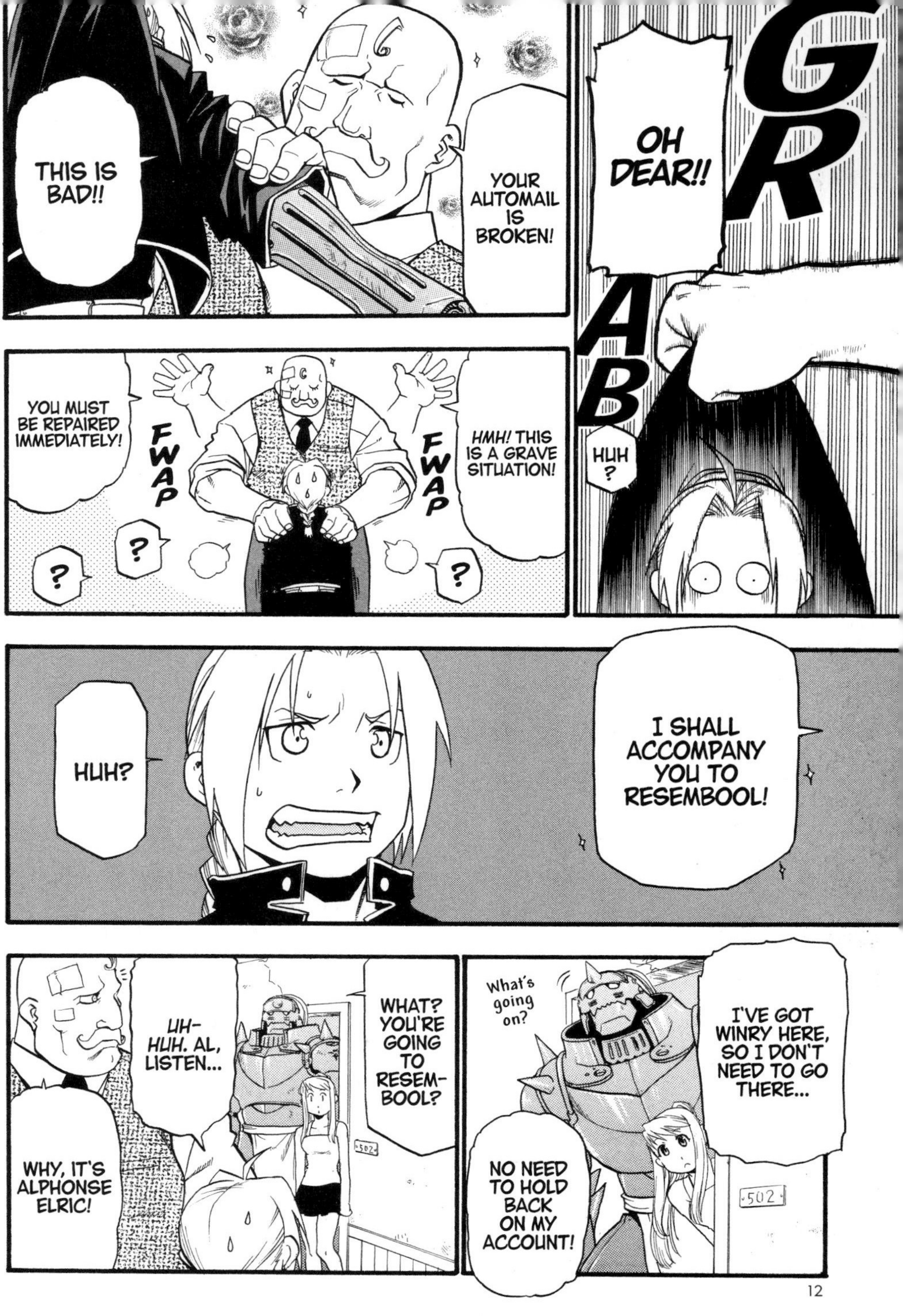
GRAB
OH DEAR!!
HUH?
YOUR AUTOMAIL IS BROKEN!
THIS IS BAD!!
HMH! THIS IS A GRAVE SITUATION!
FWAP
?
FWAP
YOU MUST BE REPAIRED IMMEDIATELY!
?
?
I SHALL ACCOMPANY YOU TO RESEMBOOL!
HUH?
I'VE GOT WINRY HERE, SO I DON'T NEED TO GO THERE...
What's going on?
NO NEED TO HOLD BACK ON MY ACCOUNT!
WHAT? YOU'RE GOING TO RESEMBOOL?
UH-HUH. AL, LISTEN...
WHY, IT'S ALPHONSE ELRIC!

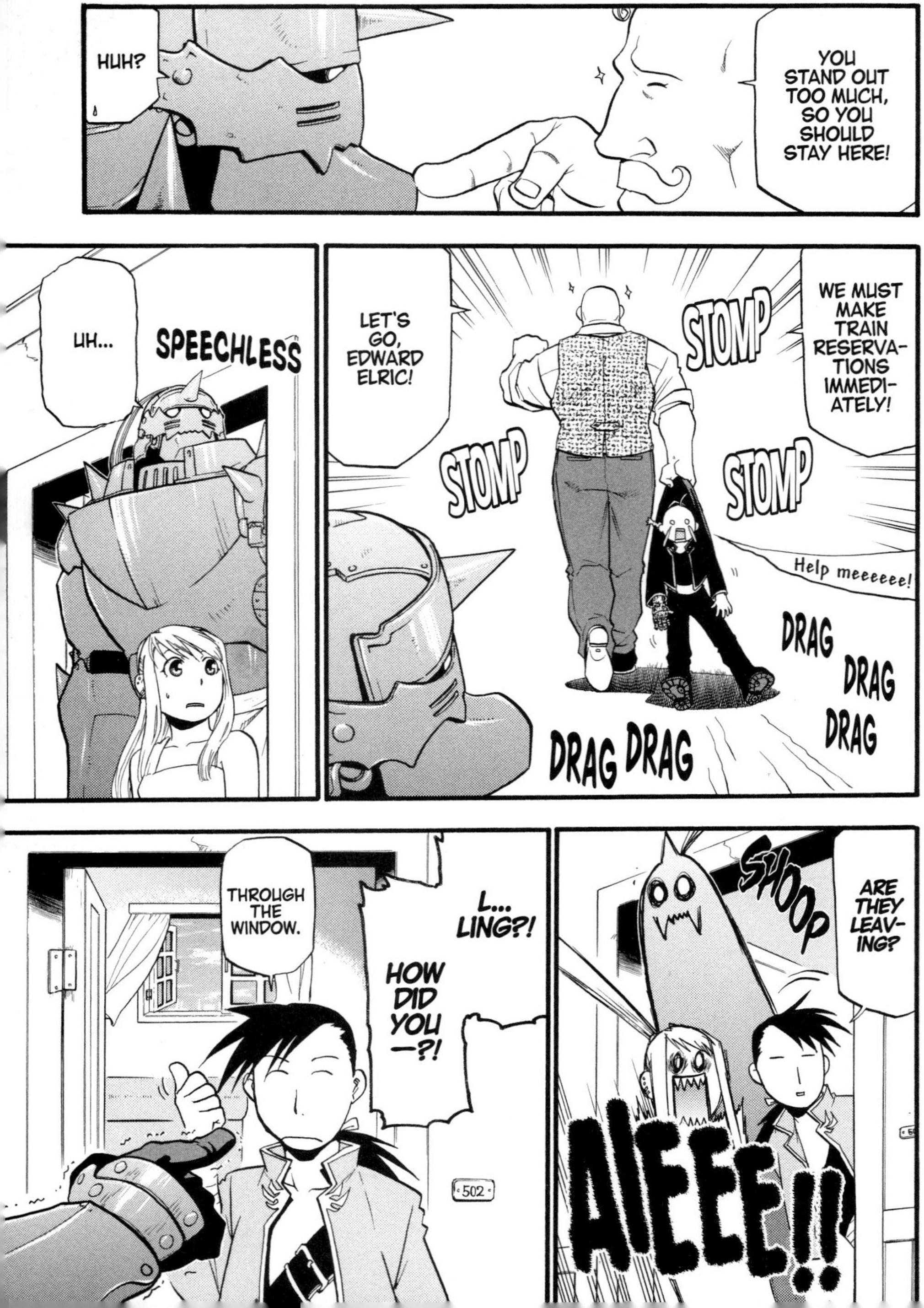

YOU STAND OUT TOO MUCH, SO YOU SHOULD STAY HERE!
HUH?
WE MUST MAKE TRAIN RESERVATIONS IMMEDIATELY!
STOMP
LET'S GO, EDWARD ELRIC!
STOMP
STOMP
Help meeeeee!
DRAG DRAG DRAG
DRAG DRAG
UH...
SPEECHLESS
SHOOP
ARE THEY LEAVING?
AIEEE!!
L... LING?!
HOW DID YOU—?!
THROUGH THE WINDOW.
502

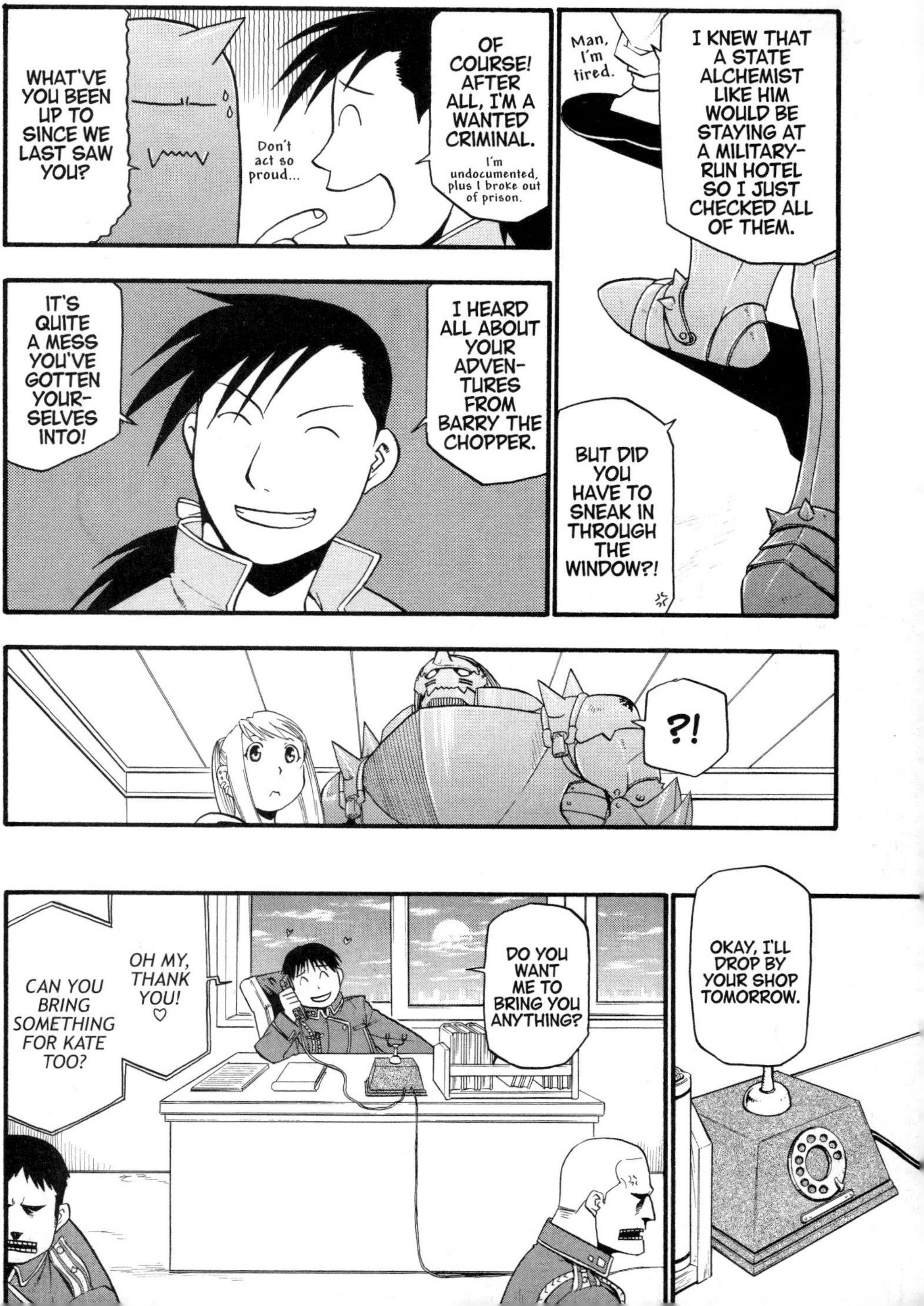
I KNEW THAT A STATE ALCHEMIST LIKE HIM WOULD BE STAYING AT A MILITARY-RUN HOTEL SO I JUST CHECKED ALL OF THEM.
Man, I'm tired.
BUT DID YOU HAVE TO SNEAK IN THROUGH THE WINDOW?!
OF COURSE! AFTER ALL, I'M A WANTED CRIMINAL.
I'm undocumented, plus I broke out of prison.
Don't act so proud...
WHAT'VE YOU BEEN UP TO SINCE WE LAST SAW YOU?
I HEARD ALL ABOUT YOUR ADVENTURES FROM BARRY THE CHOPPER.
IT'S QUITE A MESS YOU'VE GOTTEN YOURSELVES INTO!
?!
OKAY, I'LL DROP BY YOUR SHOP TOMORROW.
DO YOU WANT ME TO BRING YOU ANYTHING?
OH MY, THANK YOU! ♡
CAN YOU BRING SOMETHING FOR KATE TOO?

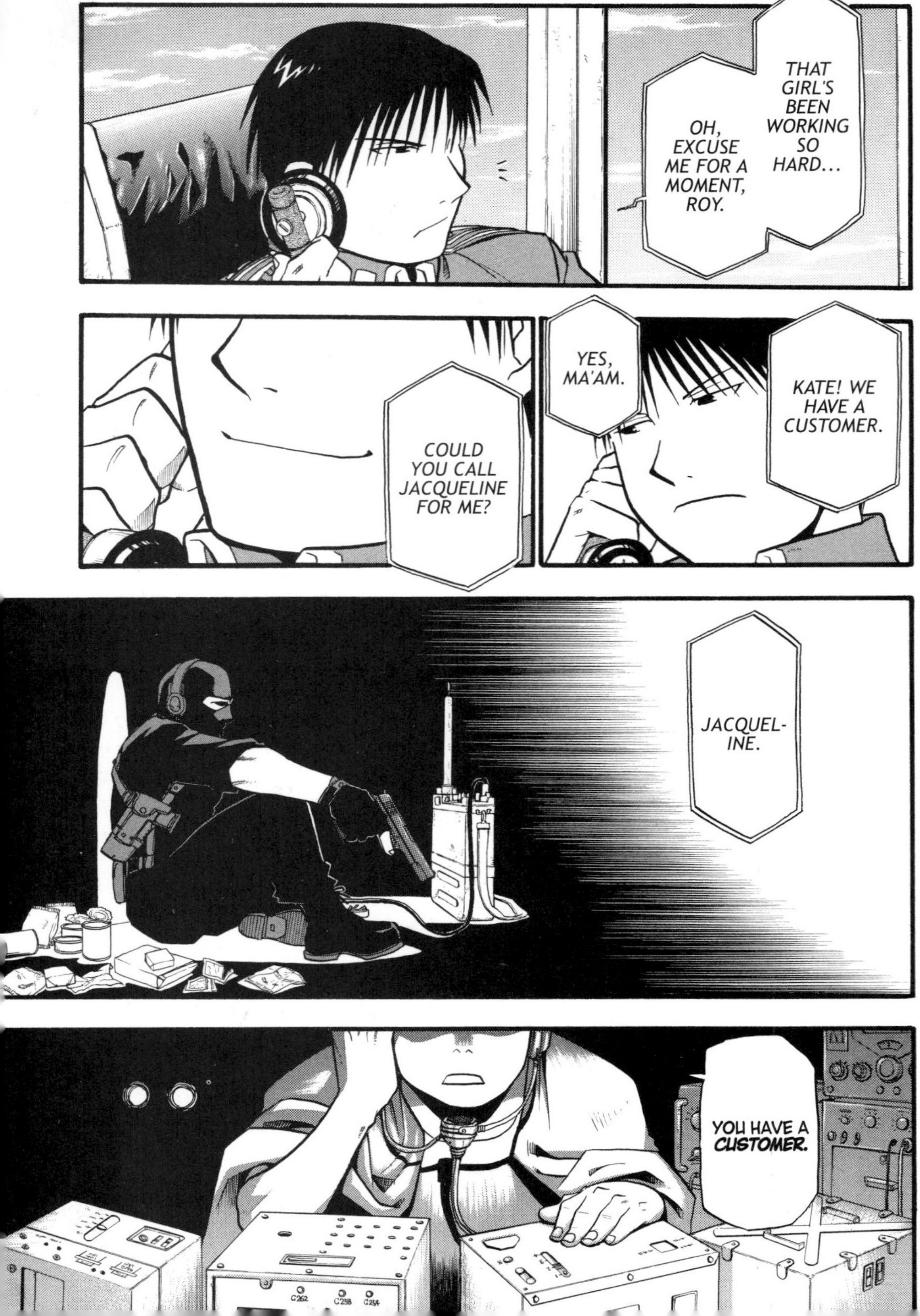
THAT GIRL'S BEEN WORKING SO HARD...
OH, EXCUSE ME FOR A MOMENT, ROY.
KATE! WE HAVE A CUSTOMER.
YES, MA'AM.
COULD YOU CALL JACQUELINE FOR ME?
JACQUEL-INE.
YOU HAVE A CUSTOMER.

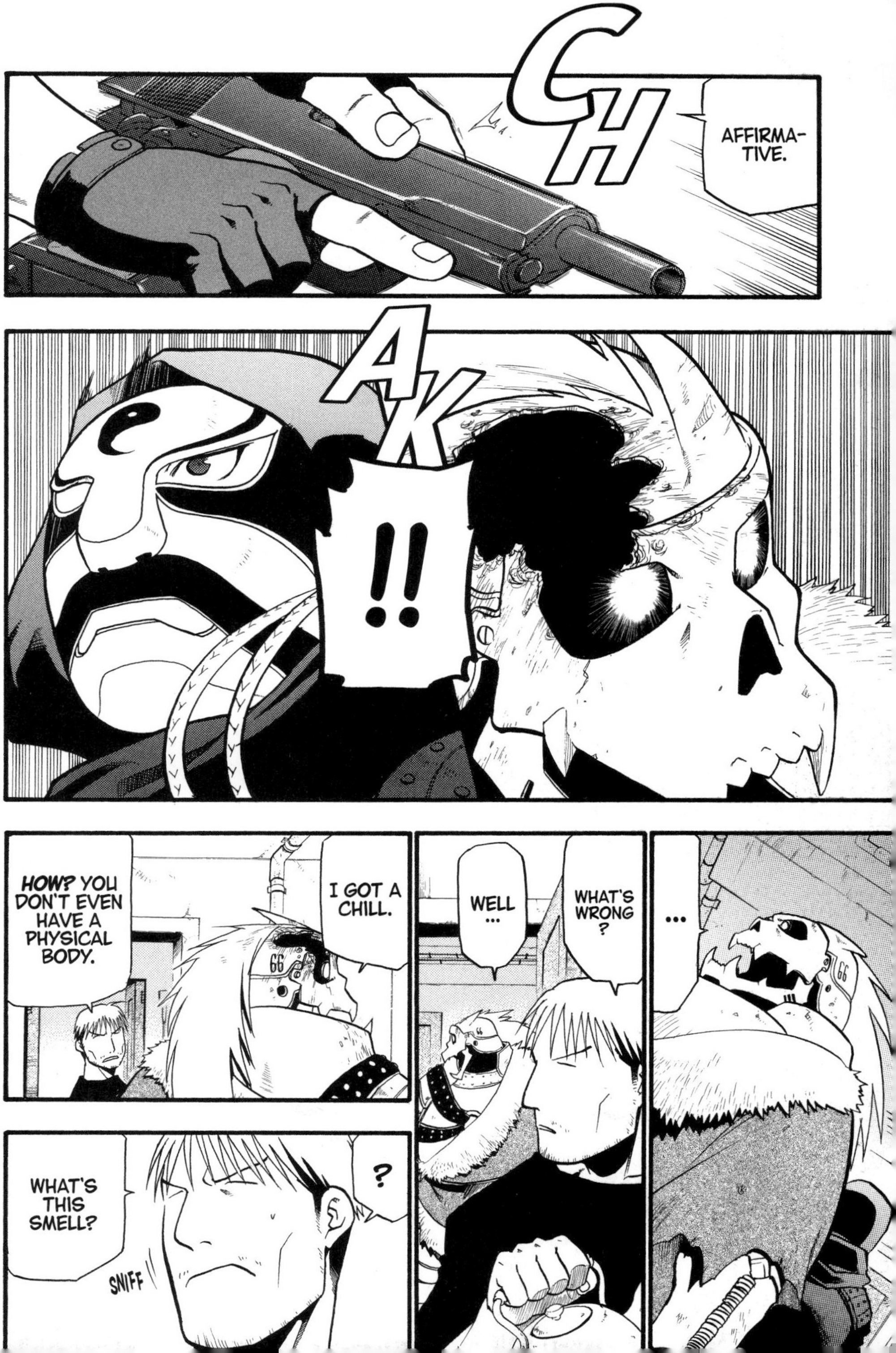
AFFIRMA-TIVE.
CH
AK
!!
...
WHAT'S WRONG?
WELL...
I GOT A CHILL.
HOW? YOU DON'T EVEN HAVE A PHYSICAL BODY.
?
WHAT'S THIS SMELL?
SNIFF

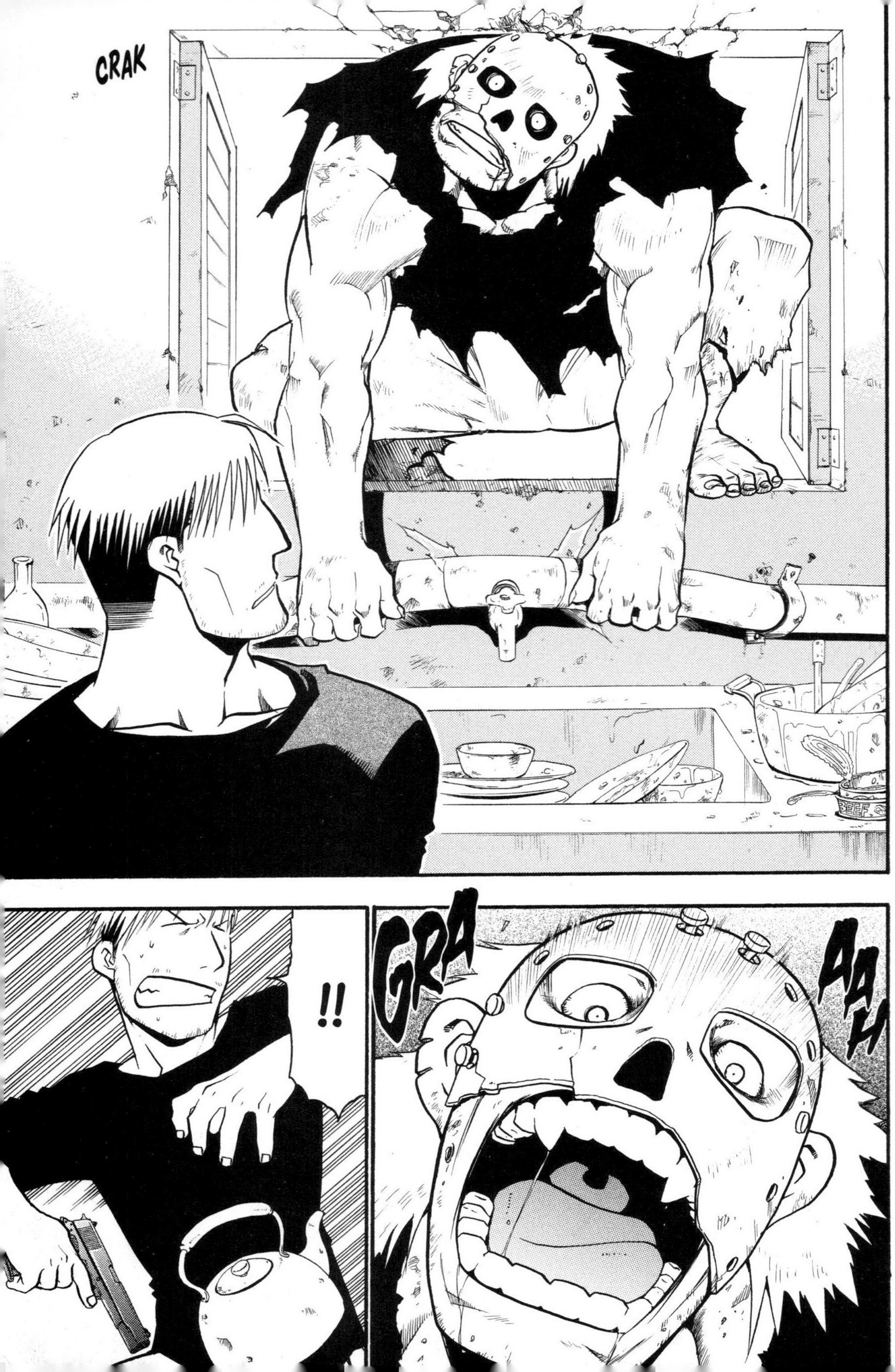
CRAK
BEEF
GRA
AAH
!!

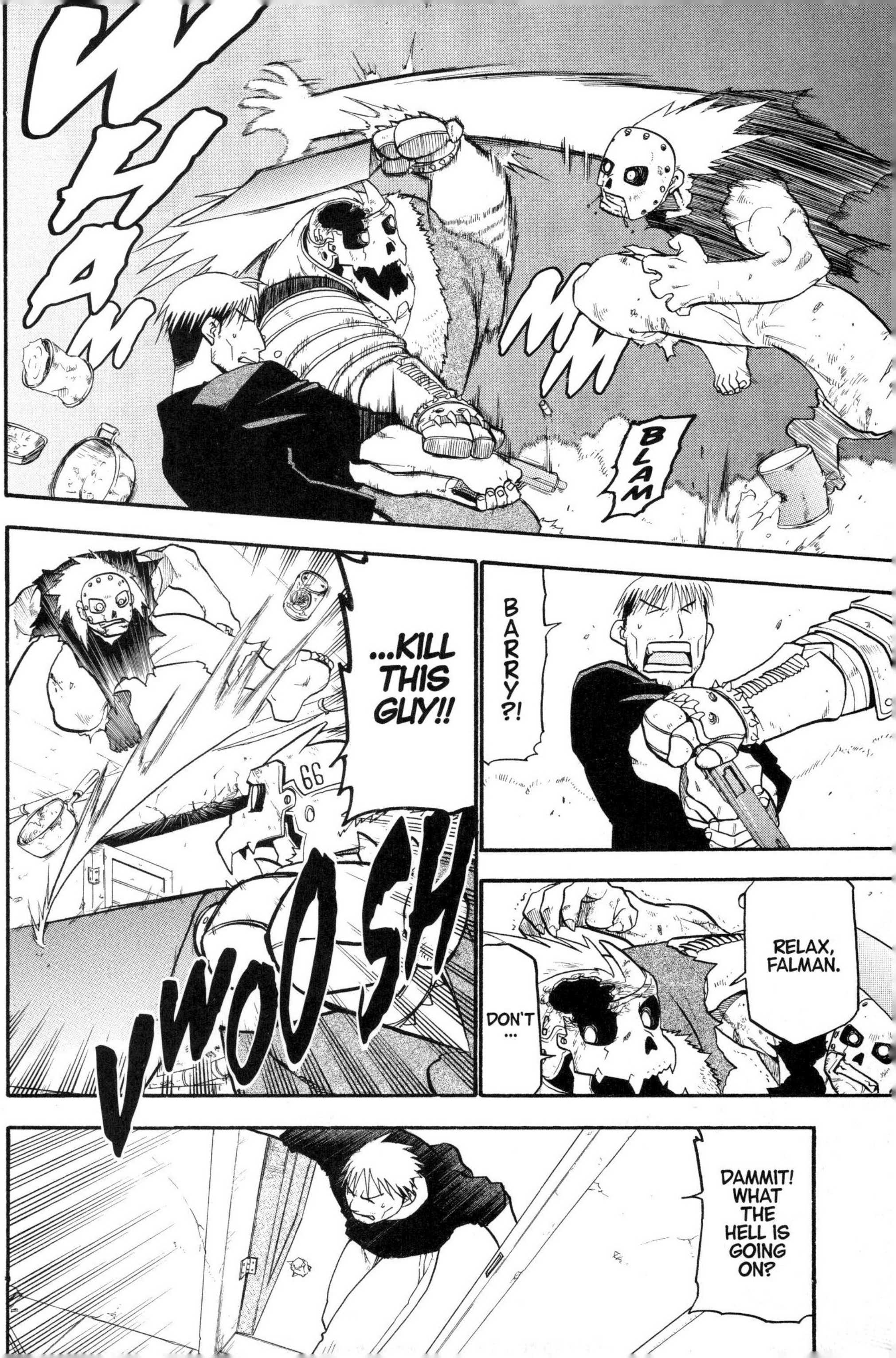
WHAMMM
BLAM
BARRY?!
RELAX, FALMAN.
DON'T ...
...KILL THIS GUY!!
VWOOSH
DAMMIT! WHAT THE HELL IS GOING ON?

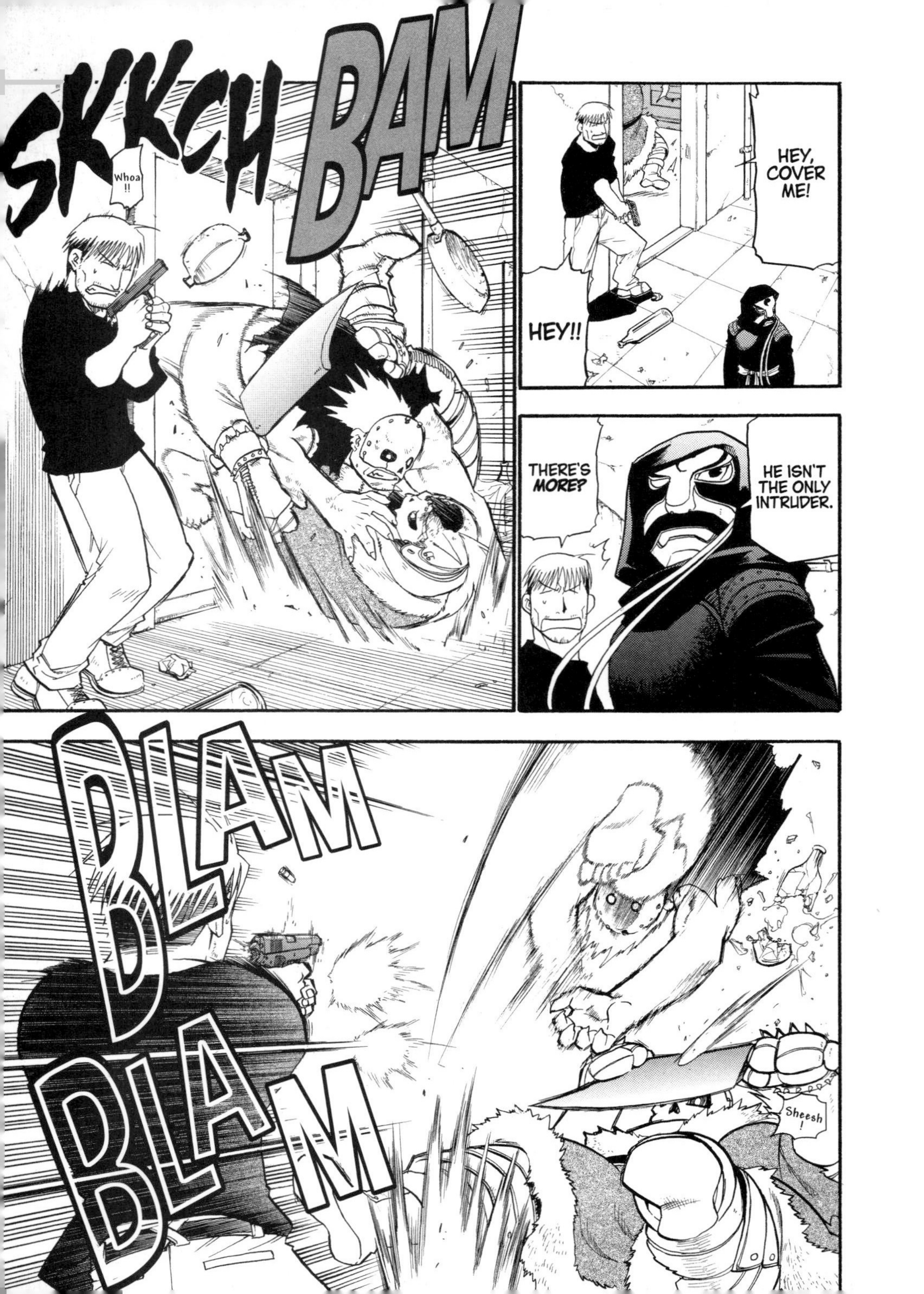
HEY, COVER ME!
HEY!!
HE ISN'T THE ONLY INTRUDER.
THERE'S MORE?
SKKCH BAM
Whoa!!
BLAM
BLAM
BLAM
Sheesh!

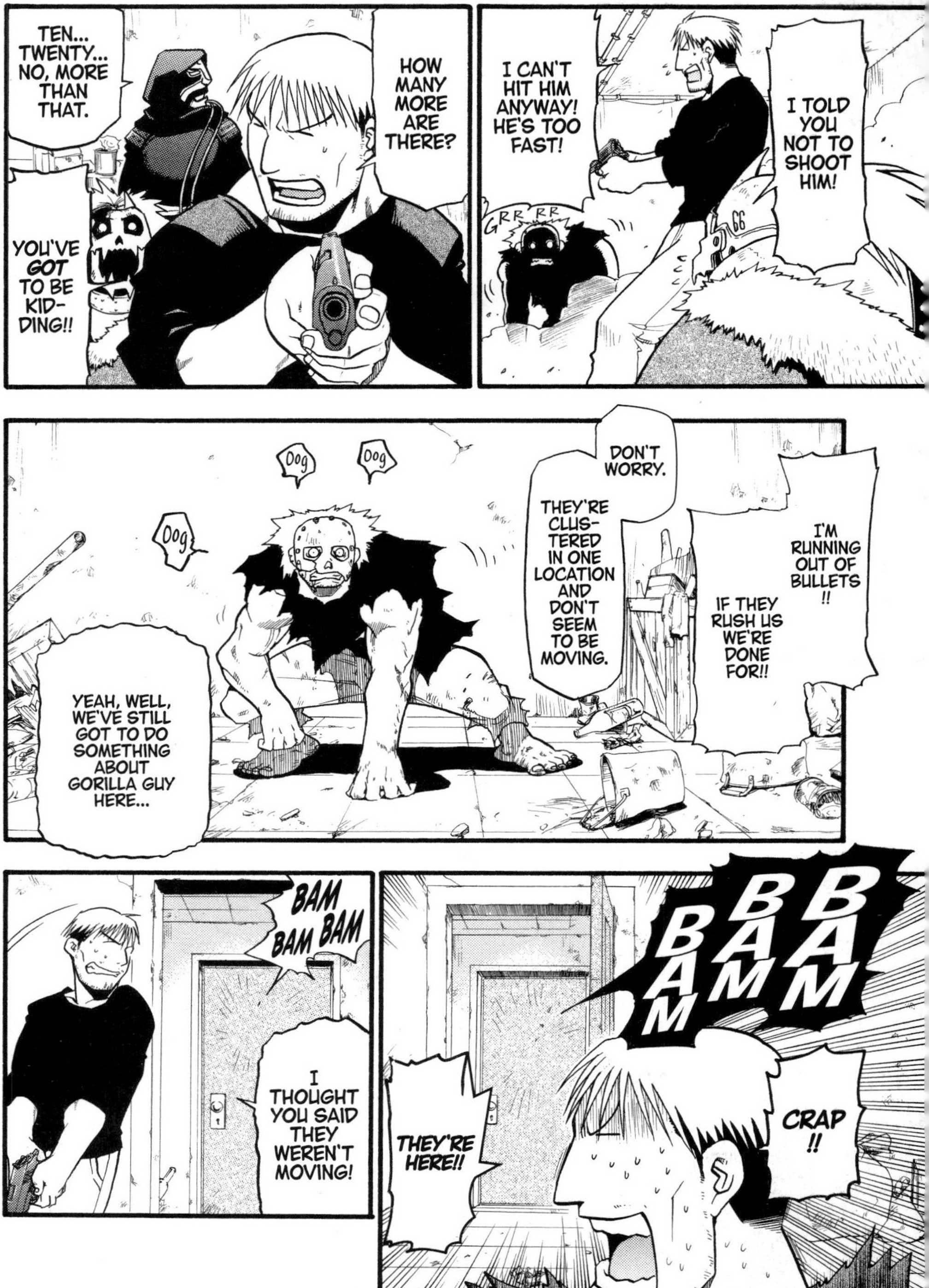
I TOLD YOU NOT TO SHOOT HIM!
I CAN'T HIT HIM ANYWAY! HE'S TOO FAST!
GRR RR
HOW MANY MORE ARE THERE?
TEN... TWENTY... NO, MORE THAN THAT.
YOU'VE GOT TO BE KID-DING!!
I'M RUNNING OUT OF BULLETS!!
IF THEY RUSH US WE'RE DONE FOR!!
DON'T WORRY.
THEY'RE CLUS-TERED IN ONE LOCATION AND DON'T SEEM TO BE MOVING.
Oog
Oog
Oog
YEAH, WELL, WE'VE STILL GOT TO DO SOMETHING ABOUT GORILLA GUY HERE...
BAM BAM BAM
CRAP!!
THEY'RE HERE!!
BAM BAM BAM
I THOUGHT YOU SAID THEY WEREN'T MOVING!

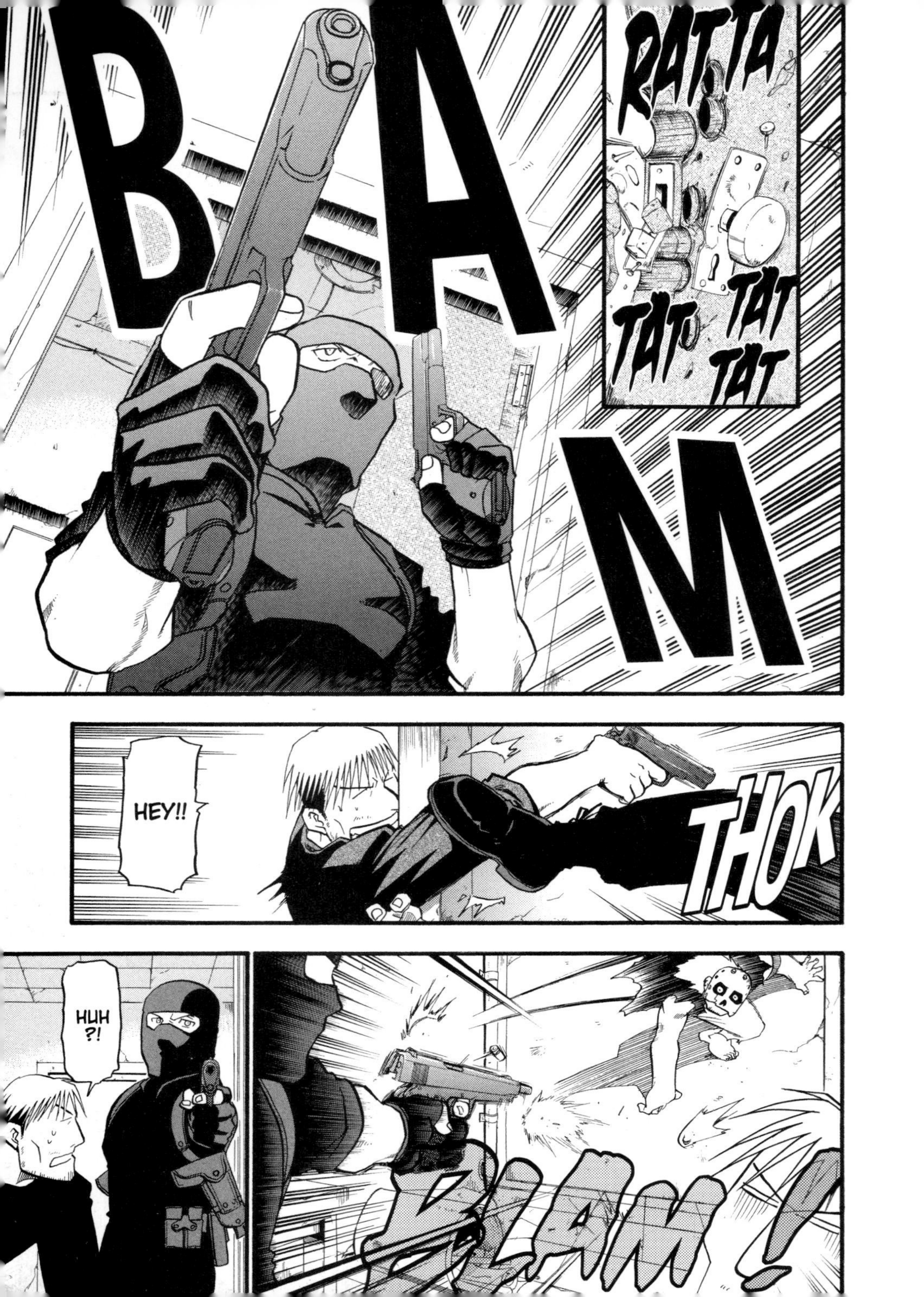
RATTA
TAT TAT TAT
BAM
THOK
HEY!!
BLAM!
HUH ?!

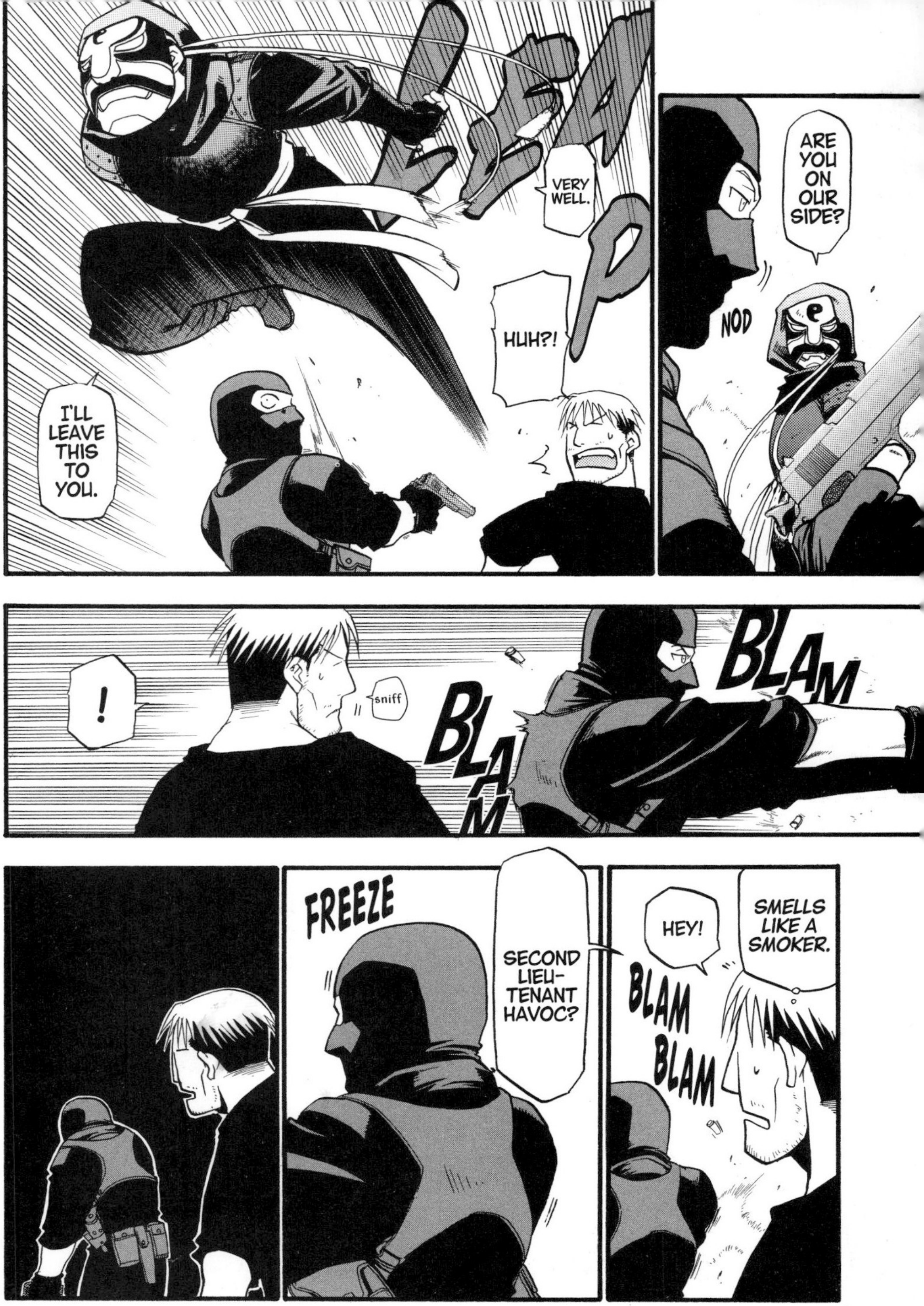
ARE YOU ON OUR SIDE?
NOD
VERY WELL.
HUH?!
I'LL LEAVE THIS TO YOU.
BLAM
BLAM
sniff
!
SMELLS LIKE A SMOKER.
HEY!
BLAM BLAM
SECOND LIEU-TENANT HAVOC?
FREEZE

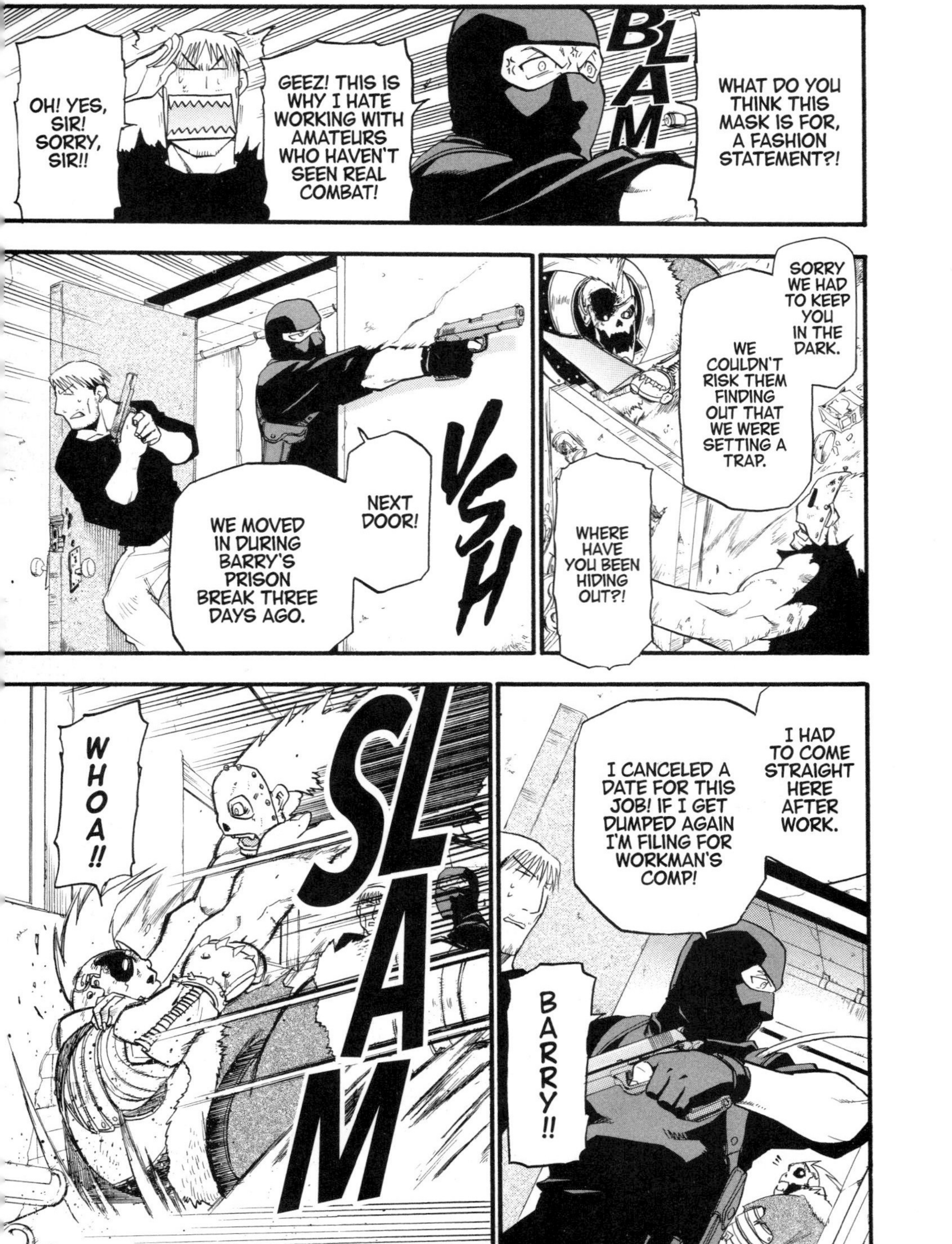
WHAT DO YOU THINK THIS MASK IS FOR, A FASHION STATEMENT?!
BLAM
GEEZ! THIS IS WHY I HATE WORKING WITH AMATEURS WHO HAVEN'T SEEN REAL COMBAT!
OH! YES, SIR! SORRY, SIR!!
SORRY WE HAD TO KEEP YOU IN THE DARK.
WE COULDN'T RISK THEM FINDING OUT THAT WE WERE SETTING A TRAP.
WHERE HAVE YOU BEEN HIDING OUT?!
VSH
NEXT DOOR!
WE MOVED IN DURING BARRY'S PRISON BREAK THREE DAYS AGO.
I HAD TO COME STRAIGHT HERE AFTER WORK.
I CANCELED A DATE FOR THIS JOB! IF I GET DUMPED AGAIN I'M FILING FOR WORKMAN'S COMP!
BARRY!!
SLAM
WHOA!!

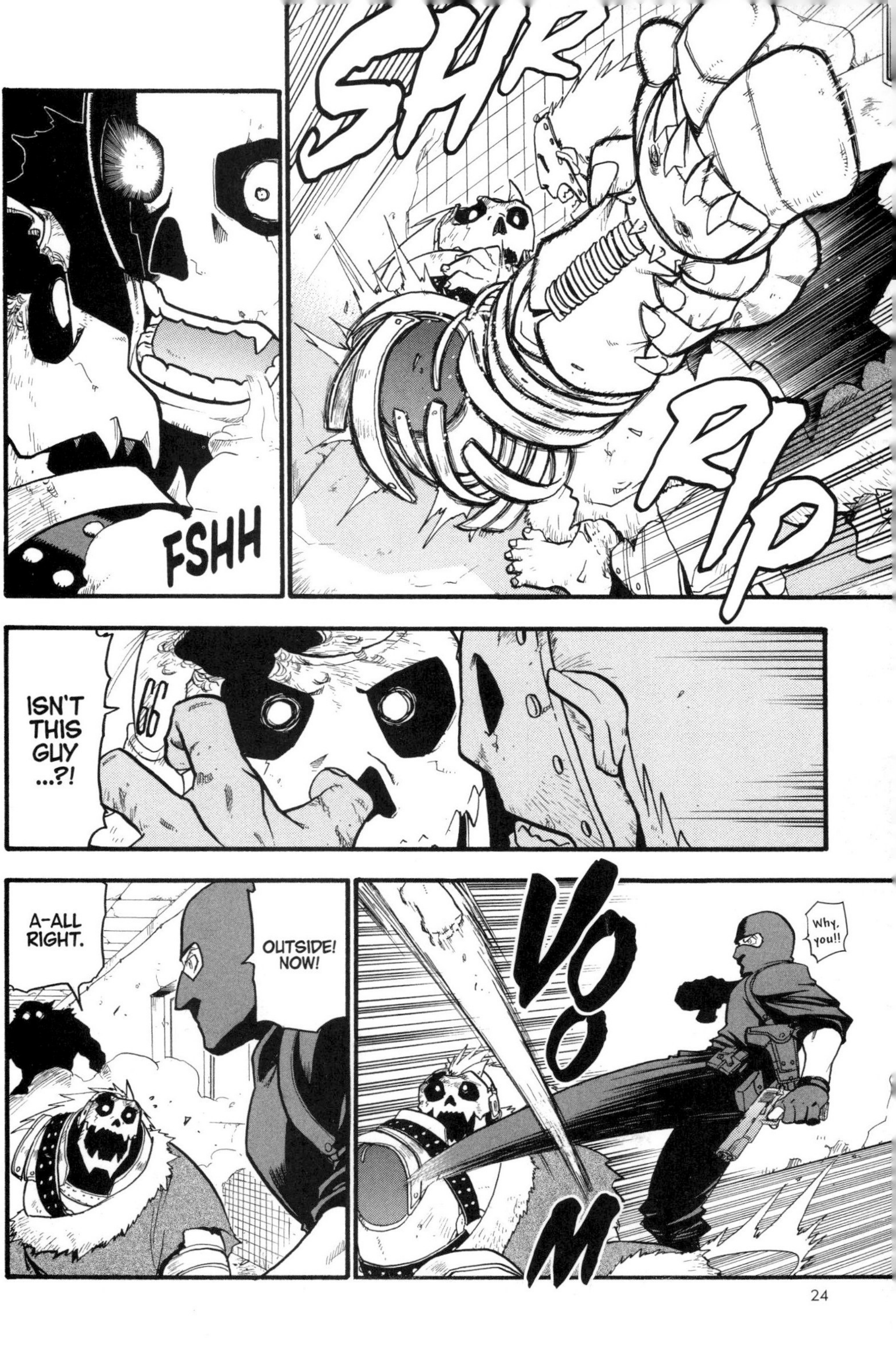
SHR
RIP
FSHH
ISN'T THIS GUY ...?!
VOOM
Why, you!!
OUTSIDE! NOW!
A-ALL RIGHT.

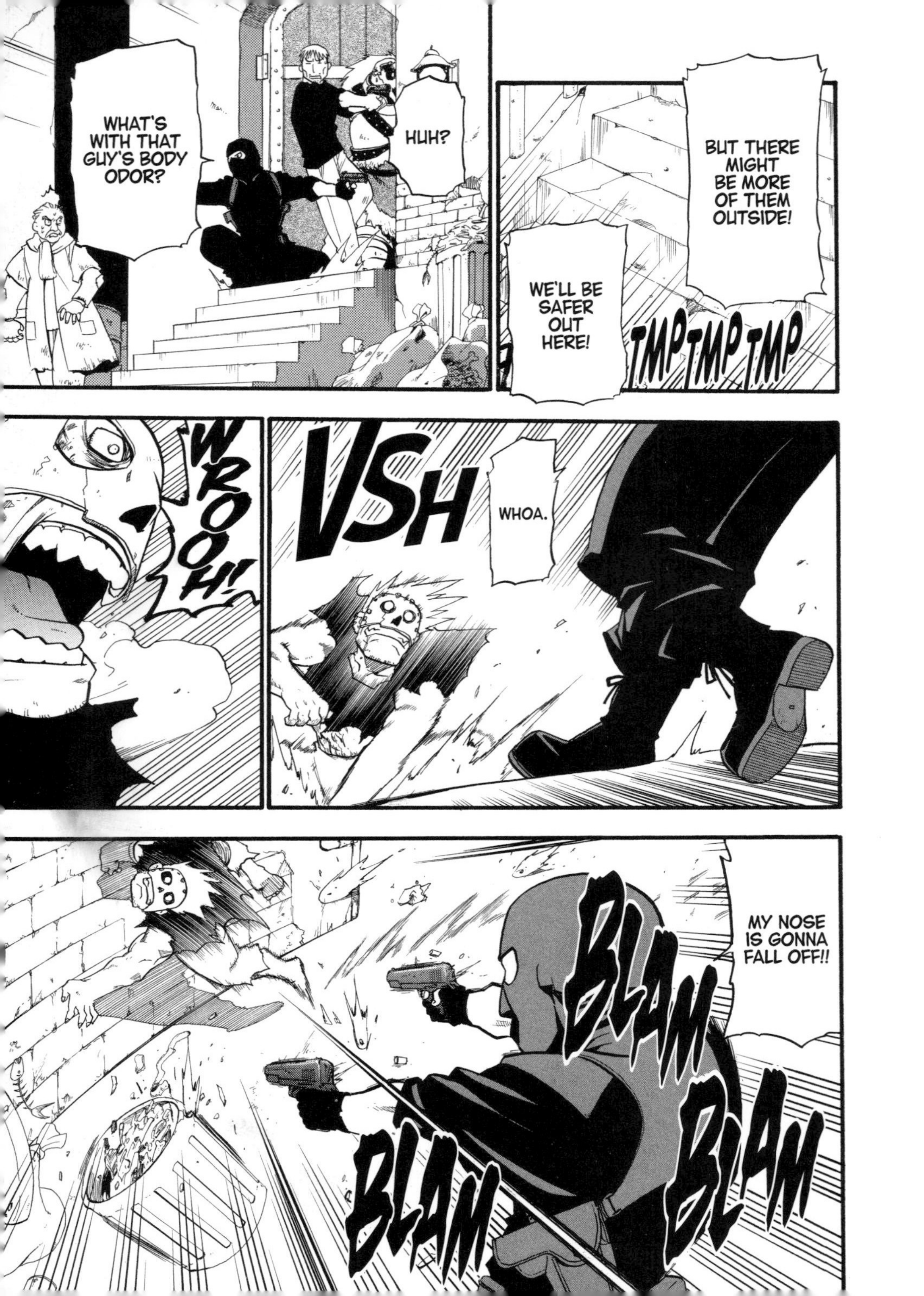
BUT THERE MIGHT BE MORE OF THEM OUTSIDE!
WE'LL BE SAFER OUT HERE!
TMP TMP TMP
HUH?
WHAT'S WITH THAT GUY'S BODY ODOR?
VSH
WHOA.
WROOOH!
MY NOSE IS GONNA FALL OFF!!
BLAM
BLAM
BLAM
BLAM

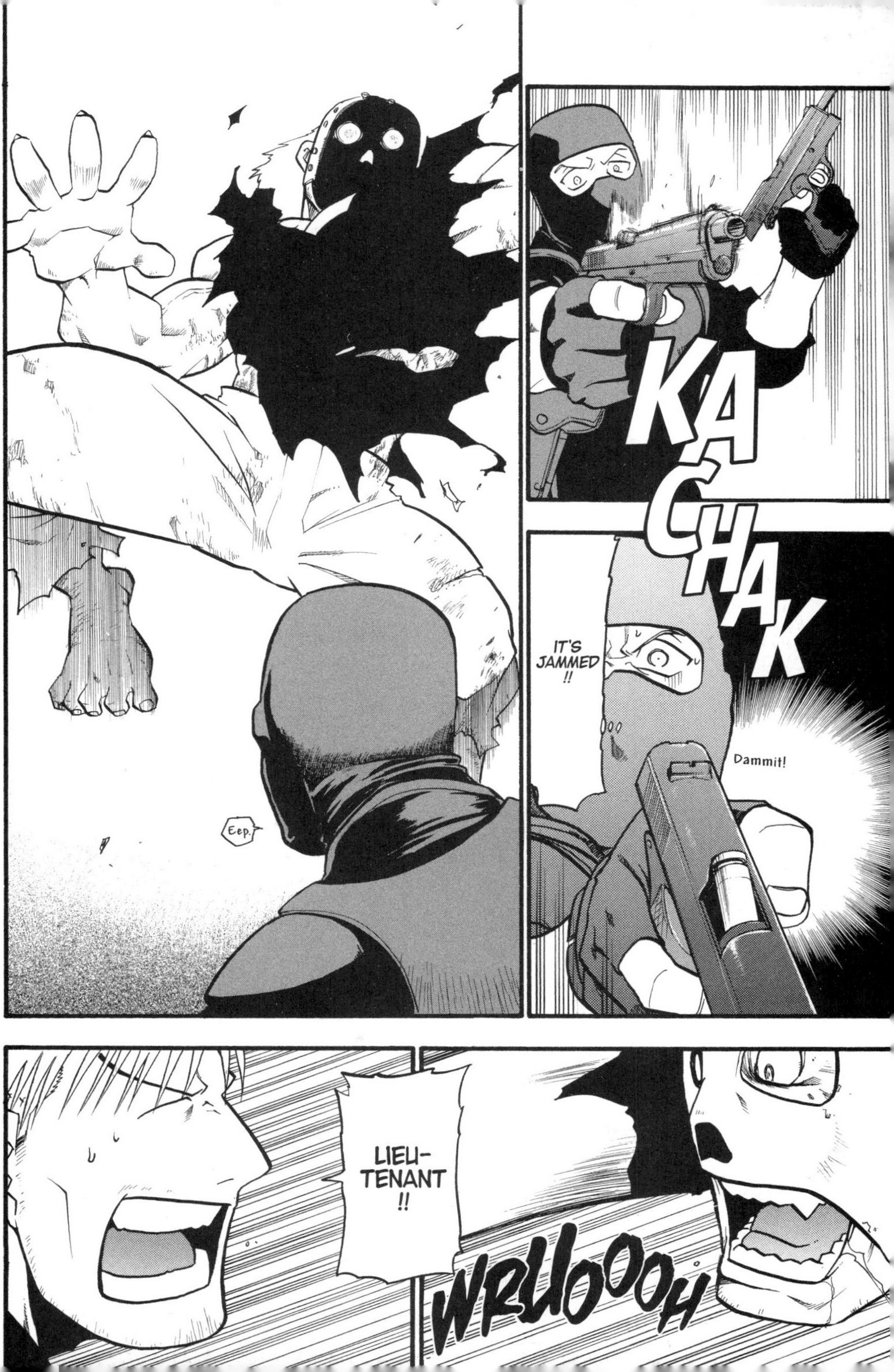
KA CHAK
IT'S JAMMED !!
Dammit!
Eep.
WRUOOOH
LIEU-TENANT !!

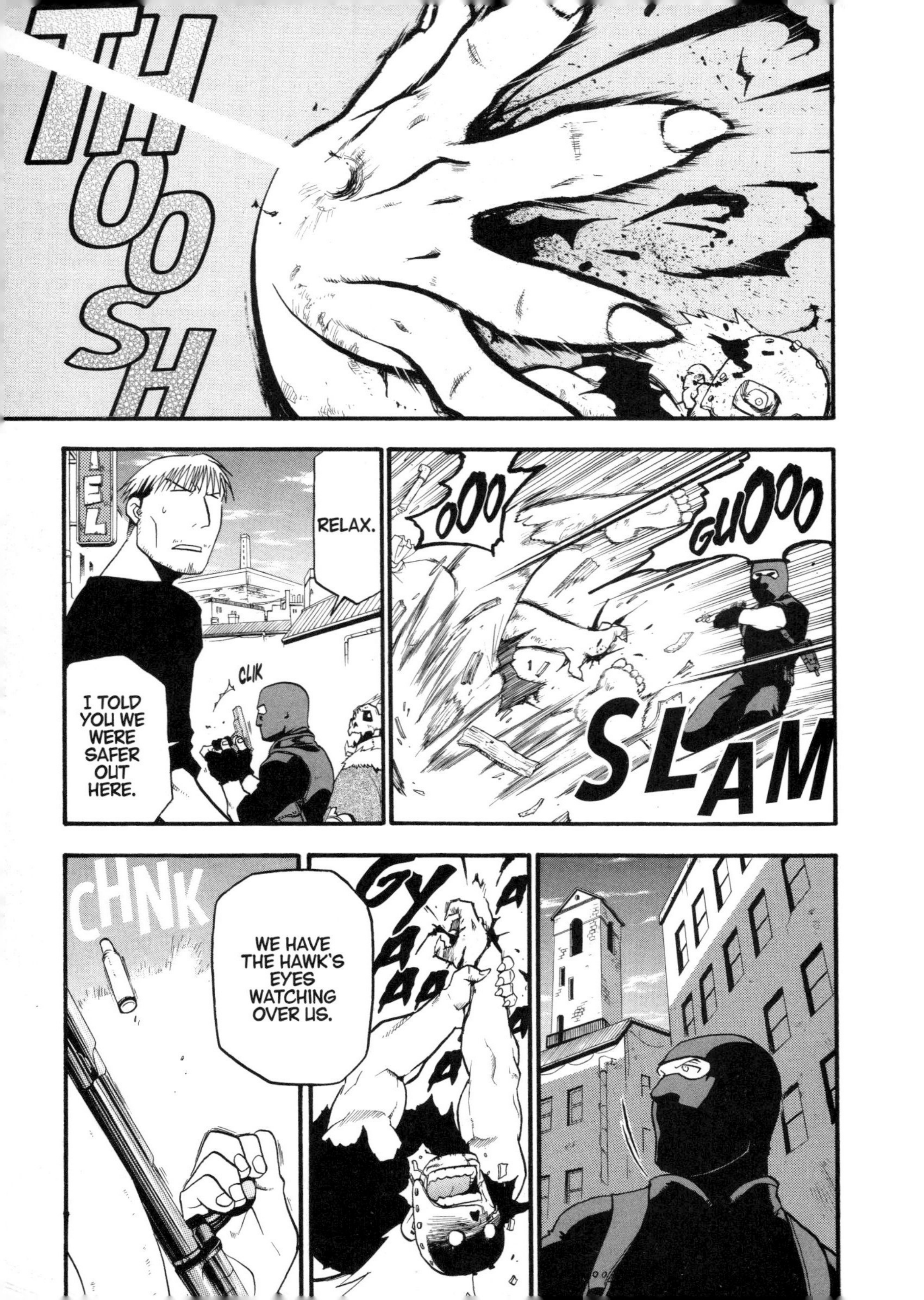
THOOSH
OOO
GUOOO
SLAM
RELAX.
CLIK
I TOLD YOU WE WERE SAFER OUT HERE.
GYAAAAAA
WE HAVE THE HAWK'S EYES WATCHING OVER US.
CHNK

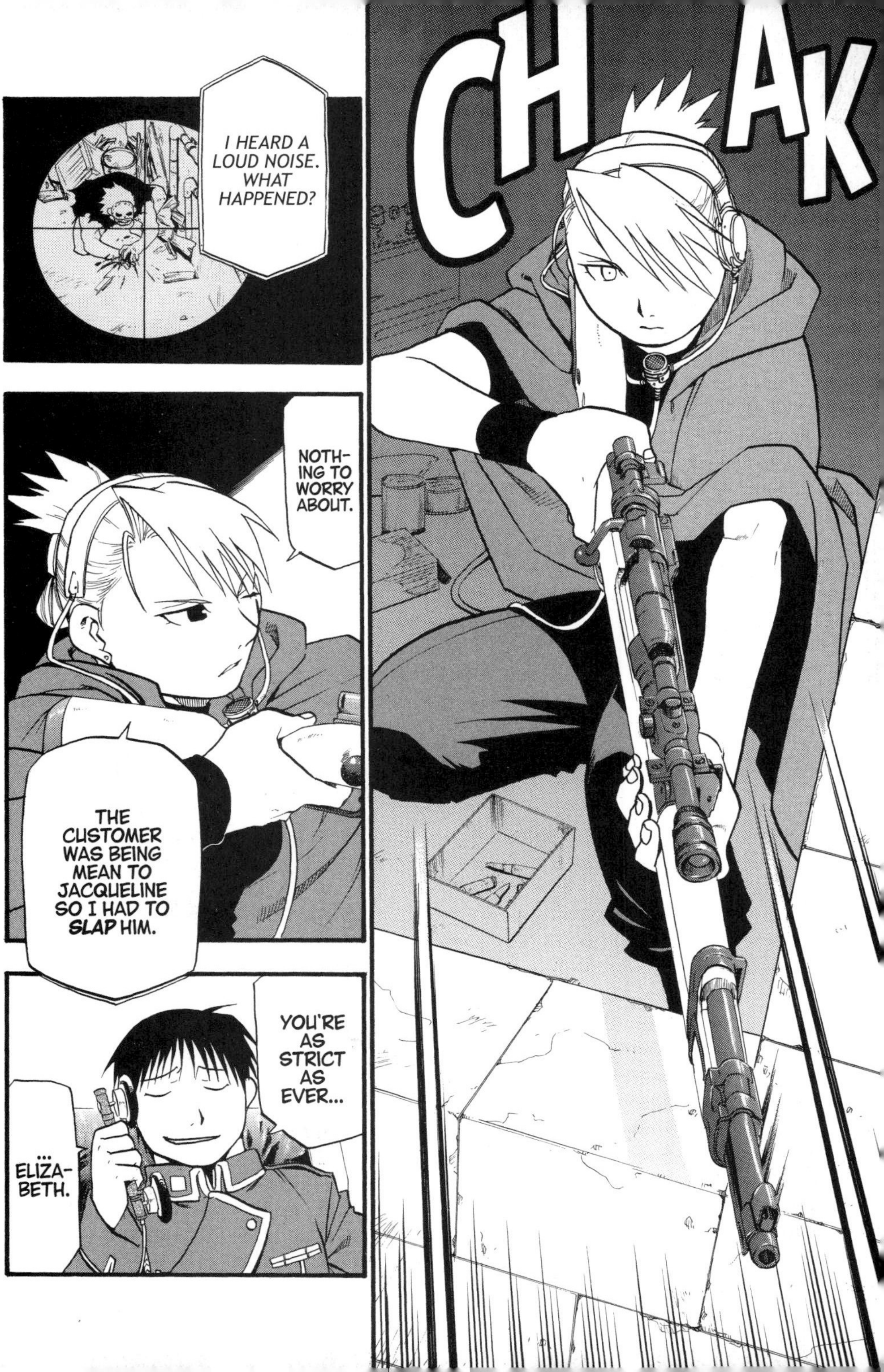
CHAK
I HEARD A LOUD NOISE. WHAT HAPPENED?
NOTH-ING TO WORRY ABOUT.
THE CUSTOMER WAS BEING MEAN TO JACQUELINE SO I HAD TO SLAP HIM.
YOU'RE AS STRICT AS EVER...
... ELIZA-BETH.

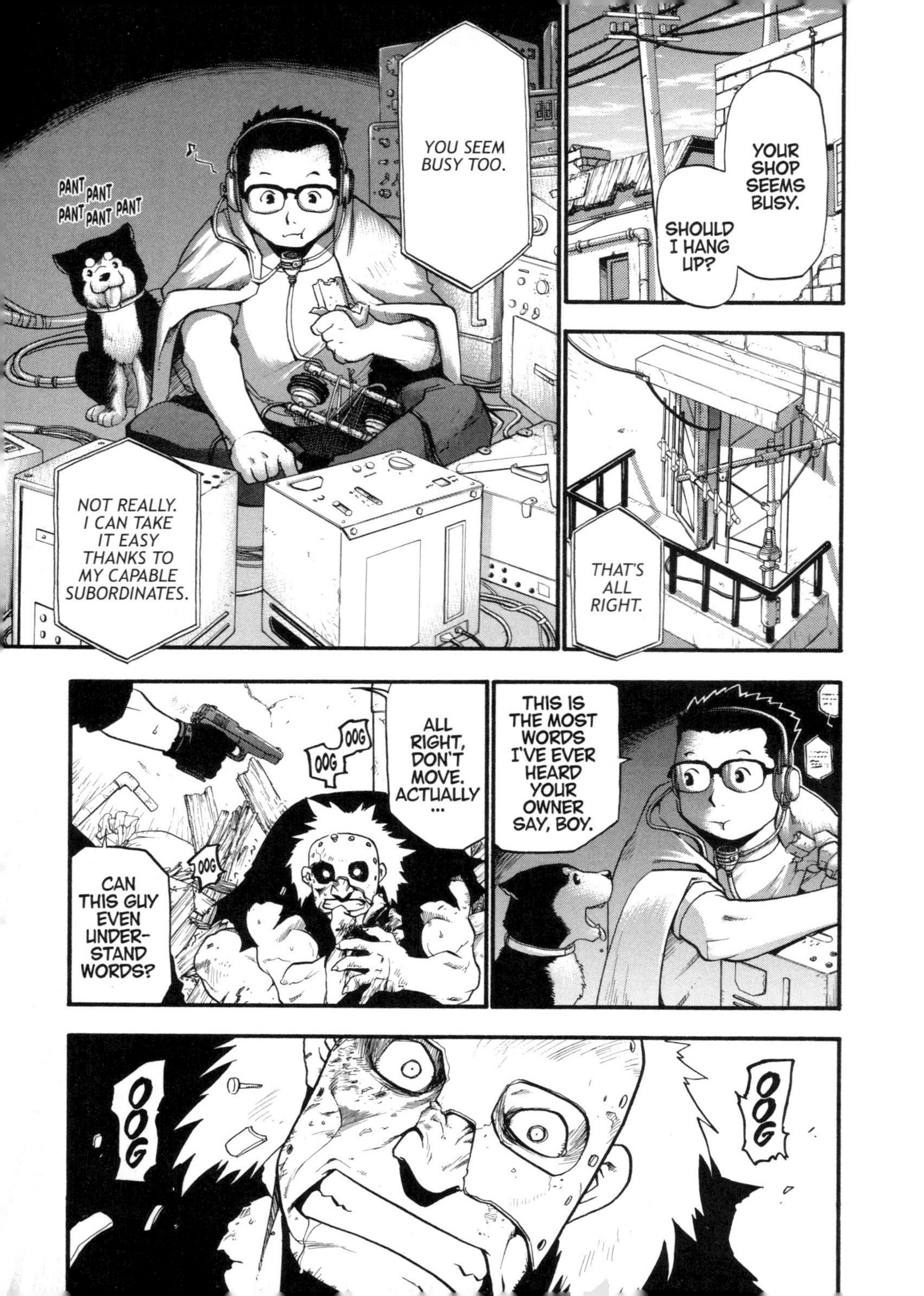
YOUR SHOP SEEMS BUSY.
SHOULD I HANG UP?
THAT'S ALL RIGHT.
YOU SEEM BUSY TOO.
PANT PANT PANT PANT PANT
NOT REALLY. I CAN TAKE IT EASY THANKS TO MY CAPABLE SUBORDINATES.
THIS IS THE MOST WORDS I'VE EVER HEARD YOUR OWNER SAY, BOY.
ALL RIGHT, DON'T MOVE. ACTUALLY...
OOG OOG
OOG
CAN THIS GUY EVEN UNDER-STAND WORDS?
OOG
OOG

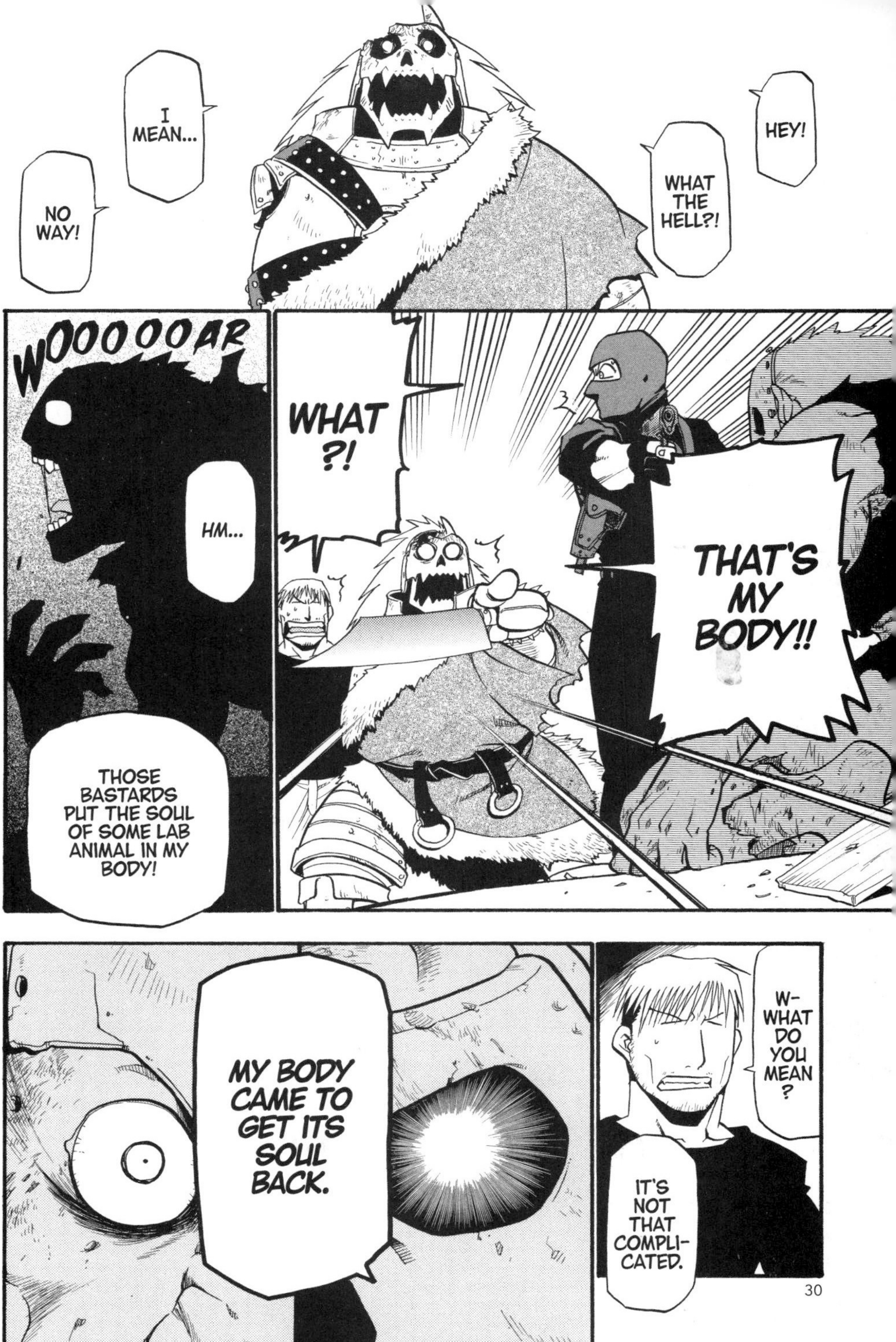
HEY!
WHAT THE HELL?!
I MEAN...
NO WAY!
WHAT ?!
THAT'S MY BODY!!
WOOOOOAR
HM...
THOSE BASTARDS PUT THE SOUL OF SOME LAB ANIMAL IN MY BODY!
W-WHAT DO YOU MEAN?
IT'S NOT THAT COMPLICATED.
MY BODY CAME TO GET ITS SOUL BACK.

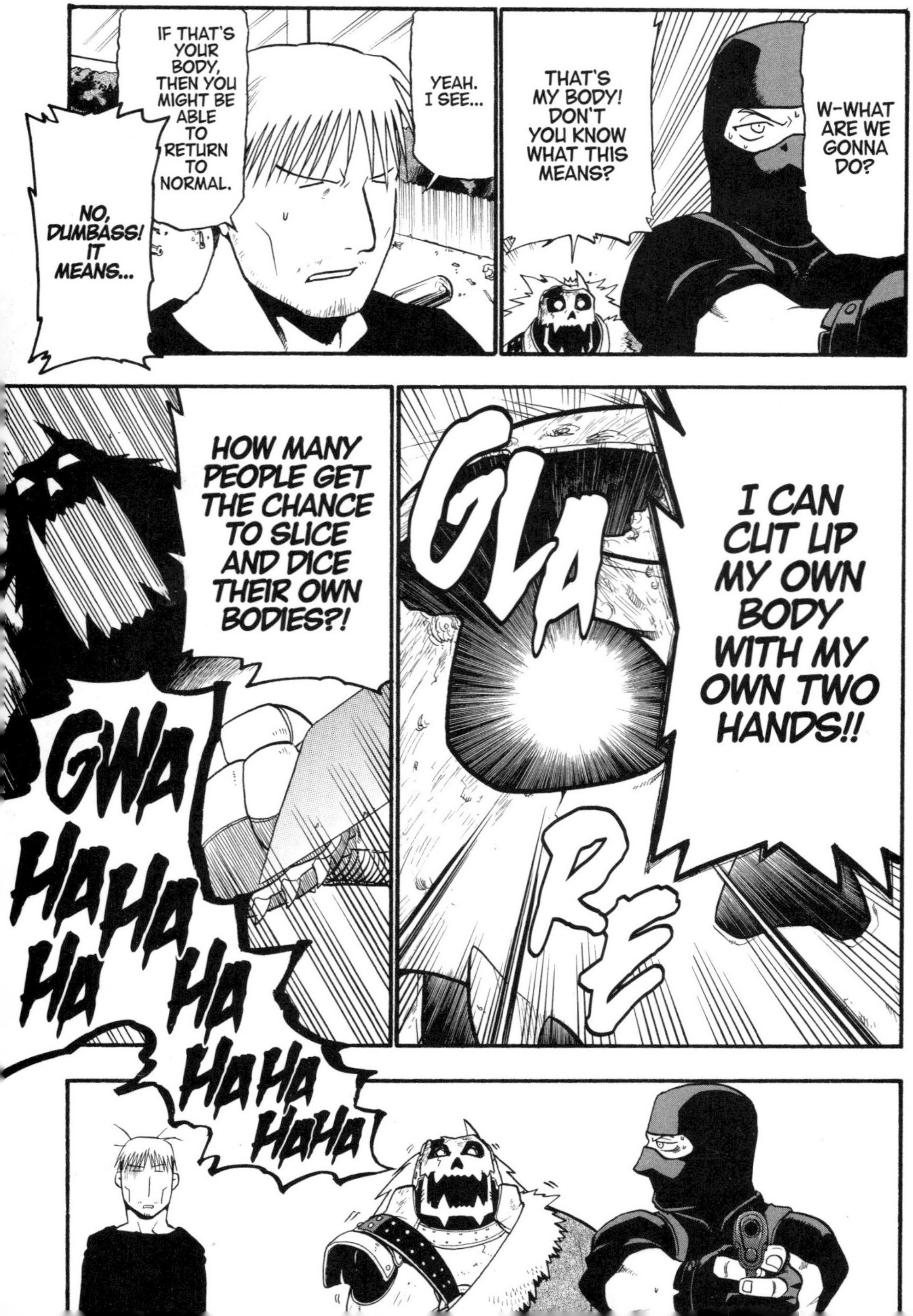
W-WHAT ARE WE GONNA DO?
THAT'S MY BODY! DON'T YOU KNOW WHAT THIS MEANS?
YEAH. I SEE...
IF THAT'S YOUR BODY, THEN YOU MIGHT BE ABLE TO RETURN TO NORMAL.
NO, DUMBASS! IT MEANS...
I CAN CUT UP MY OWN BODY WITH MY OWN TWO HANDS!!
GLARE
HOW MANY PEOPLE GET THE CHANCE TO SLICE AND DICE THEIR OWN BODIES?!
GWA HA HA HA HA HA HA HA HA HA HA

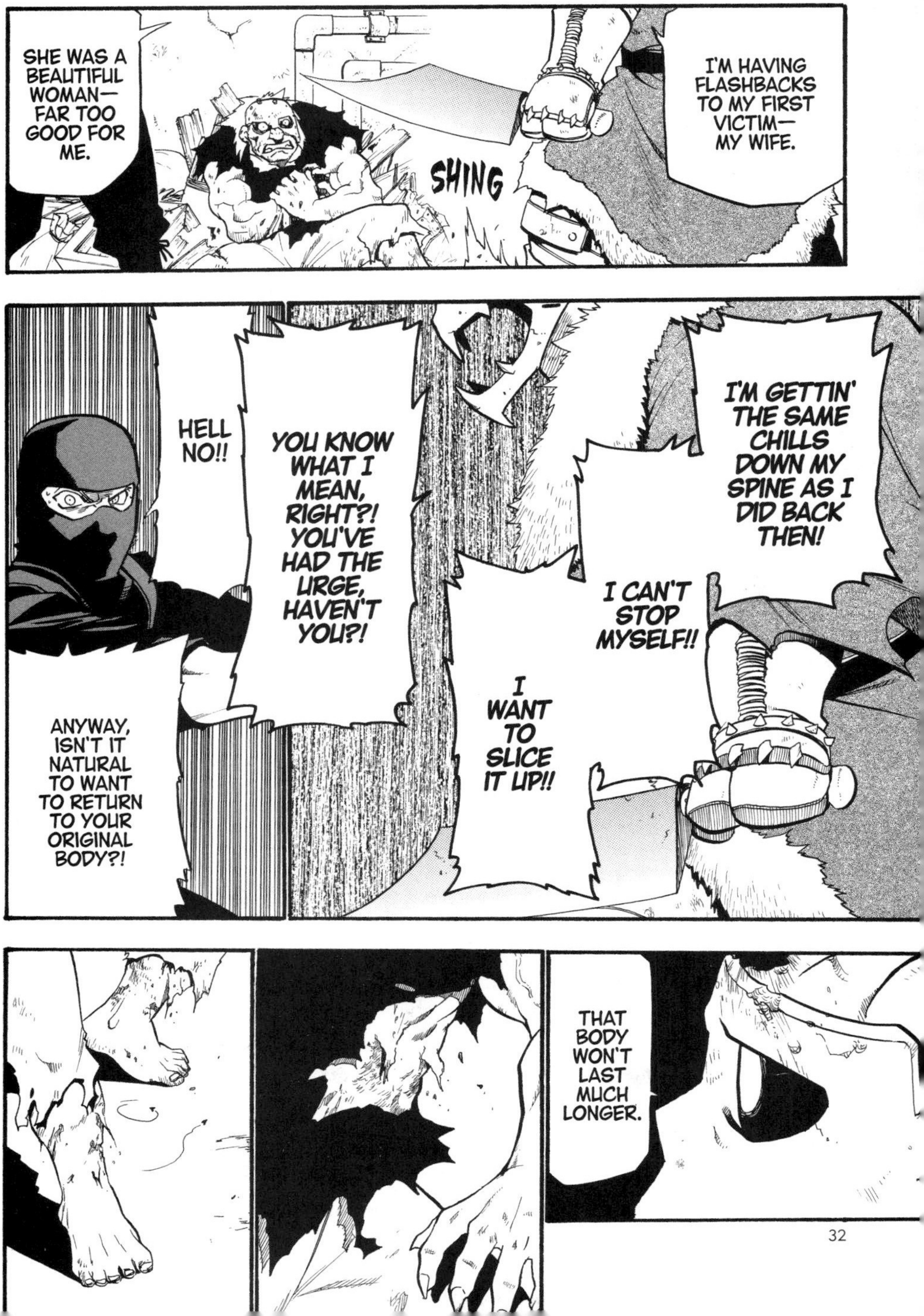
I'M HAVING FLASHBACKS TO MY FIRST VICTIM— MY WIFE.
SHE WAS A BEAUTIFUL WOMAN— FAR TOO GOOD FOR ME.
SHING
I'M GETTIN' THE SAME CHILLS DOWN MY SPINE AS I DID BACK THEN!
YOU KNOW WHAT I MEAN, RIGHT?! YOU'VE HAD THE URGE, HAVEN'T YOU?!
I CAN'T STOP MYSELF!!
I WANT TO SLICE IT UP!!
HELL NO!!
ANYWAY, ISN'T IT NATURAL TO WANT TO RETURN TO YOUR ORIGINAL BODY?!
THAT BODY WON'T LAST MUCH LONGER.

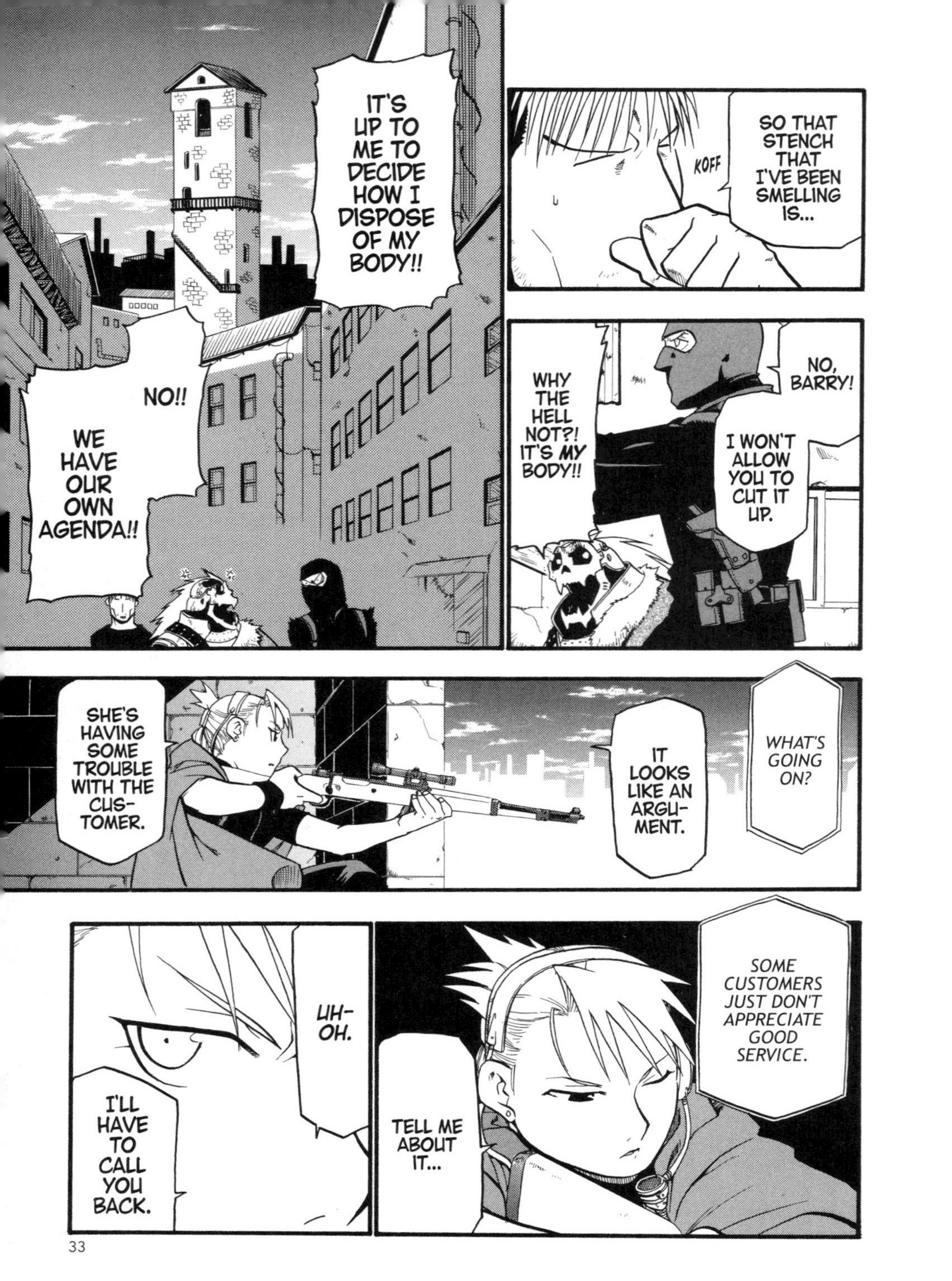
SO THAT STENCH THAT I'VE BEEN SMELLING IS...
KOFF
NO, BARRY!
I WON'T ALLOW YOU TO CUT IT UP.
WHY THE HELL NOT?! IT'S *MY* BODY!!
IT'S UP TO ME TO DECIDE HOW I DISPOSE OF MY BODY!!
NO!!
WE HAVE OUR OWN AGENDA!!
WHAT'S GOING ON?
IT LOOKS LIKE AN ARGU-MENT.
SHE'S HAVING SOME TROUBLE WITH THE CUS-TOMER.
SOME CUSTOMERS JUST DON'T APPRECIATE GOOD SERVICE.
TELL ME ABOUT IT...
UH-OH.
I'LL HAVE TO CALL YOU BACK.

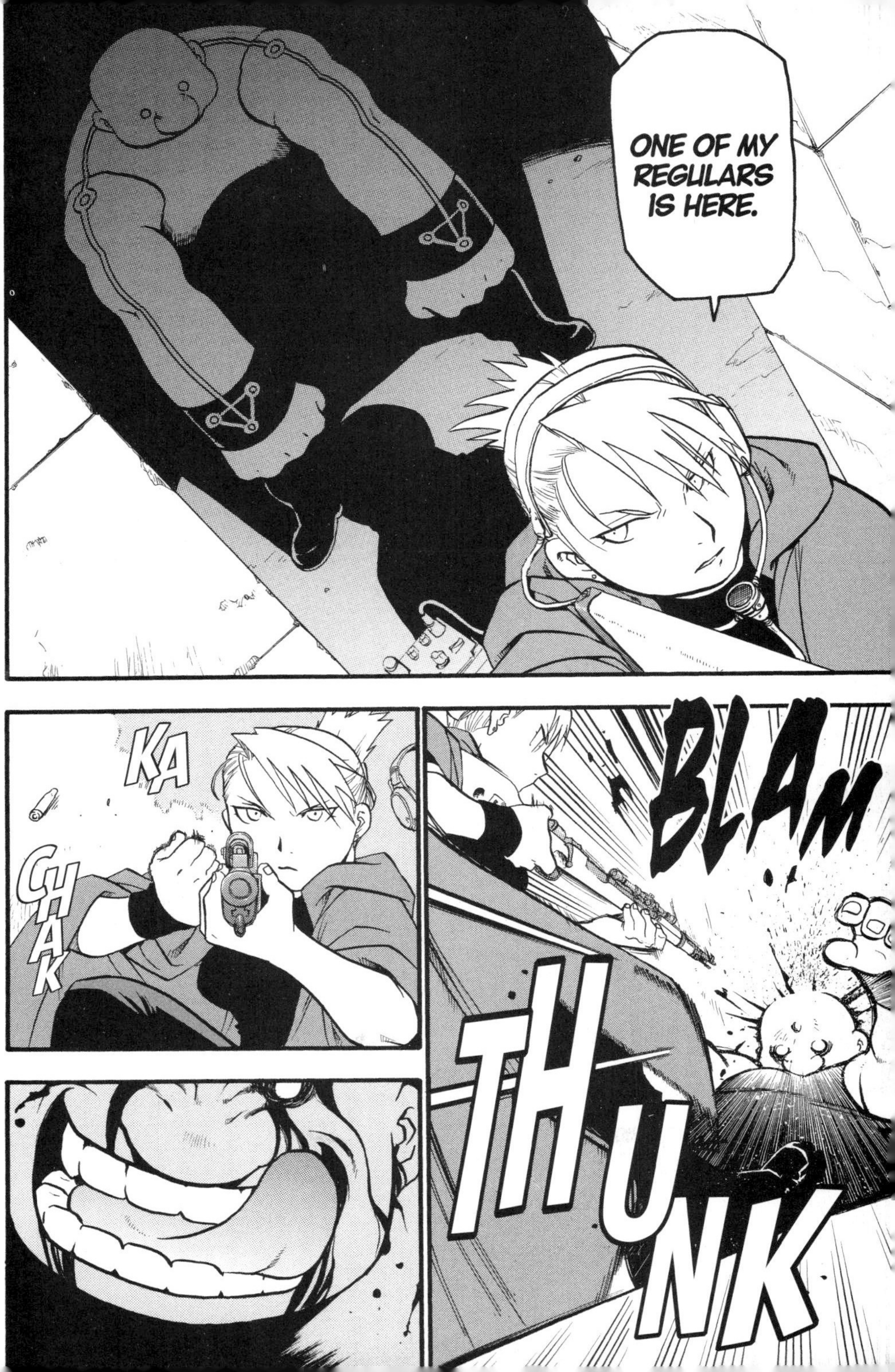

ONE OF MY REGULARS IS HERE.
BLAM
THUNK
KA
CHAK

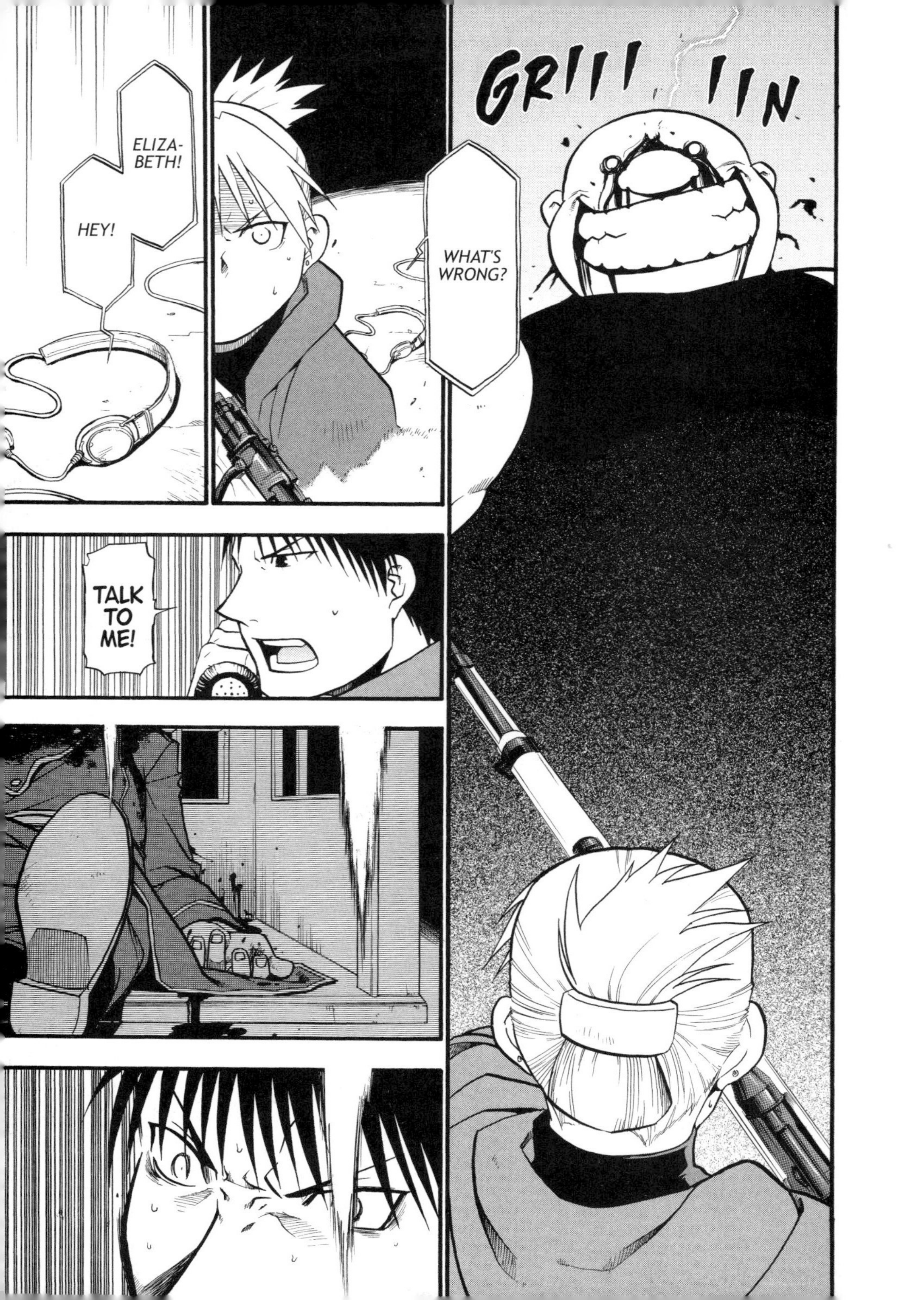
GRIII IIN
WHAT'S WRONG?
ELIZA-BETH!
HEY!
TALK TO ME!

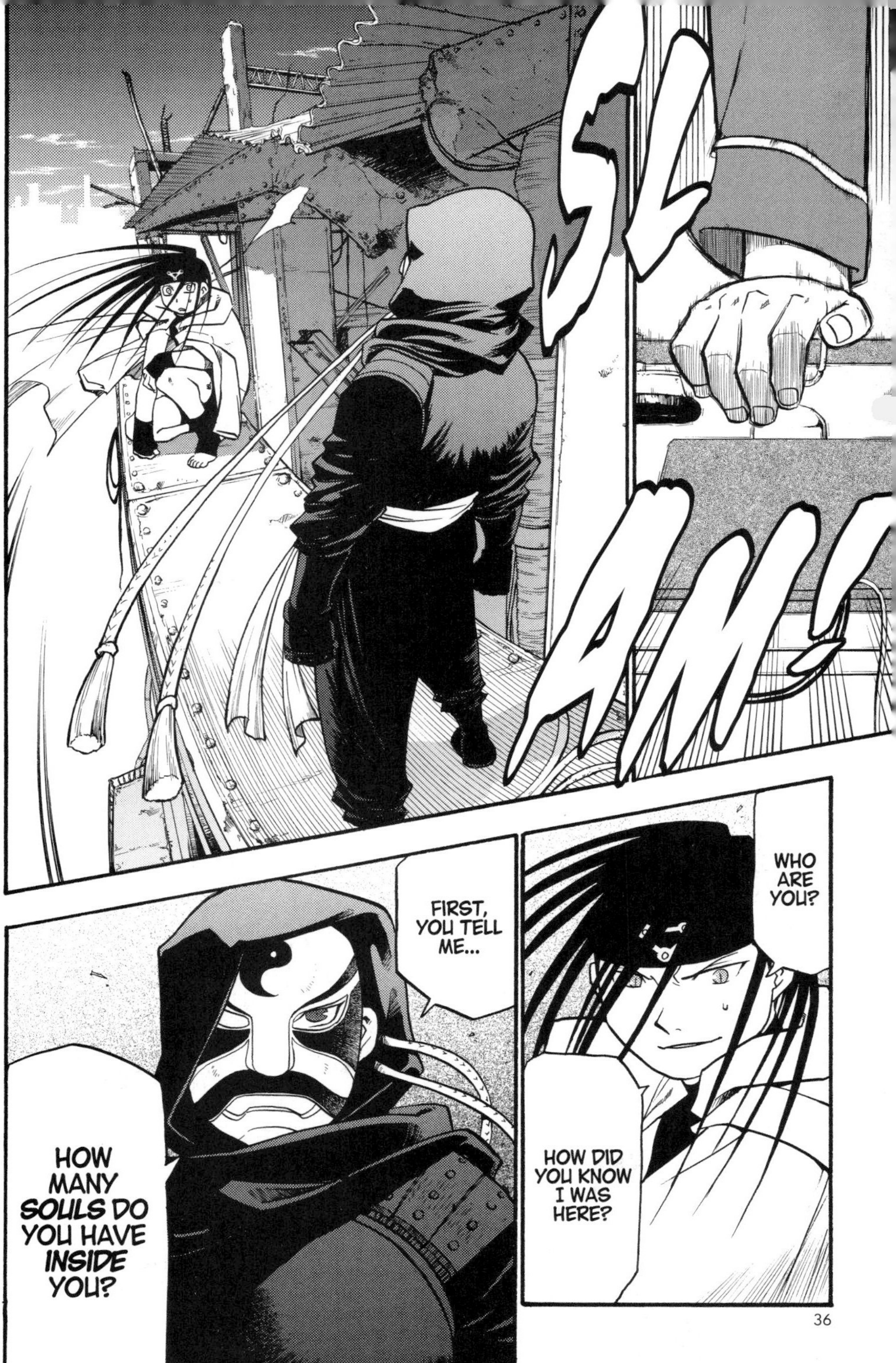
SLAM!
WHO ARE YOU?
HOW DID YOU KNOW I WAS HERE?
FIRST, YOU TELL ME...
HOW MANY **SOULS** DO YOU HAVE **INSIDE** YOU?

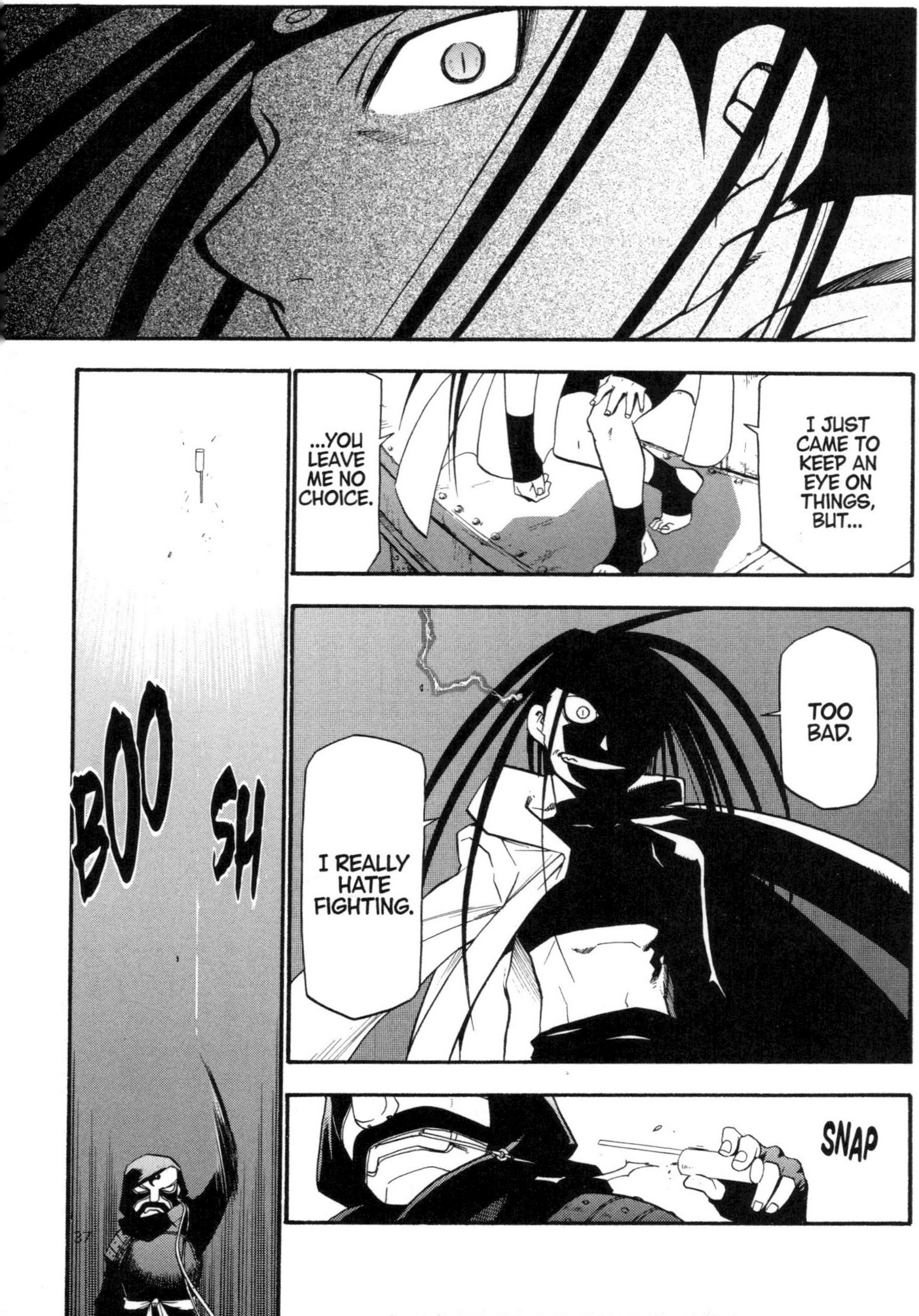
I JUST CAME TO KEEP AN EYE ON THINGS, BUT...
...YOU LEAVE ME NO CHOICE.
TOO BAD.
I REALLY HATE FIGHTING.
SNAP
BOOSH

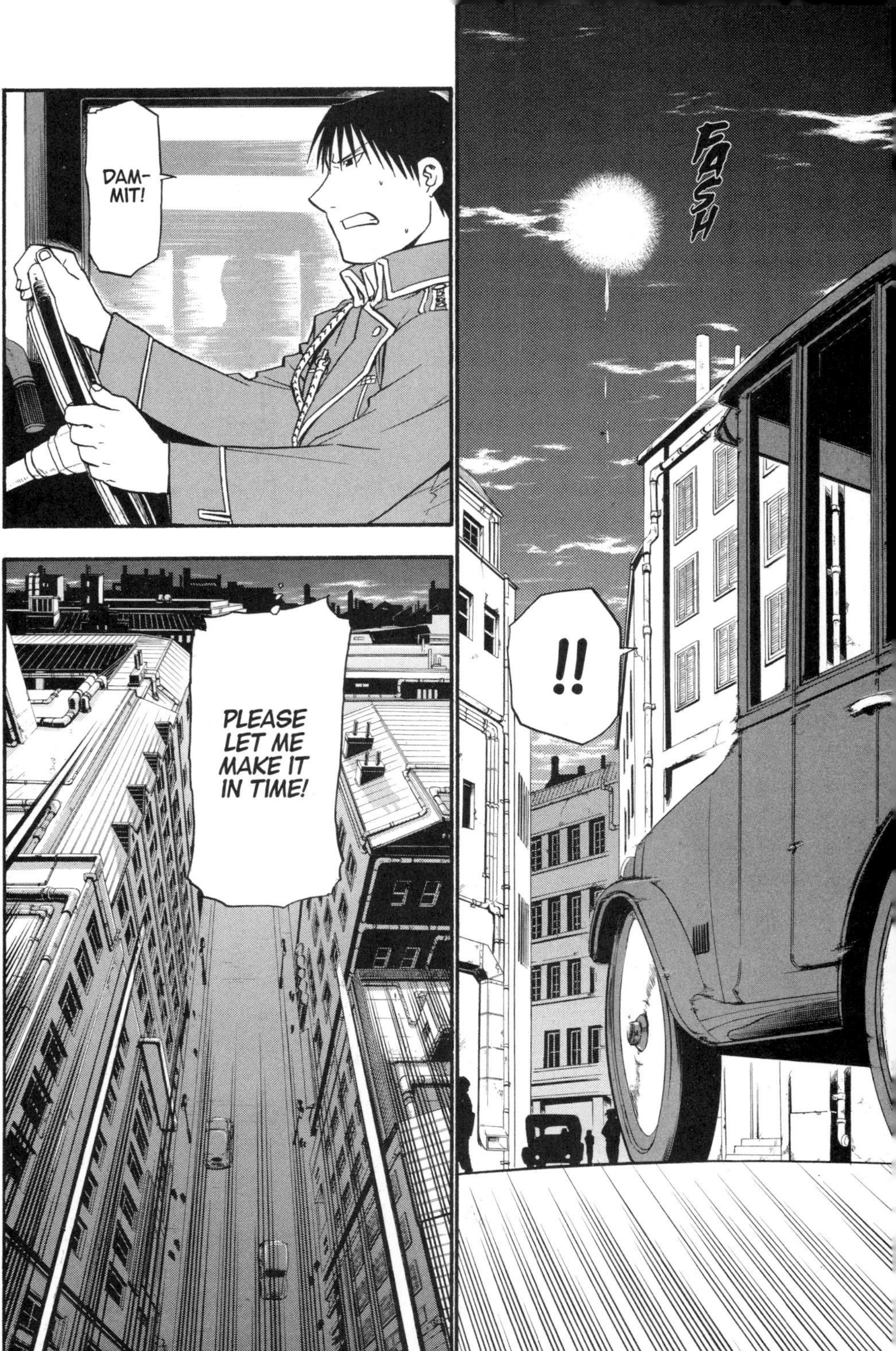
FASH
!!
DAM-MIT!
PLEASE LET ME MAKE IT IN TIME!

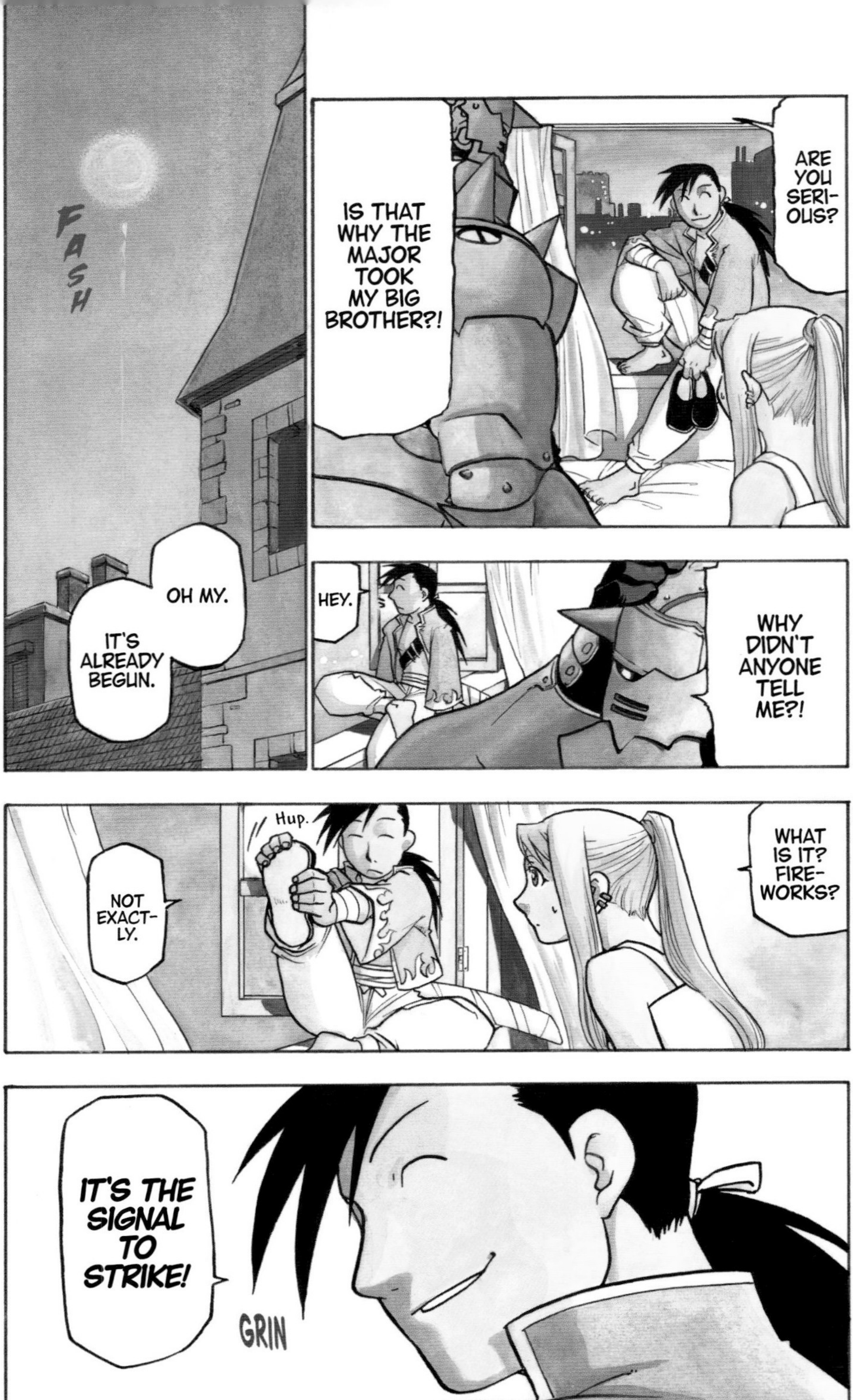
ARE YOU SERI-OUS?
IS THAT WHY THE MAJOR TOOK MY BIG BROTHER?!
WHY DIDN'T ANYONE TELL ME?!
HEY.
FASH
OH MY.
IT'S ALREADY BEGUN.
WHAT IS IT? FIRE-WORKS?
Hup.
NOT EXACT-LY.
IT'S THE SIGNAL TO STRIKE!
GRIN

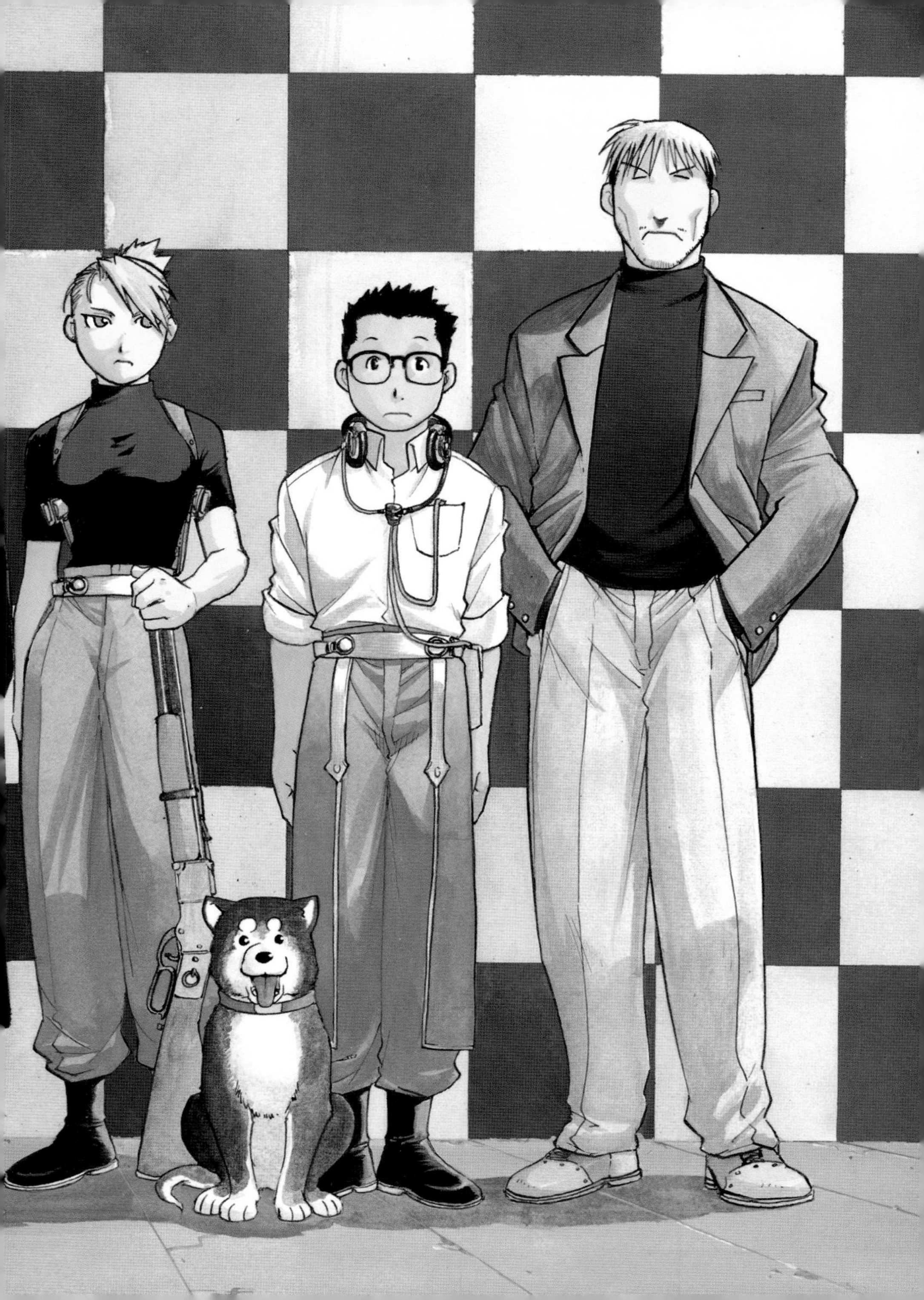

CHAPTER 38 SIGNAL TO STRIKE

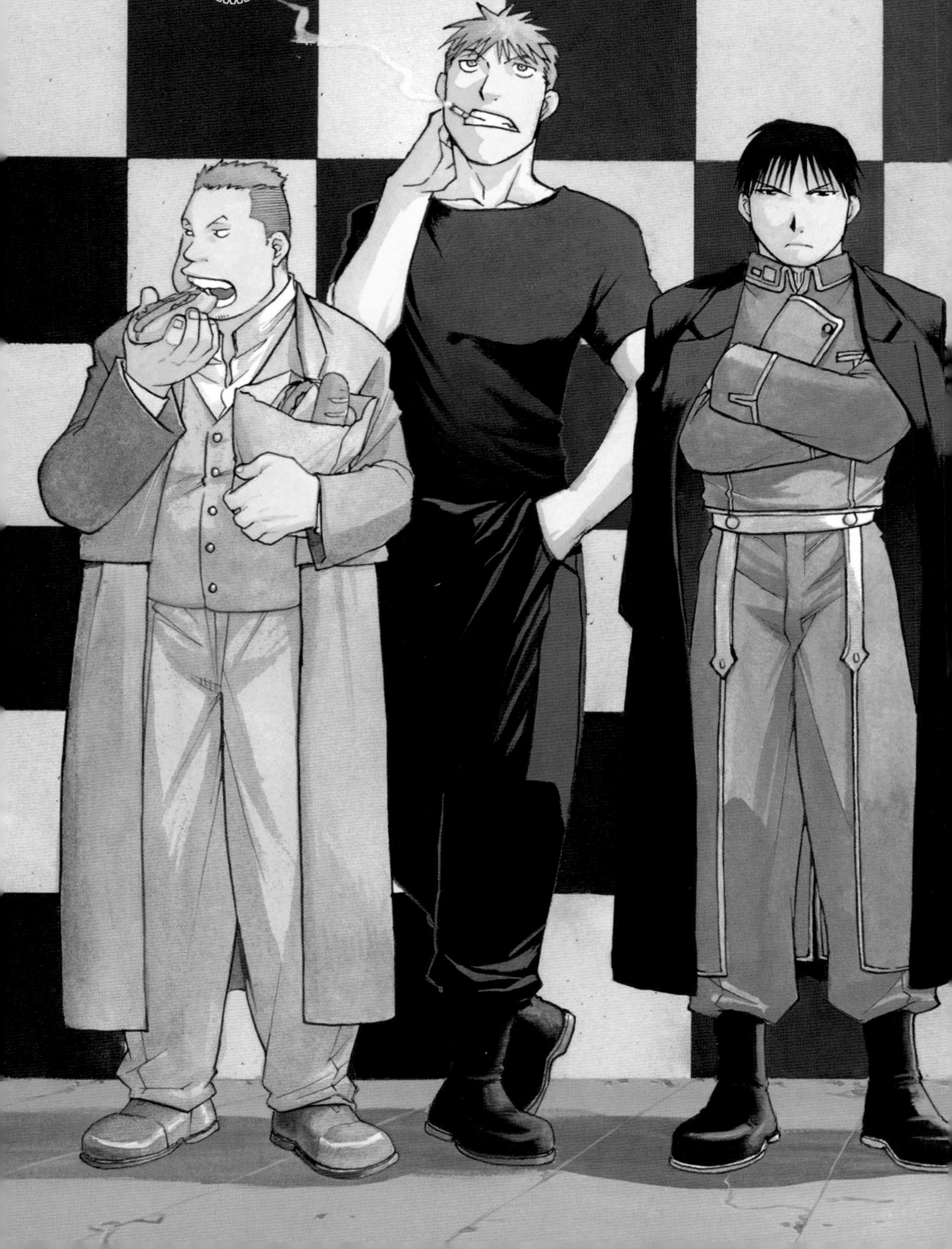

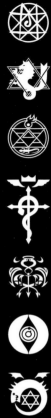

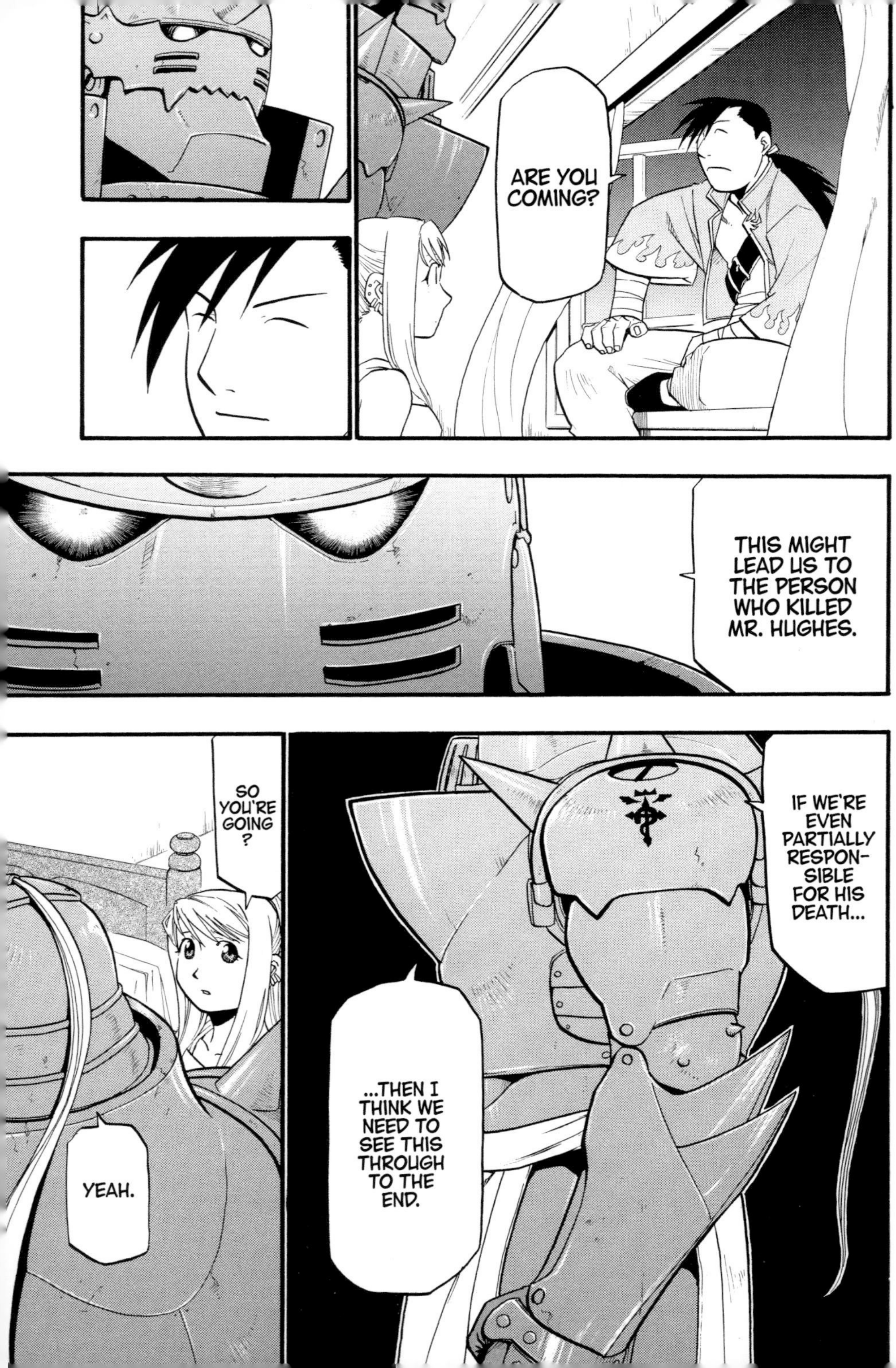
ARE YOU COMING?
THIS MIGHT LEAD US TO THE PERSON WHO KILLED MR. HUGHES.
IF WE'RE EVEN PARTIALLY RESPON-SIBLE FOR HIS DEATH...
...THEN I THINK WE NEED TO SEE THIS THROUGH TO THE END.
SO YOU'RE GOING?
YEAH.

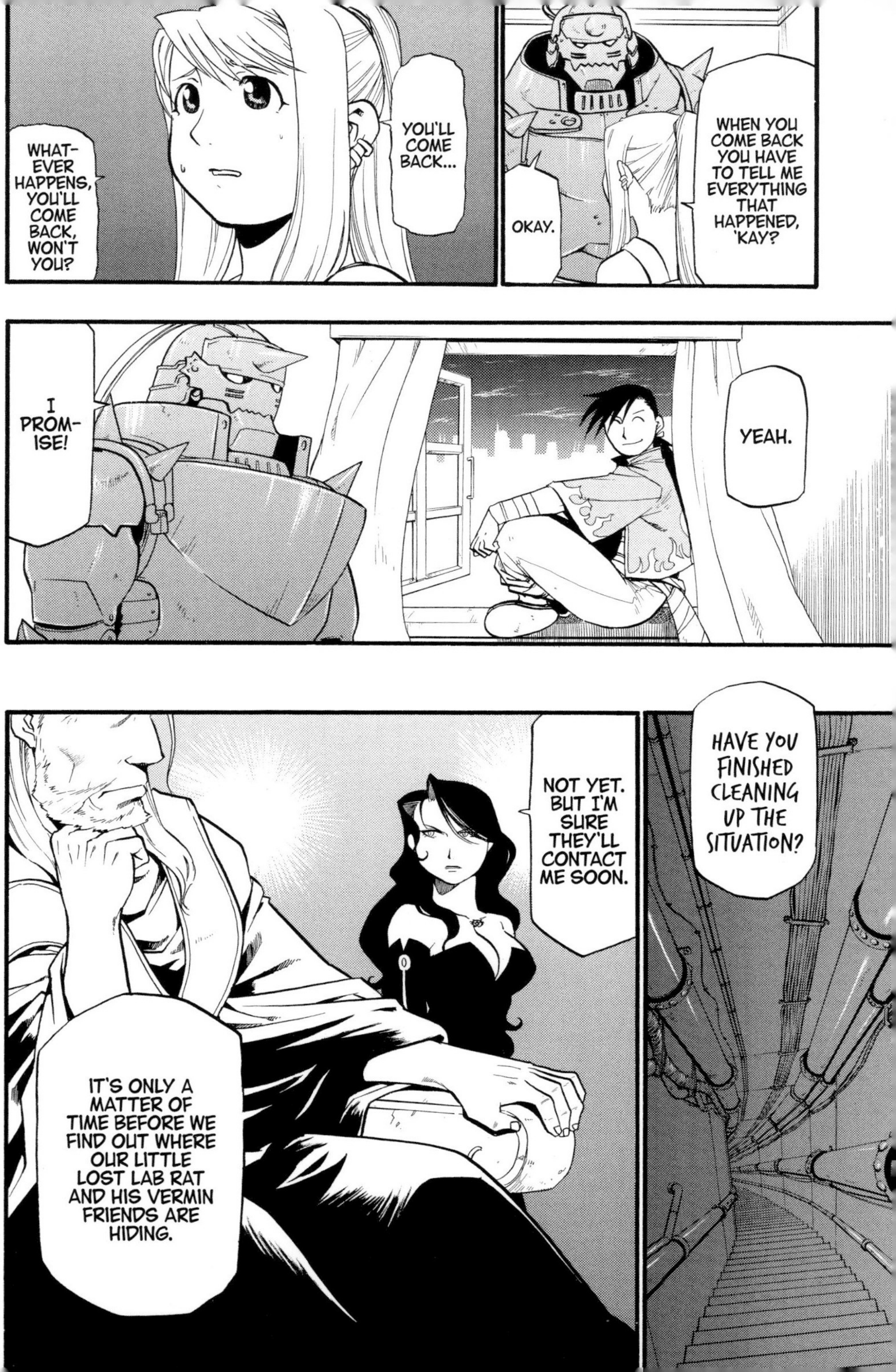
WHEN YOU COME BACK YOU HAVE TO TELL ME EVERYTHING THAT HAPPENED, 'KAY?
OKAY.
YOU'LL COME BACK...
WHAT-EVER HAPPENS, YOU'LL COME BACK, WON'T YOU?
YEAH.
I PROM-ISE!
HAVE YOU FINISHED CLEANING UP THE SITUATION?
NOT YET. BUT I'M SURE THEY'LL CONTACT ME SOON.
IT'S ONLY A MATTER OF TIME BEFORE WE FIND OUT WHERE OUR LITTLE LOST LAB RAT AND HIS VERMIN FRIENDS ARE HIDING.

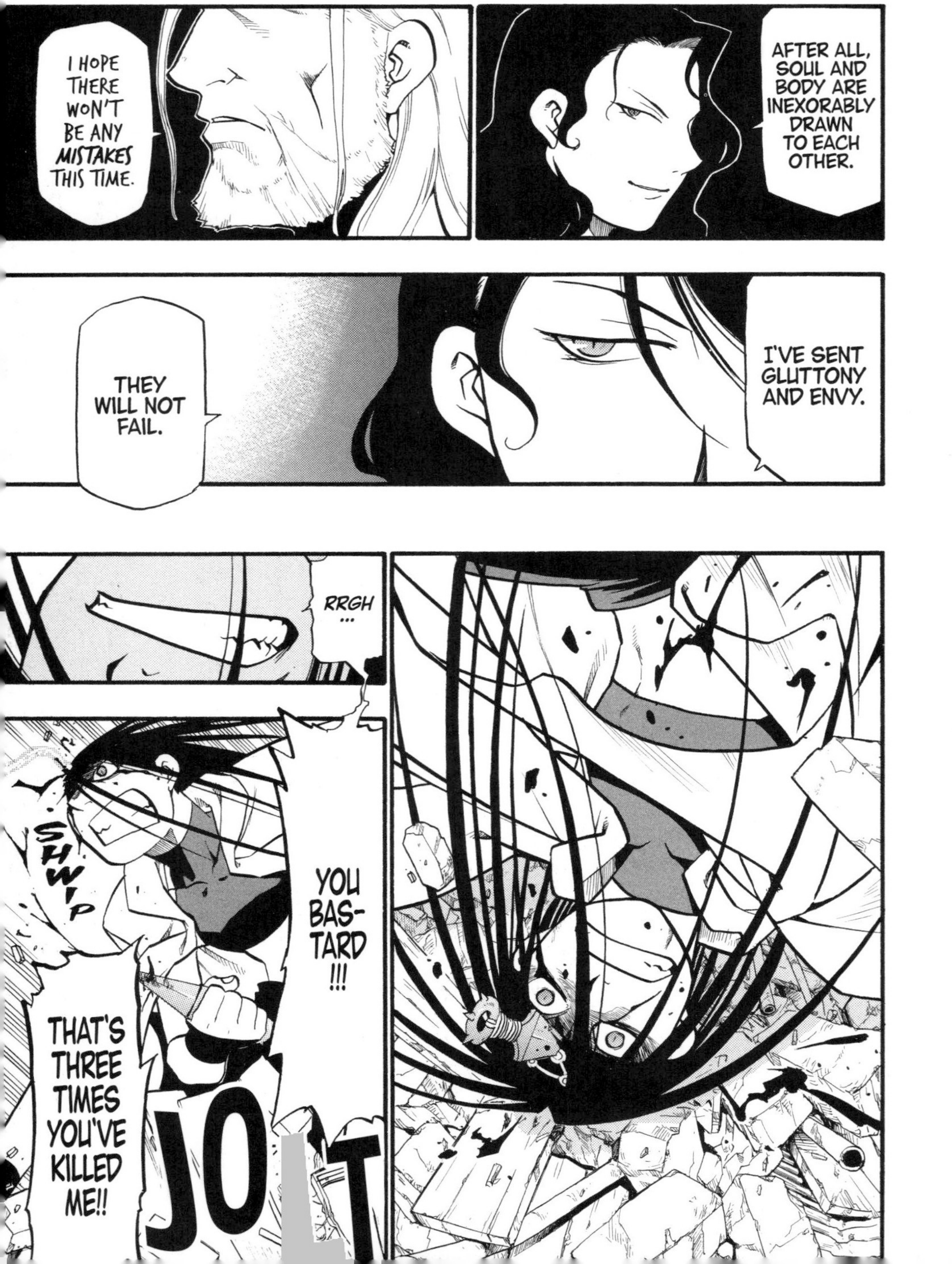
AFTER ALL, SOUL AND BODY ARE INEXORABLY DRAWN TO EACH OTHER.
I HOPE THERE WON'T BE ANY MISTAKES THIS TIME.
I'VE SENT GLUTTONY AND ENVY.
THEY WILL NOT FAIL.
RRGH ...
YOU BAS-TARD!!!
THAT'S THREE TIMES YOU'VE KILLED ME!!
SHWIP
JOLT

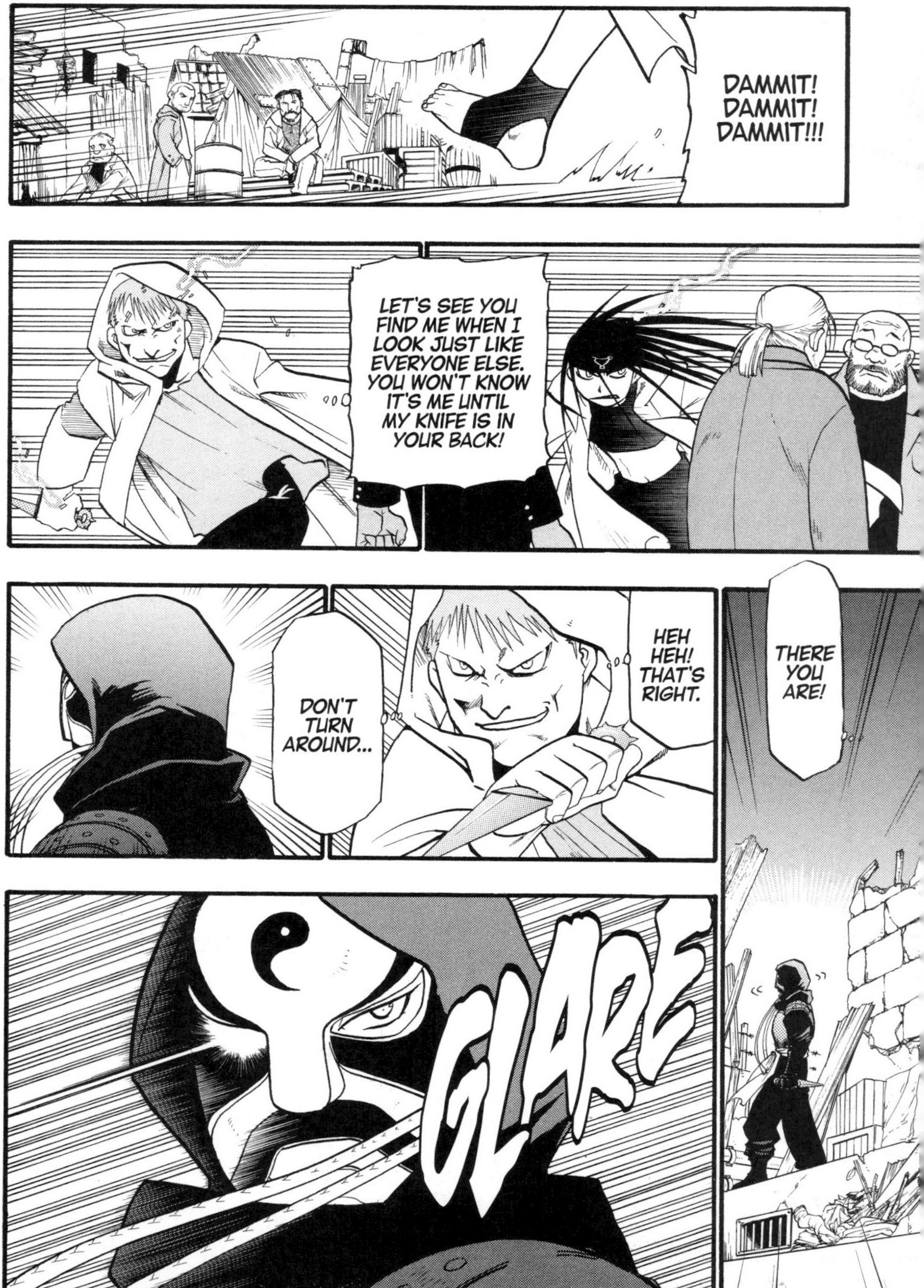
DAMMIT! DAMMIT! DAMMIT!!!
LET'S SEE YOU FIND ME WHEN I LOOK JUST LIKE EVERYONE ELSE. YOU WON'T KNOW IT'S ME UNTIL MY KNIFE IS IN YOUR BACK!
THERE YOU ARE!
HEH HEH! THAT'S RIGHT.
DON'T TURN AROUND...
GLARE

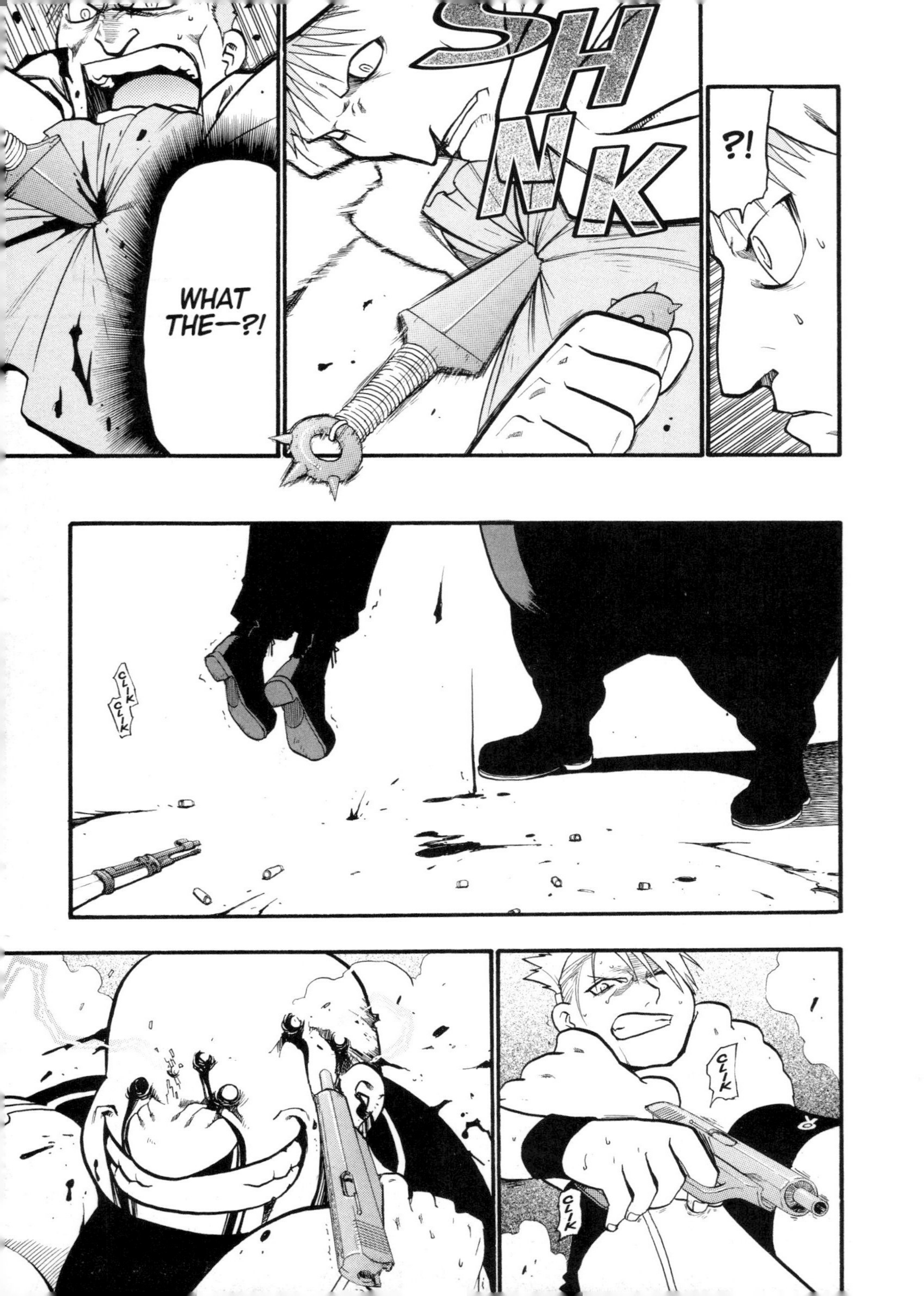
?!
SHNK
WHAT THE—?!
CLIK CLIK
CLIK
CLIK

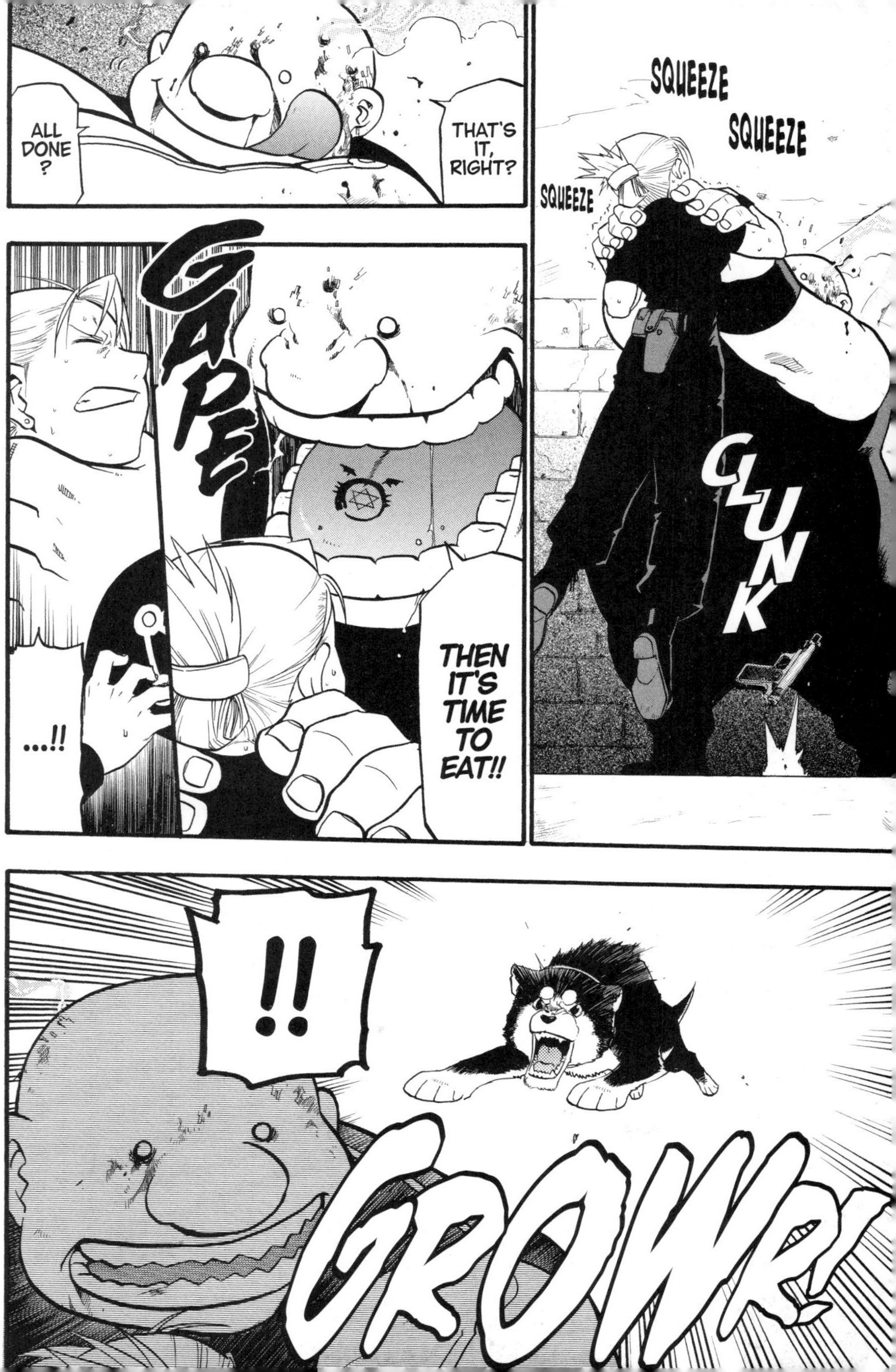
SQUEEZE
SQUEEZE
SQUEEZE
CLUNK
THAT'S IT, RIGHT?
ALL DONE?
GAPE
THEN IT'S TIME TO EAT!!
...!!
!!
GROWR!

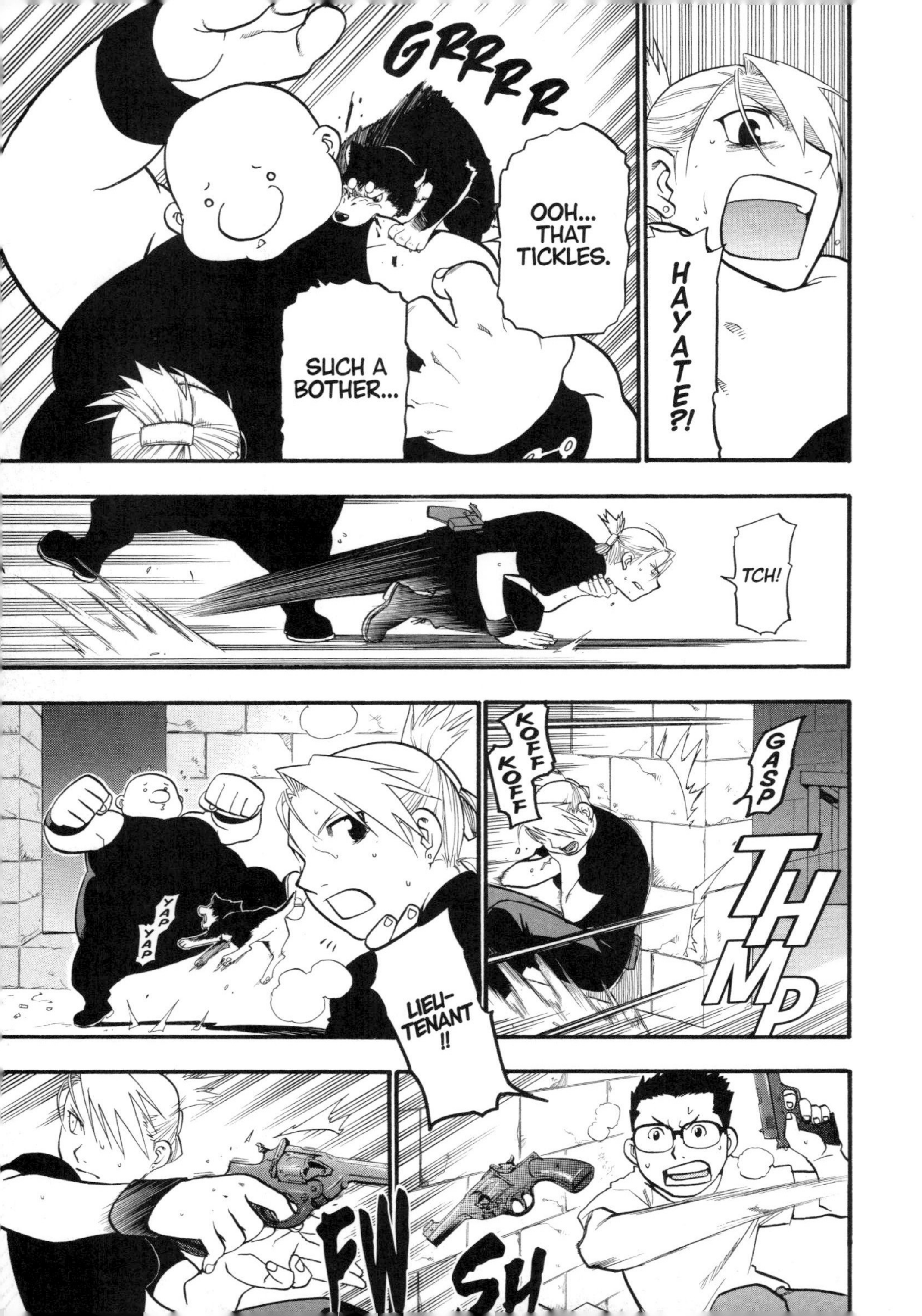
HAYATE?!
GRRRRR
OOH... THAT TICKLES.
SUCH A BOTHER...
TCH!
GASP
KOFF KOFF
THMP
YAP YAP
LIEU-TENANT!!
FWSH

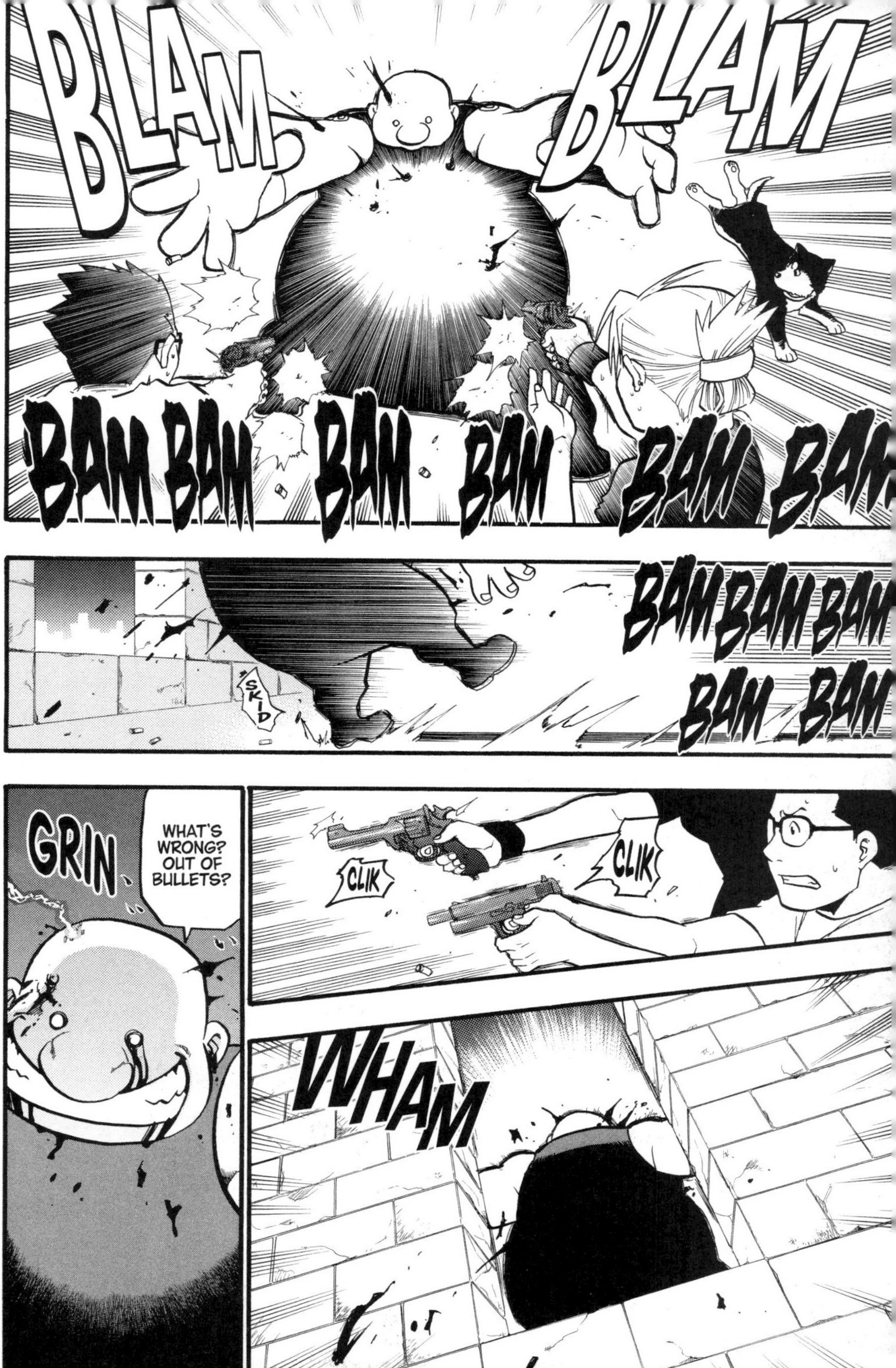
BLAM
BLAM
BAM BAM BAM BAM BAM
BAM BAM BAM
BAM BAM
SKID
CLIK
CLIK
WHAM
WHAT'S WRONG? OUT OF BULLETS?
GRIN

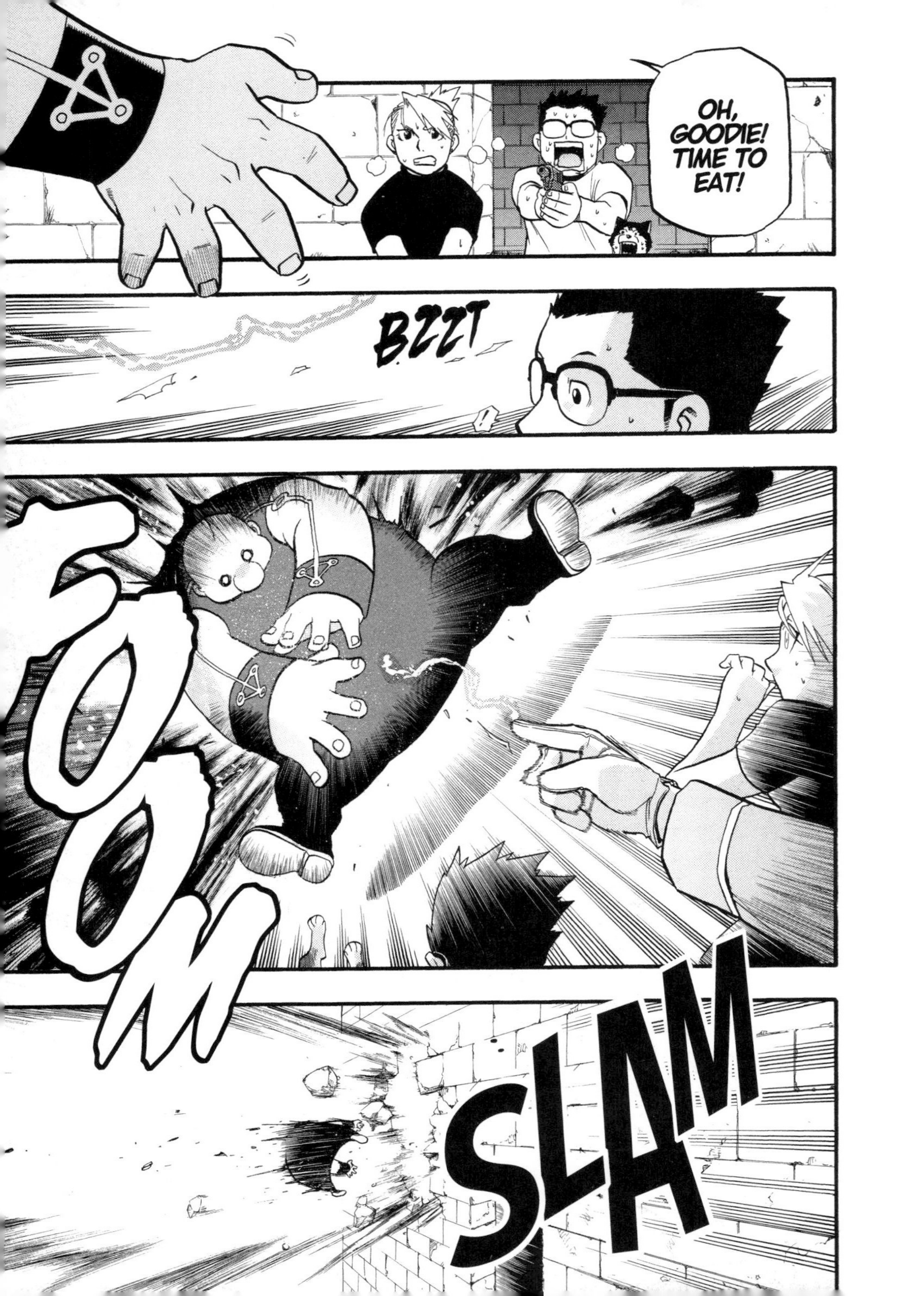
OH, GOODIE! TIME TO EAT!
BZZT
!
VOOM
SLAM

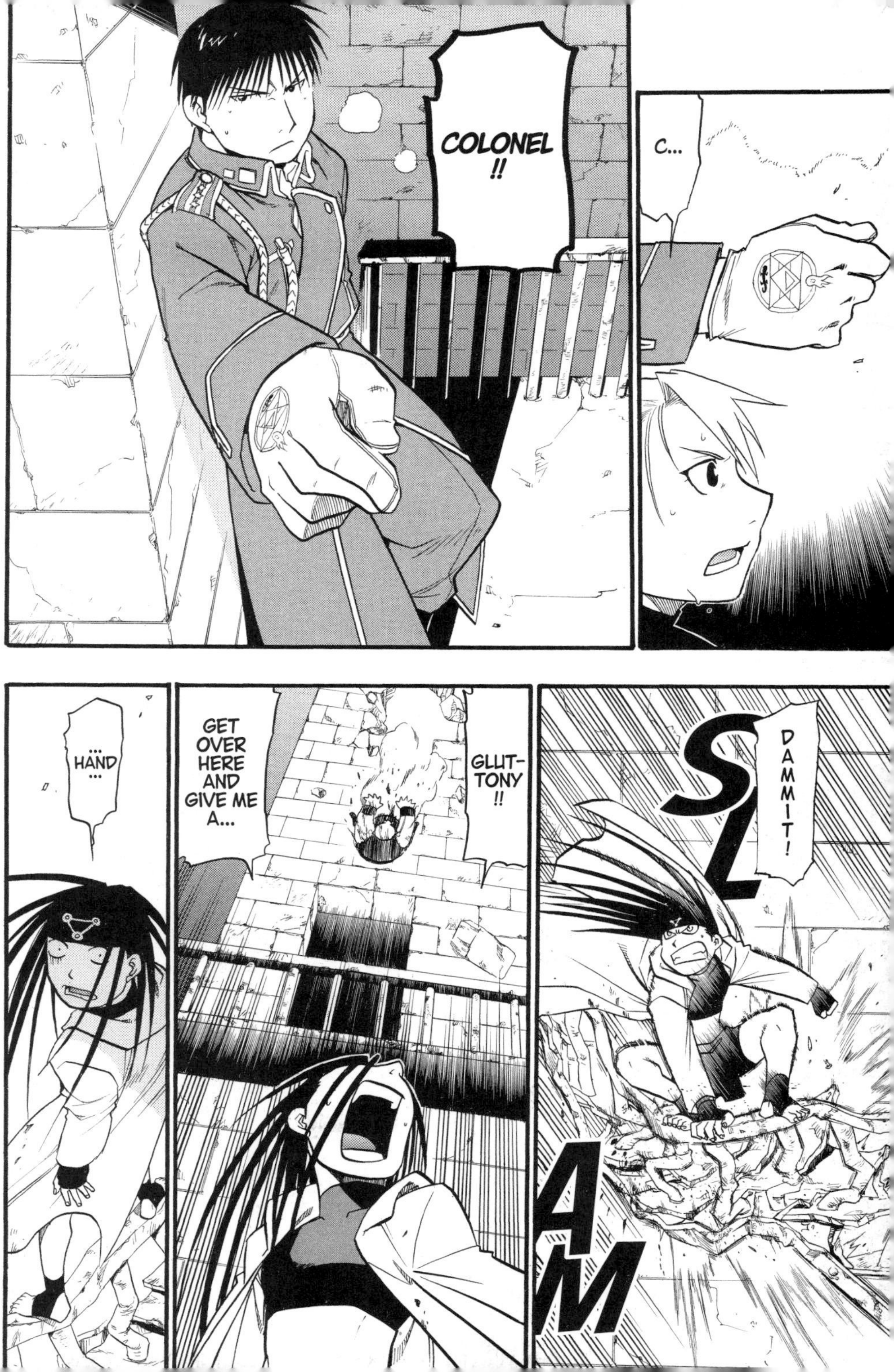
C...
COLONEL !!
DAMMIT!
SLAM
GLUT-TONY !!
GET OVER HERE AND GIVE ME A...
... HAND ...

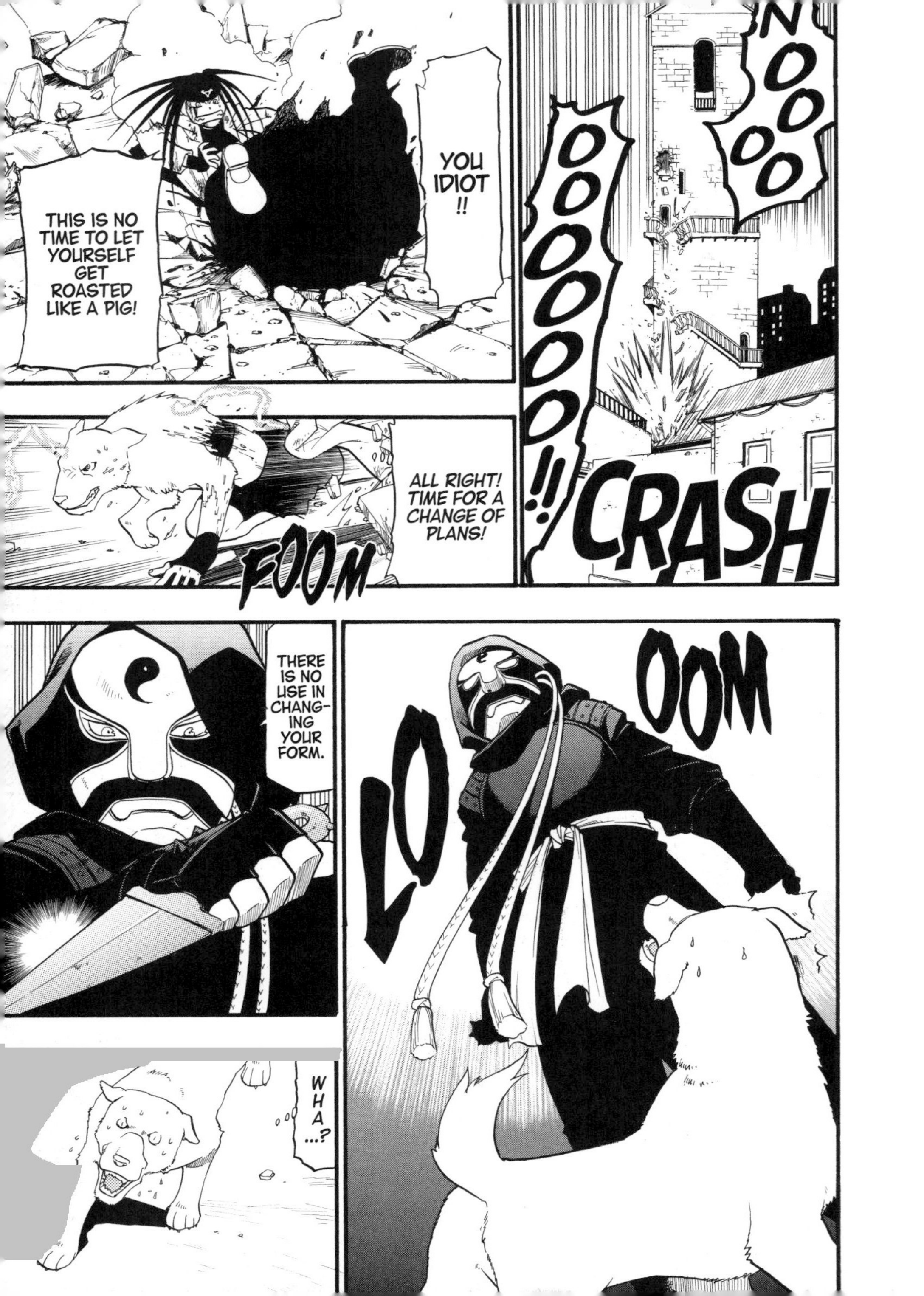
NOOOOOO
OOOOOOO!!
CRASH
YOU IDIOT!!
THIS IS NO TIME TO LET YOURSELF GET ROASTED LIKE A PIG!
ALL RIGHT! TIME FOR A CHANGE OF PLANS!
FOOM
LOOOM
THERE IS NO USE IN CHANGING YOUR FORM.
WHA...?

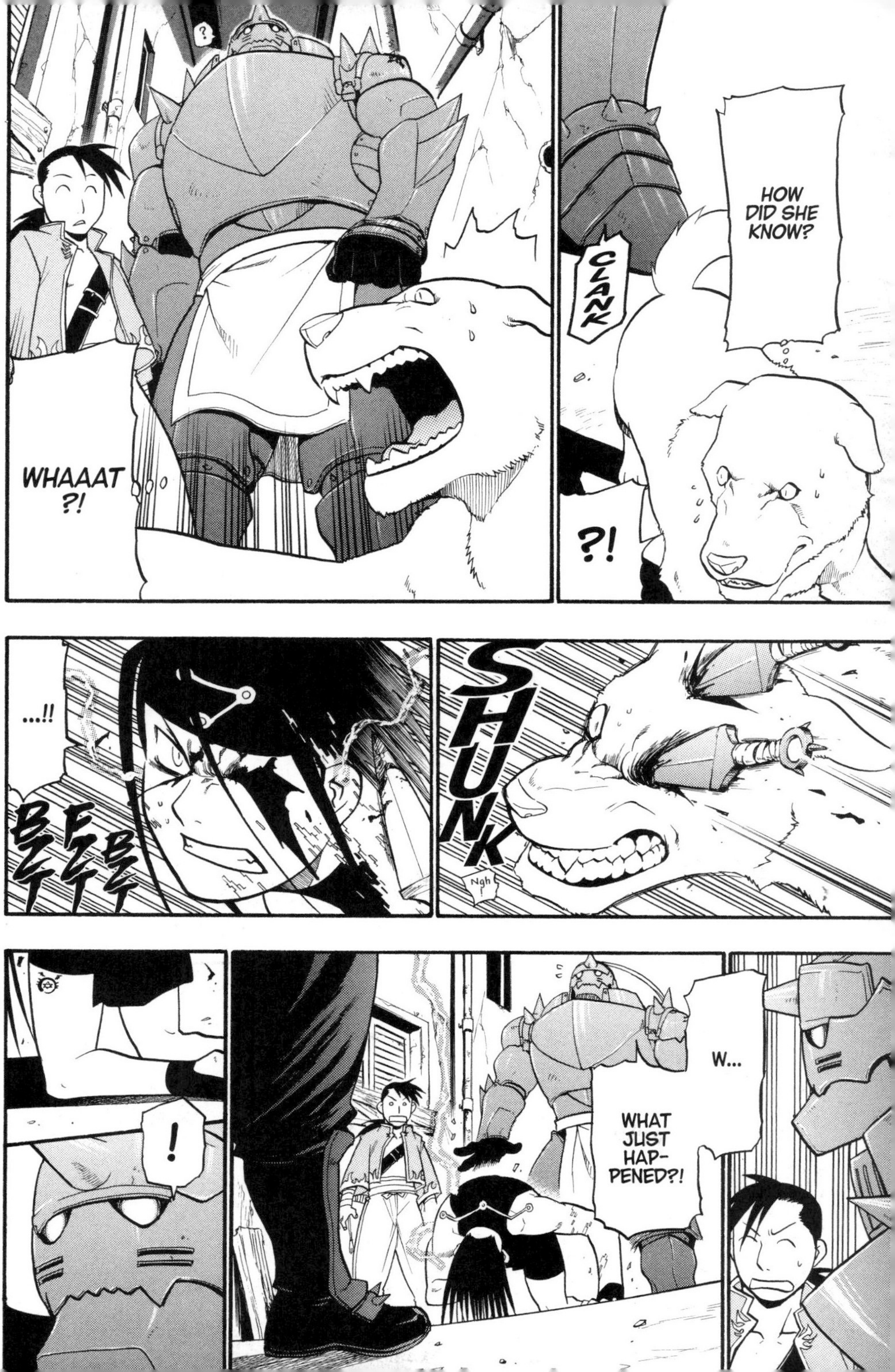
HOW DID SHE KNOW?
CLANK
?!
?
WHAAAT ?!
SHUNK
Ngh !
...!!
W...
WHAT JUST HAP-PENED?!
!

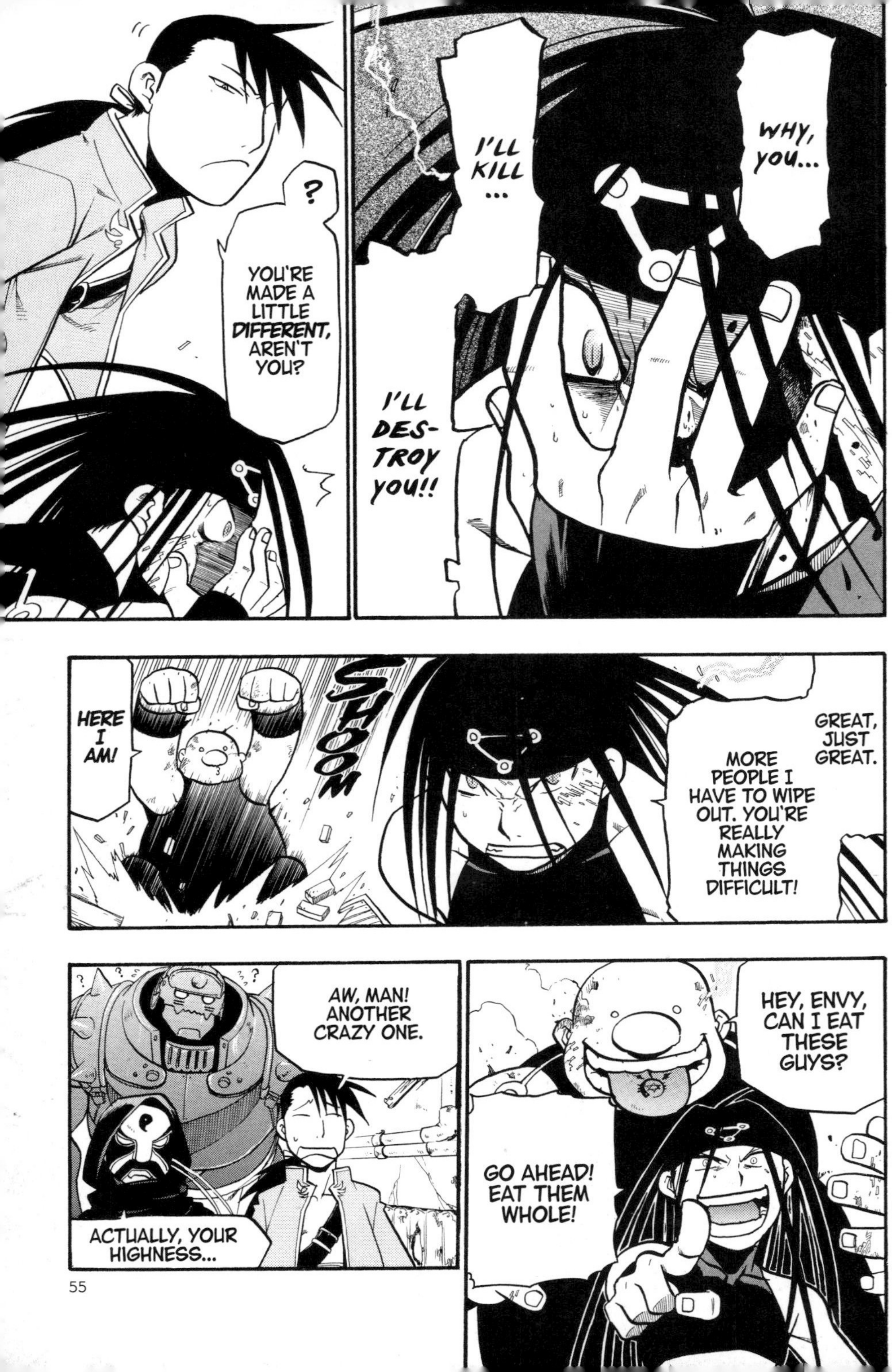
WHY, YOU...
I'LL KILL...
I'LL DES-TROY YOU!!
?
YOU'RE MADE A LITTLE DIFFERENT, AREN'T YOU?
GREAT, JUST GREAT.
MORE PEOPLE I HAVE TO WIPE OUT. YOU'RE REALLY MAKING THINGS DIFFICULT!
SHOOM
HERE I AM!
HEY, ENVY, CAN I EAT THESE GUYS?
GO AHEAD! EAT THEM WHOLE!
AW, MAN! ANOTHER CRAZY ONE.
ACTUALLY, YOUR HIGHNESS...

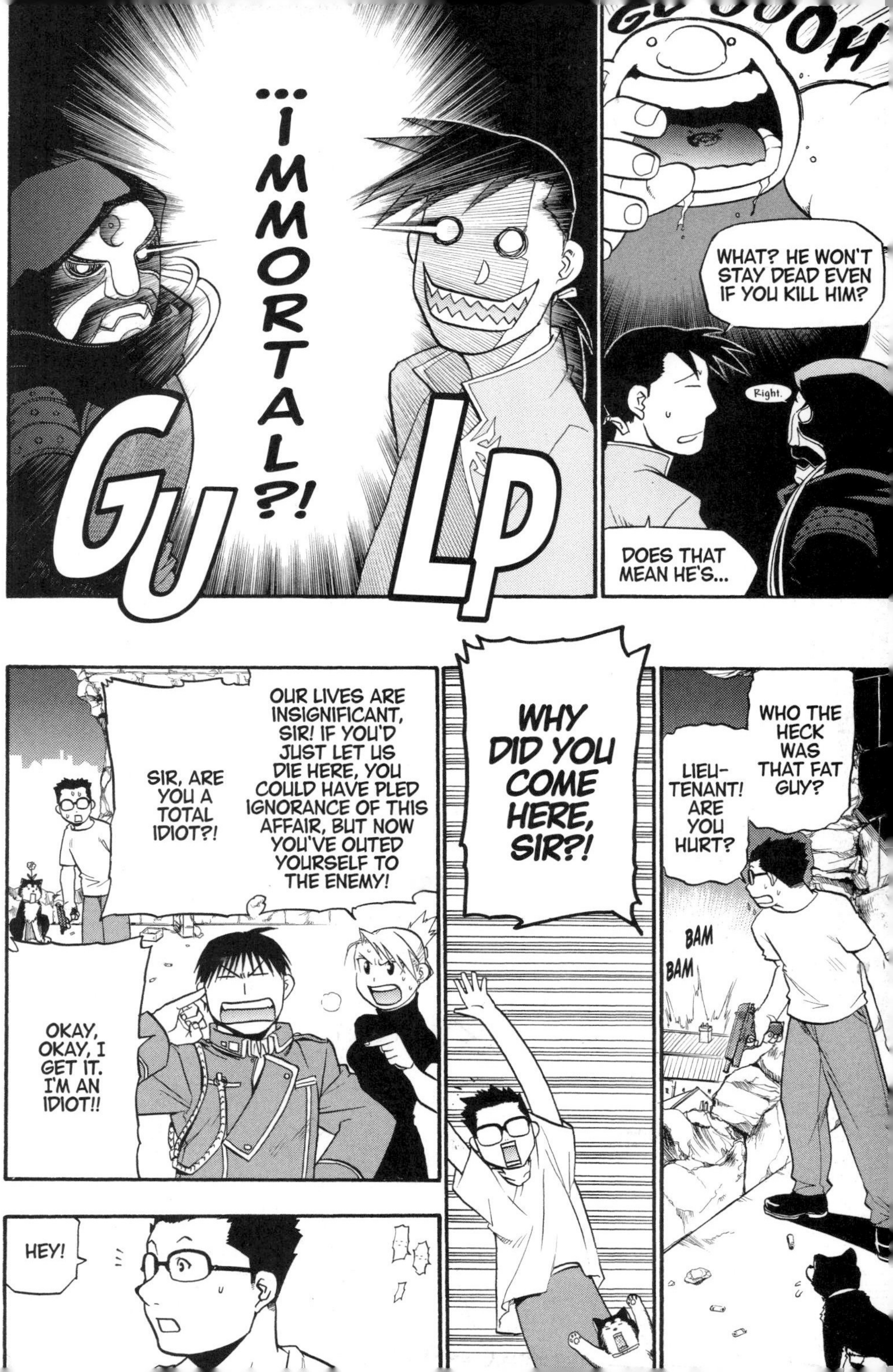
WHAT? HE WON'T STAY DEAD EVEN IF YOU KILL HIM?
Right.
DOES THAT MEAN HE'S...
...IMMORTAL?!
GULP
WHO THE HECK WAS THAT FAT GUY?
LIEU-TENANT! ARE YOU HURT?
BAM
BAM
WHY DID YOU COME HERE, SIR?!
OUR LIVES ARE INSIGNIFICANT, SIR! IF YOU'D JUST LET US DIE HERE, YOU COULD HAVE PLED IGNORANCE OF THIS AFFAIR, BUT NOW YOU'VE OUTED YOURSELF TO THE ENEMY!
SIR, ARE YOU A TOTAL IDIOT?!
OKAY, OKAY, I GET IT. I'M AN IDIOT!!
HEY!

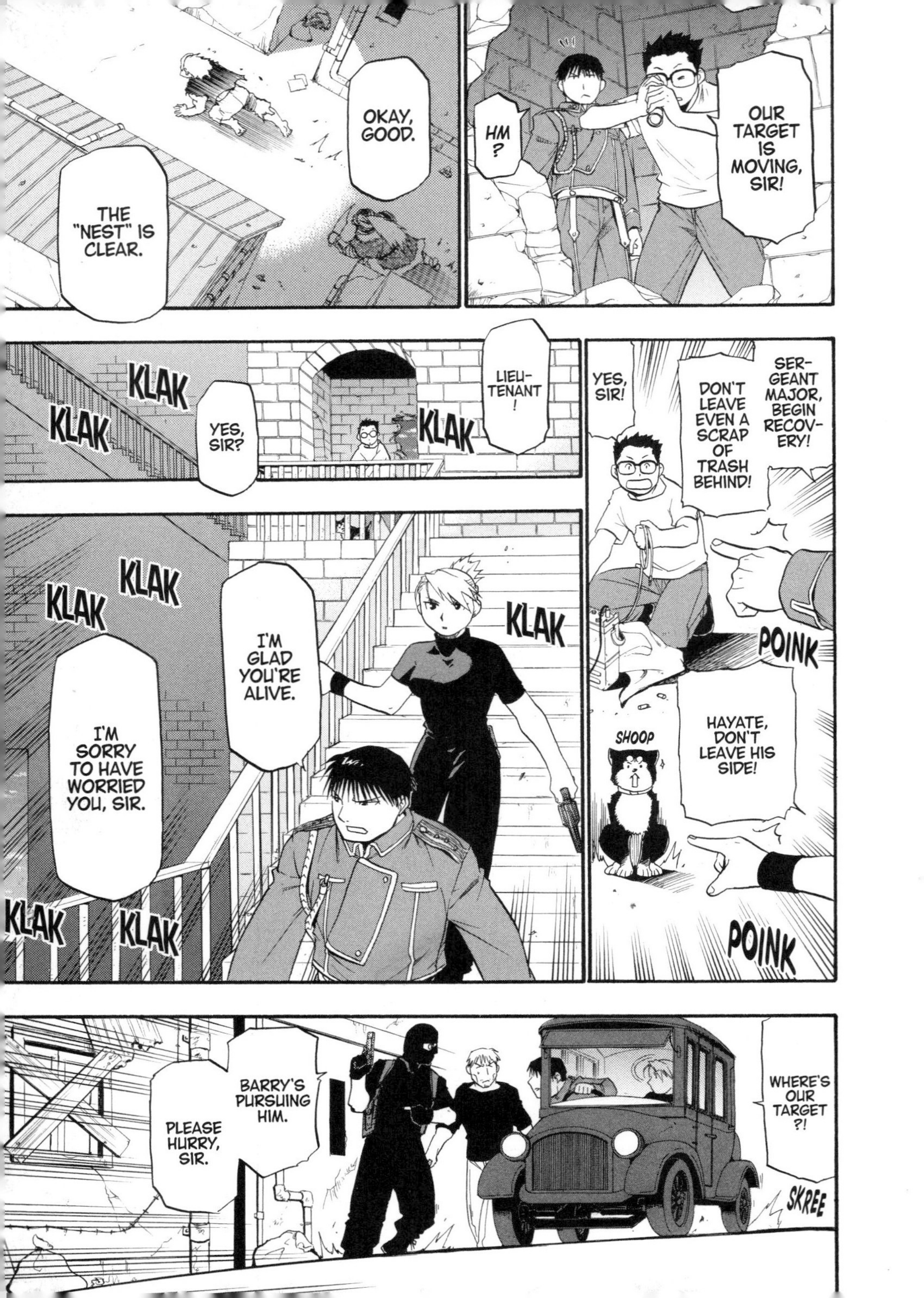
THE "NEST" IS CLEAR.
OKAY, GOOD.
OUR TARGET IS MOVING, SIR!
HM?
LIEU-TENANT!
YES, SIR?
KLAK KLAK KLAK
I'M GLAD YOU'RE ALIVE.
I'M SORRY TO HAVE WORRIED YOU, SIR.
KLAK KLAK KLAK KLAK KLAK
SER-GEANT MAJOR, BEGIN RECOV-ERY!
DON'T LEAVE EVEN A SCRAP OF TRASH BEHIND!
YES, SIR!
POINK
HAYATE, DON'T LEAVE HIS SIDE!
SHOOP
POINK
WHERE'S OUR TARGET?!
SKREE
BARRY'S PURSUING HIM.
PLEASE HURRY, SIR.

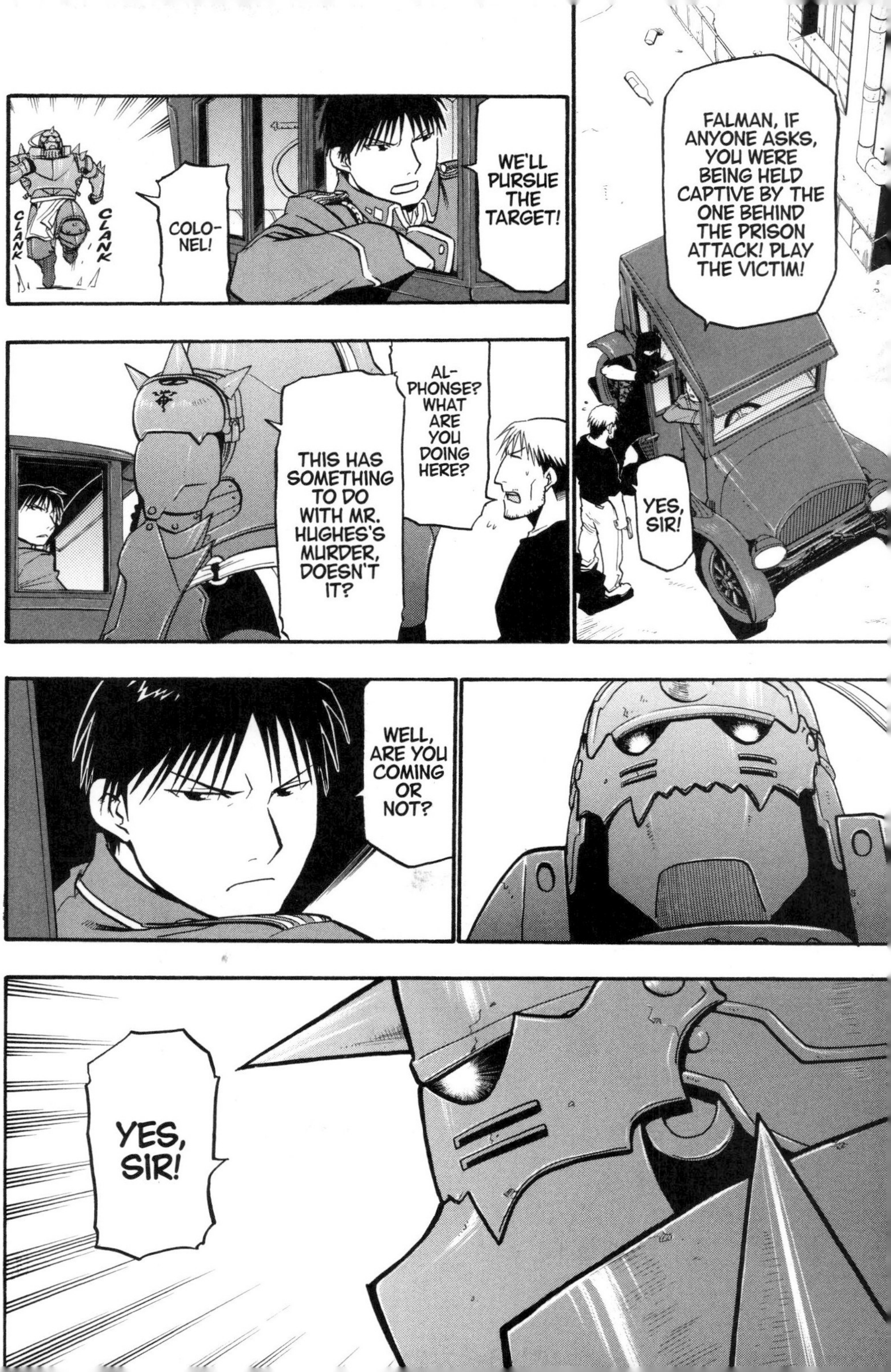
FALMAN, IF ANYONE ASKS, YOU WERE BEING HELD CAPTIVE BY THE ONE BEHIND THE PRISON ATTACK! PLAY THE VICTIM!
YES, SIR!
WE'LL PURSUE THE TARGET!
COLO-NEL!
CLANK
CLANK
AL-PHONSE? WHAT ARE YOU DOING HERE?
THIS HAS SOMETHING TO DO WITH MR. HUGHES'S MURDER, DOESN'T IT?
WELL, ARE YOU COMING OR NOT?
YES, SIR!

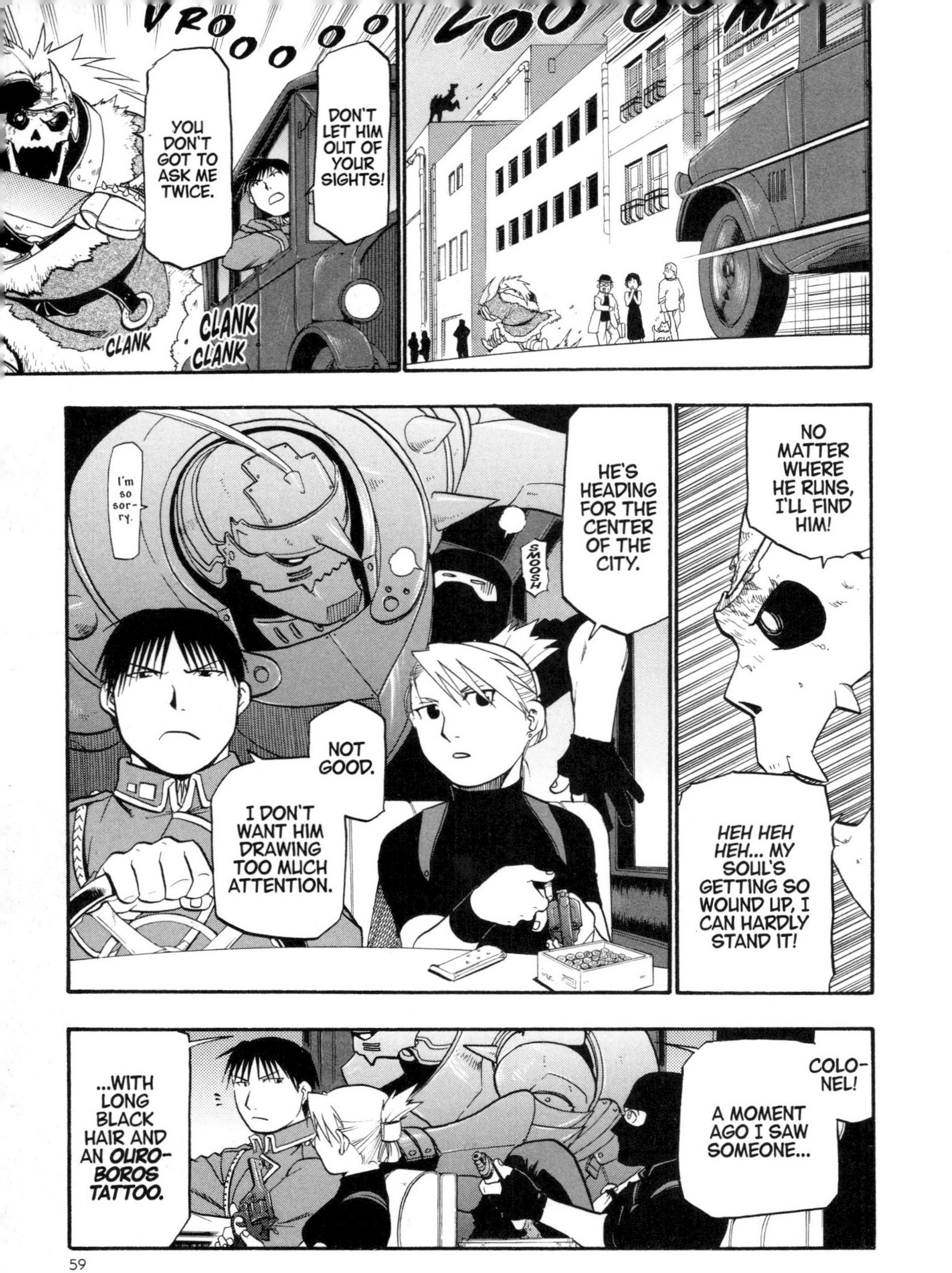
VROOOOOO
DON'T LET HIM OUT OF YOUR SIGHTS!
YOU DON'T GOT TO ASK ME TWICE.
CLANK CLANK
CLANK
NO MATTER WHERE HE RUNS, I'LL FIND HIM!
HEH HEH HEH... MY SOUL'S GETTING SO WOUND UP, I CAN HARDLY STAND IT!
HE'S HEADING FOR THE CENTER OF THE CITY.
SMOOSH
I'm so sorry.
NOT GOOD.
I DON'T WANT HIM DRAWING TOO MUCH ATTENTION.
COLONEL!
A MOMENT AGO I SAW SOMEONE...
...WITH LONG BLACK HAIR AND AN OUROBOROS TATTOO.

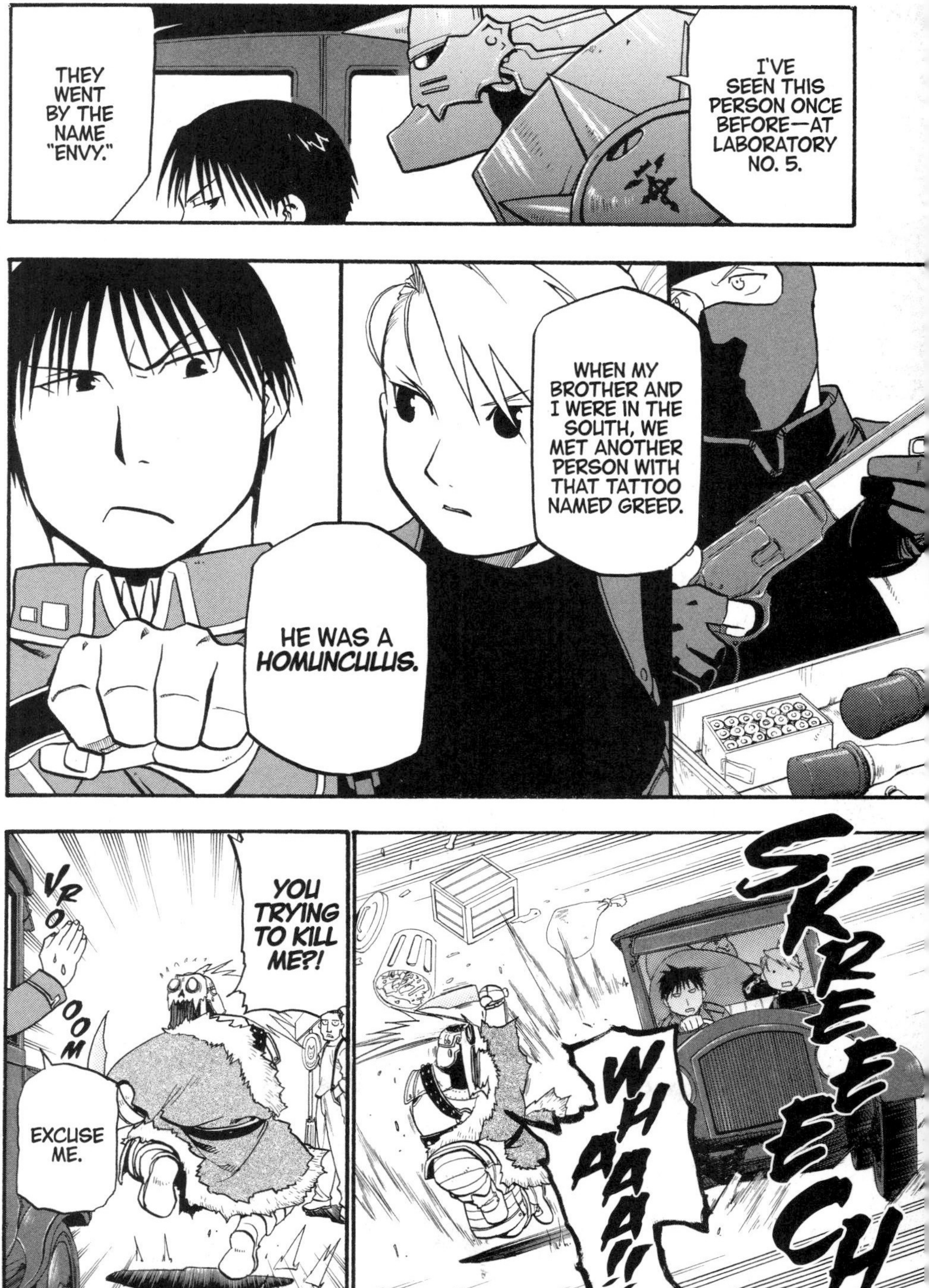
I'VE SEEN THIS PERSON ONCE BEFORE—AT LABORATORY NO. 5.
THEY WENT BY THE NAME "ENVY."
WHEN MY BROTHER AND I WERE IN THE SOUTH, WE MET ANOTHER PERSON WITH THAT TATTOO NAMED GREED.
HE WAS A *HOMUNCULUS.*
SKREEECH
WHAAAA!!
YOU TRYING TO KILL ME?!
VROOOOM
EXCUSE ME.

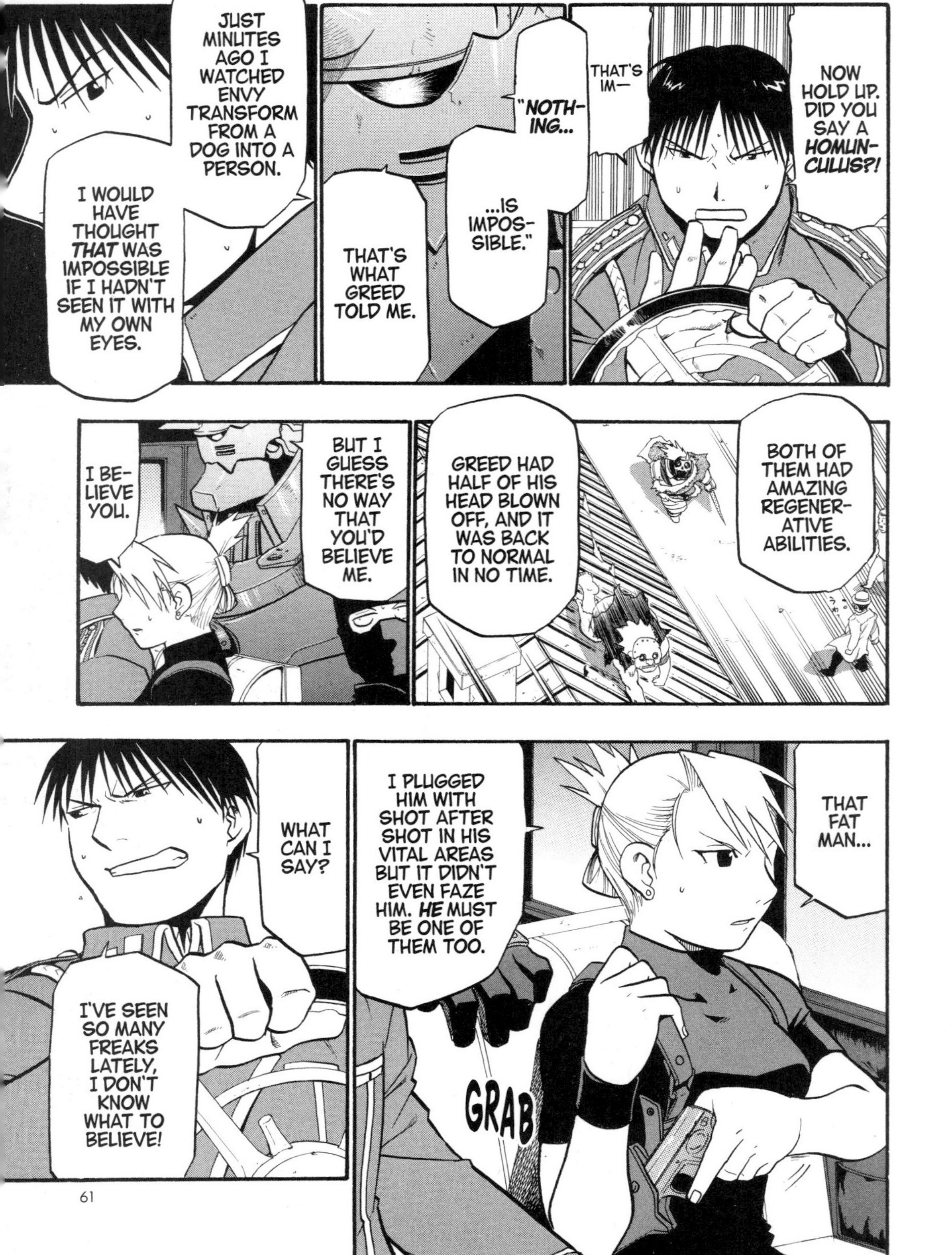
NOW HOLD UP. DID YOU SAY A *HOMUNCULUS?!*
THAT'S IM—
"*NOTHING...*
...IS IMPOSSIBLE."
THAT'S WHAT GREED TOLD ME.
JUST MINUTES AGO I WATCHED ENVY TRANSFORM FROM A DOG INTO A PERSON.
I WOULD HAVE THOUGHT *THAT* WAS IMPOSSIBLE IF I HADN'T SEEN IT WITH MY OWN EYES.
BOTH OF THEM HAD AMAZING REGENERATIVE ABILITIES.
GREED HAD HALF OF HIS HEAD BLOWN OFF, AND IT WAS BACK TO NORMAL IN NO TIME.
BUT I GUESS THERE'S NO WAY THAT YOU'D BELIEVE ME.
I BELIEVE YOU.
THAT FAT MAN...
I PLUGGED HIM WITH SHOT AFTER SHOT IN HIS VITAL AREAS BUT IT DIDN'T EVEN FAZE HIM. *HE* MUST BE ONE OF THEM TOO.
GRAB
WHAT CAN I SAY?
I'VE SEEN SO MANY FREAKS LATELY, I DON'T KNOW WHAT TO BELIEVE!

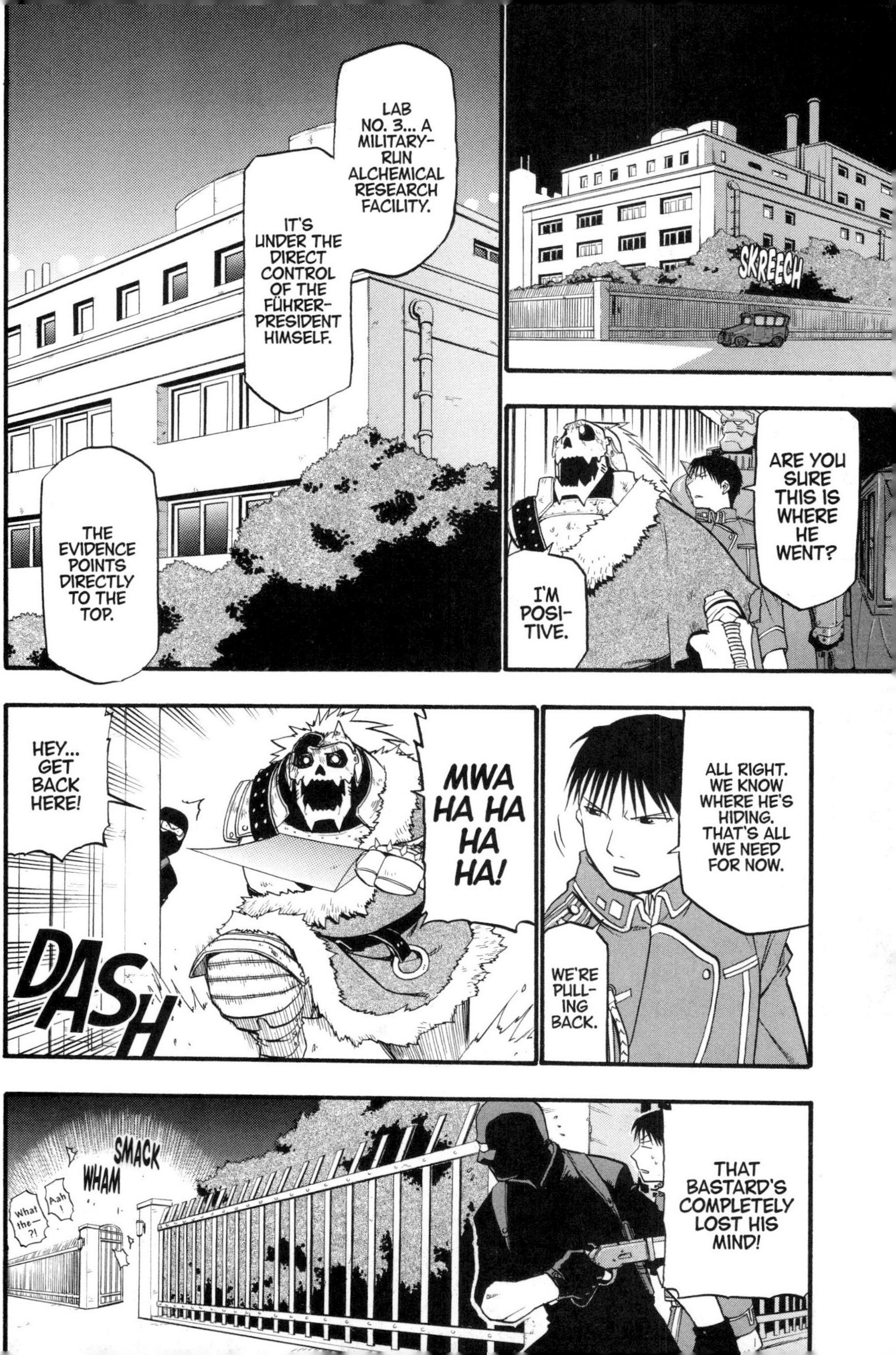
SKREECH
ARE YOU SURE THIS IS WHERE HE WENT?
I'M POSITIVE.
LAB NO. 3... A MILITARY-RUN ALCHEMICAL RESEARCH FACILITY.
IT'S UNDER THE DIRECT CONTROL OF THE FÜHRER-PRESIDENT HIMSELF.
THE EVIDENCE POINTS DIRECTLY TO THE TOP.
ALL RIGHT. WE KNOW WHERE HE'S HIDING. THAT'S ALL WE NEED FOR NOW.
WE'RE PULLING BACK.
MWA HA HA HA HA HA!
HEY... GET BACK HERE!
DASH
THAT BASTARD'S COMPLETELY LOST HIS MIND!
SMACK
WHAM
Aah!
What the—?!

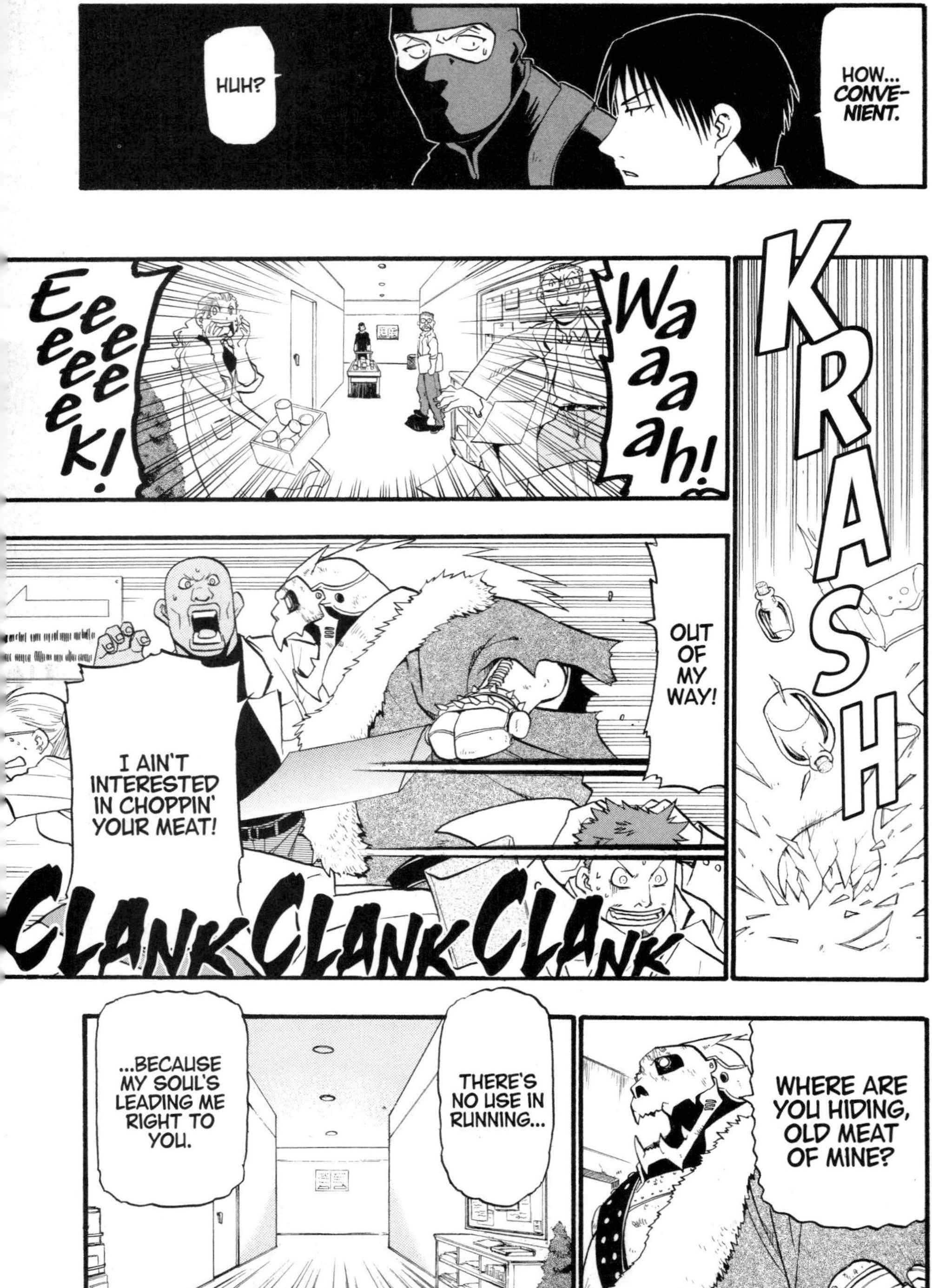
HOW... CONVE-NIENT.
HUH?
KRASH
Waaaah!
Eeeeeeek!
OUT OF MY WAY!
I AIN'T INTERESTED IN CHOPPIN' YOUR MEAT!
CLANK CLANK CLANK
WHERE ARE YOU HIDING, OLD MEAT OF MINE?
THERE'S NO USE IN RUNNING...
...BECAUSE MY SOUL'S LEADING ME RIGHT TO YOU.

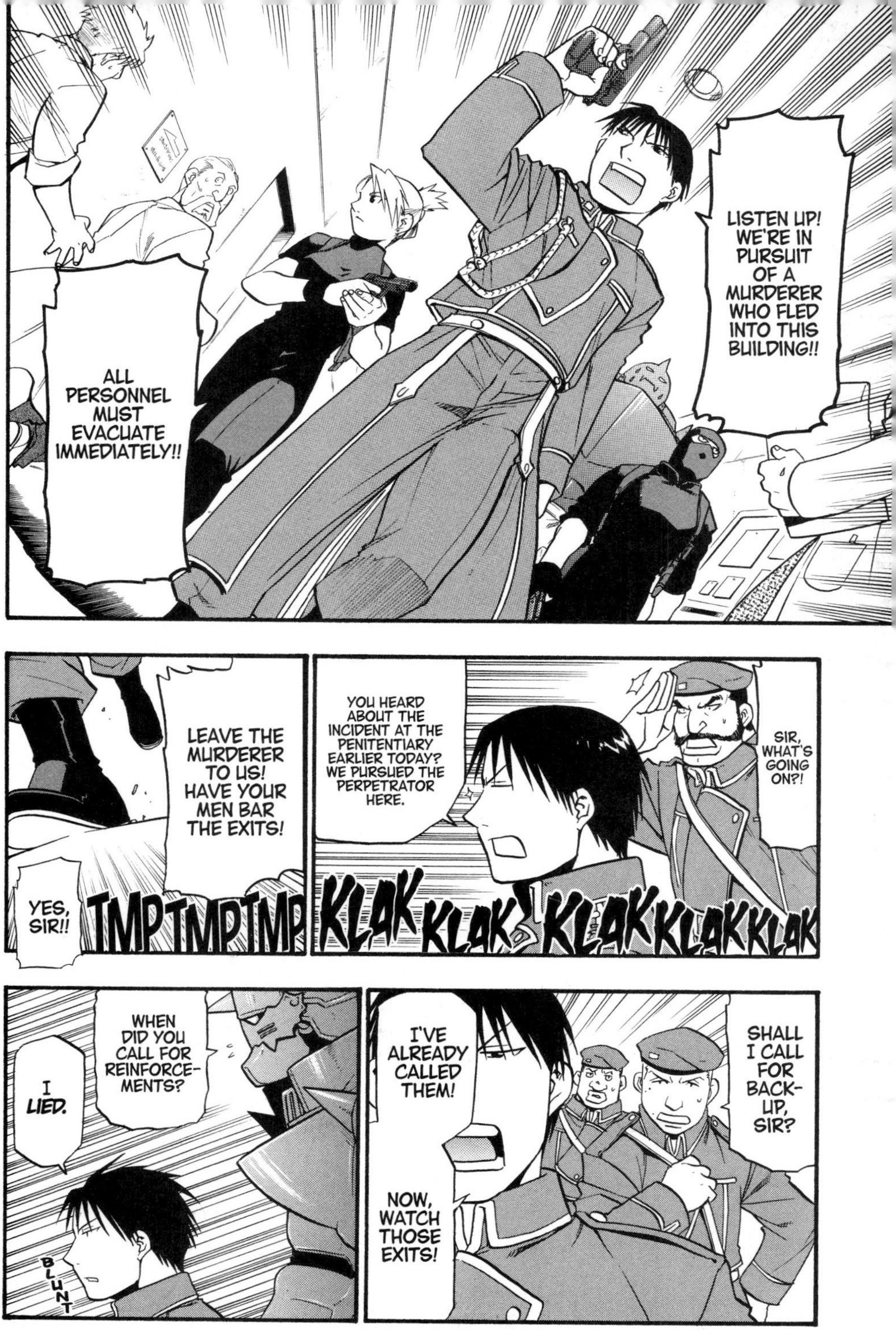
LISTEN UP! WE'RE IN PURSUIT OF A MURDERER WHO FLED INTO THIS BUILDING!!
ALL PERSONNEL MUST EVACUATE IMMEDIATELY!!
SIR, WHAT'S GOING ON?!
YOU HEARD ABOUT THE INCIDENT AT THE PENITENTIARY EARLIER TODAY? WE PURSUED THE PERPETRATOR HERE.
KLAK KLAK KLAK KLAK KLAK
LEAVE THE MURDERER TO US! HAVE YOUR MEN BAR THE EXITS!
YES, SIR!!
TMP TMP TMP
SHALL I CALL FOR BACK-UP, SIR?
I'VE ALREADY CALLED THEM!
NOW, WATCH THOSE EXITS!
WHEN DID YOU CALL FOR REINFORCEMENTS?
I LIED.
BLUNT

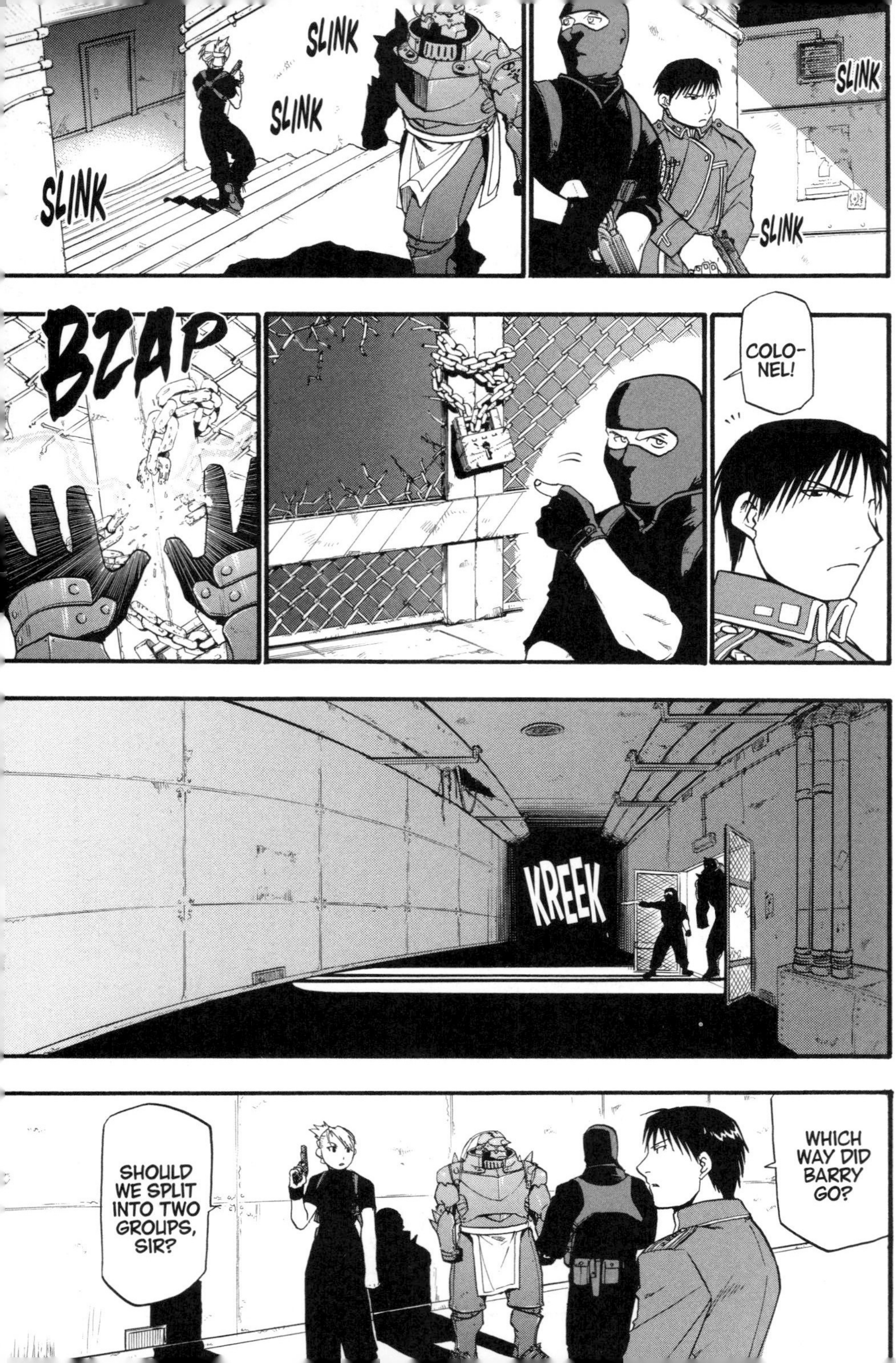
SLINK
SLINK
SLINK
SLINK
SLINK
COLO-NEL!
BZAP
KREEK
WHICH WAY DID BARRY GO?
SHOULD WE SPLIT INTO TWO GROUPS, SIR?

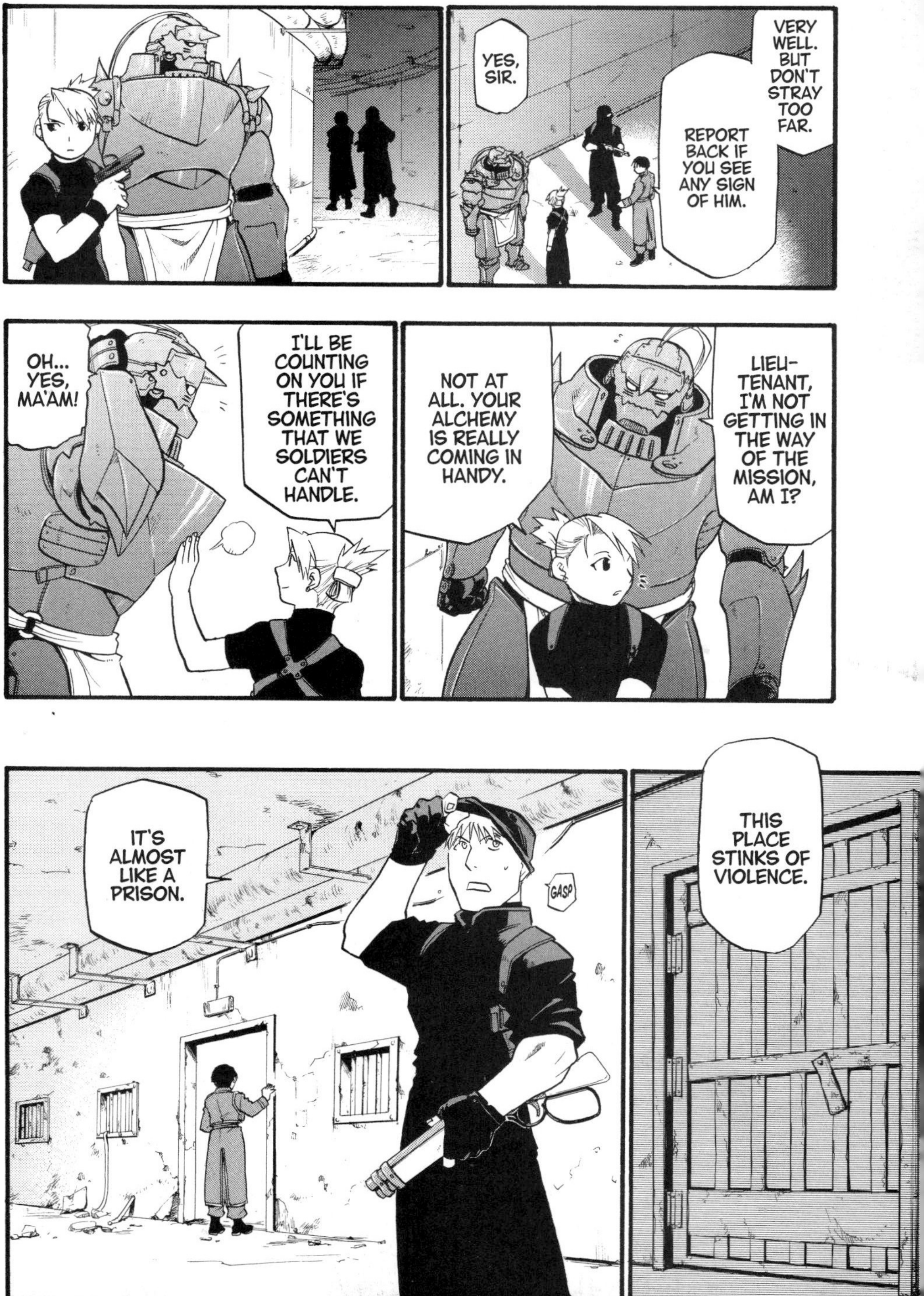
VERY WELL. BUT DON'T STRAY TOO FAR.
REPORT BACK IF YOU SEE ANY SIGN OF HIM.
YES, SIR.
LIEU-TENANT, I'M NOT GETTING IN THE WAY OF THE MISSION, AM I?
NOT AT ALL. YOUR ALCHEMY IS REALLY COMING IN HANDY.
I'LL BE COUNTING ON YOU IF THERE'S SOMETHING THAT WE SOLDIERS CAN'T HANDLE.
OH... YES, MA'AM!
THIS PLACE STINKS OF VIOLENCE.
IT'S ALMOST LIKE A PRISON.
GASP

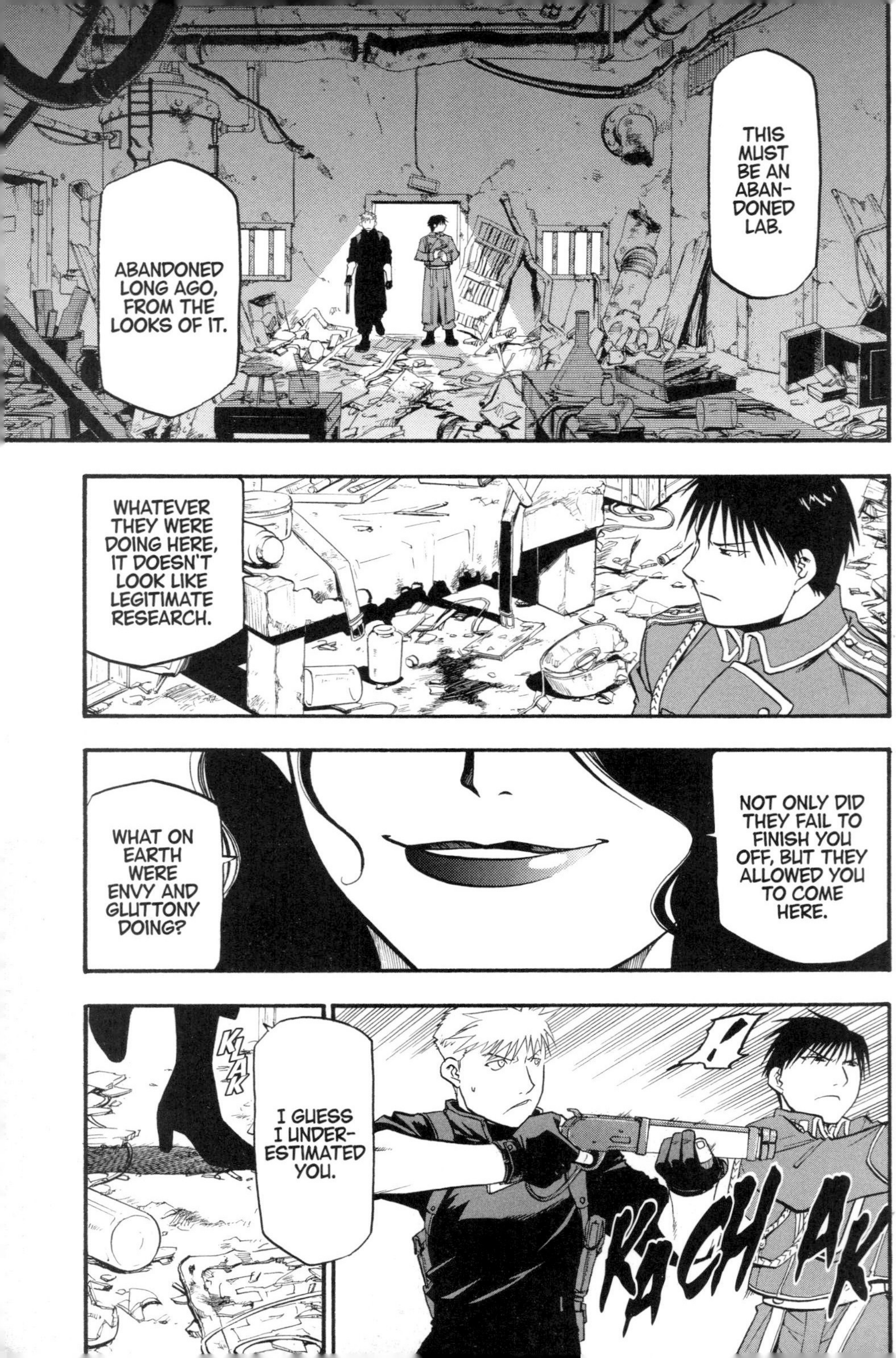
THIS MUST BE AN ABAN-DONED LAB.
ABANDONED LONG AGO, FROM THE LOOKS OF IT.
WHATEVER THEY WERE DOING HERE, IT DOESN'T LOOK LIKE LEGITIMATE RESEARCH.
NOT ONLY DID THEY FAIL TO FINISH YOU OFF, BUT THEY ALLOWED YOU TO COME HERE.
WHAT ON EARTH WERE ENVY AND GLUTTONY DOING?
!
I GUESS I UNDER-ESTIMATED YOU.
KA-CHAK
KLAK

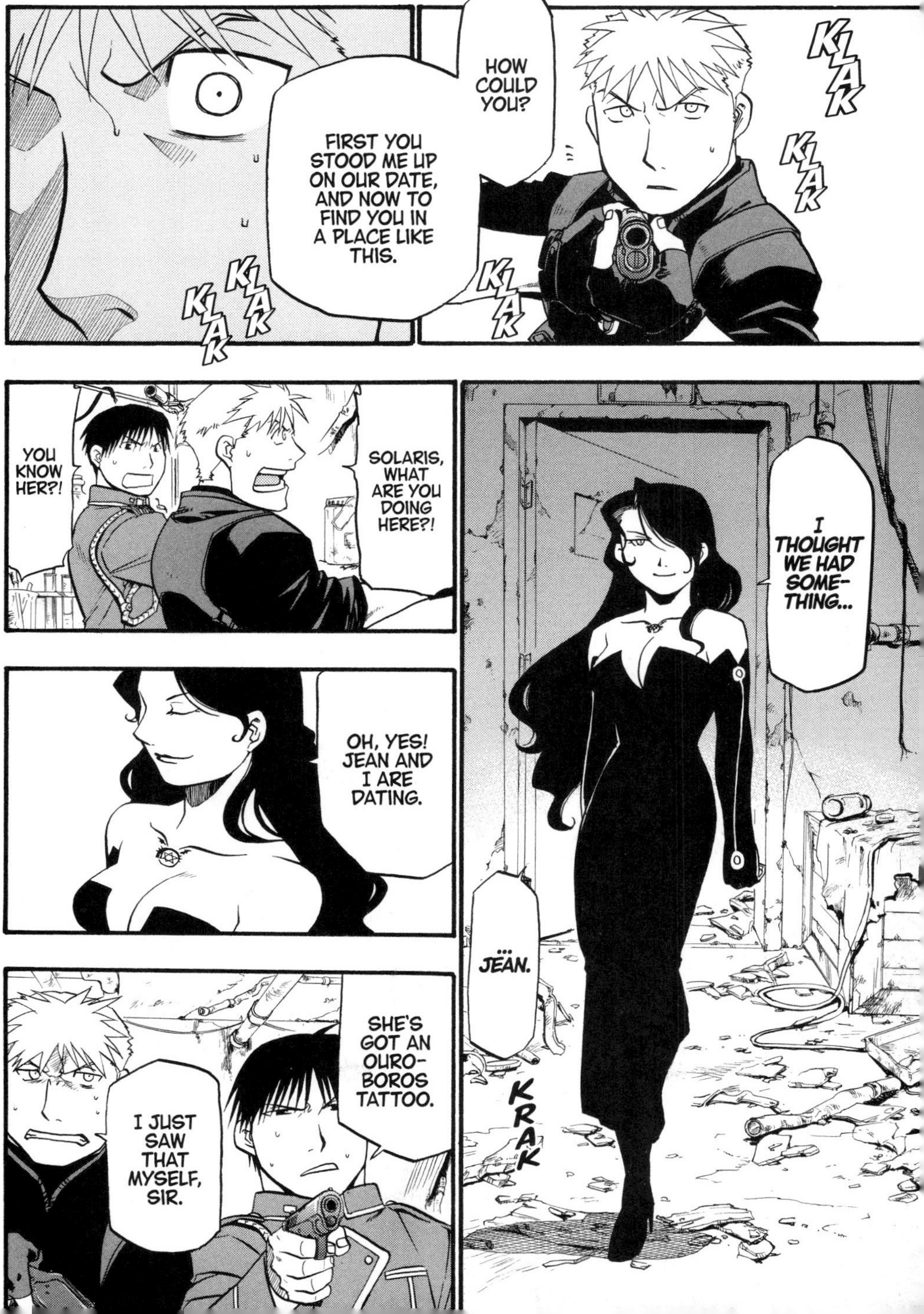
KLAK
KLAK
HOW COULD YOU?
KLAK
FIRST YOU STOOD ME UP ON OUR DATE, AND NOW TO FIND YOU IN A PLACE LIKE THIS.
KLAK
KLAK
I THOUGHT WE HAD SOME-THING...
...JEAN.
KRAK
SOLARIS, WHAT ARE YOU DOING HERE?!
YOU KNOW HER?!
OH, YES! JEAN AND I ARE DATING.
SHE'S GOT AN OURO-BOROS TATTOO.
I JUST SAW THAT MYSELF, SIR.

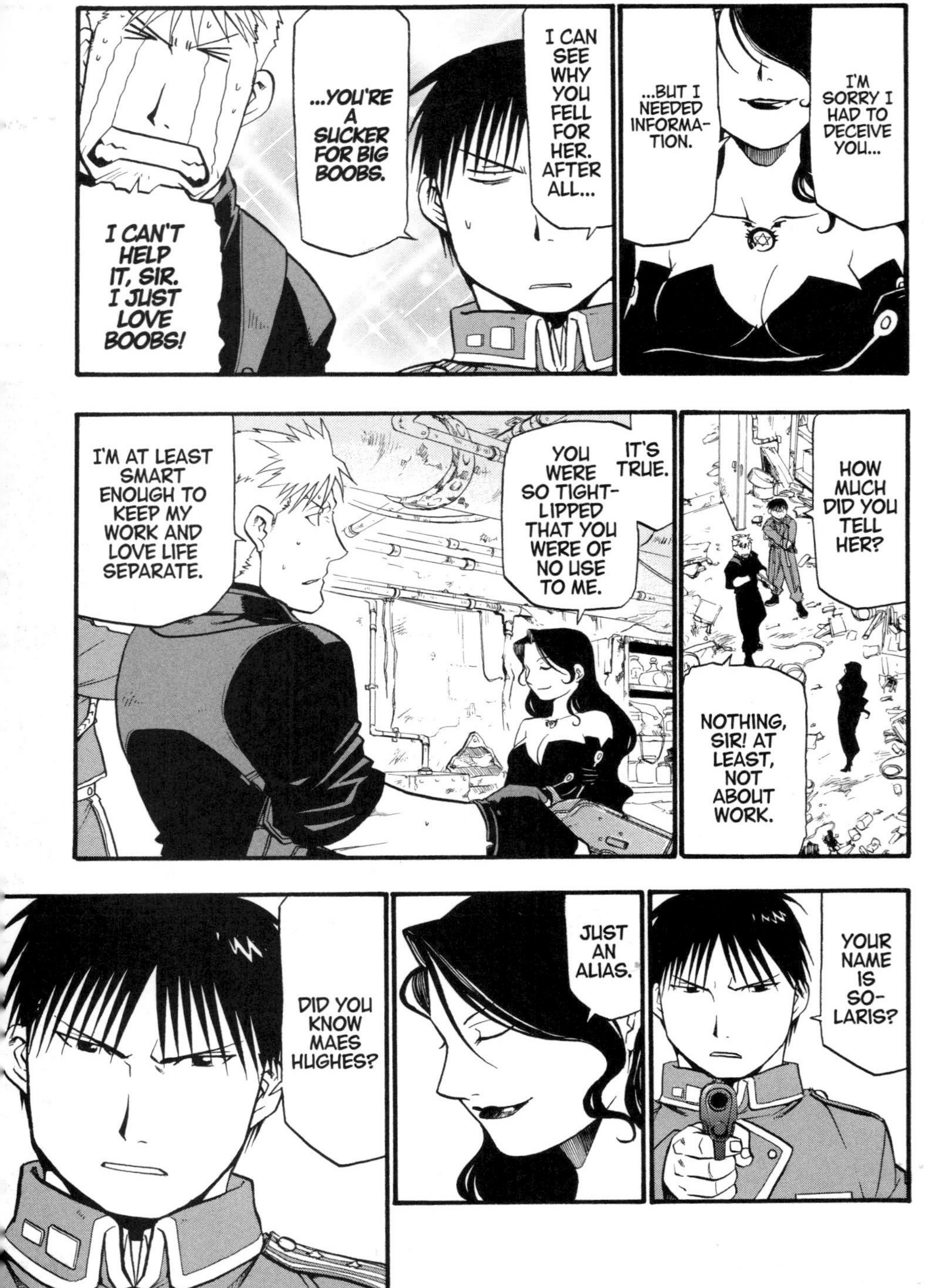
I'M SORRY I HAD TO DECEIVE YOU...
...BUT I NEEDED INFORMATION.
I CAN SEE WHY YOU FELL FOR HER. AFTER ALL...
...YOU'RE A SUCKER FOR BIG BOOBS.
I CAN'T HELP IT, SIR. I JUST LOVE BOOBS!
HOW MUCH DID YOU TELL HER?
NOTHING, SIR! AT LEAST, NOT ABOUT WORK.
IT'S TRUE.
YOU WERE SO TIGHT-LIPPED THAT YOU WERE OF NO USE TO ME.
I'M AT LEAST SMART ENOUGH TO KEEP MY WORK AND LOVE LIFE SEPARATE.
YOUR NAME IS SO-LARIS?
JUST AN ALIAS.
DID YOU KNOW MAES HUGHES?

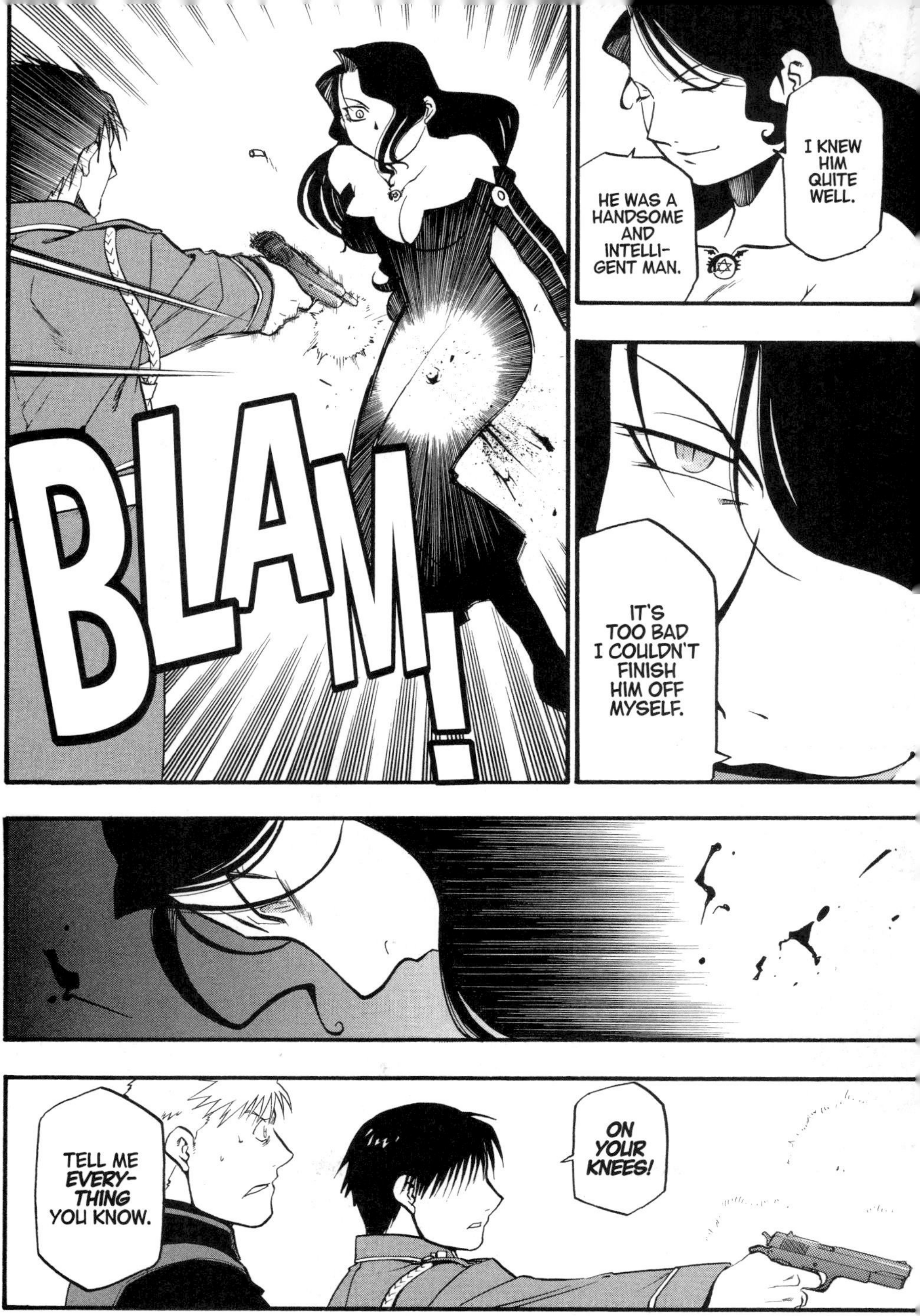
I KNEW HIM QUITE WELL.
HE WAS A HANDSOME AND INTELLIGENT MAN.
IT'S TOO BAD I COULDN'T FINISH HIM OFF MYSELF.
BLAM!
ON YOUR KNEES!
TELL ME EVERYTHING YOU KNOW.

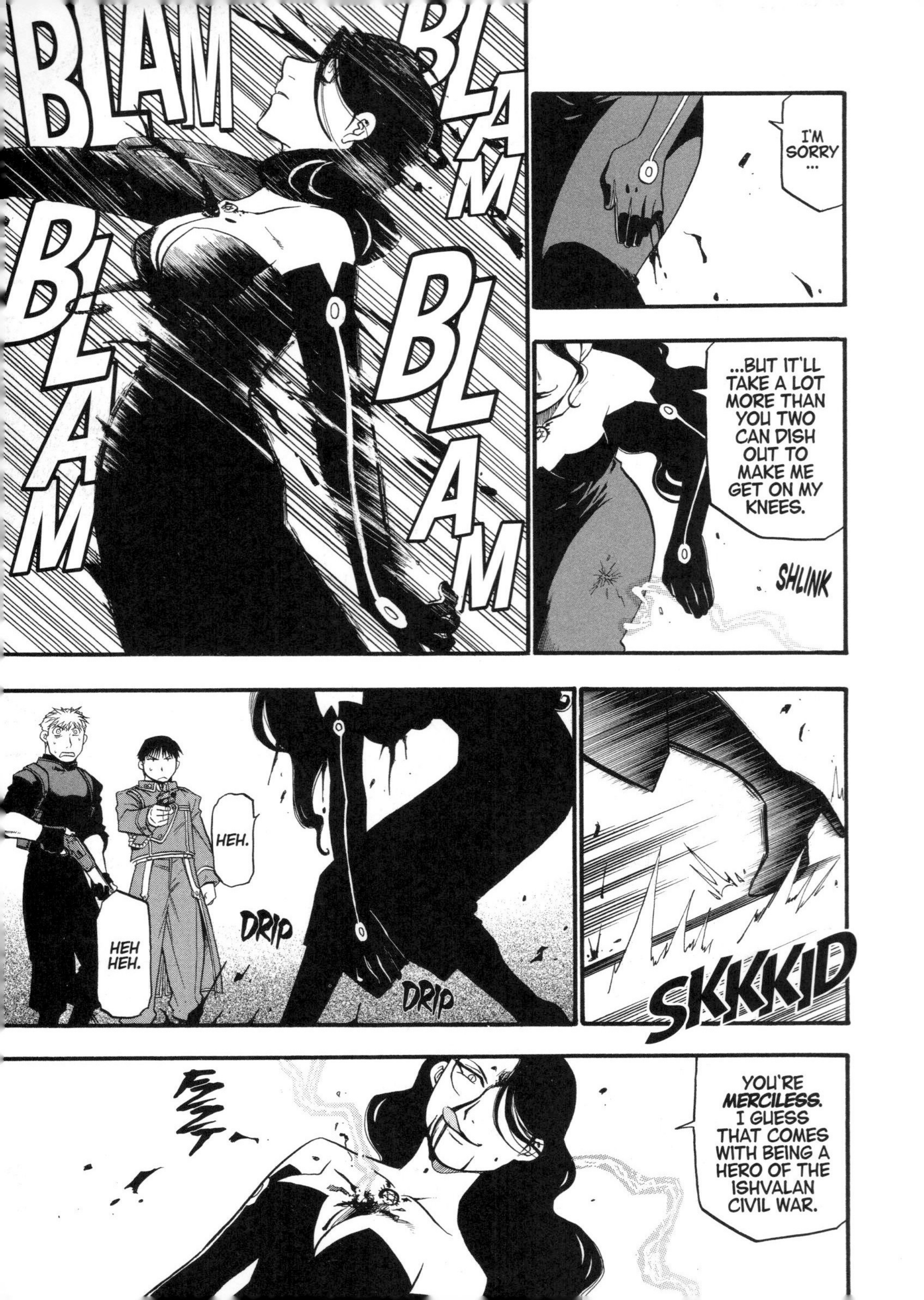
BLAM
BLAM
BLAM
BLAM
I'M SORRY...
...BUT IT'LL TAKE A LOT MORE THAN YOU TWO CAN DISH OUT TO MAKE ME GET ON MY KNEES.
SHLINK
HEH.
HEH HEH.
DRIP
DRIP
SKKKID
YOU'RE MERCILESS. I GUESS THAT COMES WITH BEING A HERO OF THE ISHVALAN CIVIL WAR.

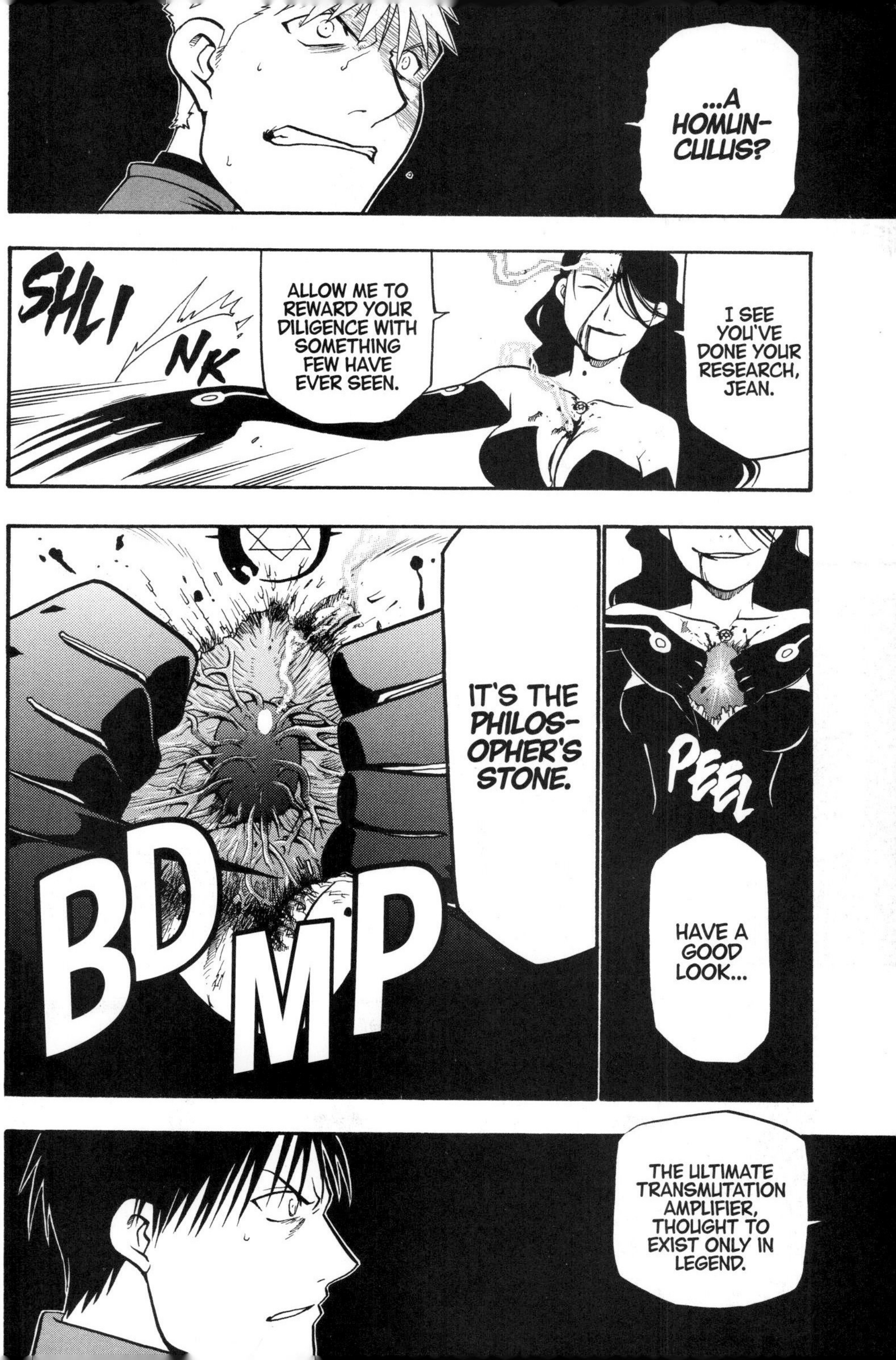
...A HOMUN-CULUS?
I SEE YOU'VE DONE YOUR RESEARCH, JEAN.
ALLOW ME TO REWARD YOUR DILIGENCE WITH SOMETHING FEW HAVE EVER SEEN.
SHLINK
PEEL
HAVE A GOOD LOOK...
IT'S THE PHILOS-OPHER'S STONE.
BDMP
THE ULTIMATE TRANSMUTATION AMPLIFIER, THOUGHT TO EXIST ONLY IN LEGEND.

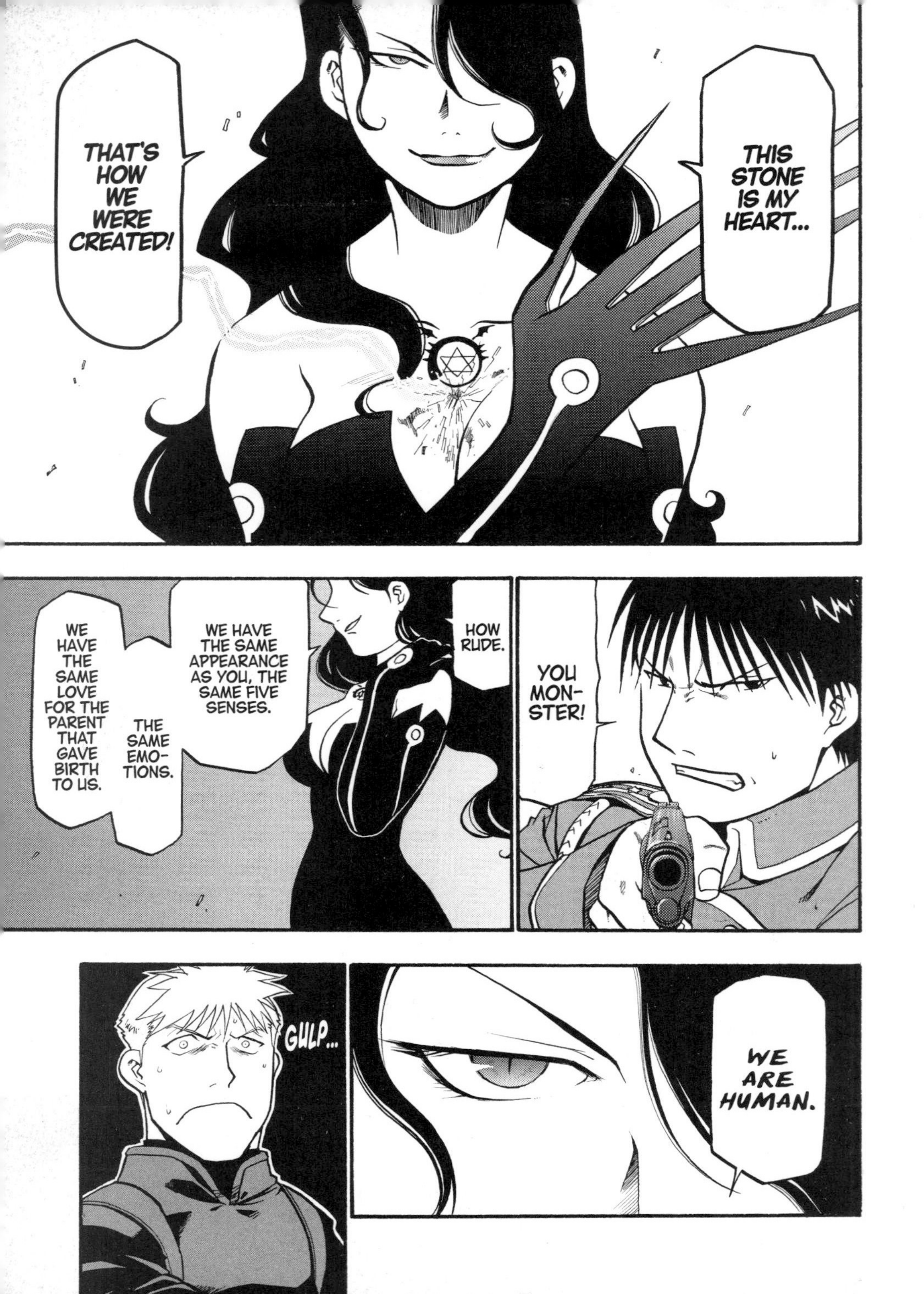
THIS STONE IS MY HEART...
THAT'S HOW WE WERE CREATED!
YOU MONSTER!
HOW RUDE.
WE HAVE THE SAME APPEARANCE AS YOU, THE SAME FIVE SENSES.
THE SAME EMOTIONS.
WE HAVE THE SAME LOVE FOR THE PARENT THAT GAVE BIRTH TO US.
WE ARE HUMAN.
GULP...

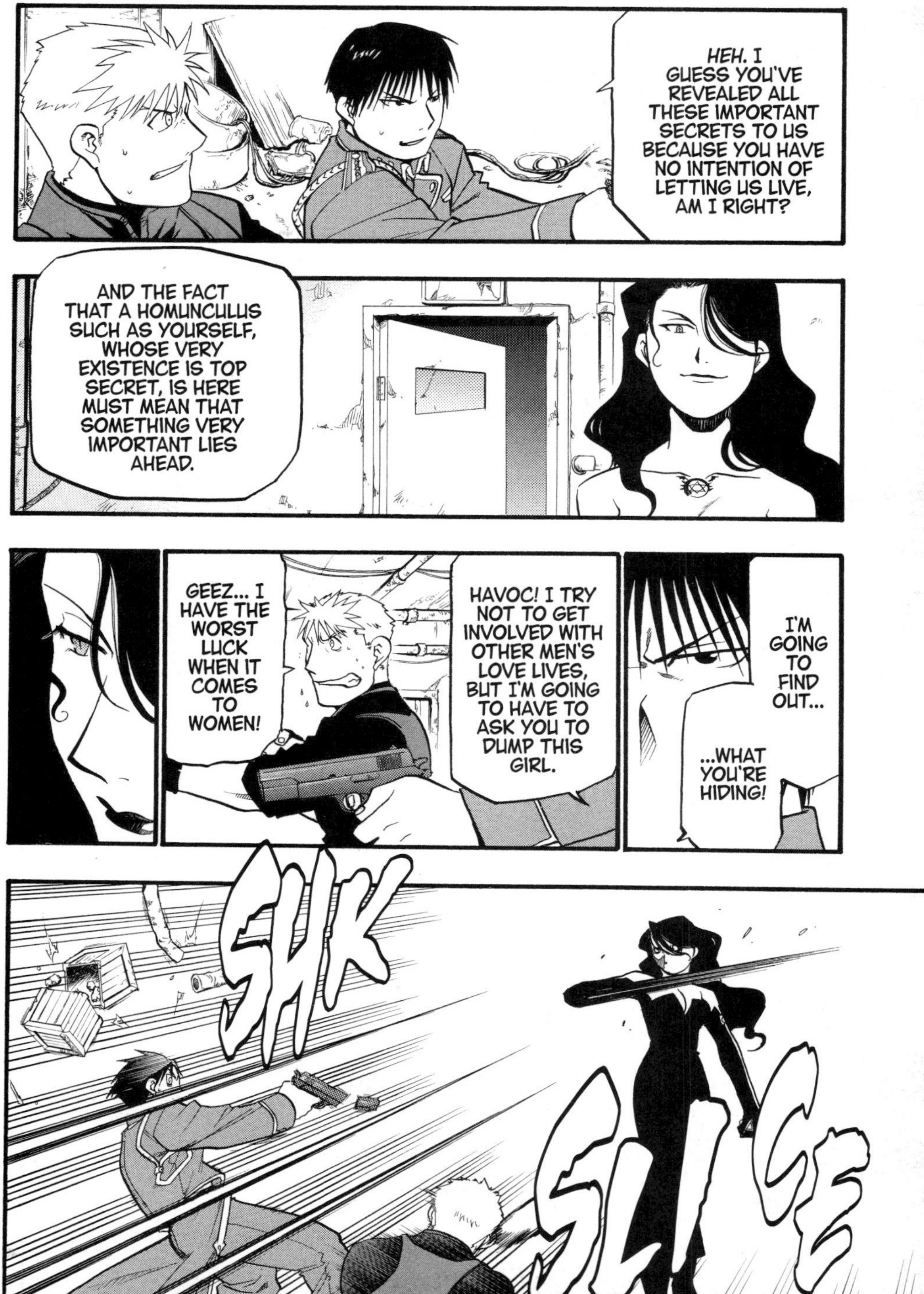
HEH. I GUESS YOU'VE REVEALED ALL THESE IMPORTANT SECRETS TO US BECAUSE YOU HAVE NO INTENTION OF LETTING US LIVE, AM I RIGHT?
AND THE FACT THAT A HOMUNCULUS SUCH AS YOURSELF, WHOSE VERY EXISTENCE IS TOP SECRET, IS HERE MUST MEAN THAT SOMETHING VERY IMPORTANT LIES AHEAD.
I'M GOING TO FIND OUT...
...WHAT YOU'RE HIDING!
HAVOC! I TRY NOT TO GET INVOLVED WITH OTHER MEN'S LOVE LIVES, BUT I'M GOING TO HAVE TO ASK YOU TO DUMP THIS GIRL.
GEEZ... I HAVE THE WORST LUCK WHEN IT COMES TO WOMEN!
SHK
SLICE

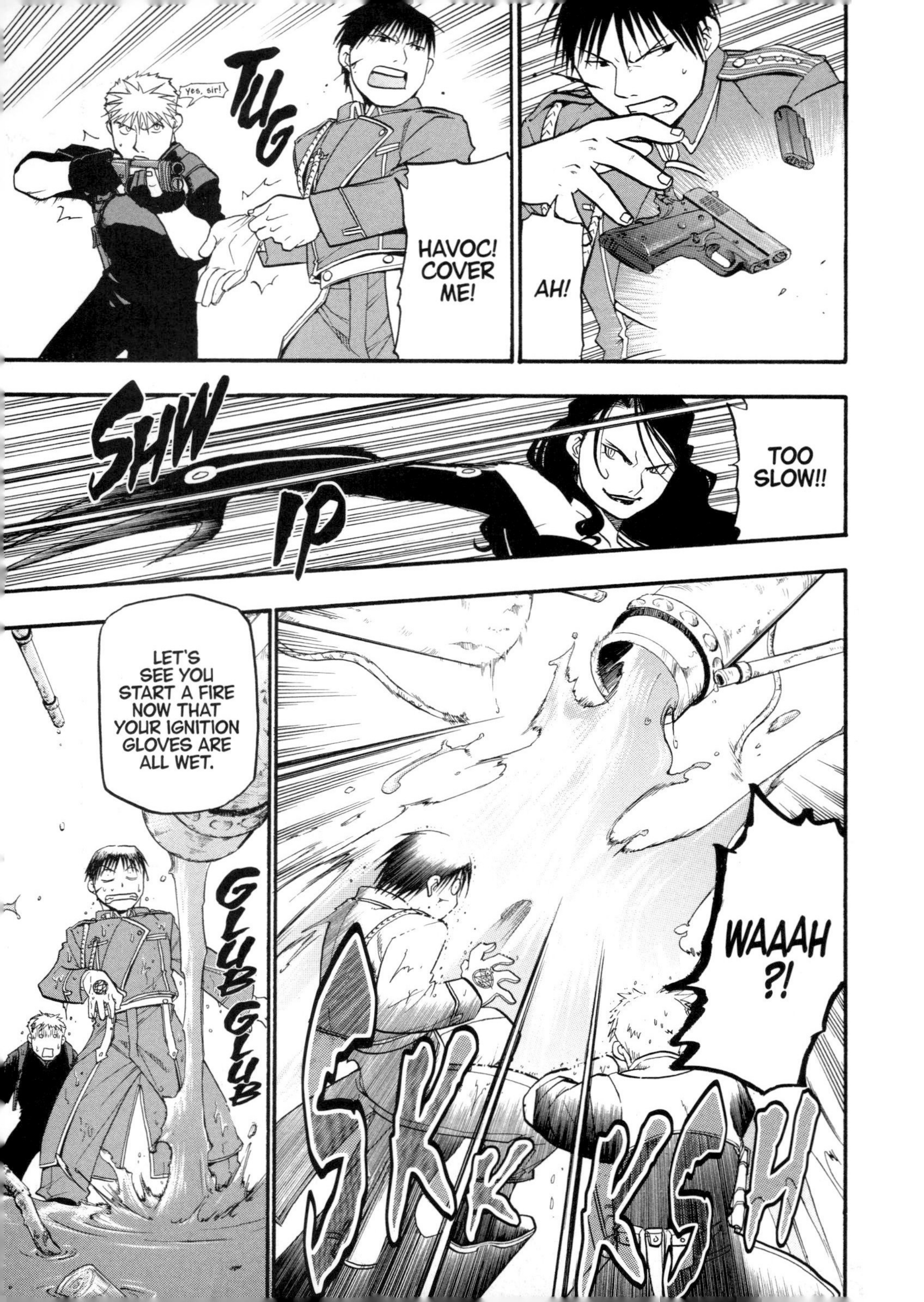
AH!
HAVOC! COVER ME!
TUG
Yes, sir!
TOO SLOW!!
SHWIP
WAAAH?!
SKKKSH
LET'S SEE YOU START A FIRE NOW THAT YOUR IGNITION GLOVES ARE ALL WET.
GLUB GLUB

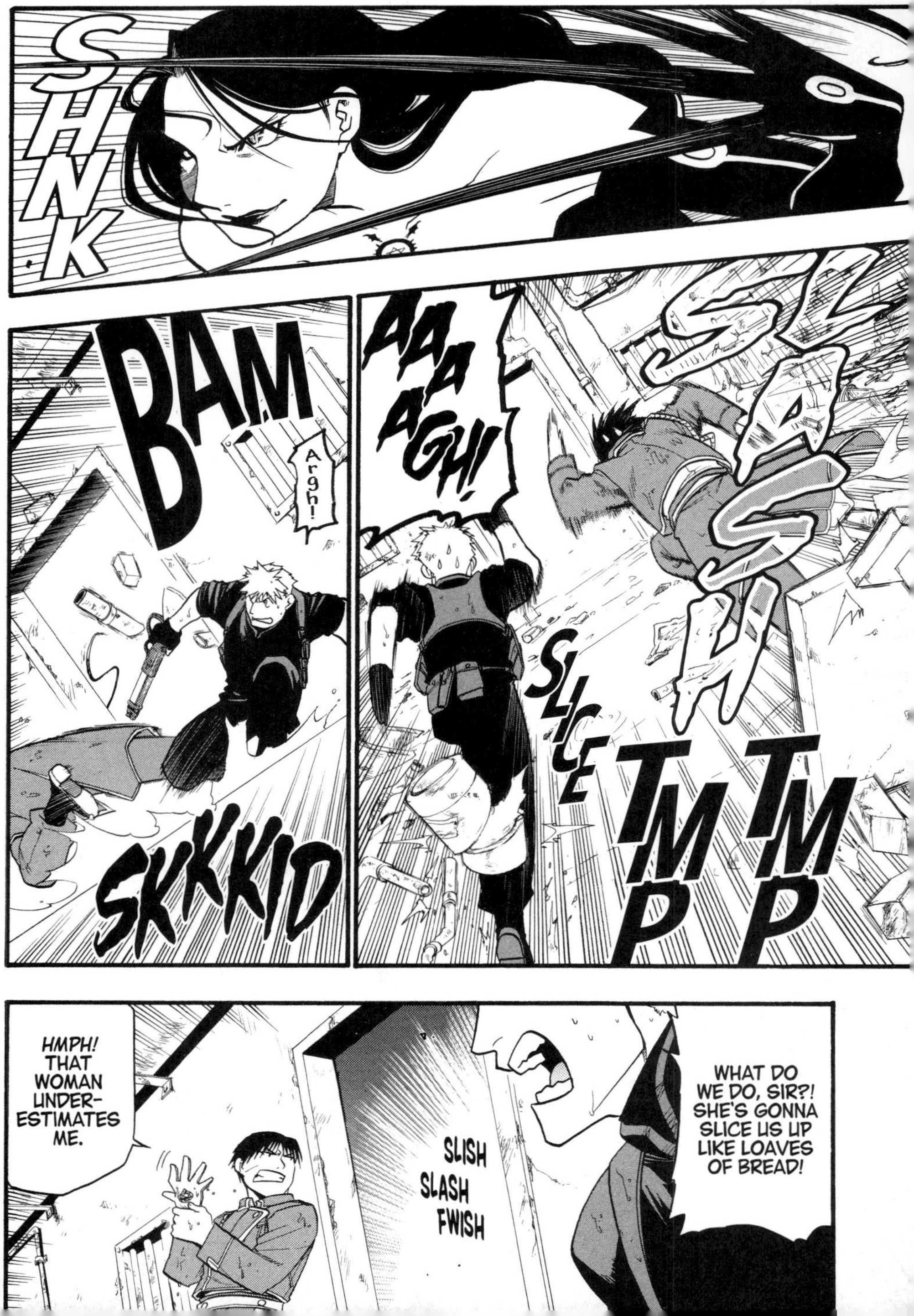
SHNK
SLASH
AAAAGH!
SLICE
TMP TMP
BAM
Argh!
SKKKID
WHAT DO WE DO, SIR?! SHE'S GONNA SLICE US UP LIKE LOAVES OF BREAD!
SLISH SLASH FWISH
HMPH! THAT WOMAN UNDER-ESTIMATES ME.

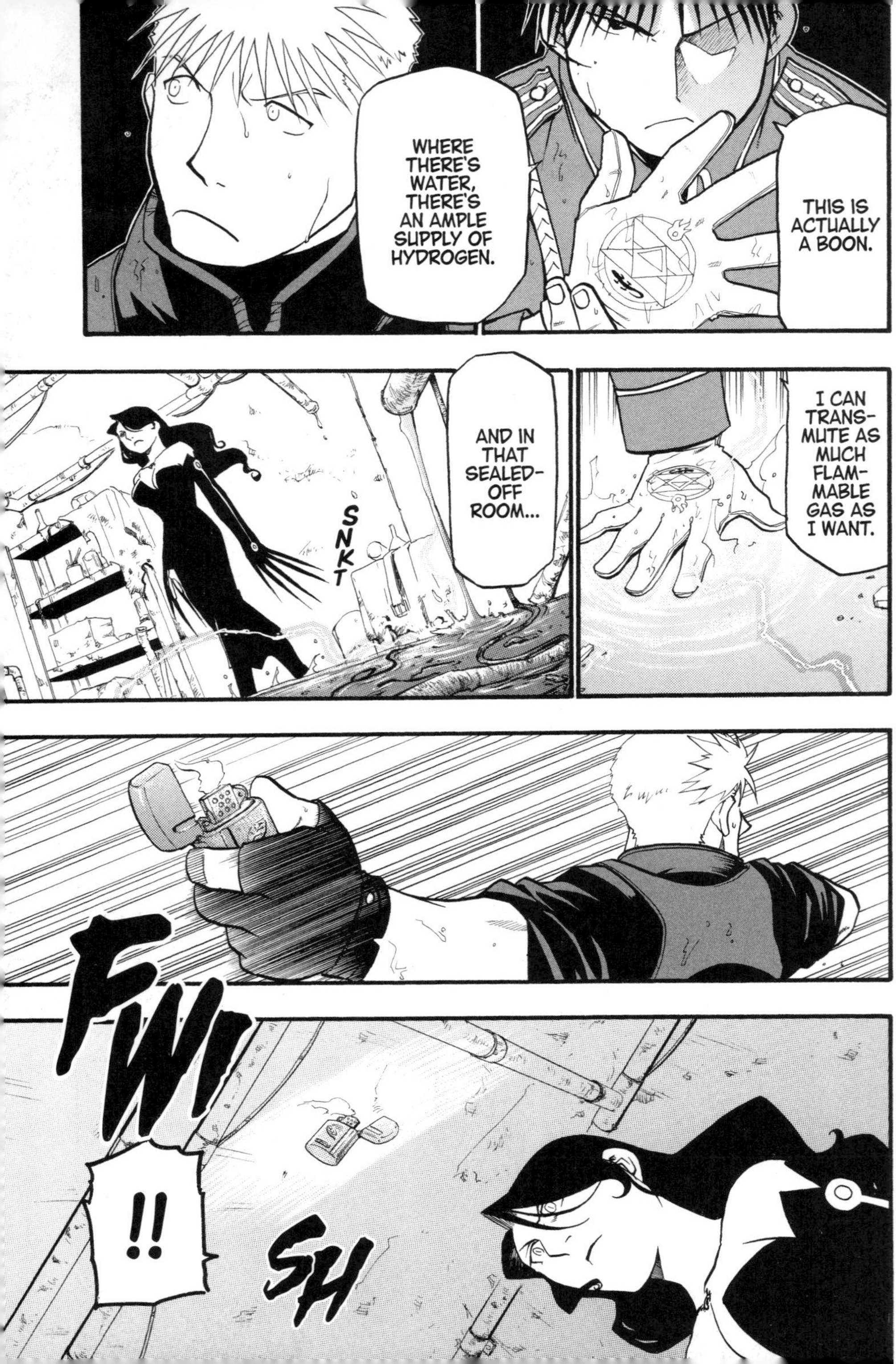
THIS IS ACTUALLY A BOON.
WHERE THERE'S WATER, THERE'S AN AMPLE SUPPLY OF HYDROGEN.
I CAN TRANSMUTE AS MUCH FLAMMABLE GAS AS I WANT.
AND IN THAT SEALED-OFF ROOM...
SNKT
FWI
!!
SH

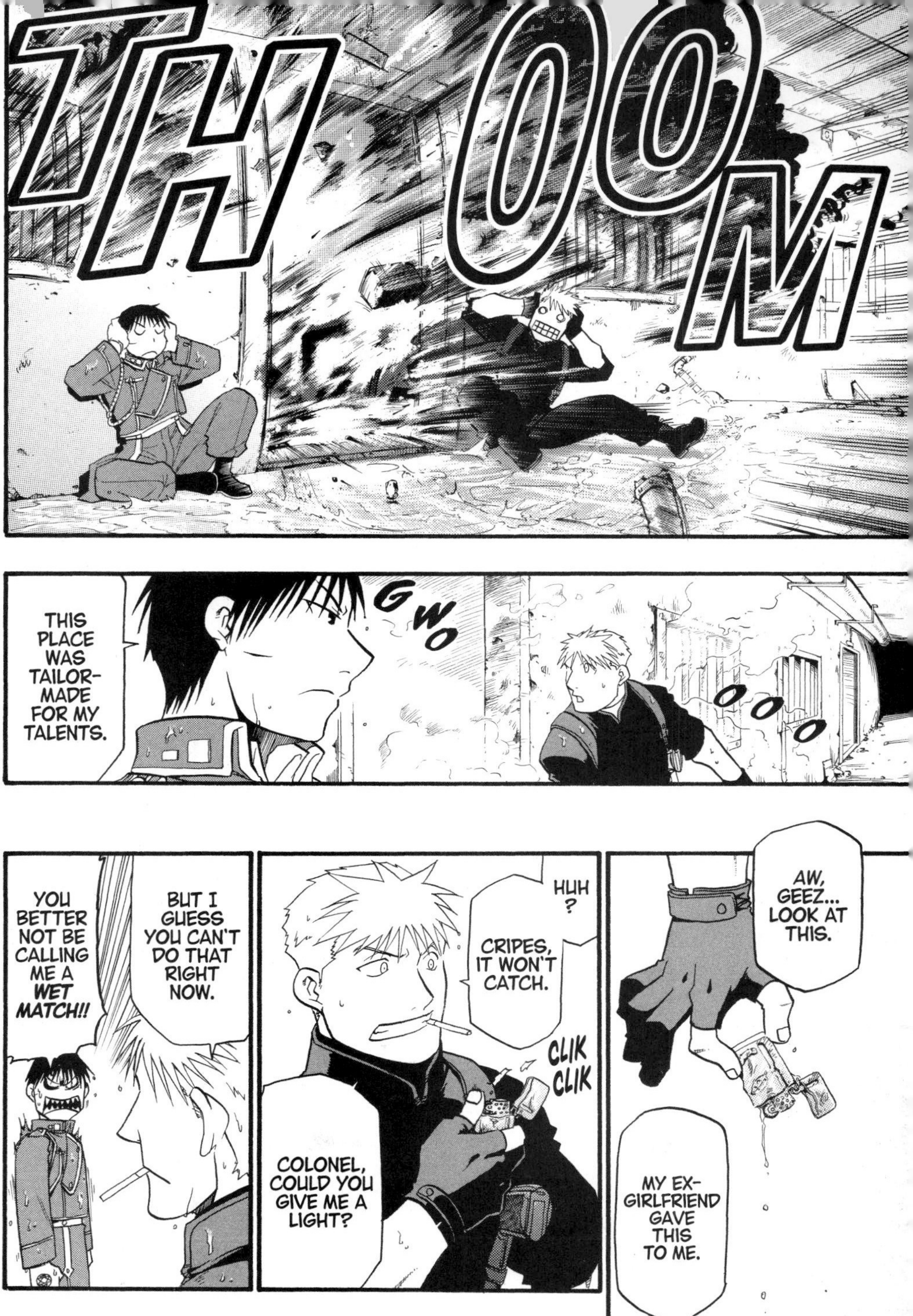
THOOOM
THIS PLACE WAS TAILOR-MADE FOR MY TALENTS.
GWOOOOO
AW, GEEZ... LOOK AT THIS.
MY EX-GIRLFRIEND GAVE THIS TO ME.
HUH?
CRIPES, IT WON'T CATCH.
CLIK CLIK
COLONEL, COULD YOU GIVE ME A LIGHT?
BUT I GUESS YOU CAN'T DO THAT RIGHT NOW.
YOU BETTER NOT BE CALLING ME A WET MATCH!!

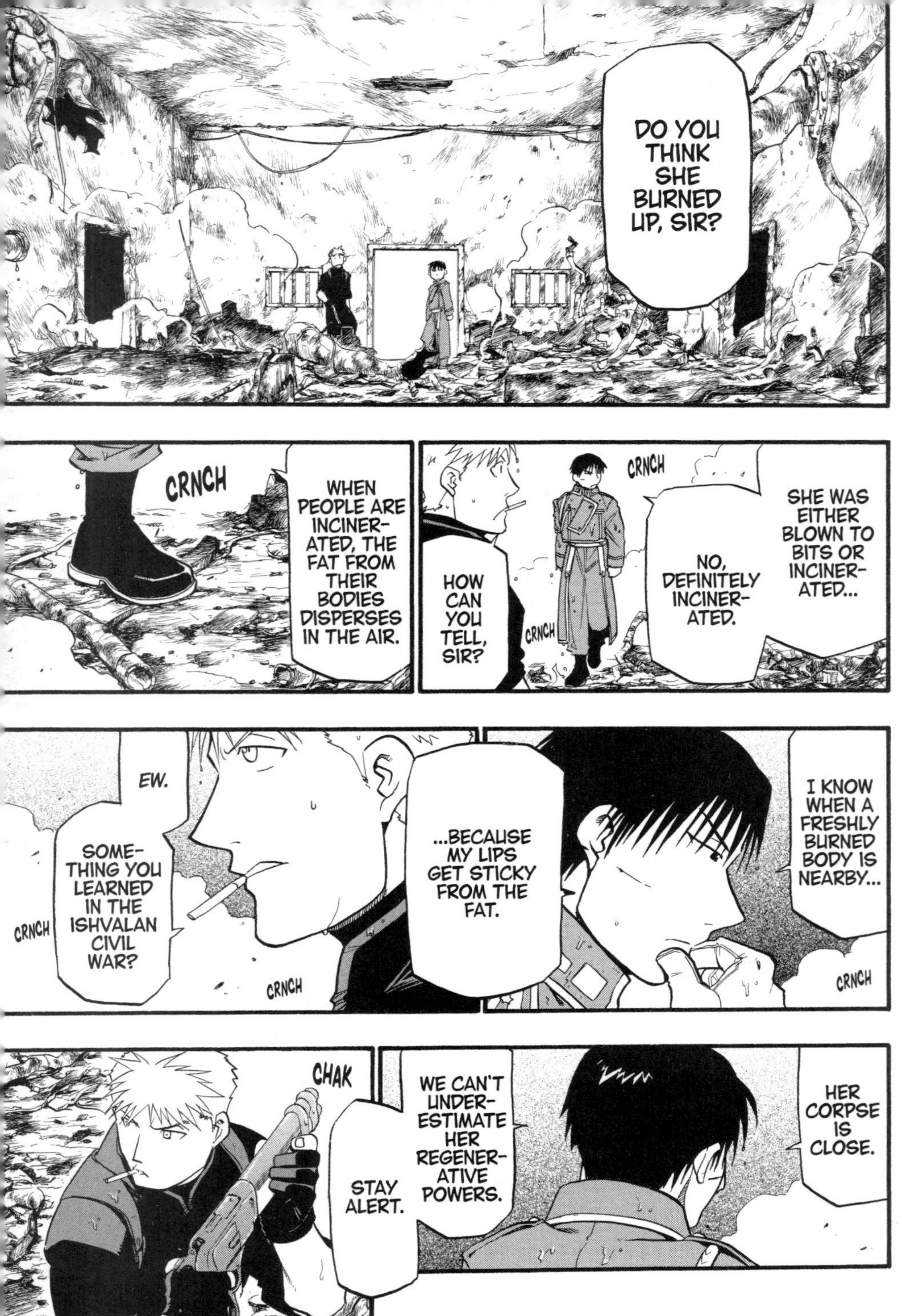
DO YOU THINK SHE BURNED UP, SIR?
SHE WAS EITHER BLOWN TO BITS OR INCINER-ATED...
NO, DEFINITELY INCINER-ATED.
CRNCH
HOW CAN YOU TELL, SIR?
CRNCH
WHEN PEOPLE ARE INCINER-ATED, THE FAT FROM THEIR BODIES DISPERSES IN THE AIR.
CRNCH
I KNOW WHEN A FRESHLY BURNED BODY IS NEARBY...
CRNCH
...BECAUSE MY LIPS GET STICKY FROM THE FAT.
EW.
SOME-THING YOU LEARNED IN THE ISHVALAN CIVIL WAR?
CRNCH
CRNCH
HER CORPSE IS CLOSE.
WE CAN'T UNDER-ESTIMATE HER REGENER-ATIVE POWERS.
STAY ALERT.
CHAK

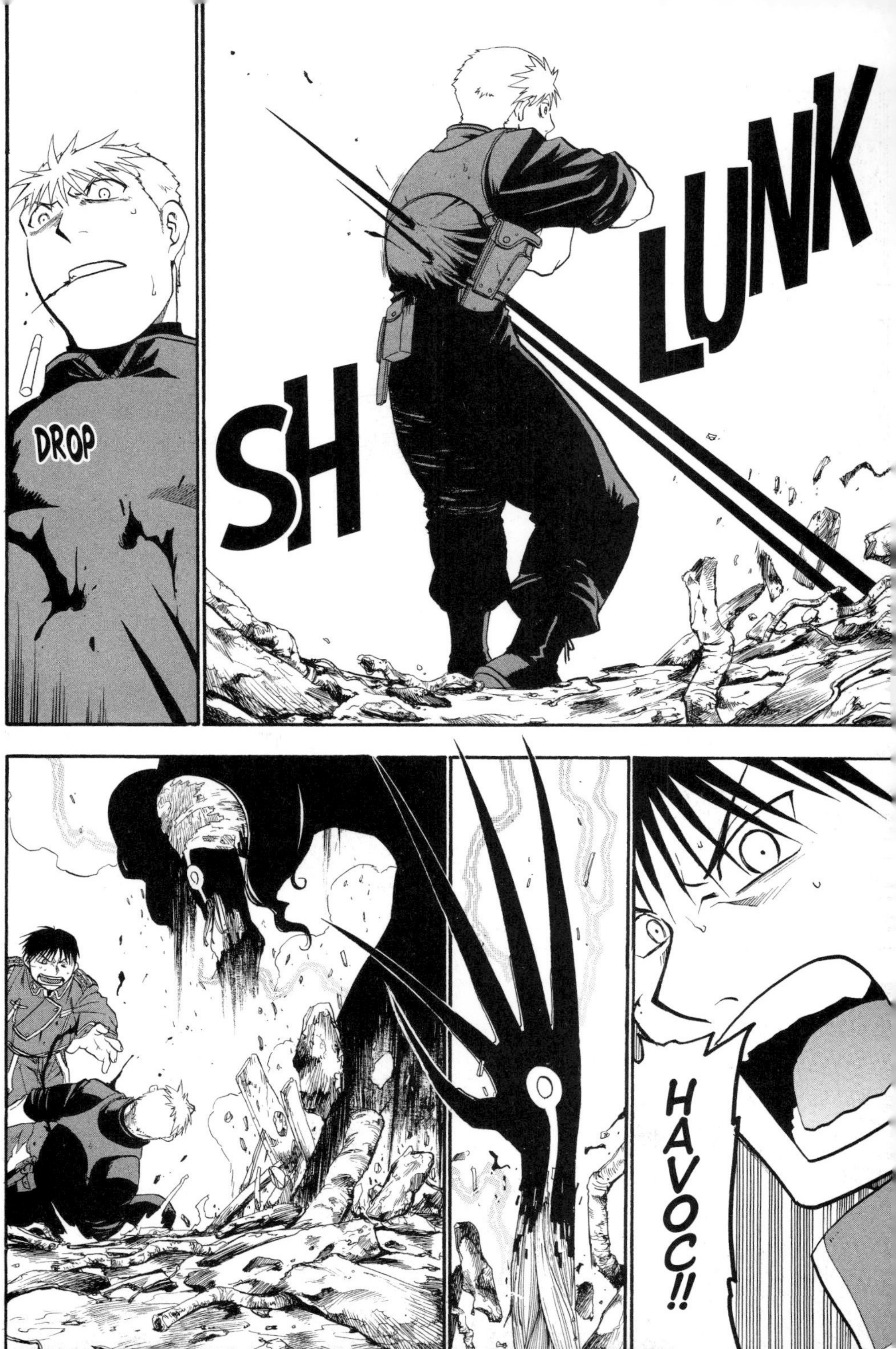
SH
LUNK
DROP
HAVOC!!

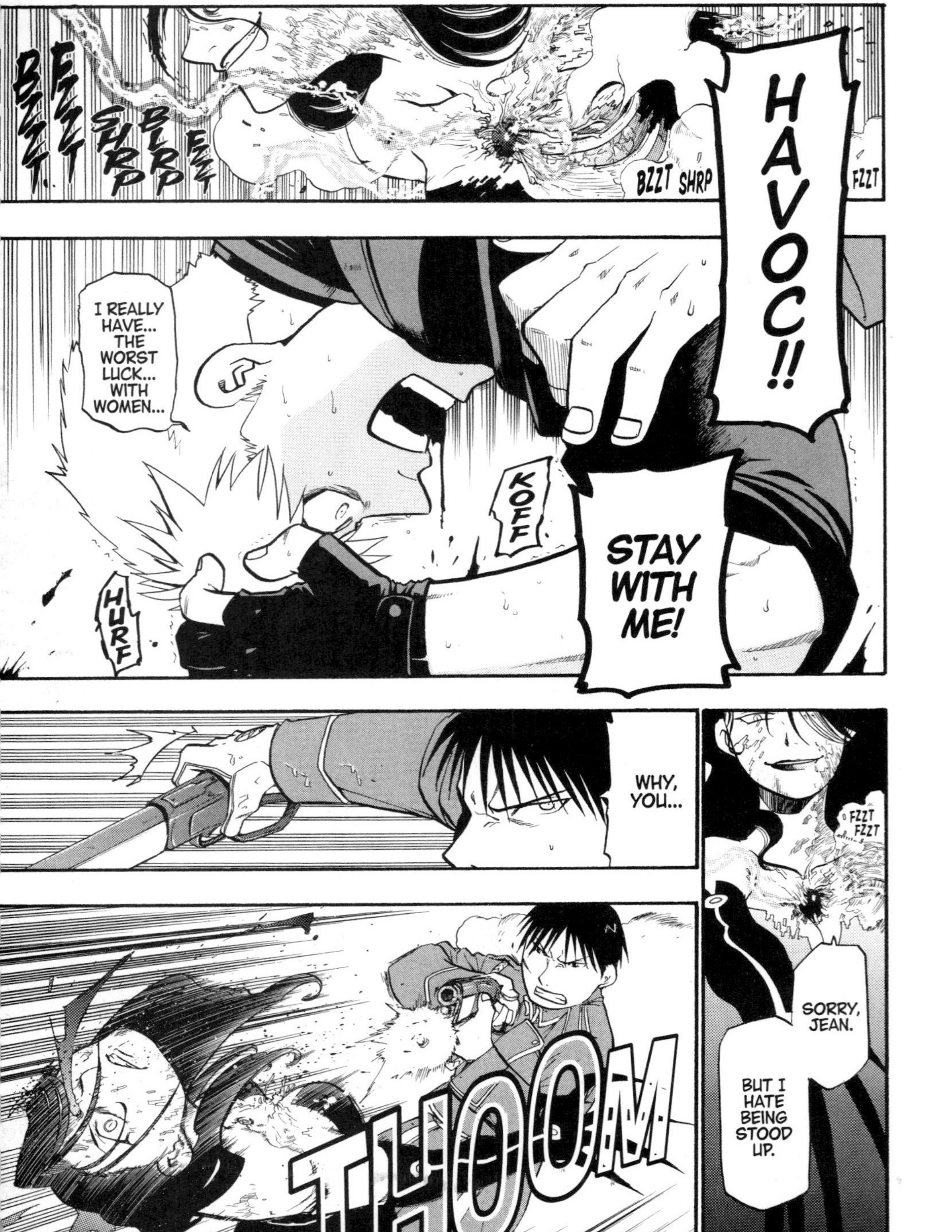
HAVOC!!
FZZT
BZZT SHRP
FZZT
BLRP
SHRP
FZZZT
BZZZT.
STAY WITH ME!
KOFF
I REALLY HAVE... THE WORST LUCK... WITH WOMEN...
HURF
FZZT FZZT
SORRY, JEAN.
BUT I HATE BEING STOOD UP.
WHY, YOU...
THOOM

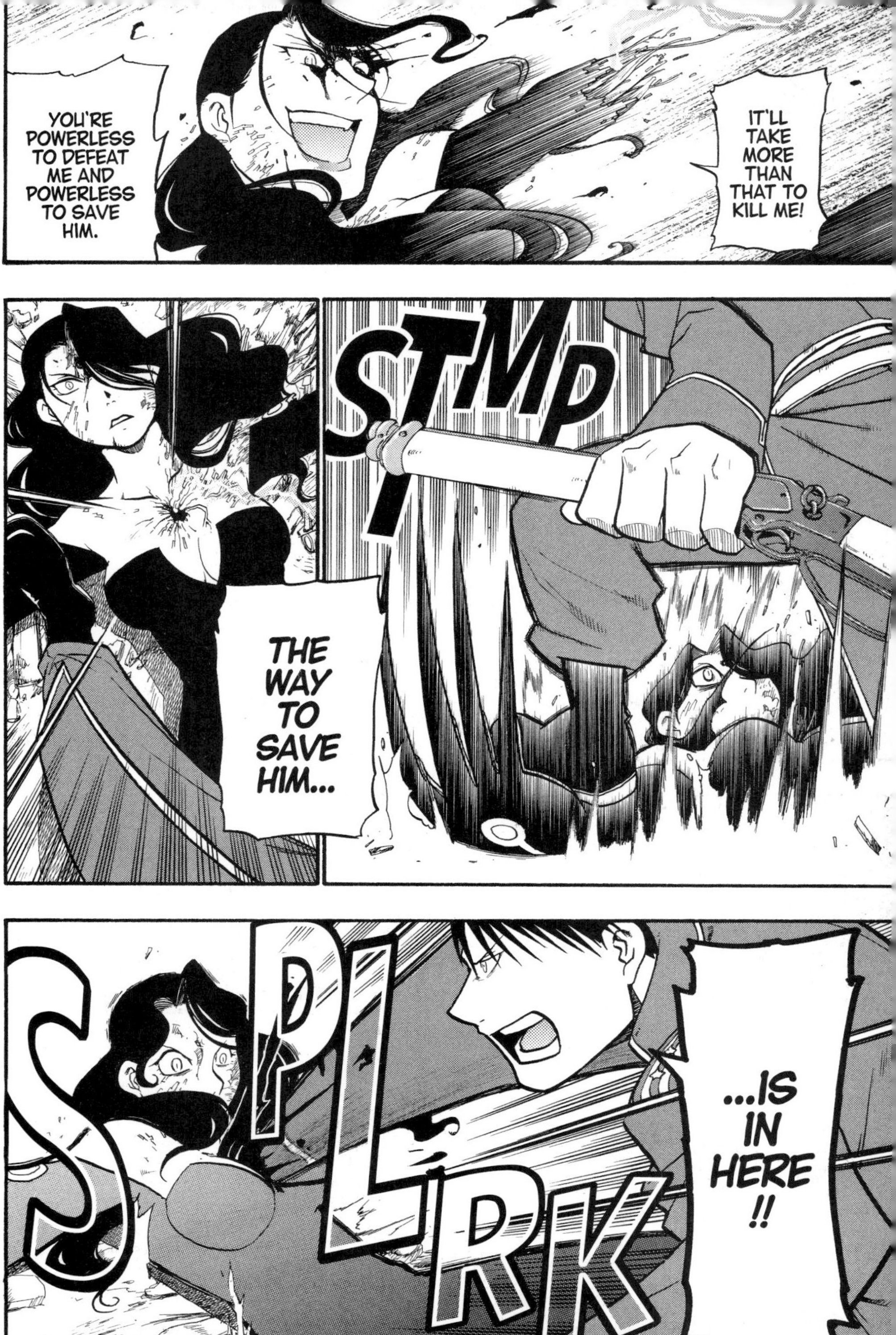
IT'LL TAKE MORE THAN THAT TO KILL ME!
YOU'RE POWERLESS TO DEFEAT ME AND POWERLESS TO SAVE HIM.
STMP
THE WAY TO SAVE HIM...
...IS IN HERE!!
SPLRK

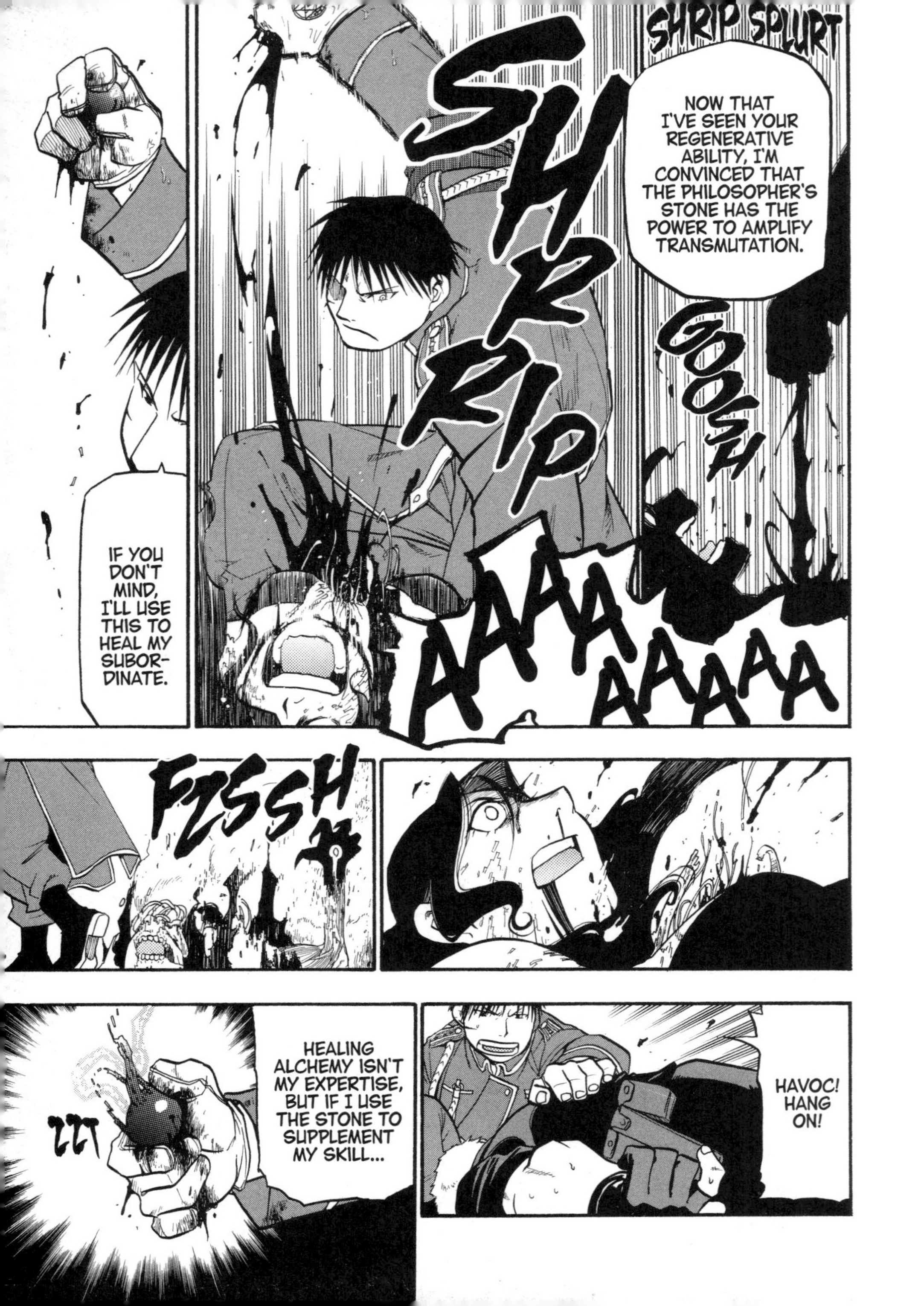
SHRIP SPLURT
NOW THAT I'VE SEEN YOUR REGENERATIVE ABILITY, I'M CONVINCED THAT THE PHILOSOPHER'S STONE HAS THE POWER TO AMPLIFY TRANSMUTATION.
SHRRIP
GOOSH
AAAAAAAAAA
IF YOU DON'T MIND, I'LL USE THIS TO HEAL MY SUBOR-DINATE.
FZSSH
HAVOC! HANG ON!
HEALING ALCHEMY ISN'T MY EXPERTISE, BUT IF I USE THE STONE TO SUPPLEMENT MY SKILL...

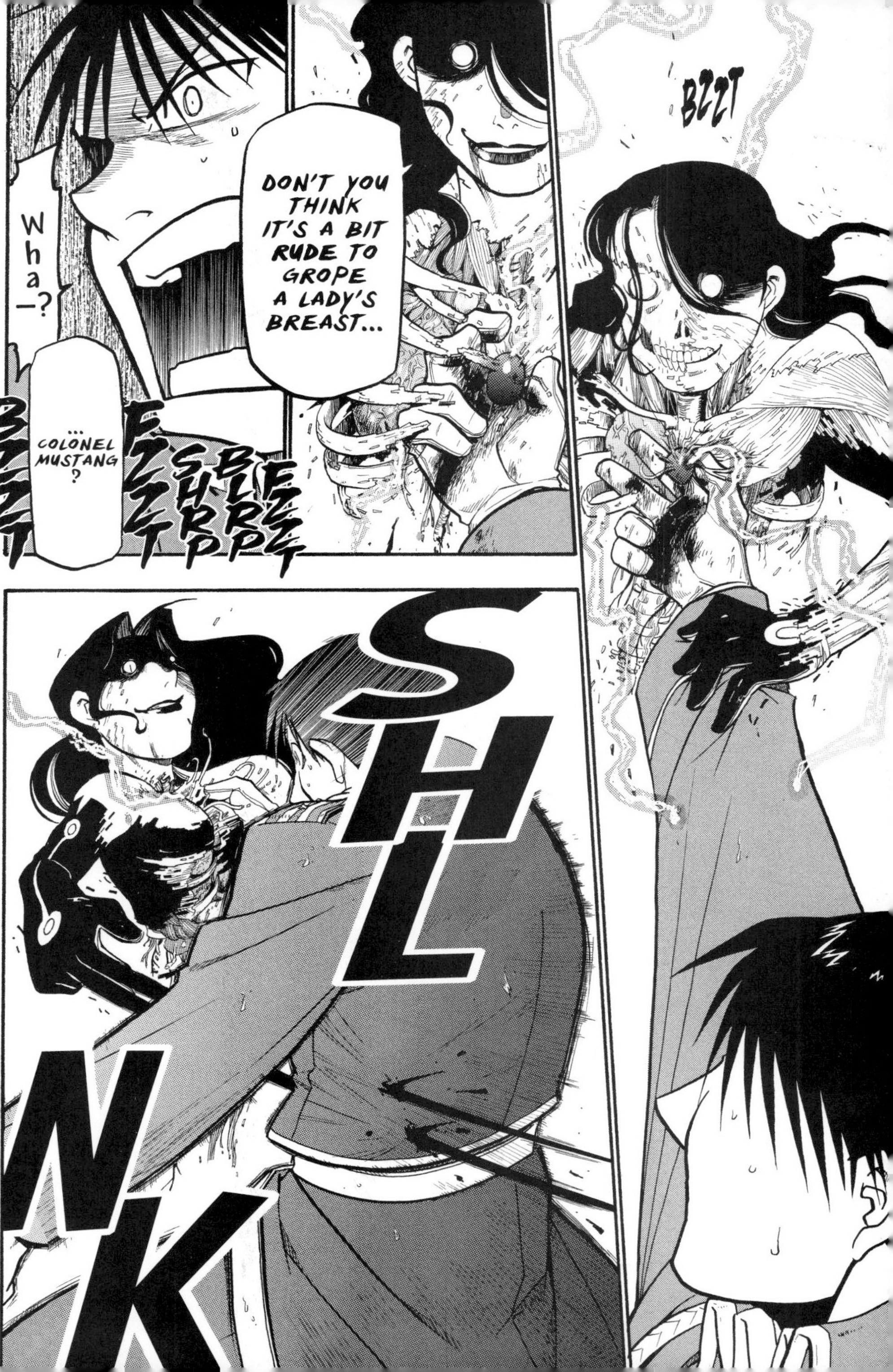
BZZT
DON'T YOU THINK IT'S A BIT RUDE TO GROPE A LADY'S BREAST...
FZZZT
BLRRP
SHRRP
FZZT
Wha—?
...COLONEL MUSTANG?
BZZZT
SHLNK

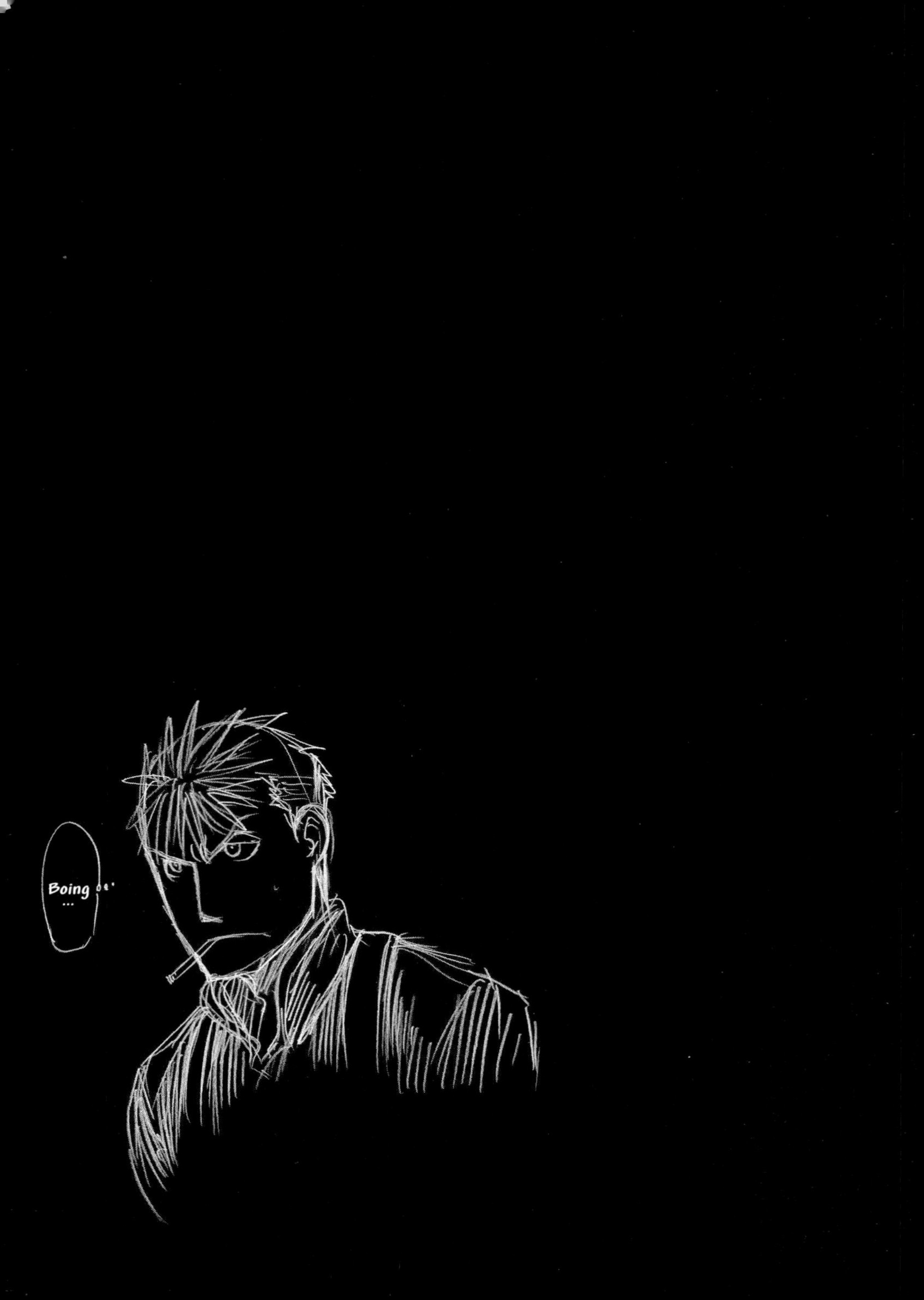
Boing
...

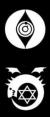

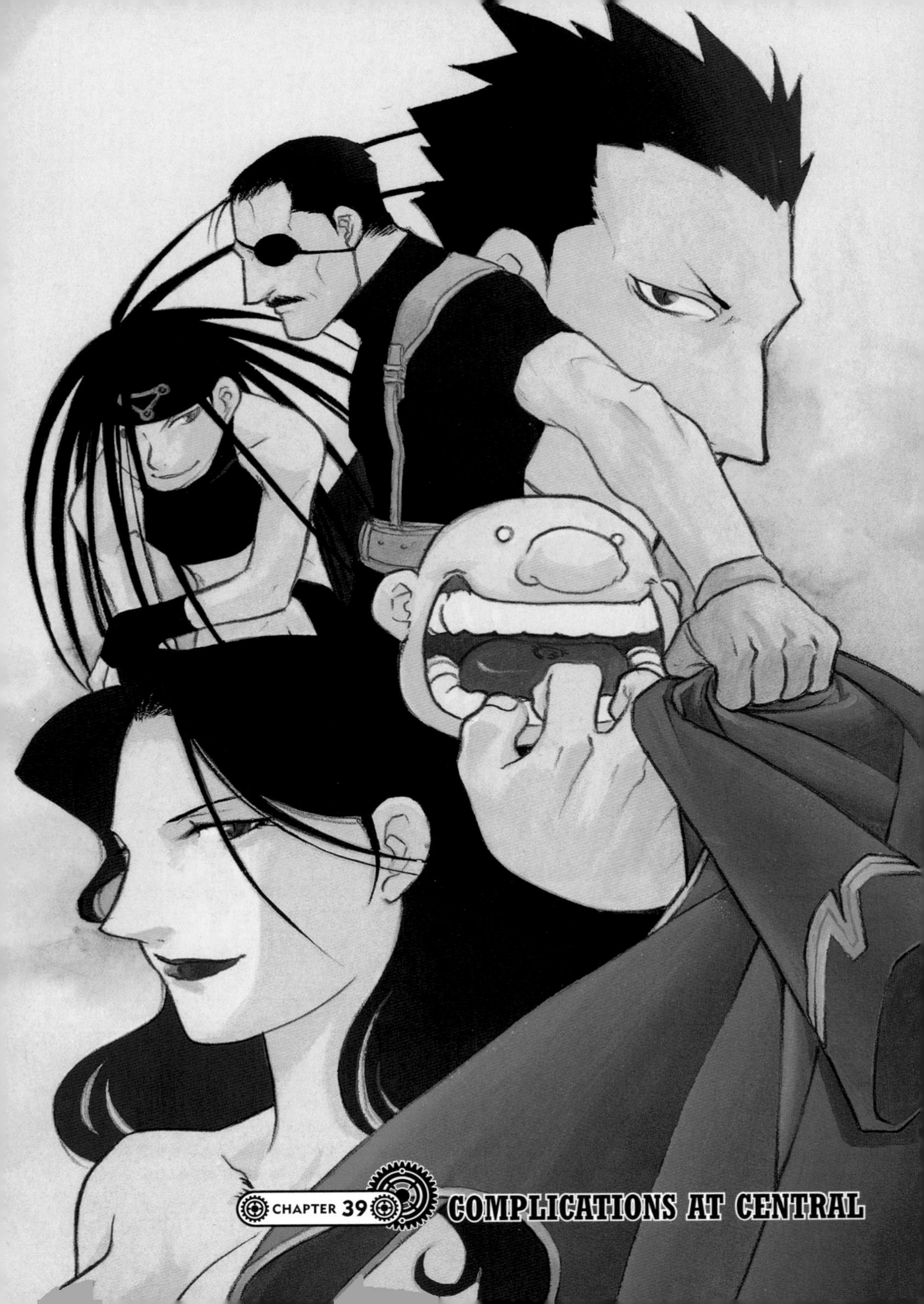
CHAPTER 39
COMPLICATIONS AT CENTRAL

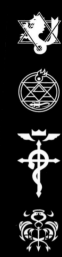
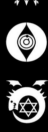

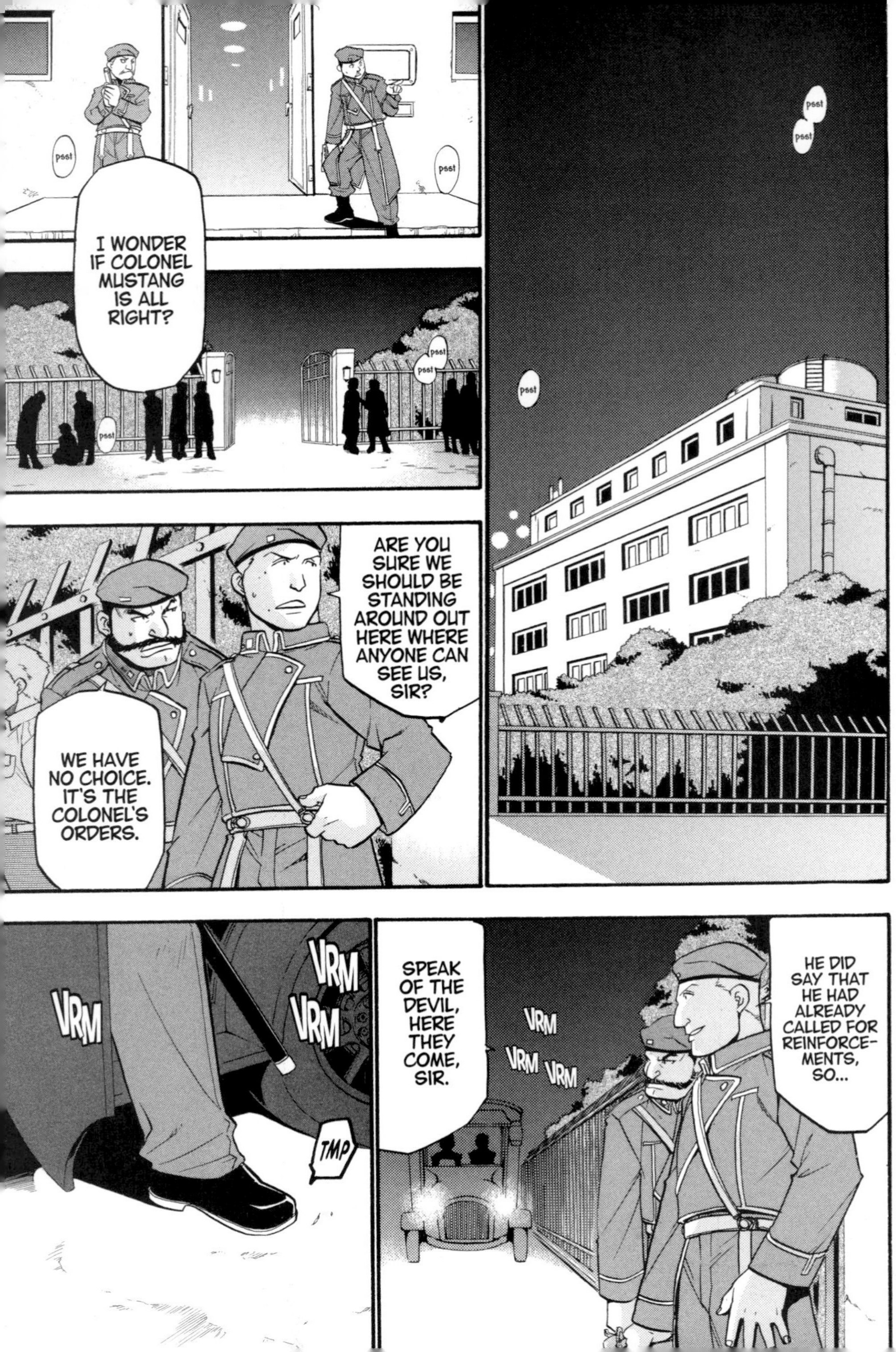
psst
psst
psst
psst
psst
I WONDER IF COLONEL MUSTANG IS ALL RIGHT?
psst
psst
psst
ARE YOU SURE WE SHOULD BE STANDING AROUND OUT HERE WHERE ANYONE CAN SEE US, SIR?
WE HAVE NO CHOICE. IT'S THE COLONEL'S ORDERS.
HE DID SAY THAT HE HAD ALREADY CALLED FOR REINFORCEMENTS, SO...
VRM
VRM
VRM
SPEAK OF THE DEVIL, HERE THEY COME, SIR.
VRM
VRM
VRM
TMP

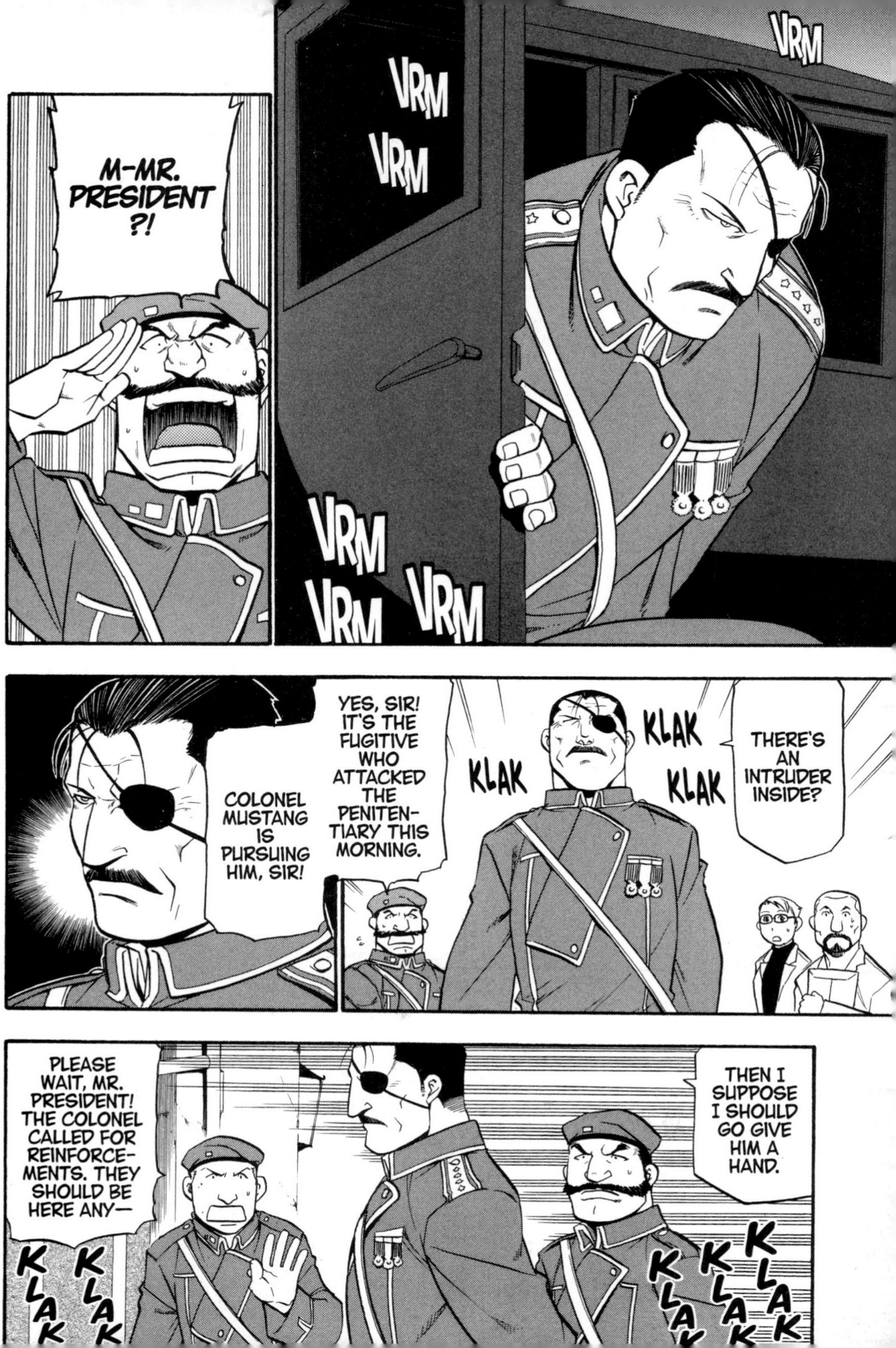
VRM
VRM
VRM
M-MR. PRESIDENT?!
VRM
VRM
VRM
THERE'S AN INTRUDER INSIDE?
KLAK
KLAK
KLAK
YES, SIR! IT'S THE FUGITIVE WHO ATTACKED THE PENITENTIARY THIS MORNING.
COLONEL MUSTANG IS PURSUING HIM, SIR!
THEN I SUPPOSE I SHOULD GO GIVE HIM A HAND.
KLAK
KLAK
KLAK
PLEASE WAIT, MR. PRESIDENT! THE COLONEL CALLED FOR REINFORCEMENTS. THEY SHOULD BE HERE ANY—
KLAK
KLAK

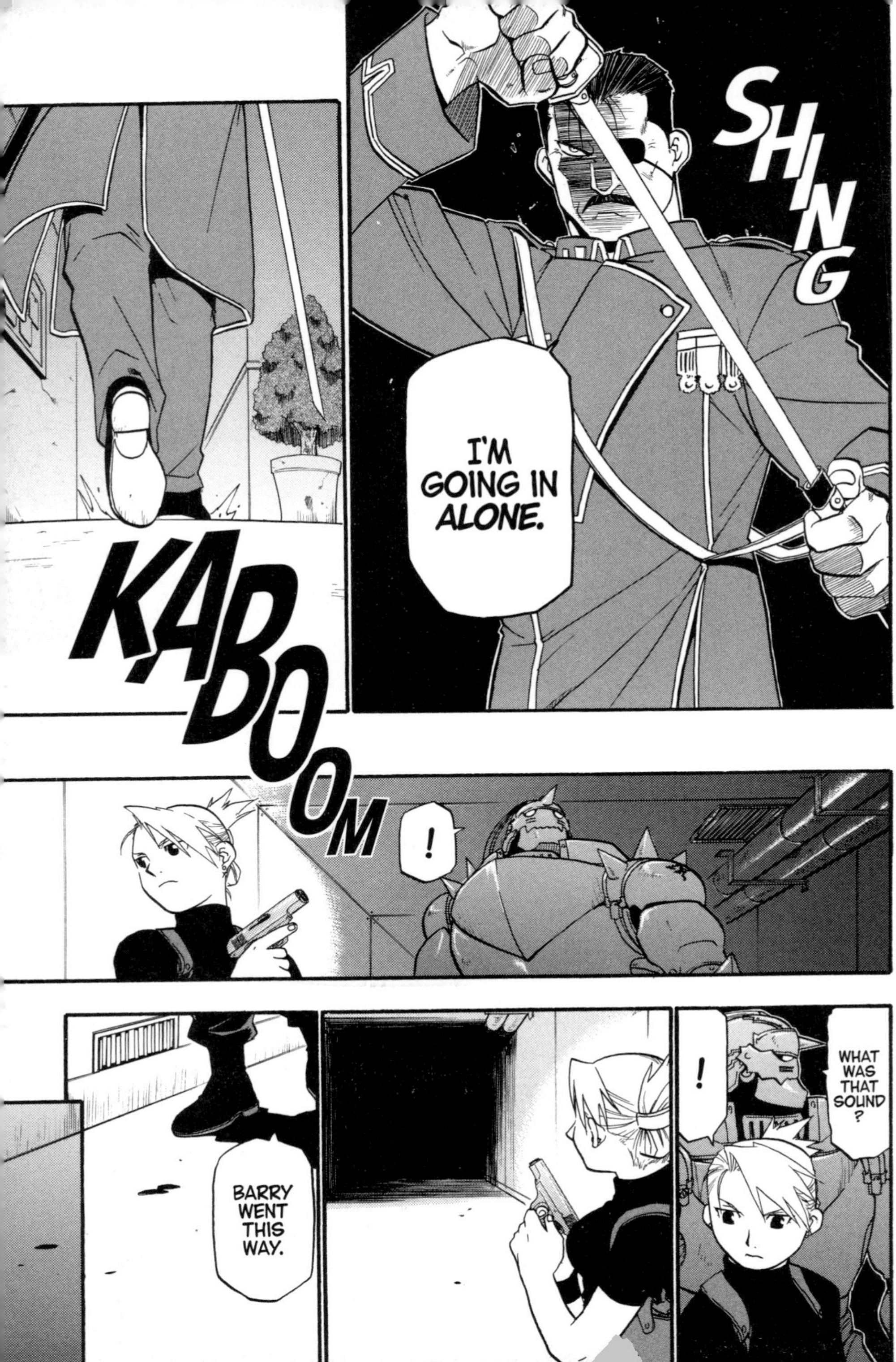
SHING
I'M GOING IN ALONE.
KABOOM
!
!
WHAT WAS THAT SOUND?
BARRY WENT THIS WAY.

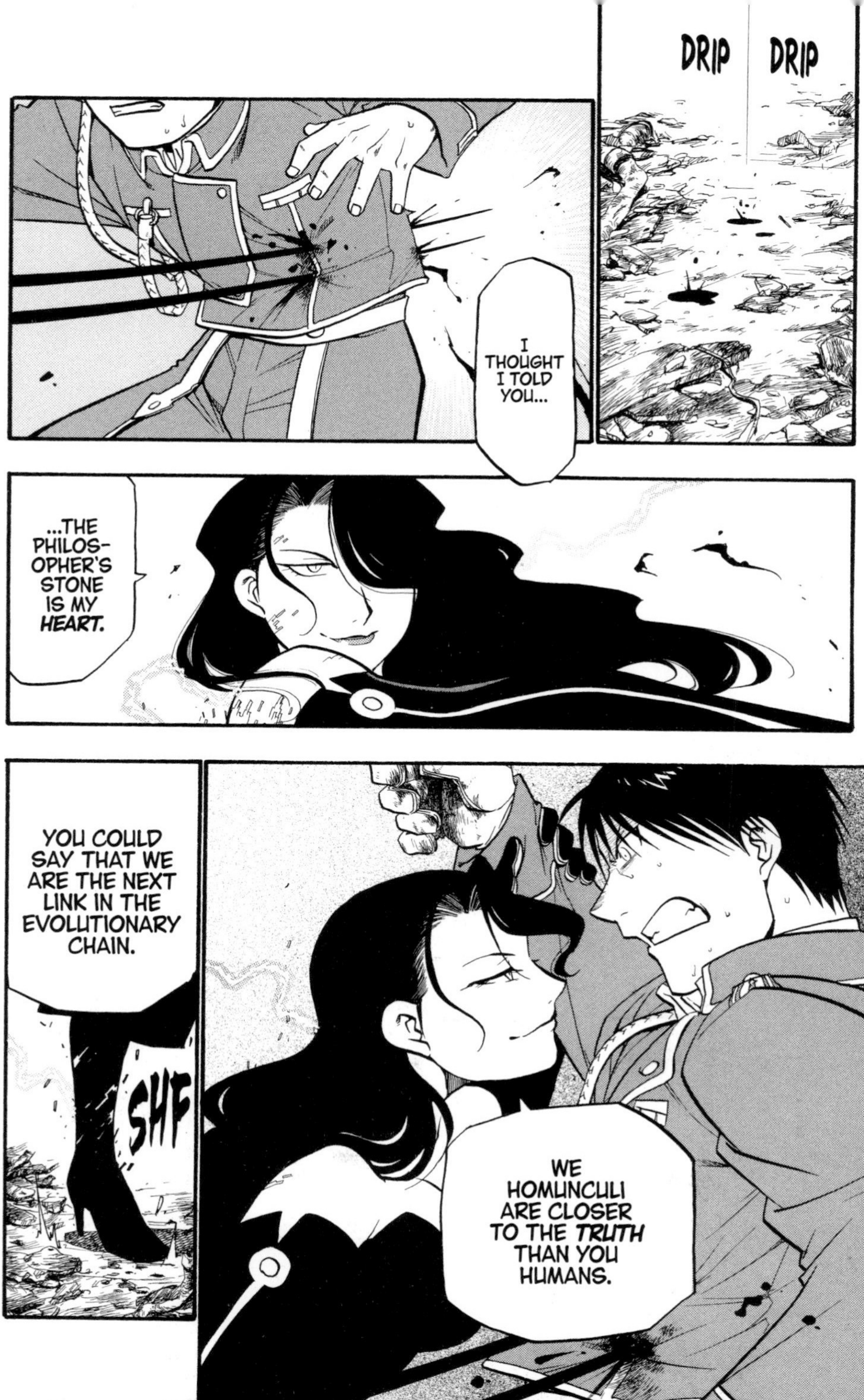
DRIP DRIP
I THOUGHT I TOLD YOU...
...THE PHILOSOPHER'S STONE IS MY HEART.
WE HOMUNCULI ARE CLOSER TO THE TRUTH THAN YOU HUMANS.
YOU COULD SAY THAT WE ARE THE NEXT LINK IN THE EVOLUTIONARY CHAIN.
SHF

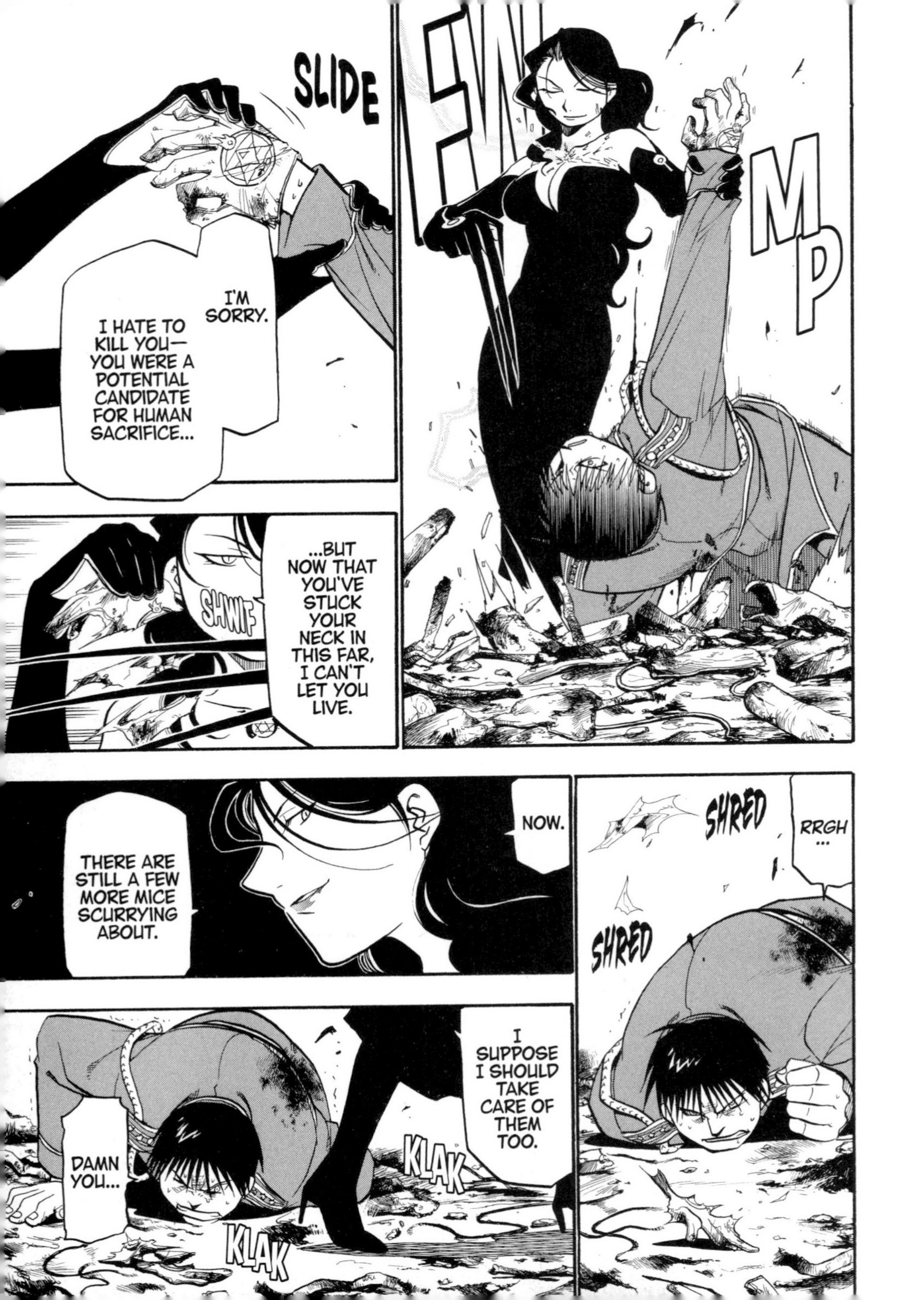
MP
SLIDE
I'M SORRY.
I HATE TO KILL YOU—YOU WERE A POTENTIAL CANDIDATE FOR HUMAN SACRIFICE...
...BUT NOW THAT YOU'VE STUCK YOUR NECK IN THIS FAR, I CAN'T LET YOU LIVE.
SHWIF
SHRED
RRGH...
SHRED
NOW.
THERE ARE STILL A FEW MORE MICE SCURRYING ABOUT.
I SUPPOSE I SHOULD TAKE CARE OF THEM TOO.
KLAK
DAMN YOU...
KLAK

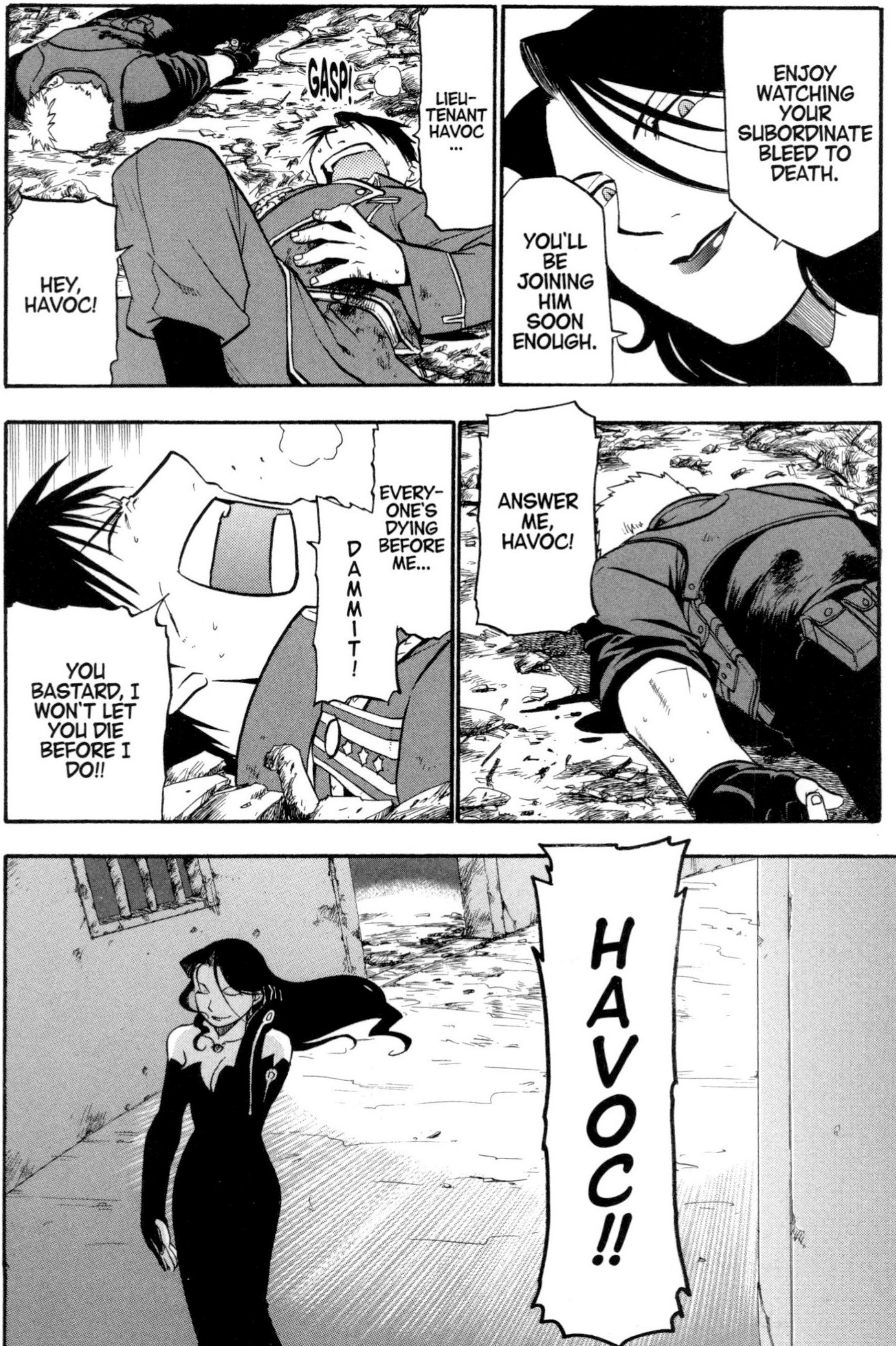
ENJOY WATCHING YOUR SUBORDINATE BLEED TO DEATH.
YOU'LL BE JOINING HIM SOON ENOUGH.
GASP!
LIEU-TENANT HAVOC ...
HEY, HAVOC!
ANSWER ME, HAVOC!
EVERY-ONE'S DYING BEFORE ME...
DAMMIT!
YOU BASTARD, I WON'T LET YOU DIE BEFORE I DO!!
HAVOC!!

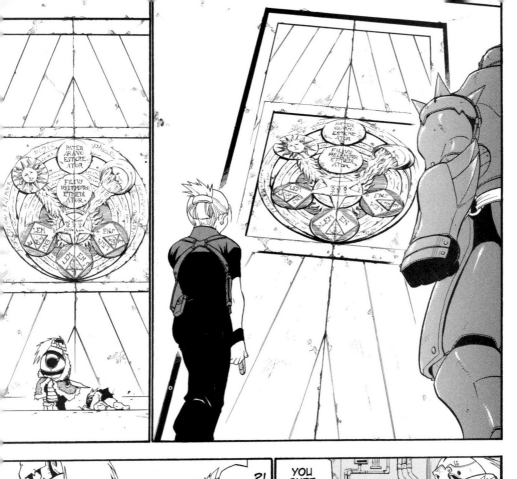

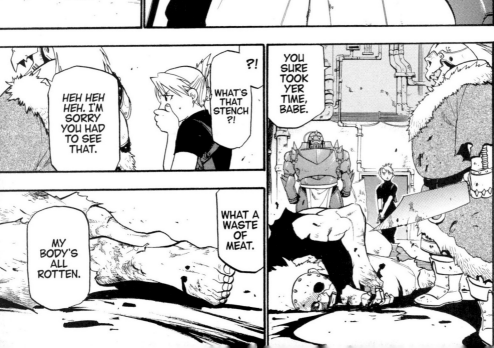

HEH HEH HEH. I'M SORRY YOU HAD TO SEE THAT.

?!

WHAT'S THAT STENCH ?!

YOU SURE TOOK YER TIME, BABE.

MY BODY'S ALL ROTTEN.

WHAT A WASTE OF MEAT.

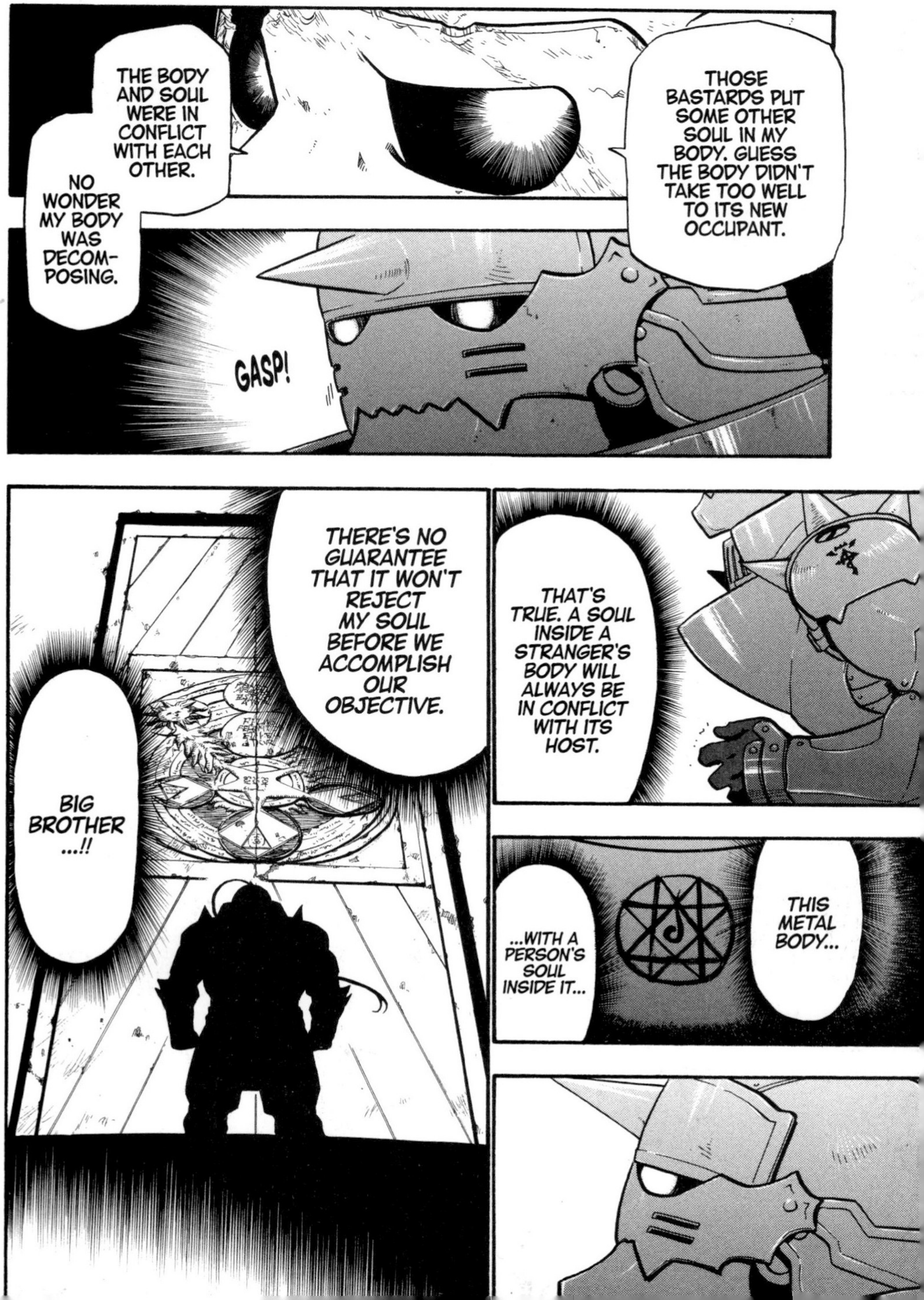
THOSE BASTARDS PUT SOME OTHER SOUL IN MY BODY. GUESS THE BODY DIDN'T TAKE TOO WELL TO ITS NEW OCCUPANT.
THE BODY AND SOUL WERE IN CONFLICT WITH EACH OTHER.
NO WONDER MY BODY WAS DECOM-POSING.
GASP!
THAT'S TRUE. A SOUL INSIDE A STRANGER'S BODY WILL ALWAYS BE IN CONFLICT WITH ITS HOST.
THIS METAL BODY...
...WITH A PERSON'S SOUL INSIDE IT...
THERE'S NO GUARANTEE THAT IT WON'T REJECT MY SOUL BEFORE WE ACCOMPLISH OUR OBJECTIVE.
BIG BROTHER ...!!

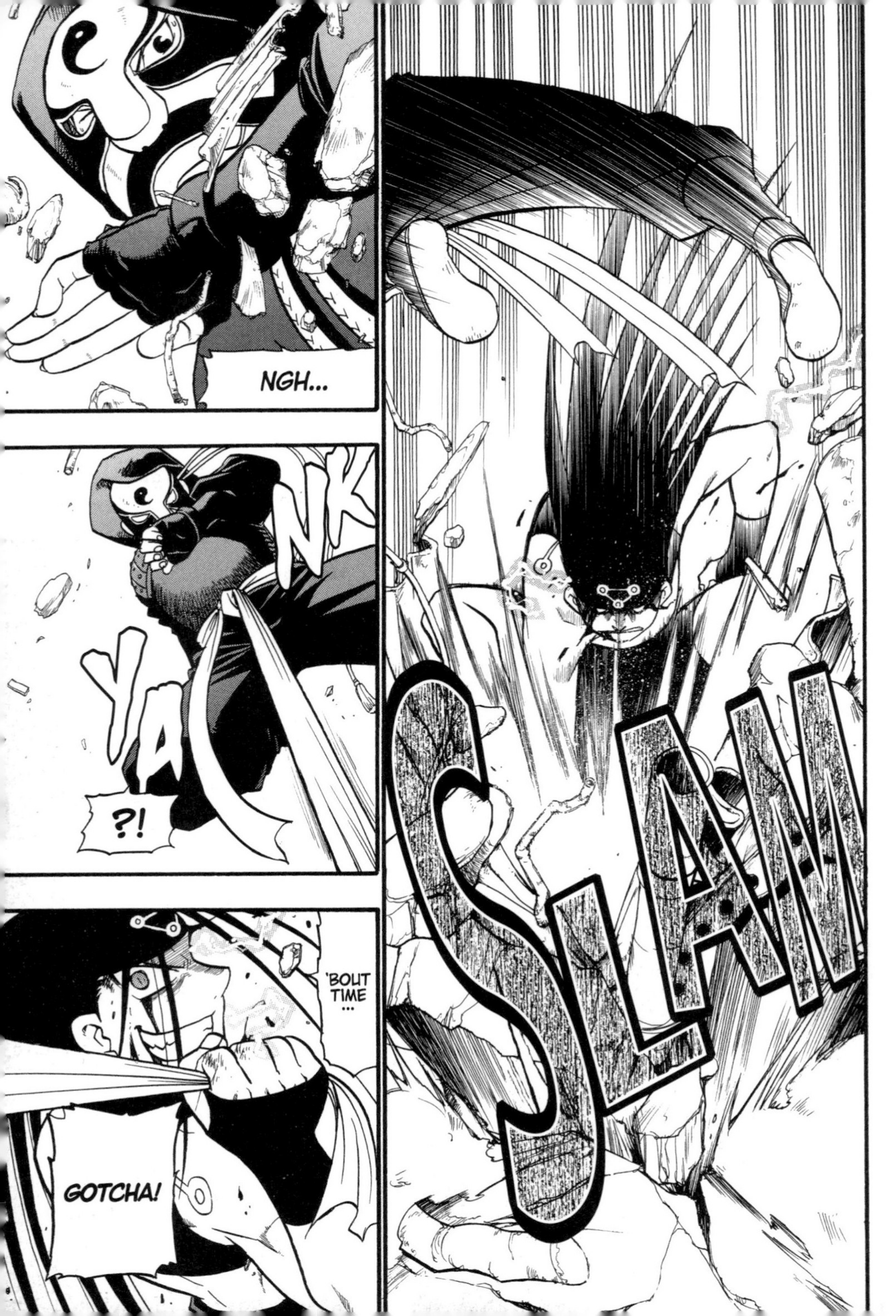
SLAM
NGH...
YANK
?!
'BOUT TIME ...
GOTCHA!

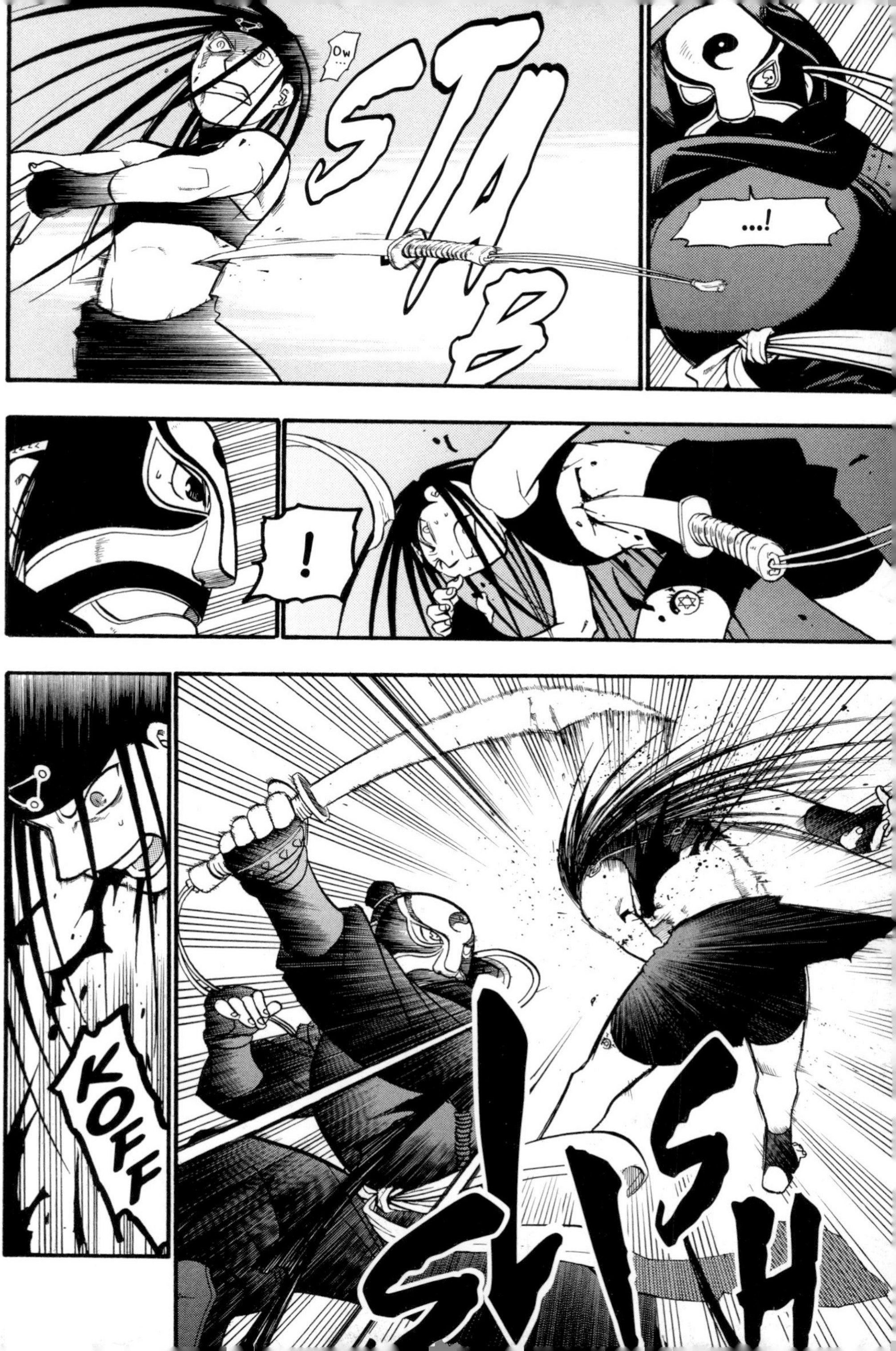

...!
OW ...
STAB
!
SHISH
KOFF

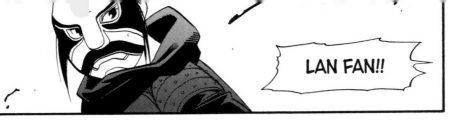

LAN FAN!!

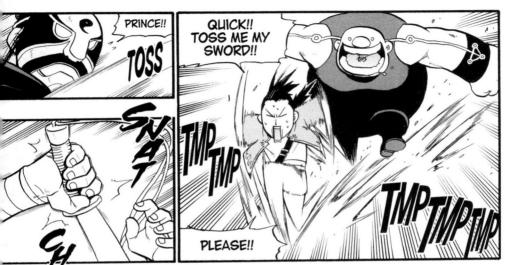

PRINCE!!

TOSS

QUICK!! TOSS ME MY SWORD!!

PLEASE!!

TMP TMP

TMPTMPTMP

SNAT

CH

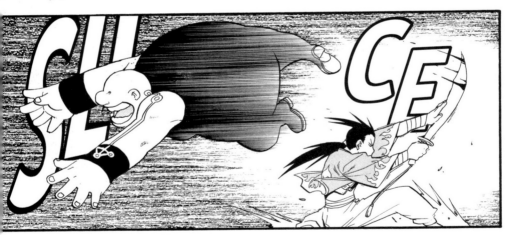

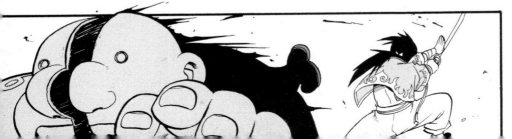

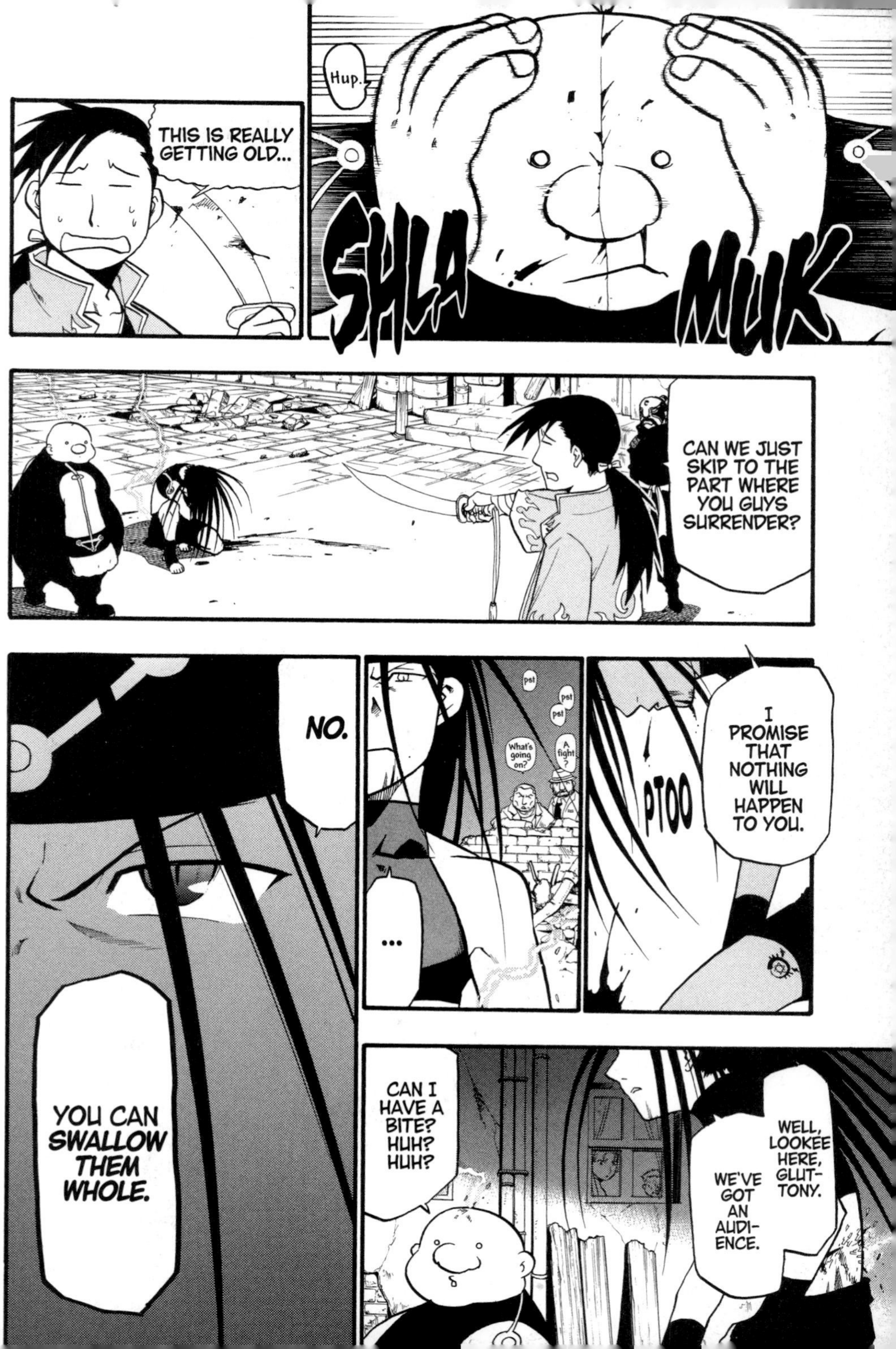
Hup..
SHLA
MUK
THIS IS REALLY GETTING OLD...
CAN WE JUST SKIP TO THE PART WHERE YOU GUYS SURRENDER?
I PROMISE THAT NOTHING WILL HAPPEN TO YOU.
PTOO
pst
pst
pst
A fight?
What's going on?
...
WELL, LOOKEE HERE, GLUTTONY.
WE'VE GOT AN AUDIENCE.
CAN I HAVE A BITE? HUH? HUH?
NO.
YOU CAN SWALLOW THEM WHOLE.

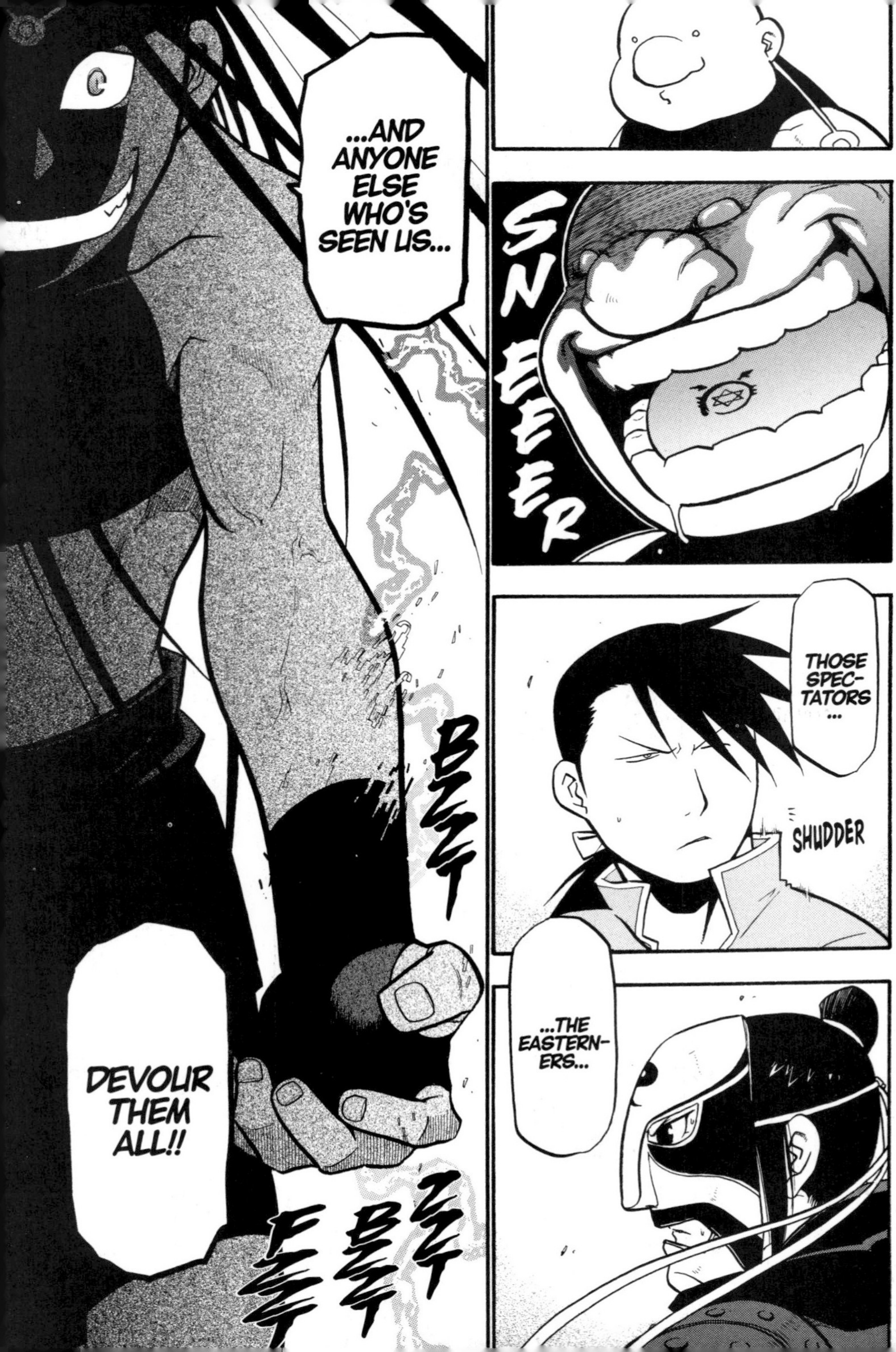
SNEEER
THOSE SPECTATORS...
SHUDDER
...THE EASTERNERS...
...AND ANYONE ELSE WHO'S SEEN US...
BZZT
DEVOUR THEM ALL!!
ZZT
BZZT
FZZT

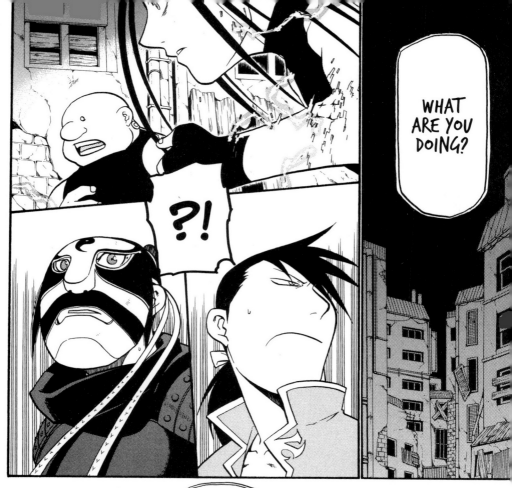

WHAT ARE YOU DOING?

?!

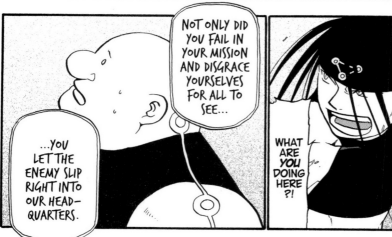

NOT ONLY DID YOU FAIL IN YOUR MISSION AND DISGRACE YOURSELVES FOR ALL TO SEE...

...YOU LET THE ENEMY SLIP RIGHT INTO OUR HEAD-QUARTERS.

PRIDE ?!

WHAT ARE *YOU* DOING HERE ?!

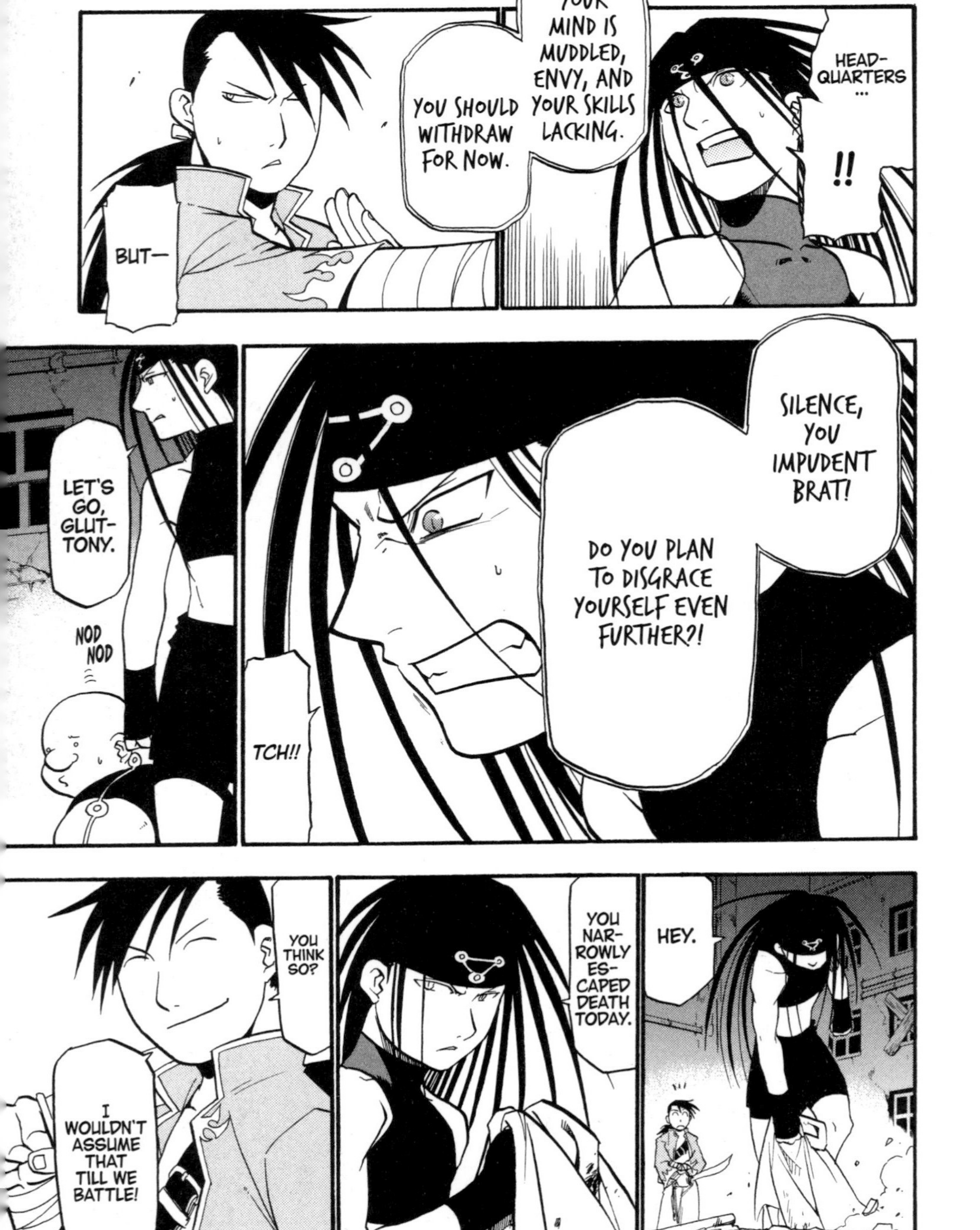
HEAD-QUARTERS ...
!!
YOUR MIND IS MUDDLED, ENVY, AND YOUR SKILLS LACKING.
YOU SHOULD WITHDRAW FOR NOW.
BUT—
SILENCE, YOU IMPUDENT BRAT!
DO YOU PLAN TO DISGRACE YOURSELF EVEN FURTHER?!
TCH!!
LET'S GO, GLUT-TONY.
NOD NOD
HEY.
YOU NAR-ROWLY ES-CAPED DEATH TODAY.
YOU THINK SO?
I WOULDN'T ASSUME THAT TILL WE BATTLE!

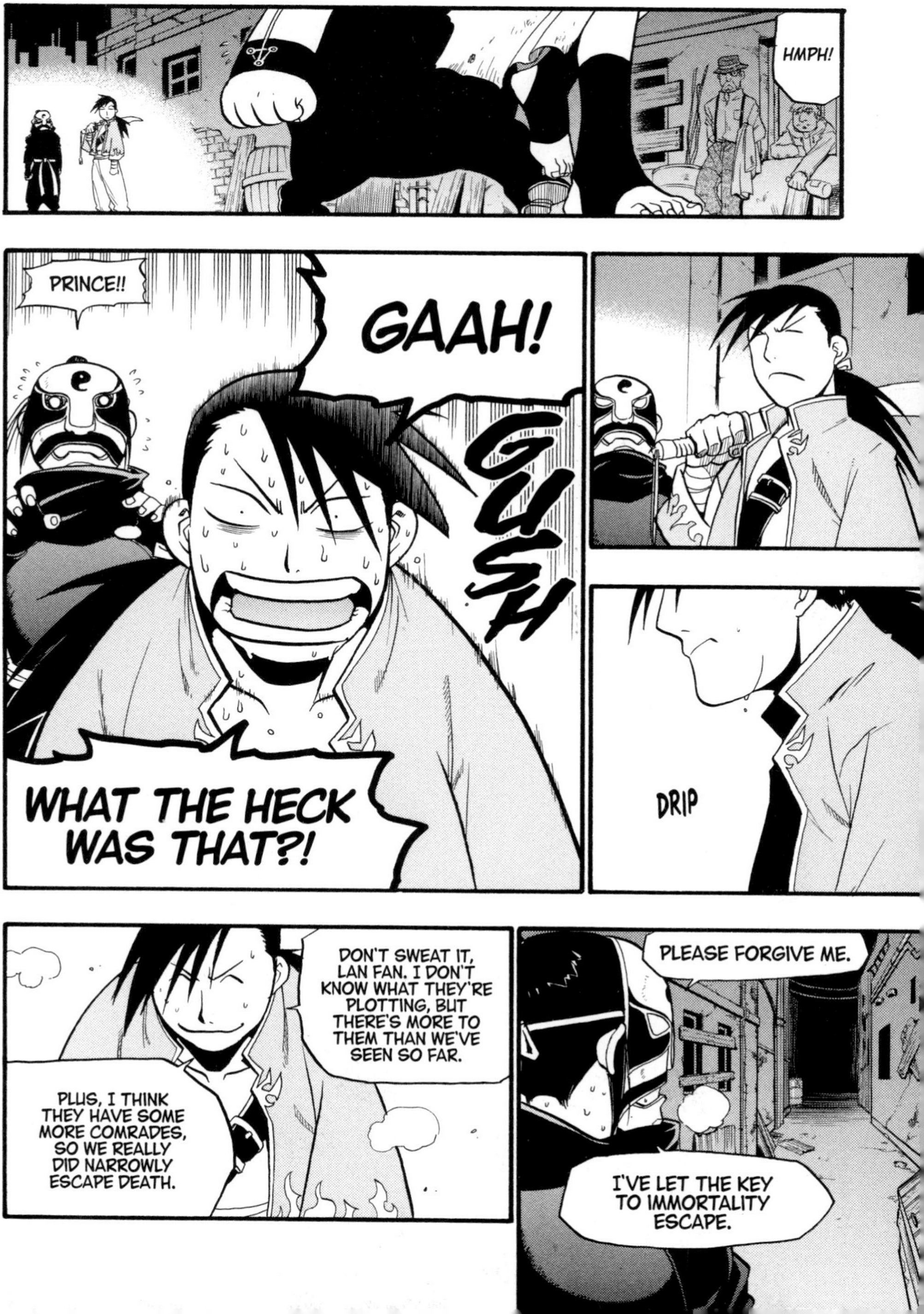
HMPH!
DRIP
PRINCE!!
GAAH!
GUSH
WHAT THE HECK WAS THAT?!
PLEASE FORGIVE ME.
I'VE LET THE KEY TO IMMORTALITY ESCAPE.
DON'T SWEAT IT, LAN FAN. I DON'T KNOW WHAT THEY'RE PLOTTING, BUT THERE'S MORE TO THEM THAN WE'VE SEEN SO FAR.
PLUS, I THINK THEY HAVE SOME MORE COMRADES, SO WE REALLY DID NARROWLY ESCAPE DEATH.

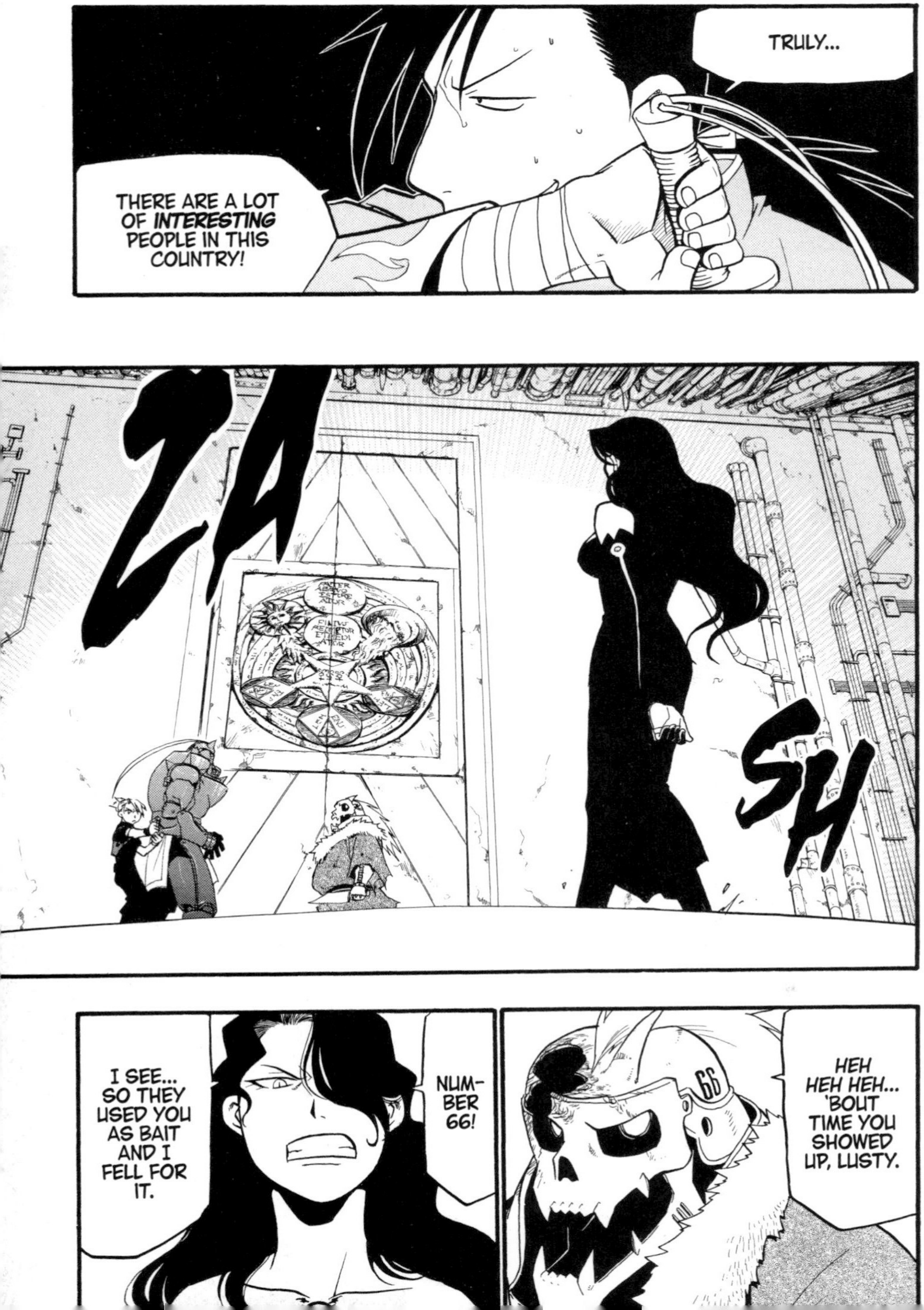
TRULY...
THERE ARE A LOT OF INTERESTING PEOPLE IN THIS COUNTRY!
ZA
SH
HEH HEH HEH... 'BOUT TIME YOU SHOWED UP, LUSTY.
NUM-BER 66!
I SEE... SO THEY USED YOU AS BAIT AND I FELL FOR IT.

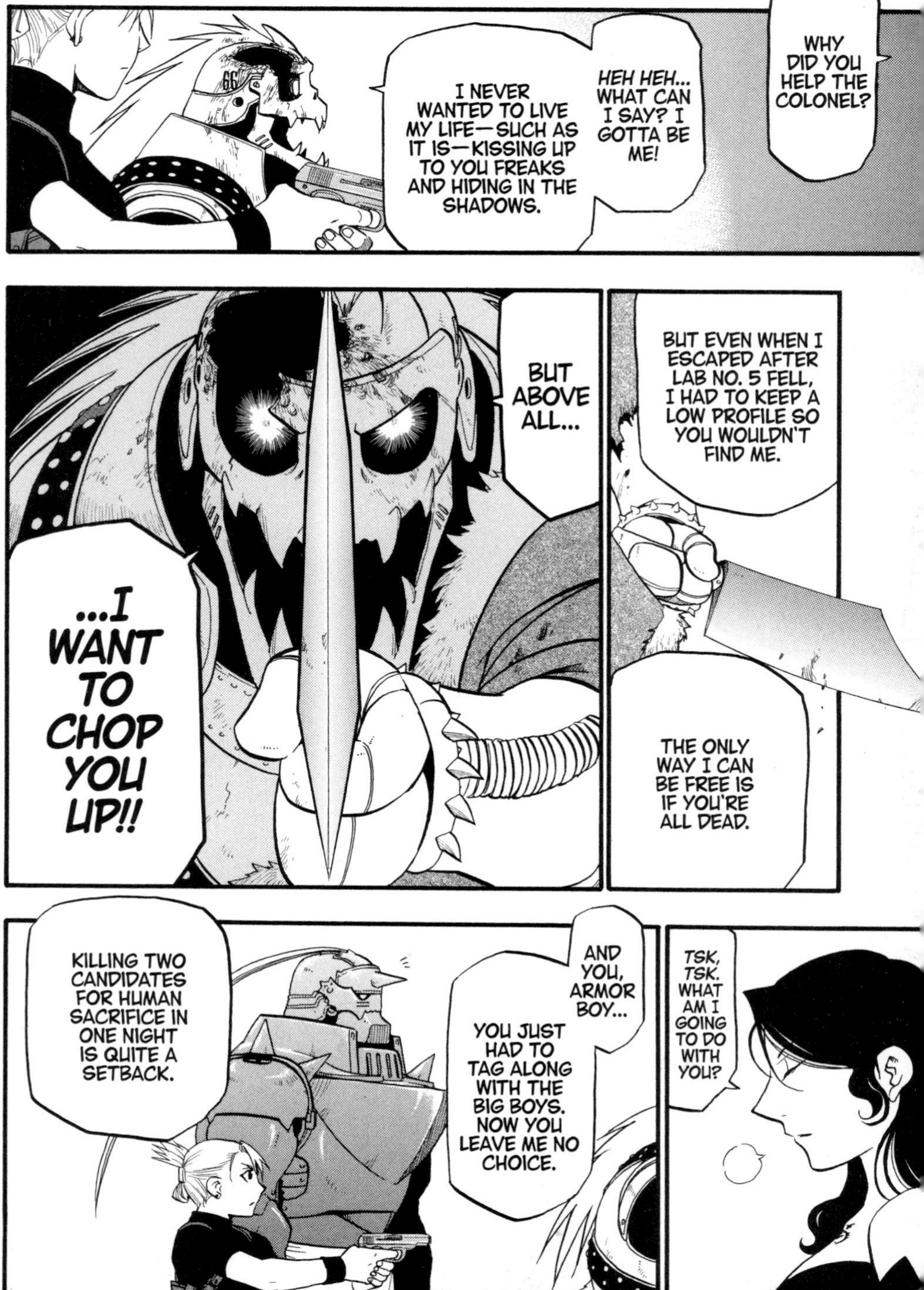
WHY DID YOU HELP THE COLONEL?
HEH HEH... WHAT CAN I SAY? I GOTTA BE ME!
I NEVER WANTED TO LIVE MY LIFE—SUCH AS IT IS—KISSING UP TO YOU FREAKS AND HIDING IN THE SHADOWS.
BUT EVEN WHEN I ESCAPED AFTER LAB NO. 5 FELL, I HAD TO KEEP A LOW PROFILE SO YOU WOULDN'T FIND ME.
THE ONLY WAY I CAN BE FREE IS IF YOU'RE ALL DEAD.
BUT ABOVE ALL...
...I WANT TO CHOP YOU UP!!
TSK, TSK. WHAT AM I GOING TO DO WITH YOU?
KILLING TWO CANDIDATES FOR HUMAN SACRIFICE IN ONE NIGHT IS QUITE A SETBACK.
AND YOU, ARMOR BOY...
YOU JUST HAD TO TAG ALONG WITH THE BIG BOYS. NOW YOU LEAVE ME NO CHOICE.

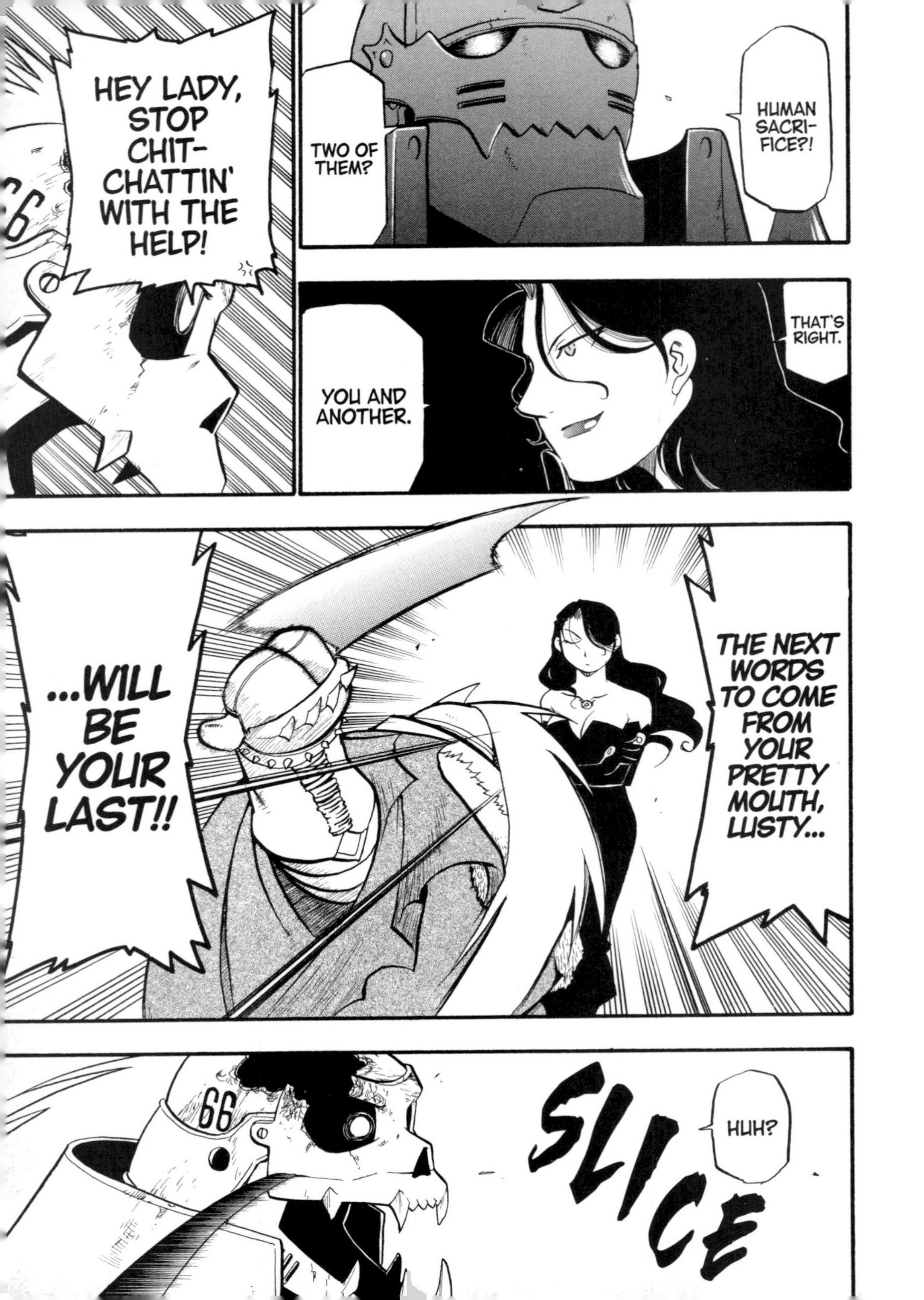
HUMAN SACRI-FICE?!
TWO OF THEM?
THAT'S RIGHT.
YOU AND ANOTHER.
HEY LADY, STOP CHIT-CHATTIN' WITH THE HELP!
THE NEXT WORDS TO COME FROM YOUR PRETTY MOUTH, LUSTY...
...WILL BE YOUR LAST!!
66
HUH?
SLICE
66

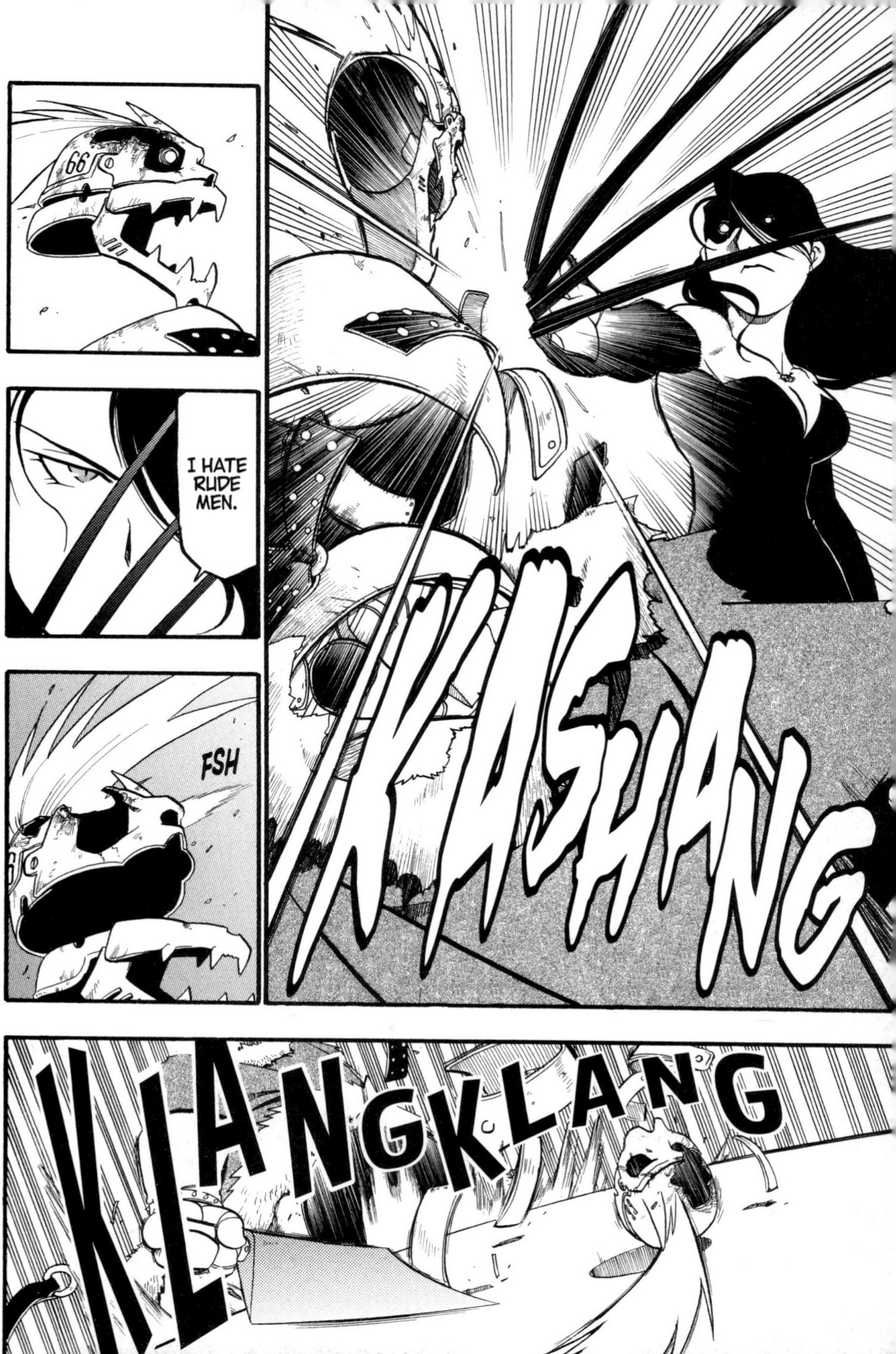
KASHANG
I HATE RUDE MEN.
FSH
KLANGKLANG

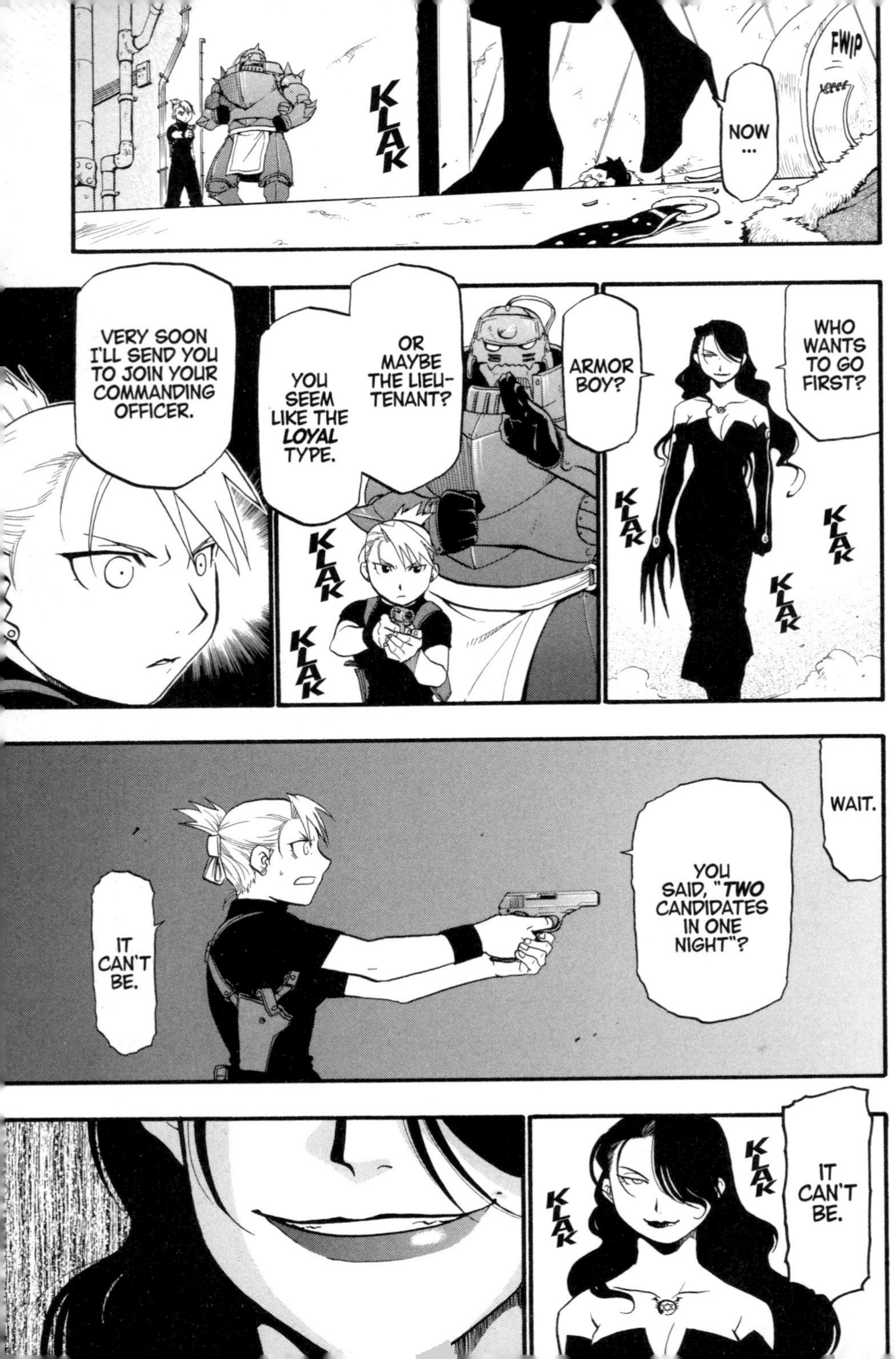
FWIP
NOW ...
KLAK
WHO WANTS TO GO FIRST?
KLAK
KLAK
KLAK
ARMOR BOY?
OR MAYBE THE LIEU-TENANT?
YOU SEEM LIKE THE LOYAL TYPE.
KLAK
KLAK
VERY SOON I'LL SEND YOU TO JOIN YOUR COMMANDING OFFICER.
WAIT.
YOU SAID, "TWO CANDIDATES IN ONE NIGHT"?
IT CAN'T BE.
IT CAN'T BE.
KLAK
KLAK

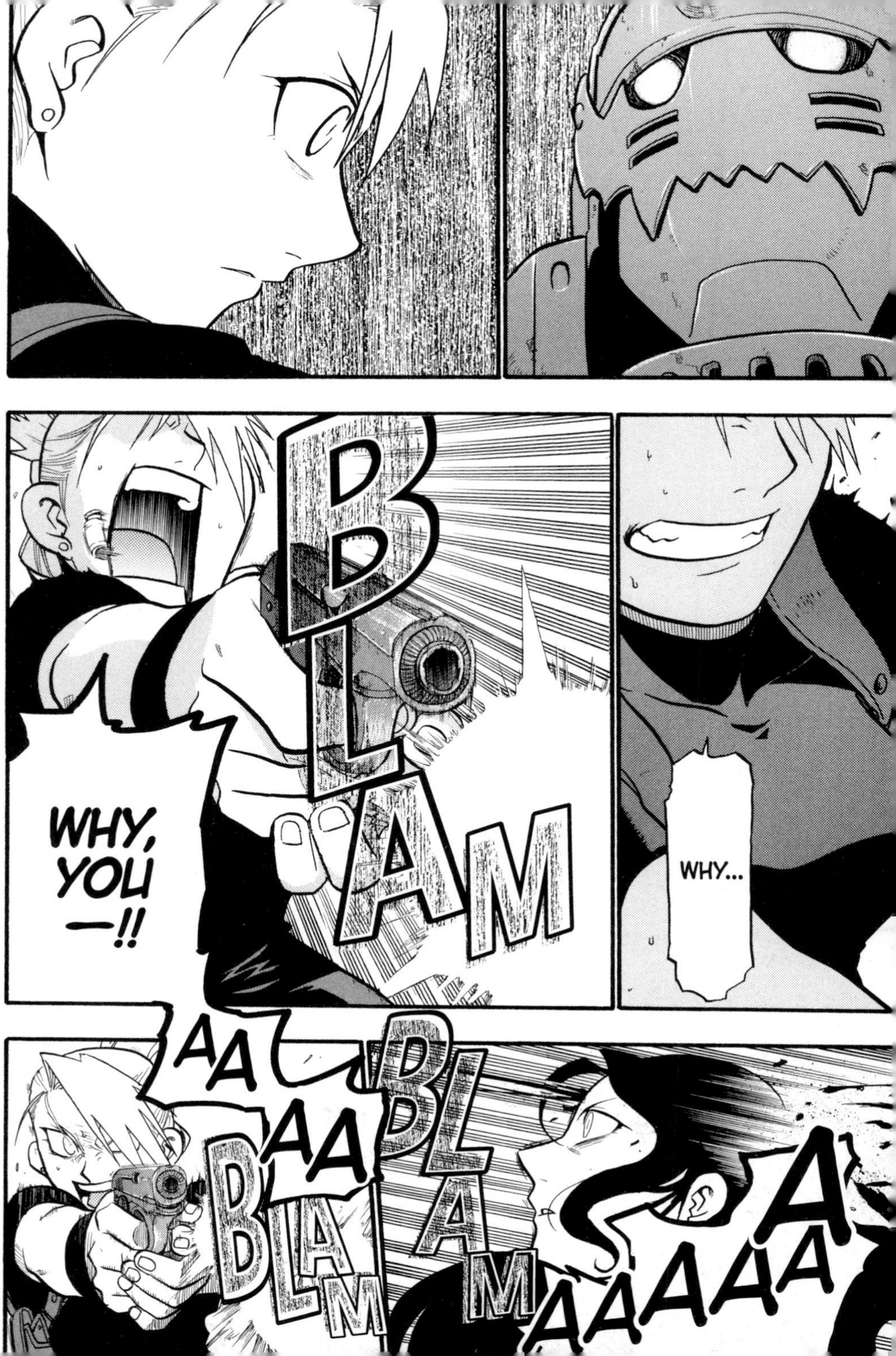
WHY...
BLAM
WHY, YOU —!!
AAAAAAA
BLAM
AAAA
BLAM
BLAM

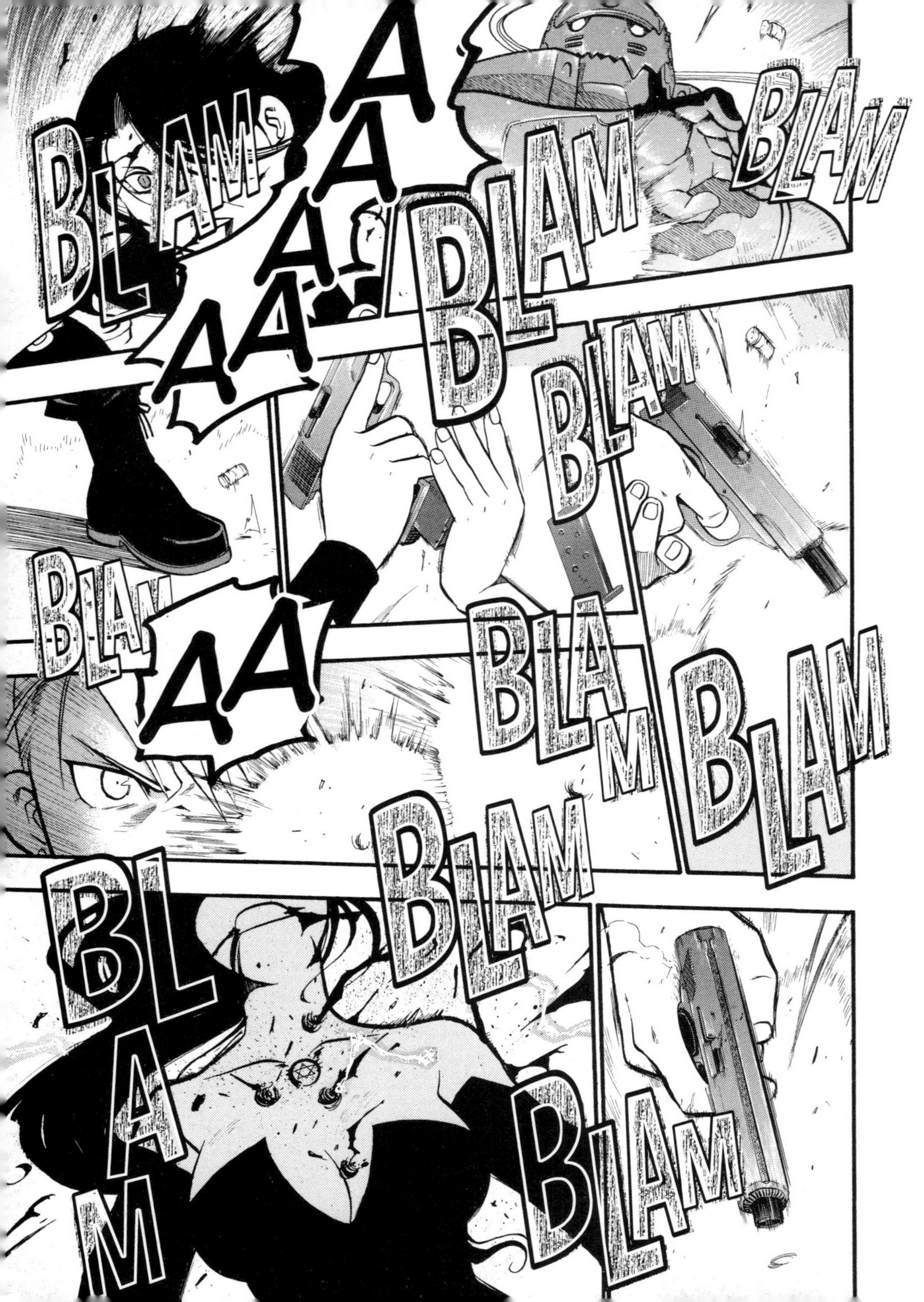

BLAM
BLAM
BLAM
BLAM
AAAAAA
BLAM
BLAM
BLAM
BLAM
BLAM
BLAM
AA
BLAM
BLAM

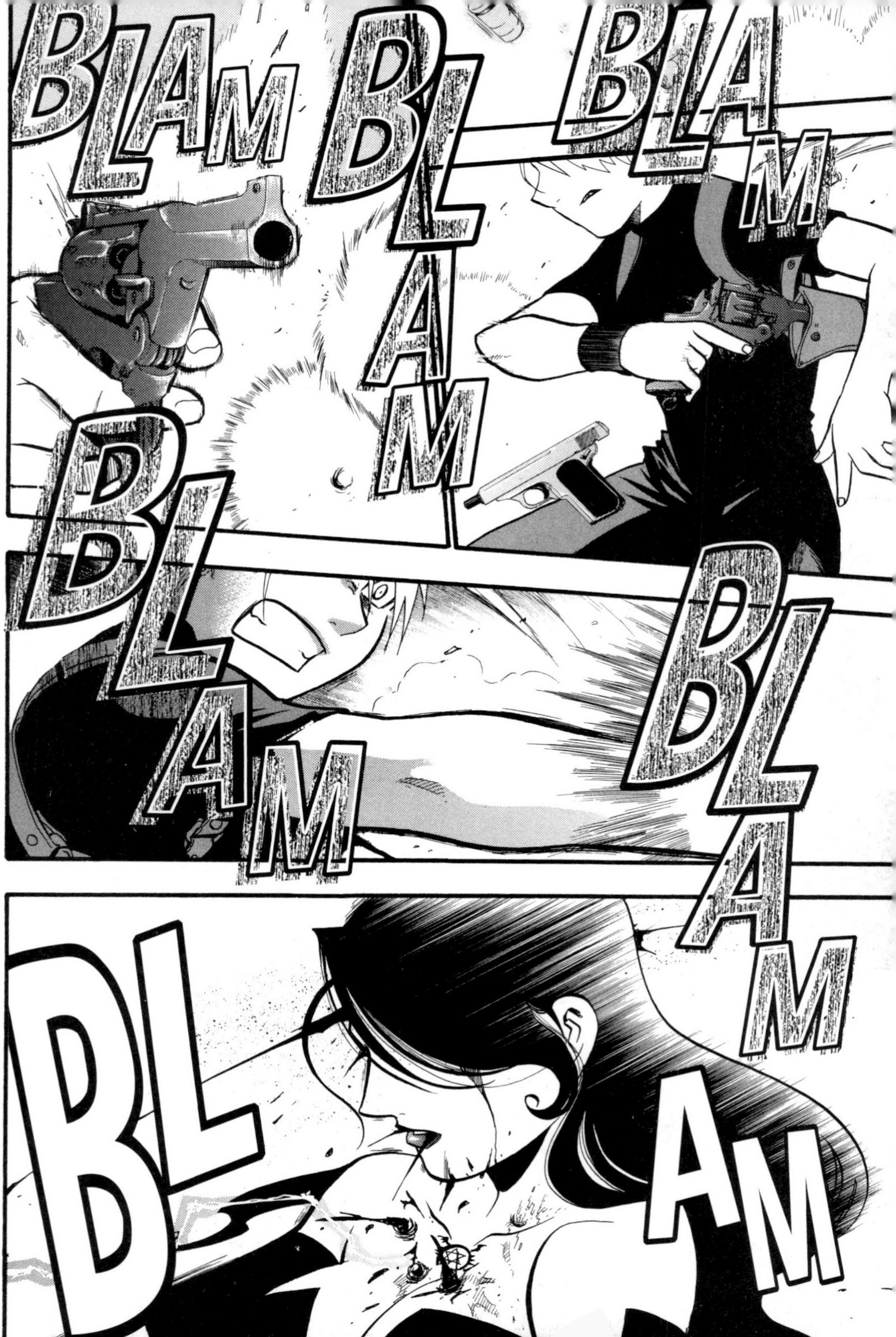
BLAM
BLAM
BLAM
BLAM
BLAM
BLAM

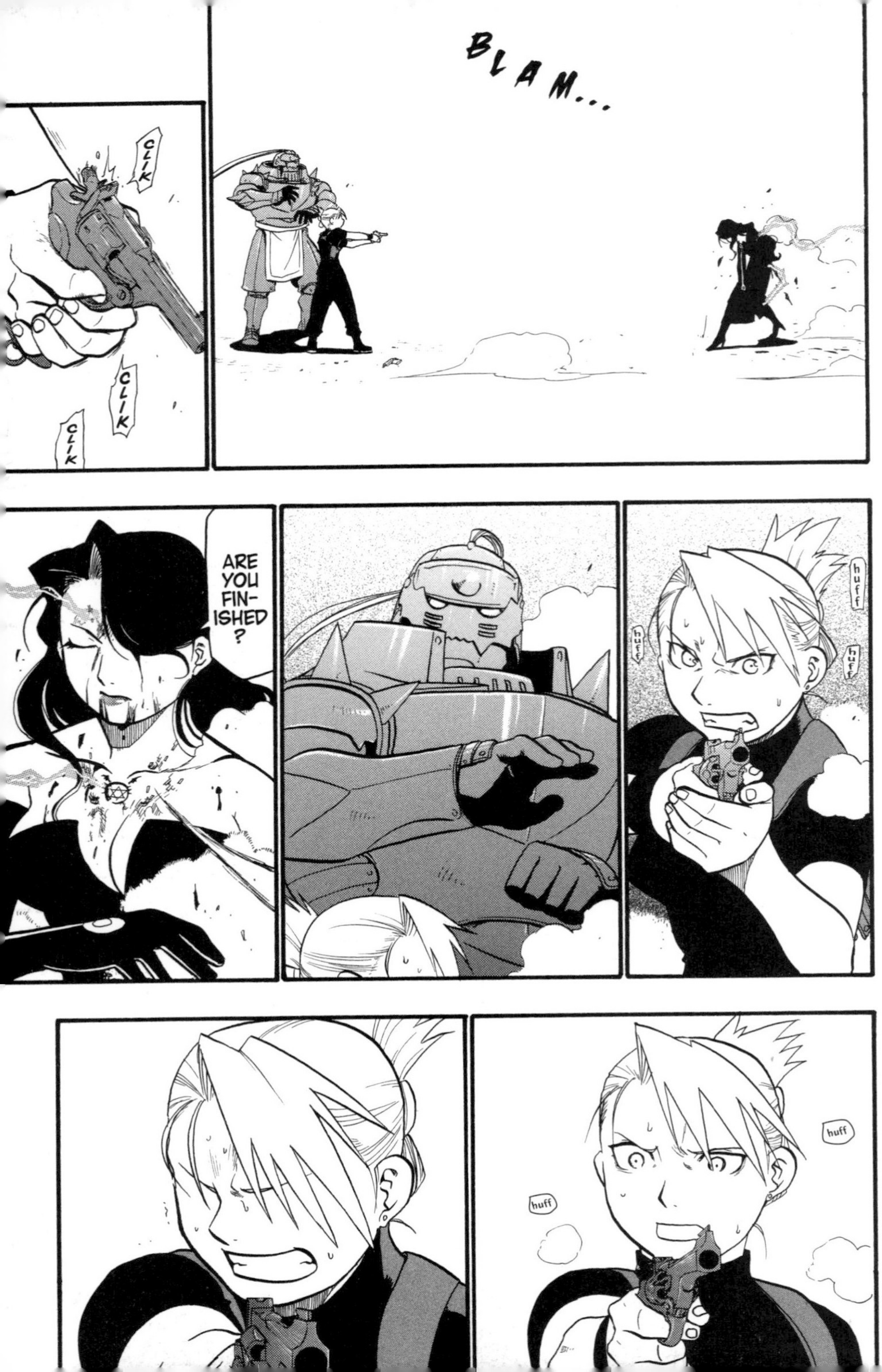
BLAM...
CLIK
CLIK
CLIK
huff
huff
huff
ARE YOU FIN-ISHED?
huff
huff

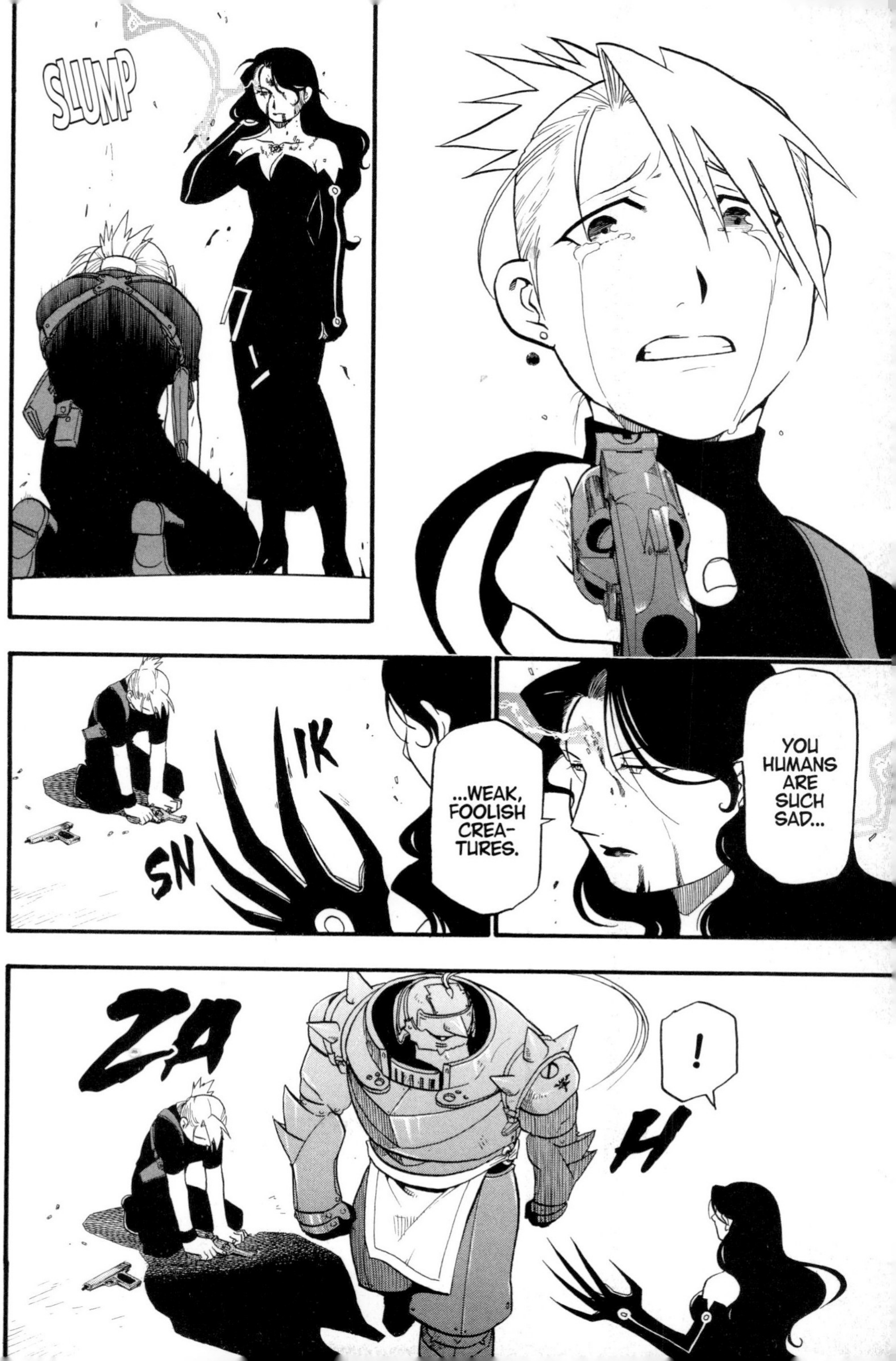
SLUMP
YOU HUMANS ARE SUCH SAD...
...WEAK, FOOLISH CREA- TURES.
SNIK
!
ZAH

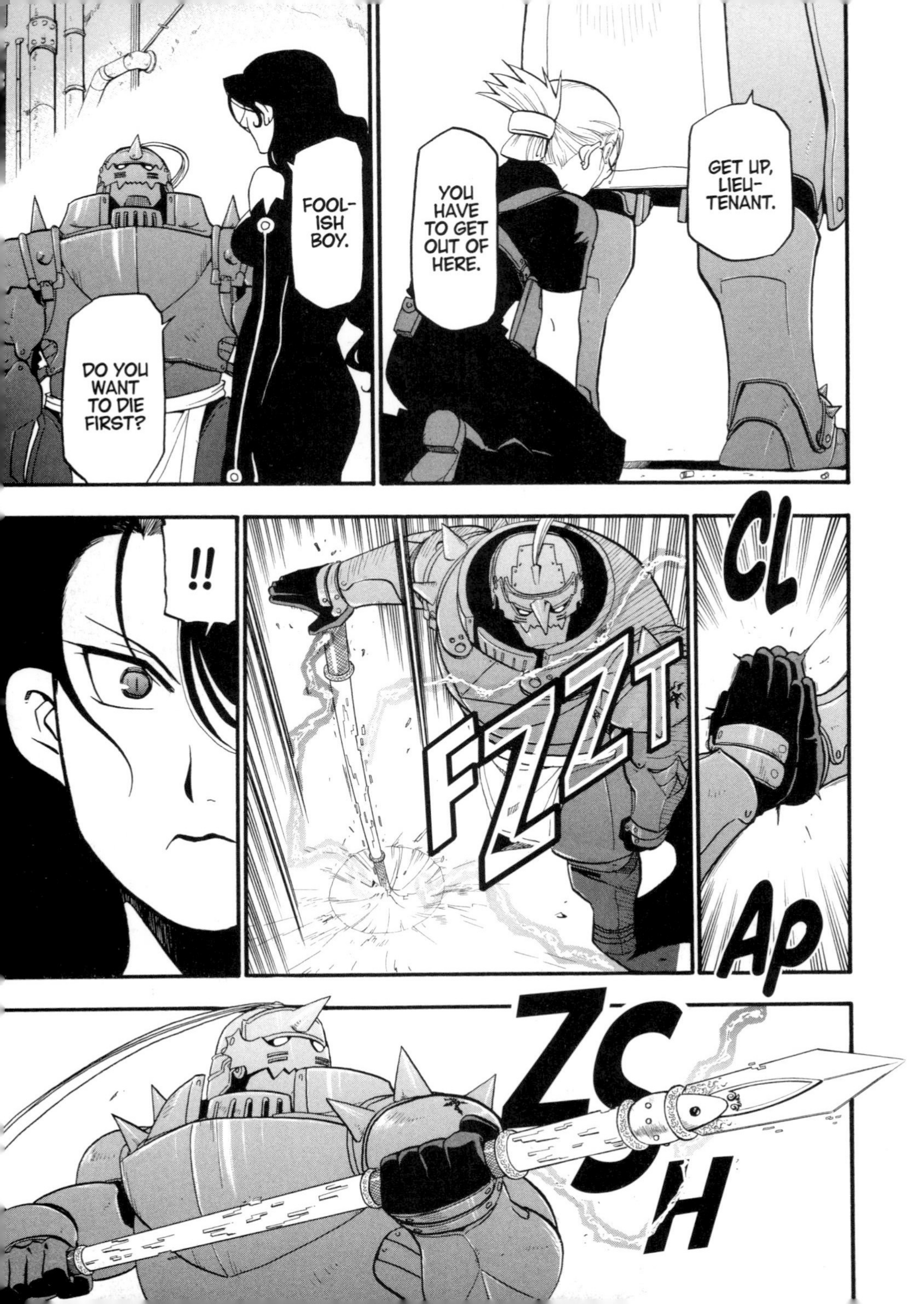
GET UP, LIEU-TENANT.
YOU HAVE TO GET OUT OF HERE.
FOOL-ISH BOY.
DO YOU WANT TO DIE FIRST?
CL
AP
FZZT
!!
ZCSH

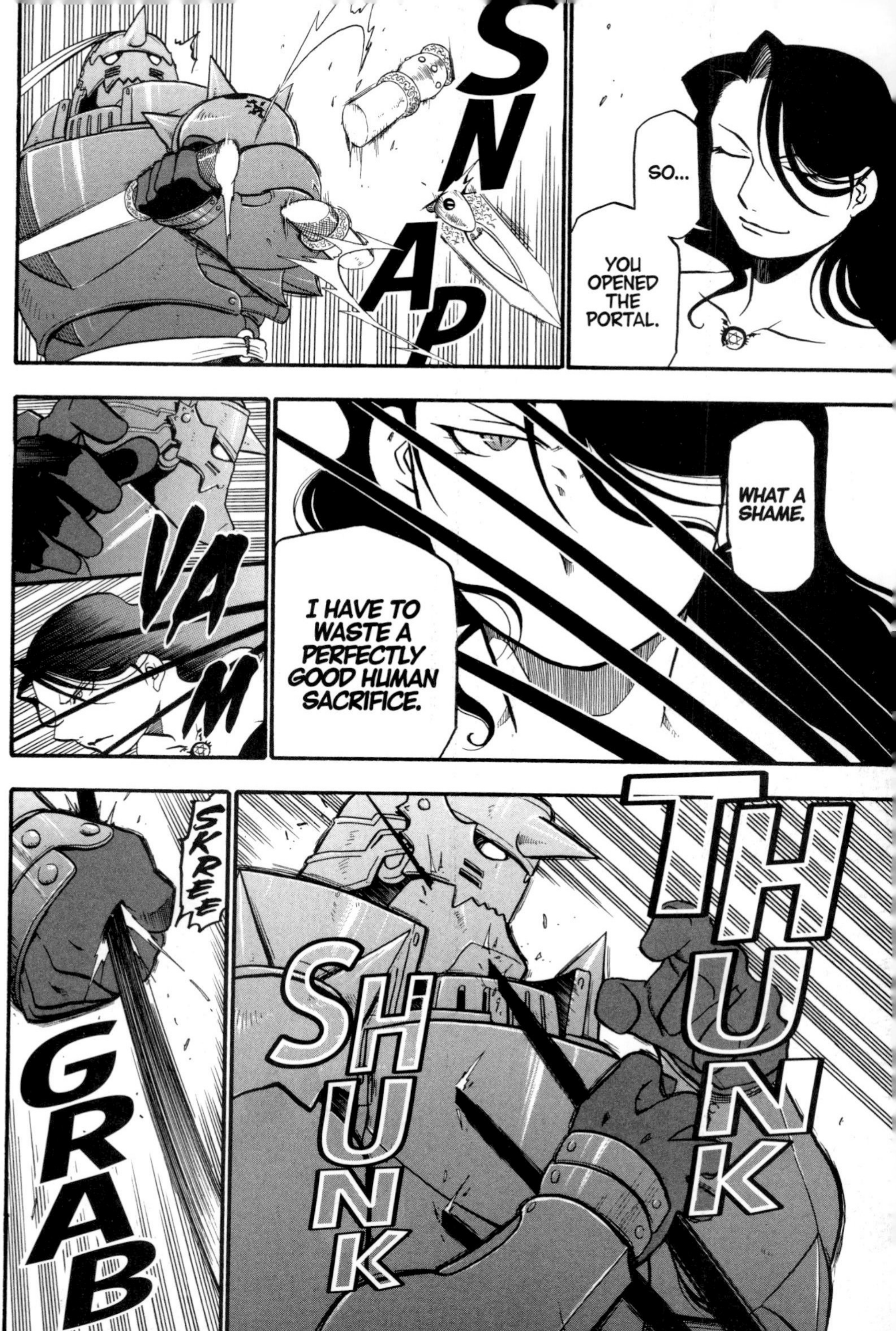
SO...
YOU OPENED THE PORTAL.
SNAP
WHAT A SHAME.
I HAVE TO WASTE A PERFECTLY GOOD HUMAN SACRIFICE.
VAMM
THUNK
SHUNK
SKREE
GRAB

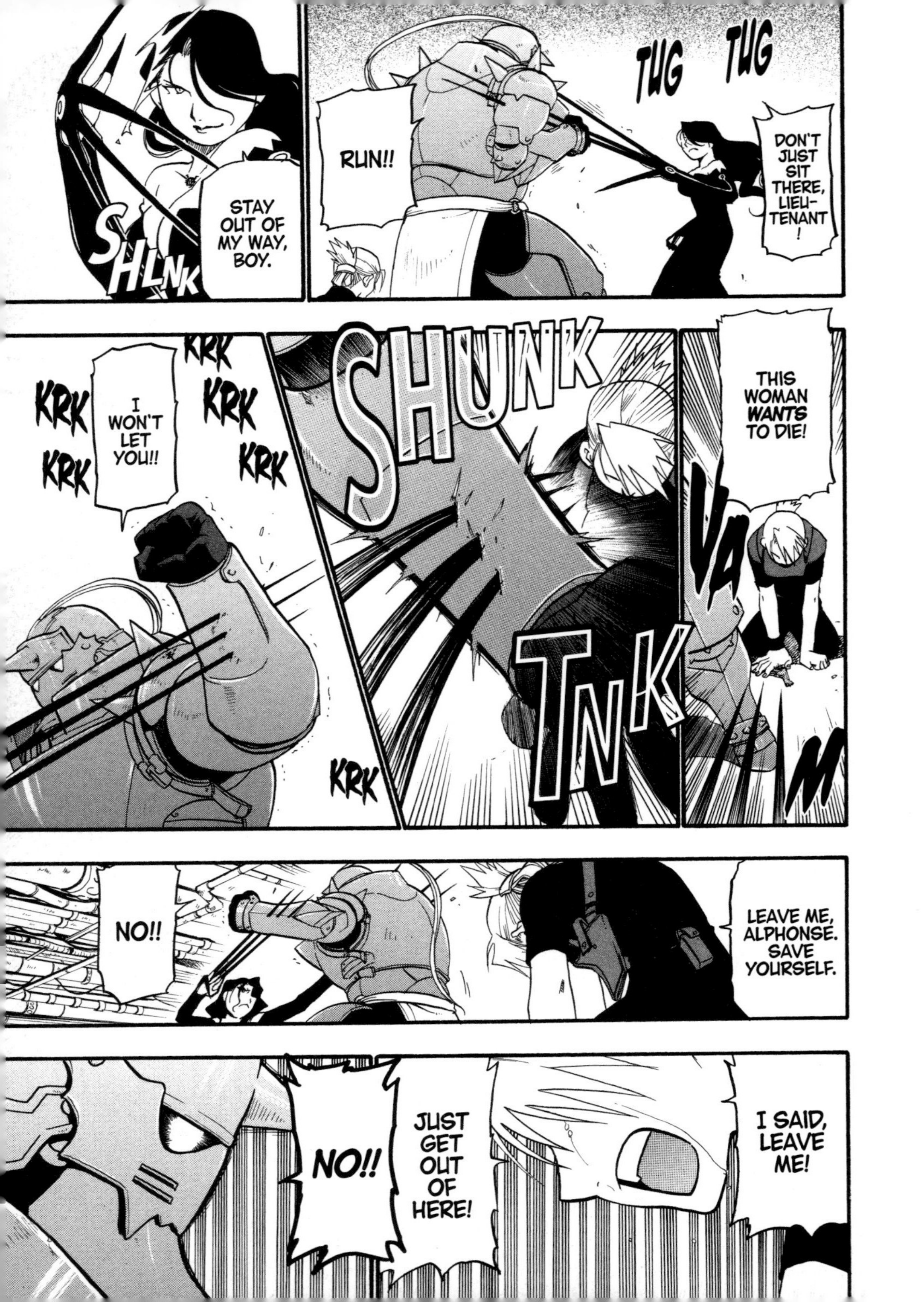
TUG TUG
DON'T JUST SIT THERE, LIEU-TENANT!
RUN!!
STAY OUT OF MY WAY, BOY.
SHLNK
THIS WOMAN WANTS TO DIE!
SHUNK
TNK
KRK KRK KRK KRK KRK KRK
I WON'T LET YOU!!
LEAVE ME, ALPHONSE. SAVE YOURSELF.
NO!!
I SAID, LEAVE ME!
JUST GET OUT OF HERE!
NO!!

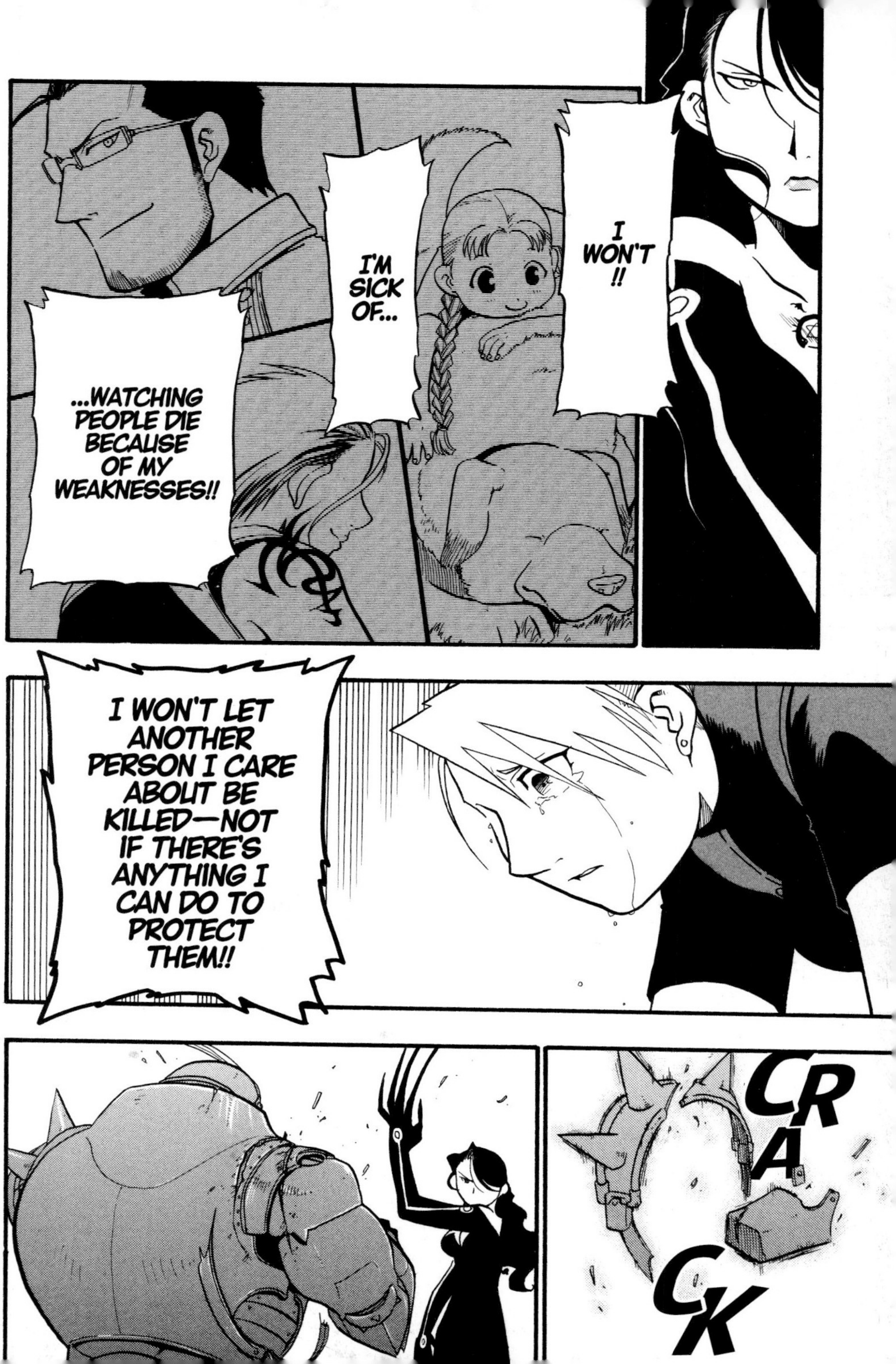
I WON'T !!
I'M SICK OF...
...WATCHING PEOPLE DIE BECAUSE OF MY WEAKNESSES!!
I WON'T LET ANOTHER PERSON I CARE ABOUT BE KILLED—NOT IF THERE'S ANYTHING I CAN DO TO PROTECT THEM!!
CRACK

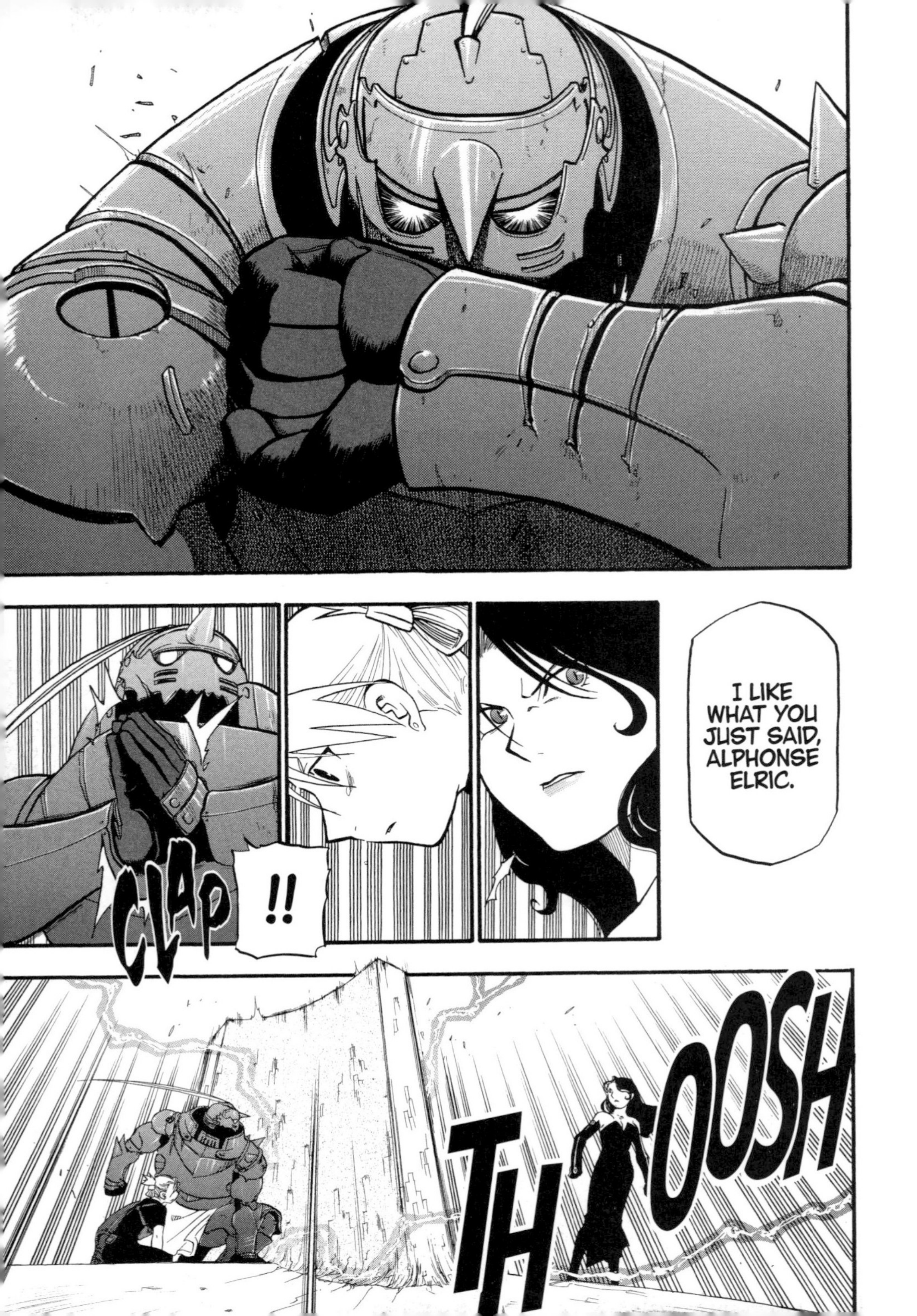
I LIKE WHAT YOU JUST SAID, ALPHONSE ELRIC.
!!
CLAP
THOOSH

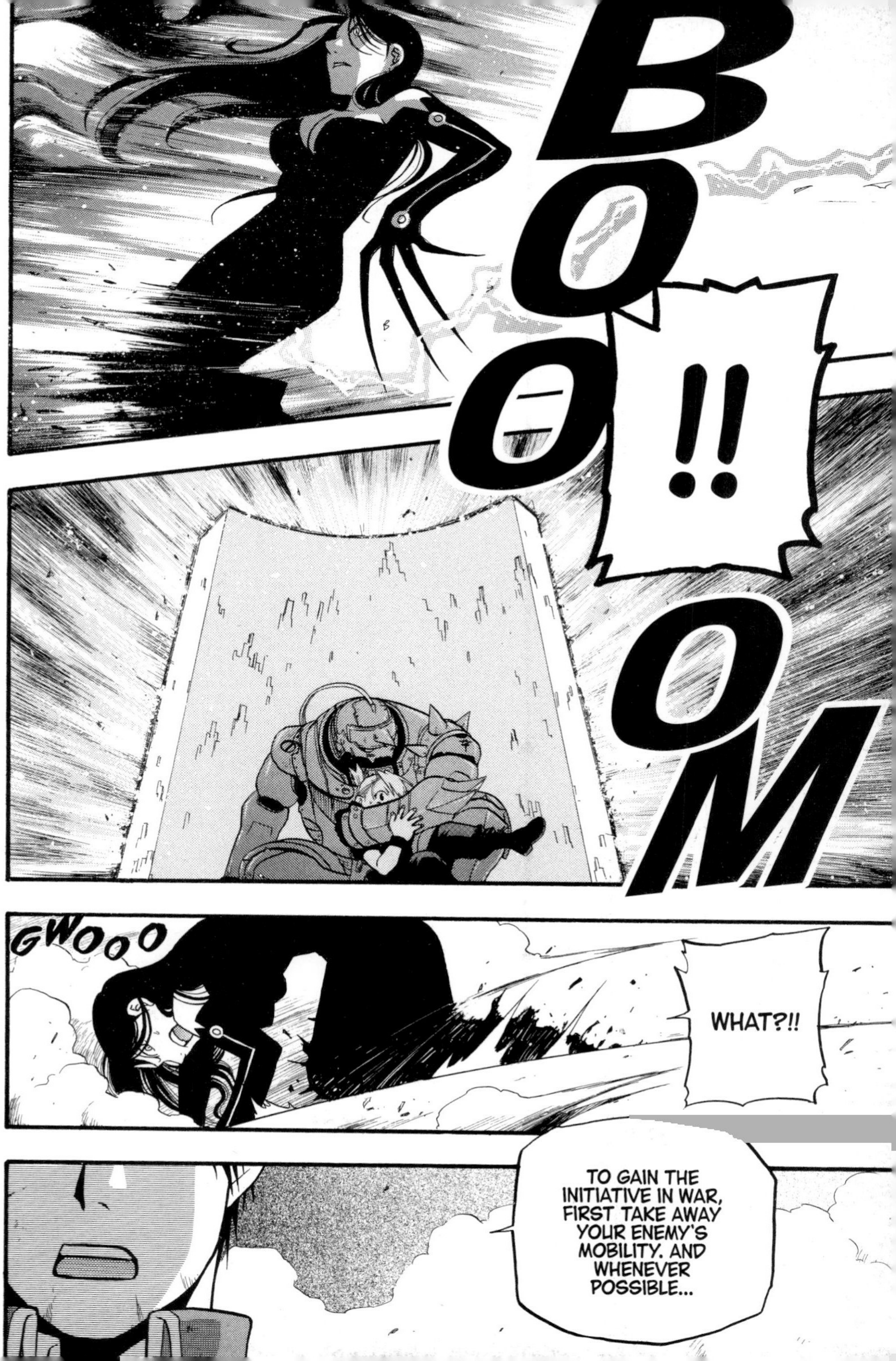
BOOOOM!!
WHAT?!!
GWOOO
TO GAIN THE INITIATIVE IN WAR, FIRST TAKE AWAY YOUR ENEMY'S MOBILITY. AND WHENEVER POSSIBLE...

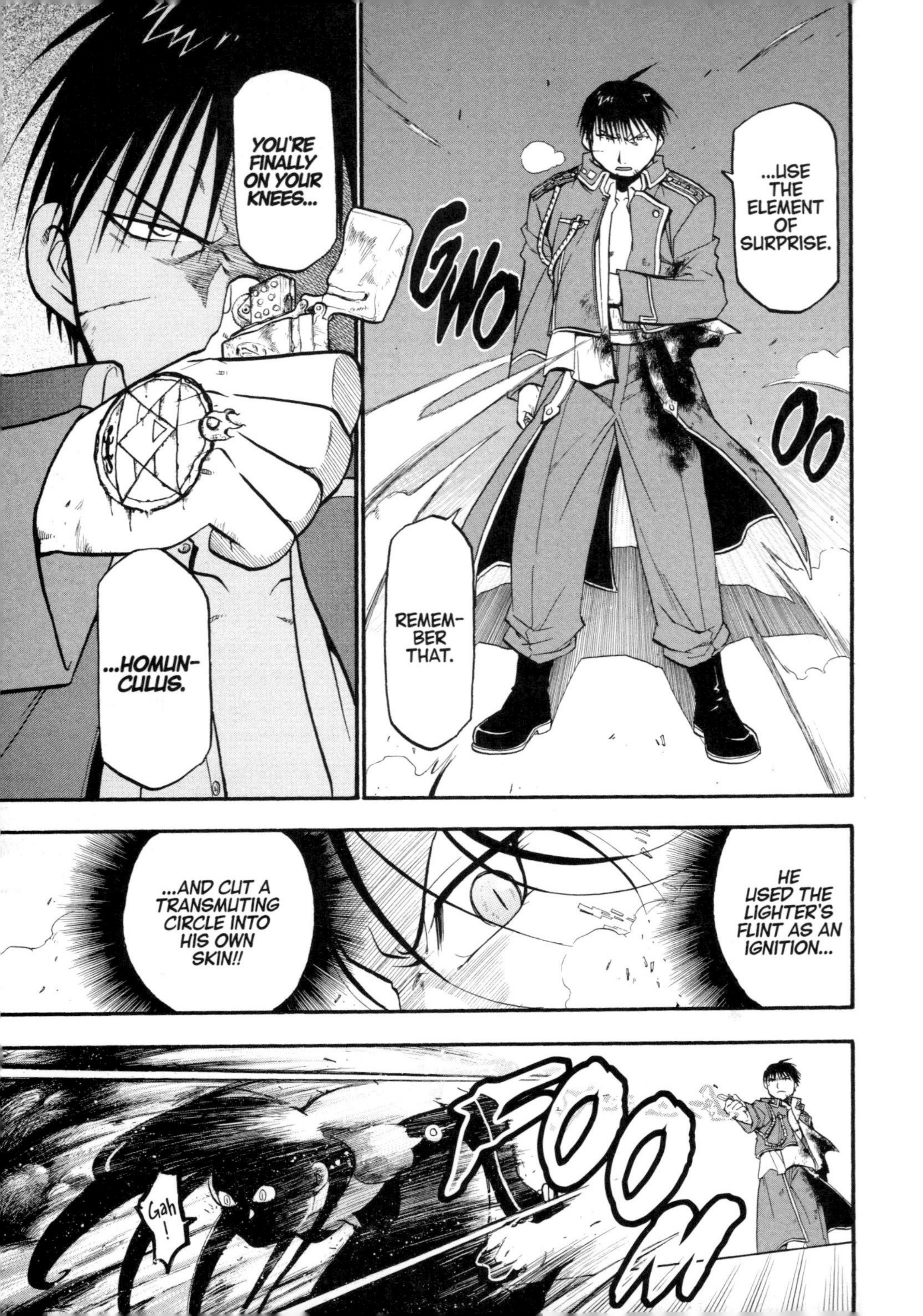
...USE THE ELEMENT OF SURPRISE.
GWOOOO
REMEMBER THAT.
YOU'RE FINALLY ON YOUR KNEES...
...HOMUNCULUS.
HE USED THE LIGHTER'S FLINT AS AN IGNITION...
...AND CUT A TRANSMUTING CIRCLE INTO HIS OWN SKIN!!
FOOOM
Gah!

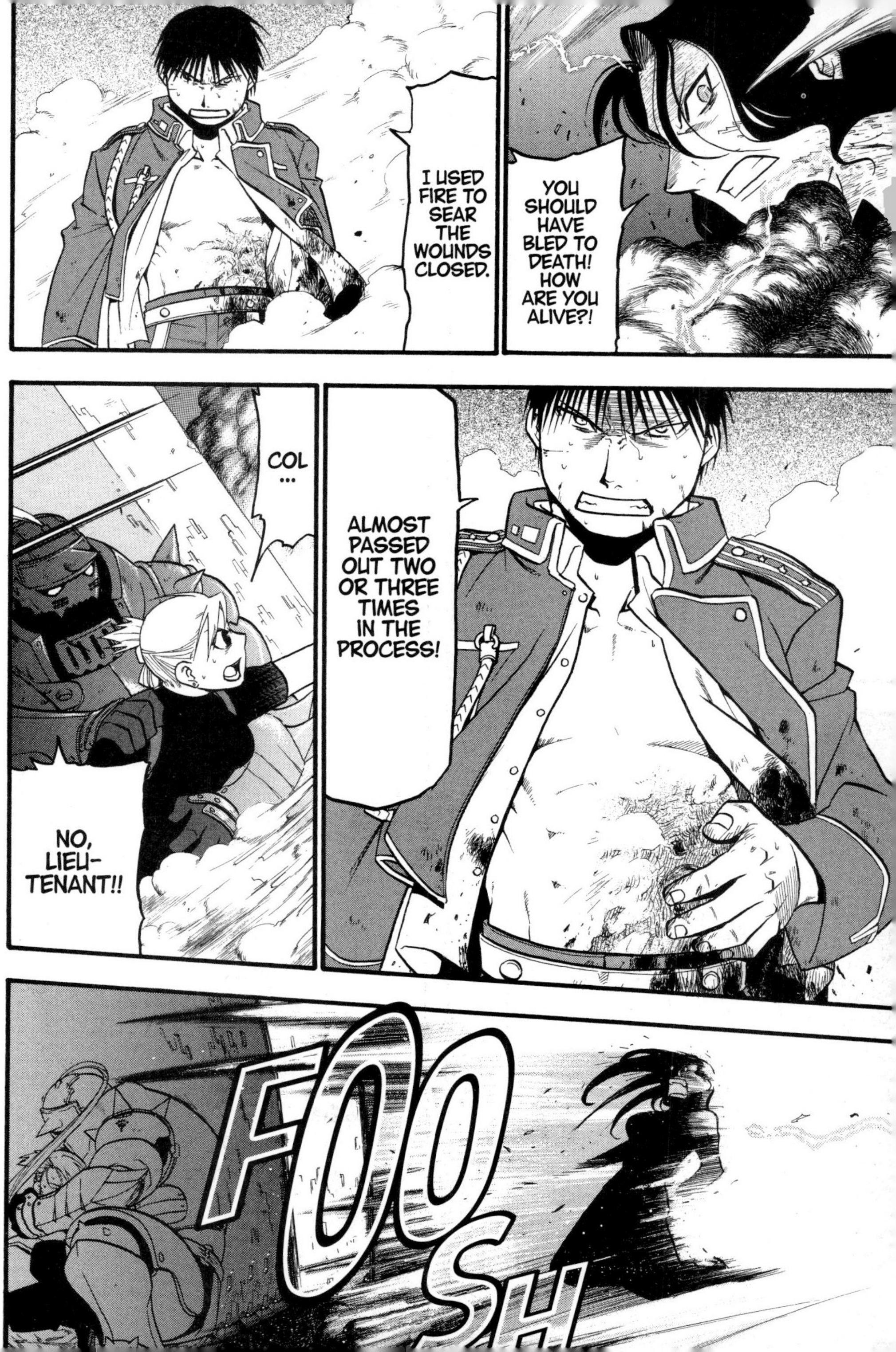
YOU SHOULD HAVE BLED TO DEATH! HOW ARE YOU ALIVE?!
I USED FIRE TO SEAR THE WOUNDS CLOSED.
ALMOST PASSED OUT TWO OR THREE TIMES IN THE PROCESS!
COL...
NO, LIEU-TENANT!!
FOOSH

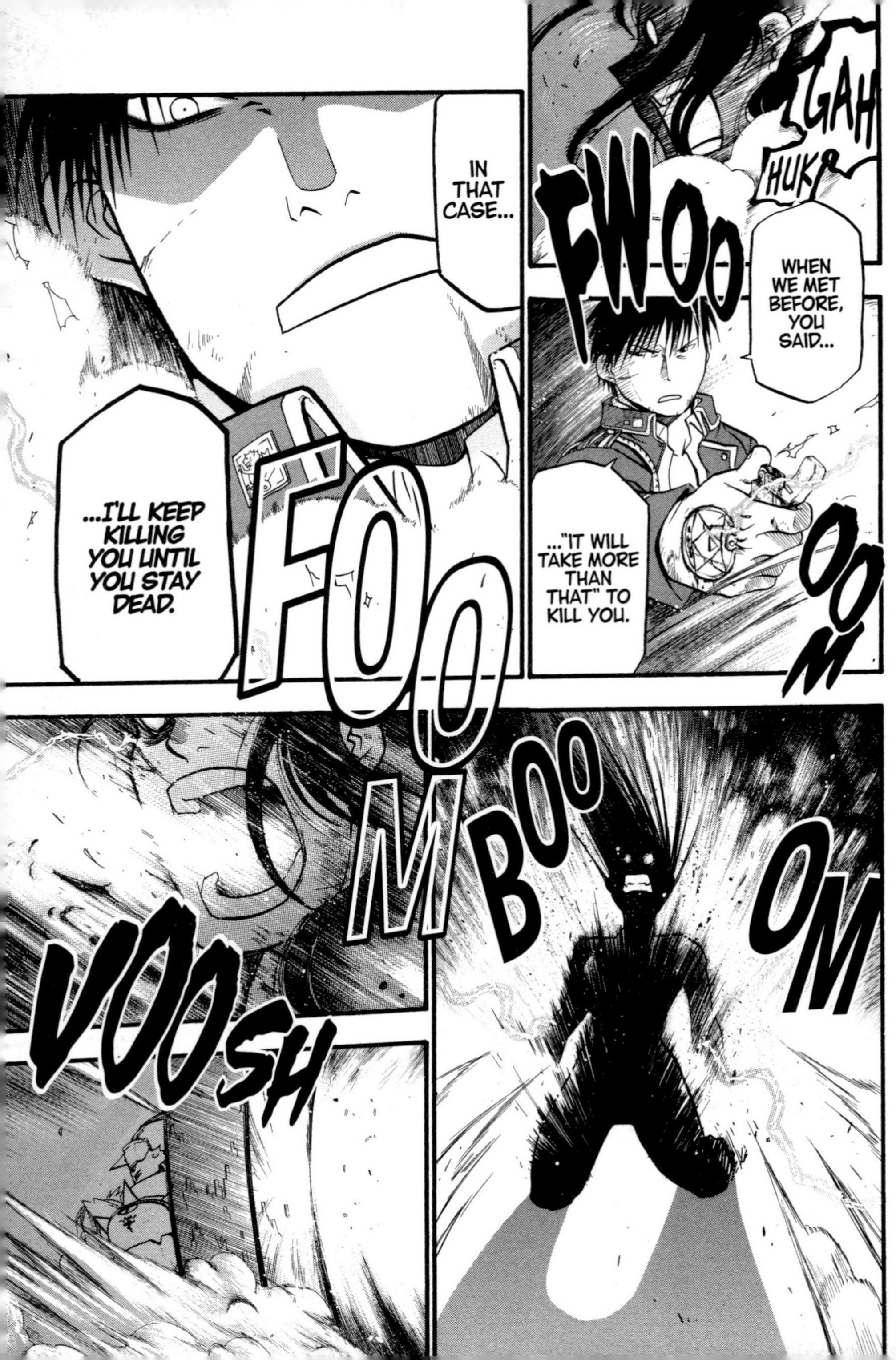
GAH
HUK
FWOO
WHEN WE MET BEFORE, YOU SAID...
..."IT WILL TAKE MORE THAN THAT" TO KILL YOU.
OOM
IN THAT CASE...
...I'LL KEEP KILLING YOU UNTIL YOU STAY DEAD.
FOOOM
BOOOM
VOOSH

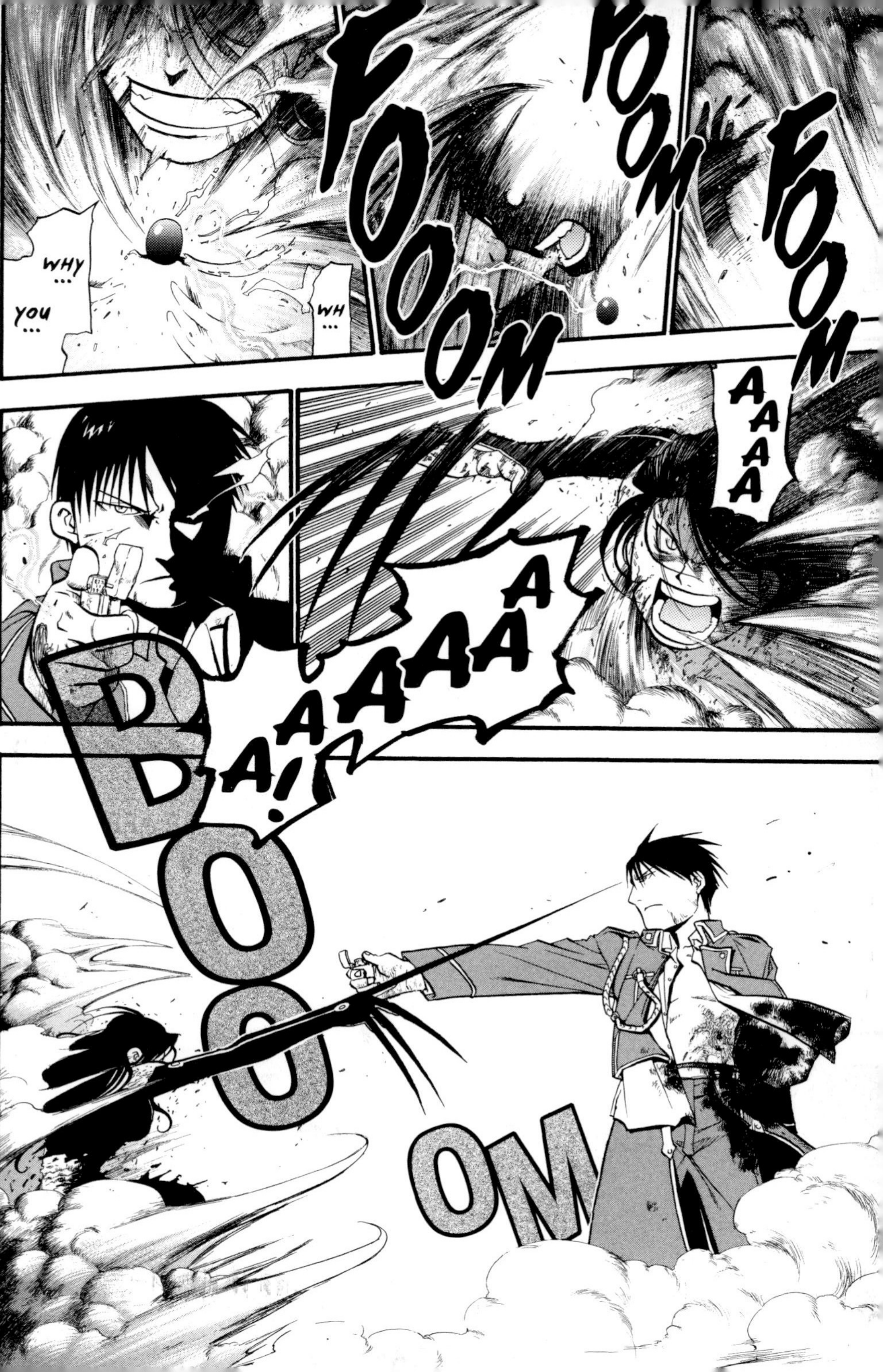

FOOM
FOOM
WH ...
FOOOOM
WHY ...
YOU ...
AAAA
AAAAAAAAA!
BOOOM

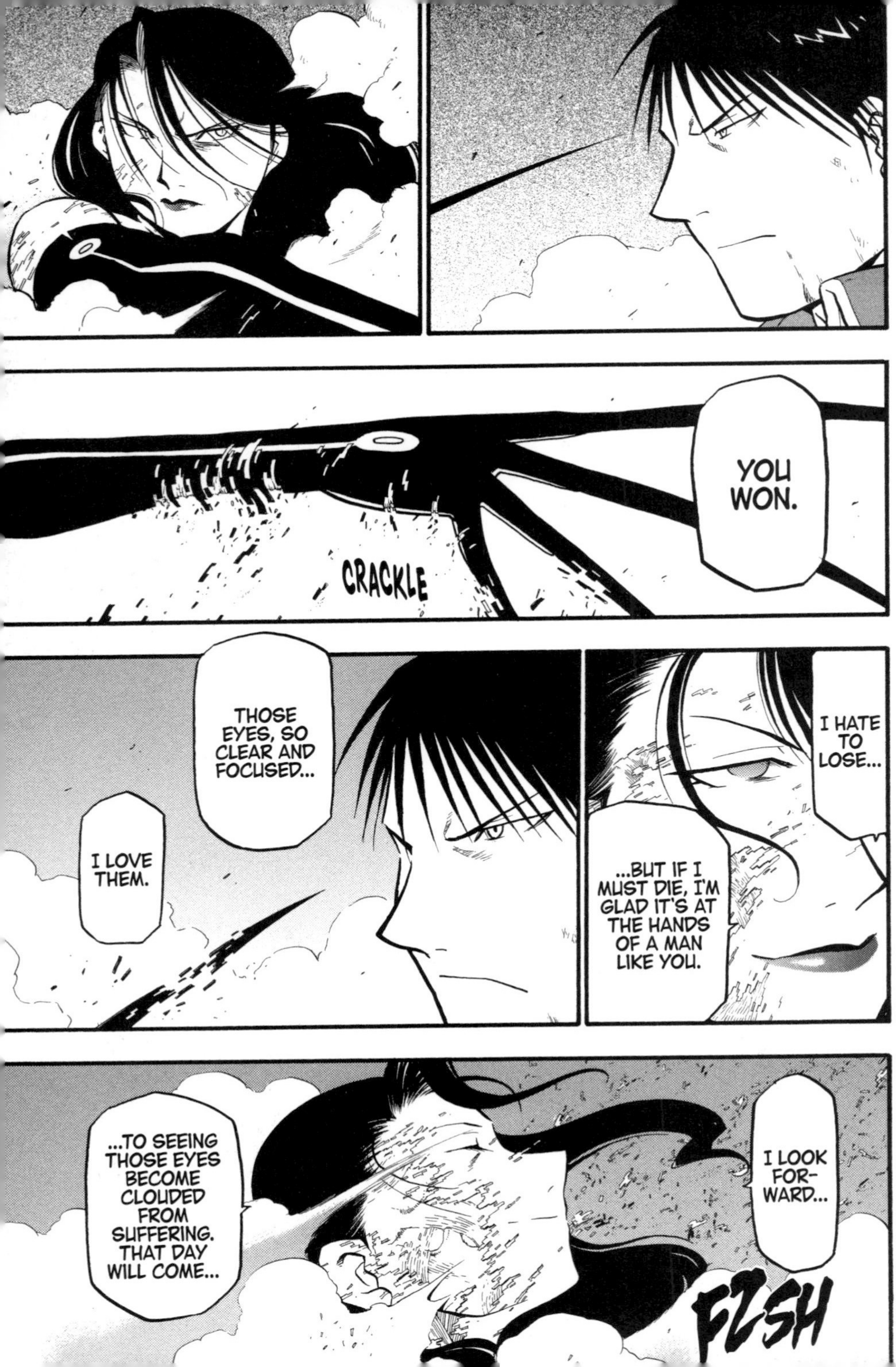
YOU WON.
CRACKLE
I HATE TO LOSE...
...BUT IF I MUST DIE, I'M GLAD IT'S AT THE HANDS OF A MAN LIKE YOU.
THOSE EYES, SO CLEAR AND FOCUSED...
I LOVE THEM.
I LOOK FOR-WARD...
...TO SEEING THOSE EYES BECOME CLOUDED FROM SUFFERING. THAT DAY WILL COME...
FZSH

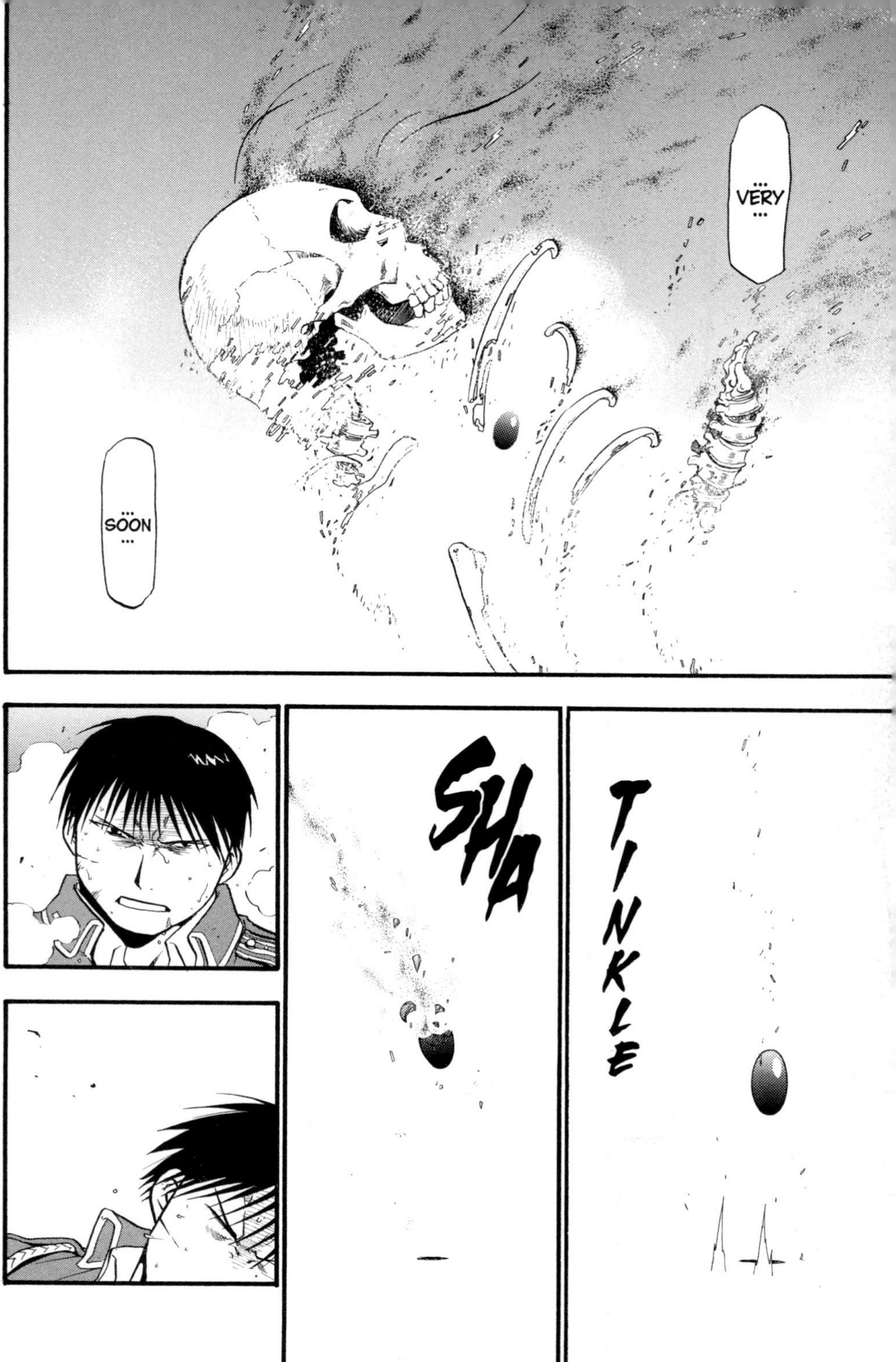
...VERY...
...SOON...
TINKLE
SHA

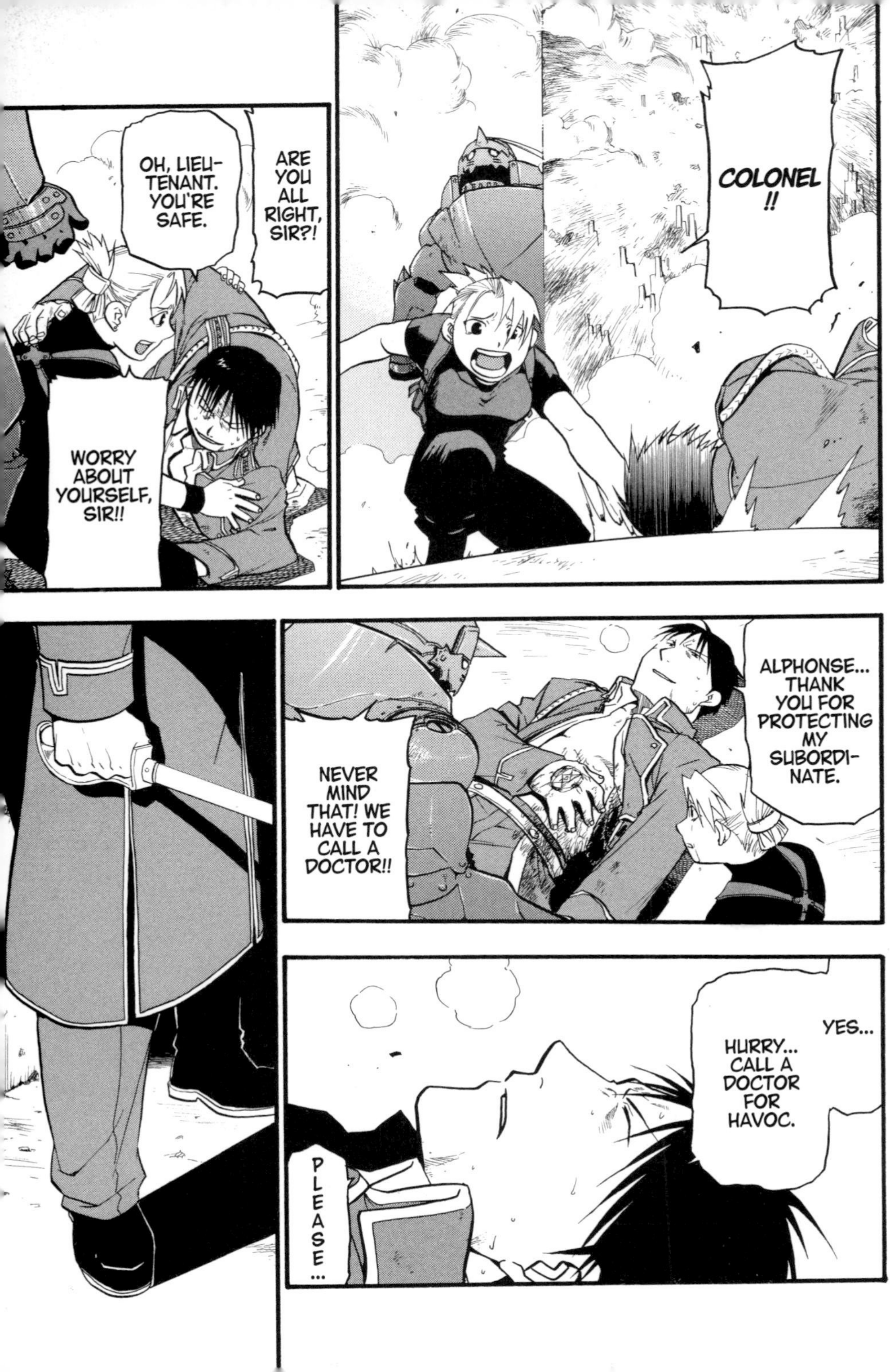
COLONEL !!
ARE YOU ALL RIGHT, SIR?!
OH, LIEU-TENANT. YOU'RE SAFE.
WORRY ABOUT YOURSELF, SIR!!
ALPHONSE... THANK YOU FOR PROTECTING MY SUBORDI-NATE.
NEVER MIND THAT! WE HAVE TO CALL A DOCTOR!!
YES...
HURRY... CALL A DOCTOR FOR HAVOC.
PLEASE...

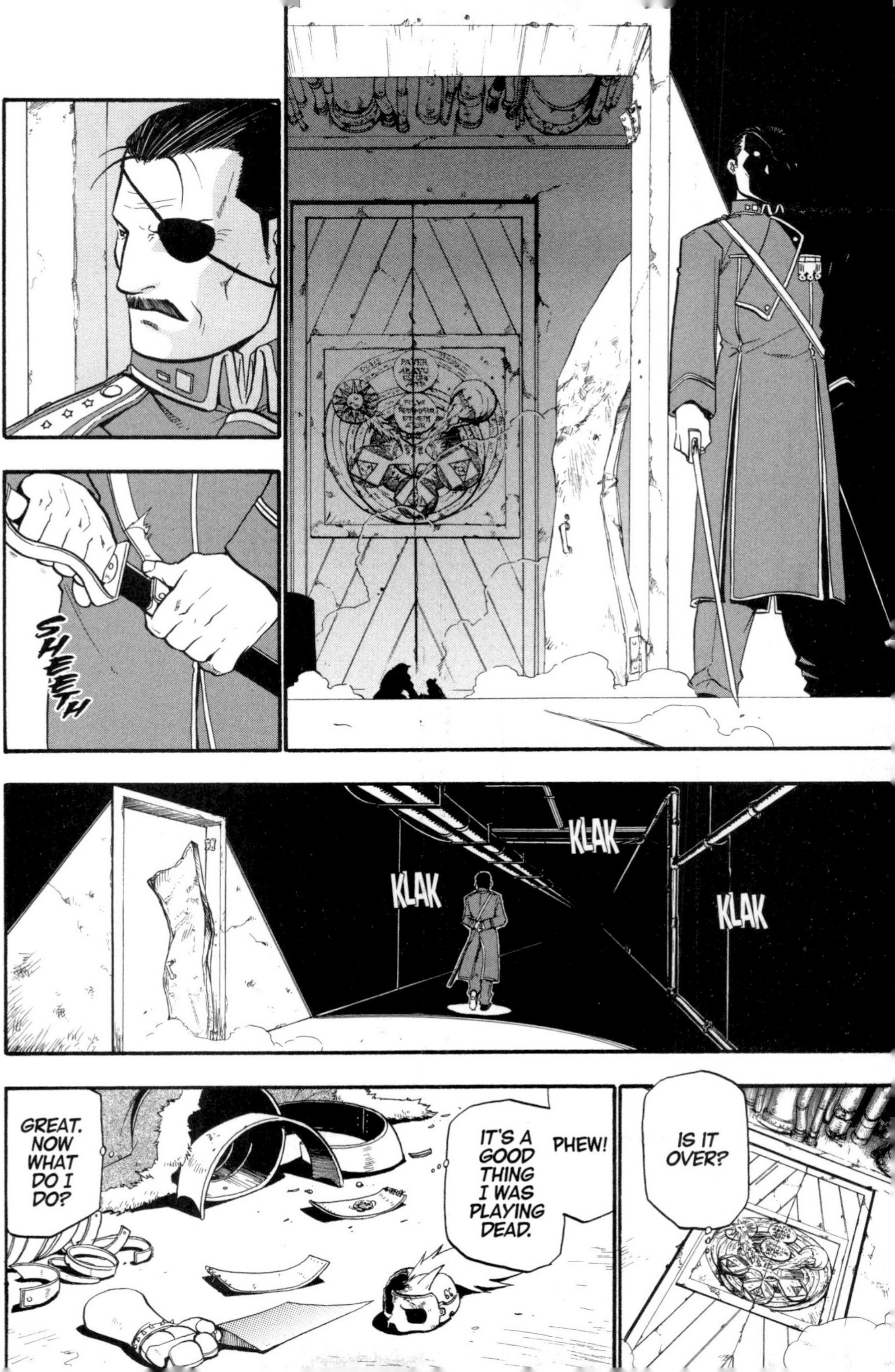
SHEETH
KLAK
KLAK
KLAK
IS IT OVER?
PHEW!
IT'S A GOOD THING I WAS PLAYING DEAD.
GREAT. NOW WHAT DO I DO?

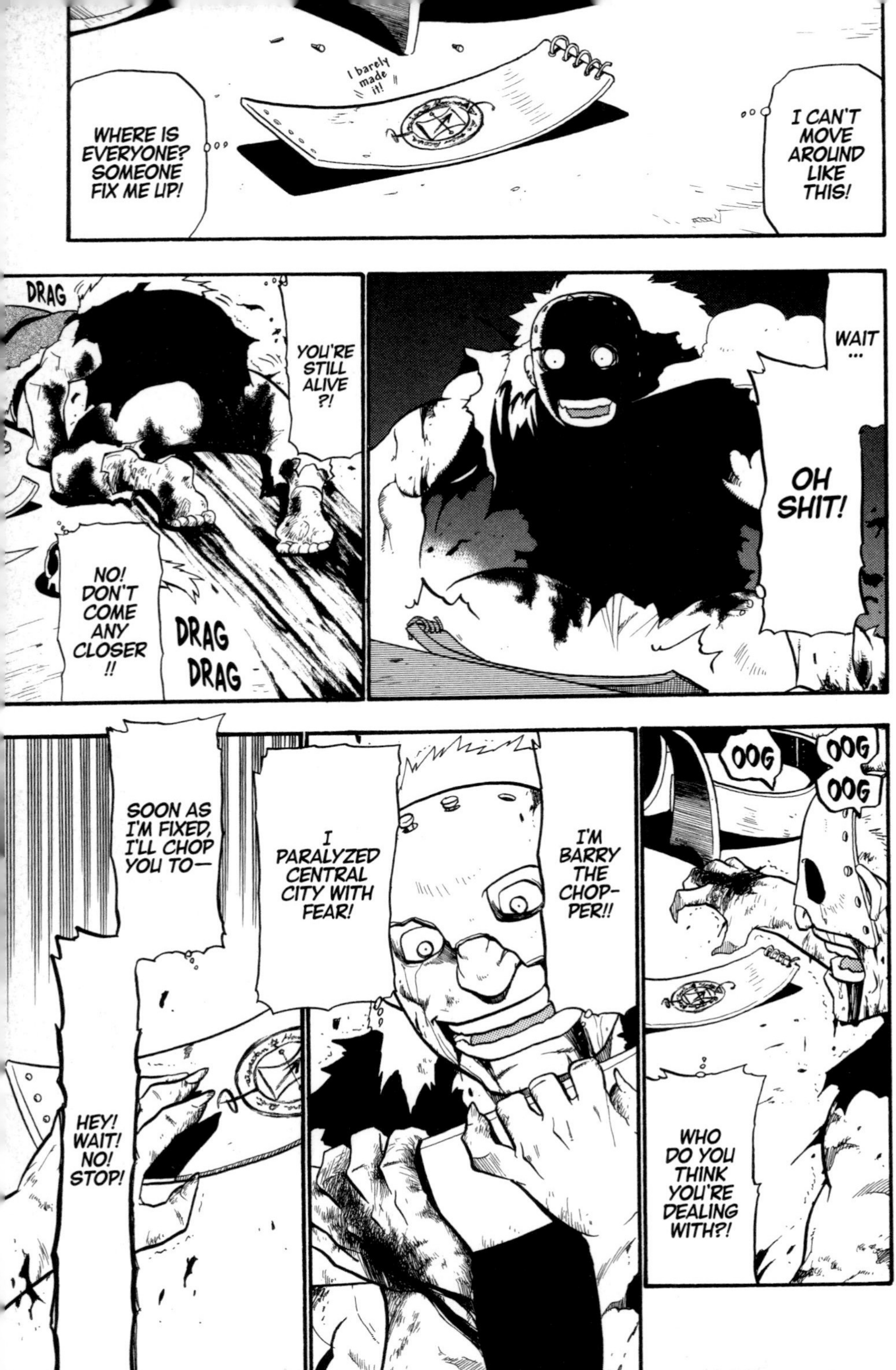
I CAN'T MOVE AROUND LIKE THIS!
I barely made it!
WHERE IS EVERYONE? SOMEONE FIX ME UP!
WAIT ...
OH SHIT!
YOU'RE STILL ALIVE ?!
DRAG
NO! DON'T COME ANY CLOSER !!
DRAG DRAG
OOG
OOG
OOG
WHO DO YOU THINK YOU'RE DEALING WITH?!
I'M BARRY THE CHOP-PER!!
I PARALYZED CENTRAL CITY WITH FEAR!
SOON AS I'M FIXED, I'LL CHOP YOU TO—
HEY! WAIT! NO! STOP!

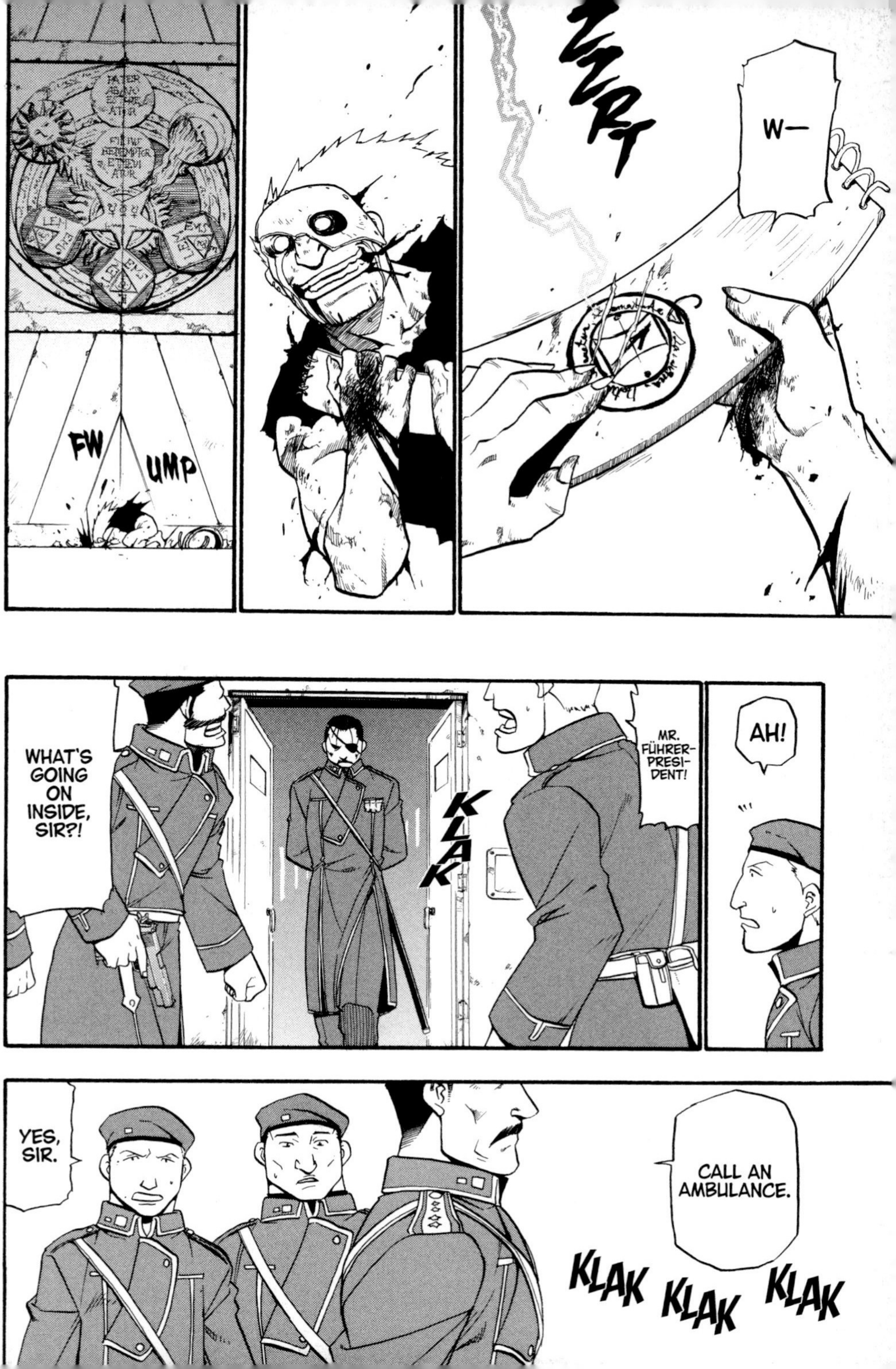
W—
ZZRT
FW UMP
AH!
MR. FÜHRER-PRESIDENT!
KLAK
WHAT'S GOING ON INSIDE, SIR?!
CALL AN AMBULANCE.
KLAK KLAK KLAK
YES, SIR.

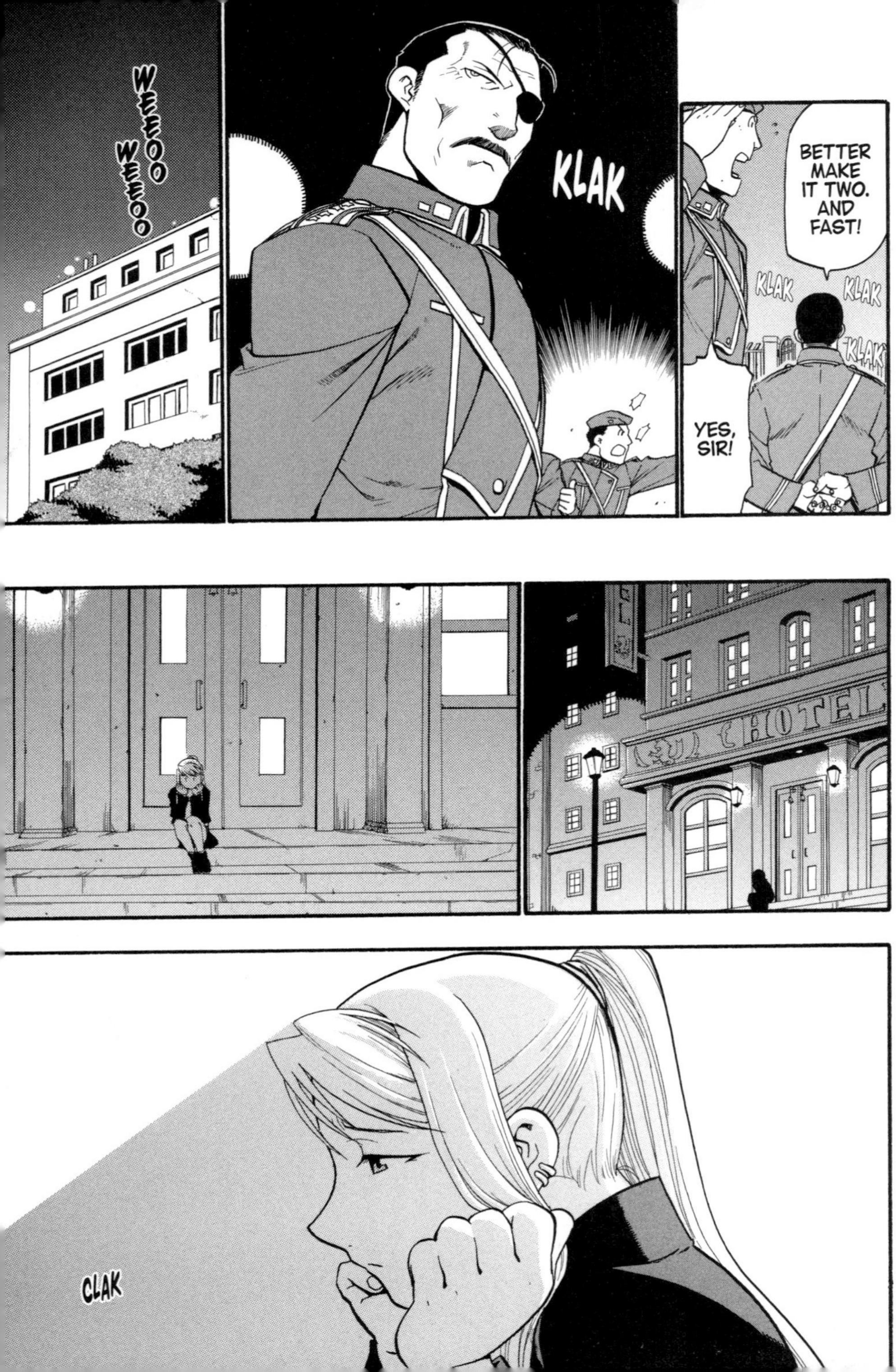
BETTER MAKE IT TWO. AND FAST!
KLAK
KLAK
KLAK
YES, SIR!
KLAK
WEEOO WEEOO
HOTEL
CLAK

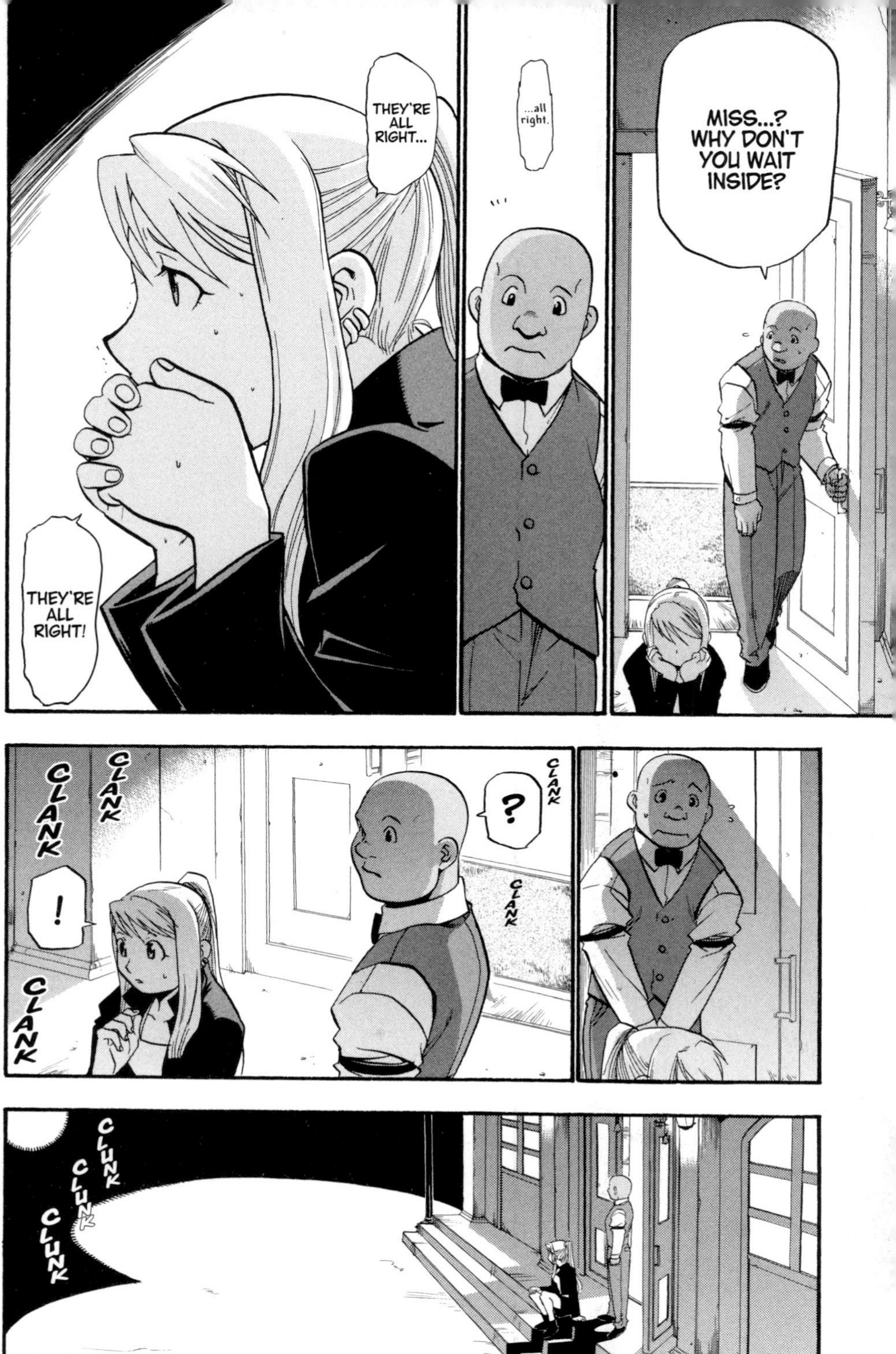
MISS...? WHY DON'T YOU WAIT INSIDE?
...all right.
THEY'RE ALL RIGHT...
THEY'RE ALL RIGHT!
CLANK
?
CLANK
CLANK
CLANK
!
CLANK
CLUNK
CLUNK
CLUNK

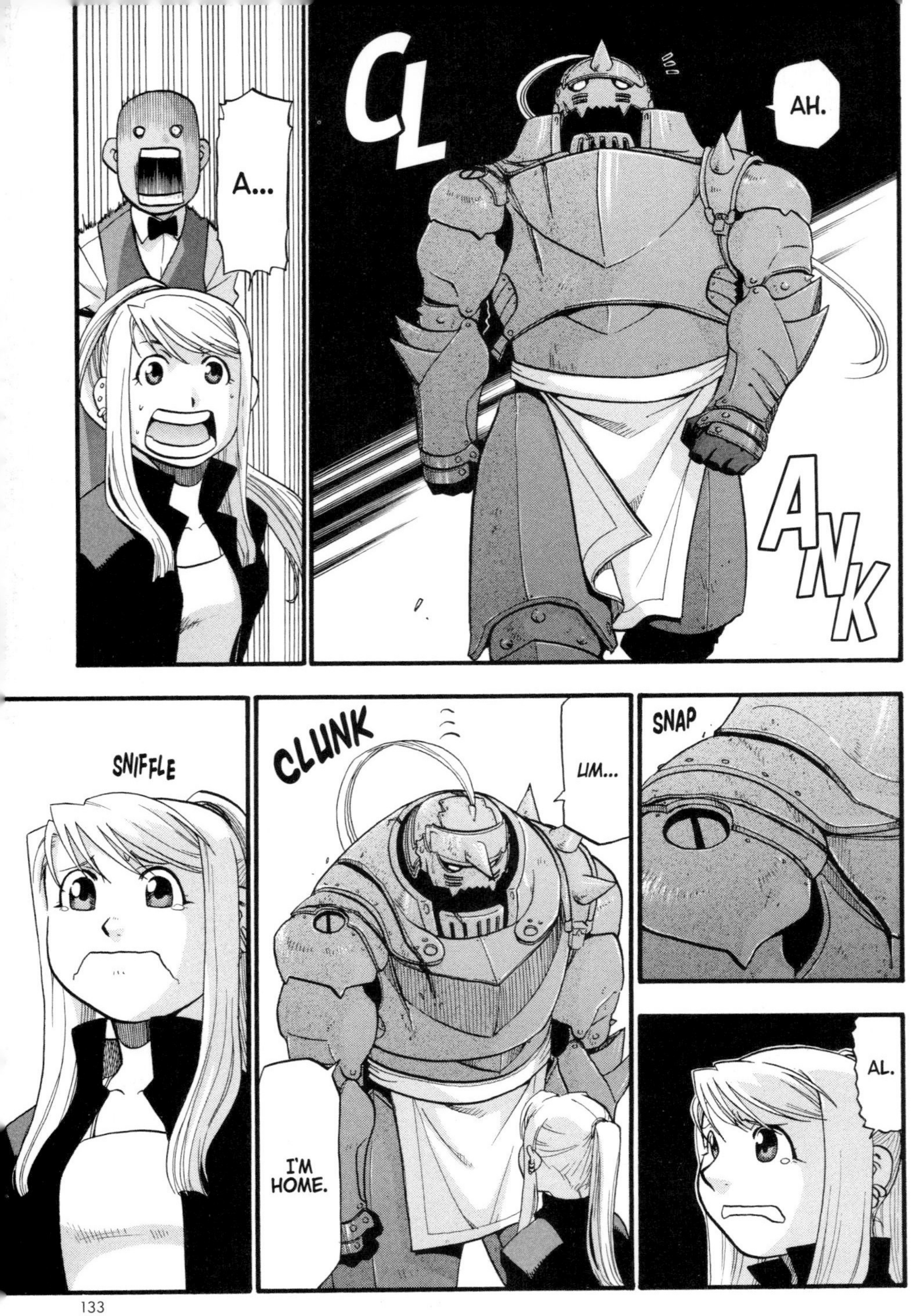

CL
AH.
ANK
A...
SNAP
AL.
CLUNK
UM...
I'M HOME.
SNIFFLE

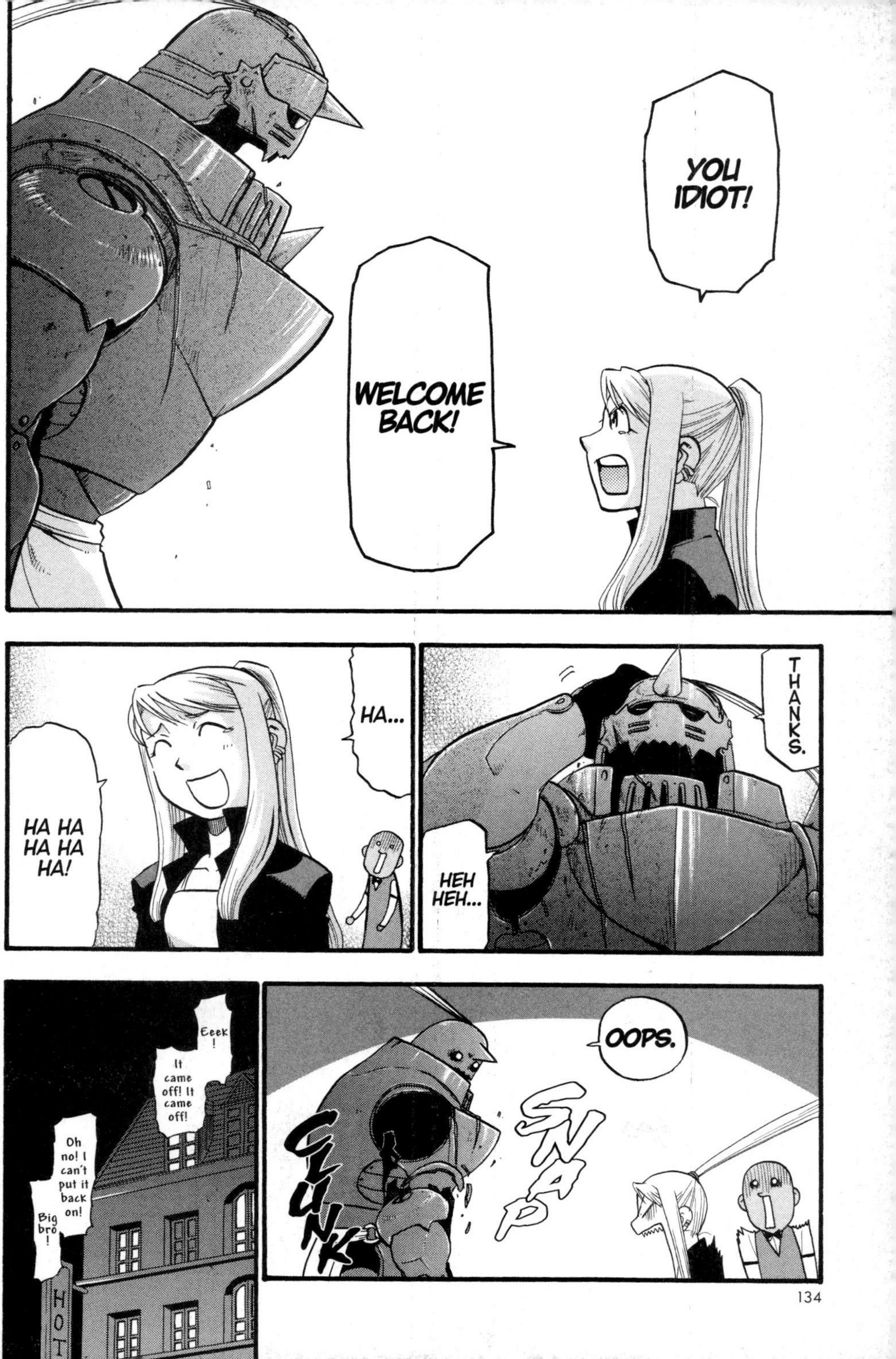
YOU IDIOT!
WELCOME BACK!
THANKS.
HEH HEH...
HA...
HA HA HA HA HA!
OOPS.
SNAP
CLUNK
Eeek!
It came off! It came off!
Oh no! I can't put it back on!
Big bro!
HOT

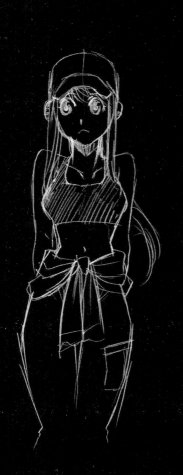

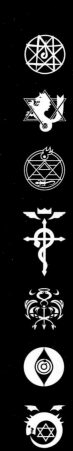

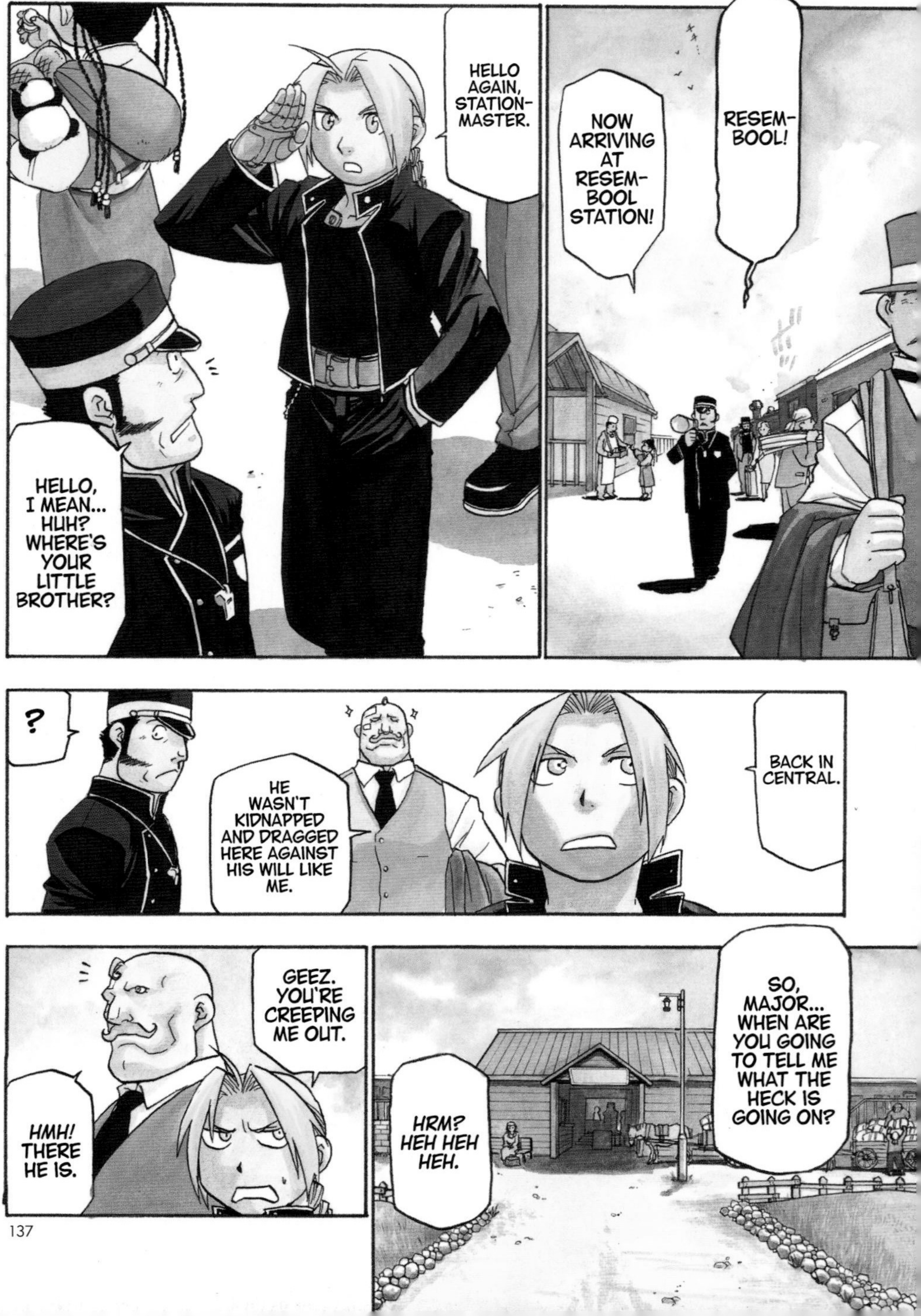
RESEM-BOOL!
NOW ARRIVING AT RESEM-BOOL STATION!
HELLO AGAIN, STATION-MASTER.
HELLO, I MEAN... HUH? WHERE'S YOUR LITTLE BROTHER?
BACK IN CENTRAL.
HE WASN'T KIDNAPPED AND DRAGGED HERE AGAINST HIS WILL LIKE ME.
?
SO, MAJOR... WHEN ARE YOU GOING TO TELL ME WHAT THE HECK IS GOING ON?
HRM? HEH HEH HEH.
GEEZ. YOU'RE CREEPING ME OUT.
HMH! THERE HE IS.

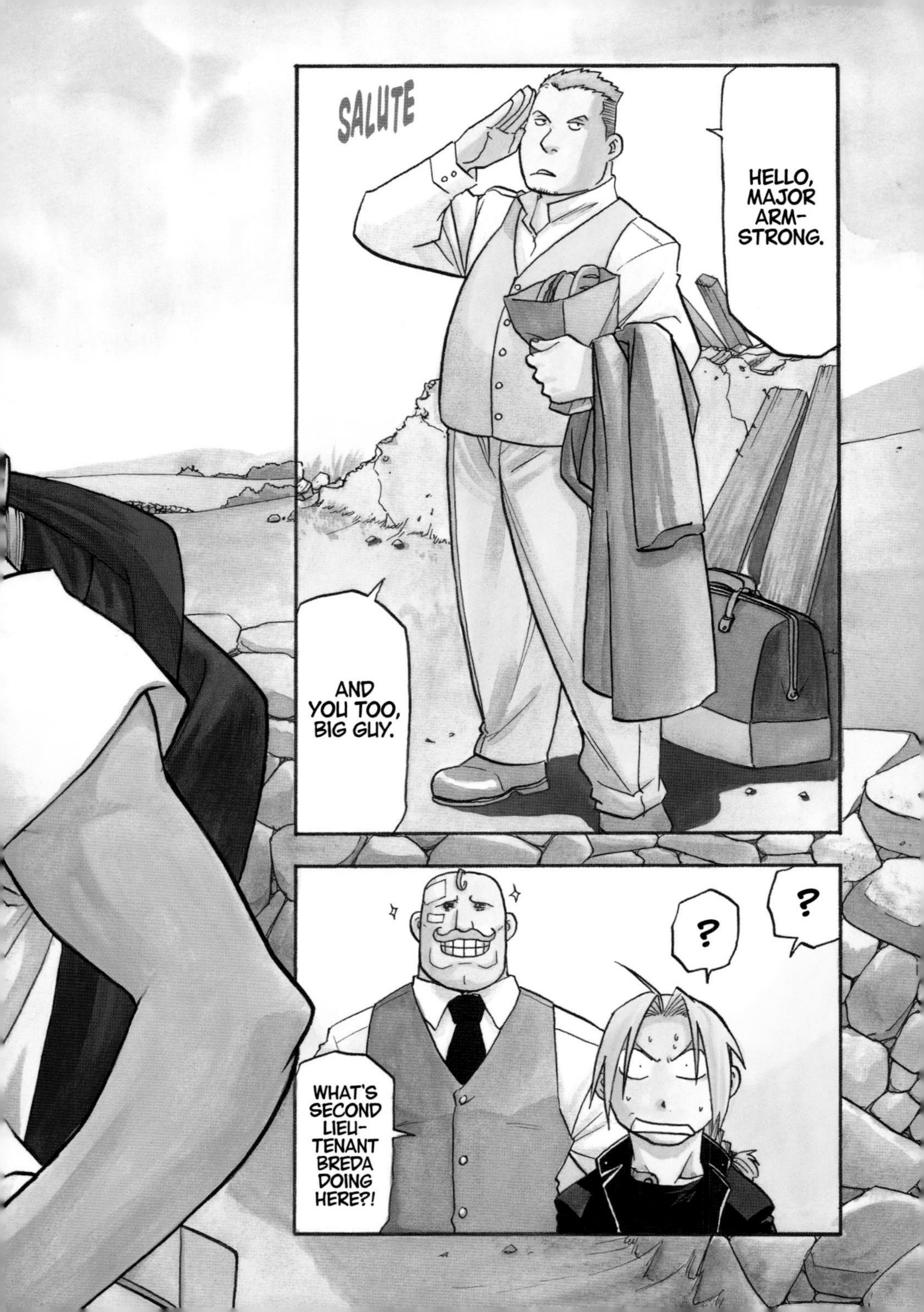
HELLO, MAJOR ARM-STRONG.
SALUTE
AND YOU TOO, BIG GUY.
?
?
WHAT'S SECOND LIEU-TENANT BREDA DOING HERE?!

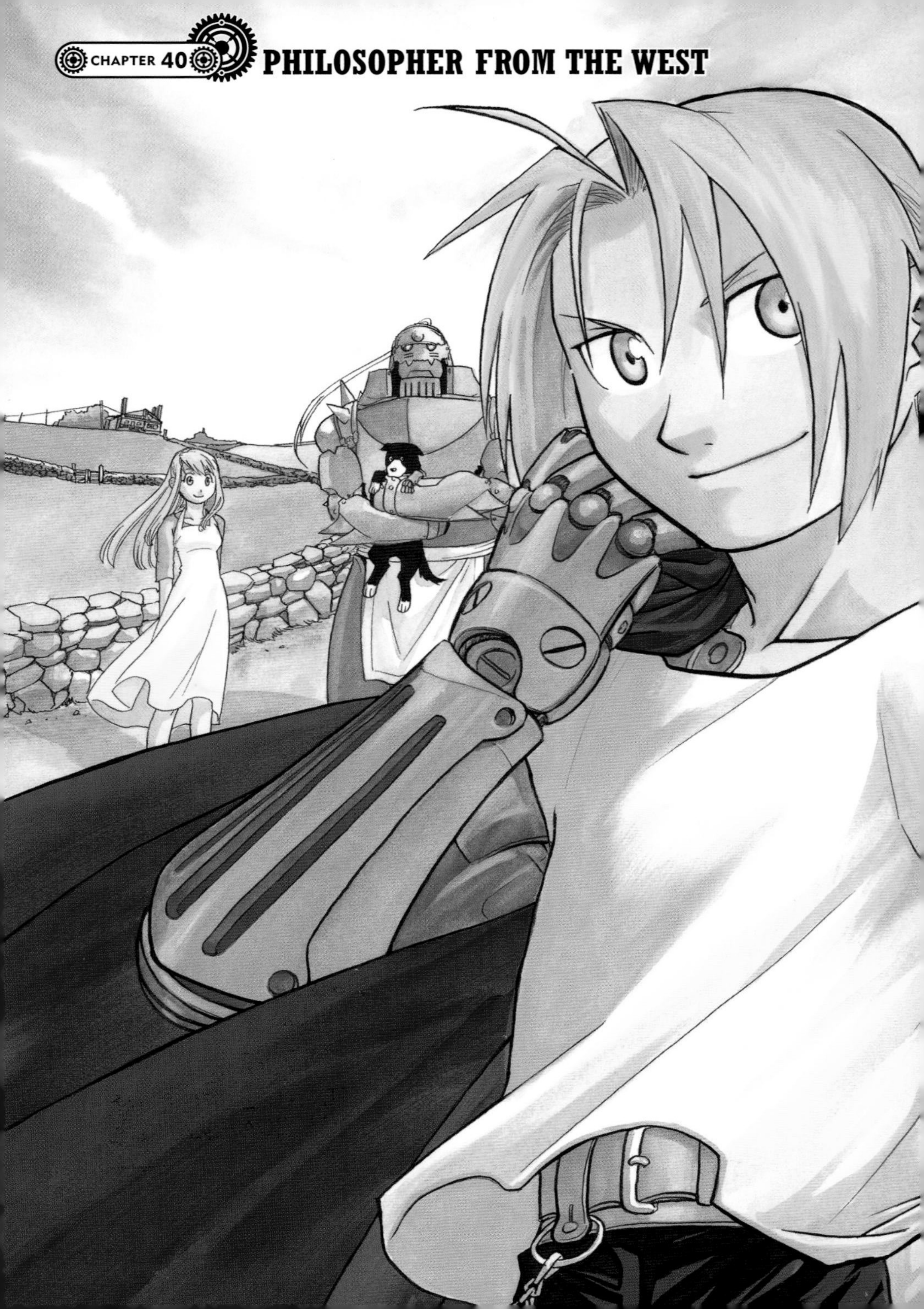
CHAPTER 40
PHILOSOPHER FROM THE WEST

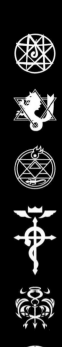

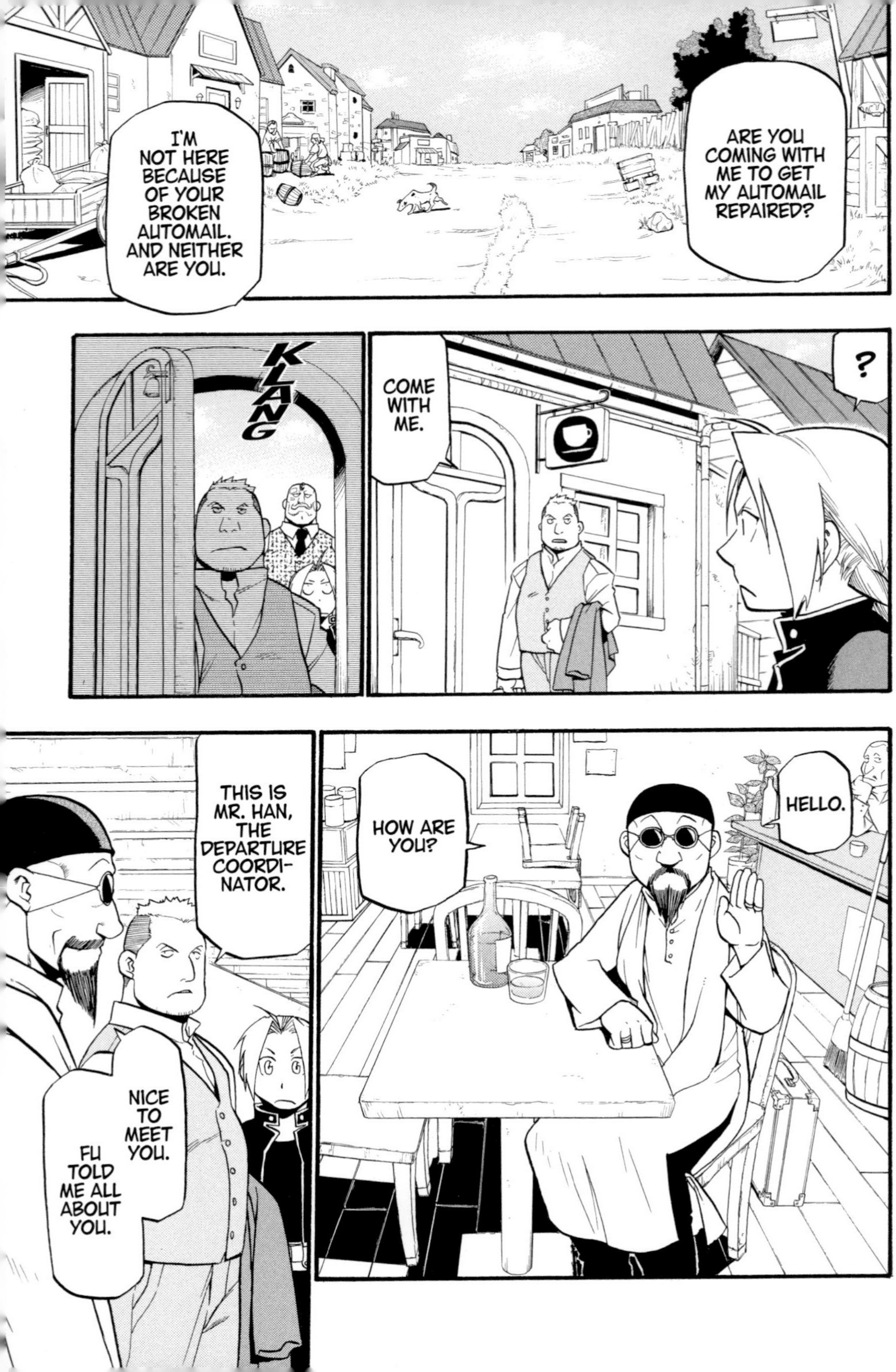
ARE YOU COMING WITH ME TO GET MY AUTOMAIL REPAIRED?
I'M NOT HERE BECAUSE OF YOUR BROKEN AUTOMAIL. AND NEITHER ARE YOU.
?
COME WITH ME.
KLANG
HELLO.
HOW ARE YOU?
THIS IS MR. HAN, THE DEPARTURE COORDINATOR.
NICE TO MEET YOU.
FU TOLD ME ALL ABOUT YOU.

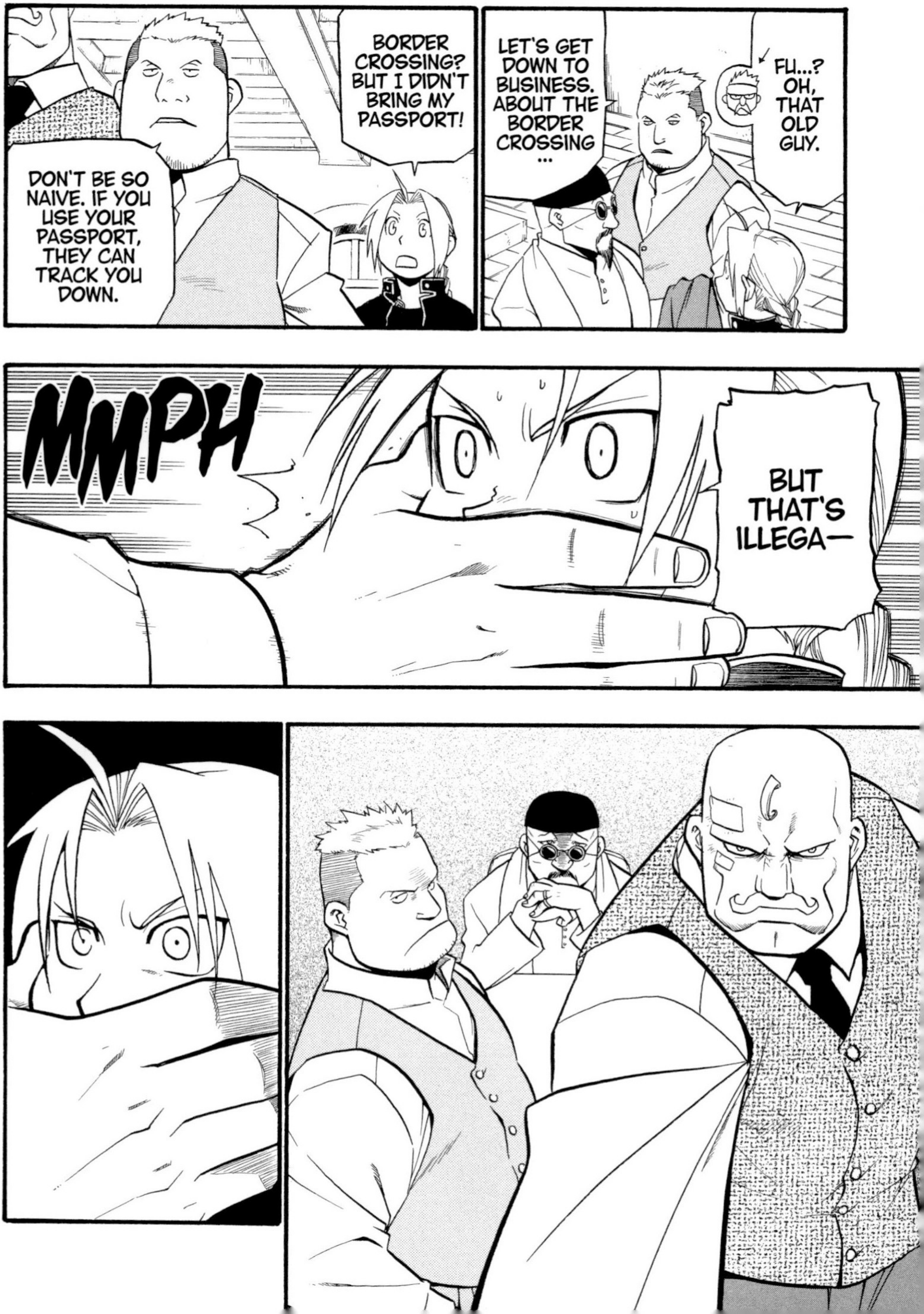
FU...? OH, THAT OLD GUY.
LET'S GET DOWN TO BUSINESS. ABOUT THE BORDER CROSSING...
BORDER CROSSING? BUT I DIDN'T BRING MY PASSPORT!
DON'T BE SO NAIVE. IF YOU USE YOUR PASSPORT, THEY CAN TRACK YOU DOWN.
BUT THAT'S ILLEGA—
MMPH

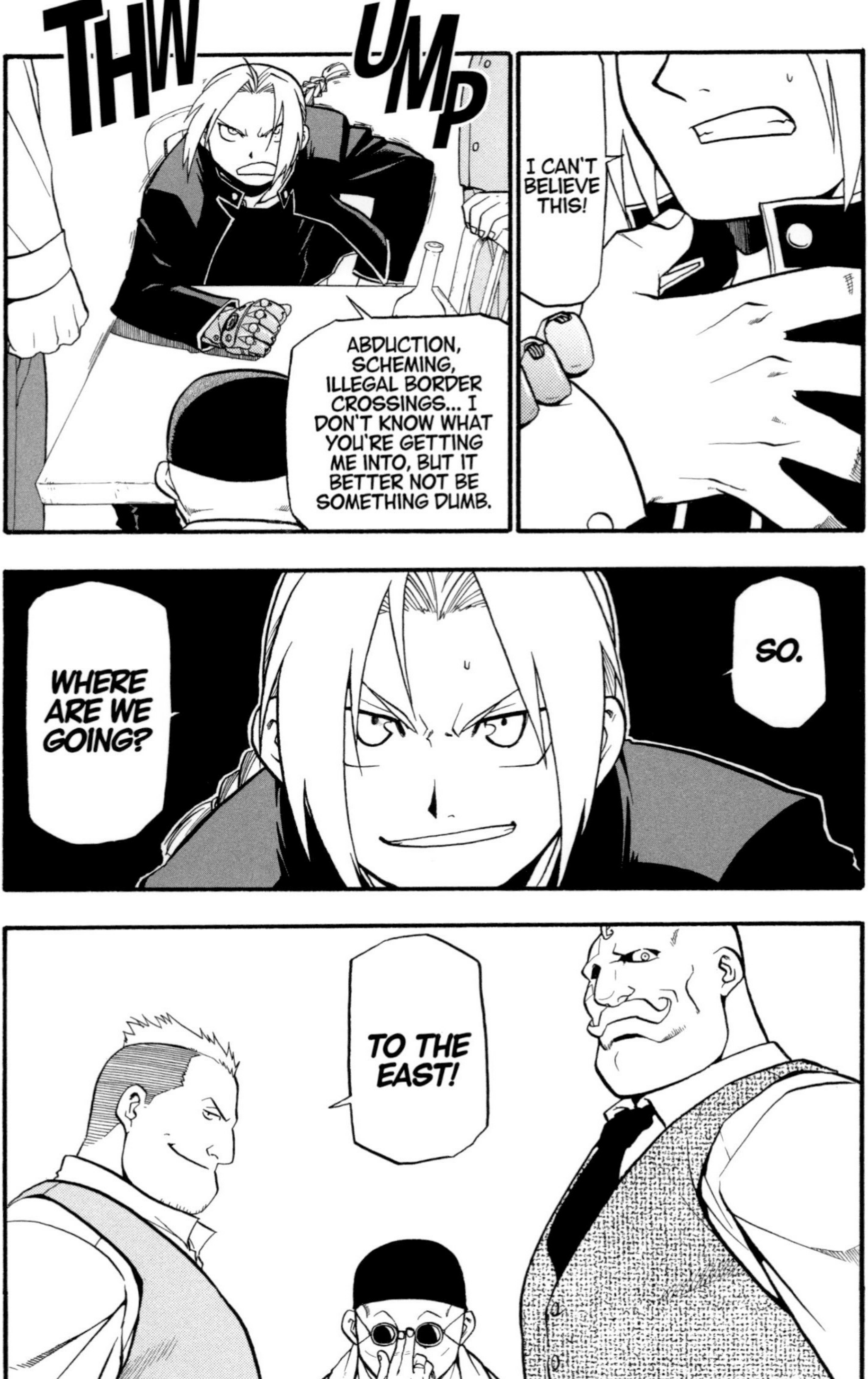
I CAN'T BELIEVE THIS!
THWUMP
ABDUCTION, SCHEMING, ILLEGAL BORDER CROSSINGS... I DON'T KNOW WHAT YOU'RE GETTING ME INTO, BUT IT BETTER NOT BE SOMETHING DUMB.
SO.
WHERE ARE WE GOING?
TO THE EAST!

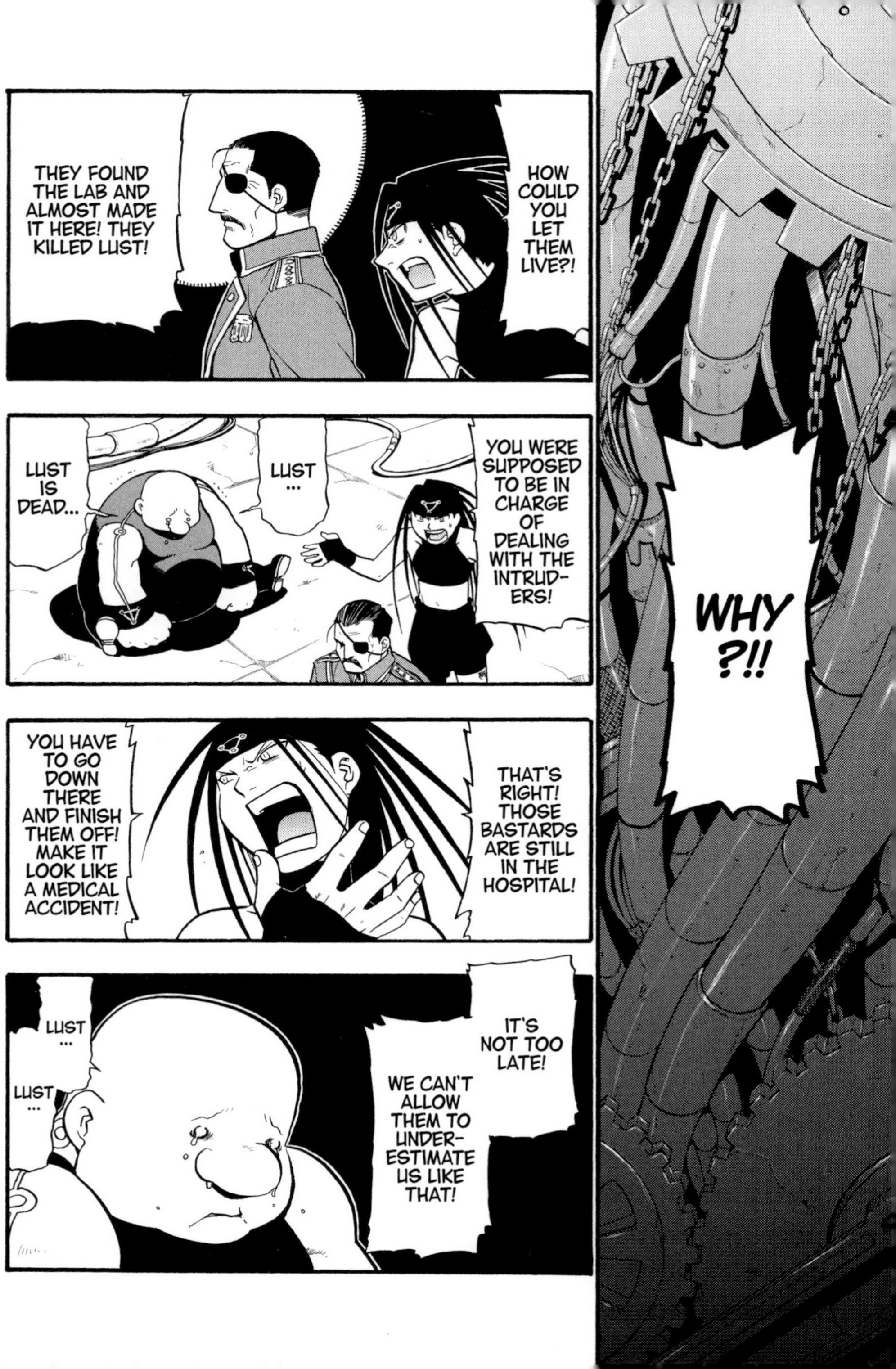
WHY ?!!
HOW COULD YOU LET THEM LIVE?!
THEY FOUND THE LAB AND ALMOST MADE IT HERE! THEY KILLED LUST!
YOU WERE SUPPOSED TO BE IN CHARGE OF DEALING WITH THE INTRUD-ERS!
LUST ...
LUST IS DEAD...
THAT'S RIGHT! THOSE BASTARDS ARE STILL IN THE HOSPITAL!
YOU HAVE TO GO DOWN THERE AND FINISH THEM OFF! MAKE IT LOOK LIKE A MEDICAL ACCIDENT!
IT'S NOT TOO LATE!
WE CAN'T ALLOW THEM TO UNDER-ESTIMATE US LIKE THAT!
LUST ...
LUST ...

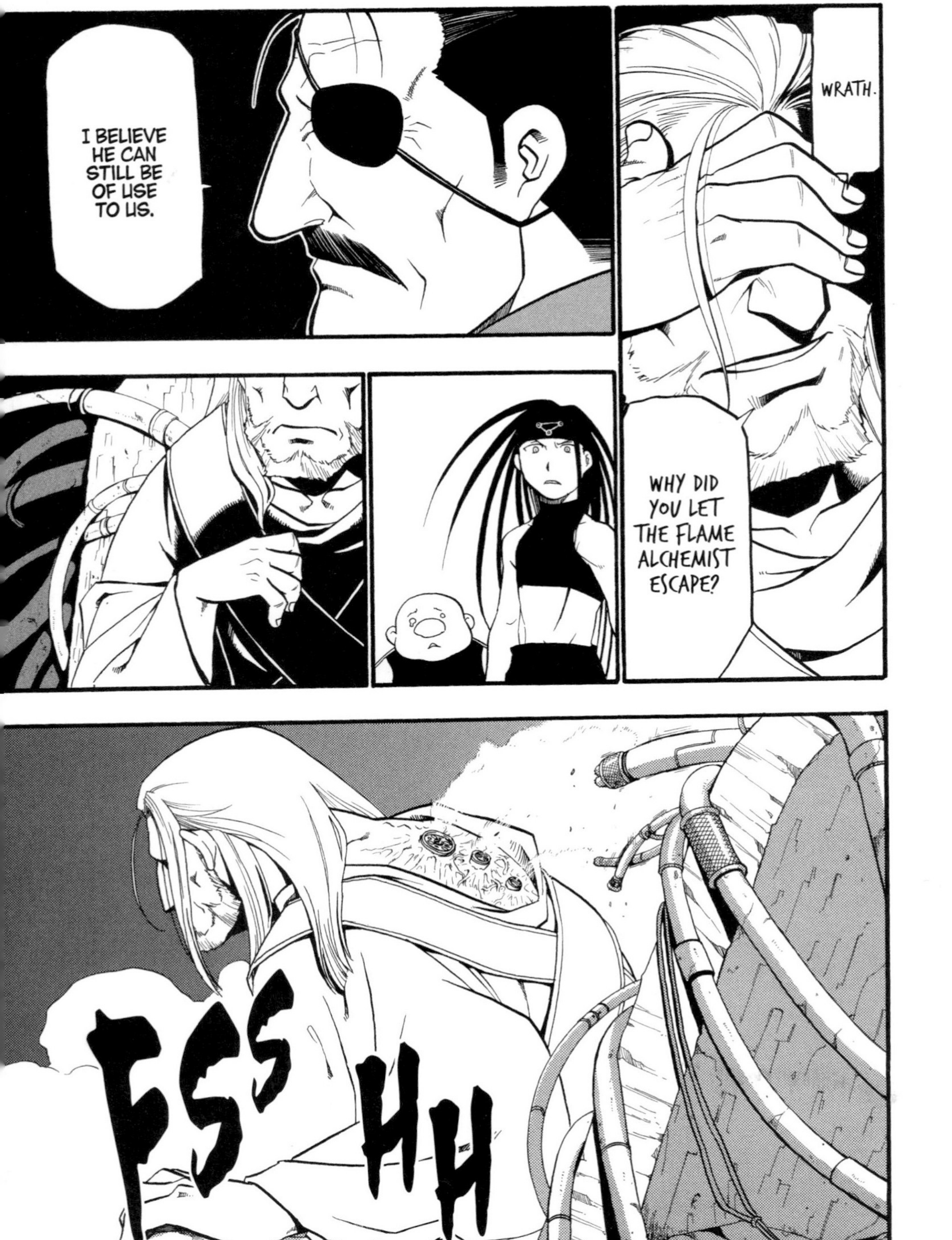
WRATH.
WHY DID YOU LET THE FLAME ALCHEMIST ESCAPE?
I BELIEVE HE CAN STILL BE OF USE TO US.
FSSHH

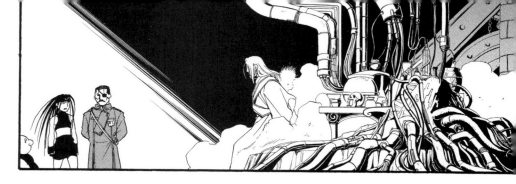

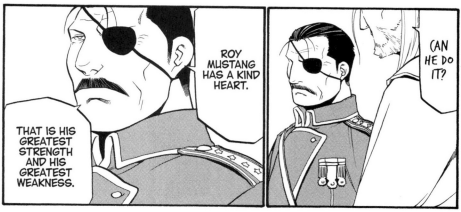

ROY MUSTANG HAS A KIND HEART.

THAT IS HIS GREATEST STRENGTH AND HIS GREATEST WEAKNESS.

CAN HE DO IT?

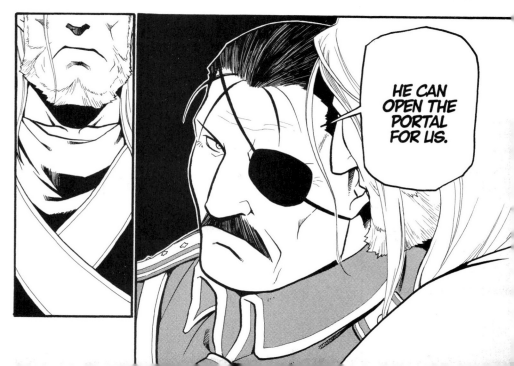

HE CAN OPEN THE PORTAL FOR US.

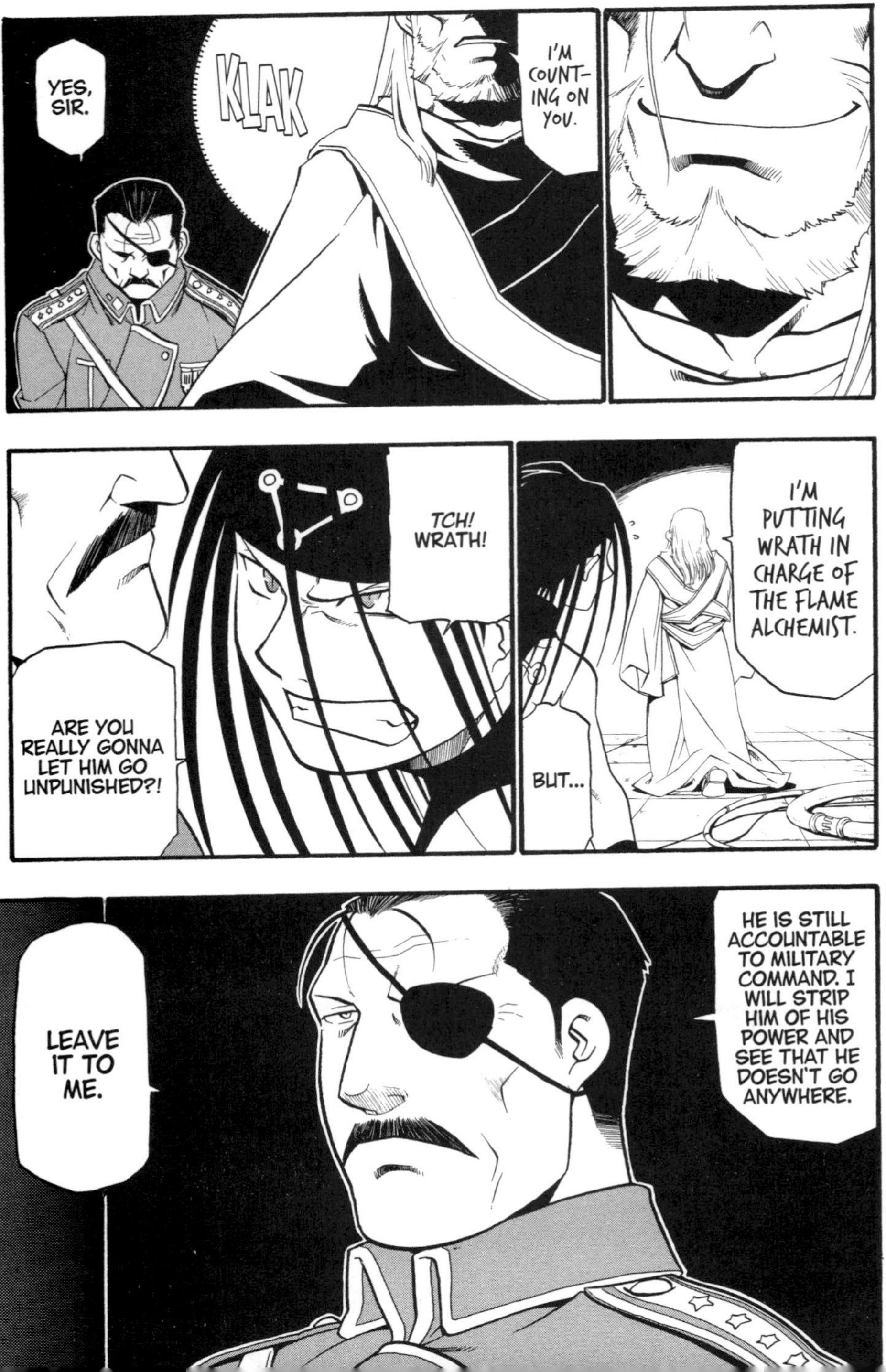
I'M COUNTING-ING ON YOU.
KLAK
YES, SIR.
I'M PUTTING WRATH IN CHARGE OF THE FLAME ALCHEMIST.
BUT...
TCH! WRATH!
ARE YOU REALLY GONNA LET HIM GO UNPUNISHED?!
HE IS STILL ACCOUNTABLE TO MILITARY COMMAND. I WILL STRIP HIM OF HIS POWER AND SEE THAT HE DOESN'T GO ANYWHERE.
LEAVE IT TO ME.

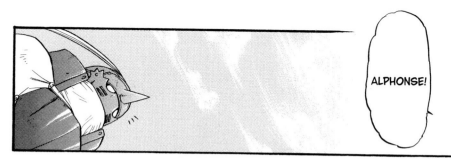

ALPHONSE!

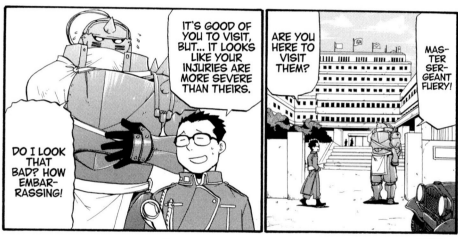

MASTER SERGEANT FUERY!

ARE YOU HERE TO VISIT THEM?

IT'S GOOD OF YOU TO VISIT, BUT... IT LOOKS LIKE YOUR INJURIES ARE MORE SEVERE THAN THEIRS.

DO I LOOK THAT BAD? HOW EMBARRASSING!

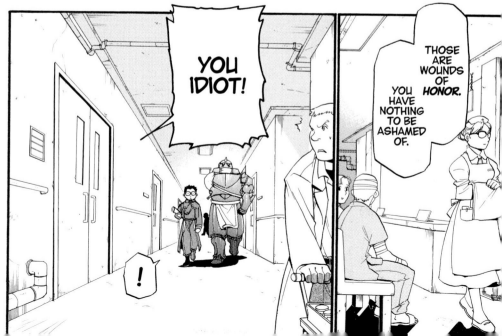

YOU IDIOT!

THOSE ARE WOUNDS OF HONOR. YOU HAVE NOTHING TO BE ASHAMED OF.

!

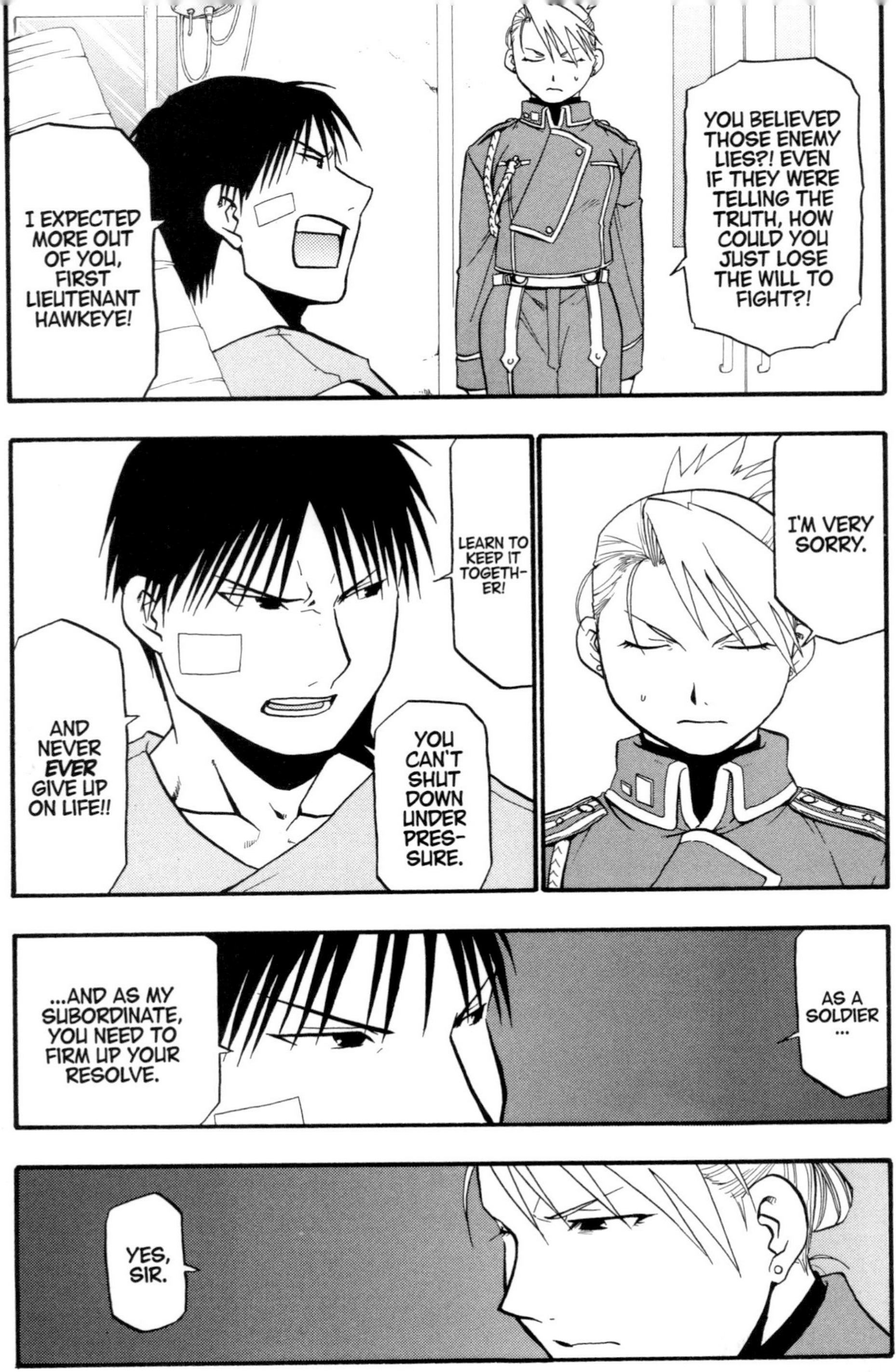
YOU BELIEVED THOSE ENEMY LIES?! EVEN IF THEY WERE TELLING THE TRUTH, HOW COULD YOU JUST LOSE THE WILL TO FIGHT?!
I EXPECTED MORE OUT OF YOU, FIRST LIEUTENANT HAWKEYE!
I'M VERY SORRY.
LEARN TO KEEP IT TOGETH-ER!
YOU CAN'T SHUT DOWN UNDER PRES-SURE.
AND NEVER EVER GIVE UP ON LIFE!!
AS A SOLDIER ...
...AND AS MY SUBORDINATE, YOU NEED TO FIRM UP YOUR RESOLVE.
YES, SIR.

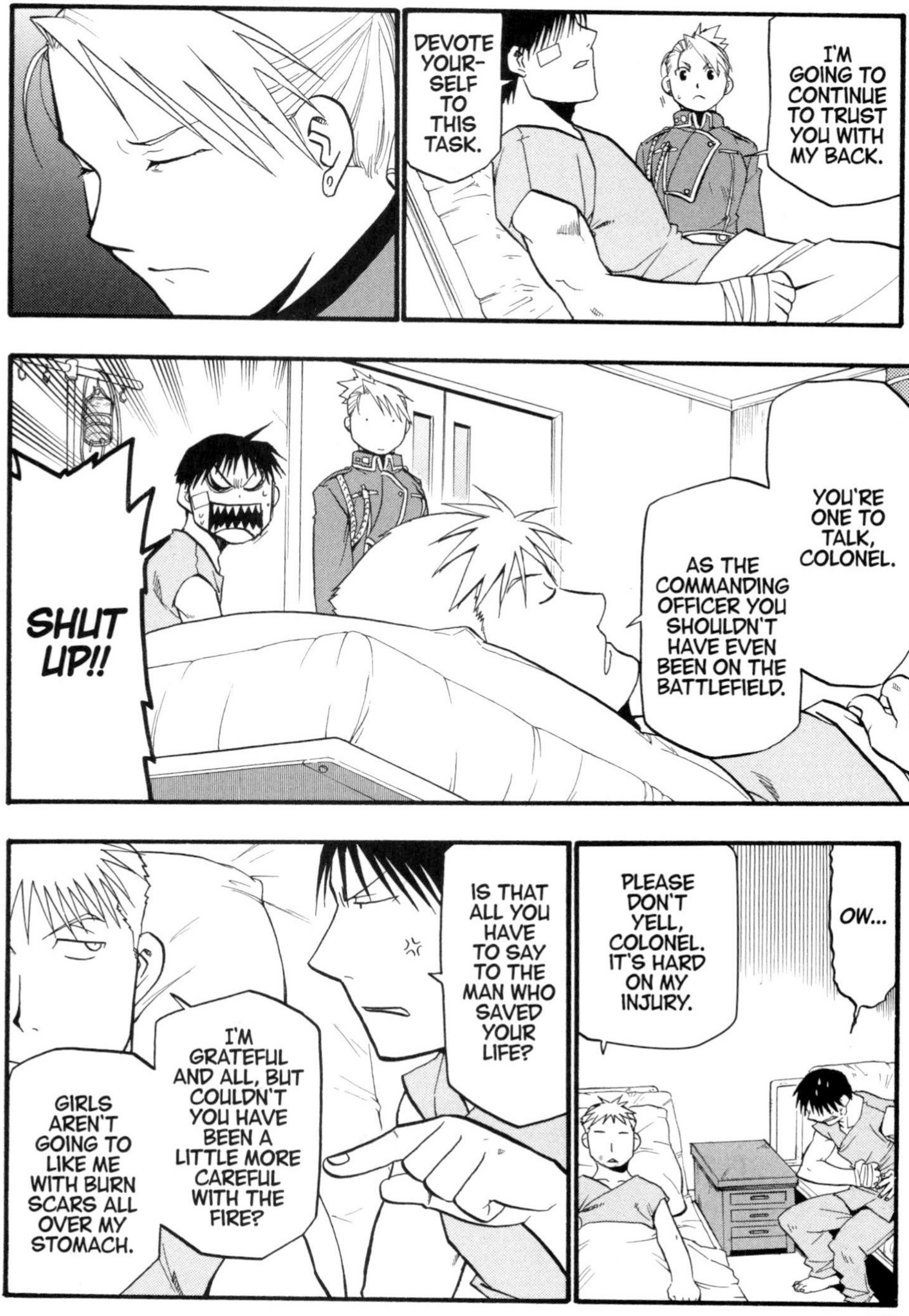
I'M GOING TO CONTINUE TO TRUST YOU WITH MY BACK.
DEVOTE YOUR-SELF TO THIS TASK.
YOU'RE ONE TO TALK, COLONEL.
AS THE COMMANDING OFFICER YOU SHOULDN'T HAVE EVEN BEEN ON THE BATTLEFIELD.
SHUT UP!!
OW...
PLEASE DON'T YELL, COLONEL. IT'S HARD ON MY INJURY.
IS THAT ALL YOU HAVE TO SAY TO THE MAN WHO SAVED YOUR LIFE?
I'M GRATEFUL AND ALL, BUT COULDN'T YOU HAVE BEEN A LITTLE MORE CAREFUL WITH THE FIRE?
GIRLS AREN'T GOING TO LIKE ME WITH BURN SCARS ALL OVER MY STOMACH.

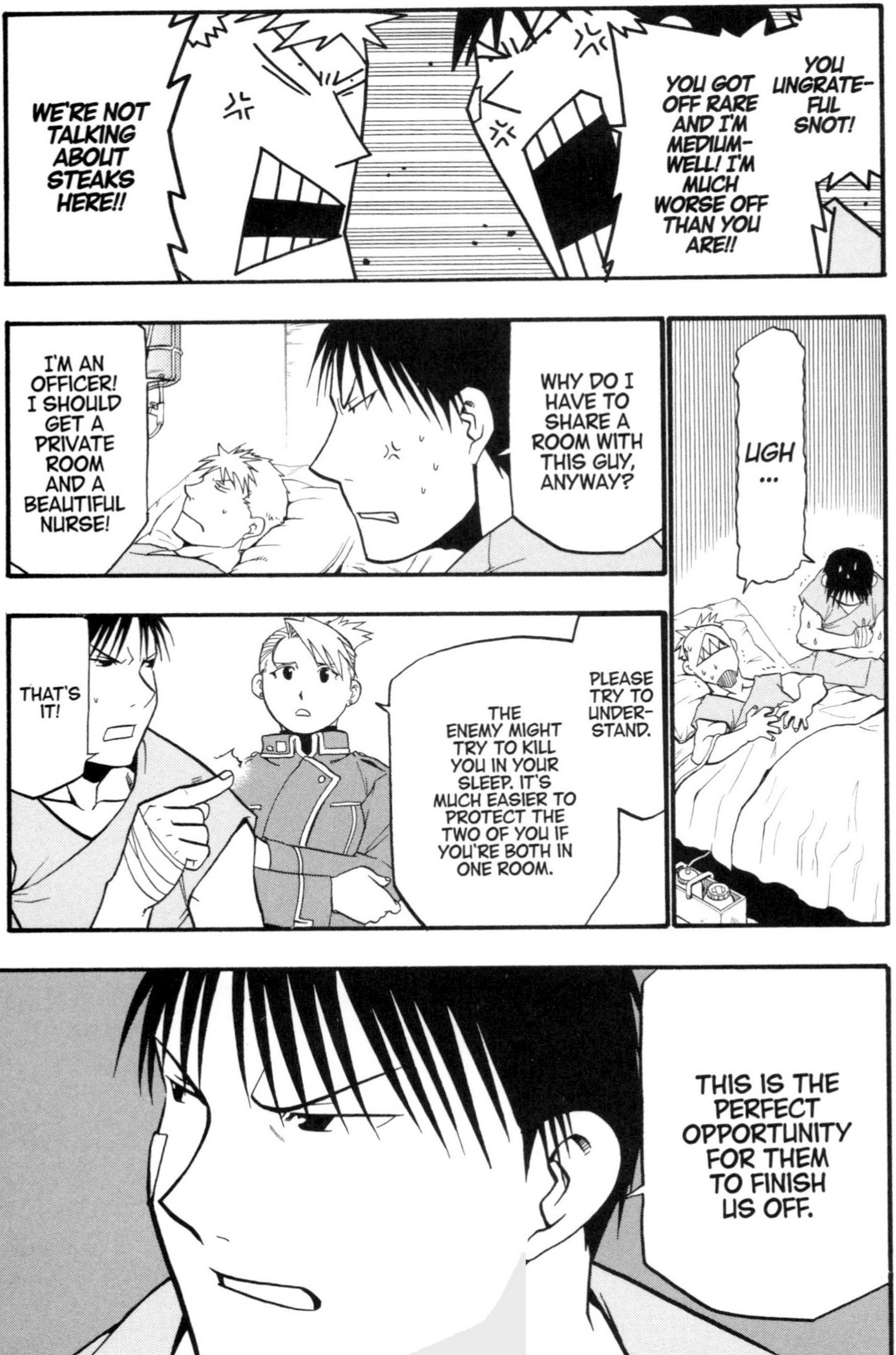

YOU UNGRATE-FUL SNOT!
YOU GOT OFF RARE AND I'M MEDIUM-WELL! I'M MUCH WORSE OFF THAN YOU ARE!!
WE'RE NOT TALKING ABOUT STEAKS HERE!!
UGH ...
WHY DO I HAVE TO SHARE A ROOM WITH THIS GUY, ANYWAY?
I'M AN OFFICER! I SHOULD GET A PRIVATE ROOM AND A BEAUTIFUL NURSE!
PLEASE TRY TO UNDER-STAND.
THE ENEMY MIGHT TRY TO KILL YOU IN YOUR SLEEP. IT'S MUCH EASIER TO PROTECT THE TWO OF YOU IF YOU'RE BOTH IN ONE ROOM.
THAT'S IT!
THIS IS THE PERFECT OPPORTUNITY FOR THEM TO FINISH US OFF.

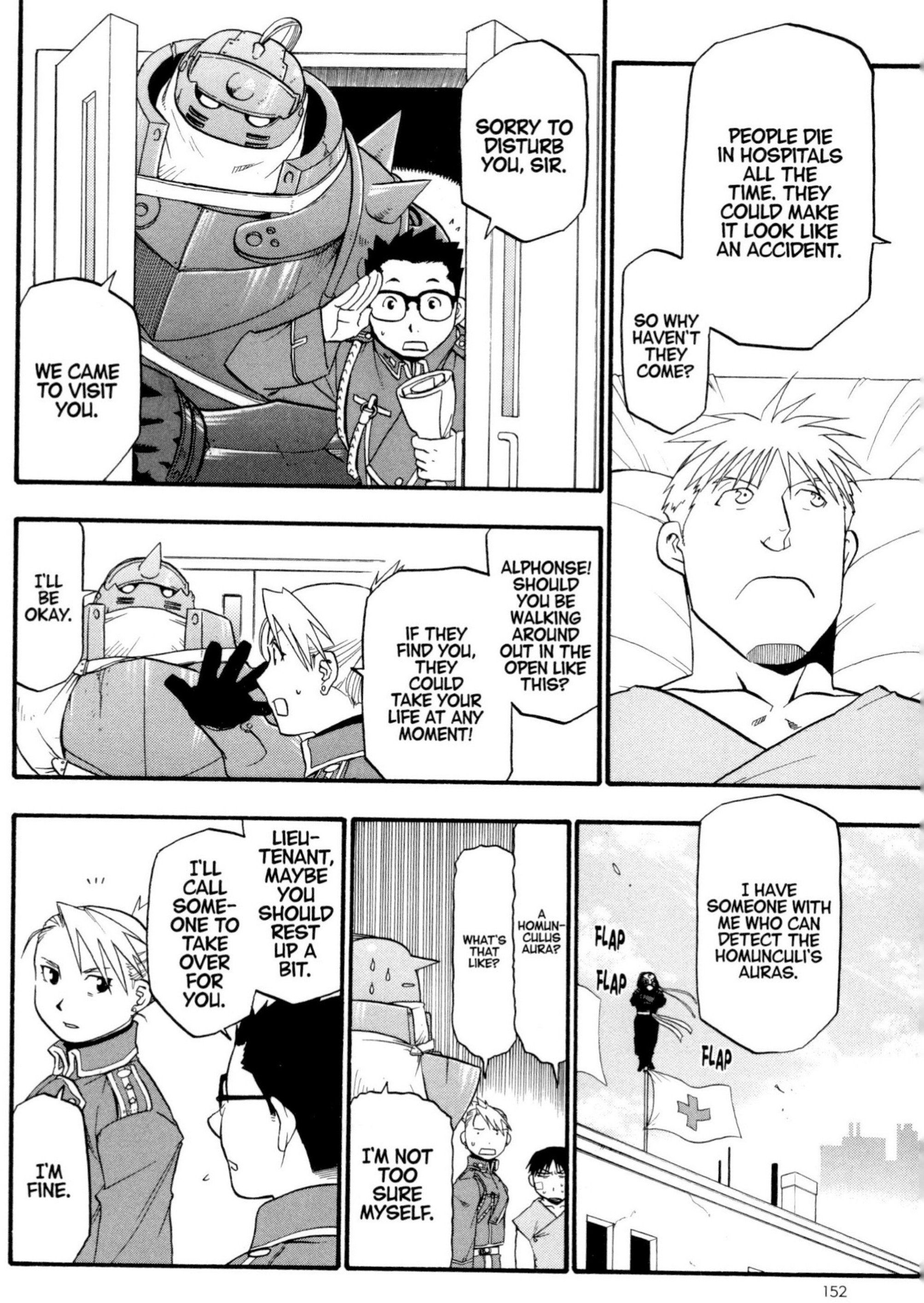

PEOPLE DIE IN HOSPITALS ALL THE TIME. THEY COULD MAKE IT LOOK LIKE AN ACCIDENT.
SO WHY HAVEN'T THEY COME?
SORRY TO DISTURB YOU, SIR.
WE CAME TO VISIT YOU.
ALPHONSE! SHOULD YOU BE WALKING AROUND OUT IN THE OPEN LIKE THIS?
IF THEY FIND YOU, THEY COULD TAKE YOUR LIFE AT ANY MOMENT!
I'LL BE OKAY.
I HAVE SOMEONE WITH ME WHO CAN DETECT THE HOMUNCULI'S AURAS.
FLAP
FLAP
FLAP
A HOMUNCULUS AURA?
WHAT'S THAT LIKE?
I'M NOT TOO SURE MYSELF.
LIEUTENANT, MAYBE YOU SHOULD REST UP A BIT.
I'LL CALL SOMEONE TO TAKE OVER FOR YOU.
I'M FINE.

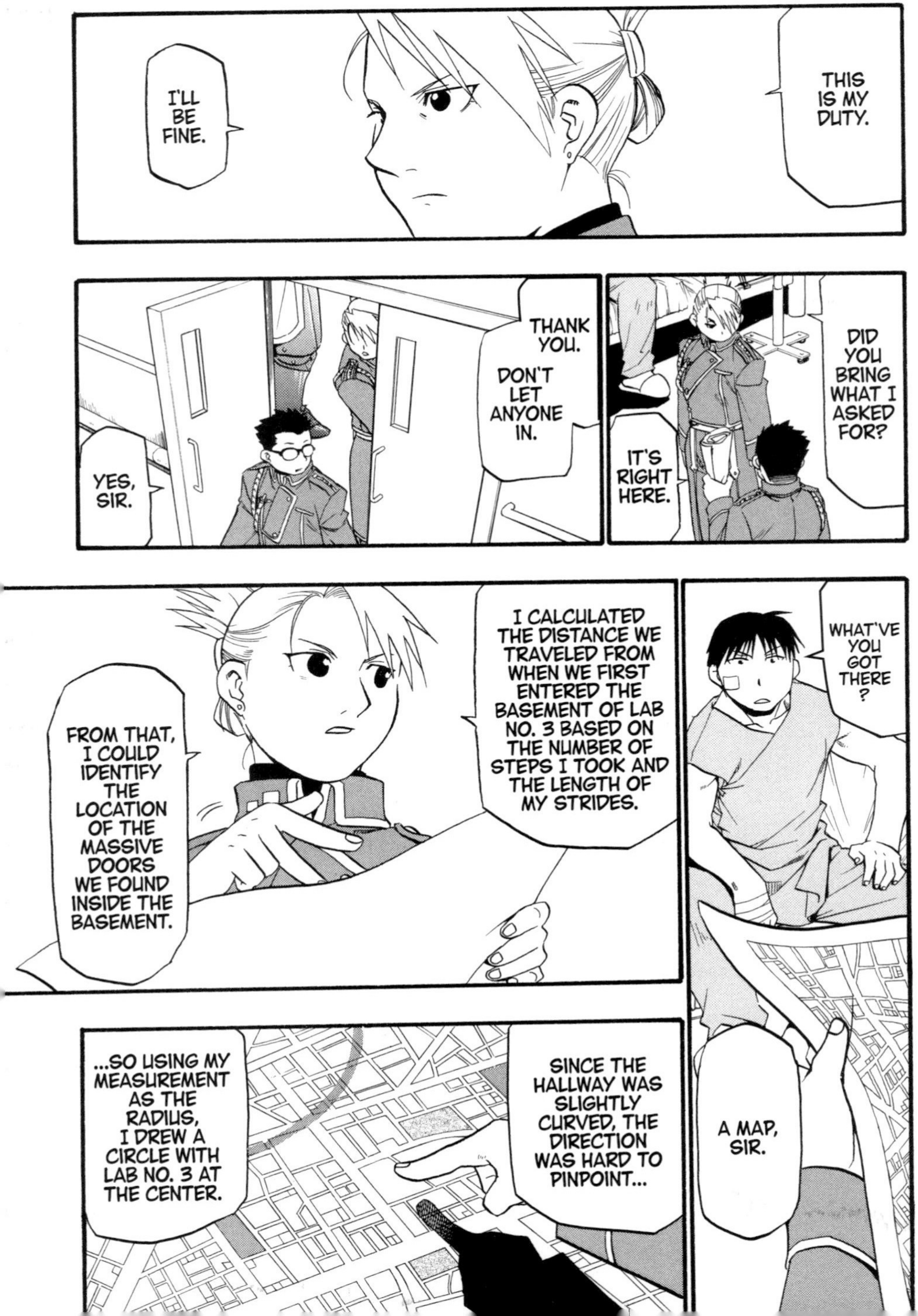
THIS IS MY DUTY.
I'LL BE FINE.
DID YOU BRING WHAT I ASKED FOR?
IT'S RIGHT HERE.
THANK YOU.
DON'T LET ANYONE IN.
YES, SIR.
WHAT'VE YOU GOT THERE?
A MAP, SIR.
I CALCULATED THE DISTANCE WE TRAVELED FROM WHEN WE FIRST ENTERED THE BASEMENT OF LAB NO. 3 BASED ON THE NUMBER OF STEPS I TOOK AND THE LENGTH OF MY STRIDES.
FROM THAT, I COULD IDENTIFY THE LOCATION OF THE MASSIVE DOORS WE FOUND INSIDE THE BASEMENT.
SINCE THE HALLWAY WAS SLIGHTLY CURVED, THE DIRECTION WAS HARD TO PINPOINT...
...SO USING MY MEASUREMENT AS THE RADIUS, I DREW A CIRCLE WITH LAB NO. 3 AT THE CENTER.

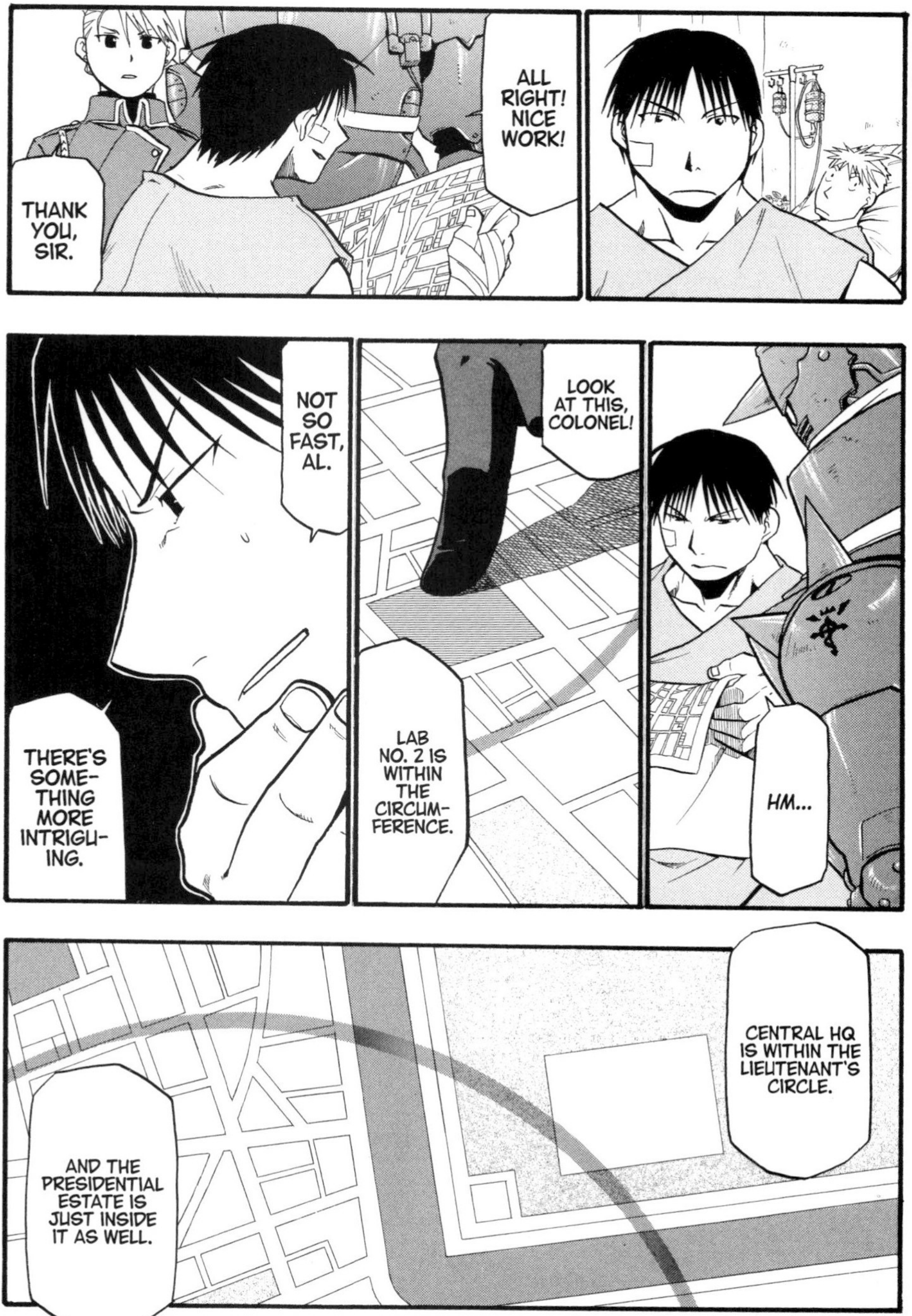
ALL RIGHT! NICE WORK!
THANK YOU, SIR.
HM...
LOOK AT THIS, COLONEL!
LAB NO. 2 IS WITHIN THE CIRCUMFERENCE.
NOT SO FAST, AL.
THERE'S SOME-THING MORE INTRIGU-ING.
CENTRAL HQ IS WITHIN THE LIEUTENANT'S CIRCLE.
AND THE PRESIDENTIAL ESTATE IS JUST INSIDE IT AS WELL.

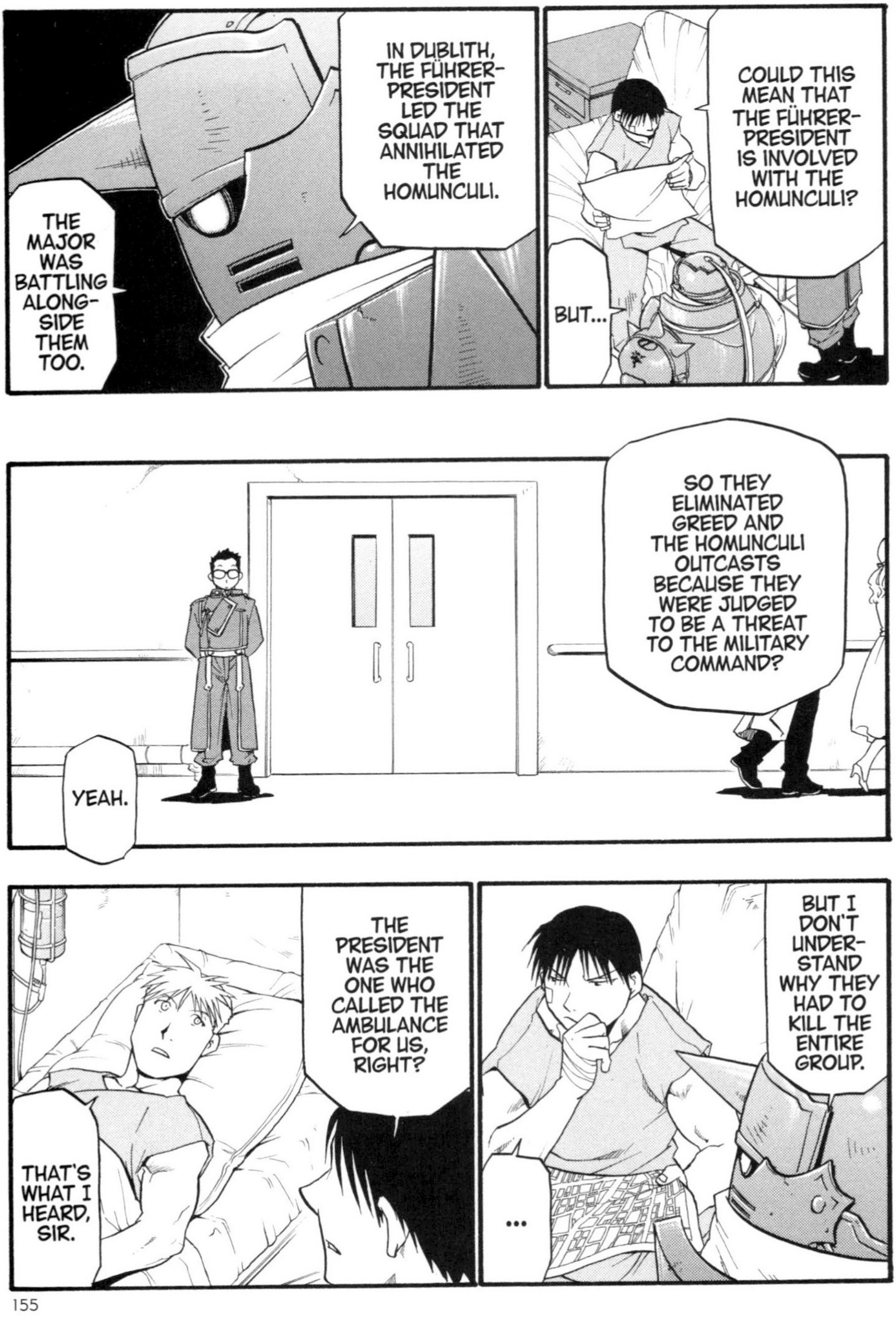
COULD THIS MEAN THAT THE FÜHRER-PRESIDENT IS INVOLVED WITH THE HOMUNCULI?
BUT...
IN DUBLITH, THE FÜHRER-PRESIDENT LED THE SQUAD THAT ANNIHILATED THE HOMUNCULI.
THE MAJOR WAS BATTLING ALONG-SIDE THEM TOO.
SO THEY ELIMINATED GREED AND THE HOMUNCULI OUTCASTS BECAUSE THEY WERE JUDGED TO BE A THREAT TO THE MILITARY COMMAND?
YEAH.
BUT I DON'T UNDER-STAND WHY THEY HAD TO KILL THE ENTIRE GROUP.
...
THE PRESIDENT WAS THE ONE WHO CALLED THE AMBULANCE FOR US, RIGHT?
THAT'S WHAT I HEARD, SIR.

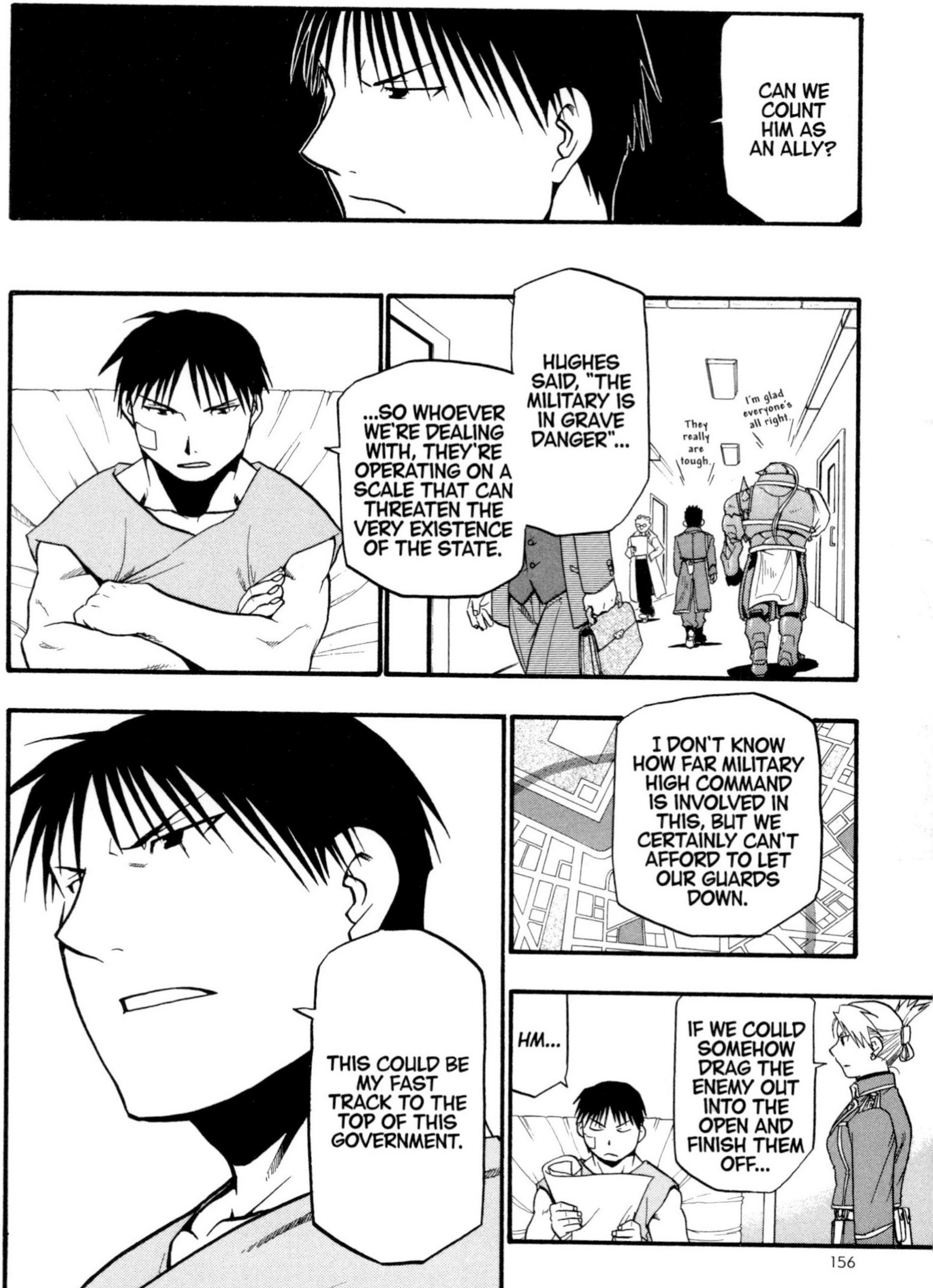
CAN WE COUNT HIM AS AN ALLY?
HUGHES SAID, "THE MILITARY IS IN GRAVE DANGER"...
I'm glad everyone's all right.
They really are tough.
...SO WHOEVER WE'RE DEALING WITH, THEY'RE OPERATING ON A SCALE THAT CAN THREATEN THE VERY EXISTENCE OF THE STATE.
I DON'T KNOW HOW FAR MILITARY HIGH COMMAND IS INVOLVED IN THIS, BUT WE CERTAINLY CAN'T AFFORD TO LET OUR GUARDS DOWN.
IF WE COULD SOMEHOW DRAG THE ENEMY OUT INTO THE OPEN AND FINISH THEM OFF...
HM...
THIS COULD BE MY FAST TRACK TO THE TOP OF THIS GOVERNMENT.

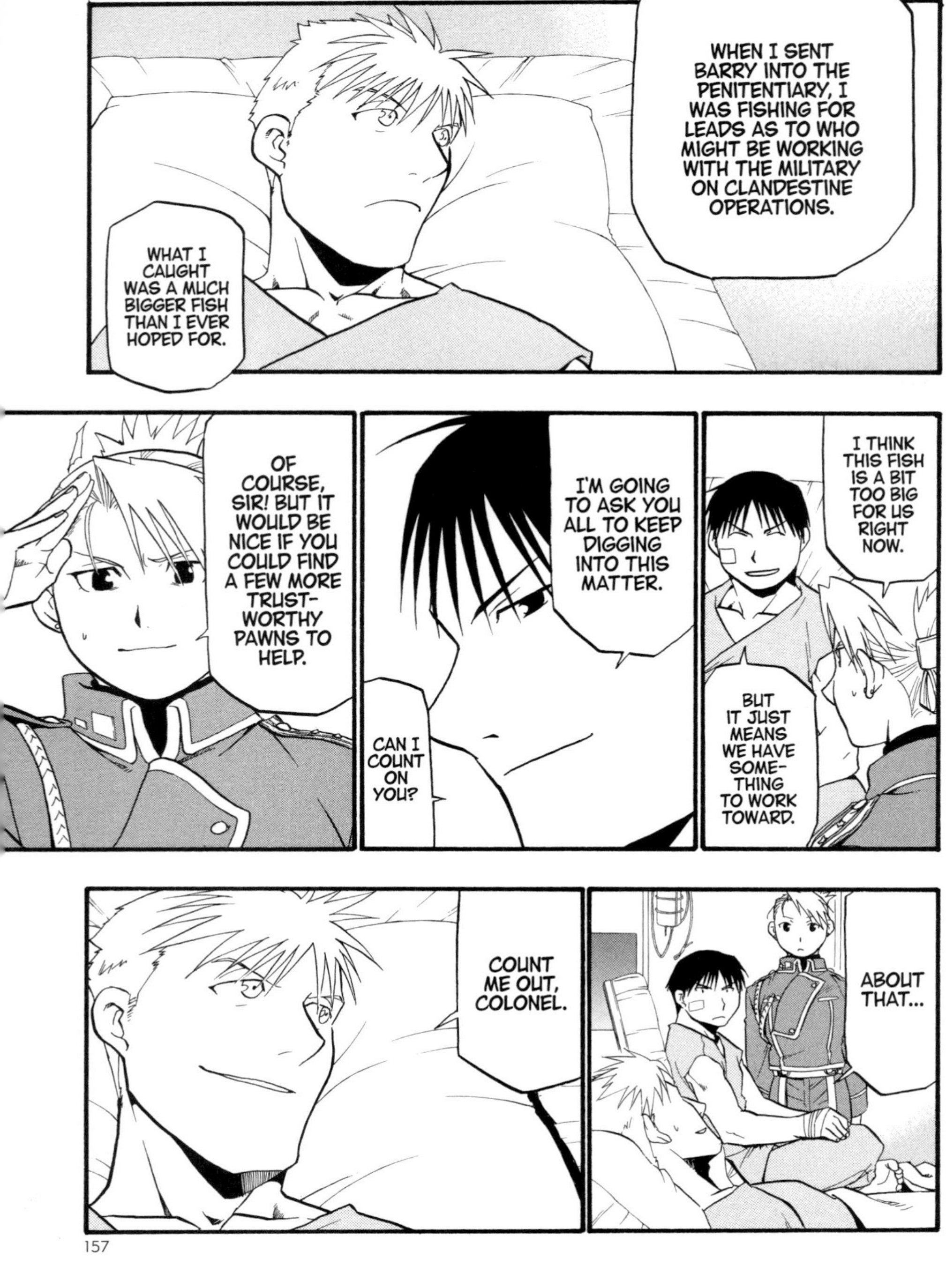
WHEN I SENT BARRY INTO THE PENITENTIARY, I WAS FISHING FOR LEADS AS TO WHO MIGHT BE WORKING WITH THE MILITARY ON CLANDESTINE OPERATIONS.
WHAT I CAUGHT WAS A MUCH BIGGER FISH THAN I EVER HOPED FOR.
I THINK THIS FISH IS A BIT TOO BIG FOR US RIGHT NOW.
BUT IT JUST MEANS WE HAVE SOME-THING TO WORK TOWARD.
I'M GOING TO ASK YOU ALL TO KEEP DIGGING INTO THIS MATTER.
CAN I COUNT ON YOU?
OF COURSE, SIR! BUT IT WOULD BE NICE IF YOU COULD FIND A FEW MORE TRUST-WORTHY PAWNS TO HELP.
ABOUT THAT...
COUNT ME OUT, COLONEL.

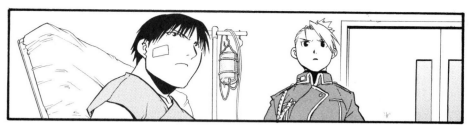

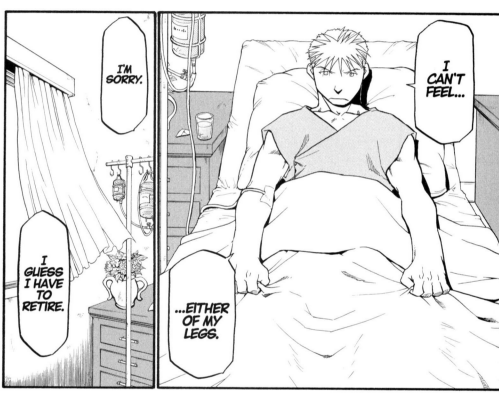

I CAN'T FEEL...
...EITHER OF MY LEGS.
I'M SORRY.
I GUESS I HAVE TO RETIRE.
I THINK I KNOW WHY BIG BROTHER DOESN'T LIKE THE COLONEL VERY MUCH.

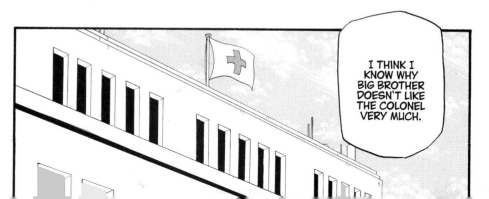

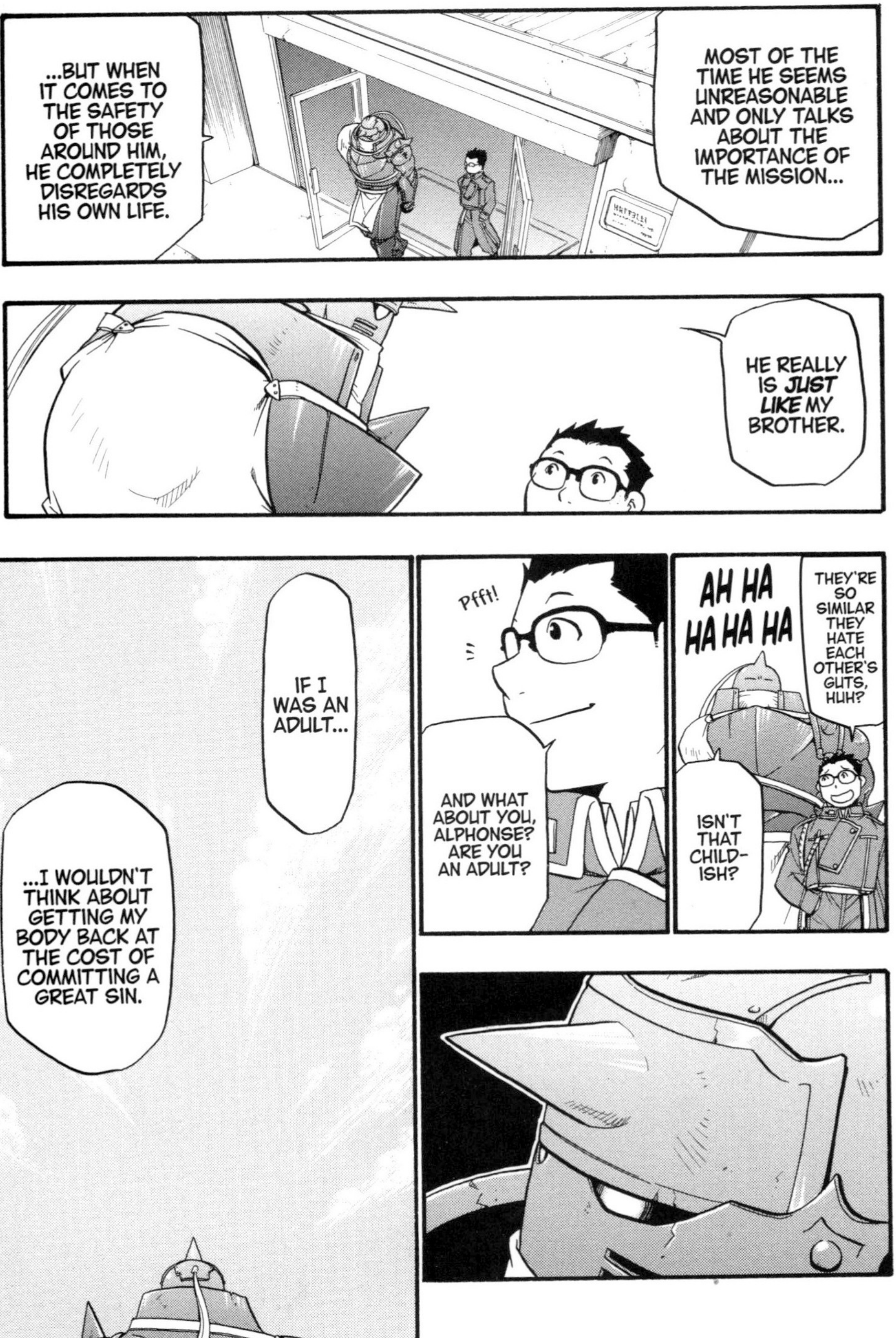
MOST OF THE TIME HE SEEMS UNREASONABLE AND ONLY TALKS ABOUT THE IMPORTANCE OF THE MISSION...
...BUT WHEN IT COMES TO THE SAFETY OF THOSE AROUND HIM, HE COMPLETELY DISREGARDS HIS OWN LIFE.
HE REALLY IS **JUST LIKE** MY BROTHER.
THEY'RE SO SIMILAR THEY HATE EACH OTHER'S GUTS, HUH?
AH HA HA HA HA
ISN'T THAT CHILD-ISH?
Pffft!
AND WHAT ABOUT YOU, ALPHONSE? ARE YOU AN ADULT?
IF I WAS AN ADULT...
...I WOULDN'T THINK ABOUT GETTING MY BODY BACK AT THE COST OF COMMITTING A GREAT SIN.

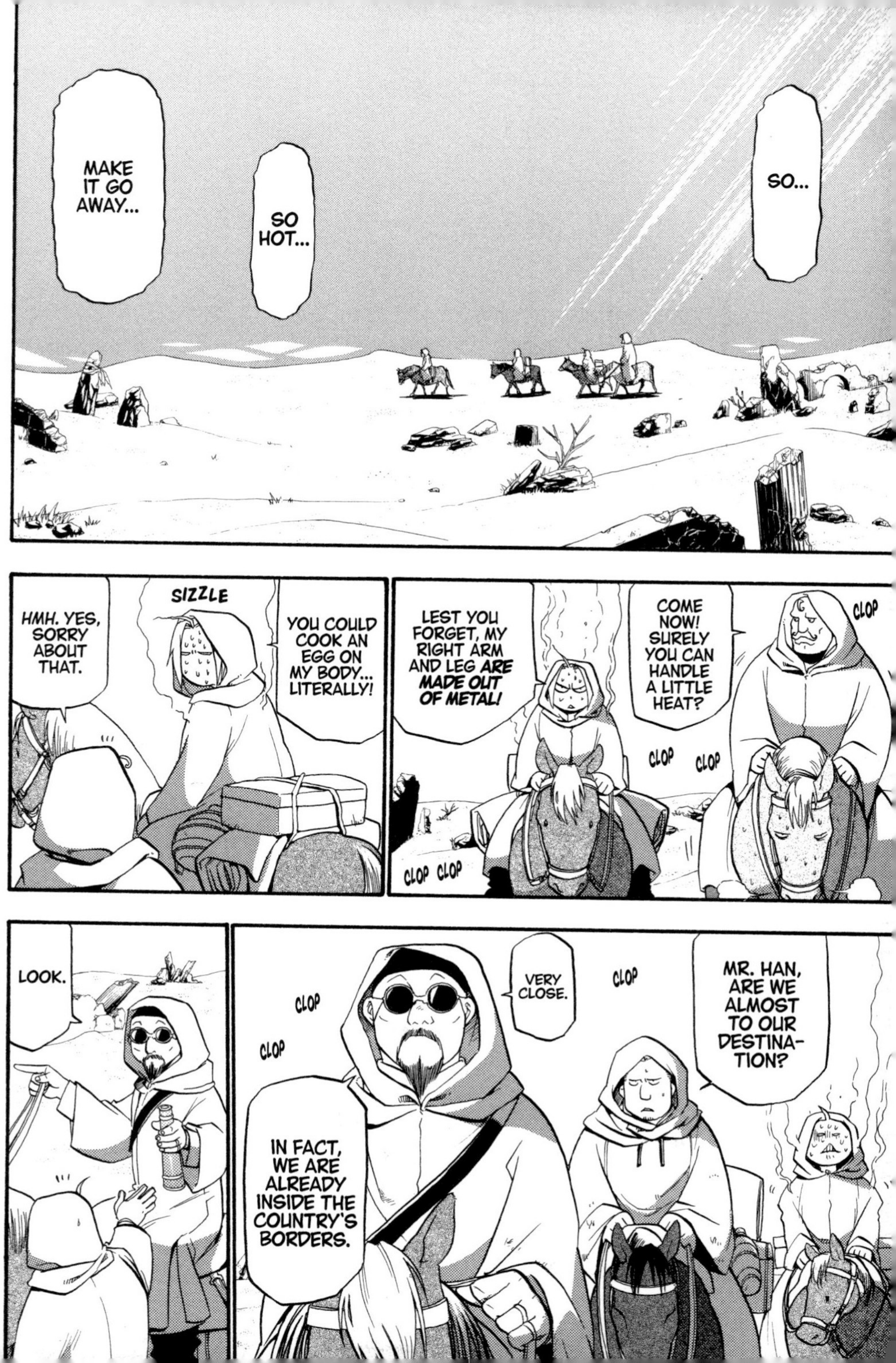
SO...
SO HOT...
MAKE IT GO AWAY...
CLOP
COME NOW! SURELY YOU CAN HANDLE A LITTLE HEAT?
LEST YOU FORGET, MY RIGHT ARM AND LEG **ARE MADE OUT OF METAL!**
CLOP CLOP
CLOP CLOP
YOU COULD COOK AN EGG ON MY BODY... LITERALLY!
SIZZLE
HMH. YES, SORRY ABOUT THAT.
MR. HAN, ARE WE ALMOST TO OUR DESTINATION?
CLOP
VERY CLOSE.
CLOP
CLOP
IN FACT, WE ARE ALREADY INSIDE THE COUNTRY'S BORDERS.
LOOK.

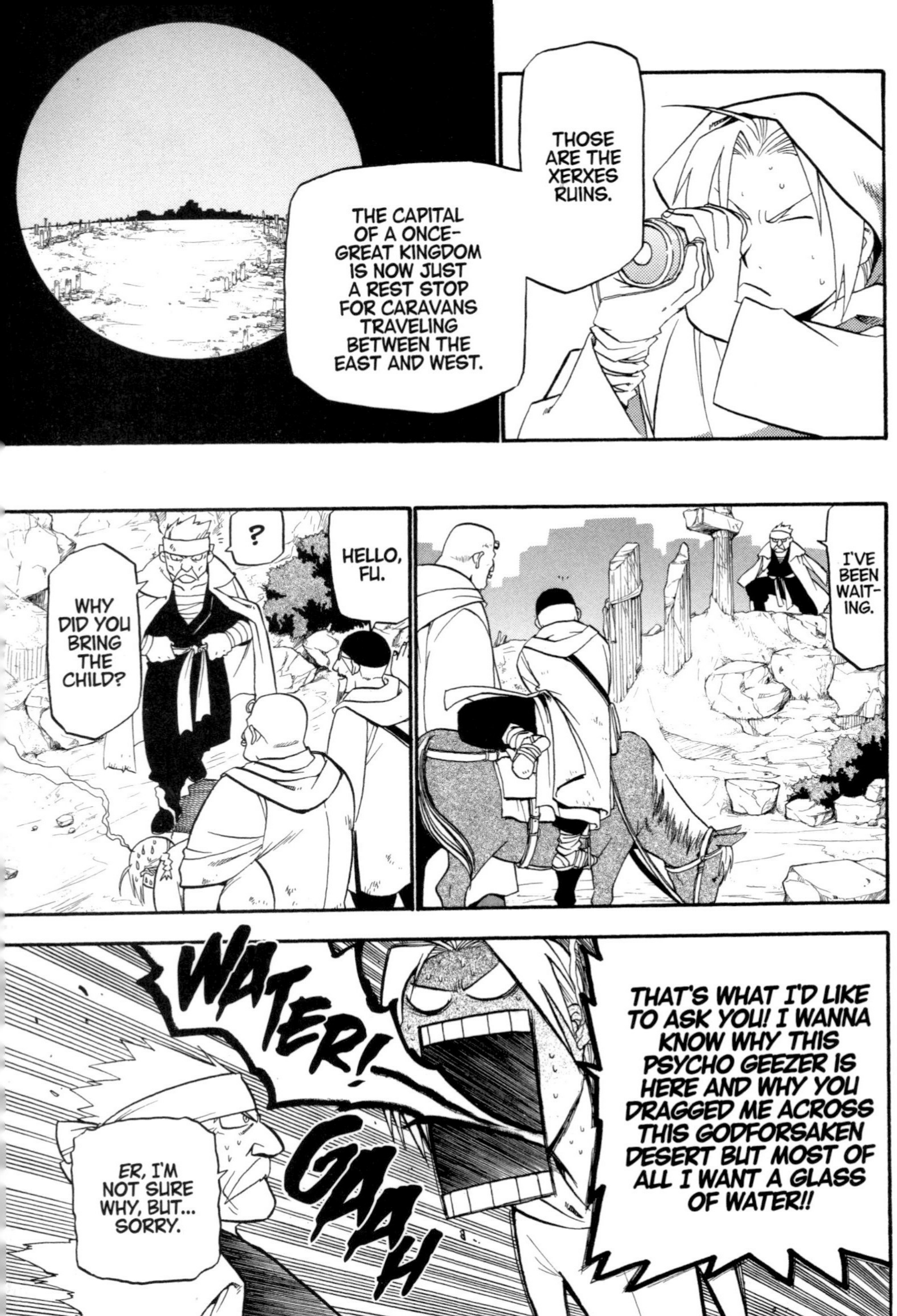
THOSE ARE THE XERXES RUINS.
THE CAPITAL OF A ONCE-GREAT KINGDOM IS NOW JUST A REST STOP FOR CARAVANS TRAVELING BETWEEN THE EAST AND WEST.
I'VE BEEN WAIT-ING.
HELLO, FU.
?
WHY DID YOU BRING THE CHILD?
THAT'S WHAT I'D LIKE TO ASK YOU! I WANNA KNOW WHY THIS PSYCHO GEEZER IS HERE AND WHY YOU DRAGGED ME ACROSS THIS GODFORSAKEN DESERT BUT MOST OF ALL I WANT A GLASS OF WATER!!
WATER!
GAAH
ER, I'M NOT SURE WHY, BUT... SORRY.

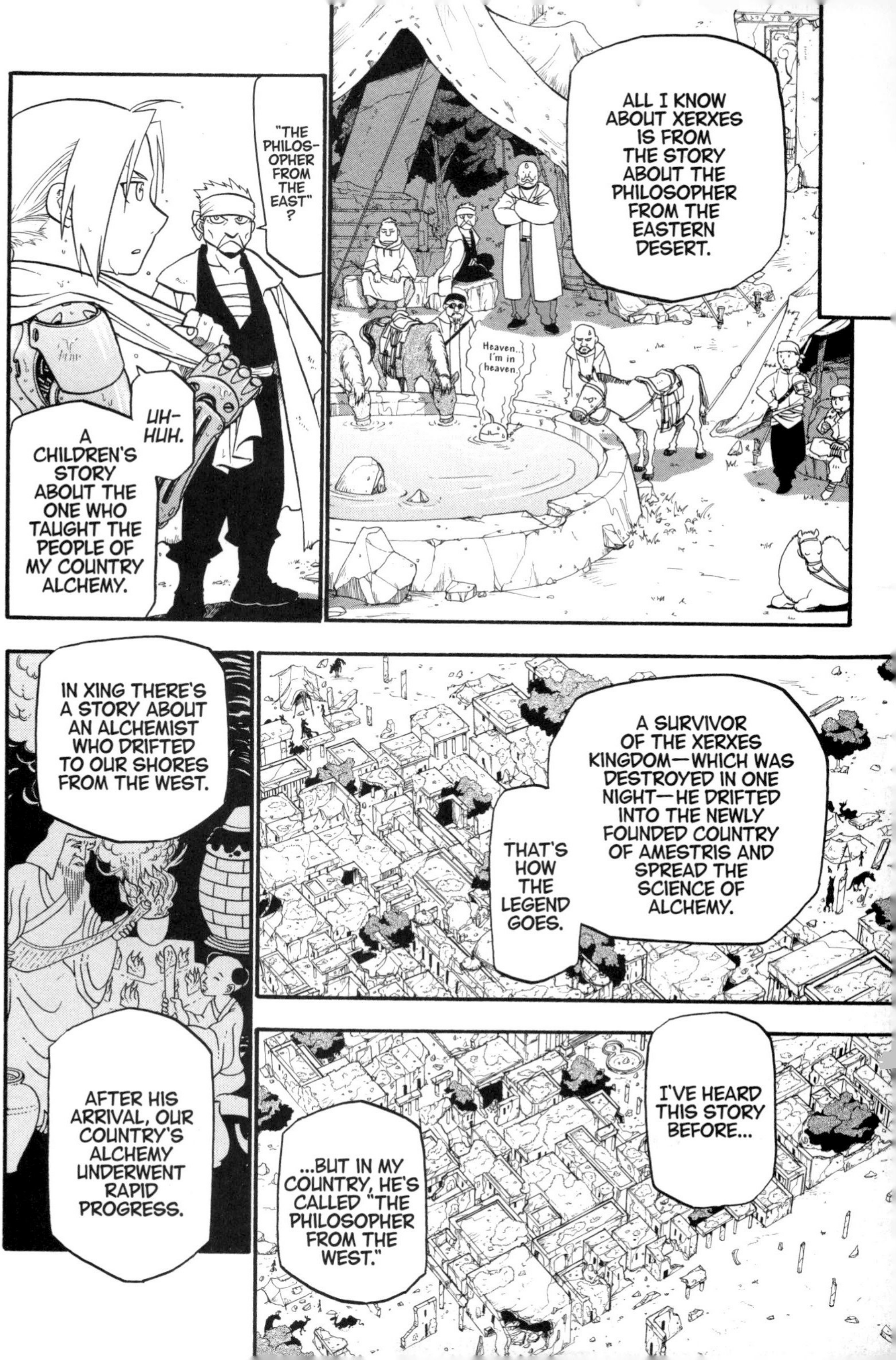

ALL I KNOW ABOUT XERXES IS FROM THE STORY ABOUT THE PHILOSOPHER FROM THE EASTERN DESERT.
Heaven... I'm in heaven.
"THE PHILOSOPHER FROM THE EAST"?
UH-HUH.
A CHILDREN'S STORY ABOUT THE ONE WHO TAUGHT THE PEOPLE OF MY COUNTRY ALCHEMY.
A SURVIVOR OF THE XERXES KINGDOM—WHICH WAS DESTROYED IN ONE NIGHT—HE DRIFTED INTO THE NEWLY FOUNDED COUNTRY OF AMESTRIS AND SPREAD THE SCIENCE OF ALCHEMY.
THAT'S HOW THE LEGEND GOES.
I'VE HEARD THIS STORY BEFORE...
...BUT IN MY COUNTRY, HE'S CALLED "THE PHILOSOPHER FROM THE WEST."
IN XING THERE'S A STORY ABOUT AN ALCHEMIST WHO DRIFTED TO OUR SHORES FROM THE WEST.
AFTER HIS ARRIVAL, OUR COUNTRY'S ALCHEMY UNDERWENT RAPID PROGRESS.

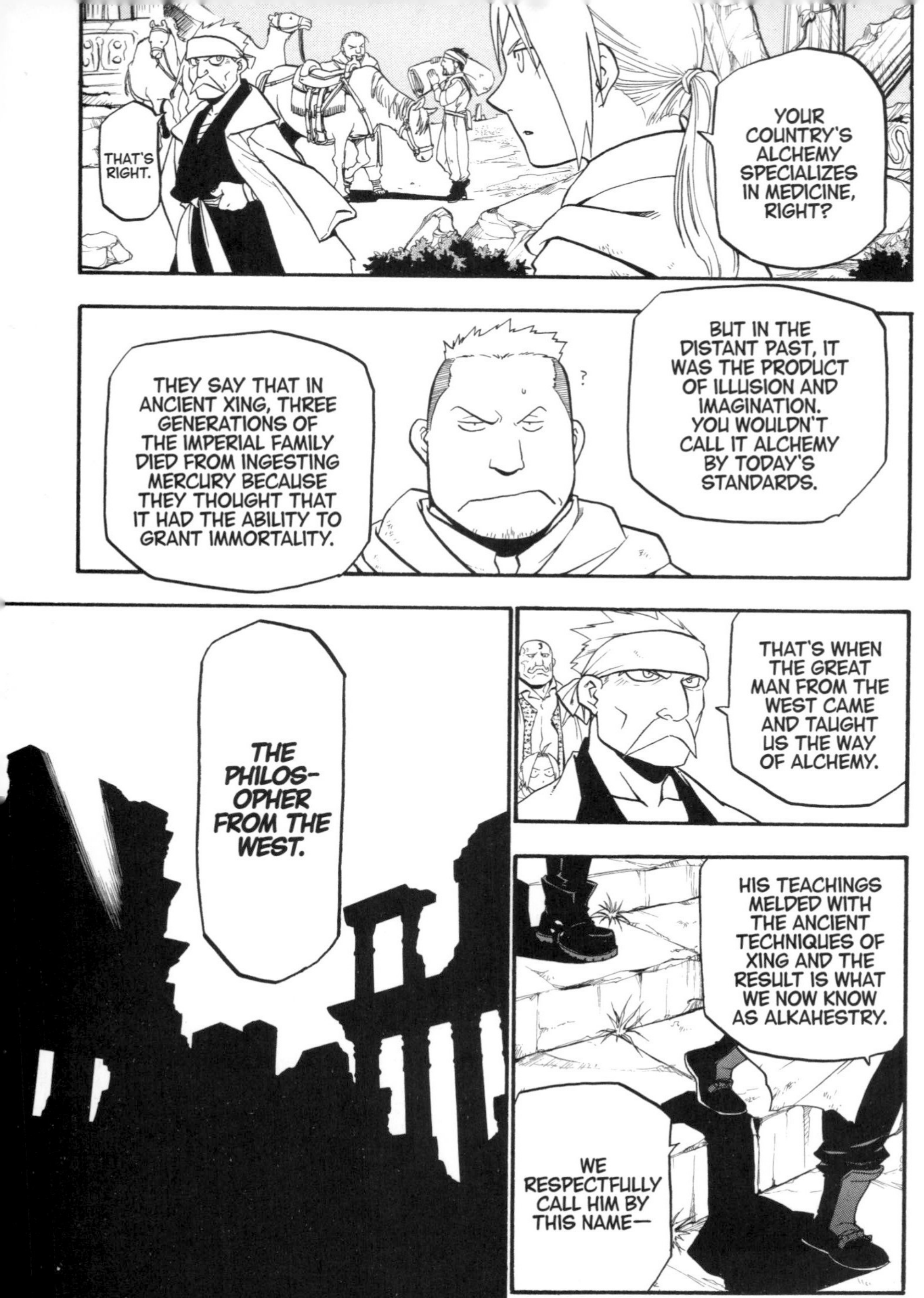
YOUR COUNTRY'S ALCHEMY SPECIALIZES IN MEDICINE, RIGHT?
THAT'S RIGHT.
BUT IN THE DISTANT PAST, IT WAS THE PRODUCT OF ILLUSION AND IMAGINATION. YOU WOULDN'T CALL IT ALCHEMY BY TODAY'S STANDARDS.
THEY SAY THAT IN ANCIENT XING, THREE GENERATIONS OF THE IMPERIAL FAMILY DIED FROM INGESTING MERCURY BECAUSE THEY THOUGHT THAT IT HAD THE ABILITY TO GRANT IMMORTALITY.
THAT'S WHEN THE GREAT MAN FROM THE WEST CAME AND TAUGHT US THE WAY OF ALCHEMY.
HIS TEACHINGS MELDED WITH THE ANCIENT TECHNIQUES OF XING AND THE RESULT IS WHAT WE NOW KNOW AS ALKAHESTRY.
WE RESPECTFULLY CALL HIM BY THIS NAME—
THE PHILOSOPHER FROM THE WEST.

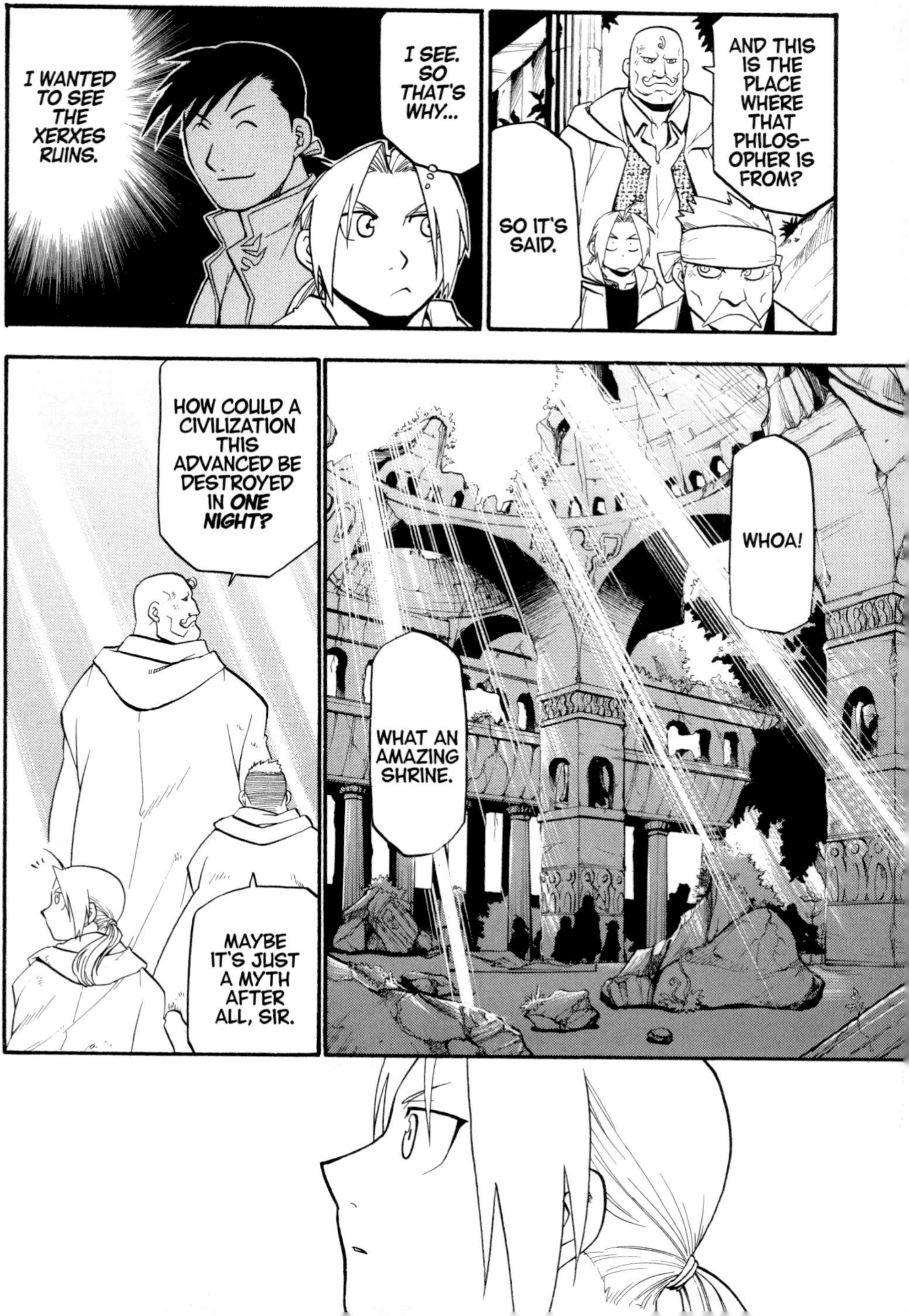
AND THIS IS THE PLACE WHERE THAT PHILOSOPHER IS FROM?
SO IT'S SAID.
I SEE. SO THAT'S WHY...
I WANTED TO SEE THE XERXES RUINS.
WHOA!
WHAT AN AMAZING SHRINE.
HOW COULD A CIVILIZATION THIS ADVANCED BE DESTROYED IN *ONE NIGHT?*
MAYBE IT'S JUST A MYTH AFTER ALL, SIR.

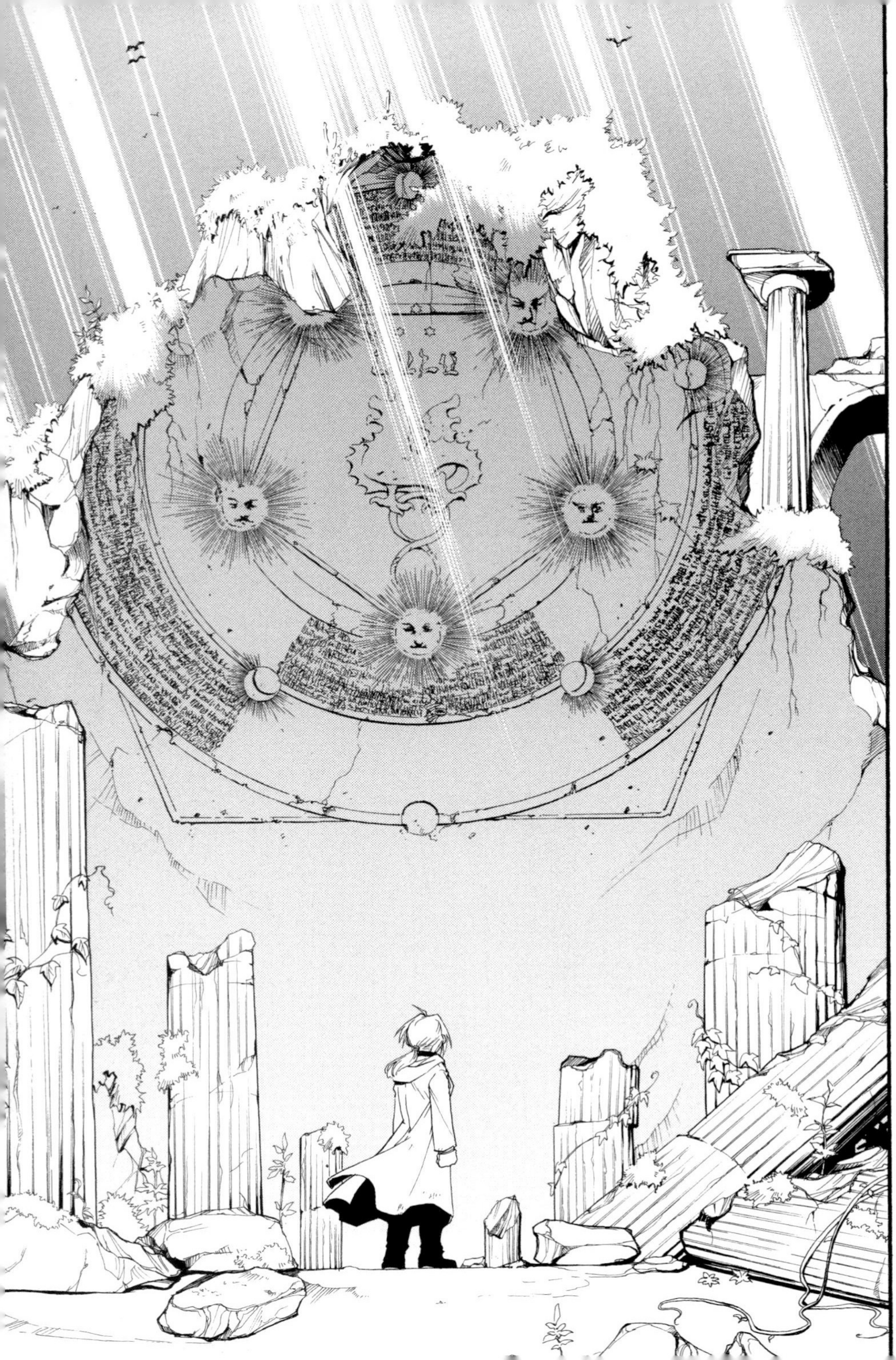

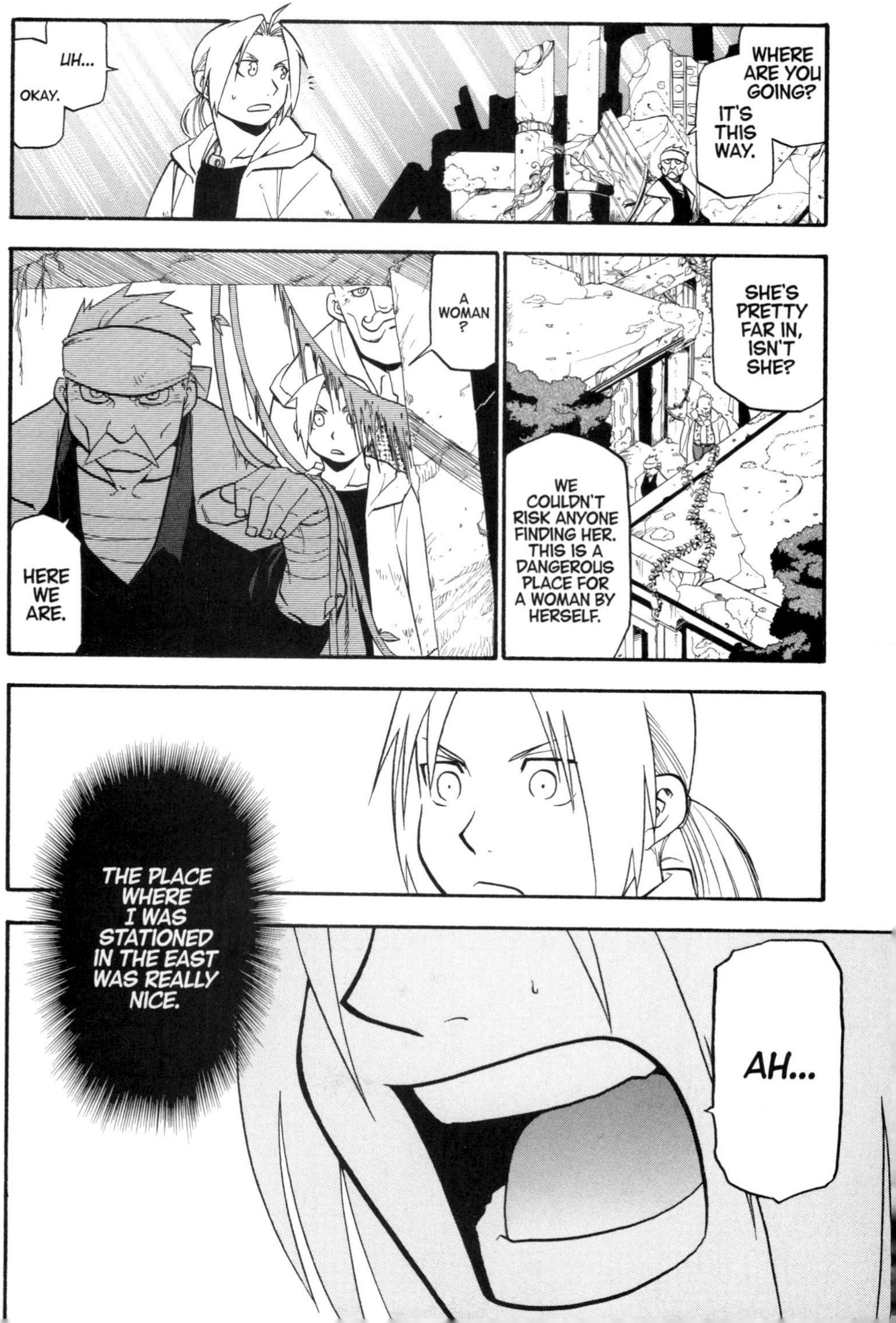
WHERE ARE YOU GOING?
IT'S THIS WAY.
UH...
OKAY.
SHE'S PRETTY FAR IN, ISN'T SHE?
WE COULDN'T RISK ANYONE FINDING HER. THIS IS A DANGEROUS PLACE FOR A WOMAN BY HERSELF.
A WOMAN?
HERE WE ARE.
THE PLACE WHERE I WAS STATIONED IN THE EAST WAS REALLY NICE.
AH...

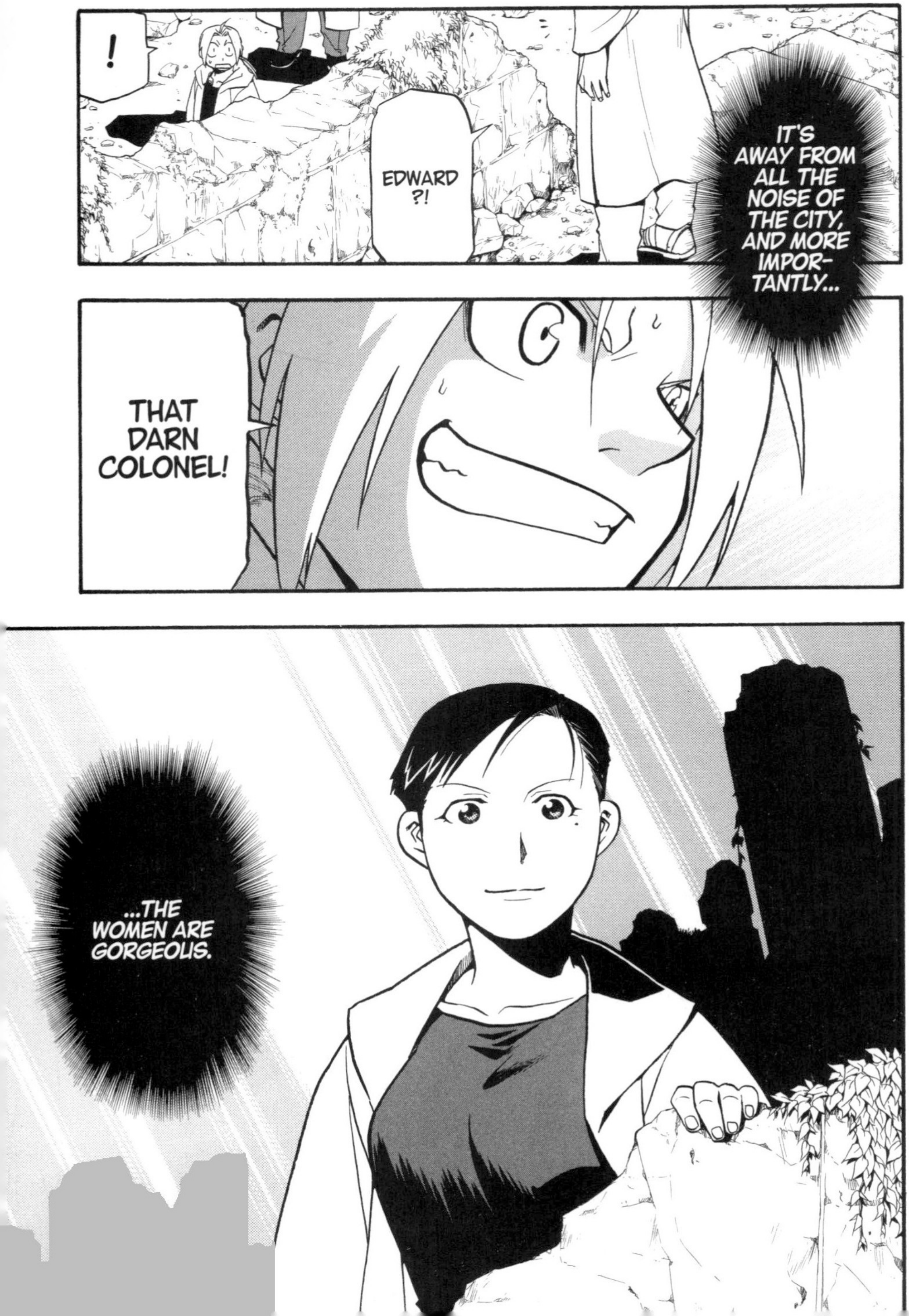
IT'S AWAY FROM ALL THE NOISE OF THE CITY, AND MORE IMPOR-TANTLY...
EDWARD ?!
!
THAT DARN COLONEL!
...THE WOMEN ARE GORGEOUS.

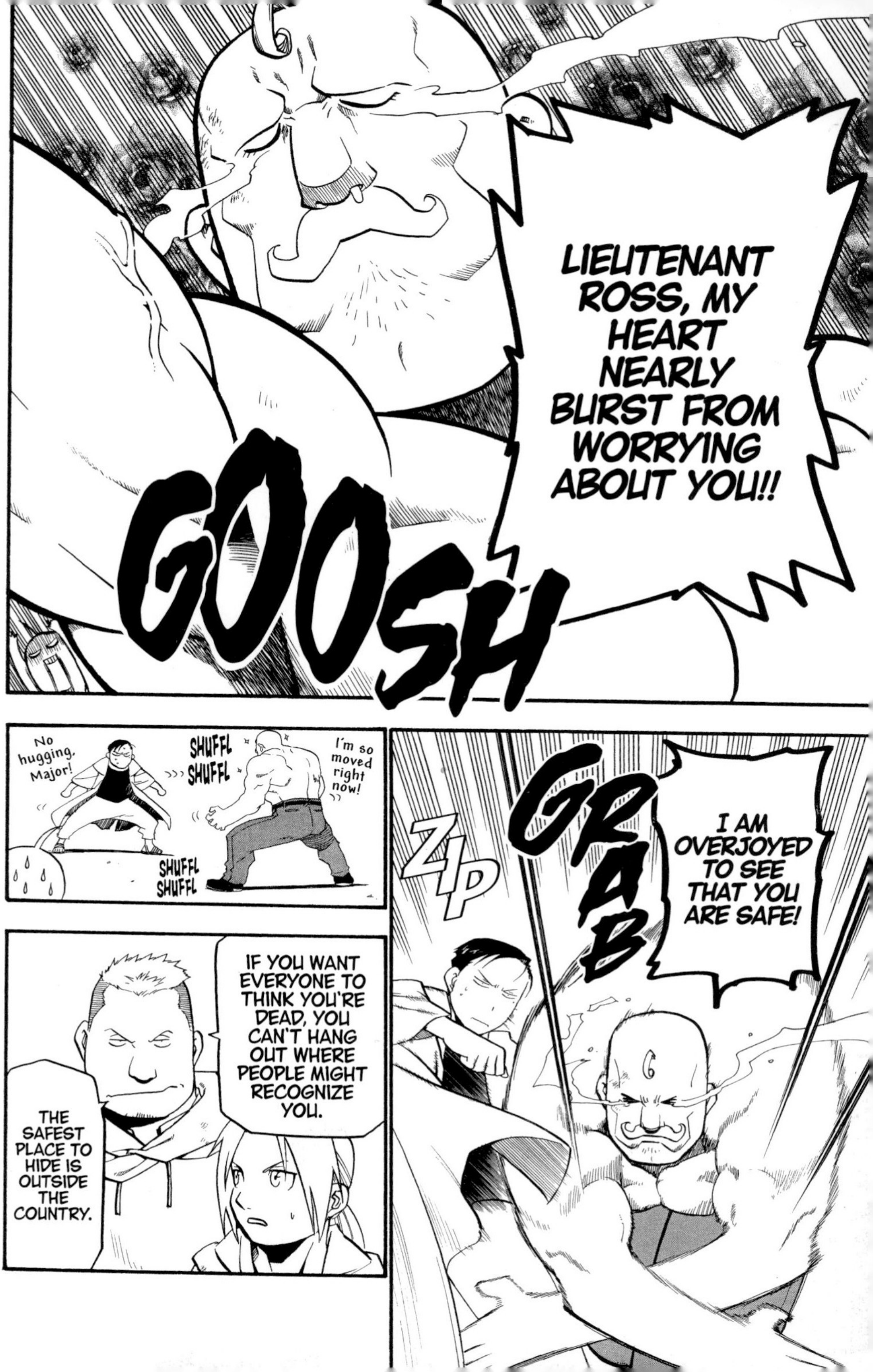
LIEUTENANT ROSS, MY HEART NEARLY BURST FROM WORRYING ABOUT YOU!!
GOOSH
GRAB
ZIP
I AM OVERJOYED TO SEE THAT YOU ARE SAFE!
I'm so moved right now!
SHUFFL SHUFFL
No hugging, Major!
SHUFFL SHUFFL
IF YOU WANT EVERYONE TO THINK YOU'RE DEAD, YOU CAN'T HANG OUT WHERE PEOPLE MIGHT RECOGNIZE YOU.
THE SAFEST PLACE TO HIDE IS OUTSIDE THE COUNTRY.

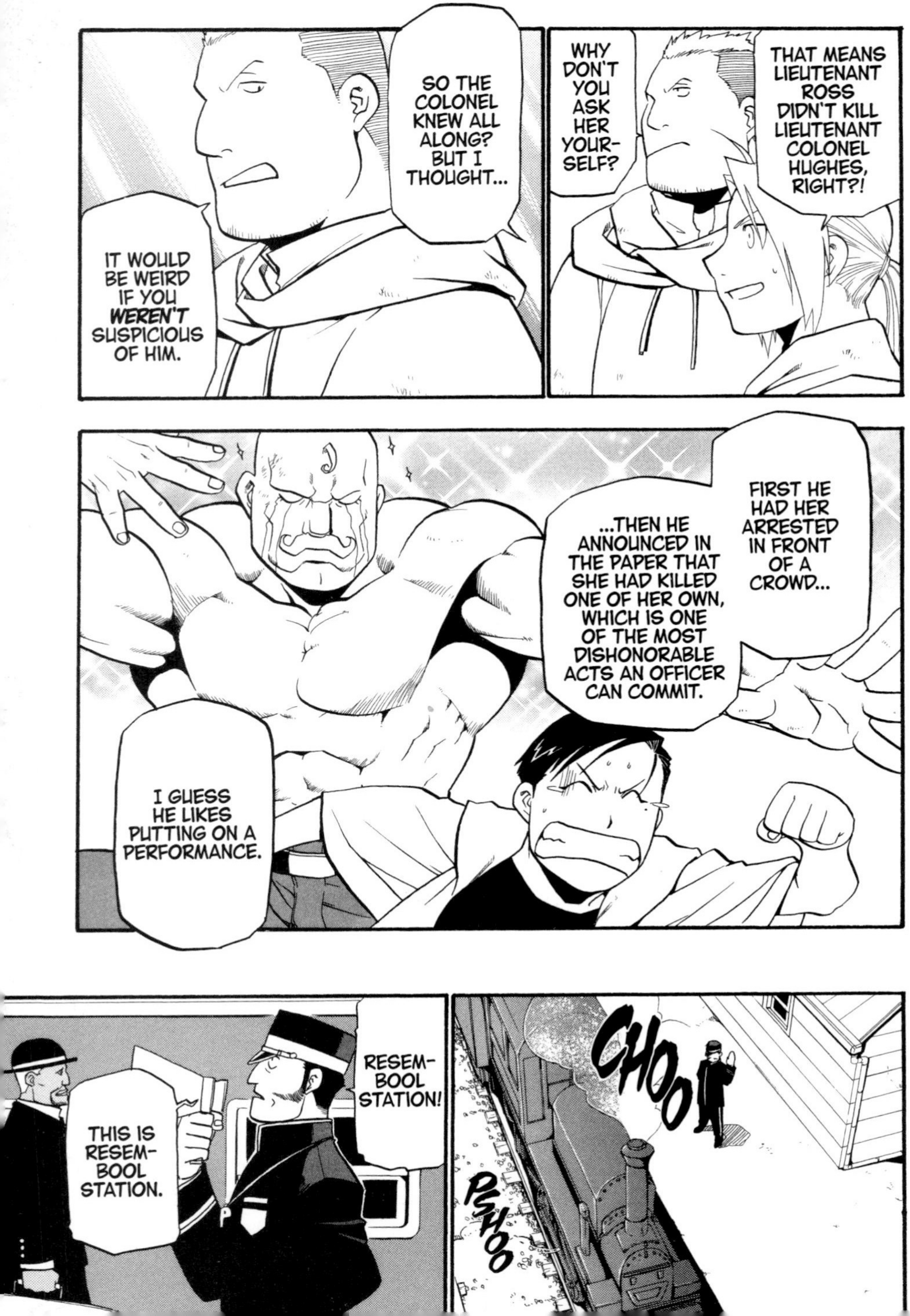
THAT MEANS LIEUTENANT ROSS DIDN'T KILL LIEUTENANT COLONEL HUGHES, RIGHT?!
WHY DON'T YOU ASK HER YOUR-SELF?
SO THE COLONEL KNEW ALL ALONG? BUT I THOUGHT...
IT WOULD BE WEIRD IF YOU ***WEREN'T*** SUSPICIOUS OF HIM.
FIRST HE HAD HER ARRESTED IN FRONT OF A CROWD...
...THEN HE ANNOUNCED IN THE PAPER THAT SHE HAD KILLED ONE OF HER OWN, WHICH IS ONE OF THE MOST DISHONORABLE ACTS AN OFFICER CAN COMMIT.
I GUESS HE LIKES PUTTING ON A PERFORMANCE.
CHOO
PSHOO
RESEM-BOOL STATION!
THIS IS RESEM-BOOL STATION.

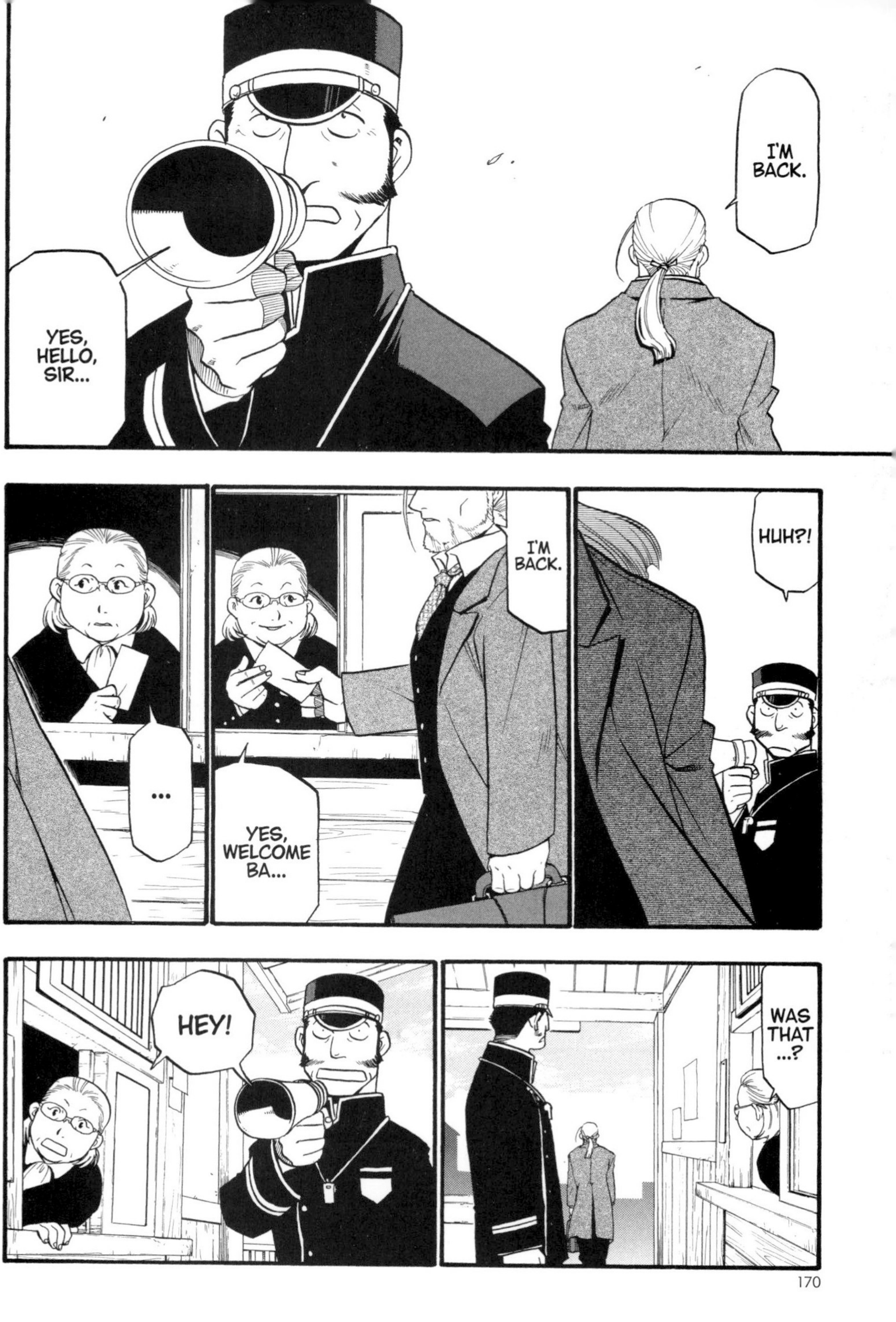
I'M BACK.
YES, HELLO, SIR...
HUH?!
I'M BACK.
YES, WELCOME BA...
...
WAS THAT ...?
HEY!

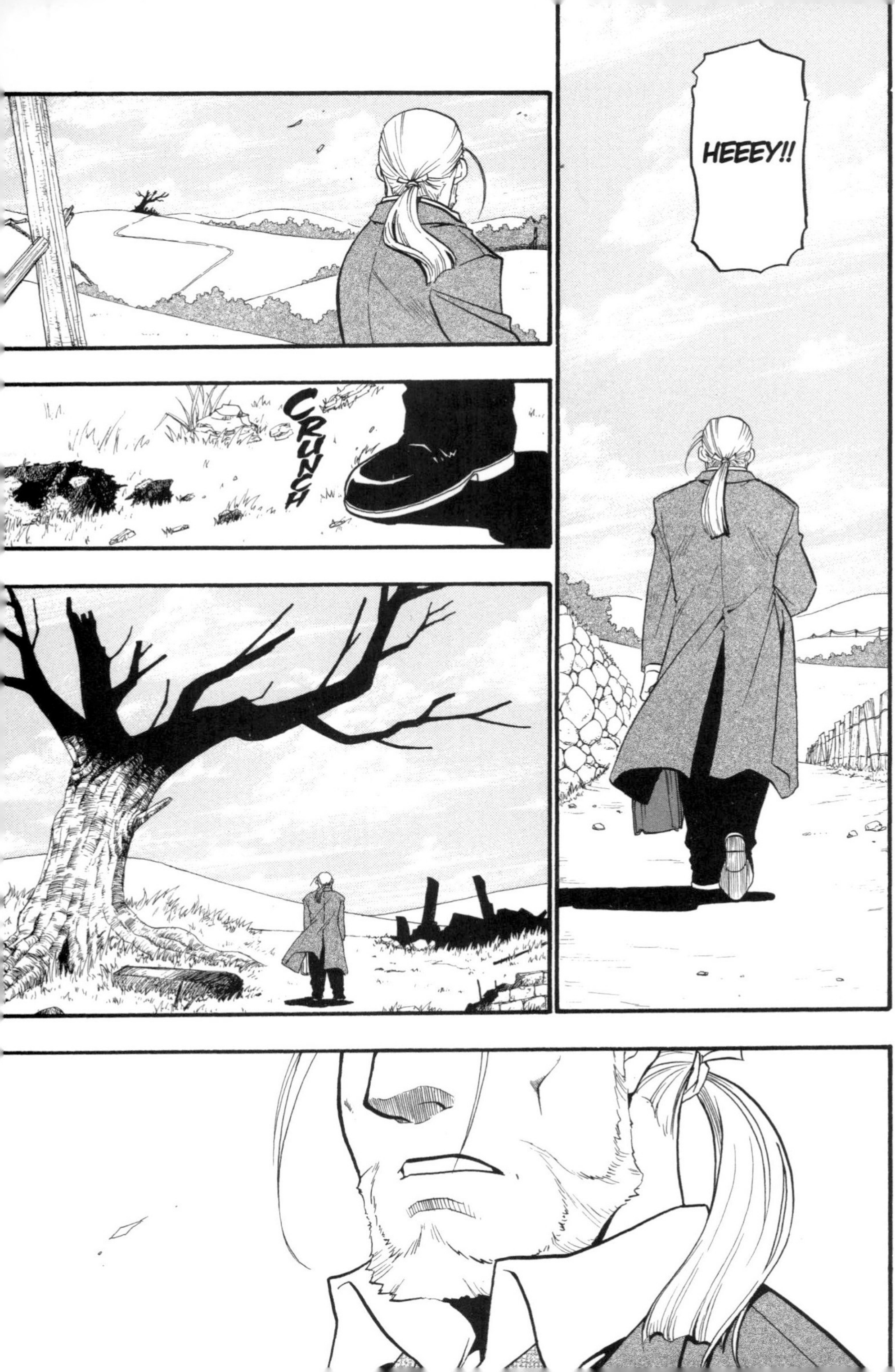
HEEEY!!
CRUNCH

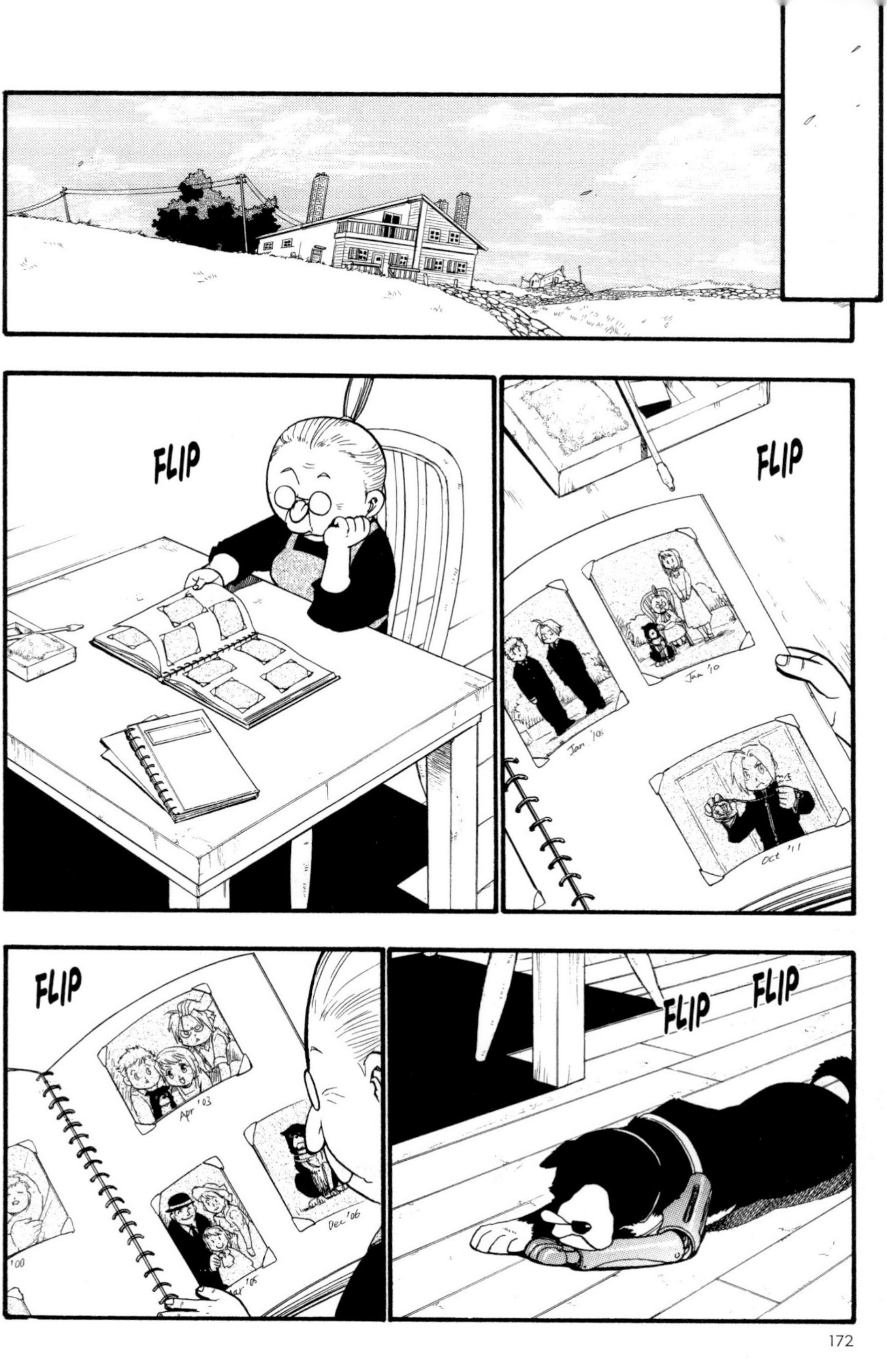
FLIP
Jan '10
Oct '11
FLIP
FLIP
FLIP
FLIP
Apr '03
Dec '06

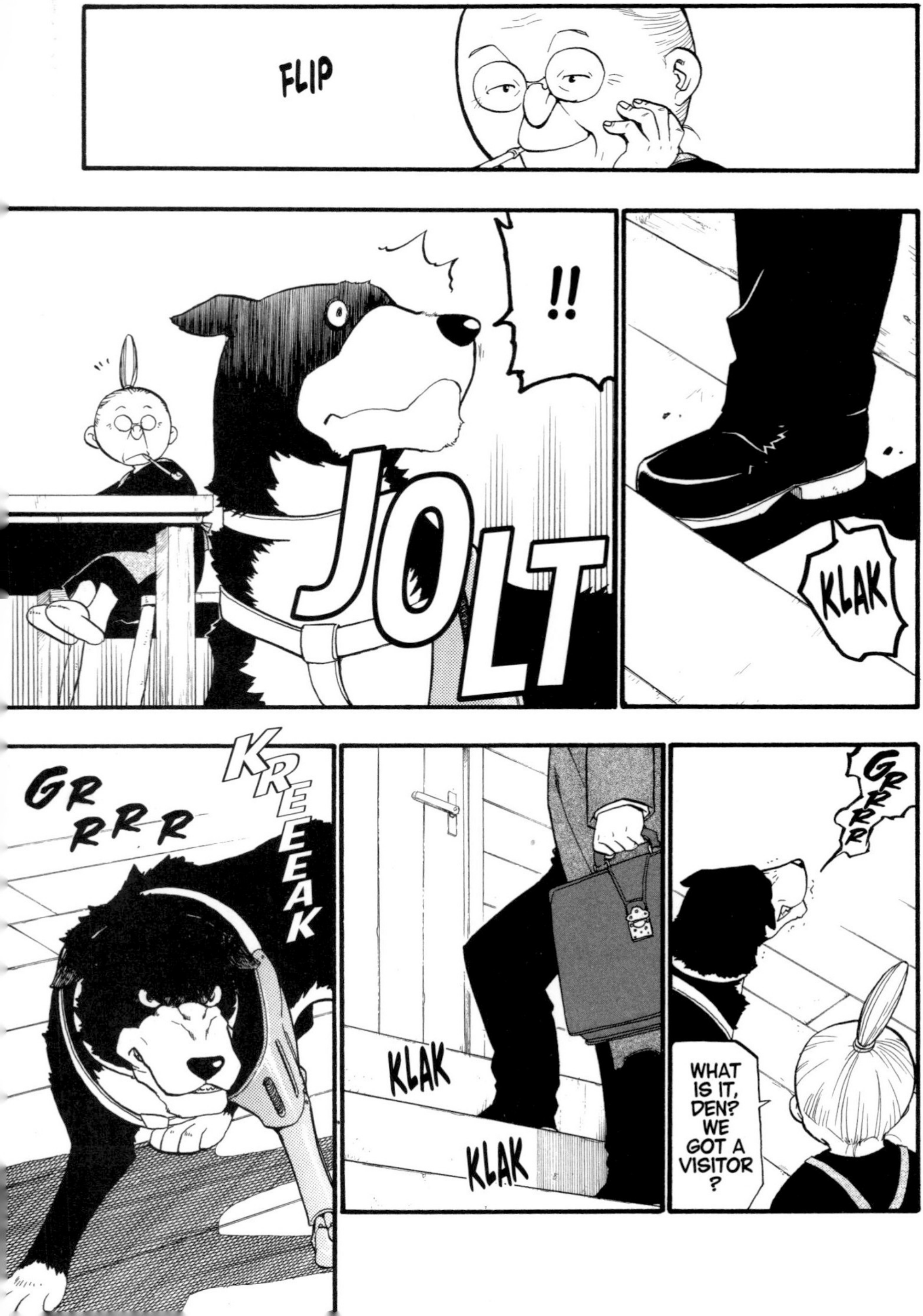
FLIP
KLAK
!!
JOLT
GRRRR
WHAT IS IT, DEN? WE GOT A VISITOR?
KLAK
KLAK
KREEEEAK
GRRRR

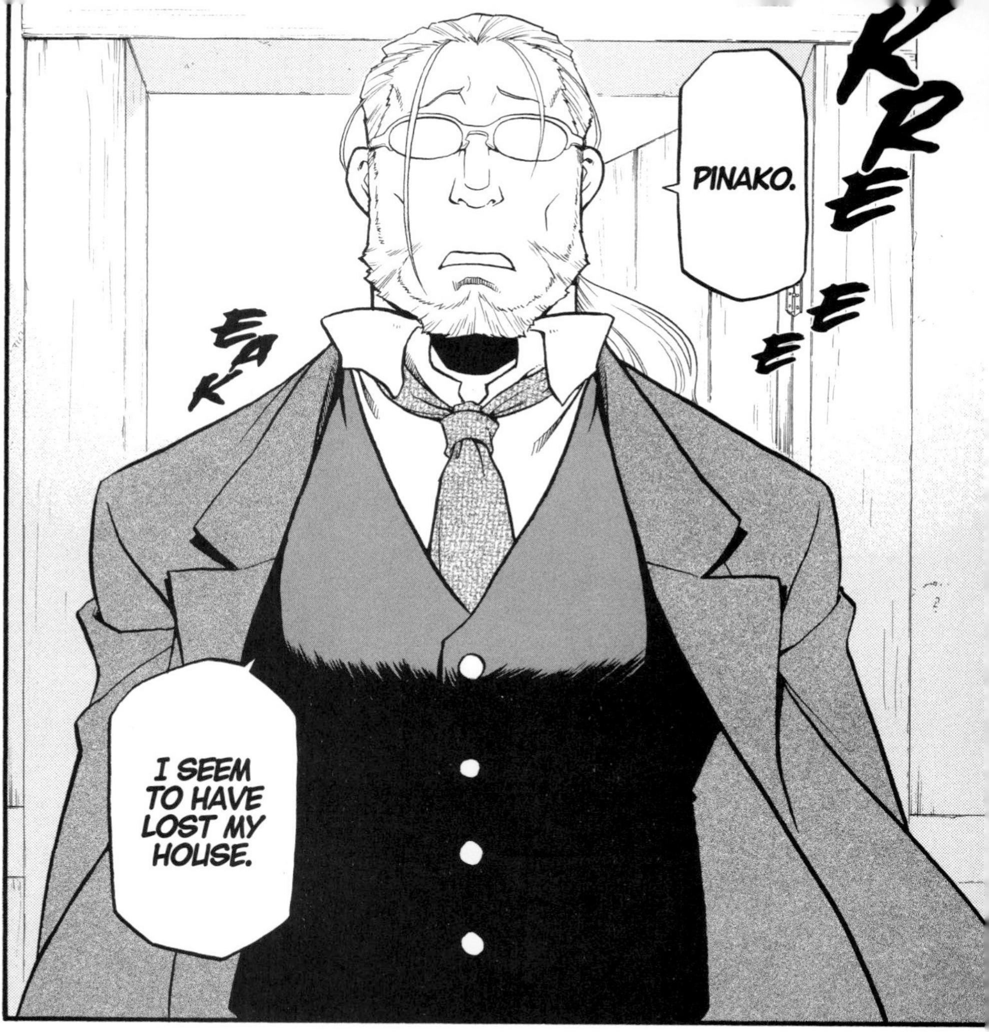
KREEEE
PINAKO.
EAK
I SEEM TO HAVE LOST MY HOUSE.

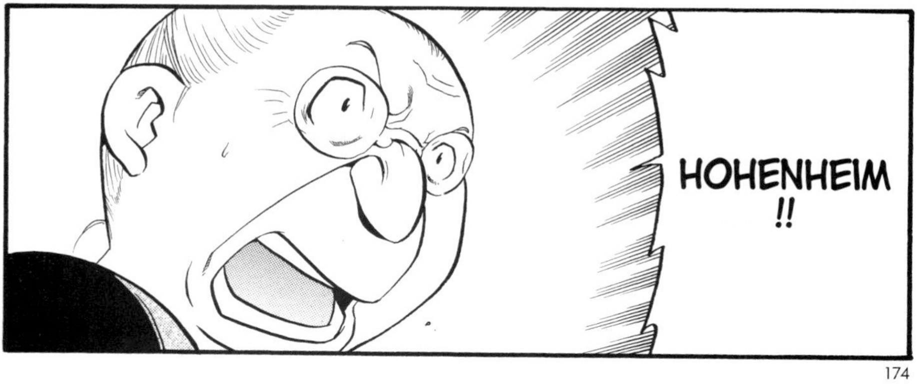
HOHENHEIM !!

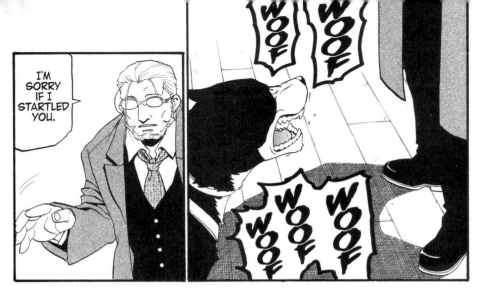

I'M SORRY IF I STARTLED YOU.

WOOF WOOF WOOF WOOF WOOF

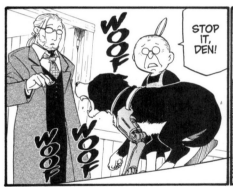

WOOF WOOF WOOF

STOP IT, DEN!

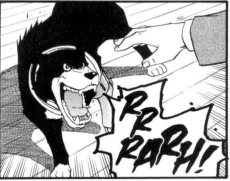

RR RARH!

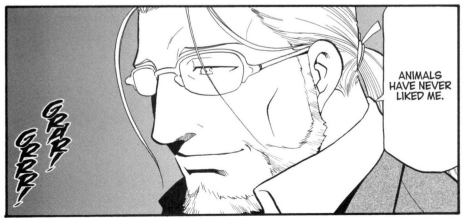

GRAR! GRRR!

ANIMALS HAVE NEVER LIKED ME.

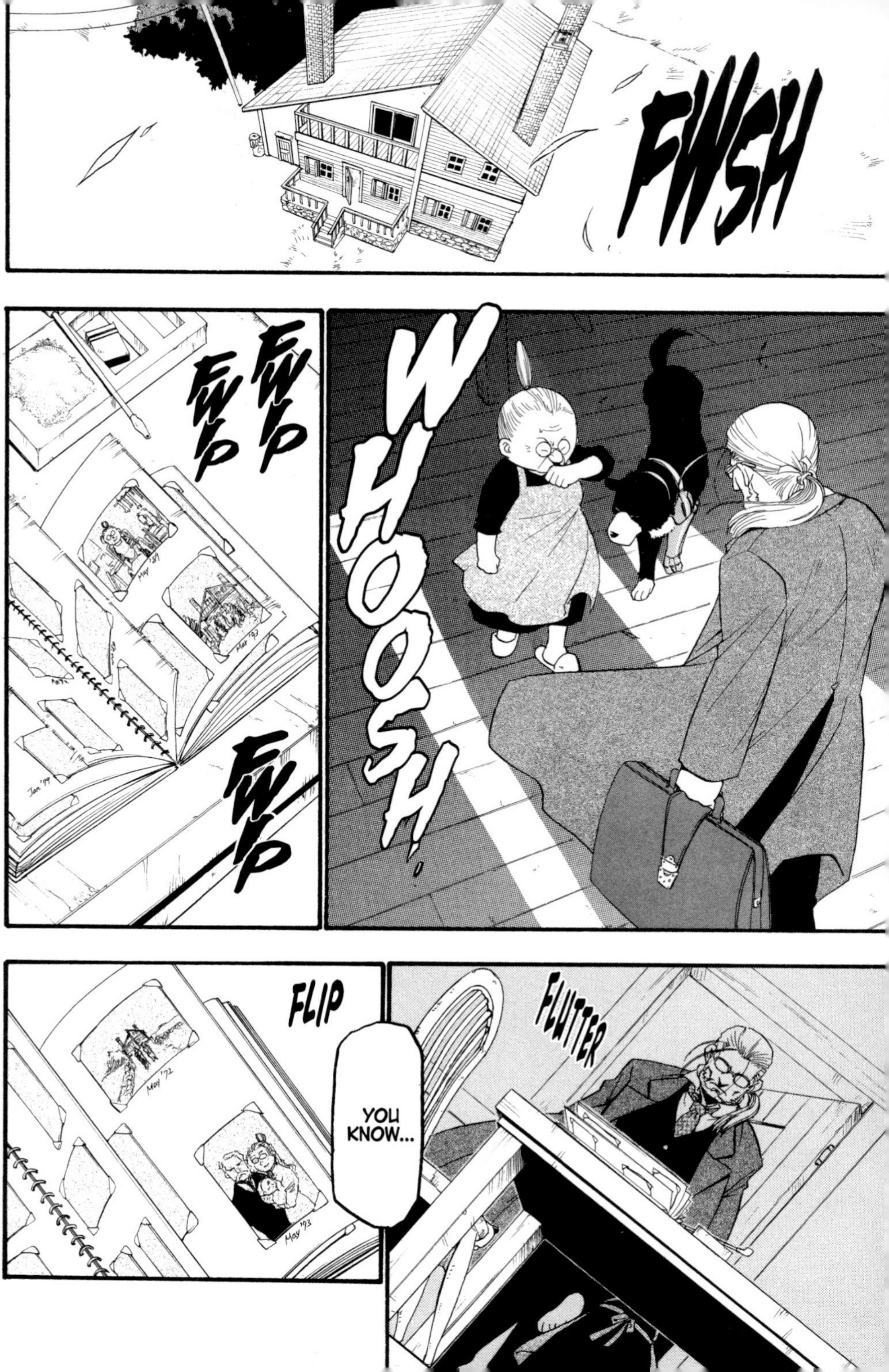
FWSH
WHOOSH
FWP
FWP
FWP
FLUTTER
YOU KNOW...
FLIP

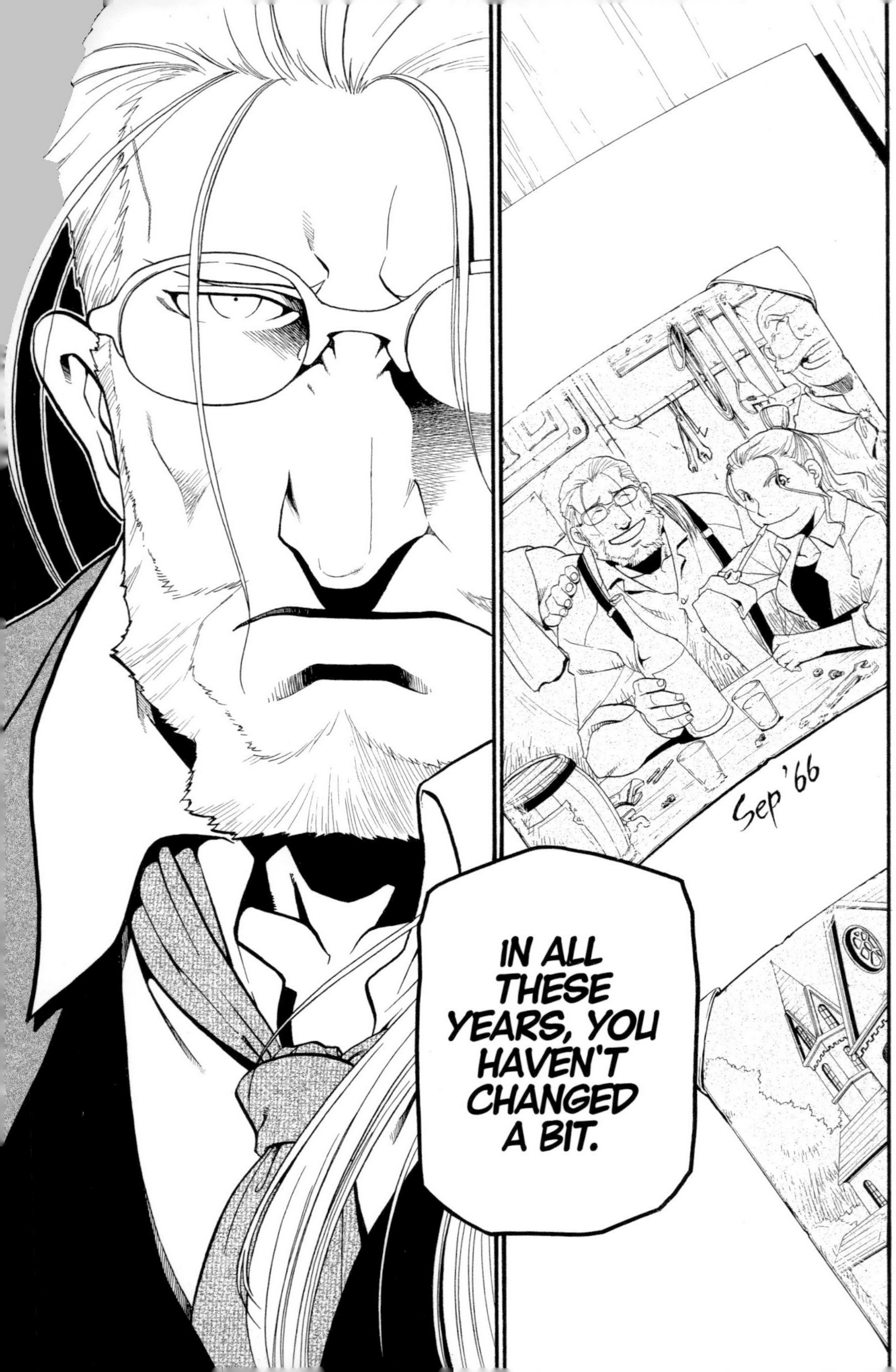
Sep '66
IN ALL THESE YEARS, YOU HAVEN'T CHANGED A BIT.

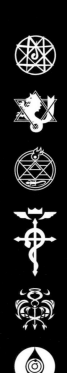

CHAPTER 41

ON THE PALM OF AN ARROGANT HUMAN BEING

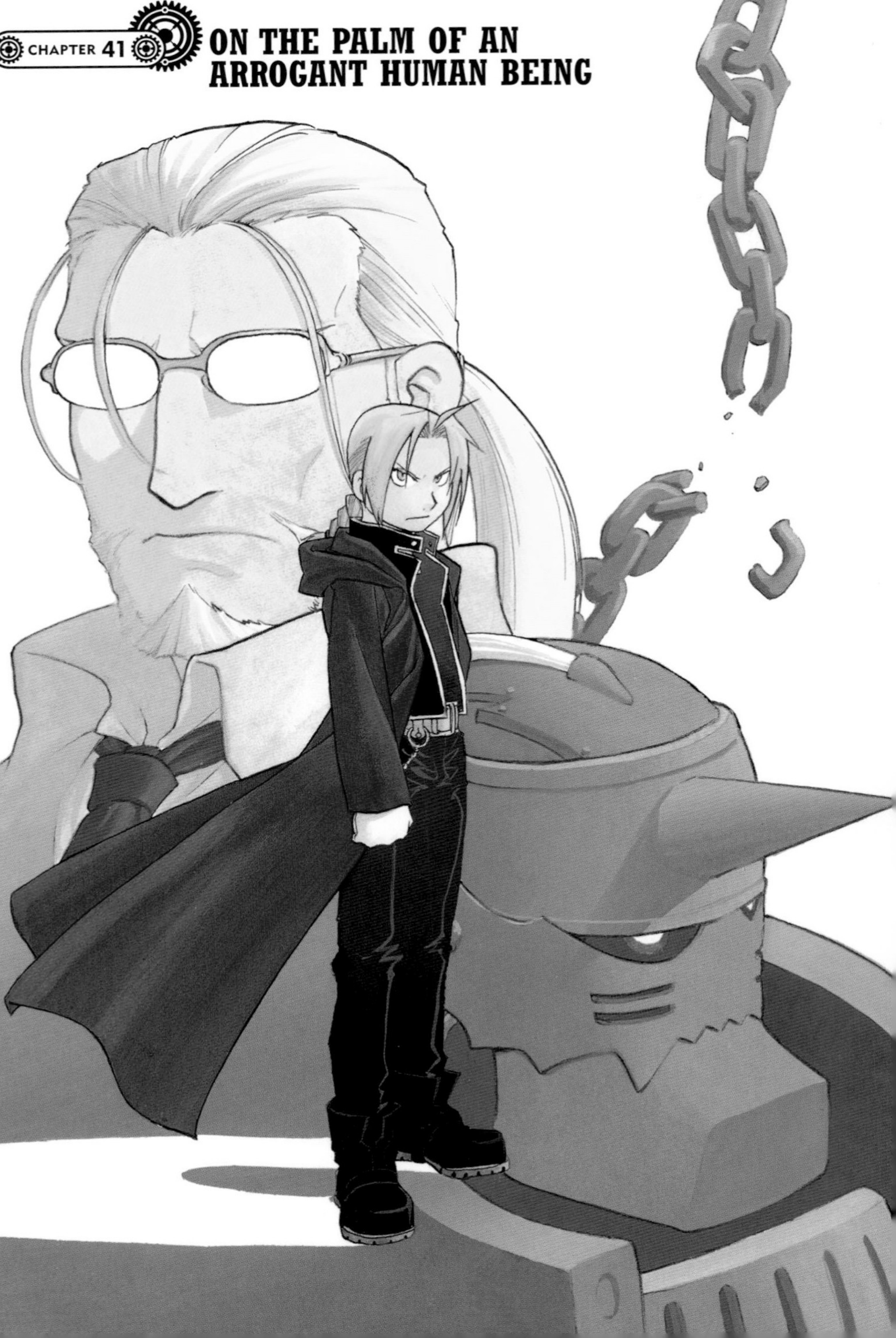

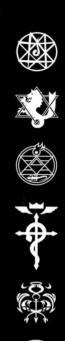

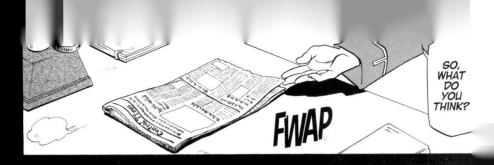

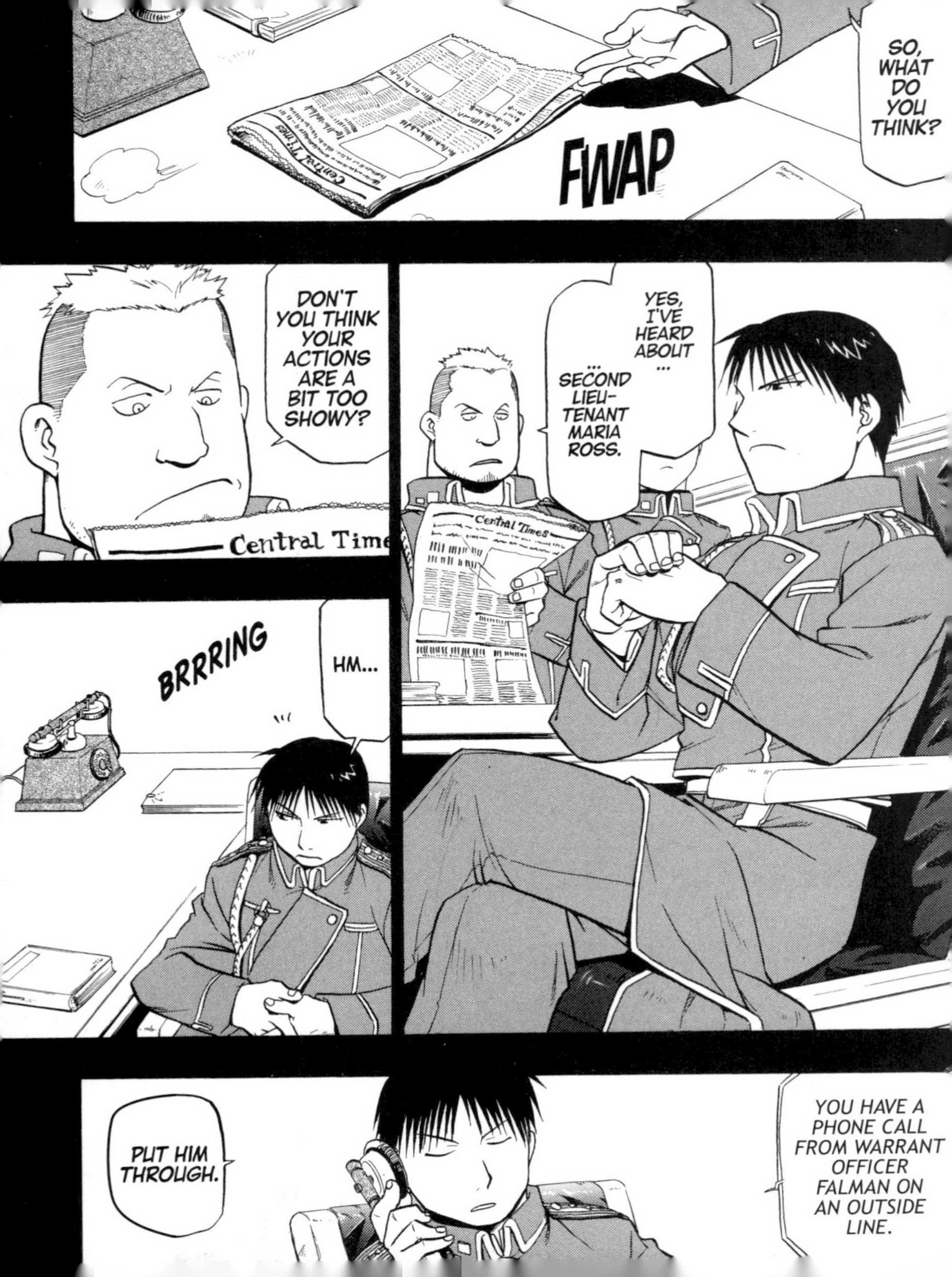
SO, WHAT DO YOU THINK?
FWAP
Central Times
YES, I'VE HEARD ABOUT ...
... SECOND LIEU-TENANT MARIA ROSS.
Central Times
DON'T YOU THINK YOUR ACTIONS ARE A BIT TOO SHOWY?
Central Time
HM...
BRRRING
YOU HAVE A PHONE CALL FROM WARRANT OFFICER FALMAN ON AN OUTSIDE LINE.
PUT HIM THROUGH.

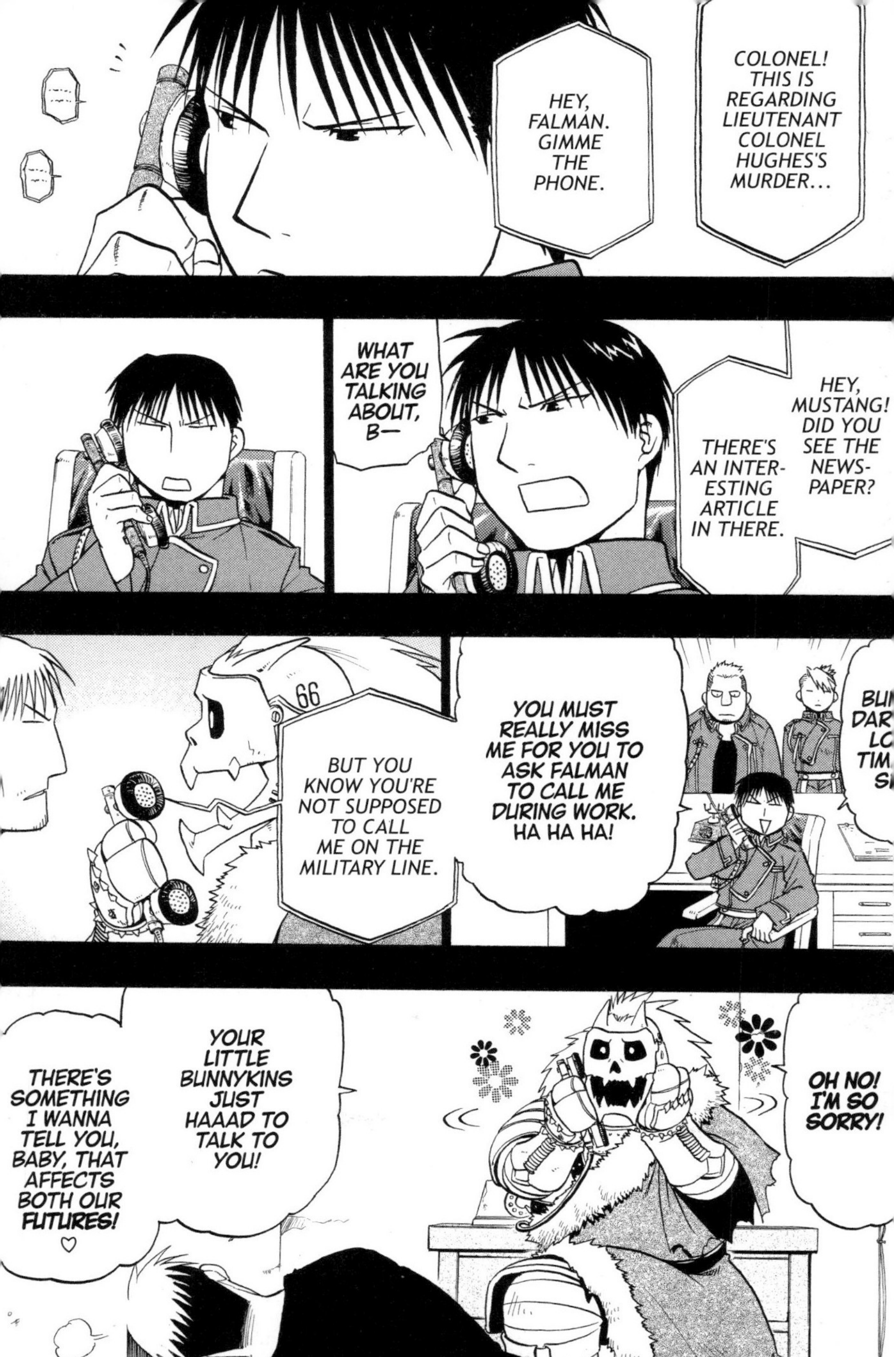
COLONEL! THIS IS REGARDING LIEUTENANT COLONEL HUGHES'S MURDER…
HEY, FALMAN. GIMME THE PHONE.
HEY, MUSTANG! DID YOU SEE THE NEWS-PAPER?
THERE'S AN INTER-ESTING ARTICLE IN THERE.
WHAT ARE YOU TALKING ABOUT, B—
YOU MUST REALLY MISS ME FOR YOU TO ASK FALMAN TO CALL ME DURING WORK. HA HA HA!
BUT YOU KNOW YOU'RE NOT SUPPOSED TO CALL ME ON THE MILITARY LINE.
66
OH NO! I'M SO SORRY!
YOUR LITTLE BUNNYKINS JUST HAAAD TO TALK TO YOU!
THERE'S SOMETHING I WANNA TELL YOU, BABY, THAT AFFECTS BOTH OUR FUTURES! ♡

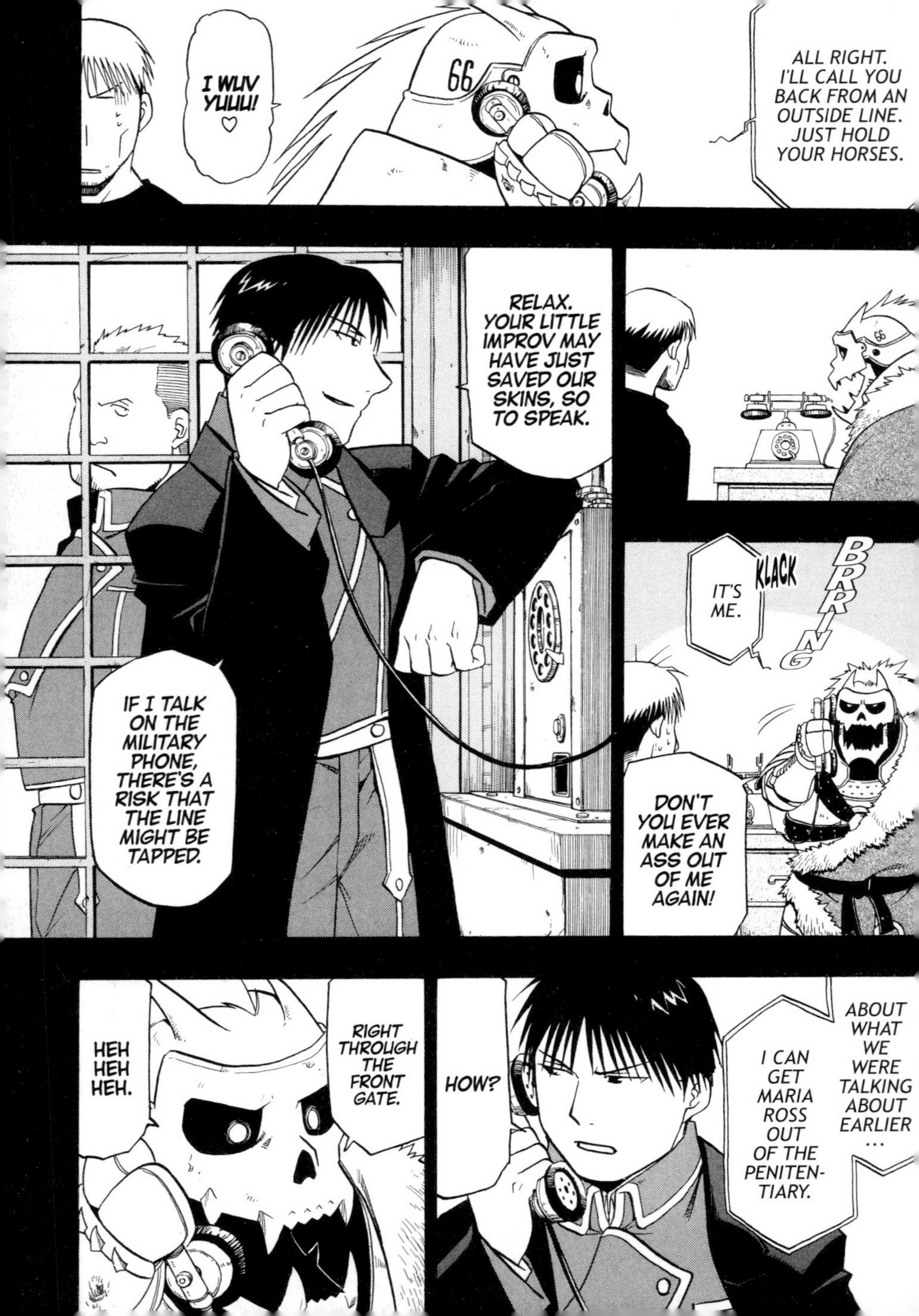
ALL RIGHT. I'LL CALL YOU BACK FROM AN OUTSIDE LINE. JUST HOLD YOUR HORSES.
I WUV YUUU! ♡
BRRING
KLACK
IT'S ME.
DON'T YOU EVER MAKE AN ASS OUT OF ME AGAIN!
RELAX. YOUR LITTLE IMPROV MAY HAVE JUST SAVED OUR SKINS, SO TO SPEAK.
IF I TALK ON THE MILITARY PHONE, THERE'S A RISK THAT THE LINE MIGHT BE TAPPED.
ABOUT WHAT WE WERE TALKING ABOUT EARLIER...
I CAN GET MARIA ROSS OUT OF THE PENITENTIARY.
HOW?
RIGHT THROUGH THE FRONT GATE.
HEH HEH HEH.

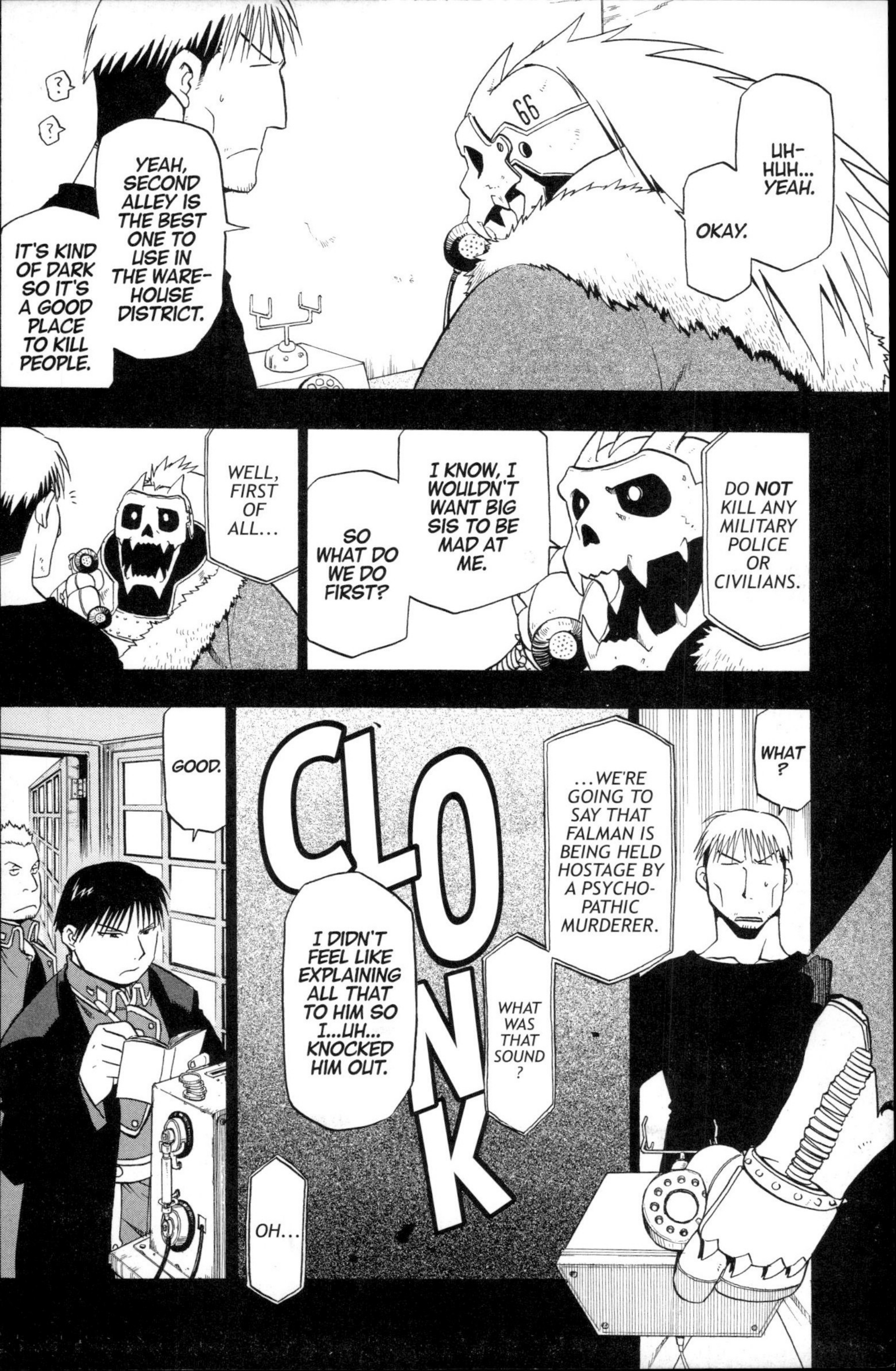
UH-HUH... YEAH.
OKAY.
?
?
YEAH, SECOND ALLEY IS THE BEST ONE TO USE IN THE WARE-HOUSE DISTRICT.
IT'S KIND OF DARK SO IT'S A GOOD PLACE TO KILL PEOPLE.
DO **NOT** KILL ANY MILITARY POLICE OR CIVILIANS.
I KNOW, I WOULDN'T WANT BIG SIS TO BE MAD AT ME.
SO WHAT DO WE DO FIRST?
WELL, FIRST OF ALL...
WHAT ?
...WE'RE GOING TO SAY THAT FALMAN IS BEING HELD HOSTAGE BY A PSYCHO-PATHIC MURDERER.
CLONK
WHAT WAS THAT SOUND ?
I DIDN'T FEEL LIKE EXPLAINING ALL THAT TO HIM SO I...UH... KNOCKED HIM OUT.
OH...
GOOD.

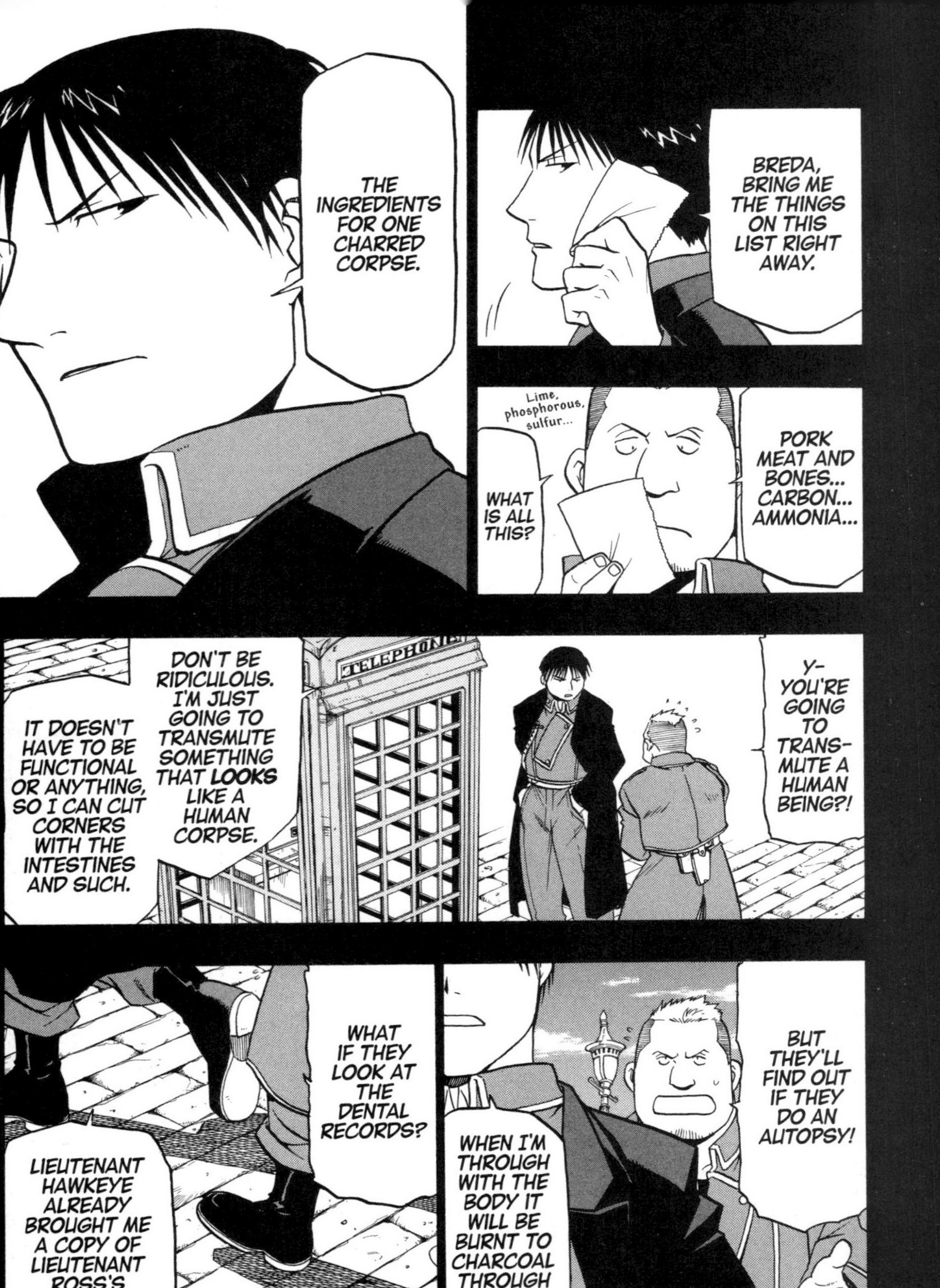
BREDA, BRING ME THE THINGS ON THIS LIST RIGHT AWAY.
PORK MEAT AND BONES... CARBON... AMMONIA...
Lime, phosphorous, sulfur...
WHAT IS ALL THIS?
THE INGREDIENTS FOR ONE CHARRED CORPSE.
Y-YOU'RE GOING TO TRANS-MUTE A HUMAN BEING?!
TELEPHONE
DON'T BE RIDICULOUS. I'M JUST GOING TO TRANSMUTE SOMETHING THAT **LOOKS** LIKE A HUMAN CORPSE.
IT DOESN'T HAVE TO BE FUNCTIONAL OR ANYTHING, SO I CAN CUT CORNERS WITH THE INTESTINES AND SUCH.
BUT THEY'LL FIND OUT IF THEY DO AN AUTOPSY!
WHEN I'M THROUGH WITH THE BODY IT WILL BE BURNT TO CHARCOAL THROUGH AND THROUGH.
WHAT IF THEY LOOK AT THE DENTAL RECORDS?
LIEUTENANT HAWKEYE ALREADY BROUGHT ME A COPY OF LIEUTENANT ROSS'S DENTAL RECORDS.

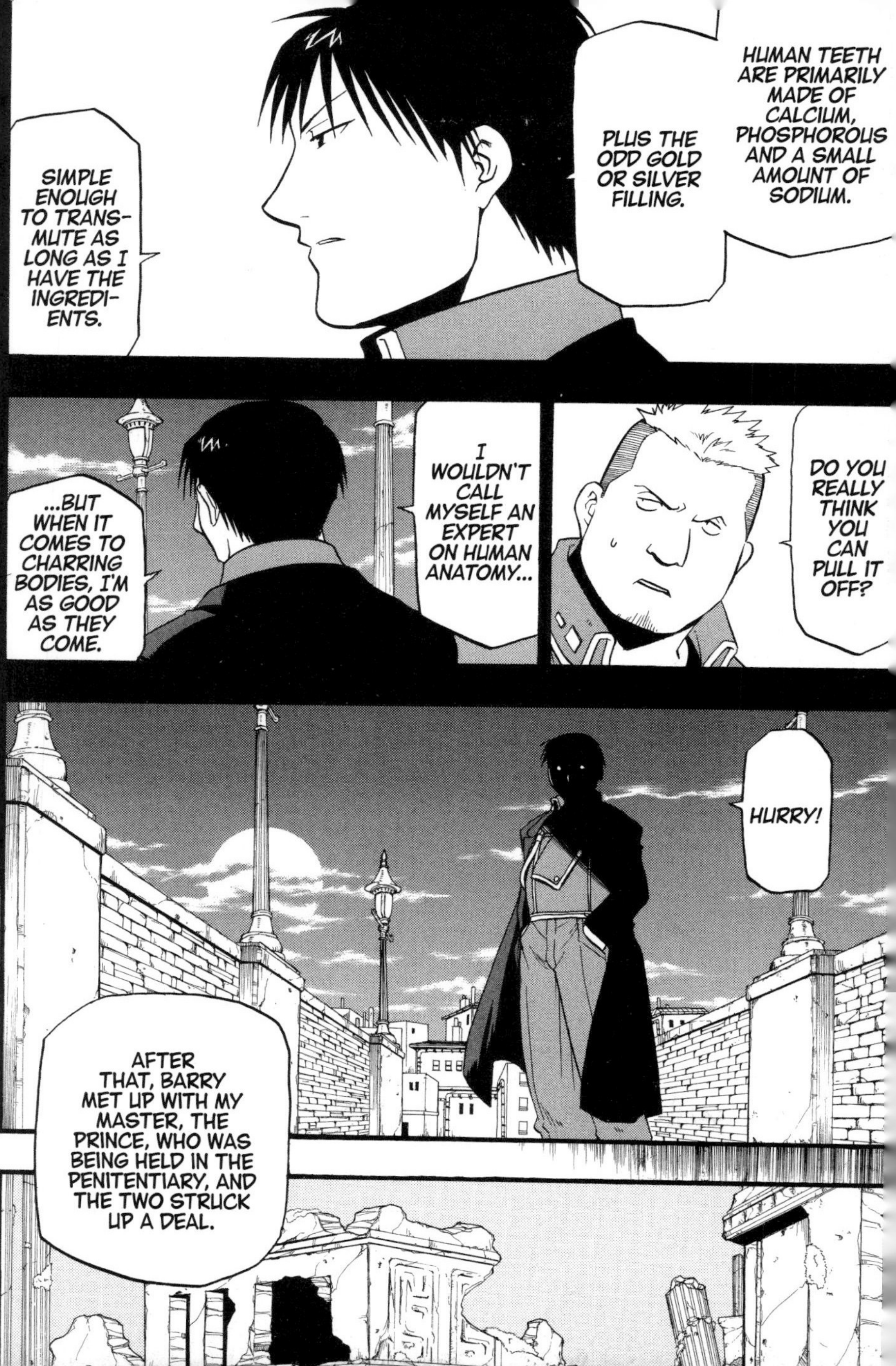
HUMAN TEETH ARE PRIMARILY MADE OF CALCIUM, PHOSPHOROUS AND A SMALL AMOUNT OF SODIUM.
PLUS THE ODD GOLD OR SILVER FILLING.
SIMPLE ENOUGH TO TRANSMUTE AS LONG AS I HAVE THE INGREDIENTS.
DO YOU REALLY THINK YOU CAN PULL IT OFF?
I WOULDN'T CALL MYSELF AN EXPERT ON HUMAN ANATOMY...
...BUT WHEN IT COMES TO CHARRING BODIES, I'M AS GOOD AS THEY COME.
HURRY!
AFTER THAT, BARRY MET UP WITH MY MASTER, THE PRINCE, WHO WAS BEING HELD IN THE PENITENTIARY, AND THE TWO STRUCK UP A DEAL.

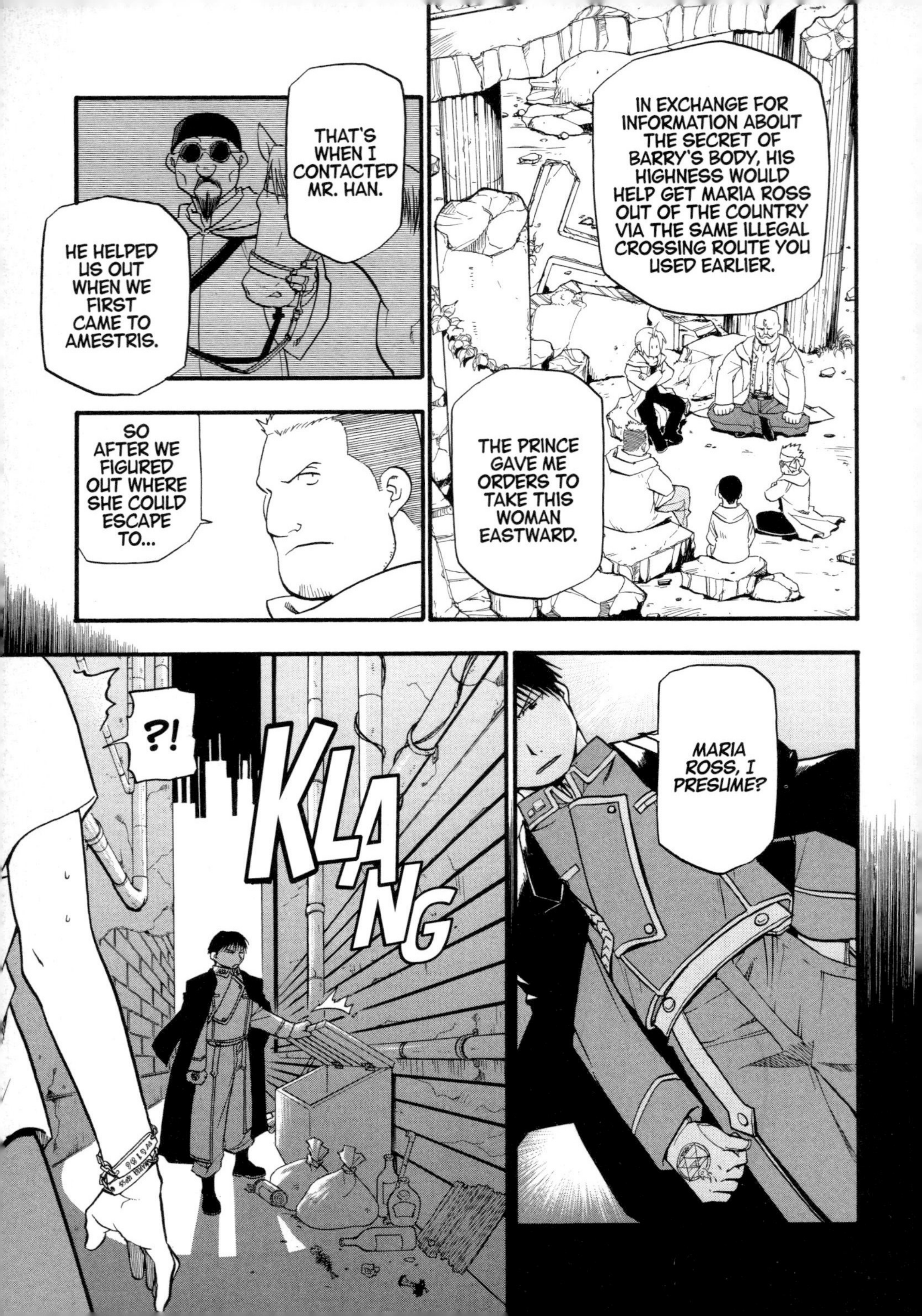
IN EXCHANGE FOR INFORMATION ABOUT THE SECRET OF BARRY'S BODY, HIS HIGHNESS WOULD HELP GET MARIA ROSS OUT OF THE COUNTRY VIA THE SAME ILLEGAL CROSSING ROUTE YOU USED EARLIER.
THE PRINCE GAVE ME ORDERS TO TAKE THIS WOMAN EASTWARD.
THAT'S WHEN I CONTACTED MR. HAN.
HE HELPED US OUT WHEN WE FIRST CAME TO AMESTRIS.
SO AFTER WE FIGURED OUT WHERE SHE COULD ESCAPE TO...
MARIA ROSS, I PRESUME?
?!
KLANG

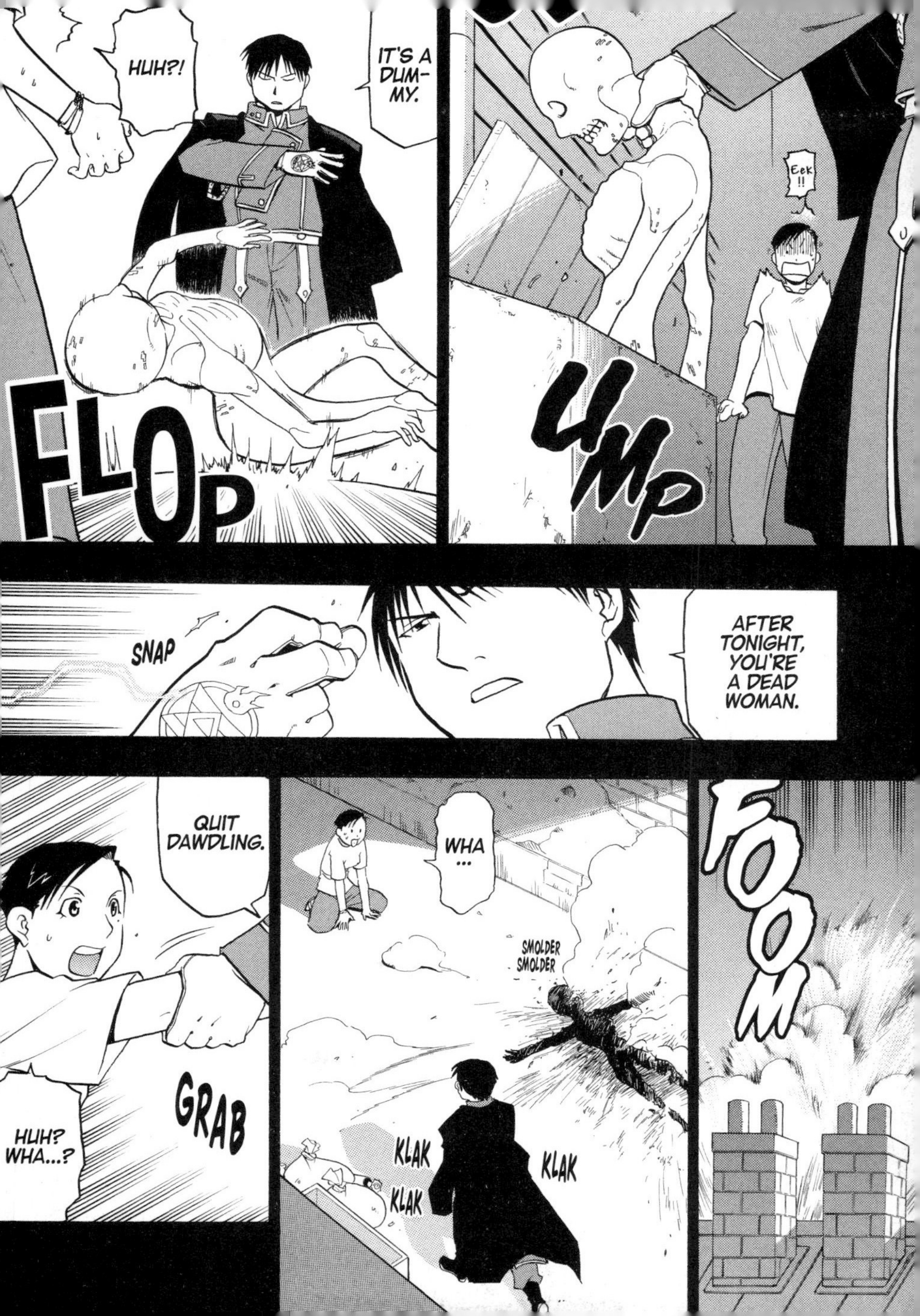
Eek !!
UMP
IT'S A DUMMY.
HUH?!
FLOP
AFTER TONIGHT, YOU'RE A DEAD WOMAN.
SNAP
FOOM
WHA ...
SMOLDER SMOLDER
KLAK
KLAK
KLAK
QUIT DAWDLING.
GRAB
HUH? WHA...?

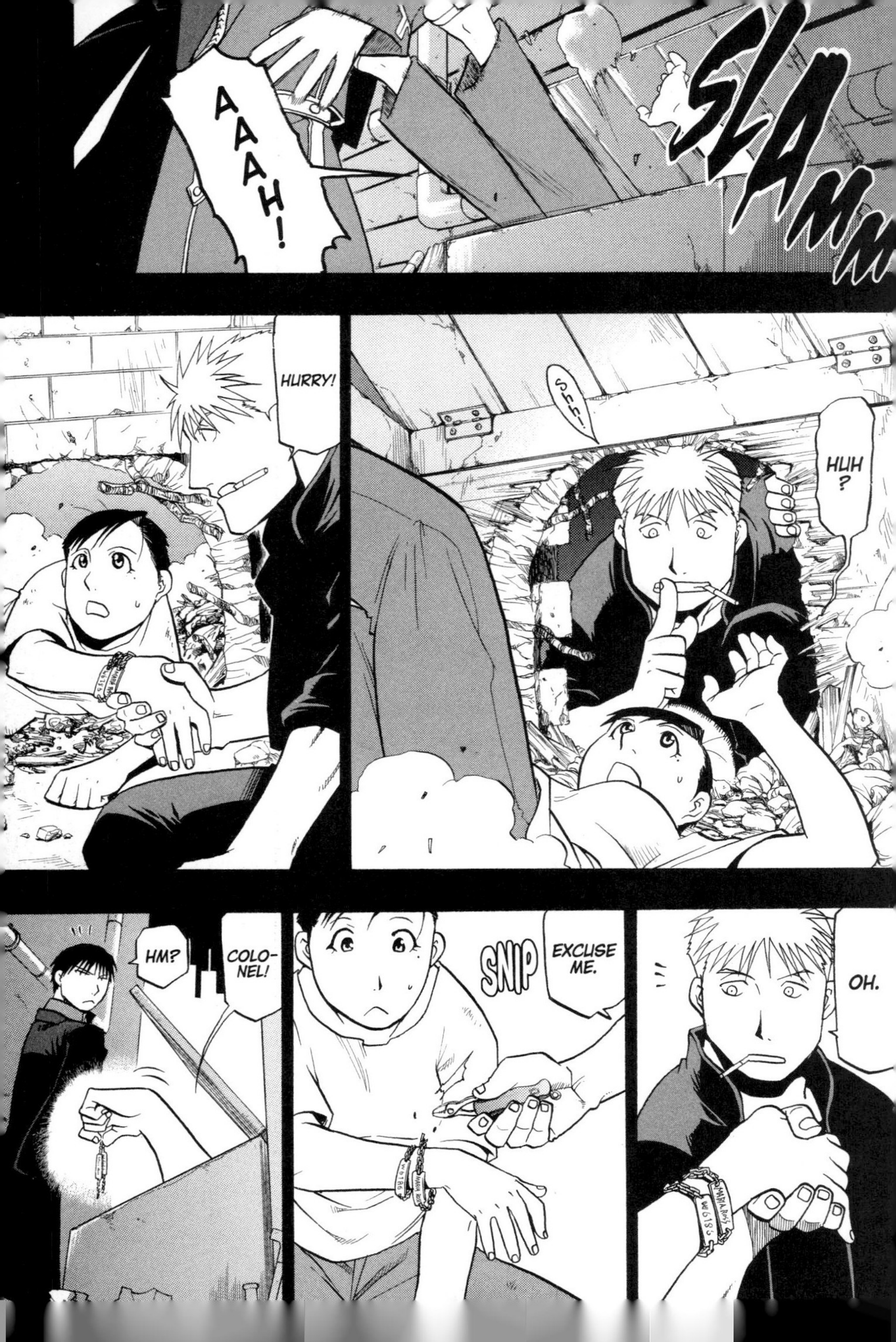
SLAMMM
AAAH!
HUH?
Shh!
HURRY!
OH.
EXCUSE ME.
SNIP
COLO-NEL!
HM?

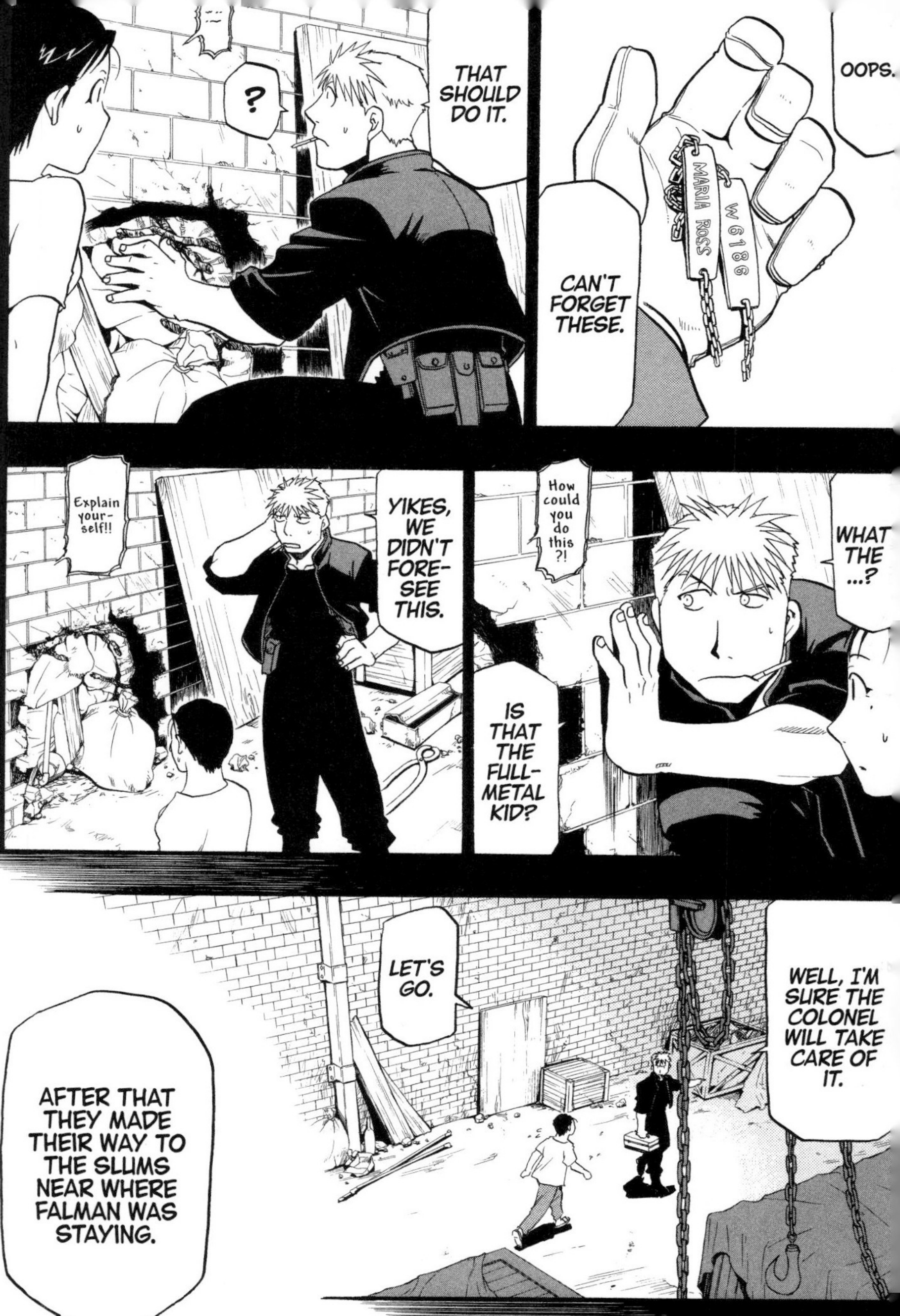
OOPS.
MARIA ROSS
W 6186
CAN'T FORGET THESE.
THAT SHOULD DO IT.
?
WHAT THE ...?
How could you do this?!
IS THAT THE FULL-METAL KID?
YIKES, WE DIDN'T FORESEE THIS.
Explain yourself!!
WELL, I'M SURE THE COLONEL WILL TAKE CARE OF IT.
LET'S GO.
AFTER THAT THEY MADE THEIR WAY TO THE SLUMS NEAR WHERE FALMAN WAS STAYING.

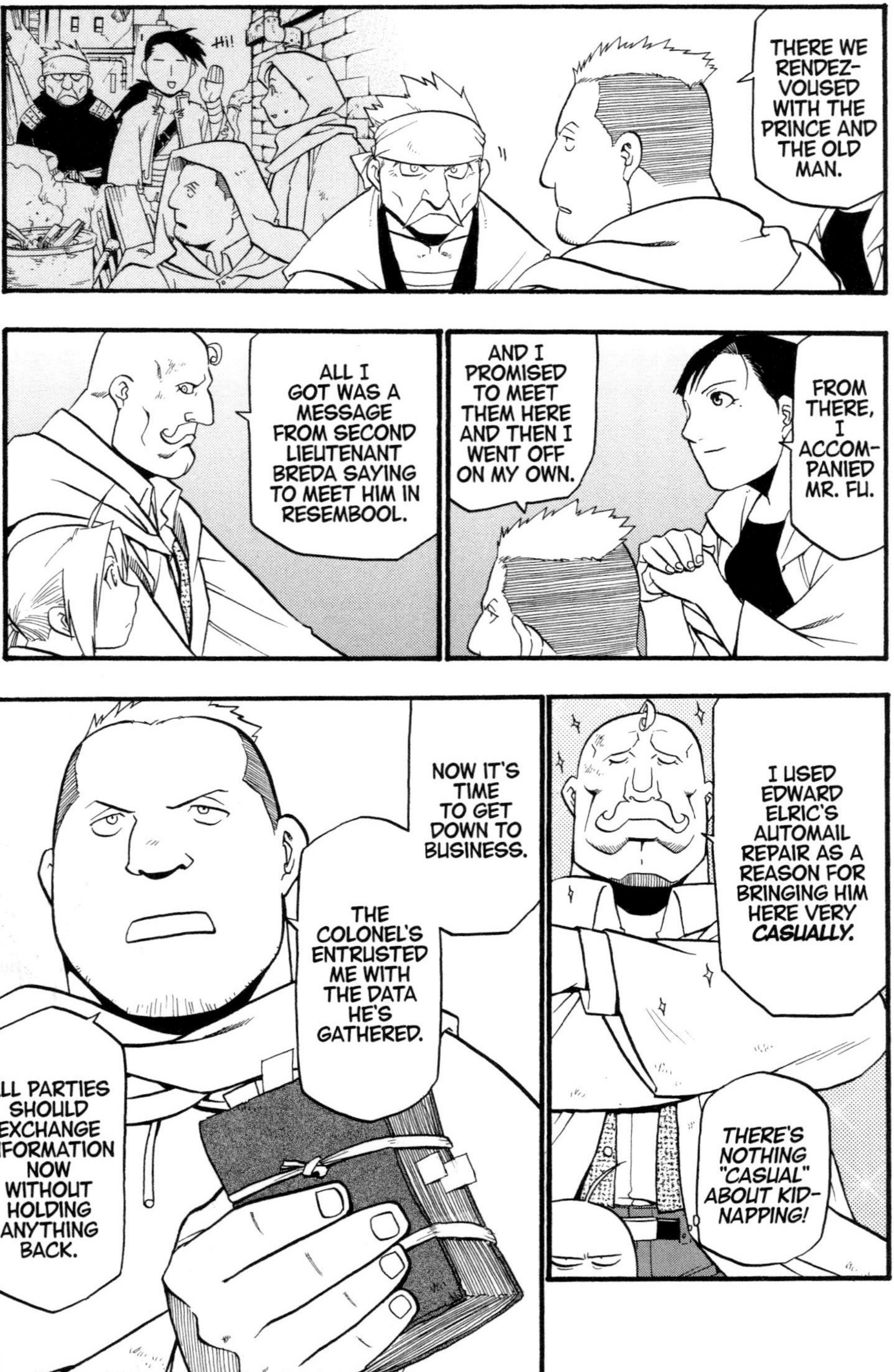
THERE WE RENDEZVOUSED WITH THE PRINCE AND THE OLD MAN.
Hi!
FROM THERE, I ACCOMPANIED MR. FU.
AND I PROMISED TO MEET THEM HERE AND THEN I WENT OFF ON MY OWN.
ALL I GOT WAS A MESSAGE FROM SECOND LIEUTENANT BREDA SAYING TO MEET HIM IN RESEMBOOL.
I USED EDWARD ELRIC'S AUTOMAIL REPAIR AS A REASON FOR BRINGING HIM HERE VERY *CASUALLY.*
THERE'S NOTHING "CASUAL" ABOUT KIDNAPPING!
NOW IT'S TIME TO GET DOWN TO BUSINESS.
THE COLONEL'S ENTRUSTED ME WITH THE DATA HE'S GATHERED.
ALL PARTIES SHOULD EXCHANGE INFORMATION NOW WITHOUT HOLDING ANYTHING BACK.

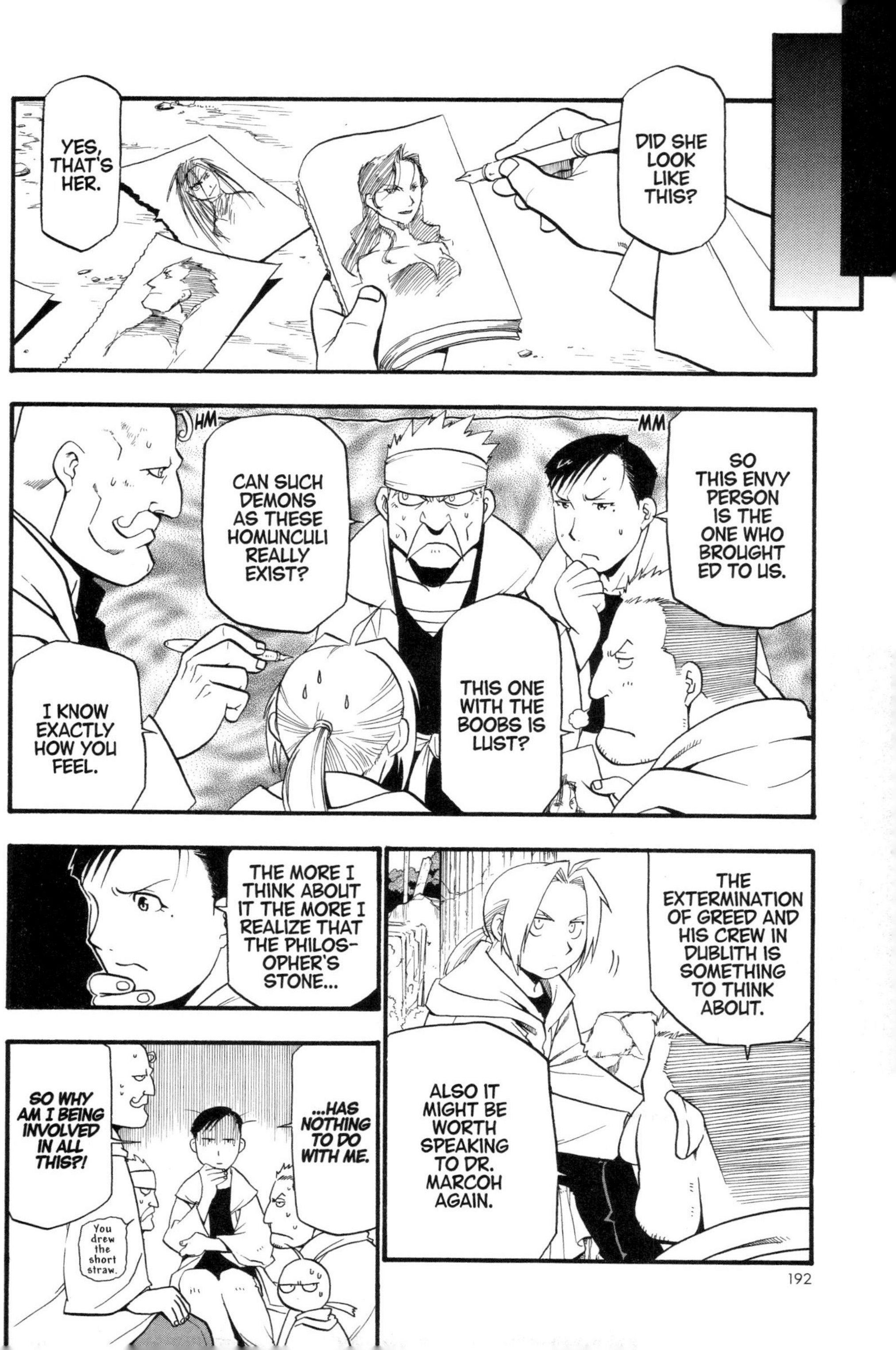
DID SHE LOOK LIKE THIS?
YES, THAT'S HER.
HM—MM
SO THIS ENVY PERSON IS THE ONE WHO BROUGHT ED TO US.
CAN SUCH DEMONS AS THESE HOMUNCULI REALLY EXIST?
THIS ONE WITH THE BOOBS IS LUST?
I KNOW EXACTLY HOW YOU FEEL.
THE EXTERMINATION OF GREED AND HIS CREW IN DUBLITH IS SOMETHING TO THINK ABOUT.
ALSO IT MIGHT BE WORTH SPEAKING TO DR. MARCOH AGAIN.
THE MORE I THINK ABOUT IT THE MORE I REALIZE THAT THE PHILOS-OPHER'S STONE...
...HAS NOTHING TO DO WITH ME.
SO WHY AM I BEING INVOLVED IN ALL THIS?!
You drew the short straw.

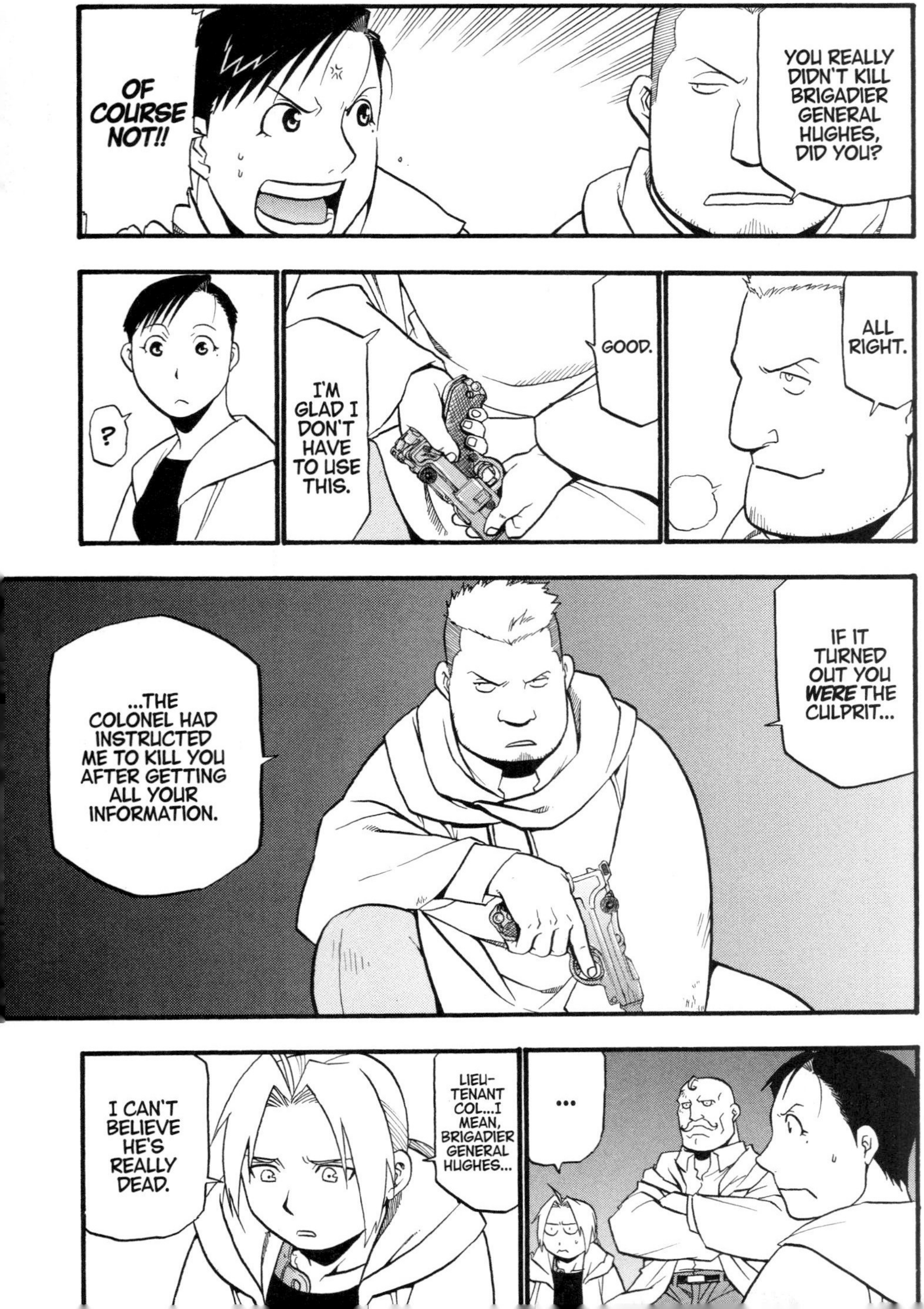
YOU REALLY DIDN'T KILL BRIGADIER GENERAL HUGHES, DID YOU?
OF COURSE NOT!!
ALL RIGHT.
GOOD.
I'M GLAD I DON'T HAVE TO USE THIS.
?
IF IT TURNED OUT YOU *WERE* THE CULPRIT...
...THE COLONEL HAD INSTRUCTED ME TO KILL YOU AFTER GETTING ALL YOUR INFORMATION.
...
LIEU-TENANT COL...I MEAN, BRIGADIER GENERAL HUGHES...
I CAN'T BELIEVE HE'S REALLY DEAD.

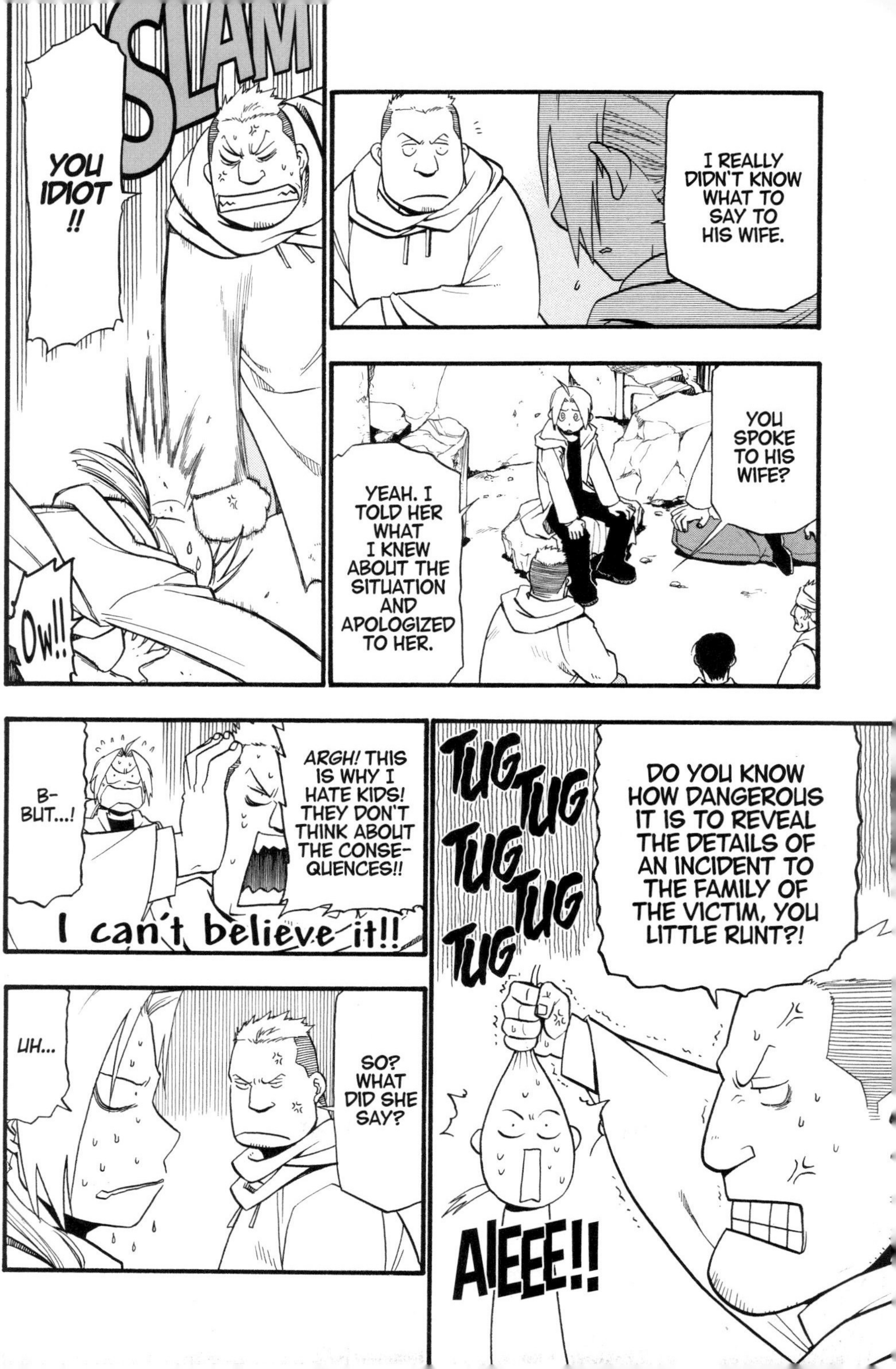
I REALLY DIDN'T KNOW WHAT TO SAY TO HIS WIFE.
YOU SPOKE TO HIS WIFE?
YEAH. I TOLD HER WHAT I KNEW ABOUT THE SITUATION AND APOLOGIZED TO HER.
SLAM
YOU IDIOT!!
Ow!!
DO YOU KNOW HOW DANGEROUS IT IS TO REVEAL THE DETAILS OF AN INCIDENT TO THE FAMILY OF THE VICTIM, YOU LITTLE RUNT?!
TUG TUG TUG TUG TUG TUG
AIEEE!!
ARGH! THIS IS WHY I HATE KIDS! THEY DON'T THINK ABOUT THE CONSE-QUENCES!!
B-BUT...!
I can't believe it!!
SO? WHAT DID SHE SAY?
UH...

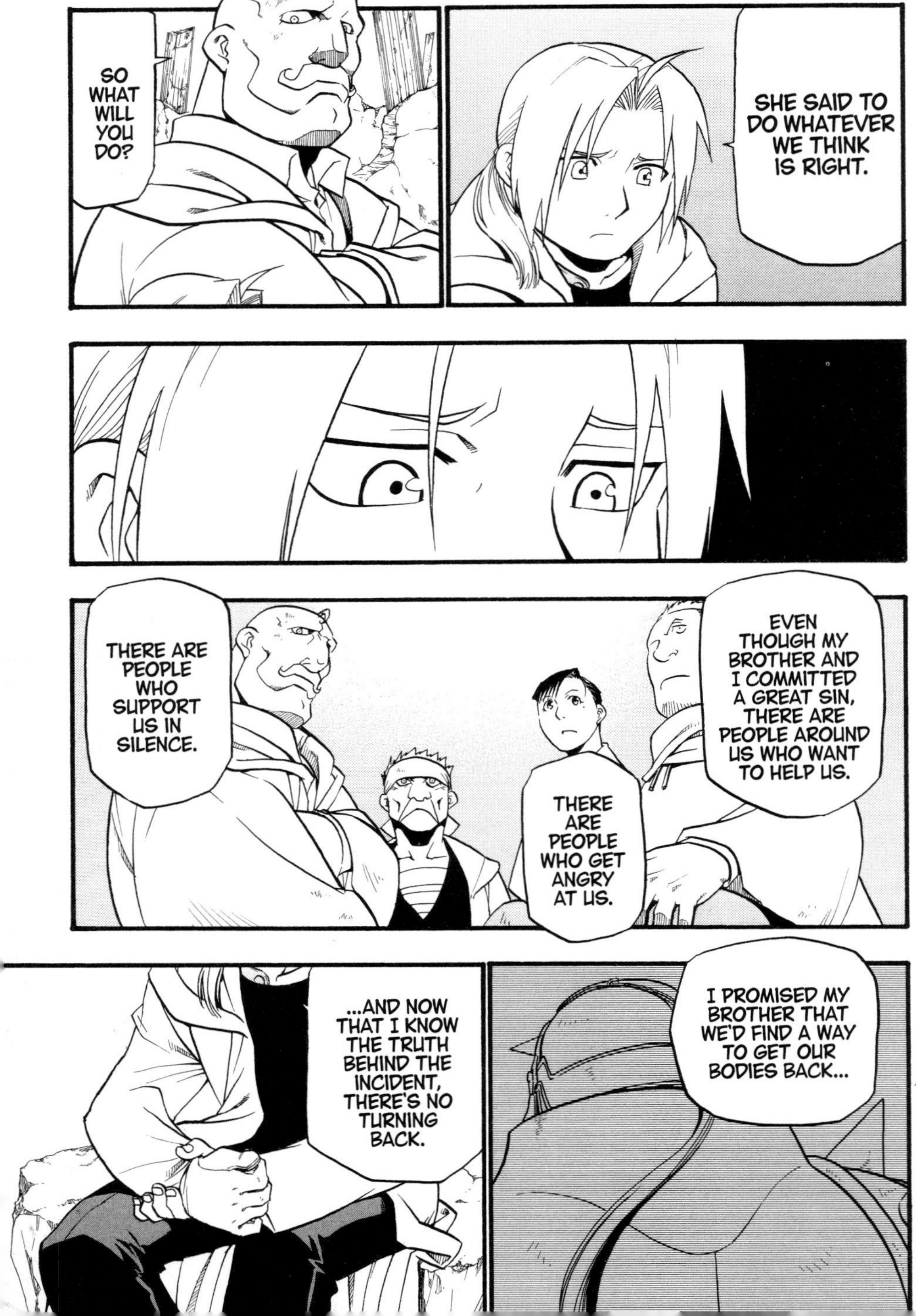
SHE SAID TO DO WHATEVER WE THINK IS RIGHT.
SO WHAT WILL YOU DO?
EVEN THOUGH MY BROTHER AND I COMMITTED A GREAT SIN, THERE ARE PEOPLE AROUND US WHO WANT TO HELP US.
THERE ARE PEOPLE WHO GET ANGRY AT US.
THERE ARE PEOPLE WHO SUPPORT US IN SILENCE.
I PROMISED MY BROTHER THAT WE'D FIND A WAY TO GET OUR BODIES BACK...
...AND NOW THAT I KNOW THE TRUTH BEHIND THE INCIDENT, THERE'S NO TURNING BACK.

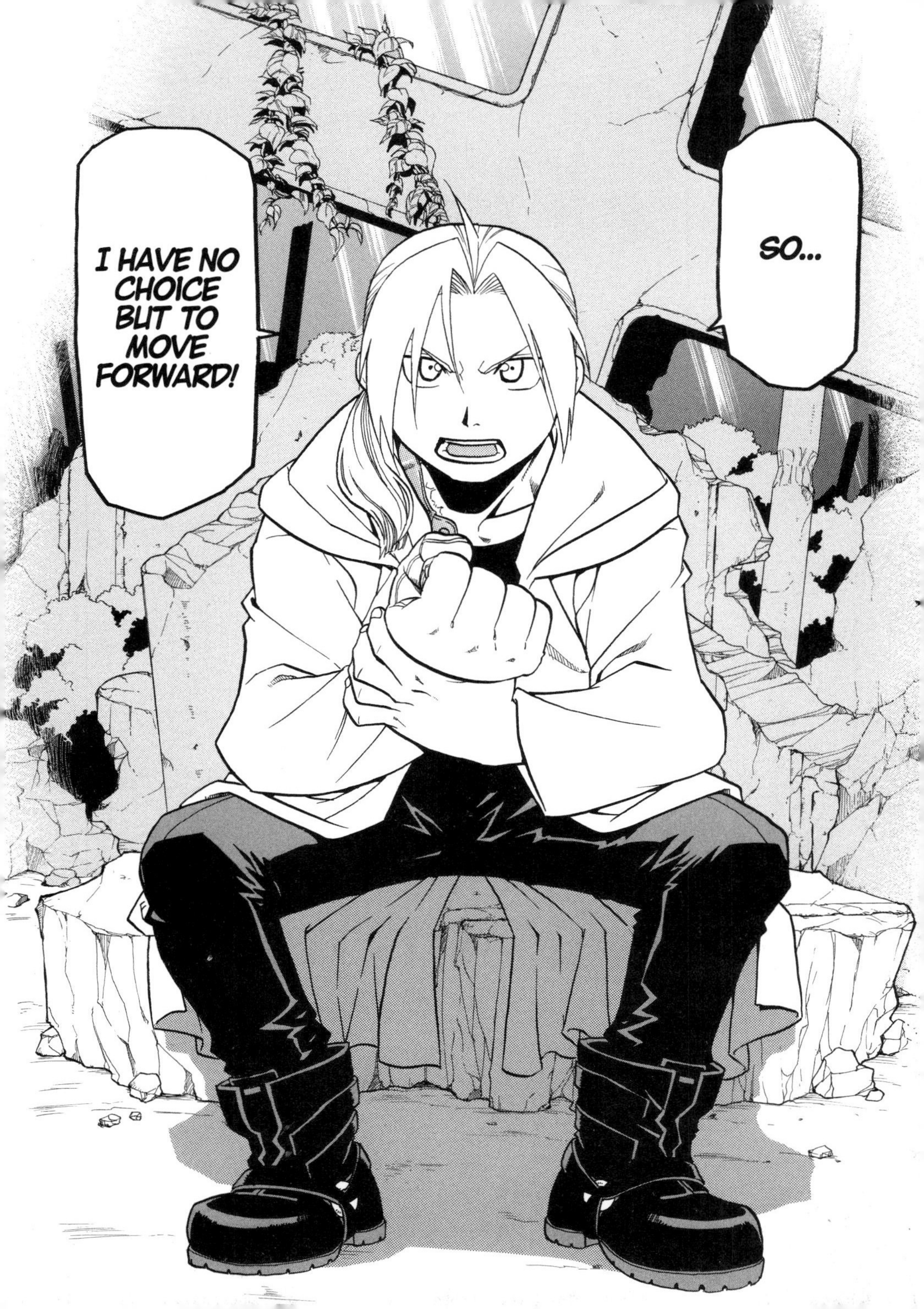
SO...
I HAVE NO CHOICE BUT TO MOVE FORWARD!

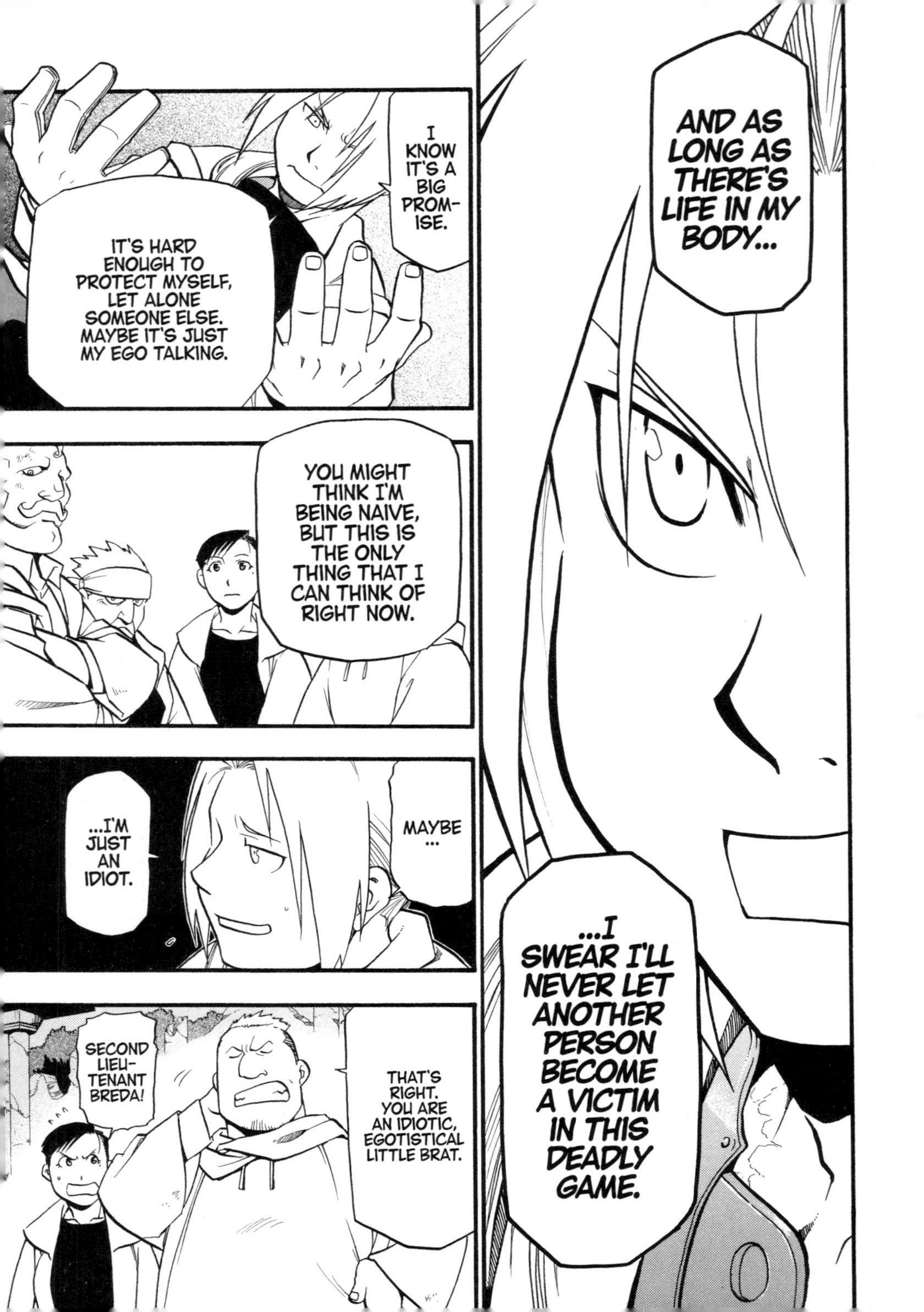
AND AS LONG AS THERE'S LIFE IN MY BODY...
...I SWEAR I'LL NEVER LET ANOTHER PERSON BECOME A VICTIM IN THIS DEADLY GAME.
I KNOW IT'S A BIG PROMISE.
IT'S HARD ENOUGH TO PROTECT MYSELF, LET ALONE SOMEONE ELSE. MAYBE IT'S JUST MY EGO TALKING.
YOU MIGHT THINK I'M BEING NAIVE, BUT THIS IS THE ONLY THING THAT I CAN THINK OF RIGHT NOW.
MAYBE...
...I'M JUST AN IDIOT.
THAT'S RIGHT. YOU ARE AN IDIOTIC, EGOTISTICAL LITTLE BRAT.
SECOND LIEUTENANT BREDA!

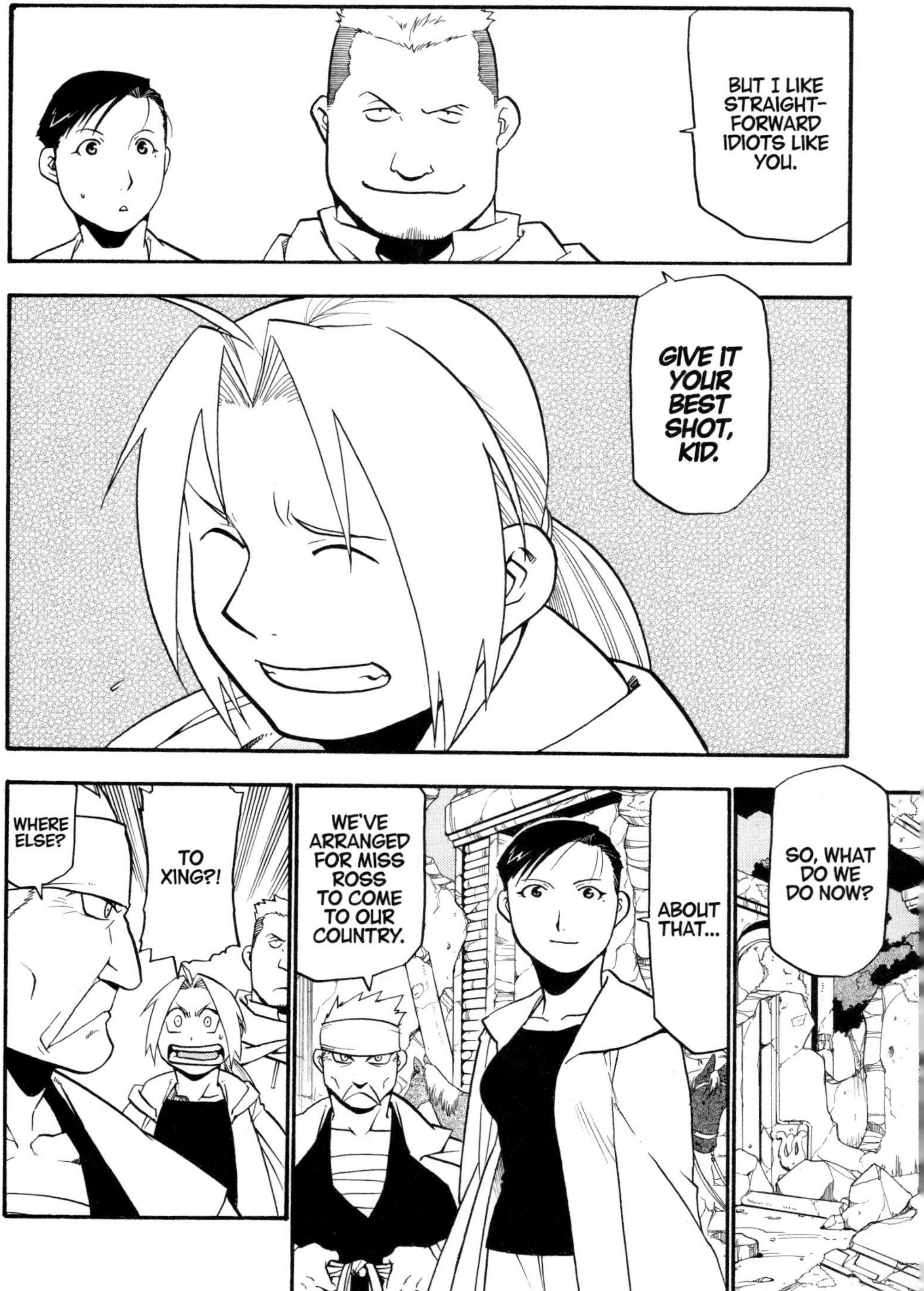
BUT I LIKE STRAIGHT-FORWARD IDIOTS LIKE YOU.
GIVE IT YOUR BEST SHOT, KID.
SO, WHAT DO WE DO NOW?
ABOUT THAT...
WE'VE ARRANGED FOR MISS ROSS TO COME TO OUR COUNTRY.
TO XING?!
WHERE ELSE?

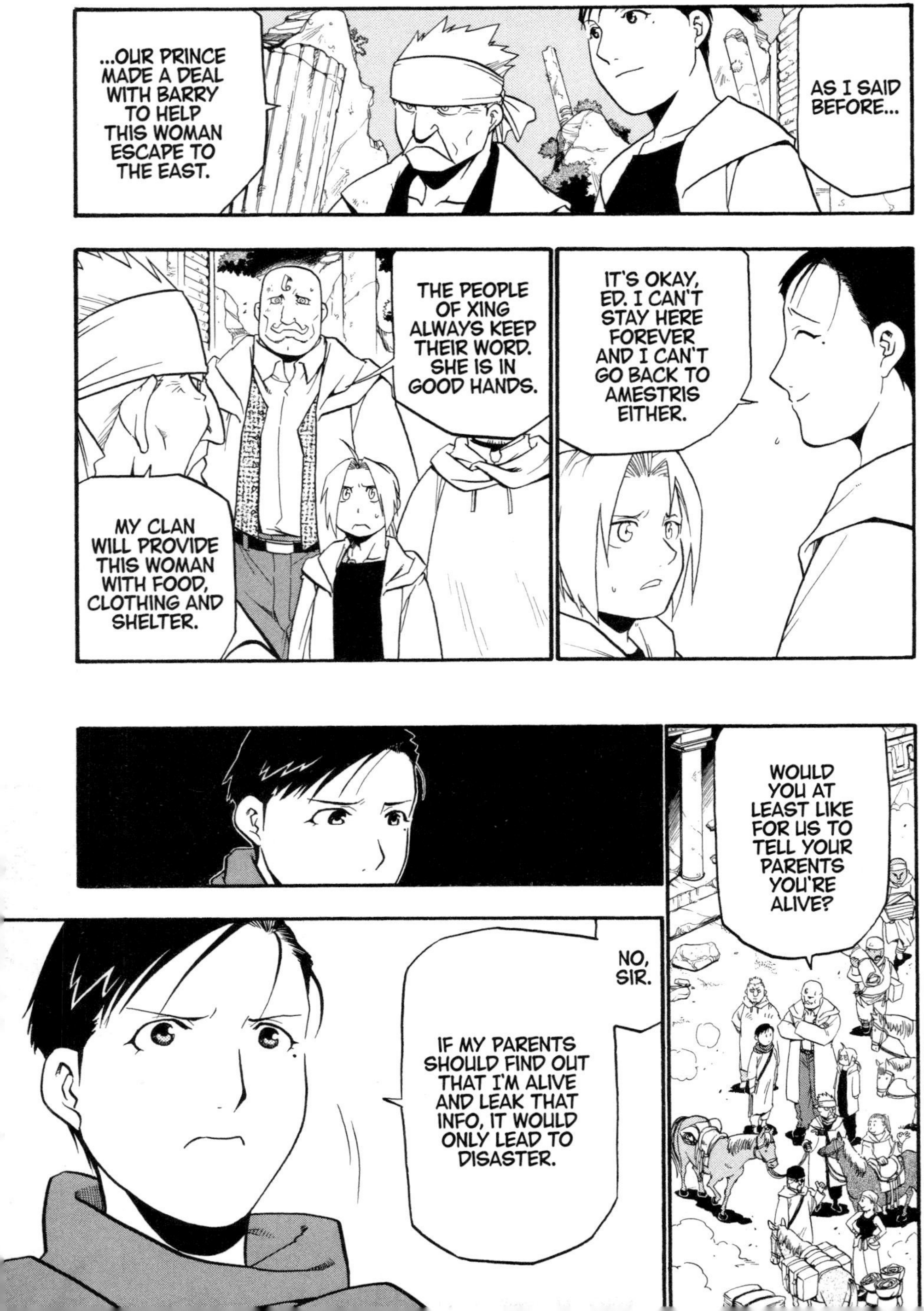
AS I SAID BEFORE...
...OUR PRINCE MADE A DEAL WITH BARRY TO HELP THIS WOMAN ESCAPE TO THE EAST.
IT'S OKAY, ED. I CAN'T STAY HERE FOREVER AND I CAN'T GO BACK TO AMESTRIS EITHER.
THE PEOPLE OF XING ALWAYS KEEP THEIR WORD. SHE IS IN GOOD HANDS.
MY CLAN WILL PROVIDE THIS WOMAN WITH FOOD, CLOTHING AND SHELTER.
WOULD YOU AT LEAST LIKE FOR US TO TELL YOUR PARENTS YOU'RE ALIVE?
NO, SIR.
IF MY PARENTS SHOULD FIND OUT THAT I'M ALIVE AND LEAK THAT INFO, IT WOULD ONLY LEAD TO DISASTER.

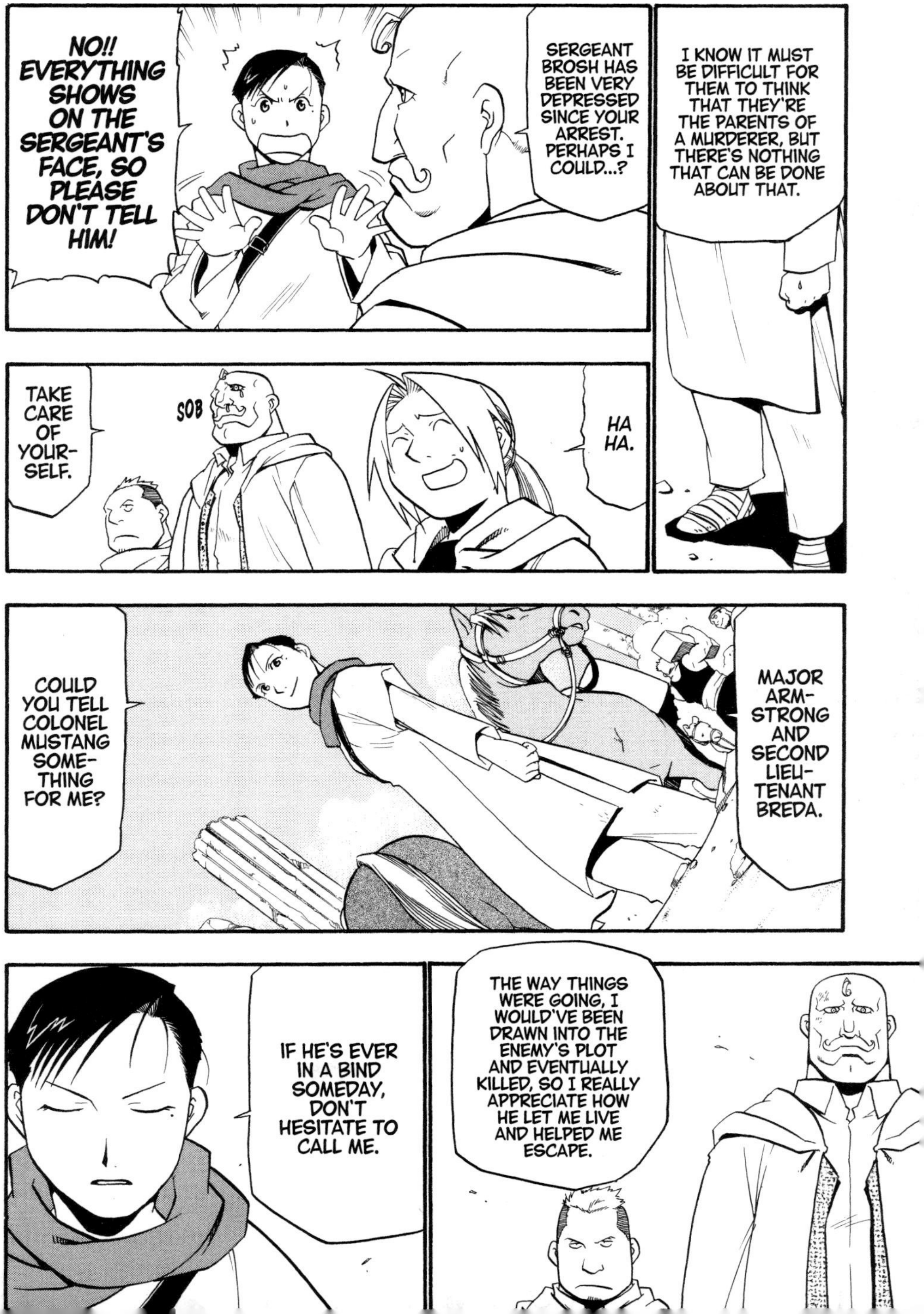
I KNOW IT MUST BE DIFFICULT FOR THEM TO THINK THAT THEY'RE THE PARENTS OF A MURDERER, BUT THERE'S NOTHING THAT CAN BE DONE ABOUT THAT.
SERGEANT BROSH HAS BEEN VERY DEPRESSED SINCE YOUR ARREST. PERHAPS I COULD...?
NO!! EVERYTHING SHOWS ON THE SERGEANT'S FACE, SO PLEASE DON'T TELL HIM!
HA HA.
SOB
TAKE CARE OF YOUR-SELF.
MAJOR ARM-STRONG AND SECOND LIEU-TENANT BREDA.
COULD YOU TELL COLONEL MUSTANG SOME-THING FOR ME?
THE WAY THINGS WERE GOING, I WOULD'VE BEEN DRAWN INTO THE ENEMY'S PLOT AND EVENTUALLY KILLED, SO I REALLY APPRECIATE HOW HE LET ME LIVE AND HELPED ME ESCAPE.
IF HE'S EVER IN A BIND SOMEDAY, DON'T HESITATE TO CALL ME.

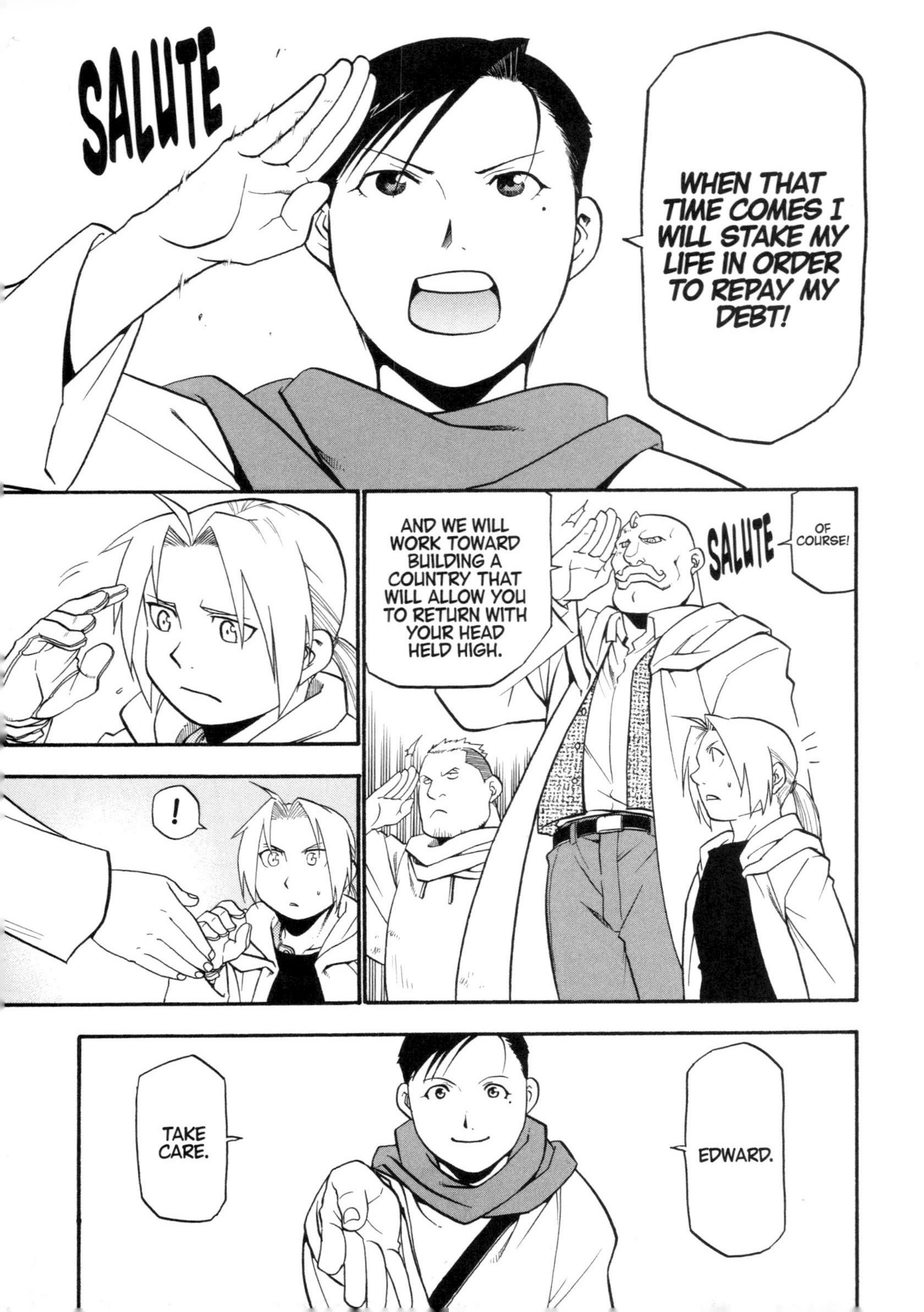
WHEN THAT TIME COMES I WILL STAKE MY LIFE IN ORDER TO REPAY MY DEBT!
SALUTE
OF COURSE!
SALUTE
AND WE WILL WORK TOWARD BUILDING A COUNTRY THAT WILL ALLOW YOU TO RETURN WITH YOUR HEAD HELD HIGH.
!
EDWARD.
TAKE CARE.

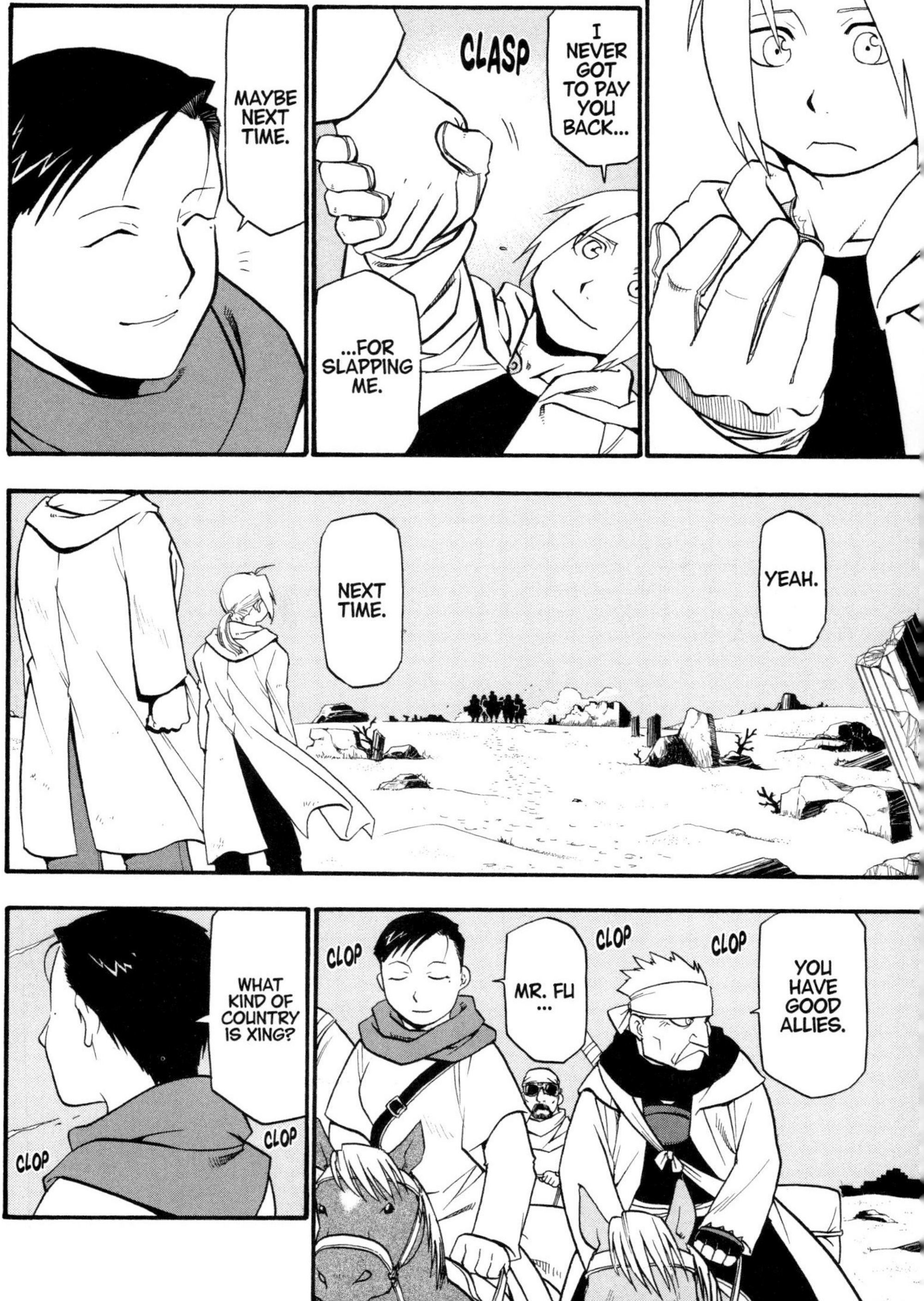
I NEVER GOT TO PAY YOU BACK...
CLASP
...FOR SLAPPING ME.
MAYBE NEXT TIME.
YEAH.
NEXT TIME.
YOU HAVE GOOD ALLIES.
CLOP
CLOP
MR. FU ...
CLOP
WHAT KIND OF COUNTRY IS XING?
CLOP
CLOP

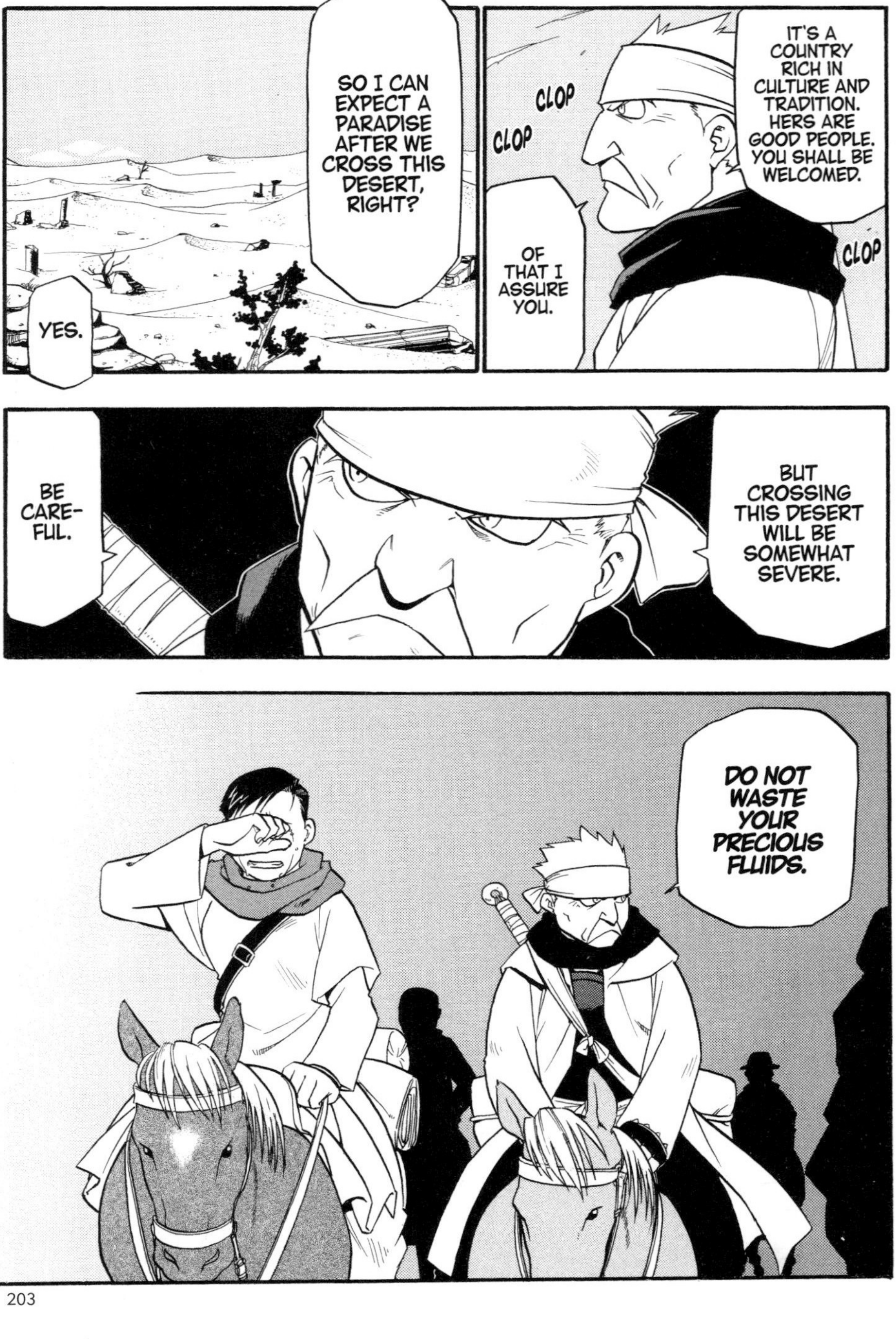
IT'S A COUNTRY RICH IN CULTURE AND TRADITION. HERS ARE GOOD PEOPLE. YOU SHALL BE WELCOMED.
CLOP
CLOP
CLOP
OF THAT I ASSURE YOU.
SO I CAN EXPECT A PARADISE AFTER WE CROSS THIS DESERT, RIGHT?
YES.
BUT CROSSING THIS DESERT WILL BE SOMEWHAT SEVERE.
BE CARE-FUL.
DO NOT WASTE YOUR PRECIOUS FLUIDS.

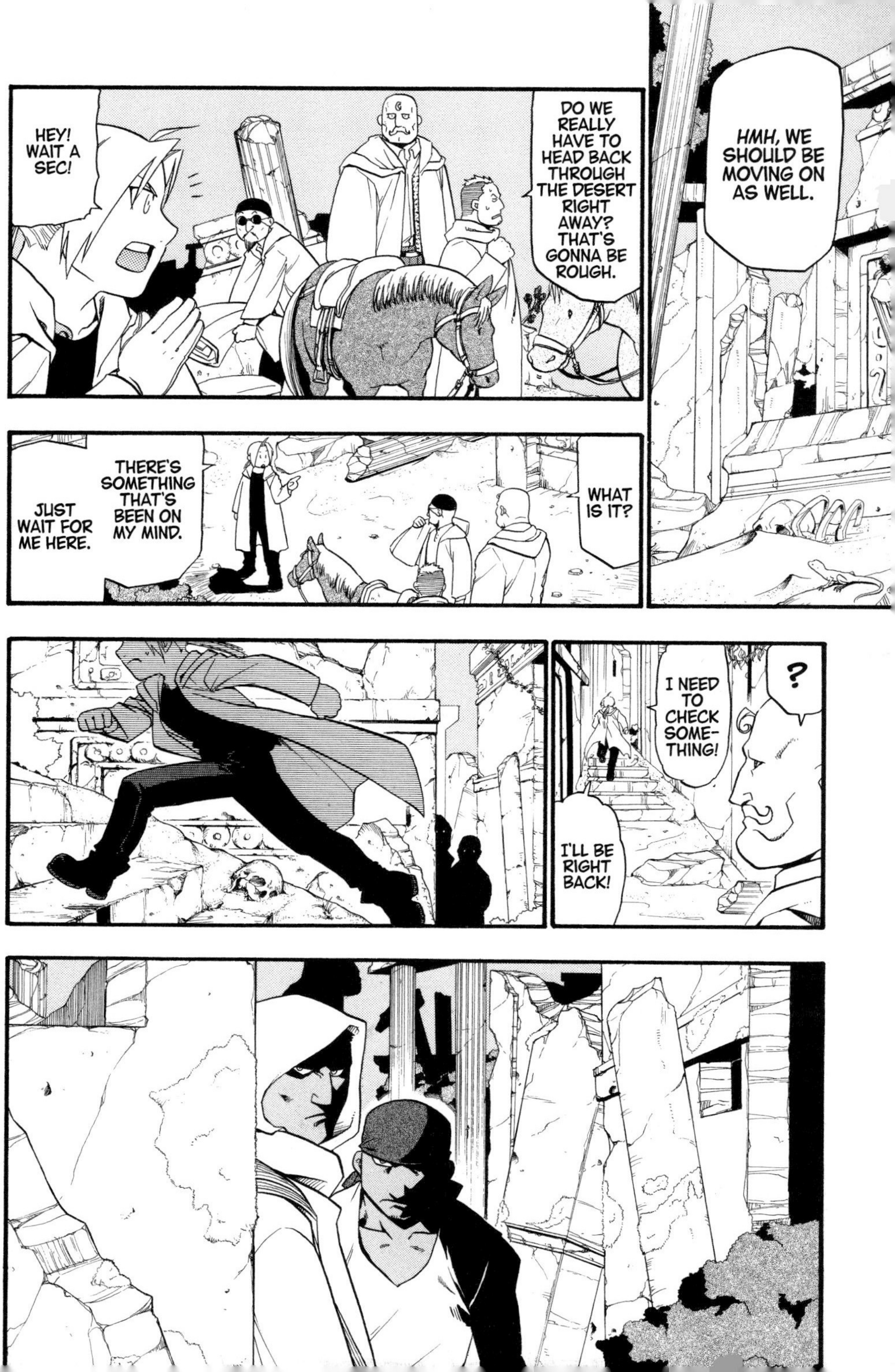
HMH, WE SHOULD BE MOVING ON AS WELL.
DO WE REALLY HAVE TO HEAD BACK THROUGH THE DESERT RIGHT AWAY? THAT'S GONNA BE ROUGH.
HEY! WAIT A SEC!
WHAT IS IT?
THERE'S SOMETHING THAT'S BEEN ON MY MIND.
JUST WAIT FOR ME HERE.
?
I NEED TO CHECK SOME-THING!
I'LL BE RIGHT BACK!

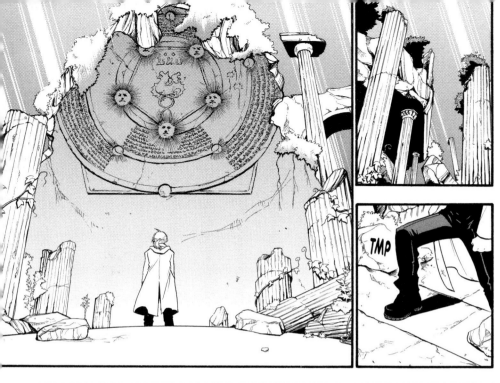

TMP

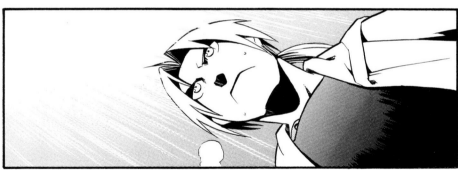

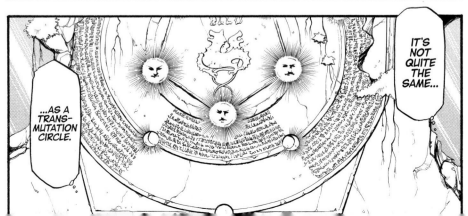

IT'S NOT QUITE THE SAME...

...AS A TRANS-MUTATION CIRCLE.

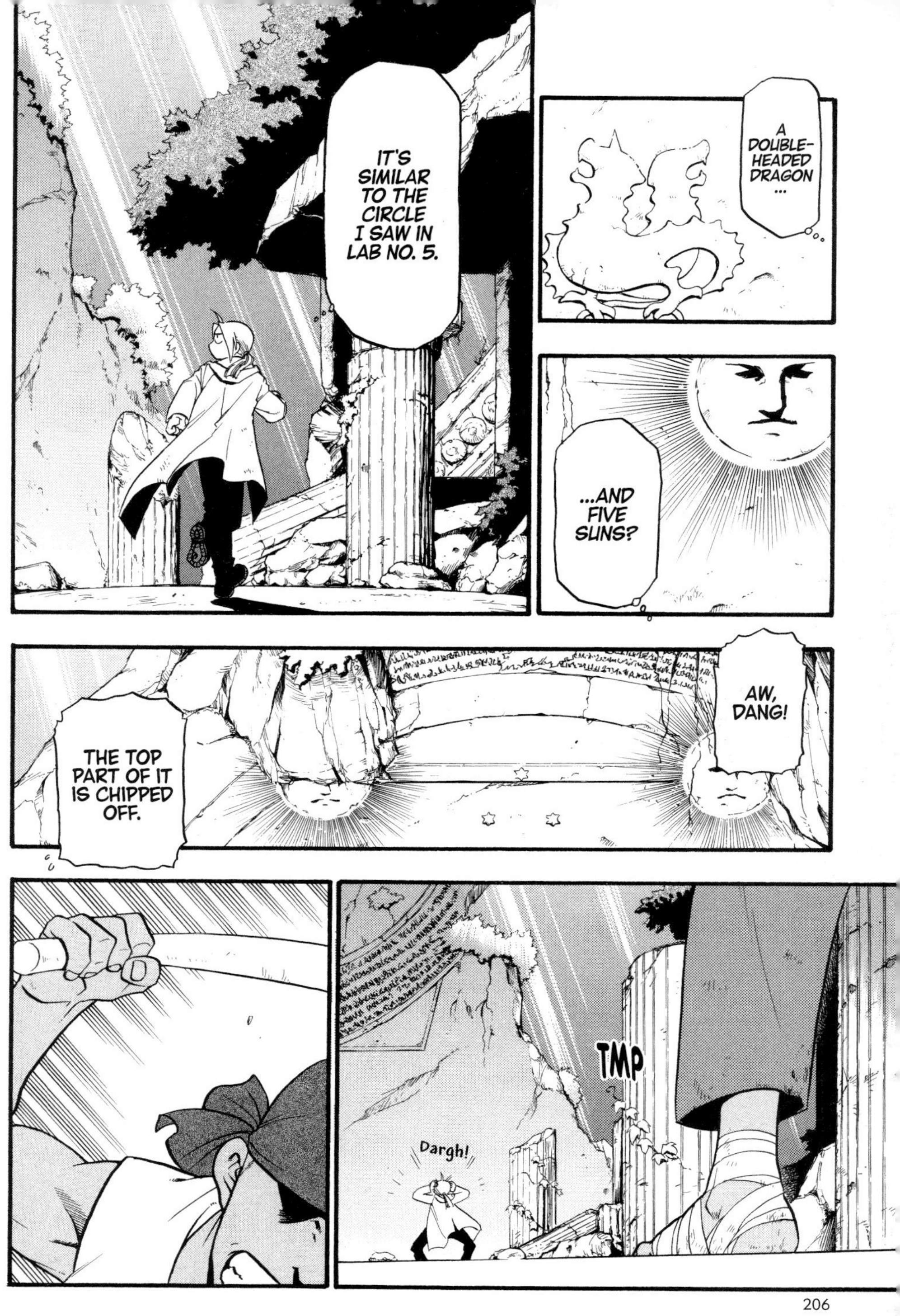
A DOUBLE-HEADED DRAGON ...
...AND FIVE SUNS?
IT'S SIMILAR TO THE CIRCLE I SAW IN LAB NO. 5.
AW, DANG!
THE TOP PART OF IT IS CHIPPED OFF.
TMP
Dargh!

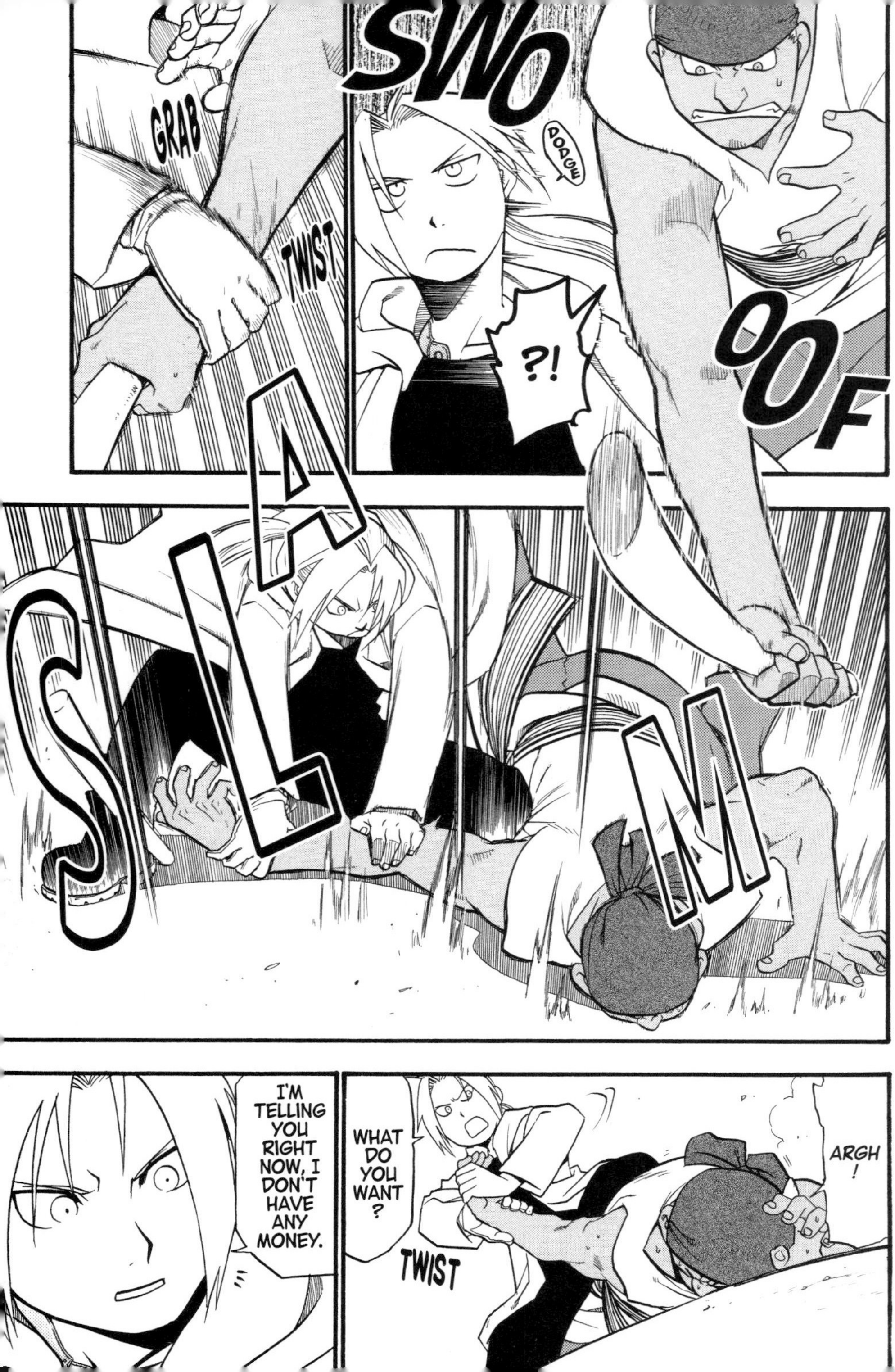
SWO
DODGE
?!
OOF
GRAB
TWIST
SLAM
ARGH!
WHAT DO YOU WANT?
TWIST
I'M TELLING YOU RIGHT NOW, I DON'T HAVE ANY MONEY.

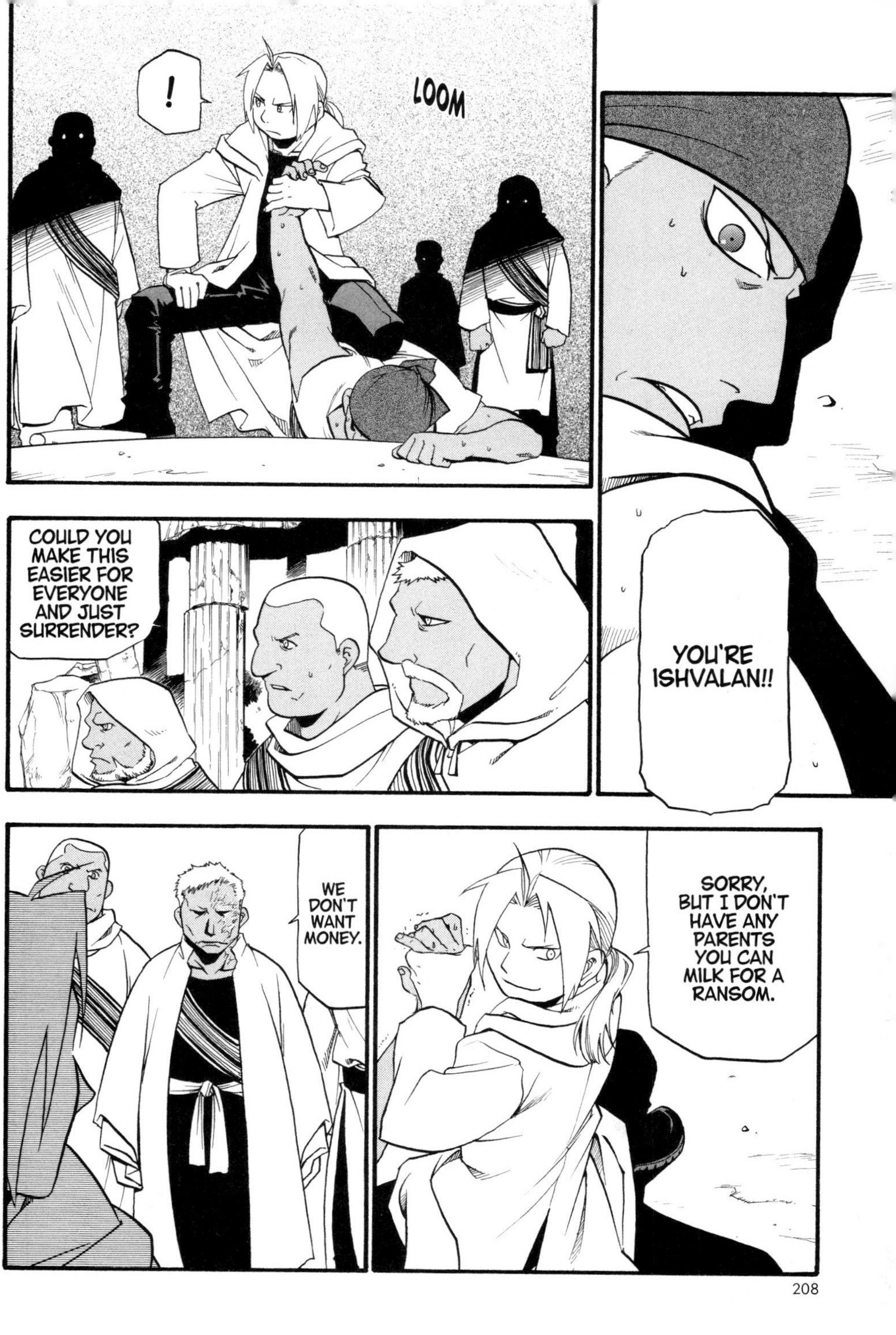
YOU'RE ISHVALAN!!
!
LOOM
COULD YOU MAKE THIS EASIER FOR EVERYONE AND JUST SURRENDER?
SORRY, BUT I DON'T HAVE ANY PARENTS YOU CAN MILK FOR A RANSOM.
WE DON'T WANT MONEY.

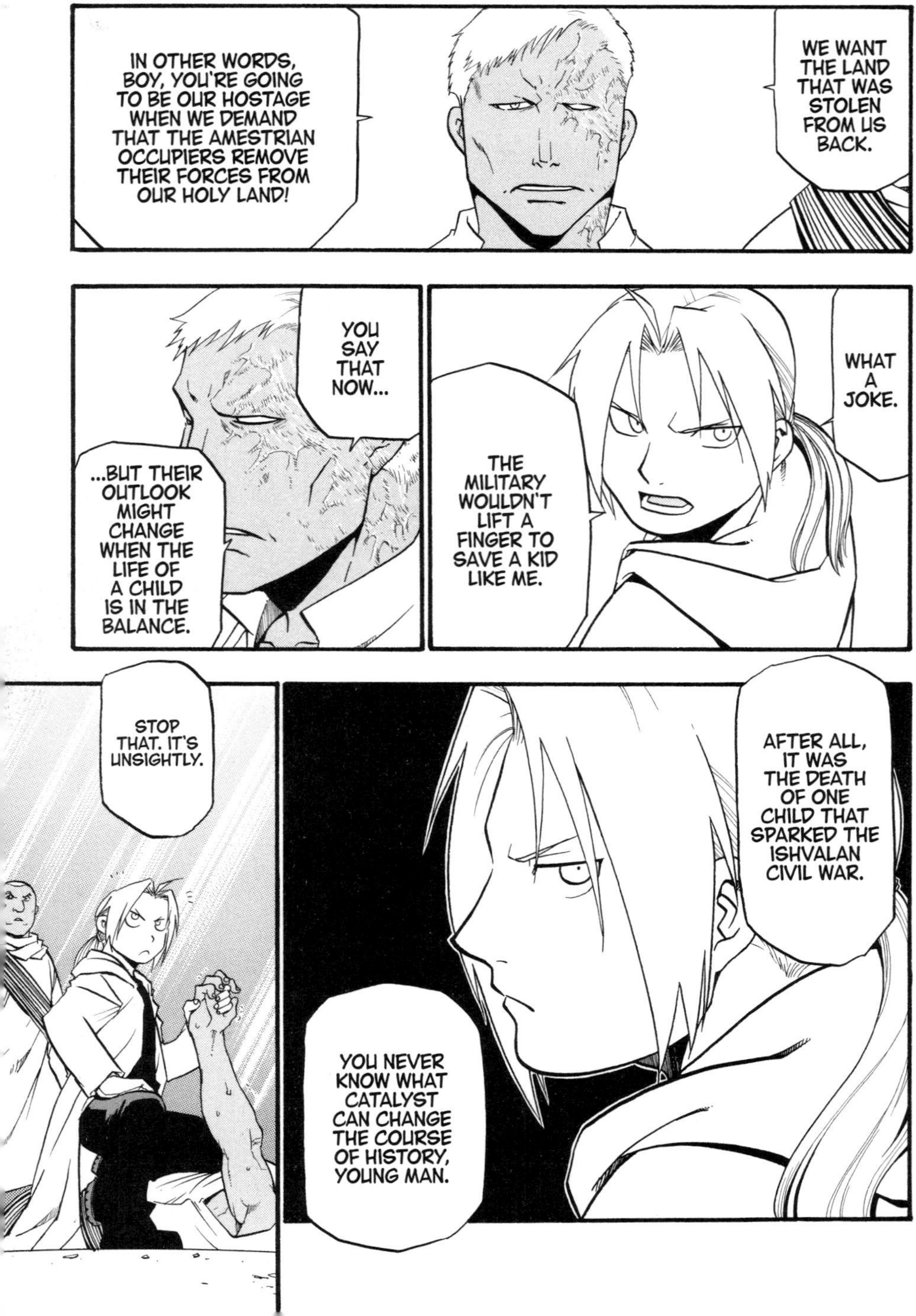
WE WANT THE LAND THAT WAS STOLEN FROM US BACK.
IN OTHER WORDS, BOY, YOU'RE GOING TO BE OUR HOSTAGE WHEN WE DEMAND THAT THE AMESTRIAN OCCUPIERS REMOVE THEIR FORCES FROM OUR HOLY LAND!
WHAT A JOKE.
THE MILITARY WOULDN'T LIFT A FINGER TO SAVE A KID LIKE ME.
YOU SAY THAT NOW...
...BUT THEIR OUTLOOK MIGHT CHANGE WHEN THE LIFE OF A CHILD IS IN THE BALANCE.
AFTER ALL, IT WAS THE DEATH OF ONE CHILD THAT SPARKED THE ISHVALAN CIVIL WAR.
YOU NEVER KNOW WHAT CATALYST CAN CHANGE THE COURSE OF HISTORY, YOUNG MAN.
STOP THAT. IT'S UNSIGHTLY.

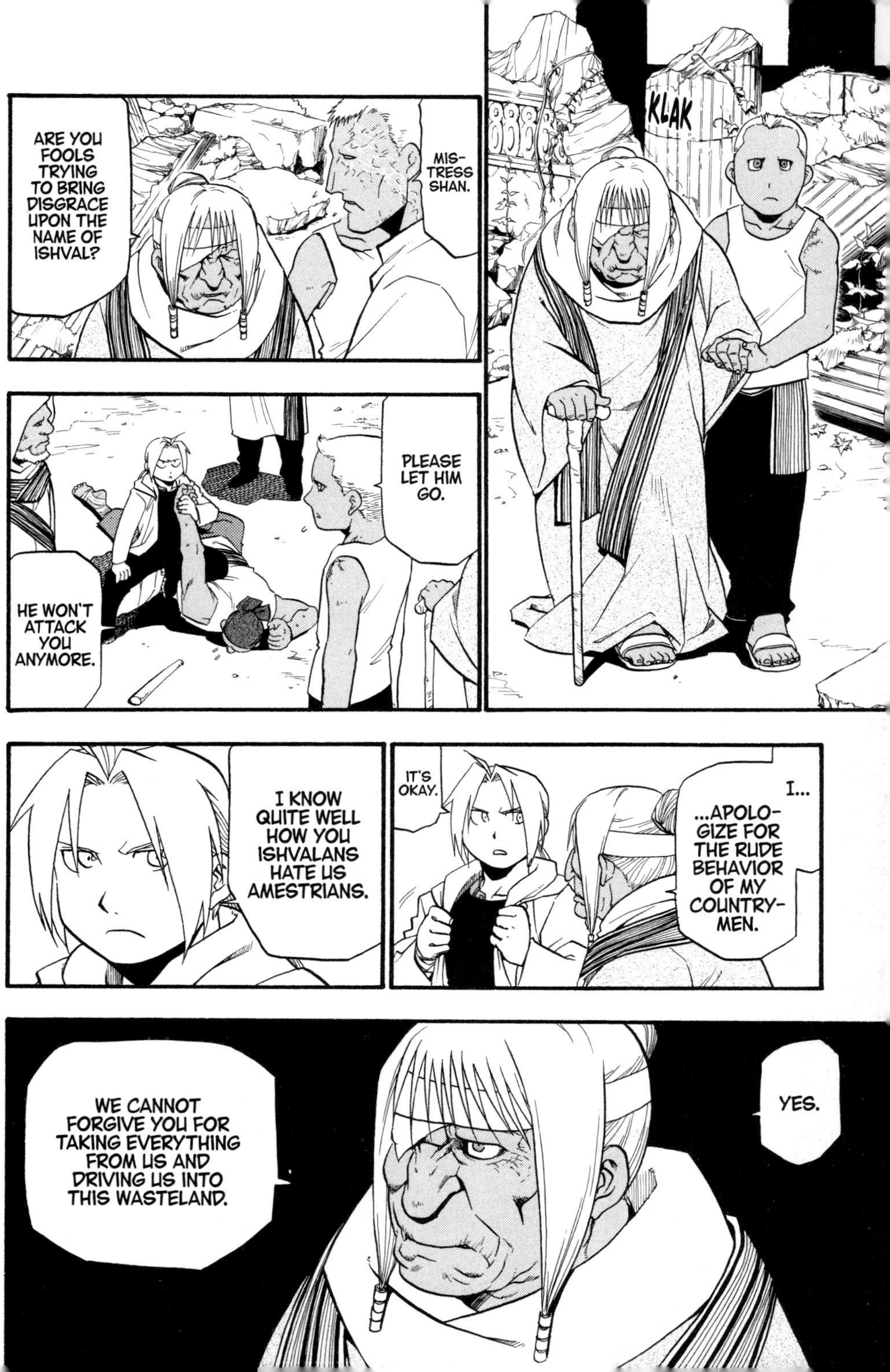
KLAK
MIS-TRESS SHAN.
ARE YOU FOOLS TRYING TO BRING DISGRACE UPON THE NAME OF ISHVAL?
PLEASE LET HIM GO.
HE WON'T ATTACK YOU ANYMORE.
I...
...APOLO-GIZE FOR THE RUDE BEHAVIOR OF MY COUNTRY-MEN.
IT'S OKAY.
I KNOW QUITE WELL HOW YOU ISHVALANS HATE US AMESTRIANS.
YES.
WE CANNOT FORGIVE YOU FOR TAKING EVERYTHING FROM US AND DRIVING US INTO THIS WASTELAND.

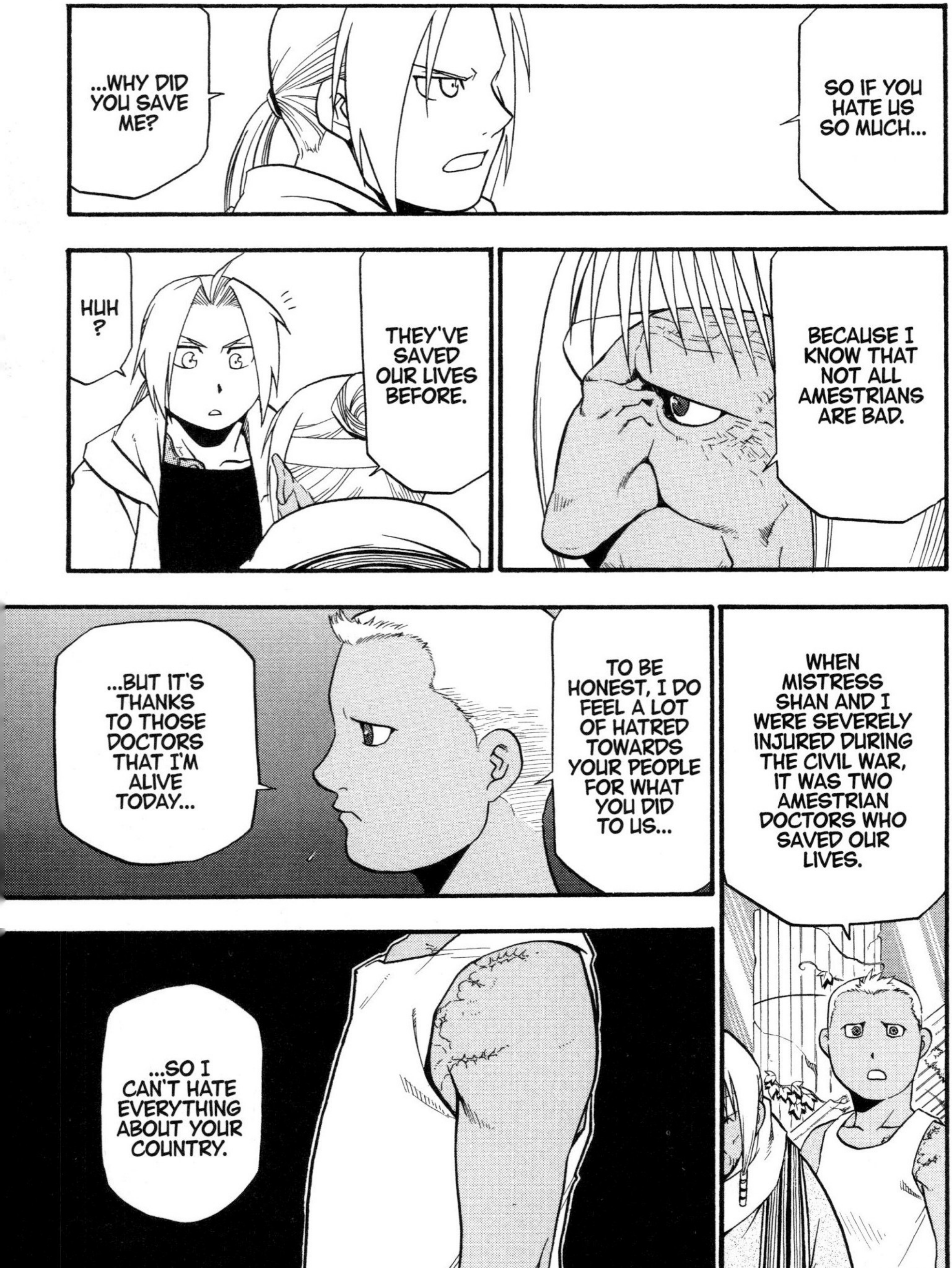
SO IF YOU HATE US SO MUCH...
...WHY DID YOU SAVE ME?
BECAUSE I KNOW THAT NOT ALL AMESTRIANS ARE BAD.
THEY'VE SAVED OUR LIVES BEFORE.
HUH ?
WHEN MISTRESS SHAN AND I WERE SEVERELY INJURED DURING THE CIVIL WAR, IT WAS TWO AMESTRIAN DOCTORS WHO SAVED OUR LIVES.
TO BE HONEST, I DO FEEL A LOT OF HATRED TOWARDS YOUR PEOPLE FOR WHAT YOU DID TO US...
...BUT IT'S THANKS TO THOSE DOCTORS THAT I'M ALIVE TODAY...
...SO I CAN'T HATE EVERYTHING ABOUT YOUR COUNTRY.

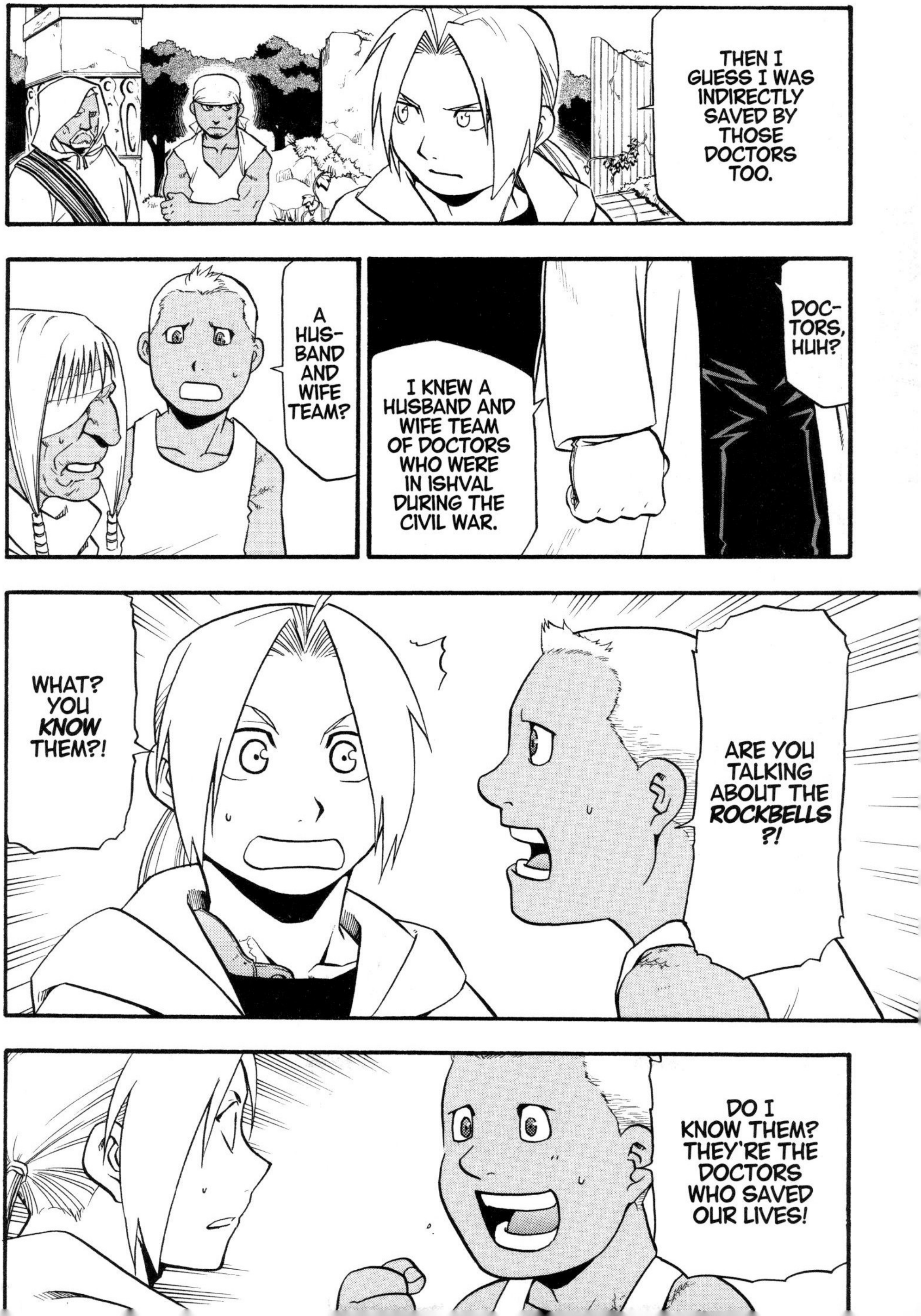
THEN I GUESS I WAS INDIRECTLY SAVED BY THOSE DOCTORS TOO.
DOCTORS, HUH?
I KNEW A HUSBAND AND WIFE TEAM OF DOCTORS WHO WERE IN ISHVAL DURING THE CIVIL WAR.
A HUSBAND AND WIFE TEAM?
ARE YOU TALKING ABOUT THE ROCKBELLS?!
WHAT? YOU KNOW THEM?!
DO I KNOW THEM? THEY'RE THE DOCTORS WHO SAVED OUR LIVES!

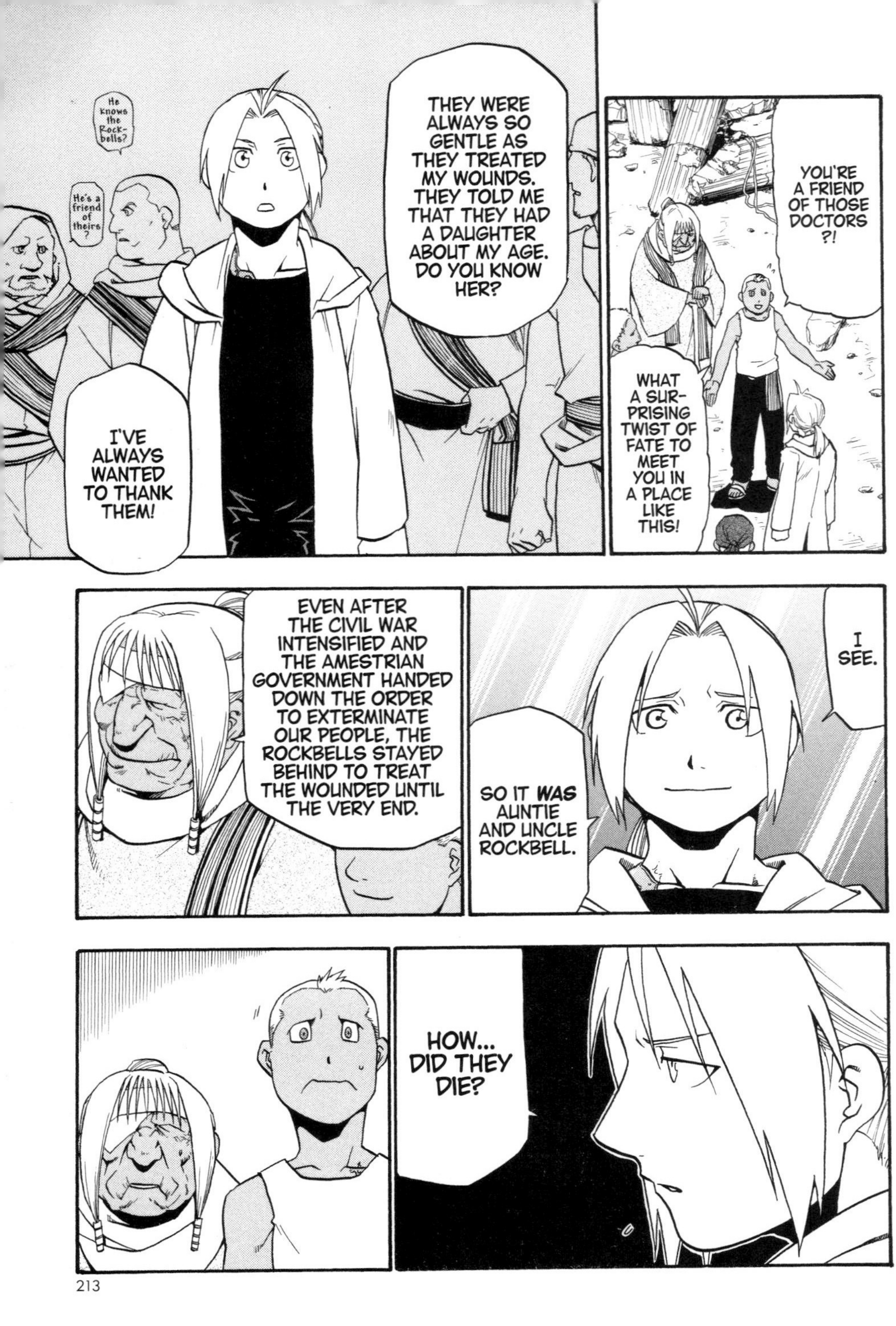
YOU'RE A FRIEND OF THOSE DOCTORS?!
WHAT A SUR-PRISING TWIST OF FATE TO MEET YOU IN A PLACE LIKE THIS!
THEY WERE ALWAYS SO GENTLE AS THEY TREATED MY WOUNDS. THEY TOLD ME THAT THEY HAD A DAUGHTER ABOUT MY AGE. DO YOU KNOW HER?
He knows the Rock-bells?
He's a friend of theirs?
I'VE ALWAYS WANTED TO THANK THEM!
I SEE.
SO IT WAS AUNTIE AND UNCLE ROCKBELL.
EVEN AFTER THE CIVIL WAR INTENSIFIED AND THE AMESTRIAN GOVERNMENT HANDED DOWN THE ORDER TO EXTERMINATE OUR PEOPLE, THE ROCKBELLS STAYED BEHIND TO TREAT THE WOUNDED UNTIL THE VERY END.
HOW... DID THEY DIE?

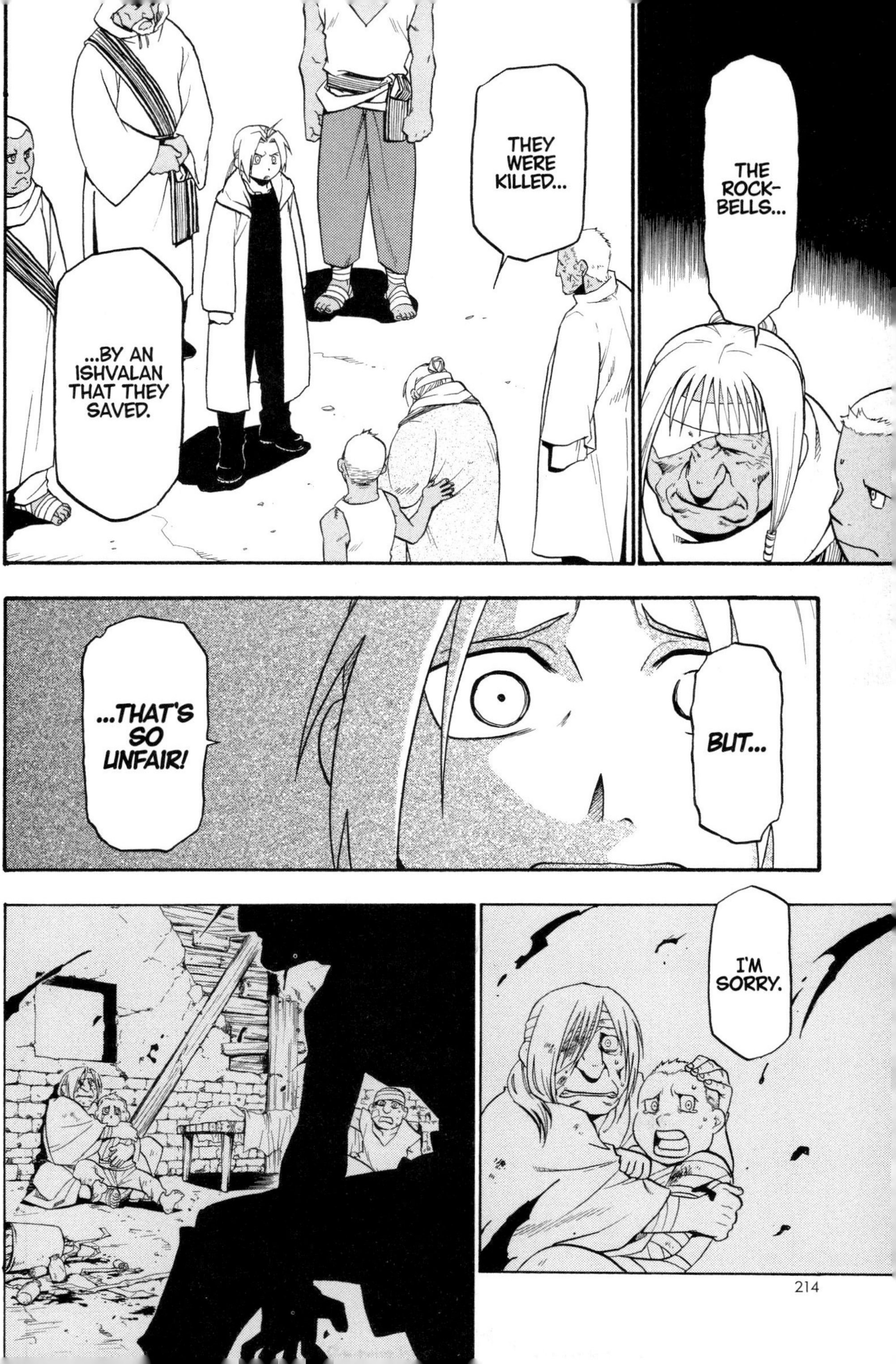
THE ROCK-BELLS...
THEY WERE KILLED...
...BY AN ISHVALAN THAT THEY SAVED.
BUT...
...THAT'S SO UNFAIR!
I'M SORRY.

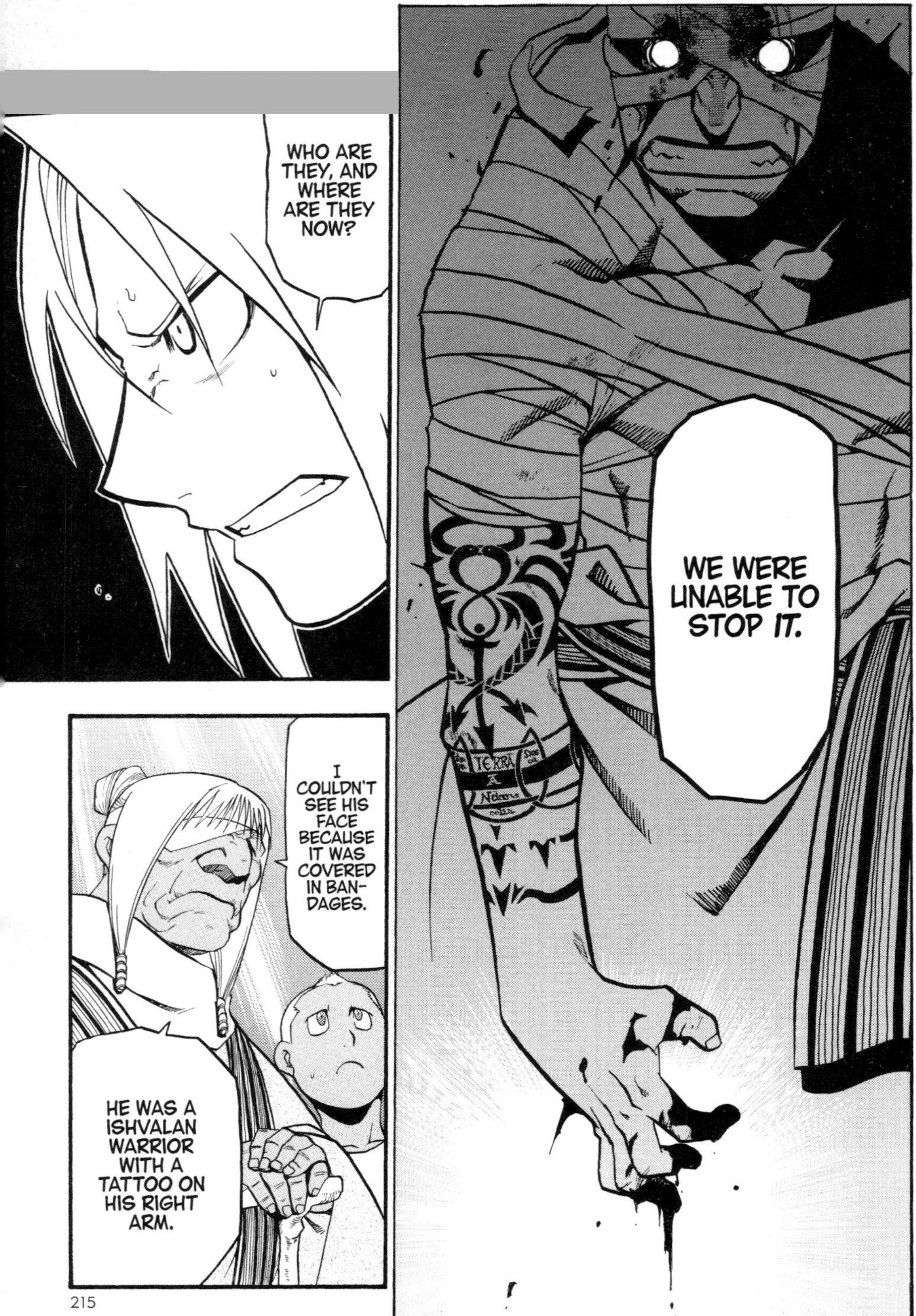
WE WERE UNABLE TO STOP IT.
WHO ARE THEY, AND WHERE ARE THEY NOW?
I COULDN'T SEE HIS FACE BECAUSE IT WAS COVERED IN BAN-DAGES.
HE WAS A ISHVALAN WARRIOR WITH A TATTOO ON HIS RIGHT ARM.

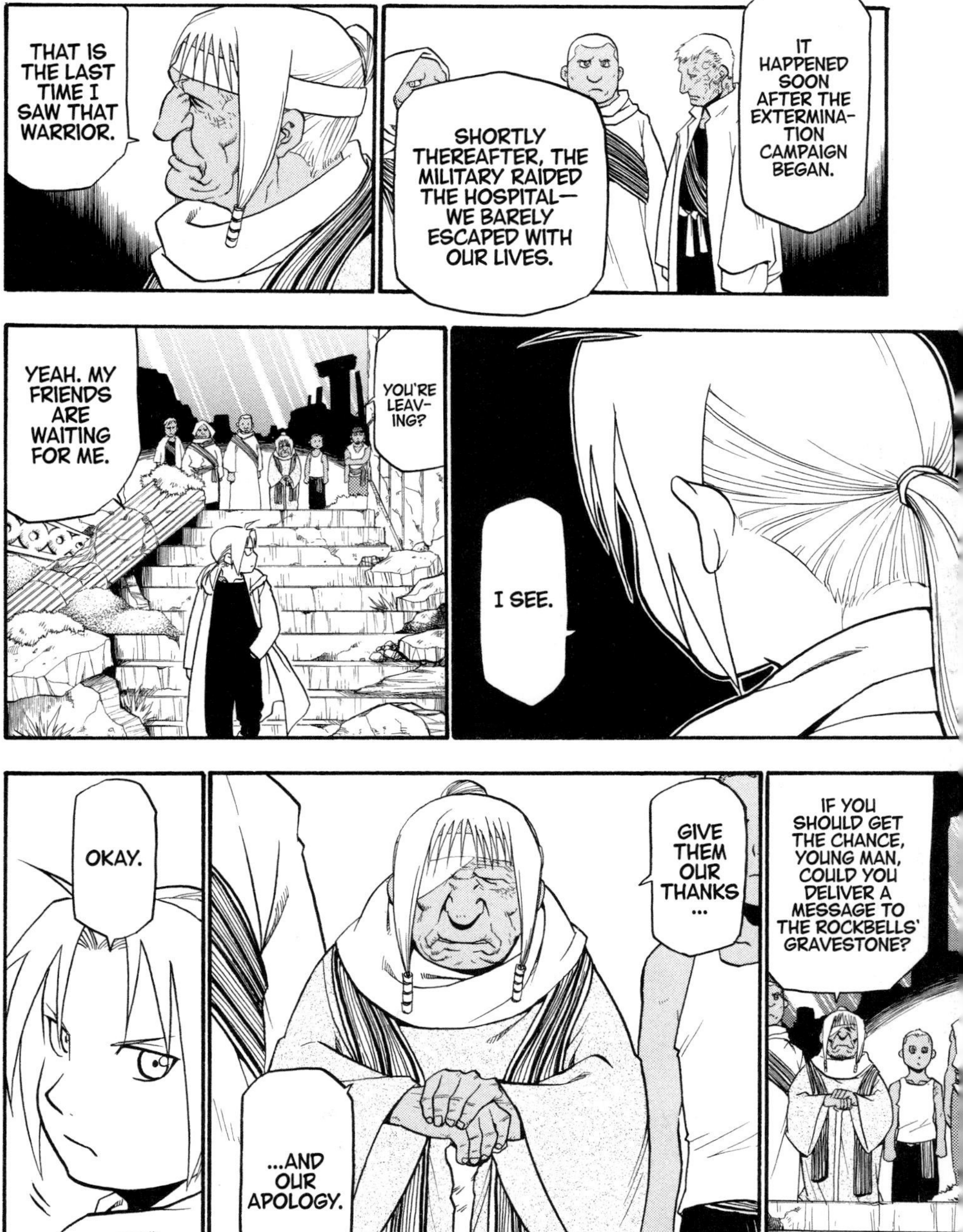
IT HAPPENED SOON AFTER THE EXTERMINATION CAMPAIGN BEGAN.
SHORTLY THEREAFTER, THE MILITARY RAIDED THE HOSPITAL—WE BARELY ESCAPED WITH OUR LIVES.
THAT IS THE LAST TIME I SAW THAT WARRIOR.
I SEE.
YOU'RE LEAVING?
YEAH. MY FRIENDS ARE WAITING FOR ME.
IF YOU SHOULD GET THE CHANCE, YOUNG MAN, COULD YOU DELIVER A MESSAGE TO THE ROCKBELLS' GRAVESTONE?
GIVE THEM OUR THANKS...
...AND OUR APOLOGY.
OKAY.

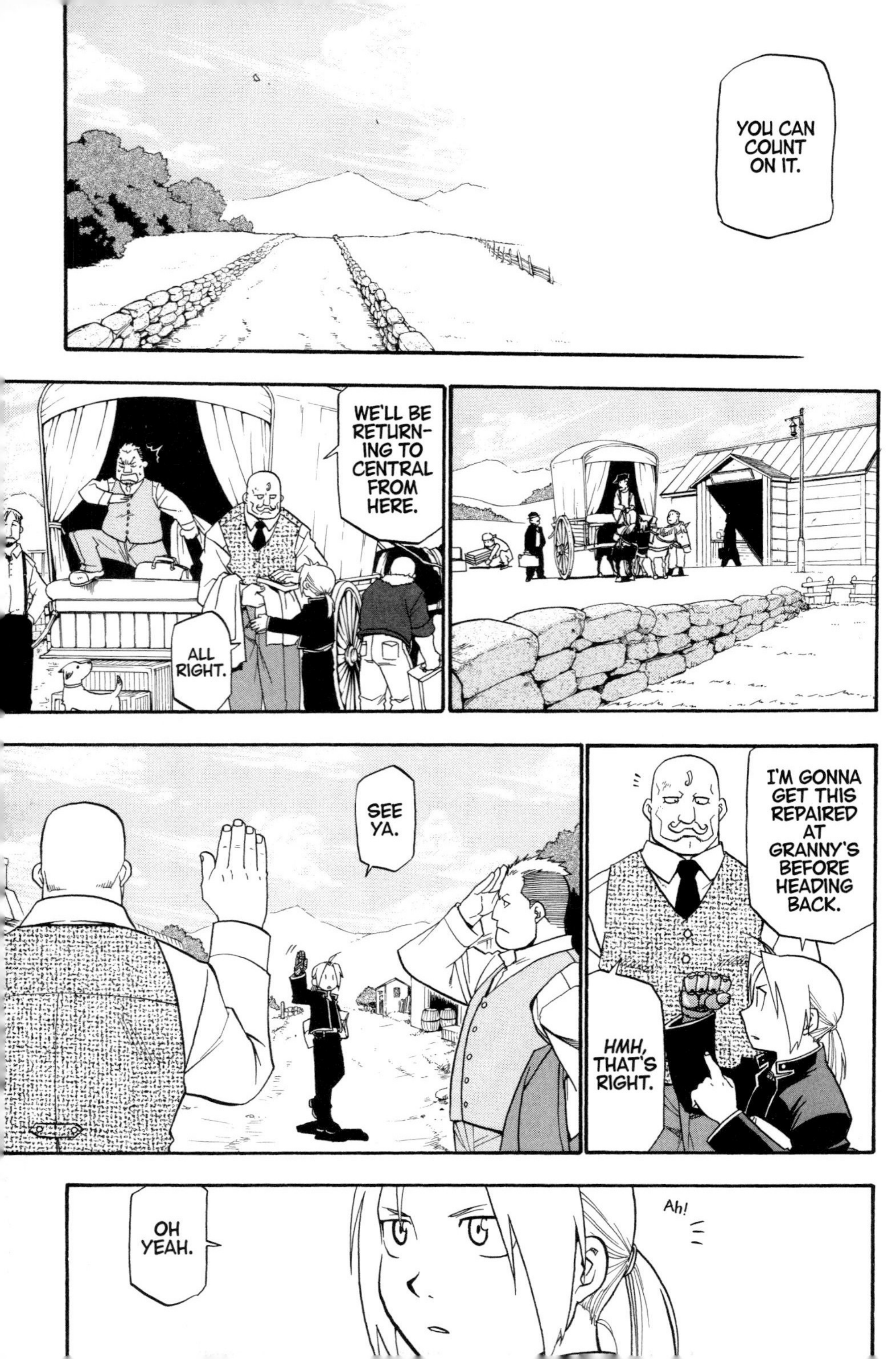
YOU CAN COUNT ON IT.
WE'LL BE RETURNING TO CENTRAL FROM HERE.
ALL RIGHT.
I'M GONNA GET THIS REPAIRED AT GRANNY'S BEFORE HEADING BACK.
HMH, THAT'S RIGHT.
SEE YA.
Ah!
OH YEAH.

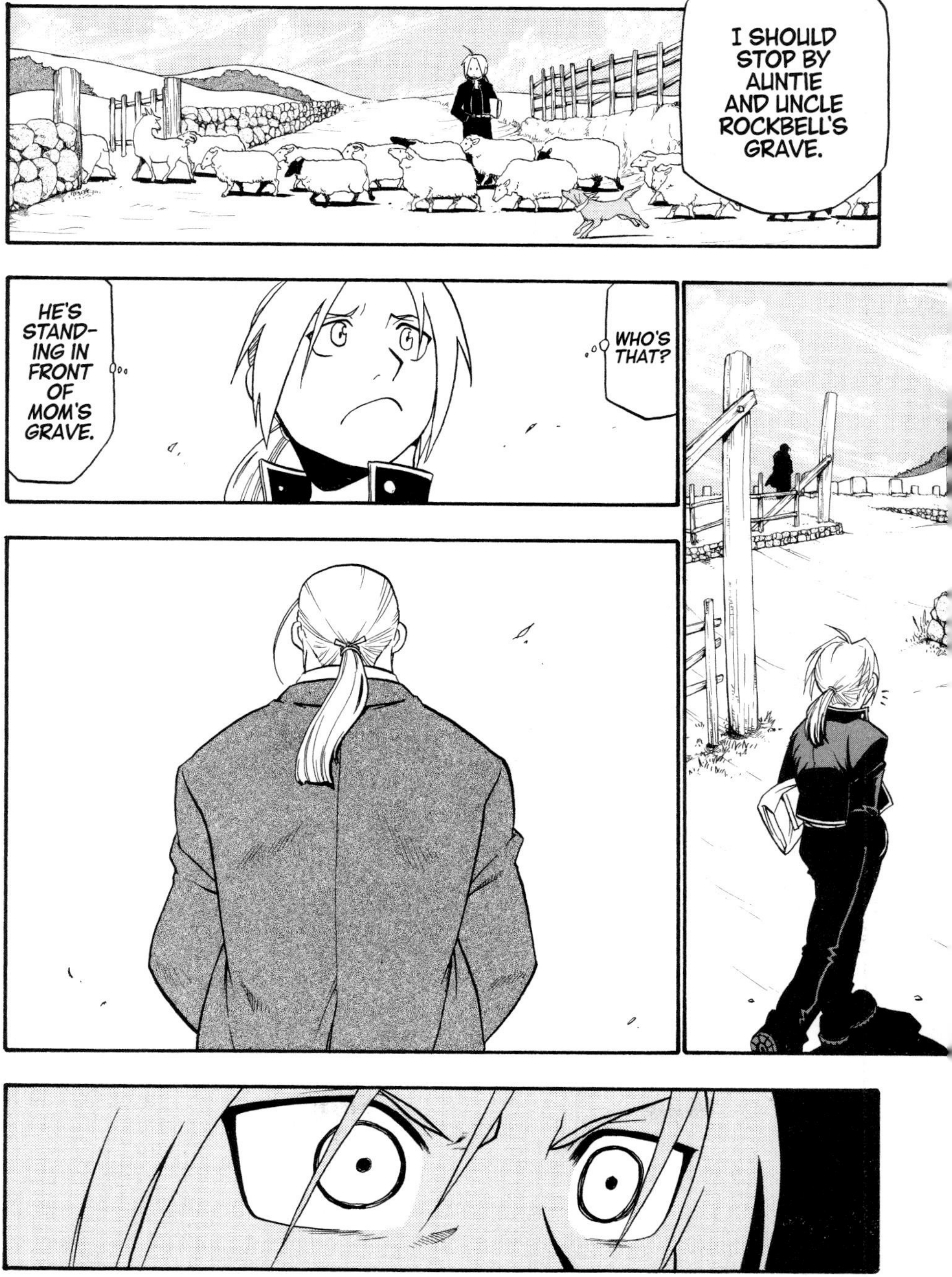
I SHOULD STOP BY AUNTIE AND UNCLE ROCKBELL'S GRAVE.
WHO'S THAT?
HE'S STANDING IN FRONT OF MOM'S GRAVE.

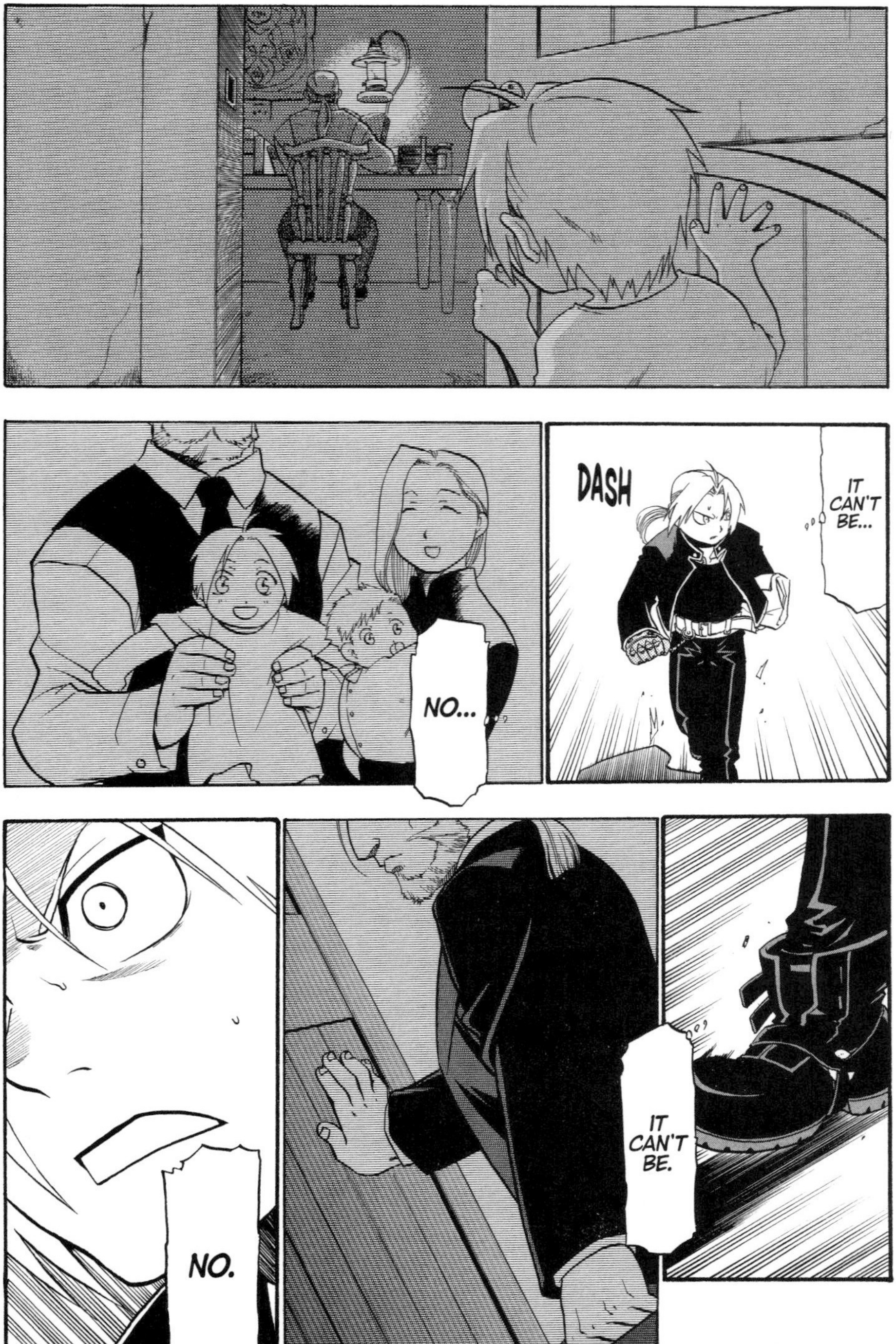
DASH
IT CAN'T BE...
NO...
IT CAN'T BE.
NO.

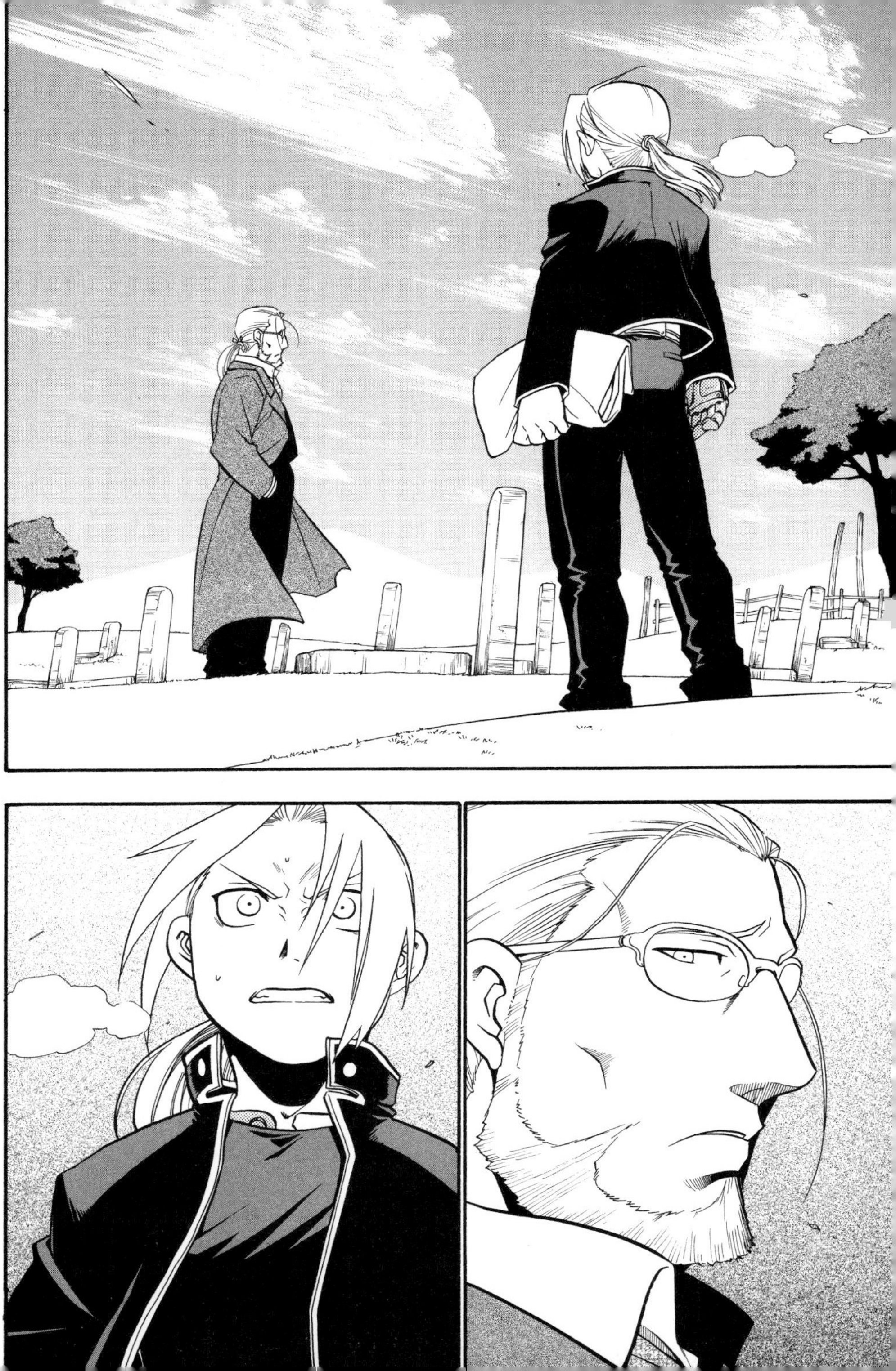

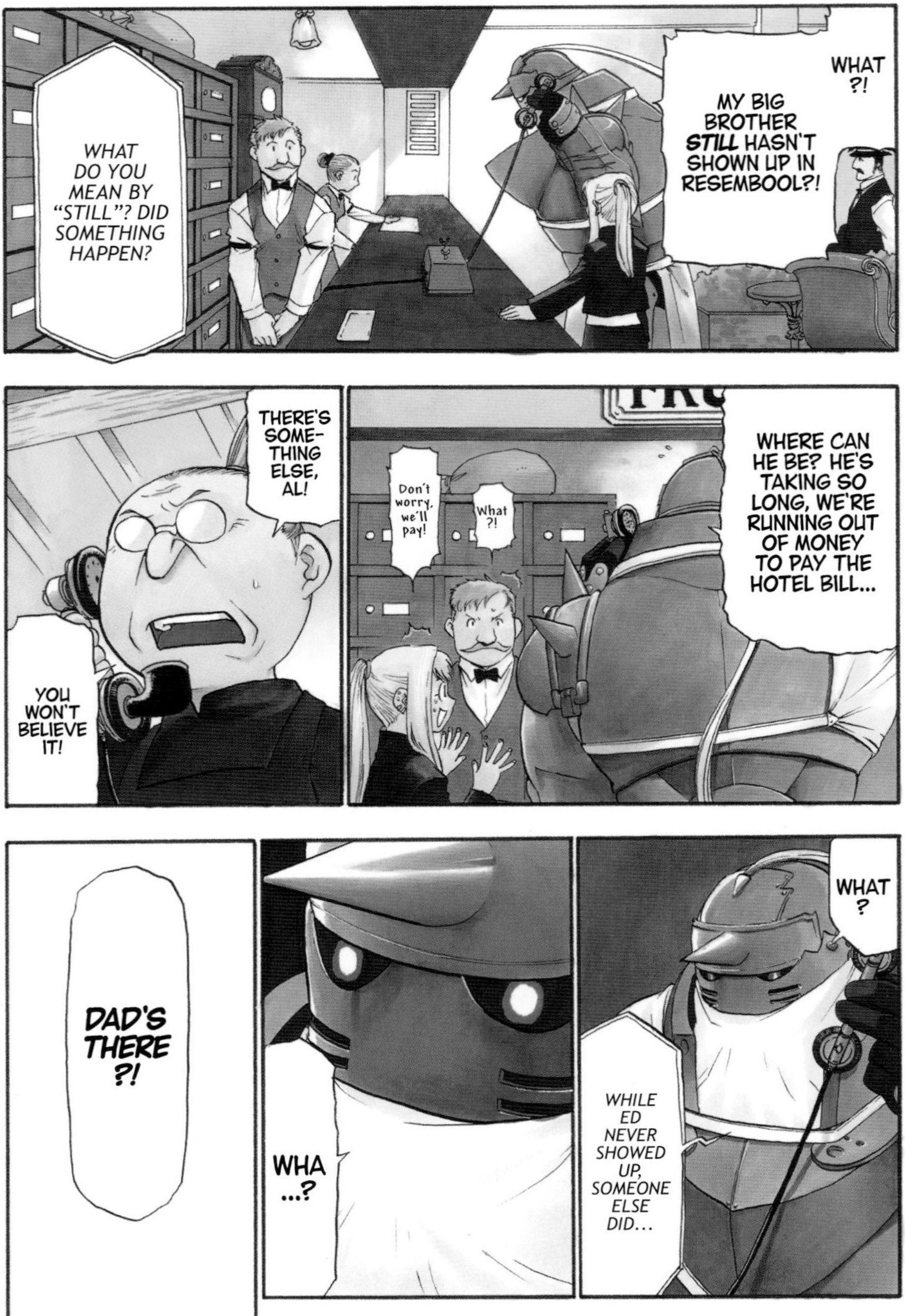
WHAT?!
MY BIG BROTHER STILL HASN'T SHOWN UP IN RESEMBOOL?!
WHAT DO YOU MEAN BY "STILL"? DID SOMETHING HAPPEN?
WHERE CAN HE BE? HE'S TAKING SO LONG, WE'RE RUNNING OUT OF MONEY TO PAY THE HOTEL BILL...
What?!
Don't worry, we'll pay!
THERE'S SOMETHING ELSE, AL!
YOU WON'T BELIEVE IT!
WHAT?
WHILE ED NEVER SHOWED UP, SOMEONE ELSE DID...
WHA...?
DAD'S THERE?!

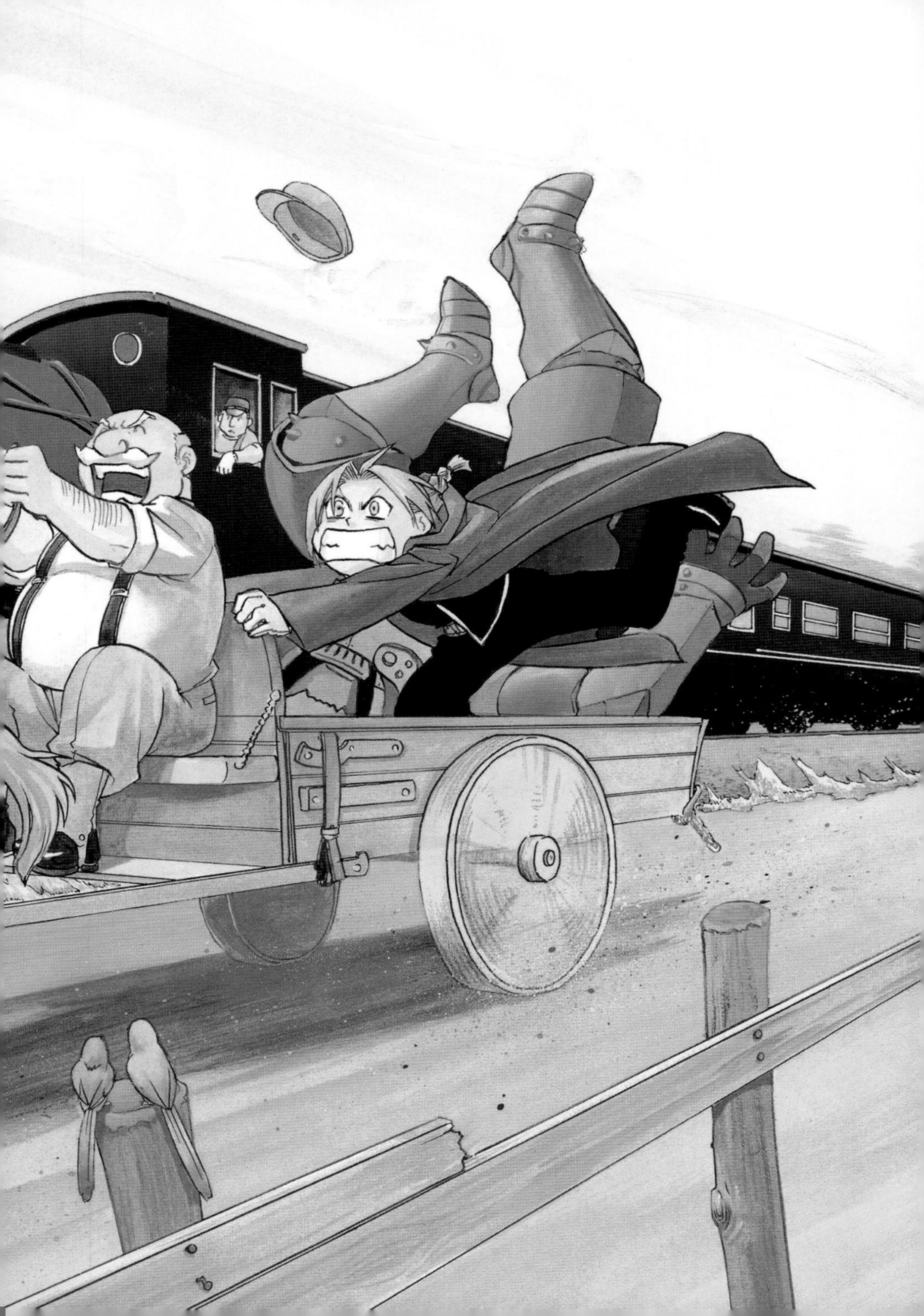

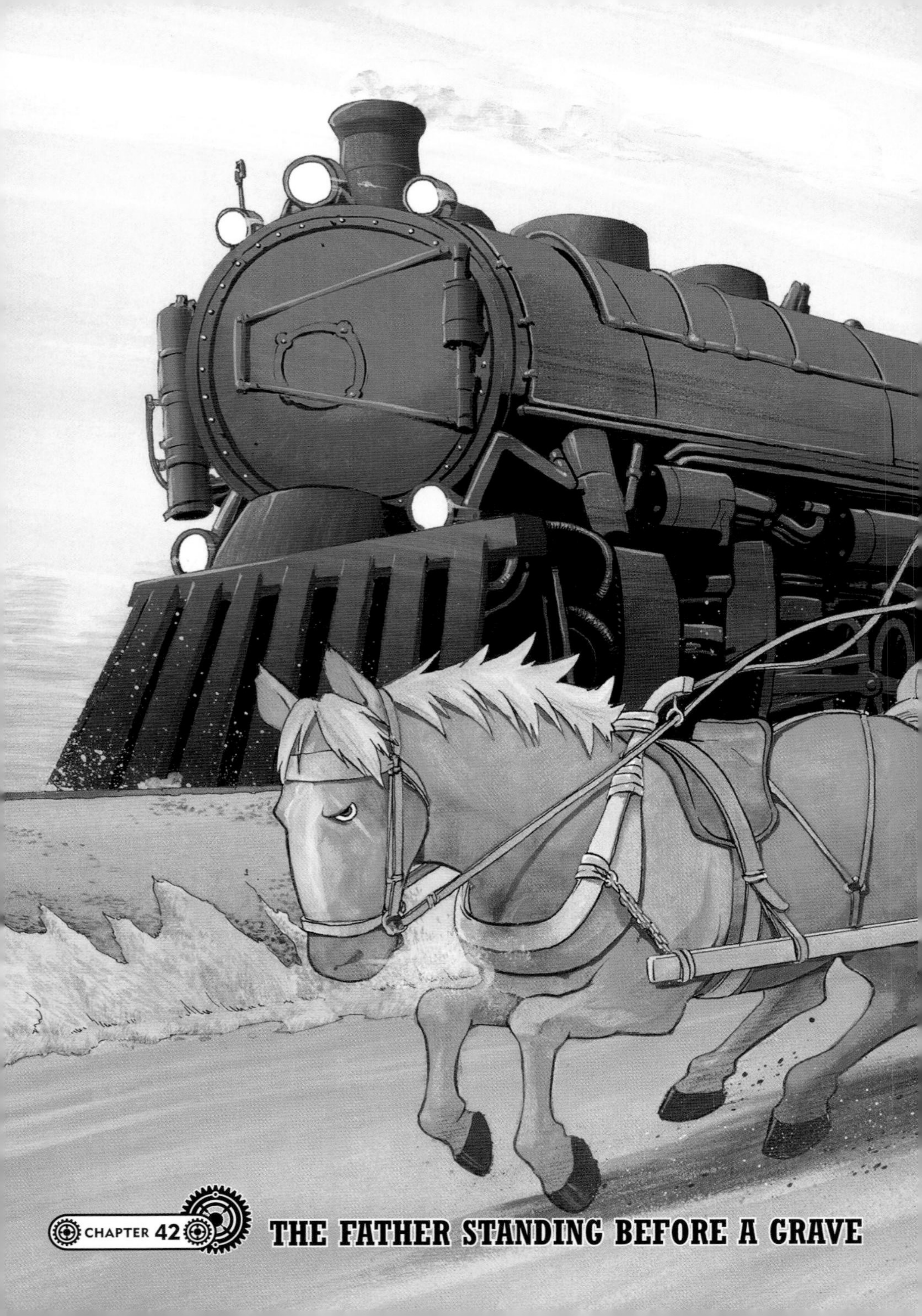

CHAPTER 42 THE FATHER STANDING BEFORE A GRAVE

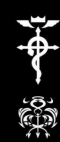

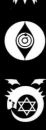

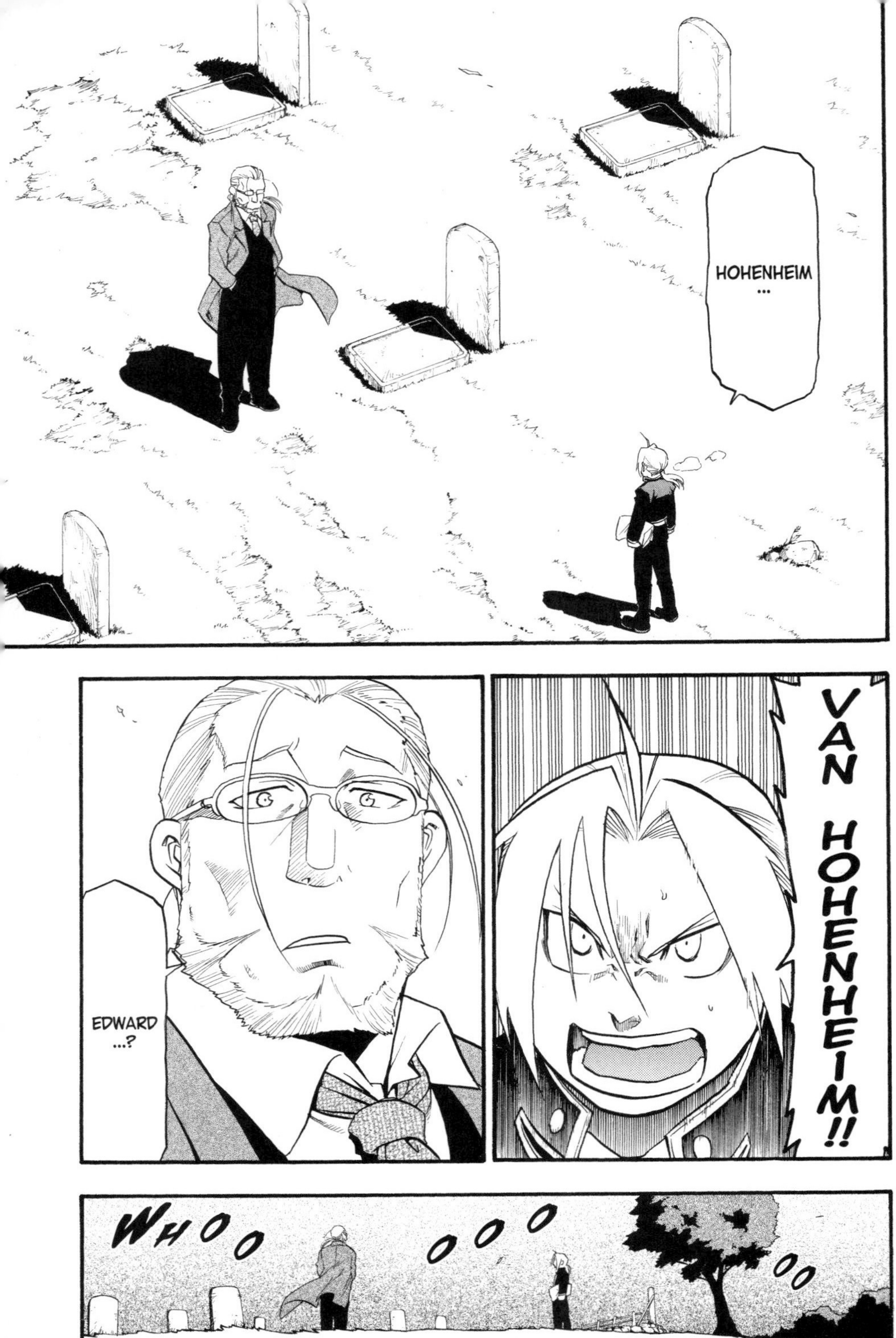
HOHENHEIM ...
VAN HOHENHEIM!!
EDWARD ...?
WHOOOOOOOOOO

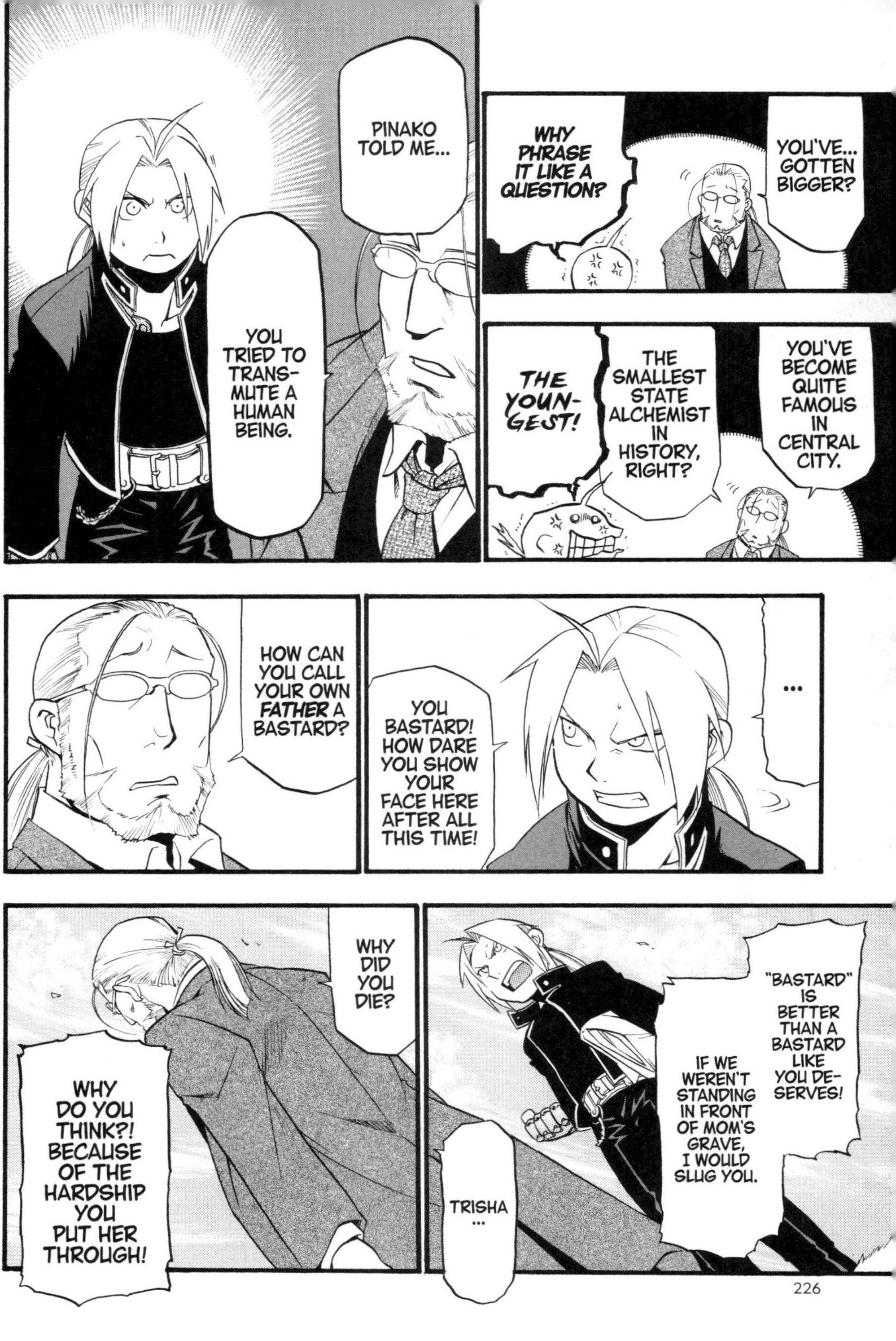
YOU'VE... GOTTEN BIGGER?
WHY PHRASE IT LIKE A QUESTION?
YOU'VE BECOME QUITE FAMOUS IN CENTRAL CITY.
THE SMALLEST STATE ALCHEMIST IN HISTORY, RIGHT?
THE YOUNGEST!
PINAKO TOLD ME...
YOU TRIED TO TRANSMUTE A HUMAN BEING.
...
YOU BASTARD! HOW DARE YOU SHOW YOUR FACE HERE AFTER ALL THIS TIME!
HOW CAN YOU CALL YOUR OWN FATHER A BASTARD?
"BASTARD" IS BETTER THAN A BASTARD LIKE YOU DESERVES!
IF WE WEREN'T STANDING IN FRONT OF MOM'S GRAVE, I WOULD SLUG YOU.
TRISHA ...
WHY DID YOU DIE?
WHY DO YOU THINK?! BECAUSE OF THE HARDSHIP YOU PUT HER THROUGH!

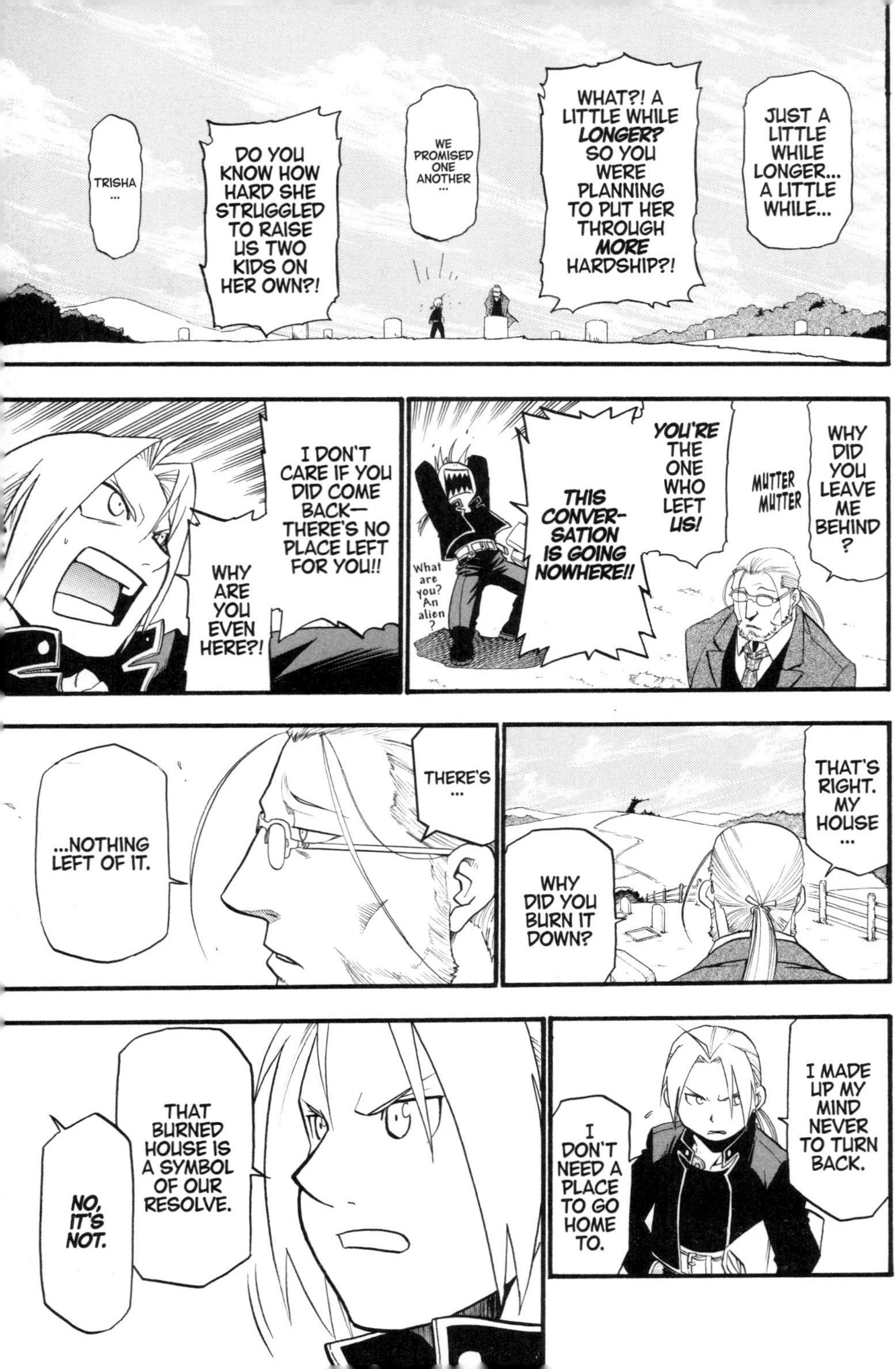

JUST A LITTLE WHILE LONGER... A LITTLE WHILE...
WHAT?! A LITTLE WHILE LONGER? SO YOU WERE PLANNING TO PUT HER THROUGH MORE HARDSHIP?!
WE PROMISED ONE ANOTHER ...
DO YOU KNOW HOW HARD SHE STRUGGLED TO RAISE US TWO KIDS ON HER OWN?!
TRISHA ...
WHY DID YOU LEAVE ME BEHIND?
MUTTER MUTTER
YOU'RE THE ONE WHO LEFT US!
THIS CONVERSATION IS GOING NOWHERE!!
What are you? An alien?
I DON'T CARE IF YOU DID COME BACK— THERE'S NO PLACE LEFT FOR YOU!!
WHY ARE YOU EVEN HERE?!
THAT'S RIGHT. MY HOUSE ...
WHY DID YOU BURN IT DOWN?
THERE'S ...
...NOTHING LEFT OF IT.
I MADE UP MY MIND NEVER TO TURN BACK.
I DON'T NEED A PLACE TO GO HOME TO.
THAT BURNED HOUSE IS A SYMBOL OF OUR RESOLVE.
NO, IT'S NOT.

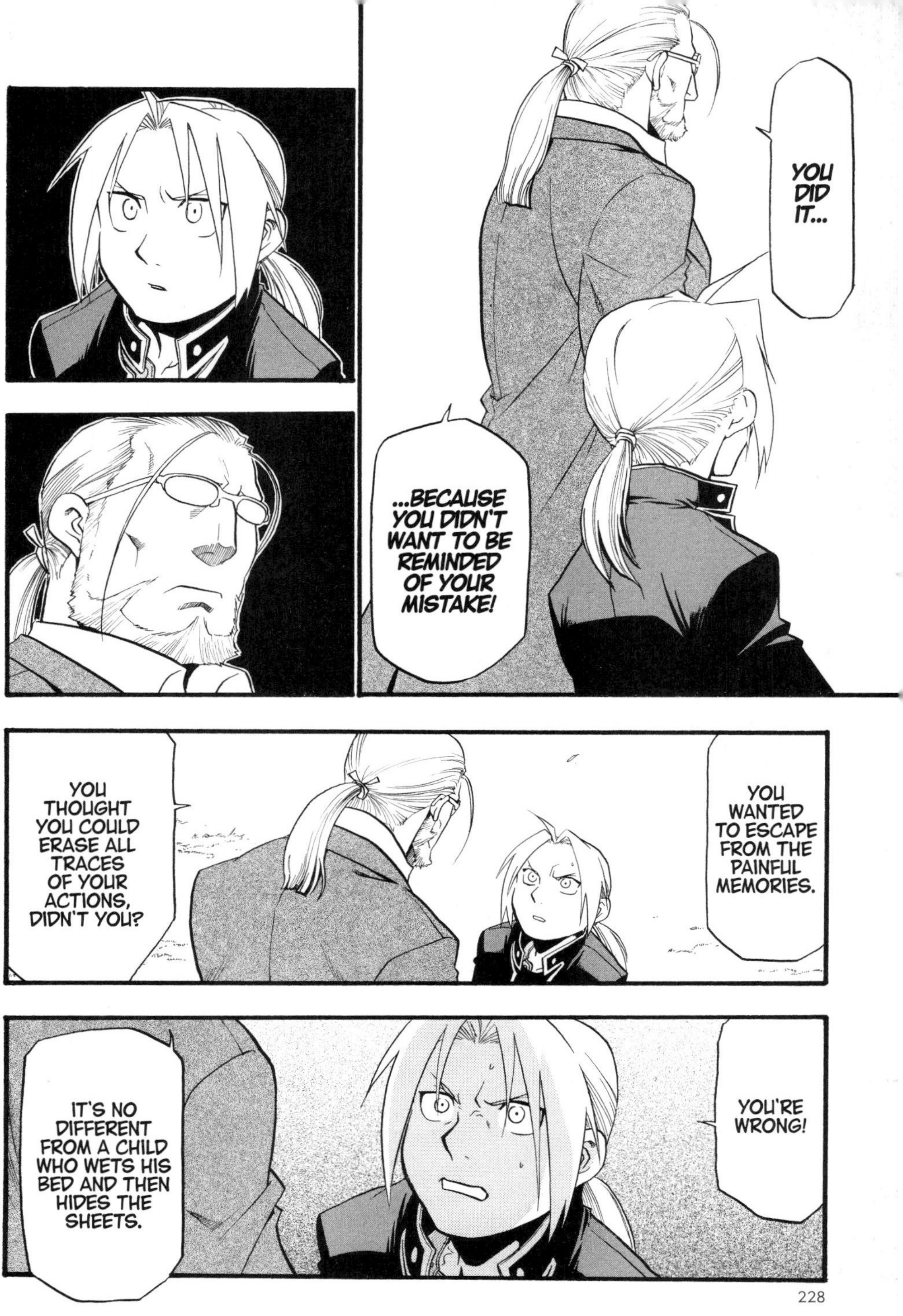
YOU DID IT...
...BECAUSE YOU DIDN'T WANT TO BE REMINDED OF YOUR MISTAKE!
YOU WANTED TO ESCAPE FROM THE PAINFUL MEMORIES.
YOU THOUGHT YOU COULD ERASE ALL TRACES OF YOUR ACTIONS, DIDN'T YOU?
YOU'RE WRONG!
IT'S NO DIFFERENT FROM A CHILD WHO WETS HIS BED AND THEN HIDES THE SHEETS.

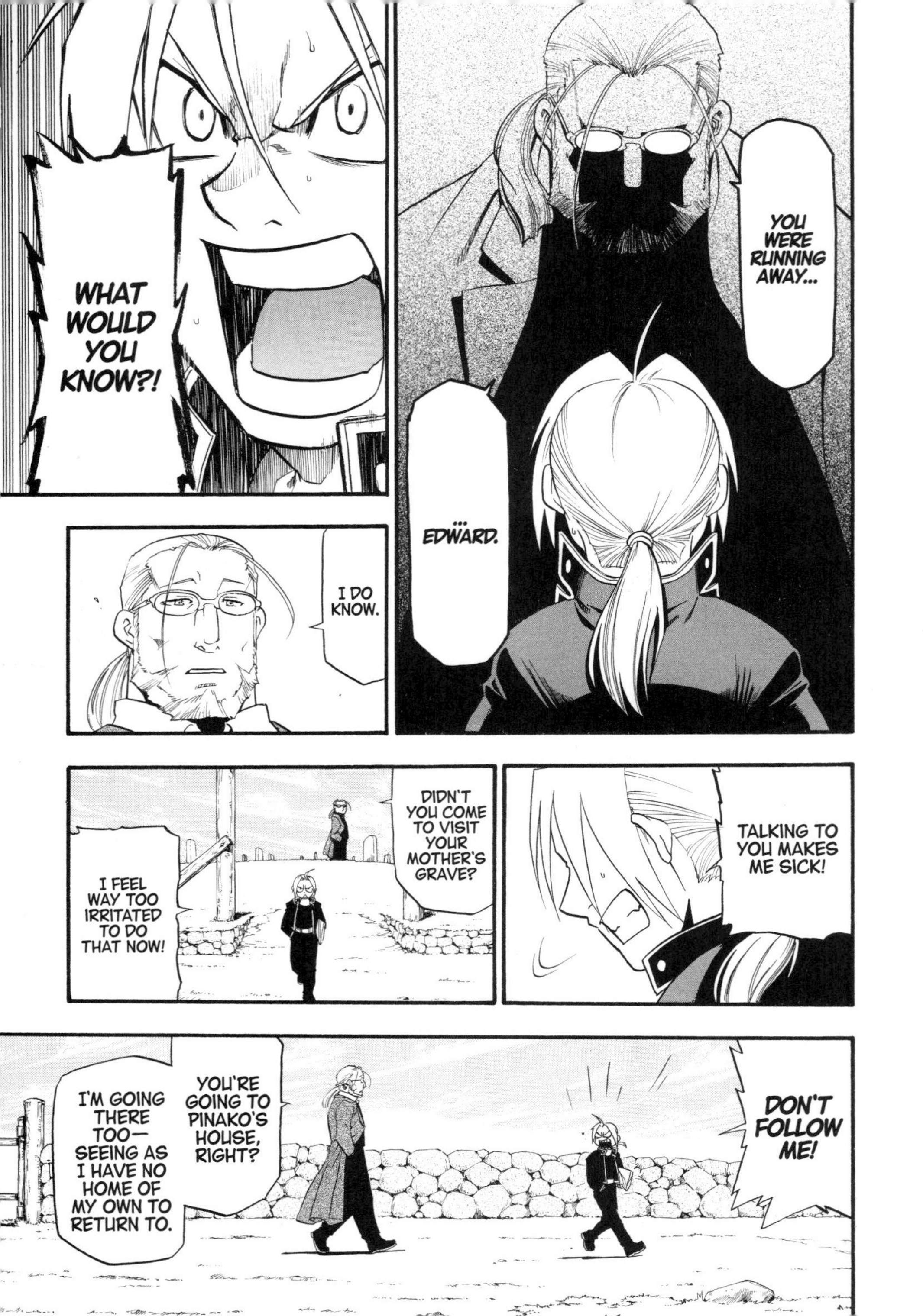
YOU WERE RUNNING AWAY...
...EDWARD.
WHAT WOULD YOU KNOW?!
I DO KNOW.
TALKING TO YOU MAKES ME SICK!
DIDN'T YOU COME TO VISIT YOUR MOTHER'S GRAVE?
I FEEL WAY TOO IRRITATED TO DO THAT NOW!
DON'T FOLLOW ME!
YOU'RE GOING TO PINAKO'S HOUSE, RIGHT?
I'M GOING THERE TOO— SEEING AS I HAVE NO HOME OF MY OWN TO RETURN TO.

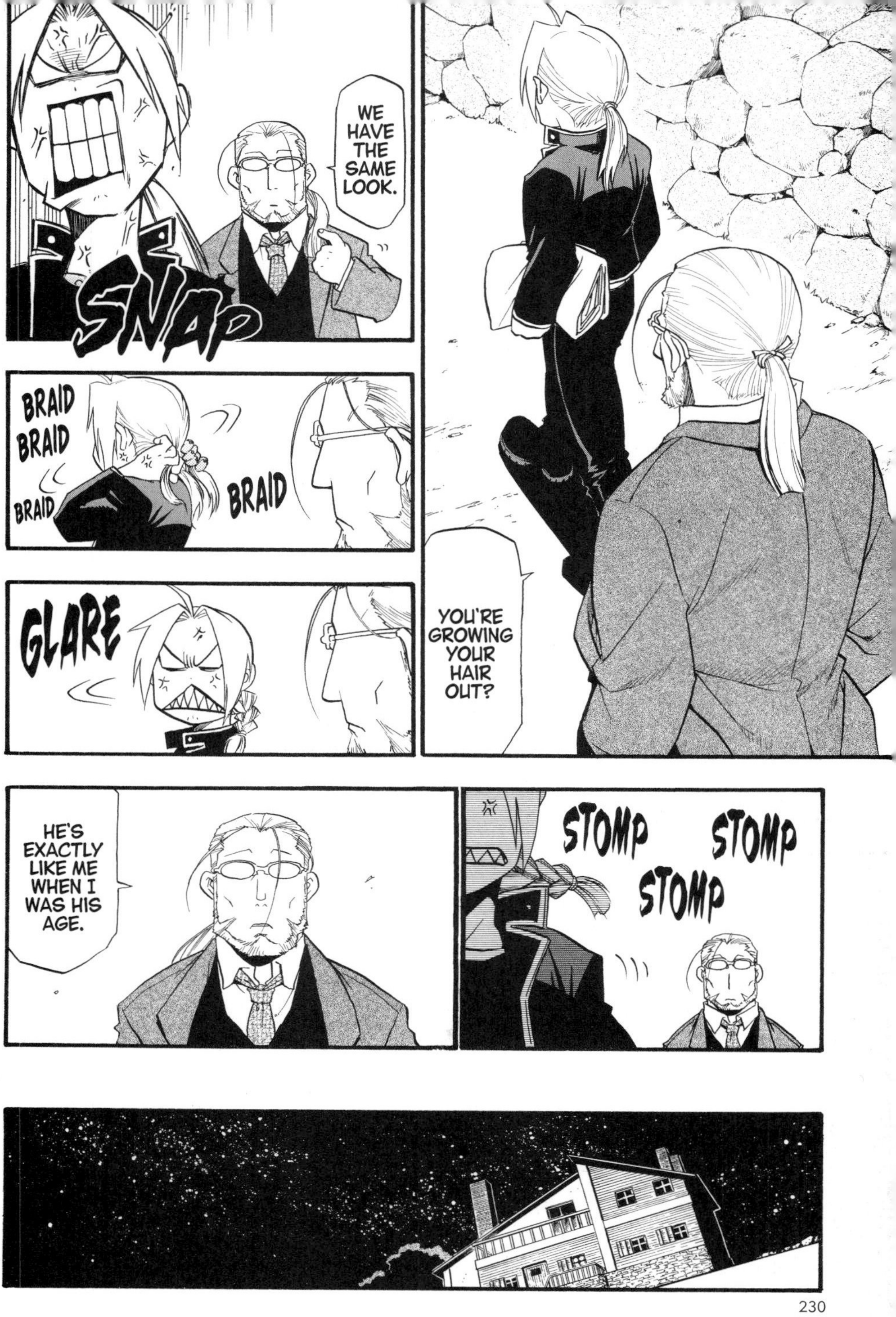
YOU'RE GROWING YOUR HAIR OUT?
WE HAVE THE SAME LOOK.
SNAP
BRAID
BRAID
BRAID
BRAID
GLARE
STOMP
STOMP
STOMP
HE'S EXACTLY LIKE ME WHEN I WAS HIS AGE.

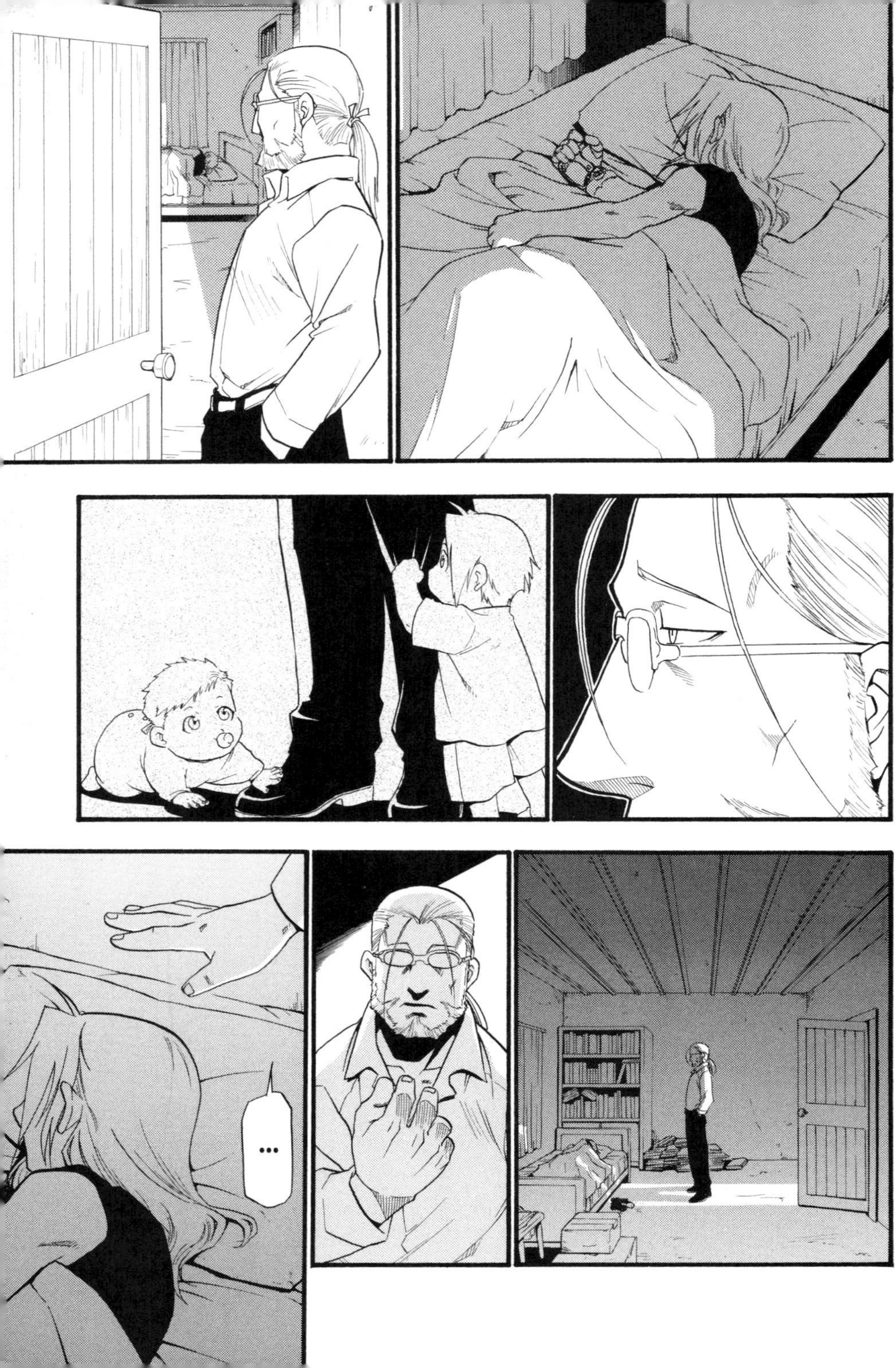
...

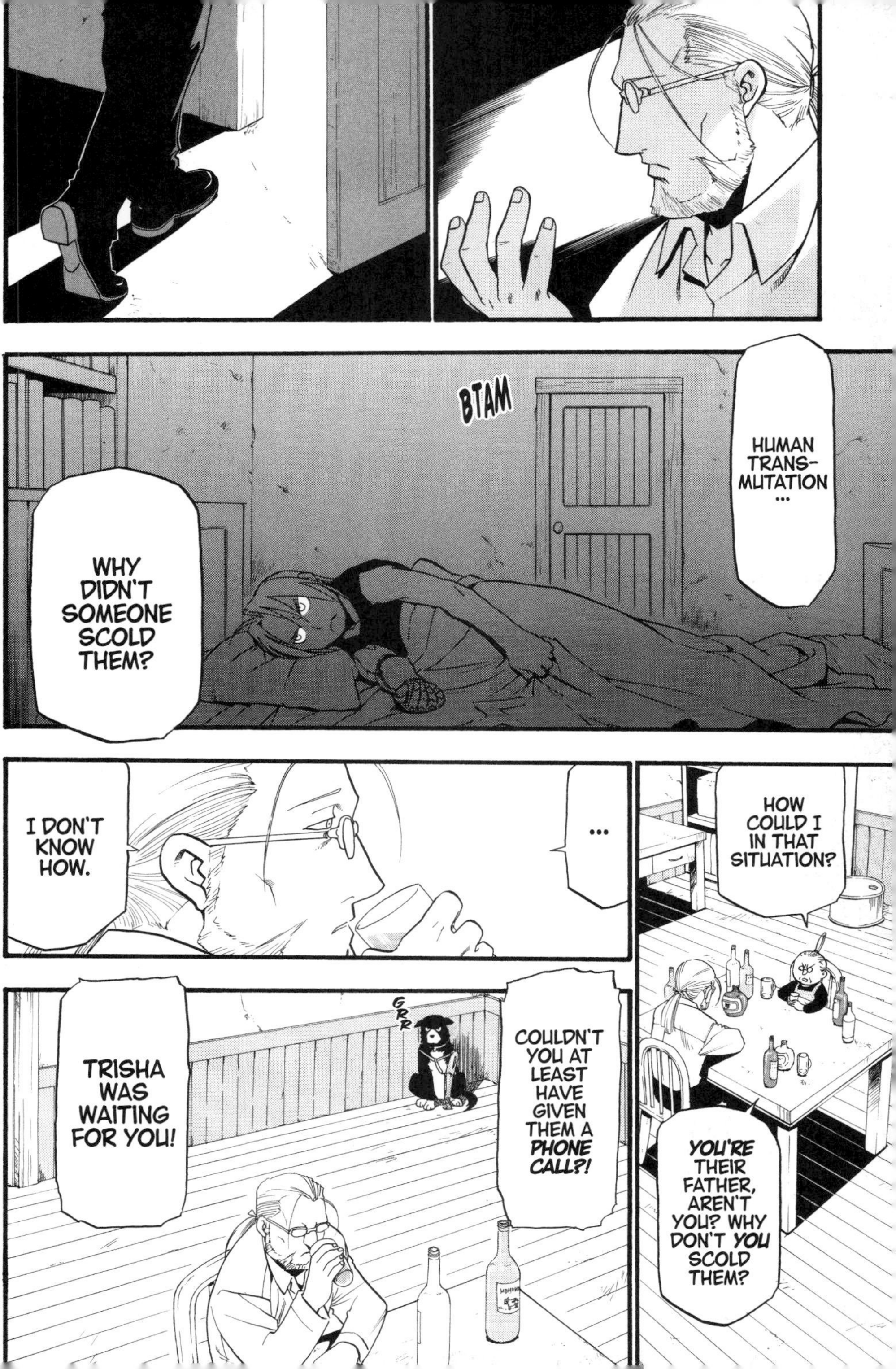
HUMAN TRANS-MUTATION ...
BTAM
WHY DIDN'T SOMEONE SCOLD THEM?
HOW COULD I IN THAT SITUATION?
YOU'RE THEIR FATHER, AREN'T YOU? WHY DON'T *YOU* SCOLD THEM?
...
I DON'T KNOW HOW.
COULDN'T YOU AT LEAST HAVE GIVEN THEM A *PHONE CALL?!*
GRR
TRISHA WAS WAITING FOR YOU!

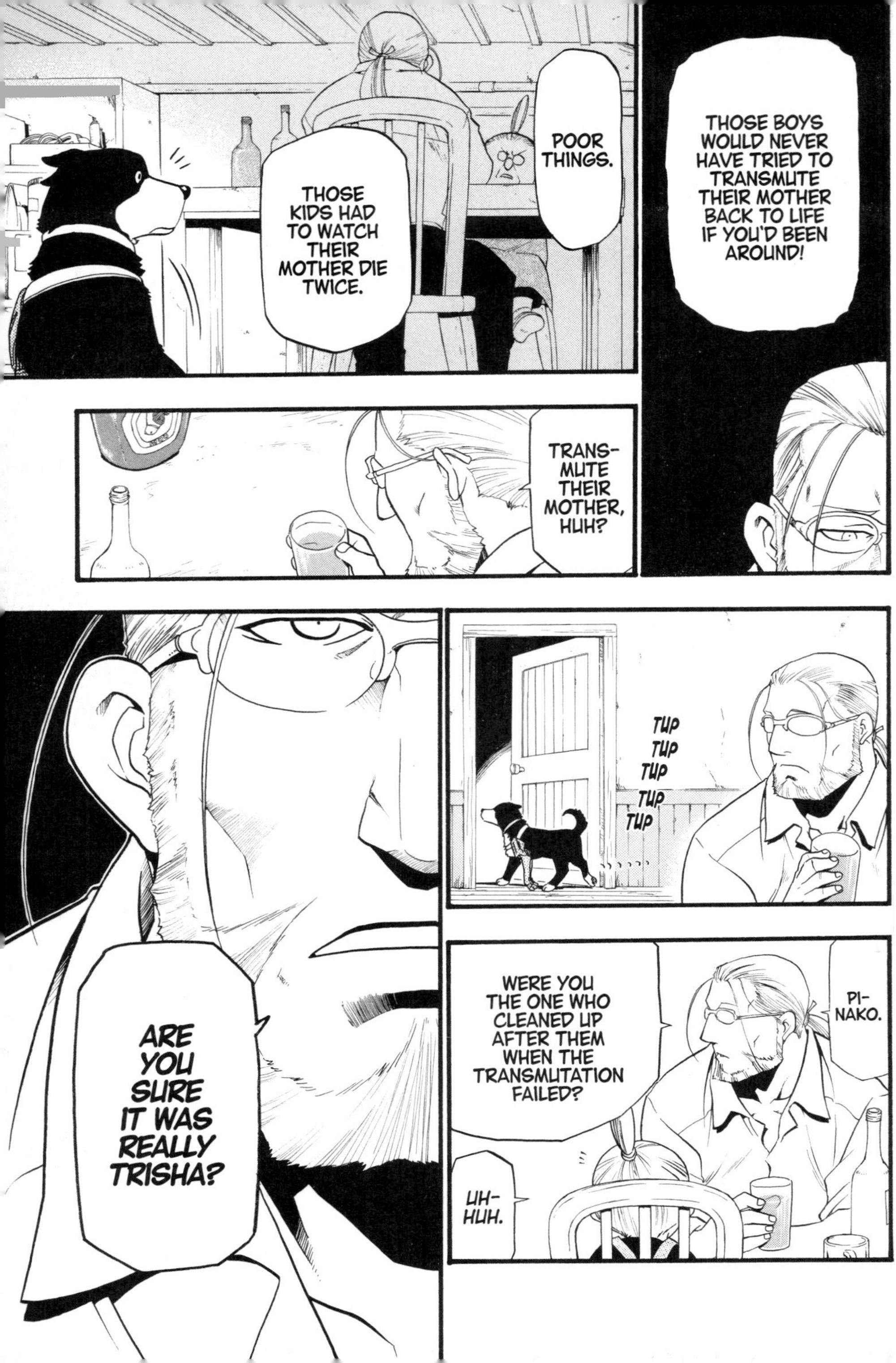
THOSE BOYS WOULD NEVER HAVE TRIED TO TRANSMUTE THEIR MOTHER BACK TO LIFE IF YOU'D BEEN AROUND!
POOR THINGS.
THOSE KIDS HAD TO WATCH THEIR MOTHER DIE TWICE.
TRANS-MUTE THEIR MOTHER, HUH?
TUP TUP TUP TUP TUP
PI-NAKO.
WERE YOU THE ONE WHO CLEANED UP AFTER THEM WHEN THE TRANSMUTATION FAILED?
UH-HUH.
ARE YOU SURE IT WAS REALLY TRISHA?

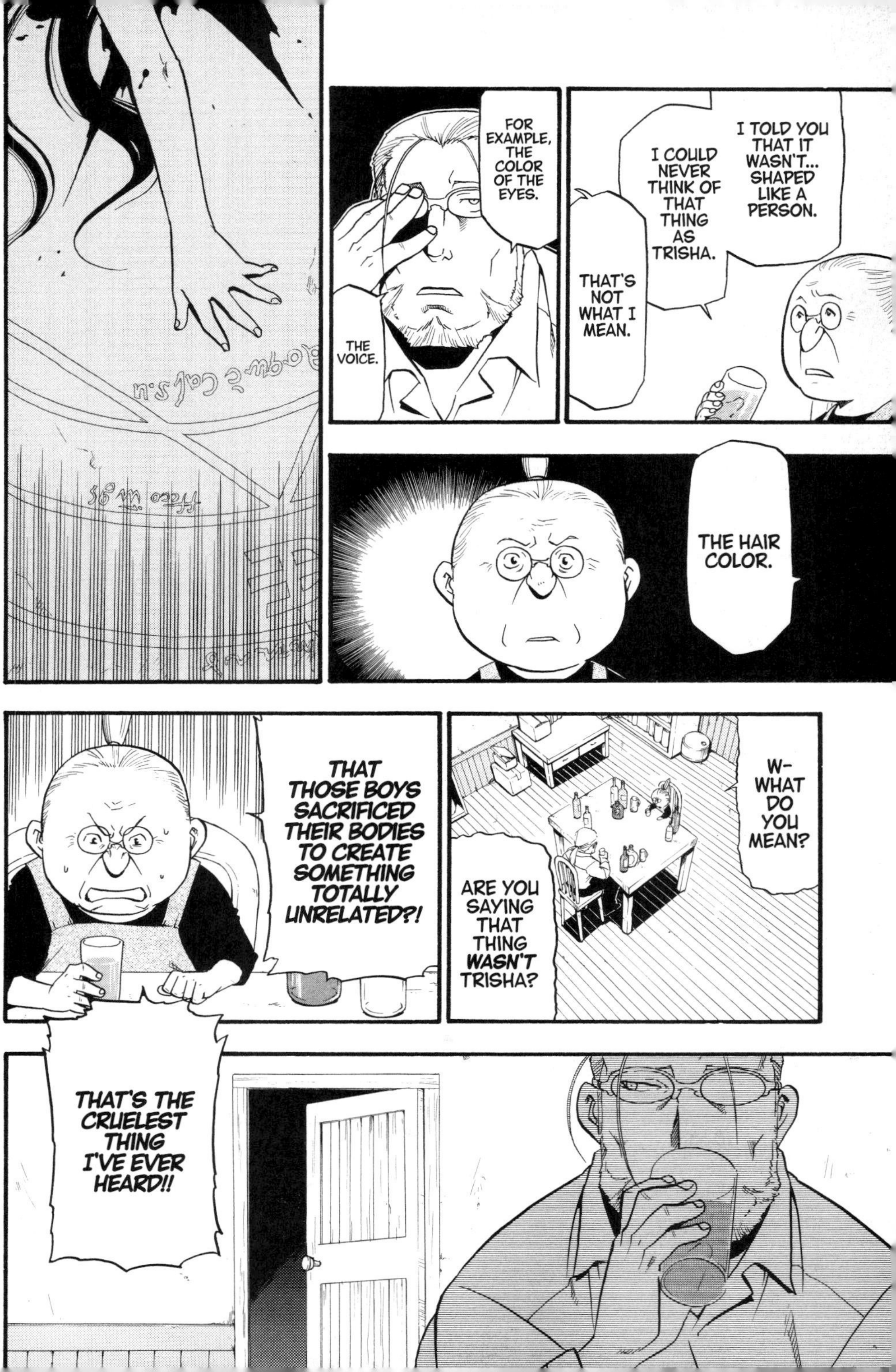
I TOLD YOU THAT IT WASN'T... SHAPED LIKE A PERSON.
I COULD NEVER THINK OF THAT THING AS TRISHA.
THAT'S NOT WHAT I MEAN.
FOR EXAMPLE, THE COLOR OF THE EYES.
THE VOICE.
THE HAIR COLOR.
W-WHAT DO YOU MEAN?
ARE YOU SAYING THAT THING *WASN'T* TRISHA?
THAT THOSE BOYS SACRIFICED THEIR BODIES TO CREATE SOMETHING TOTALLY UNRELATED?!
THAT'S THE CRUELEST THING I'VE EVER HEARD!!

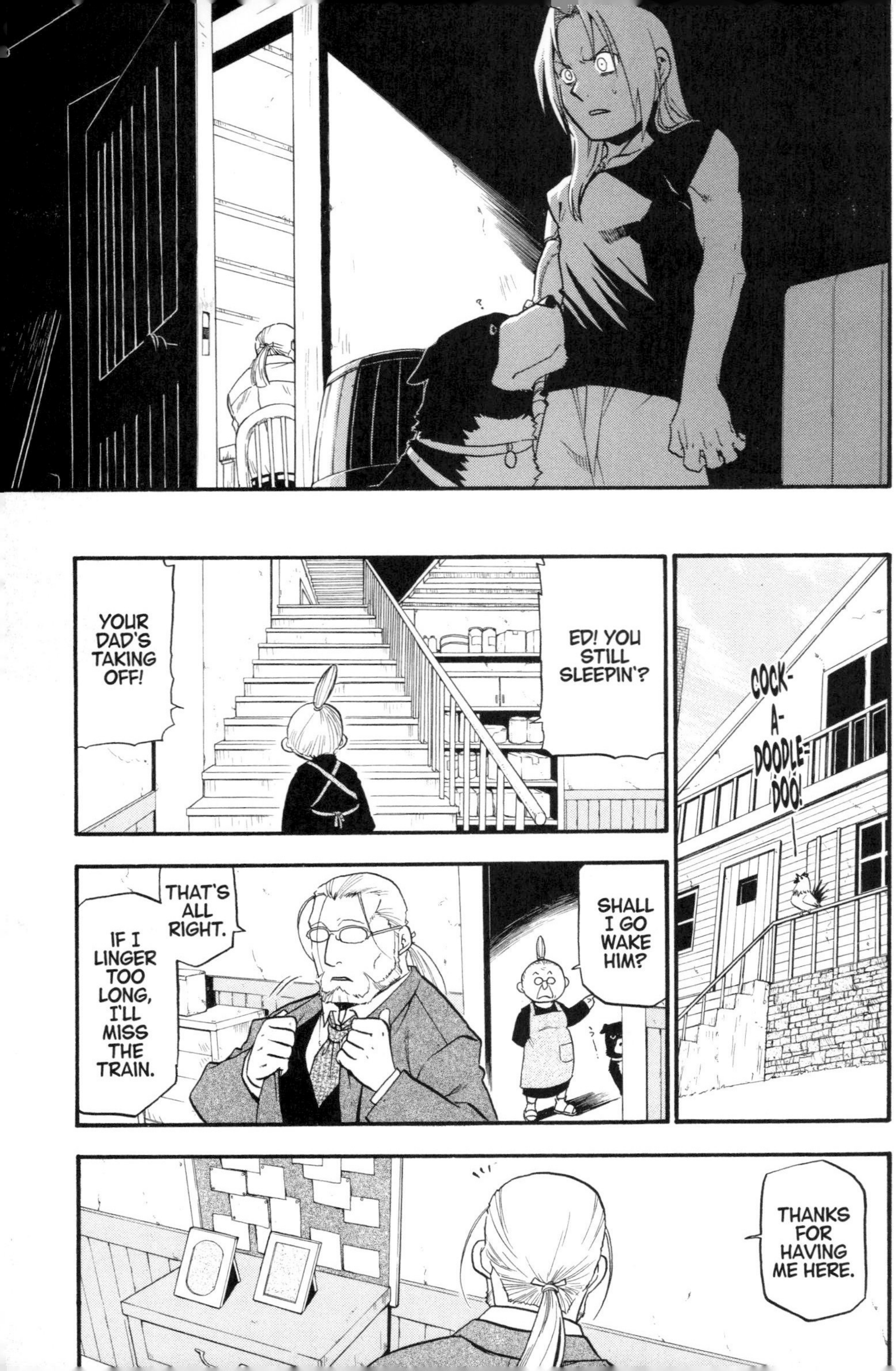
COCK-A-DOODLE-DOO!
ED! YOU STILL SLEEPIN'?
YOUR DAD'S TAKING OFF!
SHALL I GO WAKE HIM?
THAT'S ALL RIGHT.
IF I LINGER TOO LONG, I'LL MISS THE TRAIN.
THANKS FOR HAVING ME HERE.

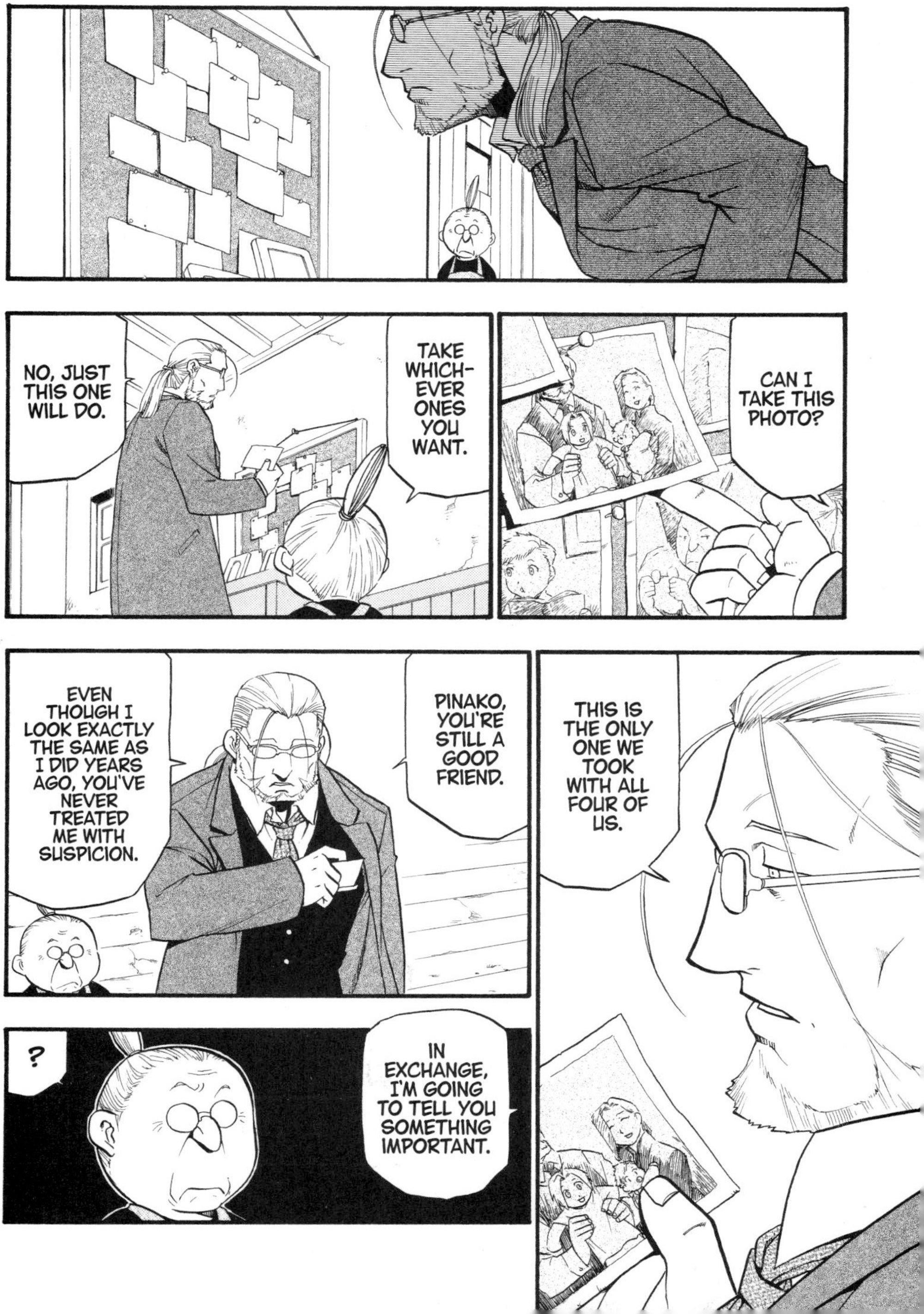
CAN I TAKE THIS PHOTO?
TAKE WHICH-EVER ONES YOU WANT.
NO, JUST THIS ONE WILL DO.
THIS IS THE ONLY ONE WE TOOK WITH ALL FOUR OF US.
PINAKO, YOU'RE STILL A GOOD FRIEND.
EVEN THOUGH I LOOK EXACTLY THE SAME AS I DID YEARS AGO, YOU'VE NEVER TREATED ME WITH SUSPICION.
IN EXCHANGE, I'M GOING TO TELL YOU SOMETHING IMPORTANT.
?

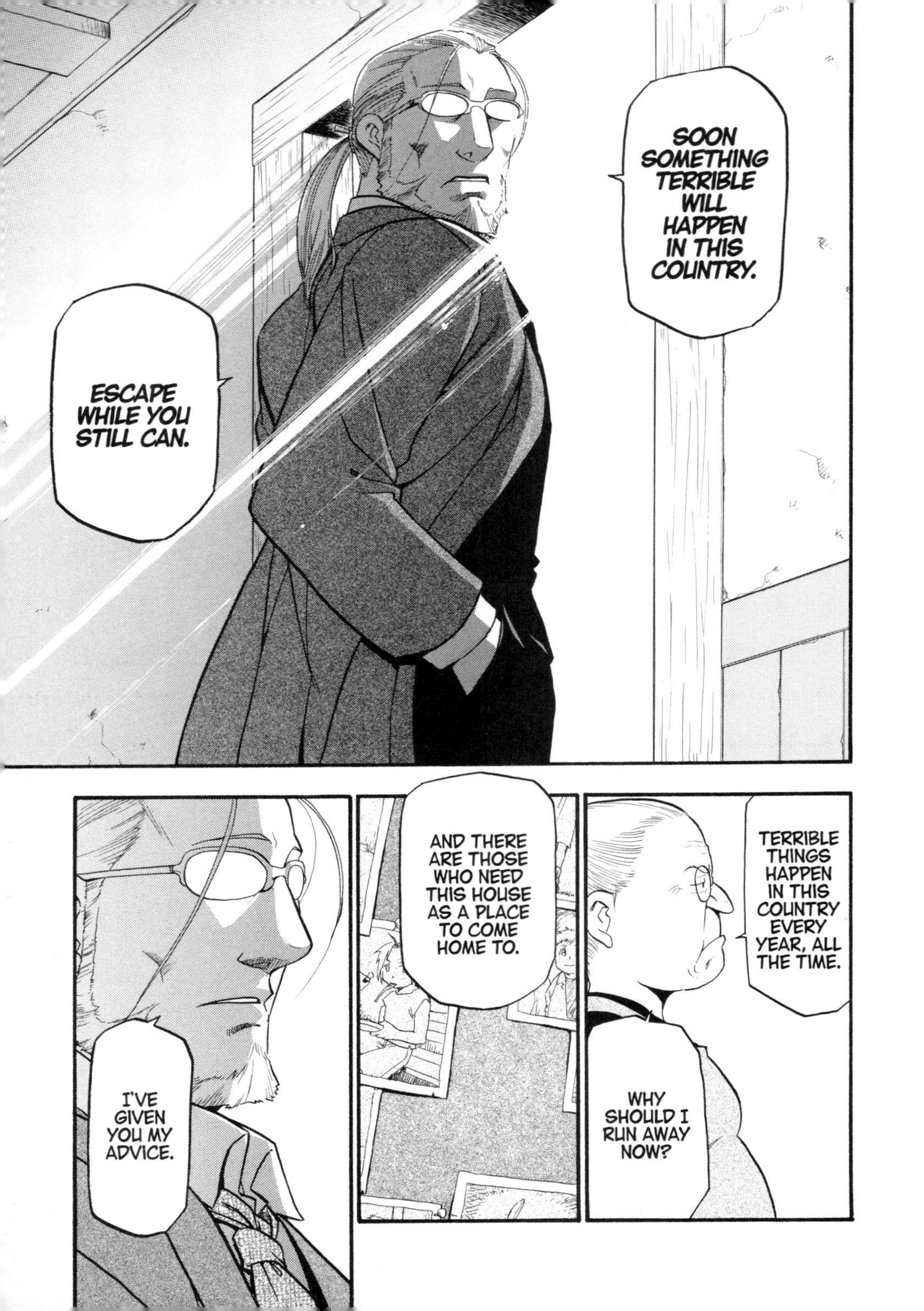
SOON SOMETHING TERRIBLE WILL HAPPEN IN THIS COUNTRY.
ESCAPE WHILE YOU STILL CAN.
TERRIBLE THINGS HAPPEN IN THIS COUNTRY EVERY YEAR, ALL THE TIME.
WHY SHOULD I RUN AWAY NOW?
AND THERE ARE THOSE WHO NEED THIS HOUSE AS A PLACE TO COME HOME TO.
I'VE GIVEN YOU MY ADVICE.

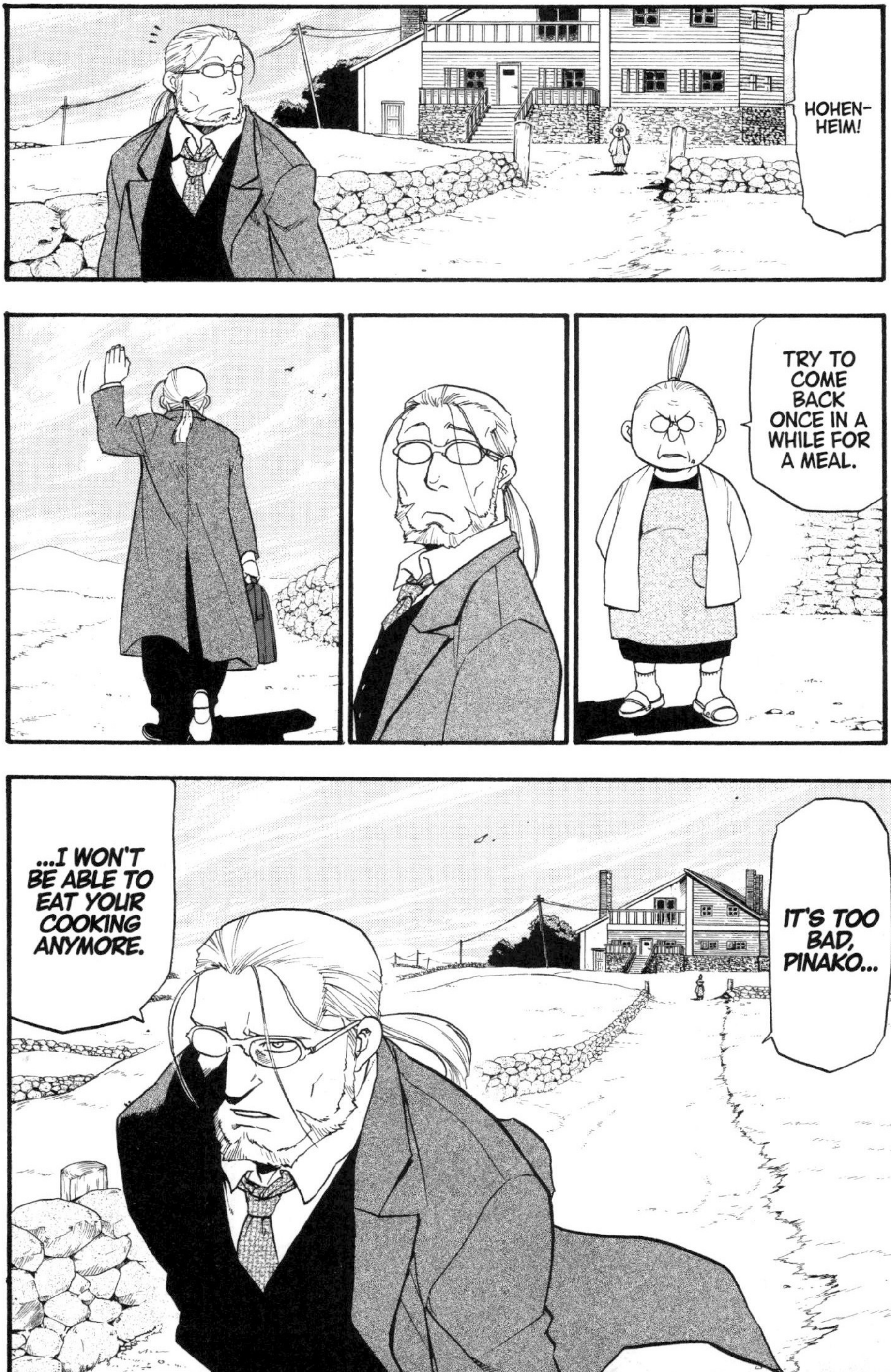
HOHEN-HEIM!
TRY TO COME BACK ONCE IN A WHILE FOR A MEAL.
IT'S TOO BAD, PINAKO...
...I WON'T BE ABLE TO EAT YOUR COOKING ANYMORE.

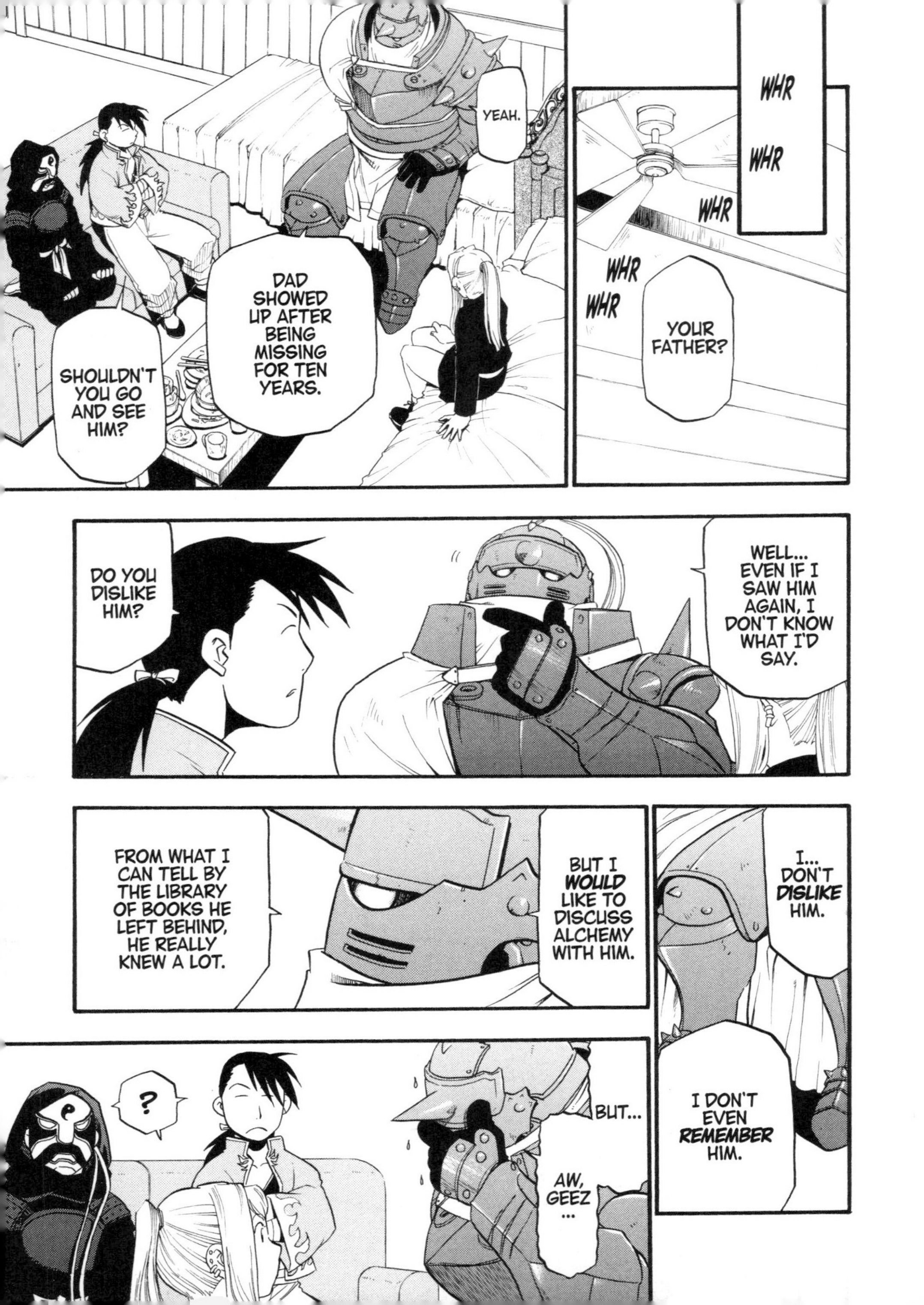
WHR
WHR
WHR
WHR
WHR
YOUR FATHER?
YEAH.
DAD SHOWED UP AFTER BEING MISSING FOR TEN YEARS.
SHOULDN'T YOU GO AND SEE HIM?
WELL... EVEN IF I SAW HIM AGAIN, I DON'T KNOW WHAT I'D SAY.
DO YOU DISLIKE HIM?
I... DON'T **DISLIKE** HIM.
I DON'T EVEN **REMEMBER** HIM.
BUT I **WOULD** LIKE TO DISCUSS ALCHEMY WITH HIM.
FROM WHAT I CAN TELL BY THE LIBRARY OF BOOKS HE LEFT BEHIND, HE REALLY KNEW A LOT.
BUT...
AW, GEEZ...
?

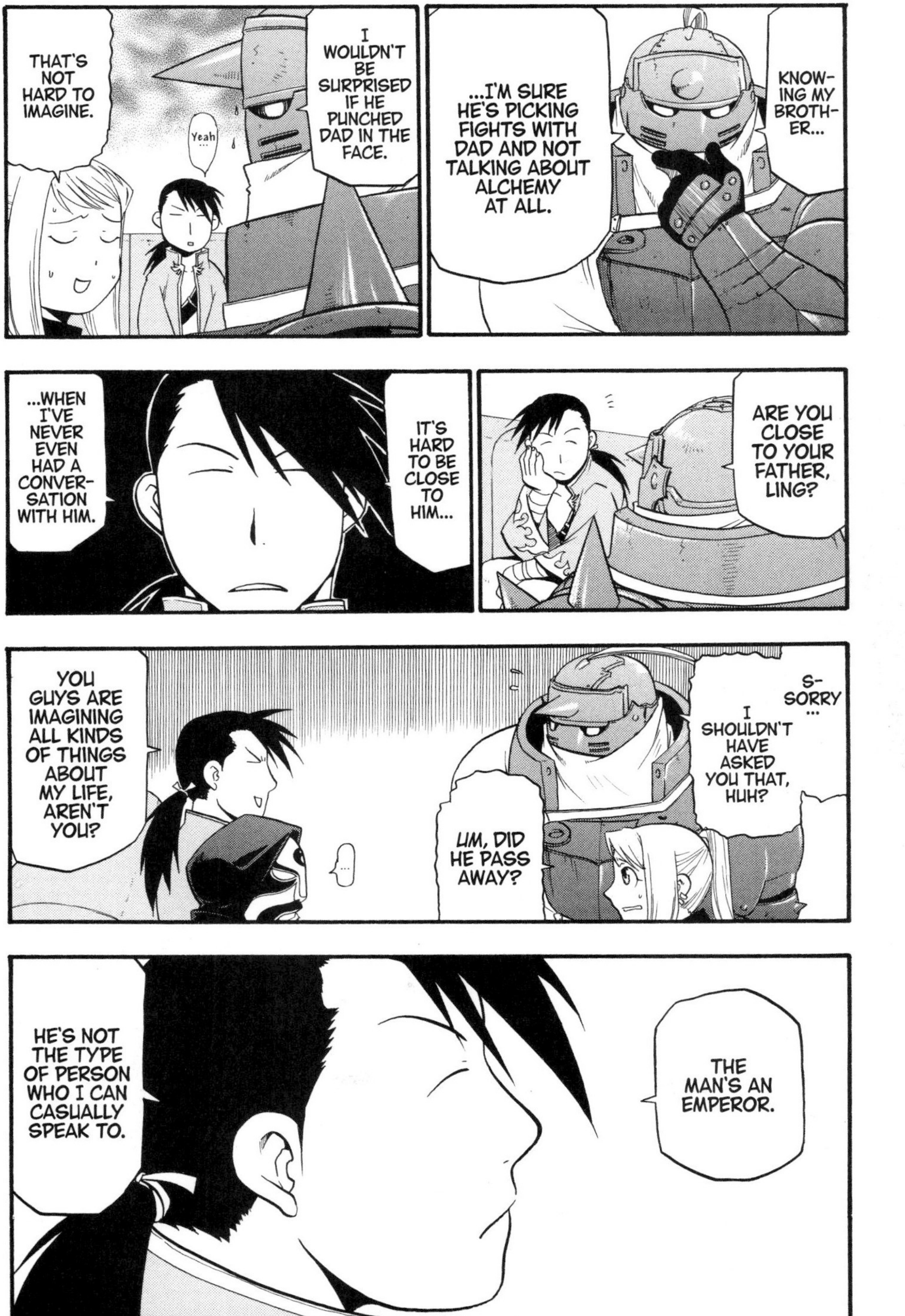
KNOWING MY BROTHER...
...I'M SURE HE'S PICKING FIGHTS WITH DAD AND NOT TALKING ABOUT ALCHEMY AT ALL.
I WOULDN'T BE SURPRISED IF HE PUNCHED DAD IN THE FACE.
Yeah...
THAT'S NOT HARD TO IMAGINE.
ARE YOU CLOSE TO YOUR FATHER, LING?
IT'S HARD TO BE CLOSE TO HIM...
...WHEN I'VE NEVER EVEN HAD A CONVERSATION WITH HIM.
S-SORRY... I SHOULDN'T HAVE ASKED YOU THAT, HUH?
UM, DID HE PASS AWAY?
...
YOU GUYS ARE IMAGINING ALL KINDS OF THINGS ABOUT MY LIFE, AREN'T YOU?
THE MAN'S AN EMPEROR.
HE'S NOT THE TYPE OF PERSON WHO I CAN CASUALLY SPEAK TO.

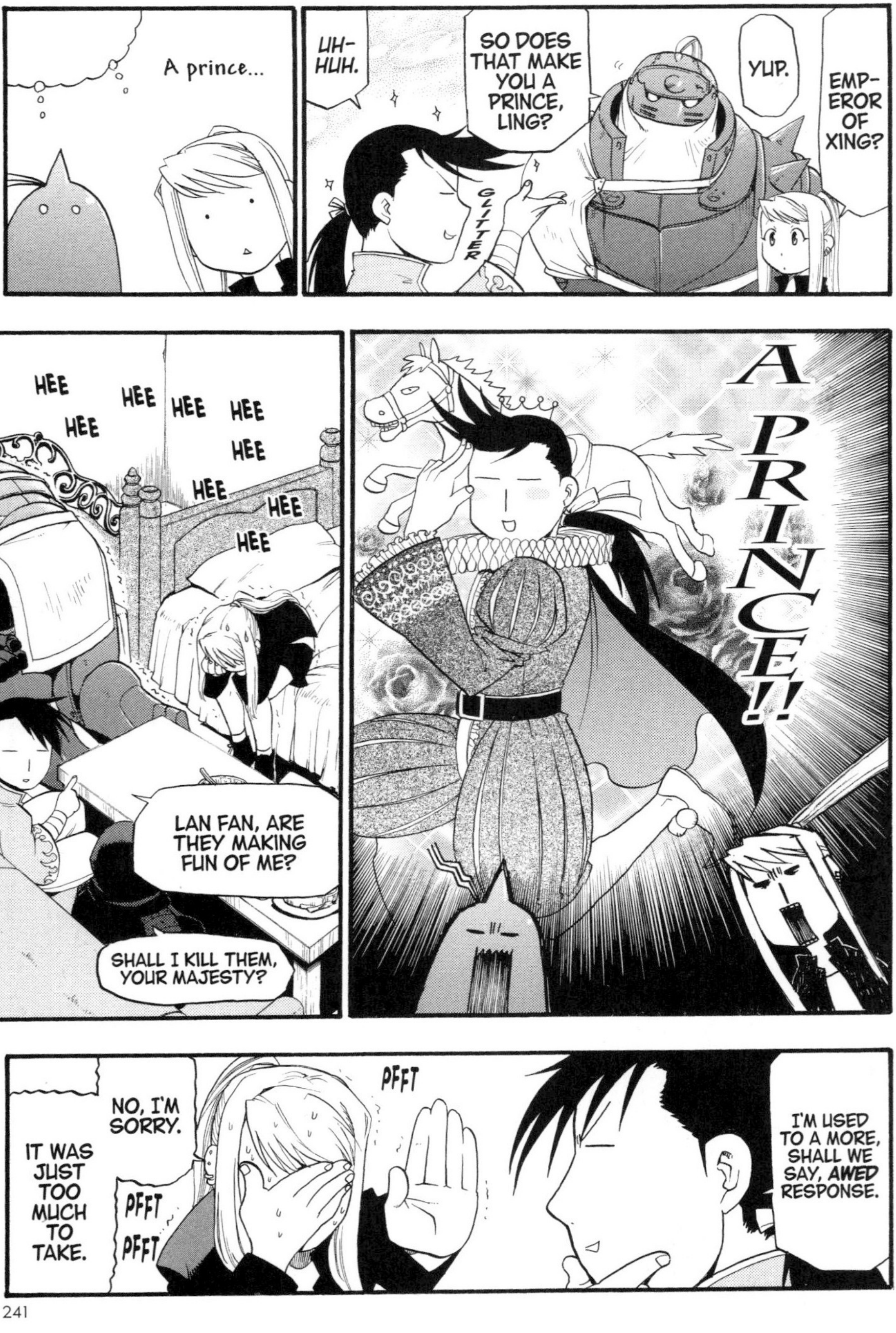
EMP-EROR OF XING?
YUP.
SO DOES THAT MAKE YOU A PRINCE, LING?
UH-HUH.
GLITTER
A prince...
A PRINCE!!
HEE HEE HEE HEE HEE HEE HEE HEE HEE
LAN FAN, ARE THEY MAKING FUN OF ME?
SHALL I KILL THEM, YOUR MAJESTY?
I'M USED TO A MORE, SHALL WE SAY, AWED RESPONSE.
PFFT
NO, I'M SORRY.
IT WAS JUST TOO MUCH TO TAKE.
PFFT
PFFT

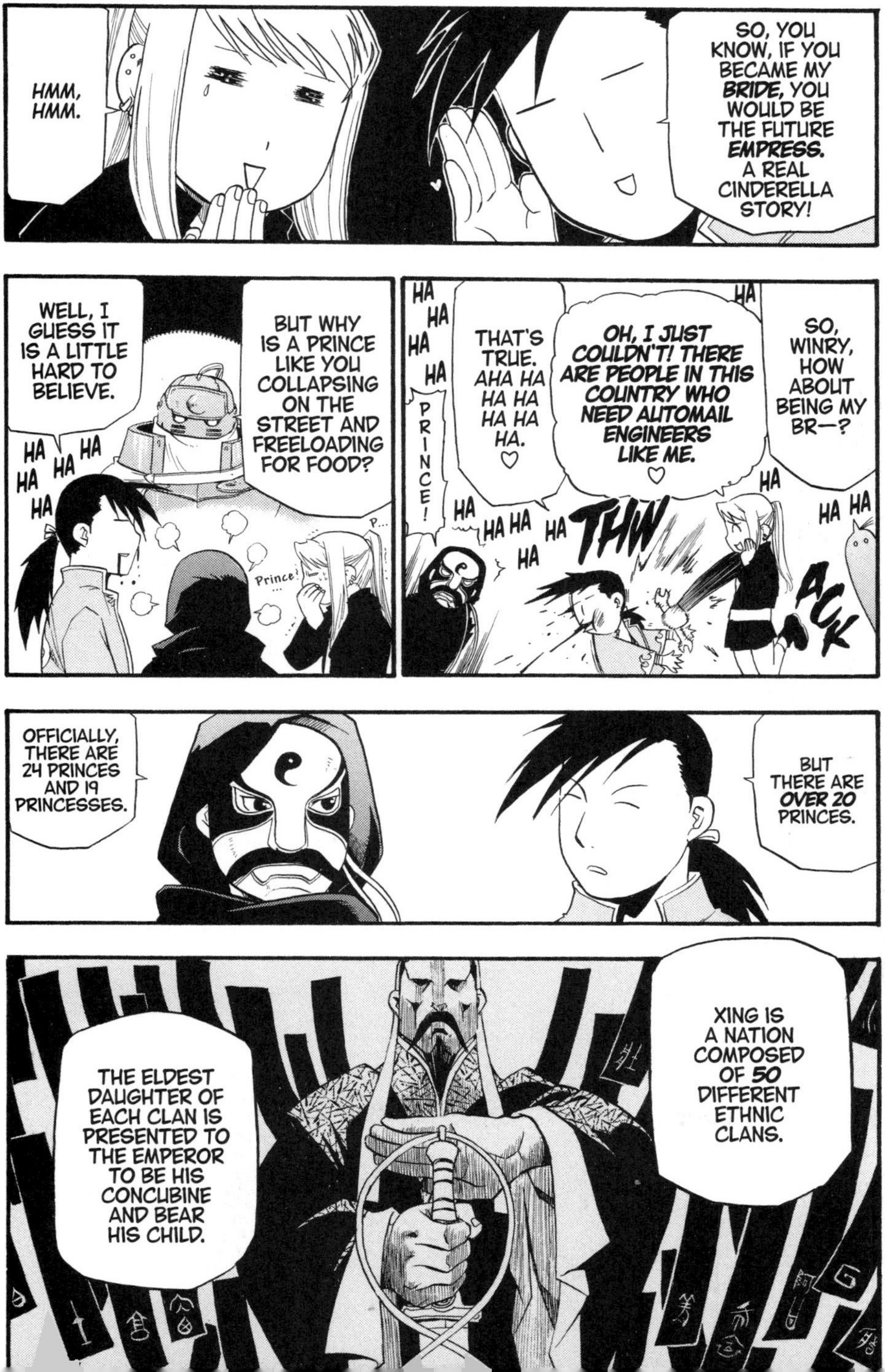
SO, YOU KNOW, IF YOU BECAME MY BRIDE, YOU WOULD BE THE FUTURE EMPRESS. A REAL CINDERELLA STORY!
HMM, HMM.
SO, WINRY, HOW ABOUT BEING MY BR—?
HA HA HA
OH, I JUST COULDN'T! THERE ARE PEOPLE IN THIS COUNTRY WHO NEED AUTOMAIL ENGINEERS LIKE ME.
THAT'S TRUE. AHA HA HA HA HA HA HA.
HA HA HA HA HA HA HA HA HA
PRINCE!
THW
ACK
BUT WHY IS A PRINCE LIKE YOU COLLAPSING ON THE STREET AND FREELOADING FOR FOOD?
WELL, I GUESS IT IS A LITTLE HARD TO BELIEVE.
HA HA HA HA HA HA
P...
Prince!
BUT THERE ARE OVER 20 PRINCES.
OFFICIALLY, THERE ARE 24 PRINCES AND 19 PRINCESSES.
XING IS A NATION COMPOSED OF 50 DIFFERENT ETHNIC CLANS.
THE ELDEST DAUGHTER OF EACH CLAN IS PRESENTED TO THE EMPEROR TO BE HIS CONCUBINE AND BEAR HIS CHILD.

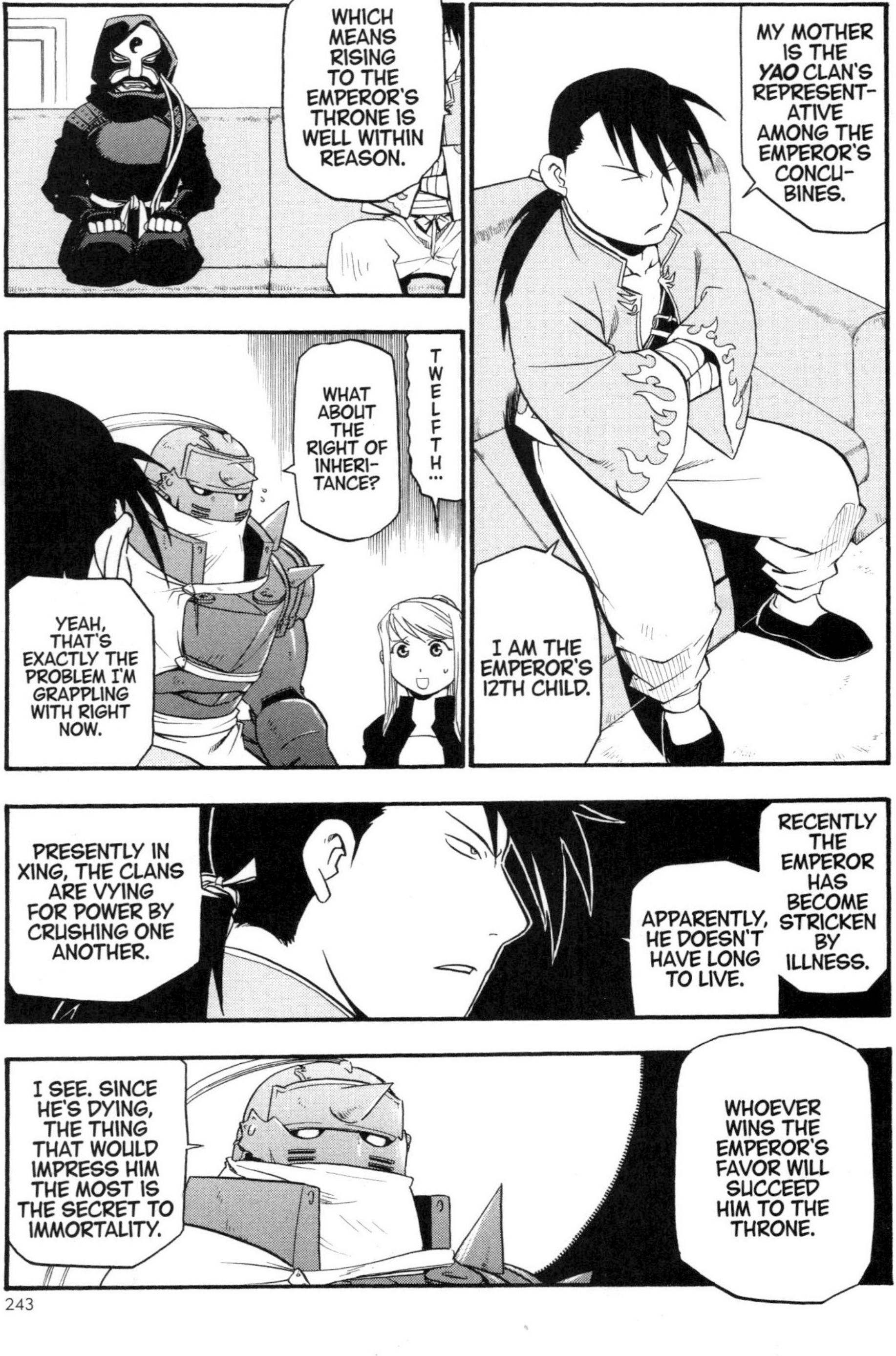
MY MOTHER IS THE *YAO* CLAN'S REPRESENTATIVE AMONG THE EMPEROR'S CONCUBINES.
I AM THE EMPEROR'S 12TH CHILD.
WHICH MEANS RISING TO THE EMPEROR'S THRONE IS WELL WITHIN REASON.
TWELFTH...
WHAT ABOUT THE RIGHT OF INHERITANCE?
YEAH, THAT'S EXACTLY THE PROBLEM I'M GRAPPLING WITH RIGHT NOW.
RECENTLY THE EMPEROR HAS BECOME STRICKEN BY ILLNESS.
APPARENTLY, HE DOESN'T HAVE LONG TO LIVE.
PRESENTLY IN XING, THE CLANS ARE VYING FOR POWER BY CRUSHING ONE ANOTHER.
WHOEVER WINS THE EMPEROR'S FAVOR WILL SUCCEED HIM TO THE THRONE.
I SEE. SINCE HE'S DYING, THE THING THAT WOULD IMPRESS HIM THE MOST IS THE SECRET TO IMMORTALITY.

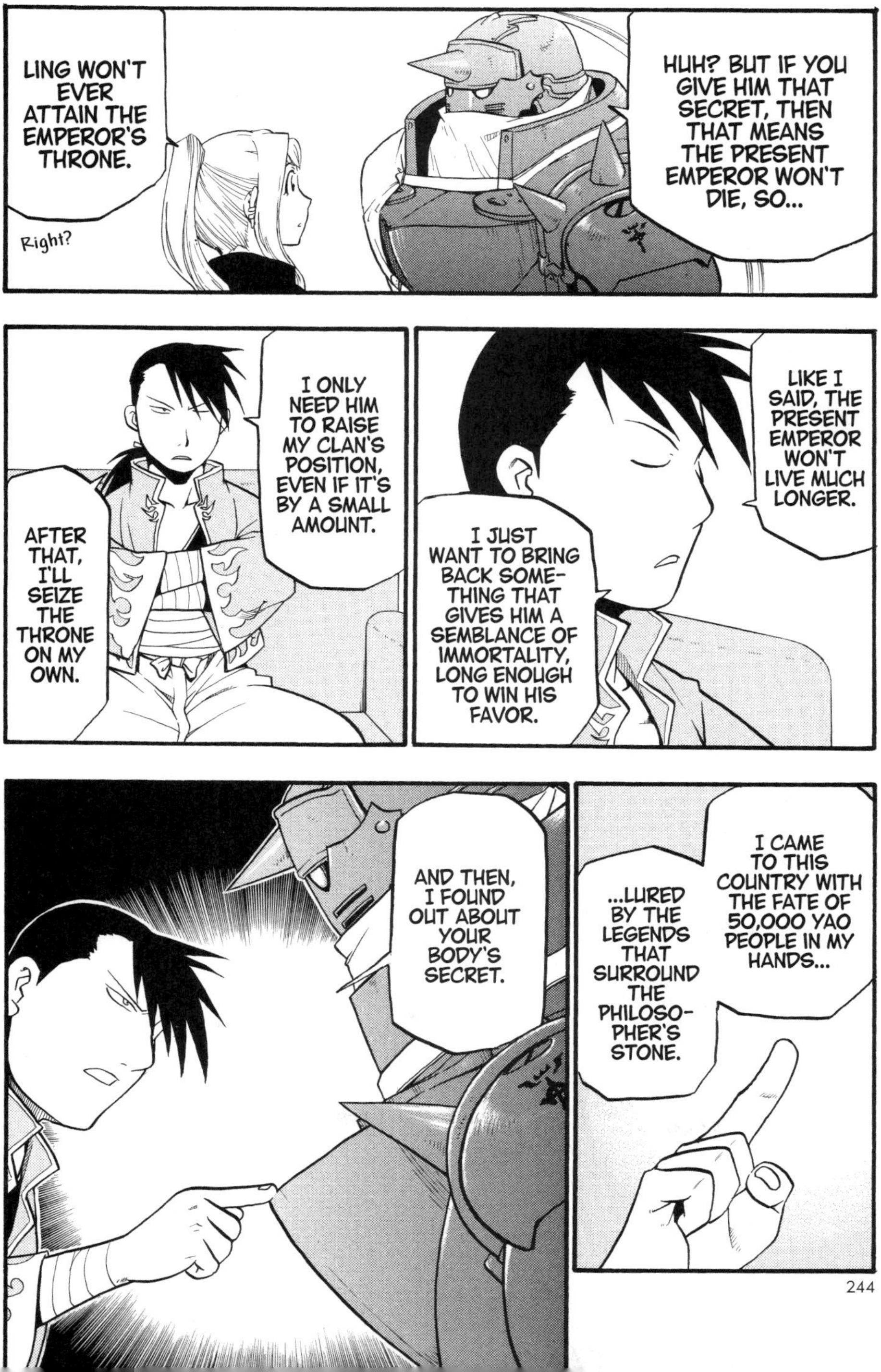
HUH? BUT IF YOU GIVE HIM THAT SECRET, THEN THAT MEANS THE PRESENT EMPEROR WON'T DIE, SO...
LING WON'T EVER ATTAIN THE EMPEROR'S THRONE.
Right?
LIKE I SAID, THE PRESENT EMPEROR WON'T LIVE MUCH LONGER.
I JUST WANT TO BRING BACK SOME-THING THAT GIVES HIM A SEMBLANCE OF IMMORTALITY, LONG ENOUGH TO WIN HIS FAVOR.
I ONLY NEED HIM TO RAISE MY CLAN'S POSITION, EVEN IF IT'S BY A SMALL AMOUNT.
AFTER THAT, I'LL SEIZE THE THRONE ON MY OWN.
I CAME TO THIS COUNTRY WITH THE FATE OF 50,000 YAO PEOPLE IN MY HANDS...
...LURED BY THE LEGENDS THAT SURROUND THE PHILOSO-PHER'S STONE.
AND THEN, I FOUND OUT ABOUT YOUR BODY'S SECRET.

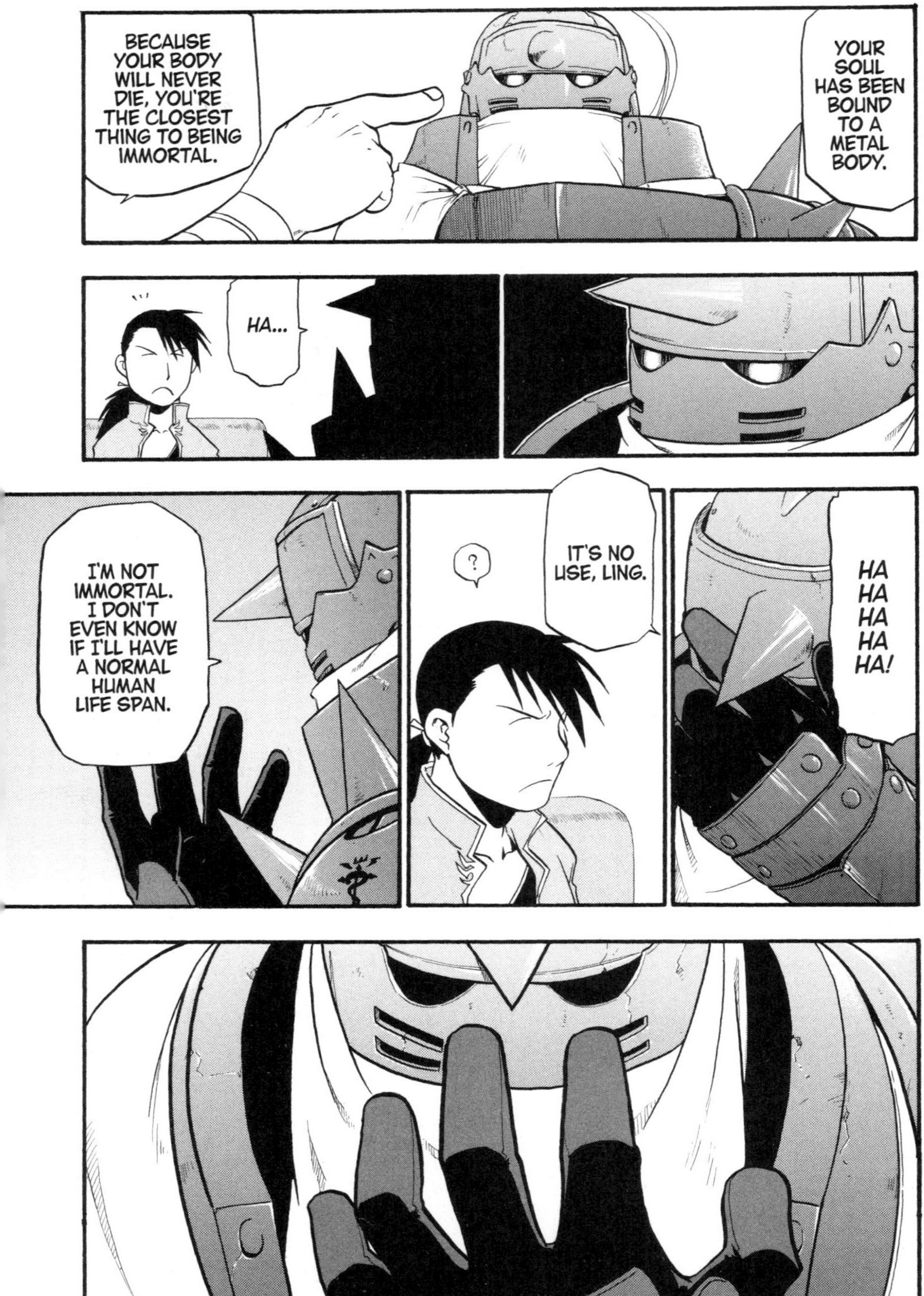
YOUR SOUL HAS BEEN BOUND TO A METAL BODY.
BECAUSE YOUR BODY WILL NEVER DIE, YOU'RE THE CLOSEST THING TO BEING IMMORTAL.
HA...
HA HA HA HA HA!
IT'S NO USE, LING.
?
I'M NOT IMMORTAL. I DON'T EVEN KNOW IF I'LL HAVE A NORMAL HUMAN LIFE SPAN.

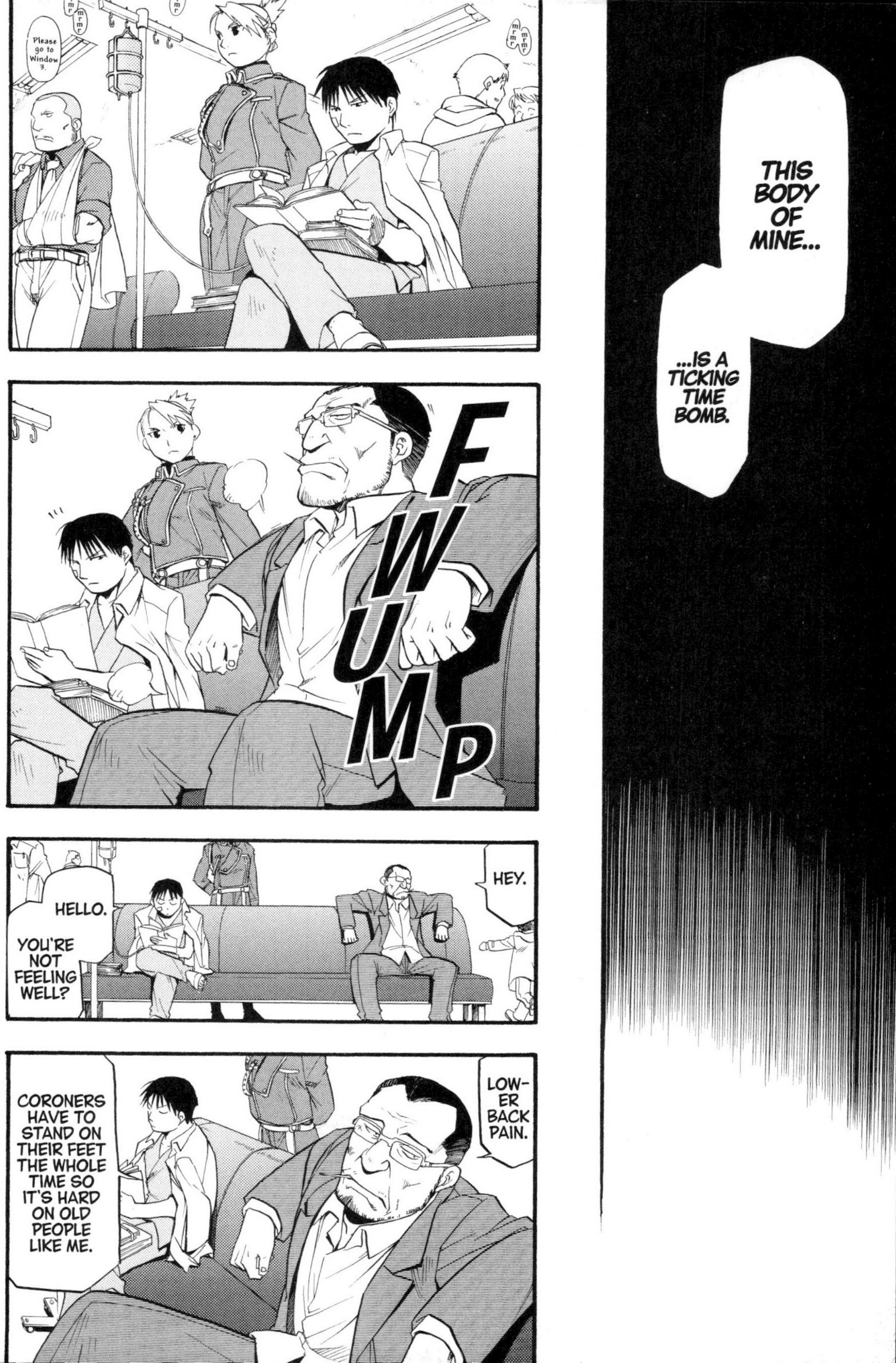
THIS BODY OF MINE...
...IS A TICKING TIME BOMB.
mrmr
mrmr
mrmr
Please go to Window 3.
FWUMP
HEY.
HELLO.
YOU'RE NOT FEELING WELL?
LOW-ER BACK PAIN.
CORONERS HAVE TO STAND ON THEIR FEET THE WHOLE TIME SO IT'S HARD ON OLD PEOPLE LIKE ME.

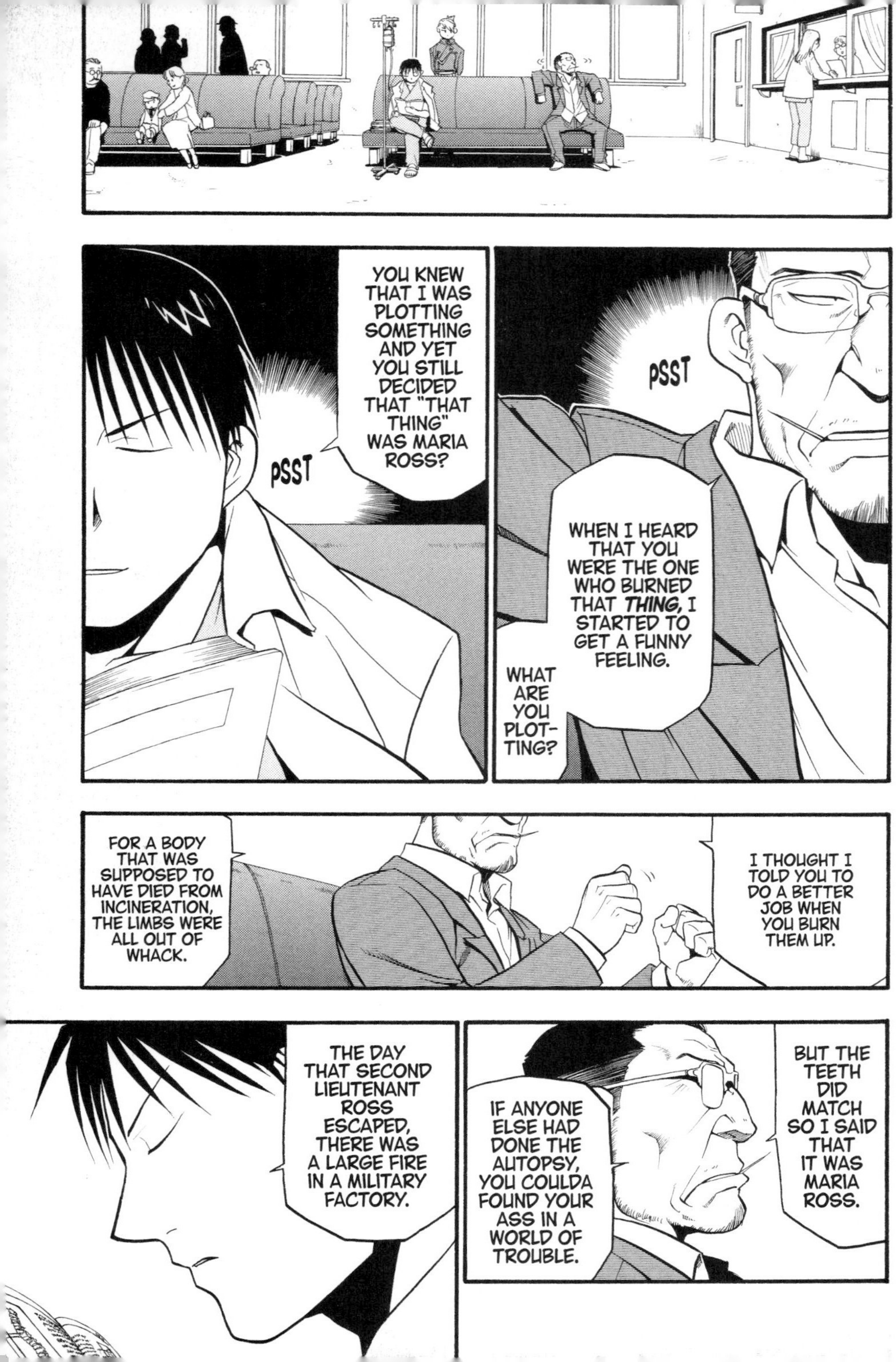
PSST
WHEN I HEARD THAT YOU WERE THE ONE WHO BURNED THAT ***THING,*** I STARTED TO GET A FUNNY FEELING.
WHAT ARE YOU PLOT-TING?
YOU KNEW THAT I WAS PLOTTING SOMETHING AND YET YOU STILL DECIDED THAT "THAT THING" WAS MARIA ROSS?
PSST
I THOUGHT I TOLD YOU TO DO A BETTER JOB WHEN YOU BURN THEM UP.
FOR A BODY THAT WAS SUPPOSED TO HAVE DIED FROM INCINERATION, THE LIMBS WERE ALL OUT OF WHACK.
BUT THE TEETH DID MATCH SO I SAID THAT IT WAS MARIA ROSS.
IF ANYONE ELSE HAD DONE THE AUTOPSY, YOU COULDA FOUND YOUR ASS IN A WORLD OF TROUBLE.
THE DAY THAT SECOND LIEUTENANT ROSS ESCAPED, THERE WAS A LARGE FIRE IN A MILITARY FACTORY.

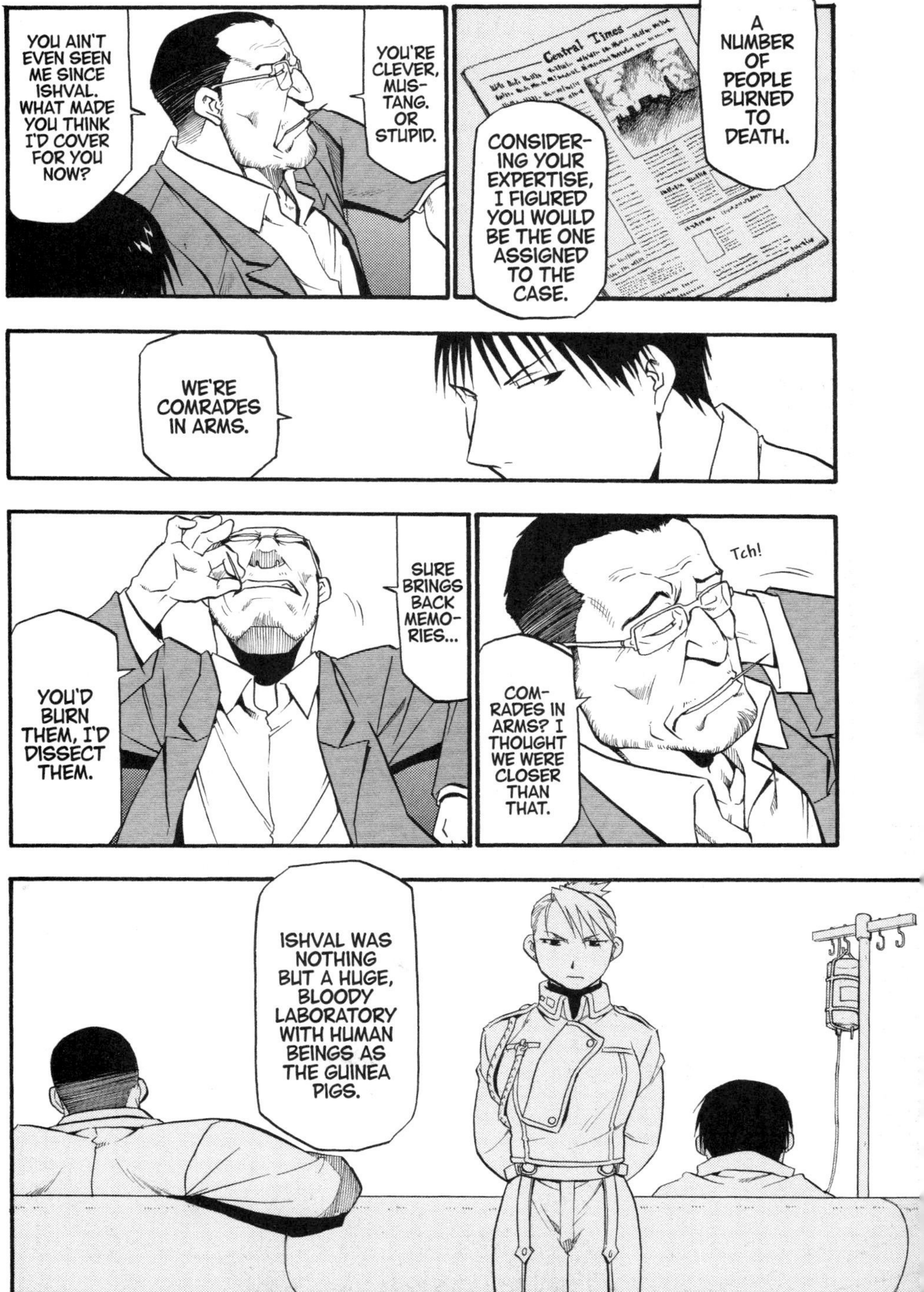
A NUMBER OF PEOPLE BURNED TO DEATH.
Central Times
CONSIDERING YOUR EXPERTISE, I FIGURED YOU WOULD BE THE ONE ASSIGNED TO THE CASE.
YOU'RE CLEVER, MUSTANG. OR STUPID.
YOU AIN'T EVEN SEEN ME SINCE ISHVAL. WHAT MADE YOU THINK I'D COVER FOR YOU NOW?
WE'RE COMRADES IN ARMS.
Tch!
COMRADES IN ARMS? I THOUGHT WE WERE CLOSER THAN THAT.
SURE BRINGS BACK MEMORIES...
YOU'D BURN THEM, I'D DISSECT THEM.
ISHVAL WAS NOTHING BUT A HUGE, BLOODY LABORATORY WITH HUMAN BEINGS AS THE GUINEA PIGS.

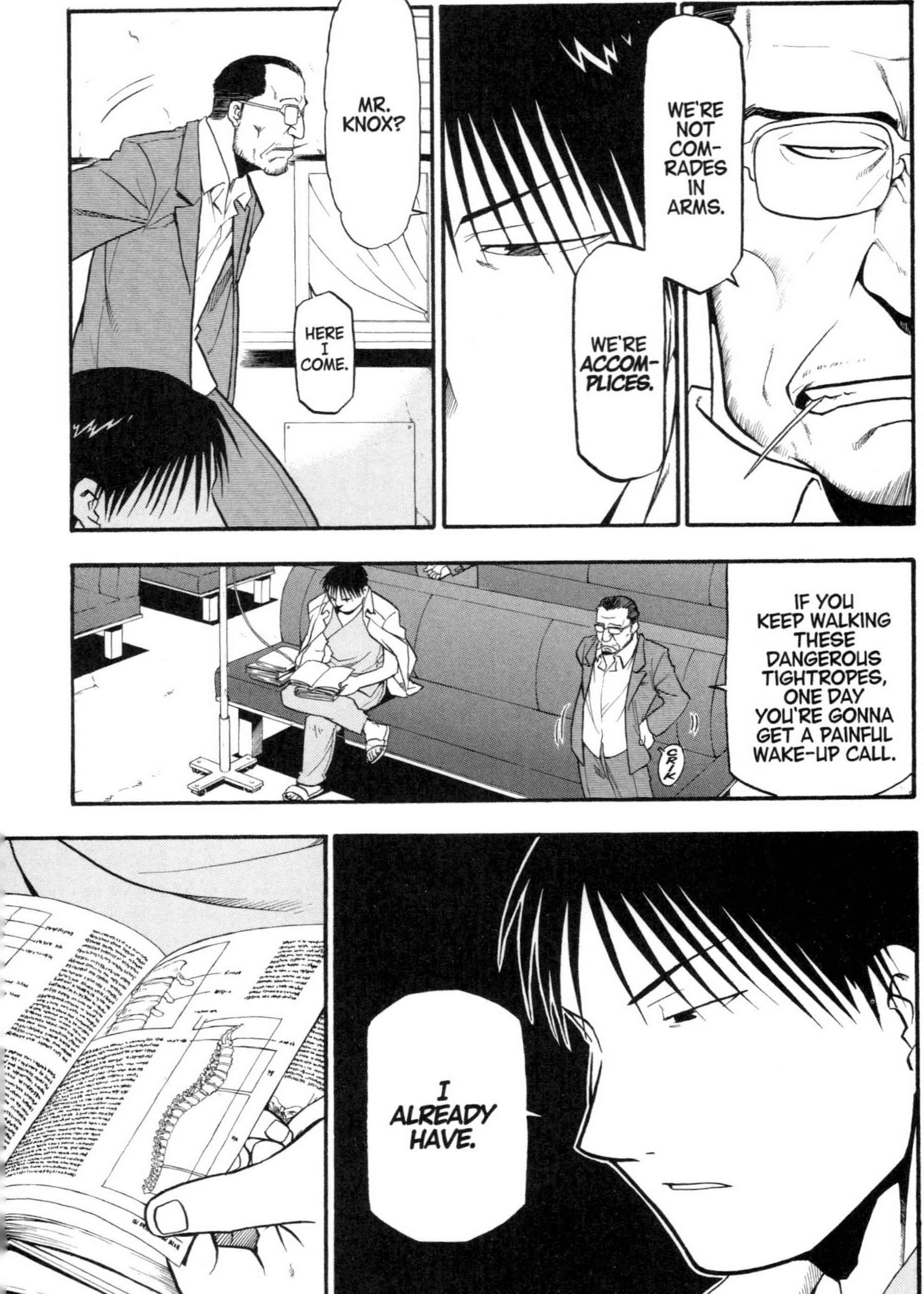
WE'RE NOT COM-RADES IN ARMS.
WE'RE ACCOMPLICES.
MR. KNOX?
HERE I COME.
IF YOU KEEP WALKING THESE DANGEROUS TIGHTROPES, ONE DAY YOU'RE GONNA GET A PAINFUL WAKE-UP CALL.
CRIK
I ALREADY HAVE.

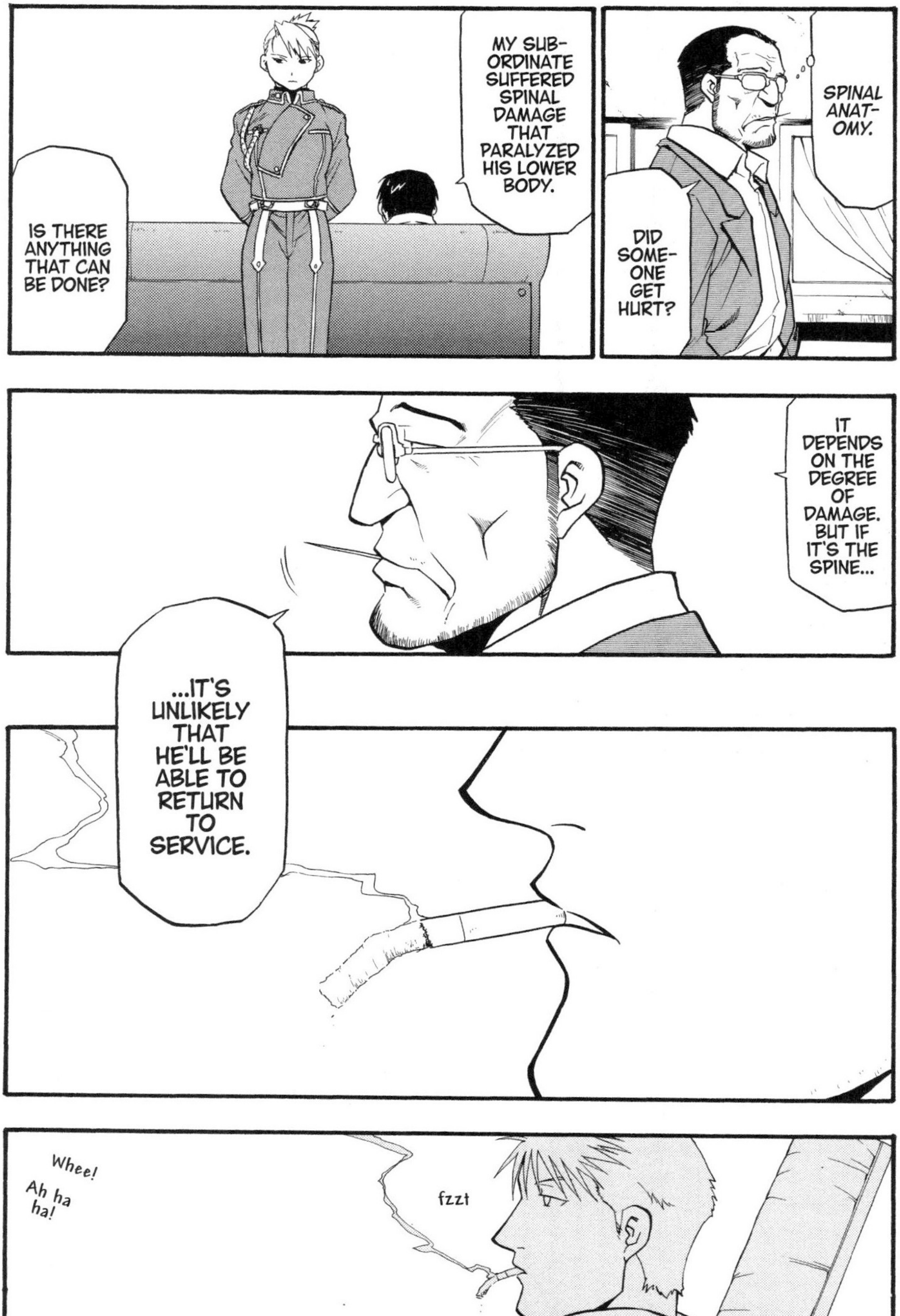
SPINAL ANATOMY.
DID SOMEONE GET HURT?
MY SUBORDINATE SUFFERED SPINAL DAMAGE THAT PARALYZED HIS LOWER BODY.
IS THERE ANYTHING THAT CAN BE DONE?
IT DEPENDS ON THE DEGREE OF DAMAGE. BUT IF IT'S THE SPINE...
...IT'S UNLIKELY THAT HE'LL BE ABLE TO RETURN TO SERVICE.
fzzt
Whee!
Ah ha ha!

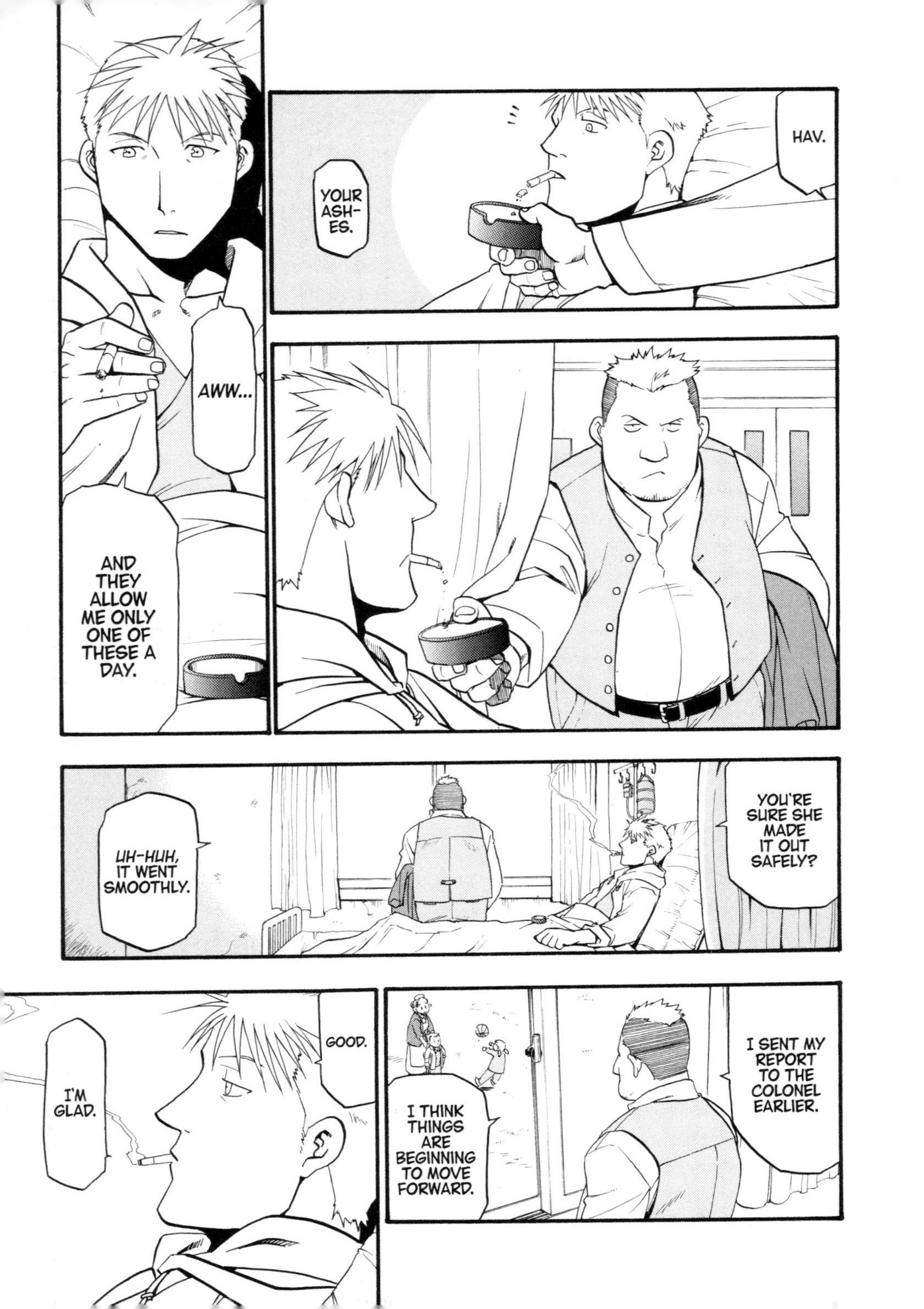
HAV.
YOUR ASHES.
AWW...
AND THEY ALLOW ME ONLY ONE OF THESE A DAY.
YOU'RE SURE SHE MADE IT OUT SAFELY?
UH-HUH, IT WENT SMOOTHLY.
I SENT MY REPORT TO THE COLONEL EARLIER.
I THINK THINGS ARE BEGINNING TO MOVE FORWARD.
GOOD.
I'M GLAD.

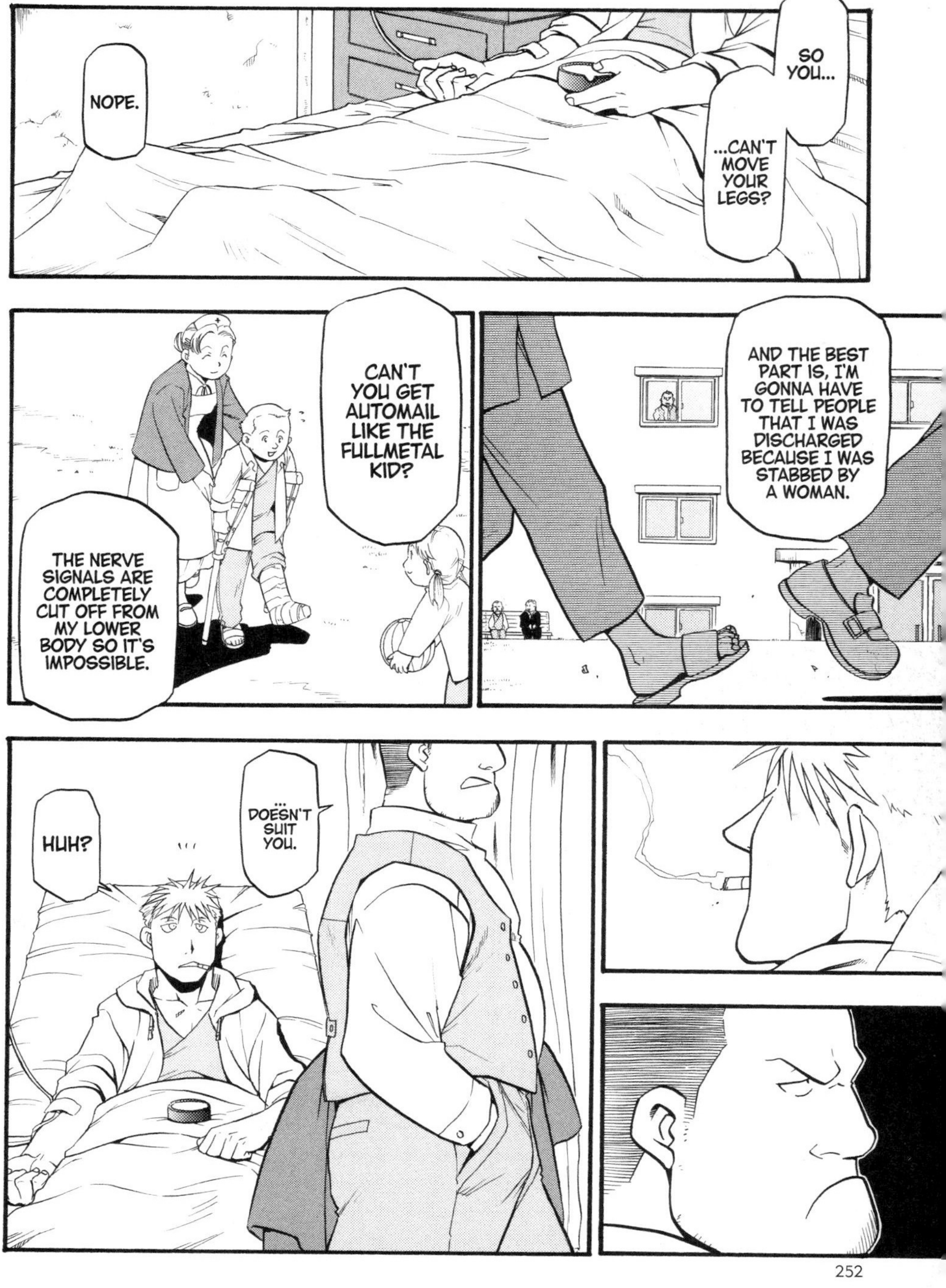
SO YOU...
...CAN'T MOVE YOUR LEGS?
NOPE.
AND THE BEST PART IS, I'M GONNA HAVE TO TELL PEOPLE THAT I WAS DISCHARGED BECAUSE I WAS STABBED BY A WOMAN.
CAN'T YOU GET AUTOMAIL LIKE THE FULLMETAL KID?
THE NERVE SIGNALS ARE COMPLETELY CUT OFF FROM MY LOWER BODY SO IT'S IMPOSSIBLE.
...DOESN'T SUIT YOU.
HUH?

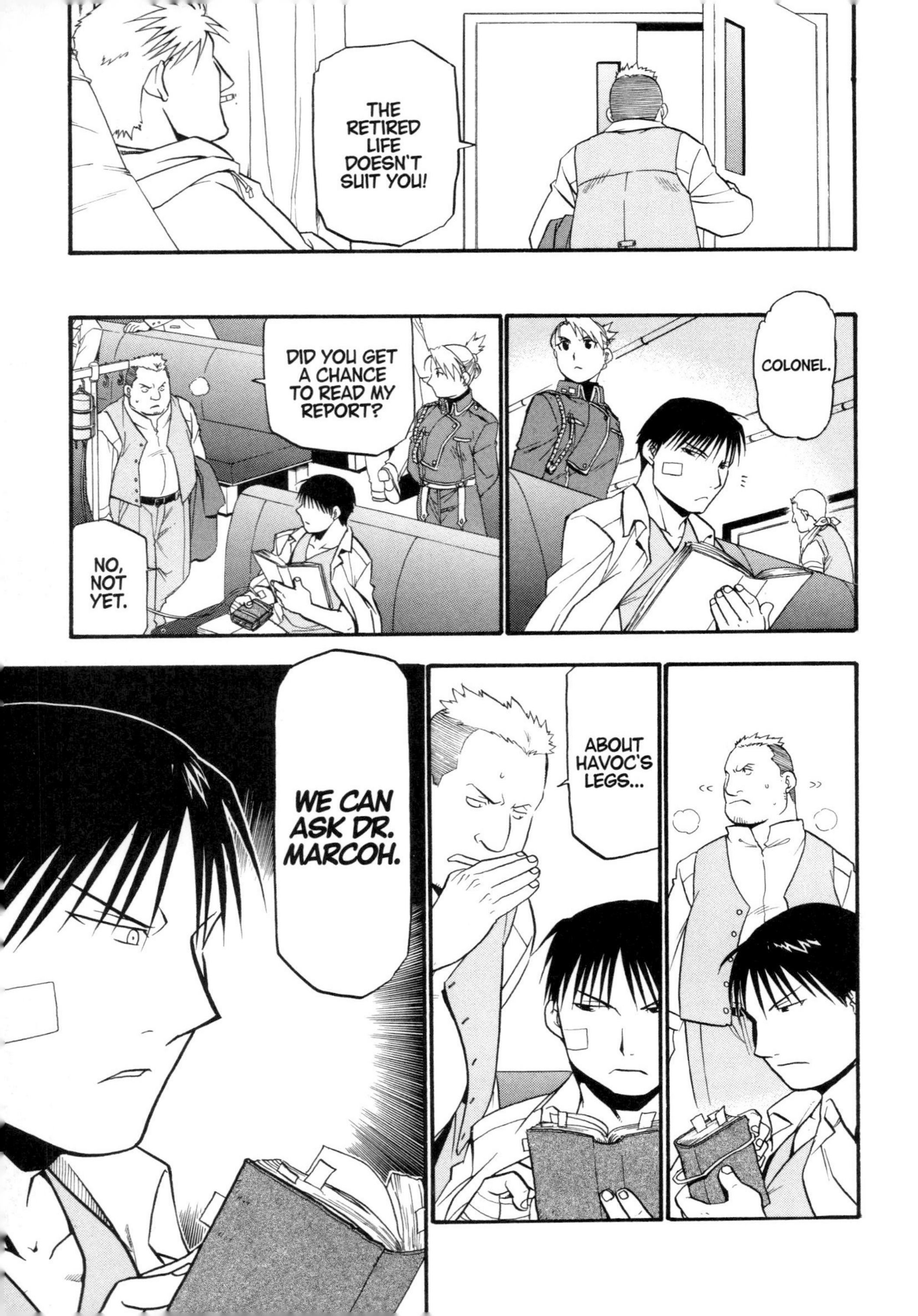
THE RETIRED LIFE DOESN'T SUIT YOU!
COLONEL.
DID YOU GET A CHANCE TO READ MY REPORT?
NO, NOT YET.
ABOUT HAVOC'S LEGS...
WE CAN ASK DR. MARCOH.

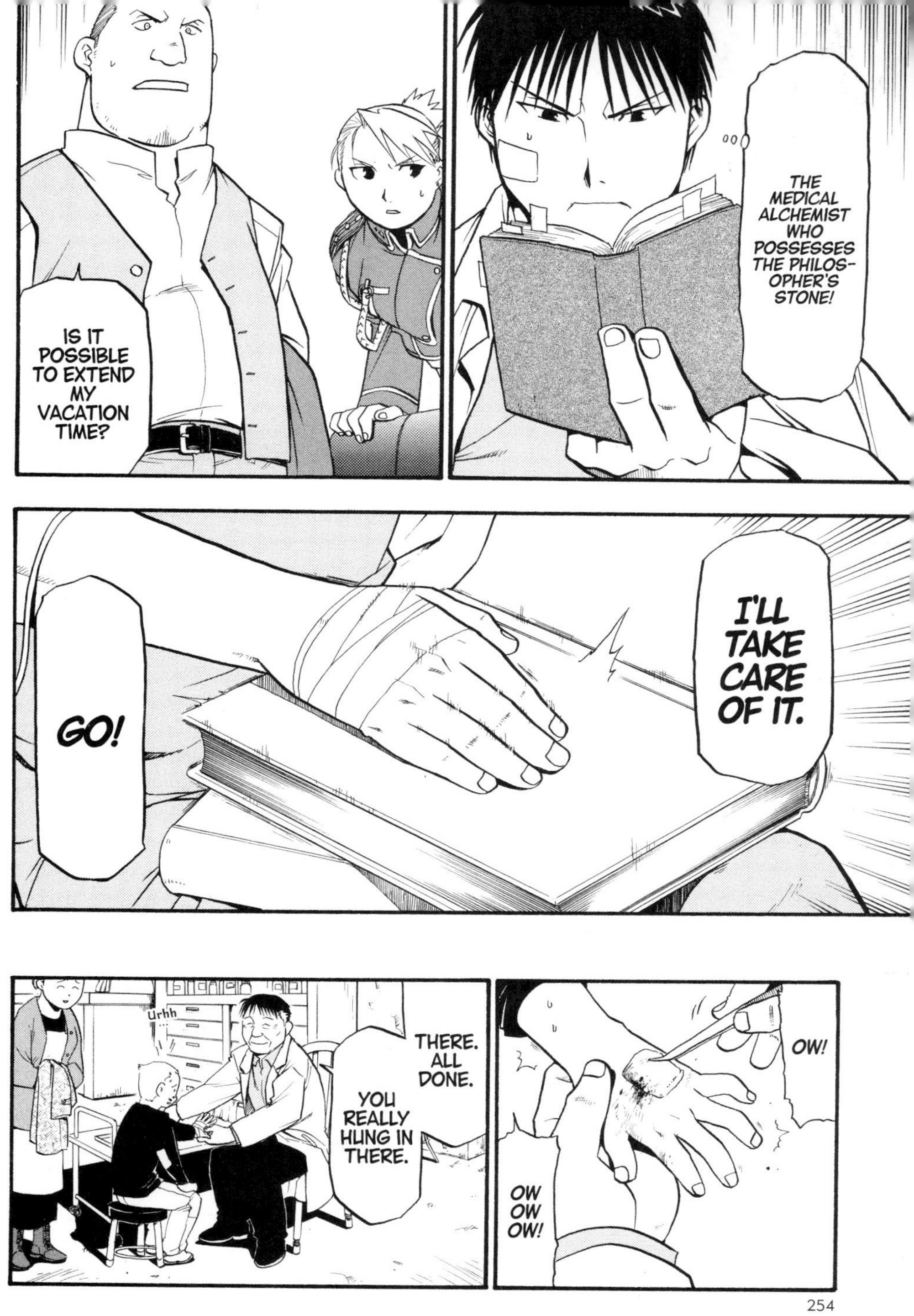
THE MEDICAL ALCHEMIST WHO POSSESSES THE PHILOSOPHER'S STONE!
IS IT POSSIBLE TO EXTEND MY VACATION TIME?
I'LL TAKE CARE OF IT.
GO!
OW!
OW OW OW!
THERE. ALL DONE.
YOU REALLY HUNG IN THERE.
Urhh...

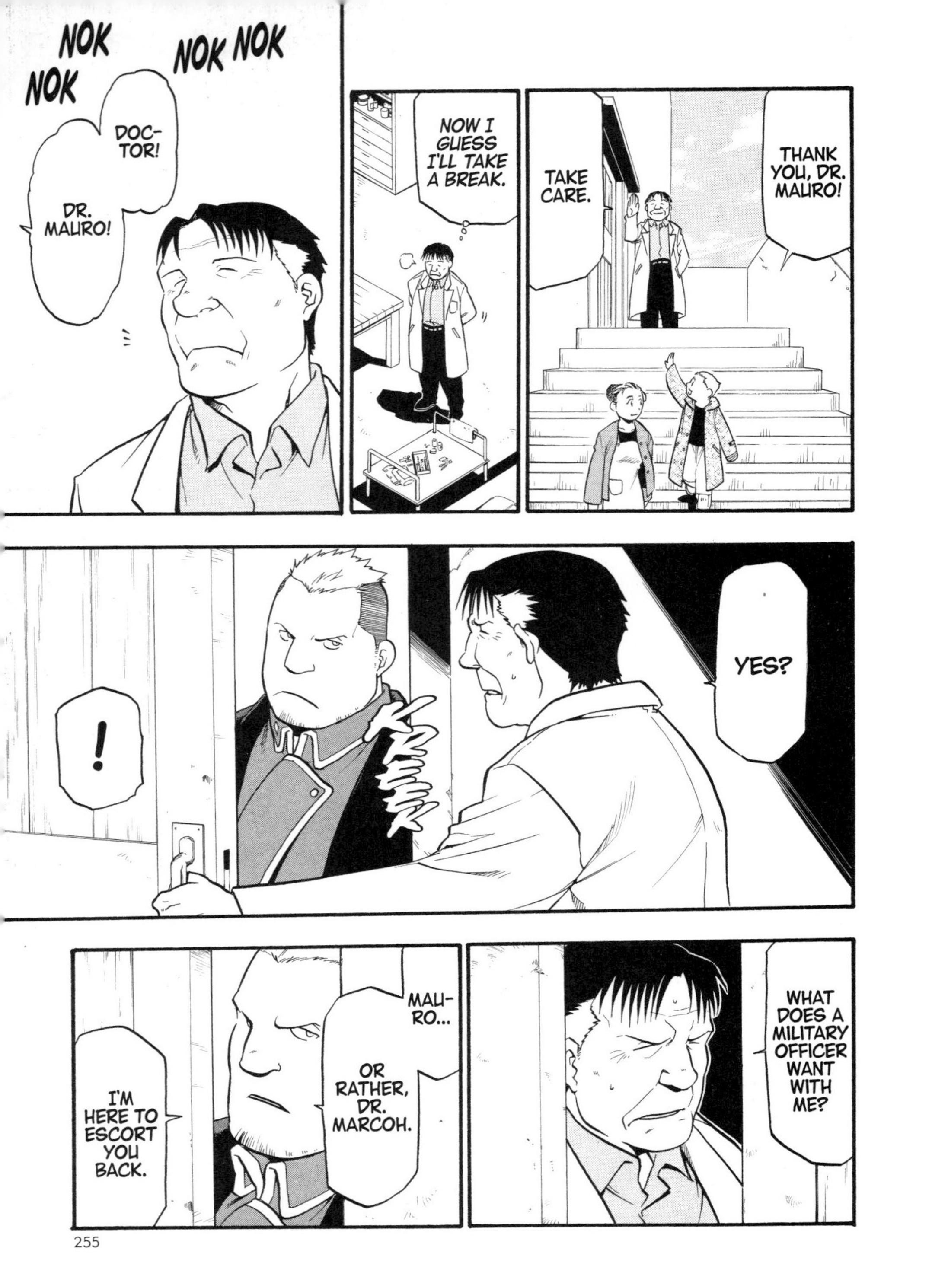
THANK YOU, DR. MAURO!
TAKE CARE.
NOW I GUESS I'LL TAKE A BREAK.
NOK NOK
NOK NOK
DOC-TOR!
DR. MAURO!
YES?
!
WHAT DOES A MILITARY OFFICER WANT WITH ME?
MAU-RO...
OR RATHER, DR. MARCOH.
I'M HERE TO ESCORT YOU BACK.

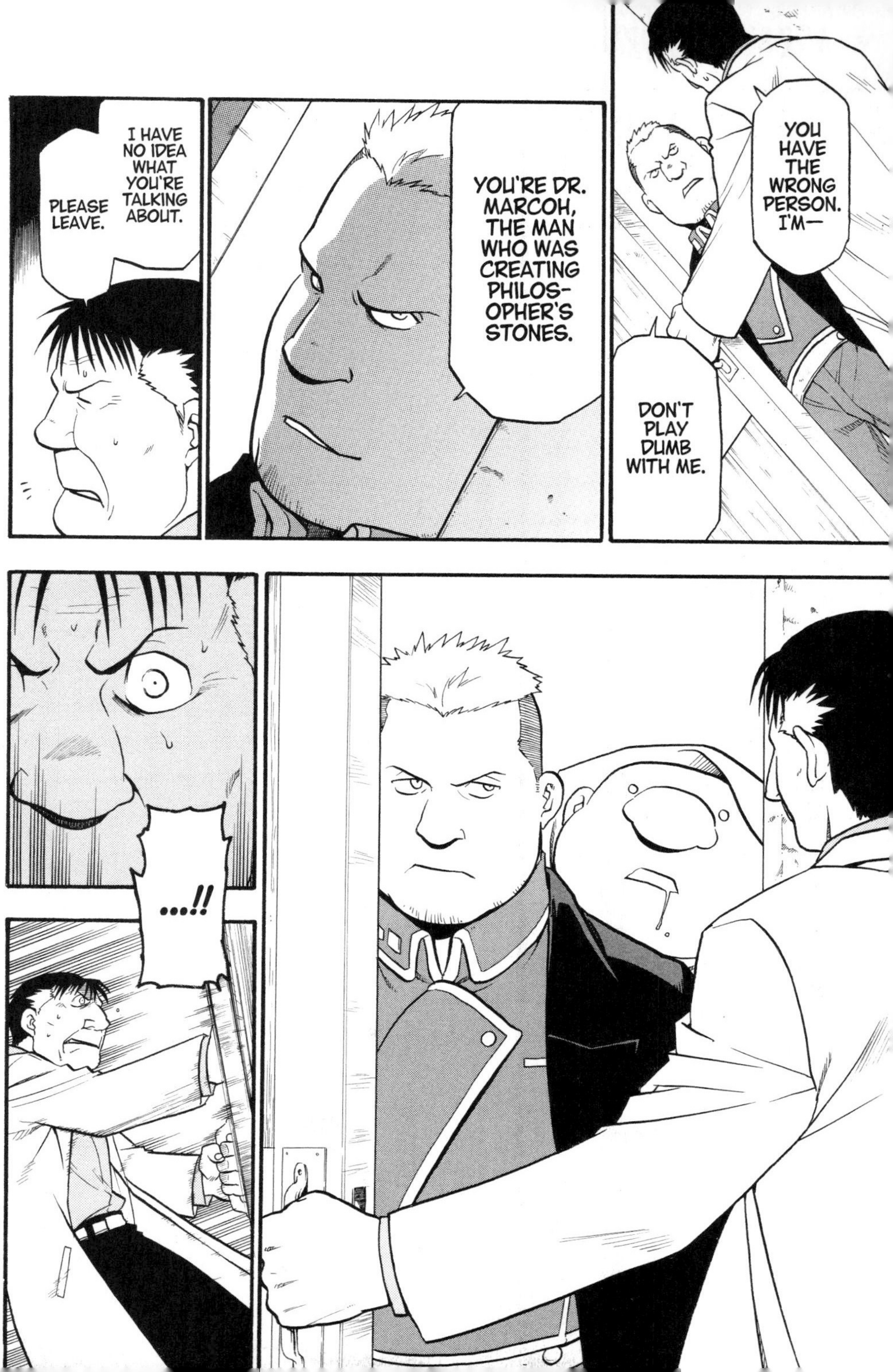
YOU HAVE THE WRONG PERSON. I'M—
DON'T PLAY DUMB WITH ME.
YOU'RE DR. MARCOH, THE MAN WHO WAS CREATING PHILOS-OPHER'S STONES.
I HAVE NO IDEA WHAT YOU'RE TALKING ABOUT.
PLEASE LEAVE.
...!!

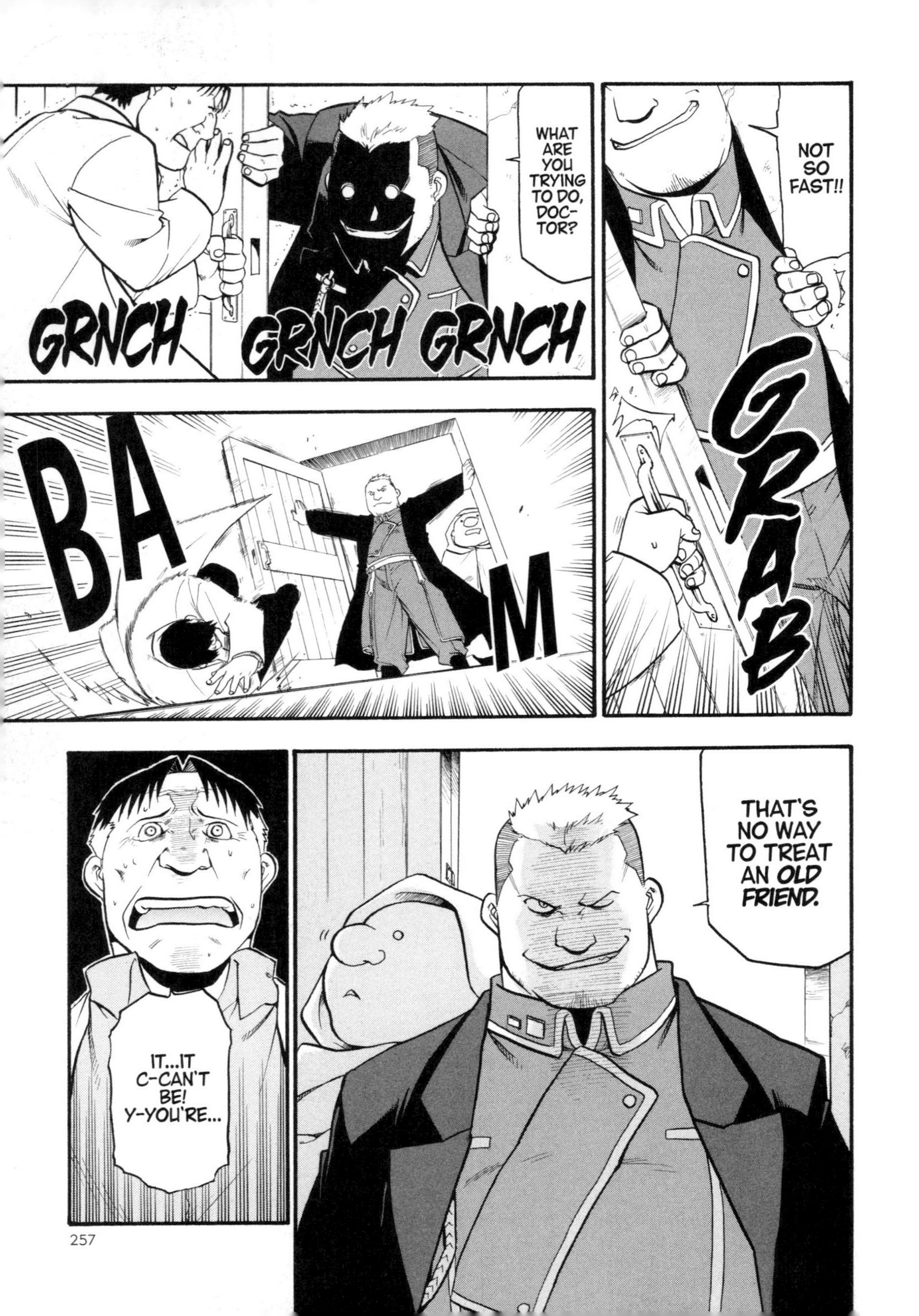
NOT SO FAST!!
GRAB
WHAT ARE YOU TRYING TO DO, DOCTOR?
GRNCH GRNCH
GRNCH
BAM
THAT'S NO WAY TO TREAT AN **OLD FRIEND.**
IT...IT C-CAN'T BE! Y-YOU'RE...

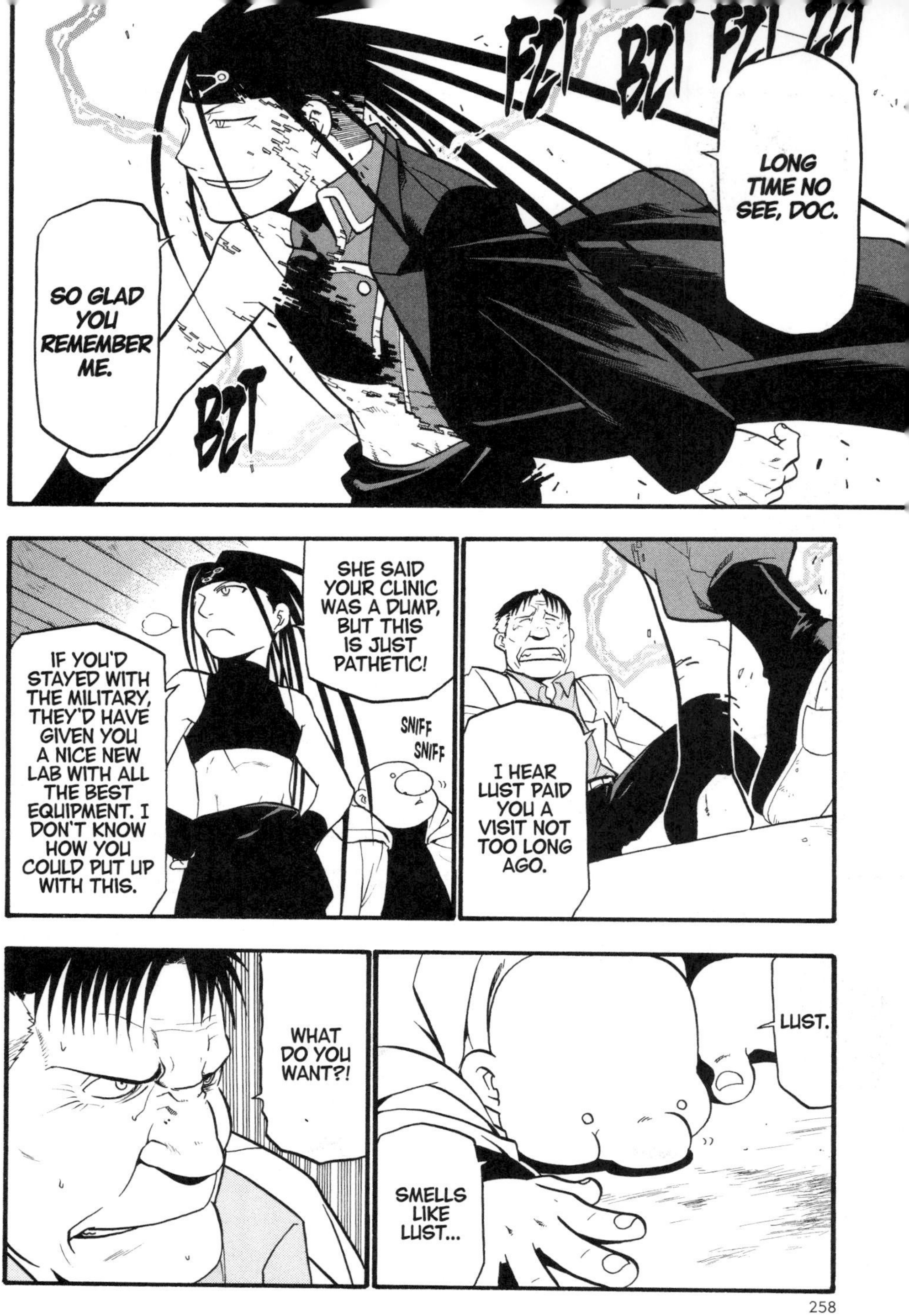
FZT BZT FZT ZZT
LONG TIME NO SEE, DOC.
SO GLAD YOU REMEMBER ME.
BZT
I HEAR LUST PAID YOU A VISIT NOT TOO LONG AGO.
SHE SAID YOUR CLINIC WAS A DUMP, BUT THIS IS JUST PATHETIC!
IF YOU'D STAYED WITH THE MILITARY, THEY'D HAVE GIVEN YOU A NICE NEW LAB WITH ALL THE BEST EQUIPMENT. I DON'T KNOW HOW YOU COULD PUT UP WITH THIS.
SNIFF SNIFF
LUST.
SMELLS LIKE LUST...
WHAT DO YOU WANT?!

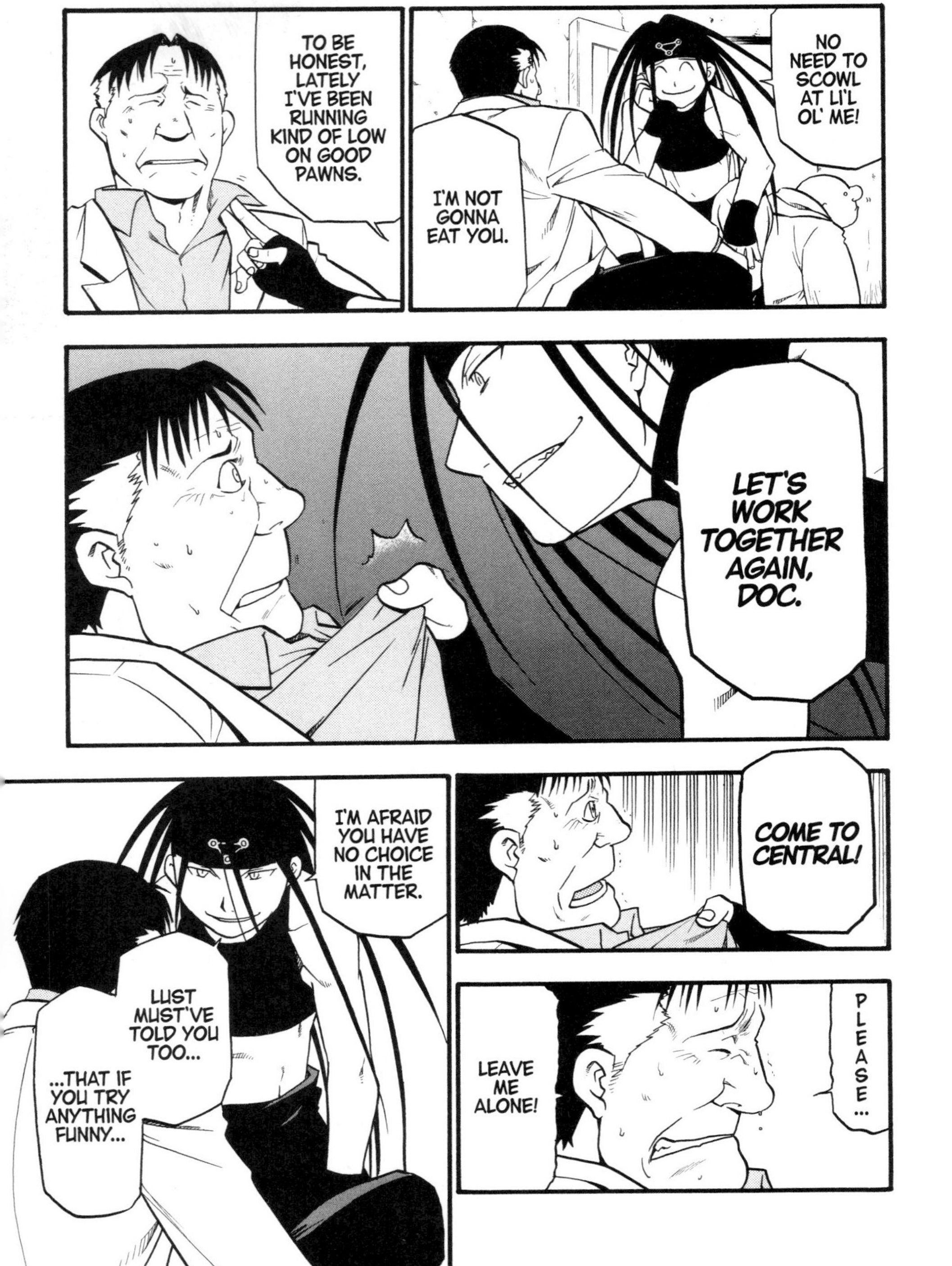
NO NEED TO SCOWL AT LI'L OL' ME!
I'M NOT GONNA EAT YOU.
TO BE HONEST, LATELY I'VE BEEN RUNNING KIND OF LOW ON GOOD PAWNS.
LET'S WORK TOGETHER AGAIN, DOC.
COME TO CENTRAL!
PLEASE...
LEAVE ME ALONE!
I'M AFRAID YOU HAVE NO CHOICE IN THE MATTER.
LUST MUST'VE TOLD YOU TOO...
...THAT IF YOU TRY ANYTHING FUNNY...

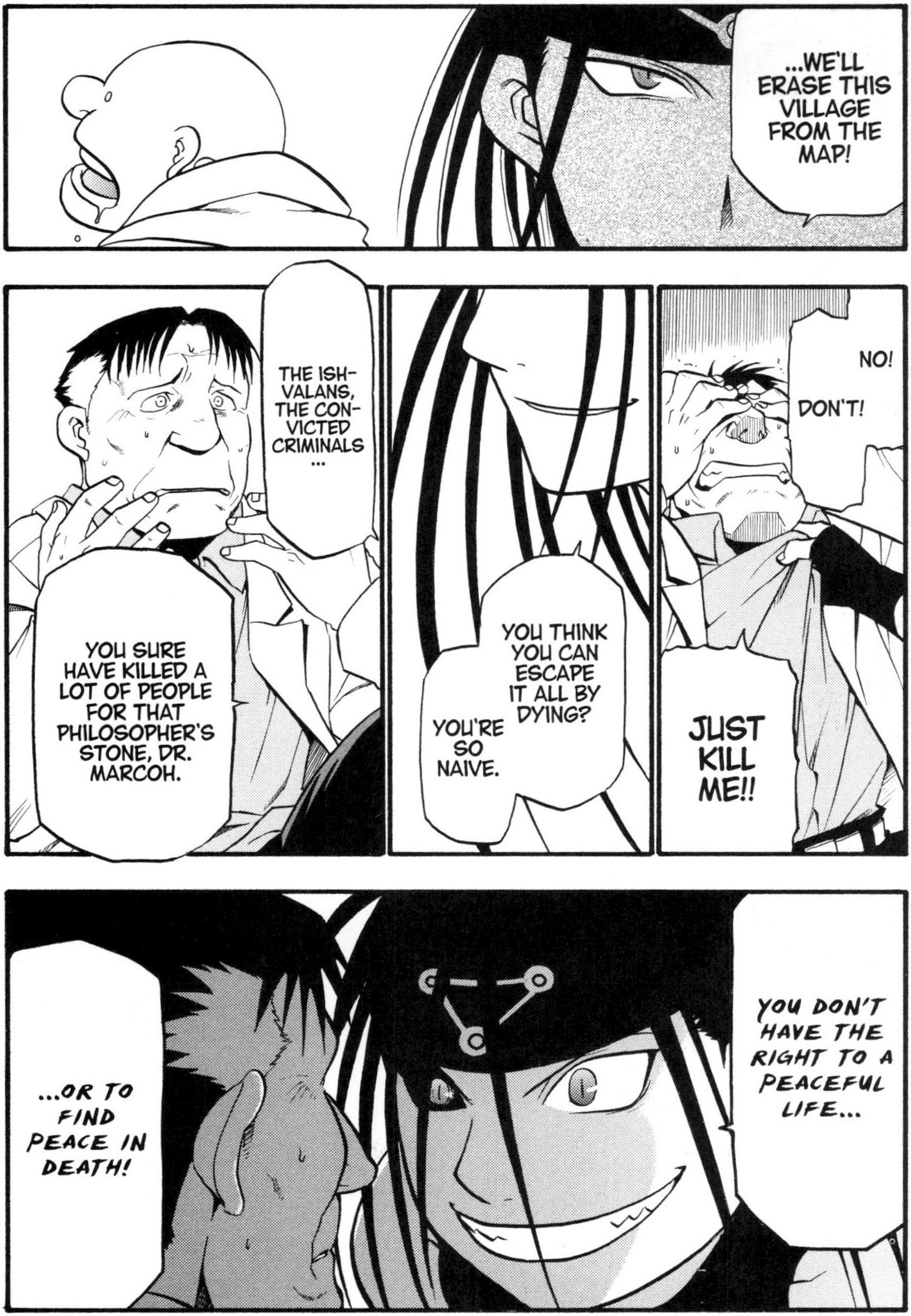
...WE'LL ERASE THIS VILLAGE FROM THE MAP!
NO!
DON'T!
JUST KILL ME!!
YOU THINK YOU CAN ESCAPE IT ALL BY DYING?
YOU'RE SO NAIVE.
THE ISH-VALANS, THE CON-VICTED CRIMINALS...
YOU SURE HAVE KILLED A LOT OF PEOPLE FOR THAT PHILOSOPHER'S STONE, DR. MARCOH.
YOU DON'T HAVE THE RIGHT TO A PEACEFUL LIFE...
...OR TO FIND PEACE IN DEATH!

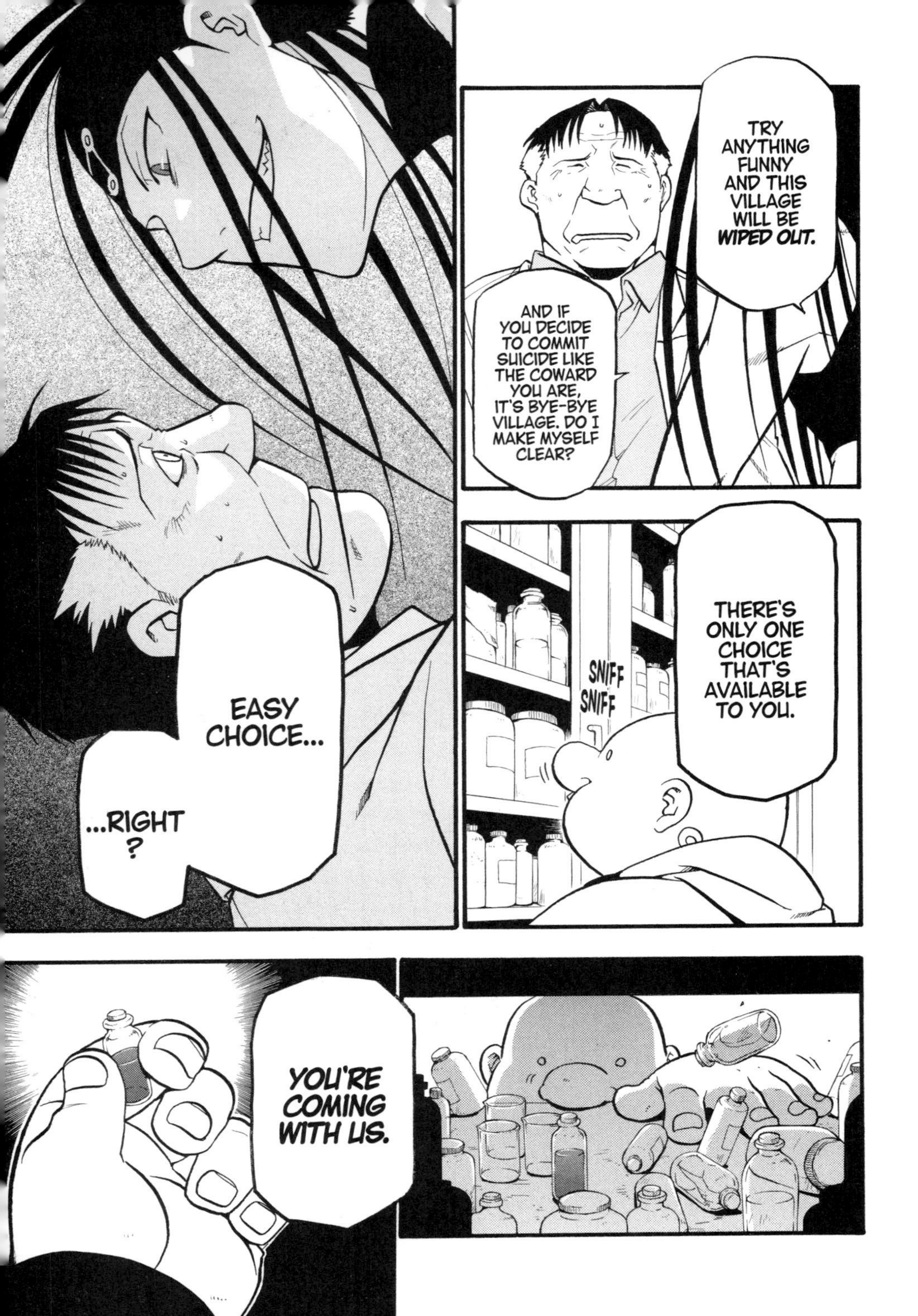
TRY ANYTHING FUNNY AND THIS VILLAGE WILL BE **WIPED OUT.**
AND IF YOU DECIDE TO COMMIT SUICIDE LIKE THE COWARD YOU ARE, IT'S BYE-BYE VILLAGE. DO I MAKE MYSELF CLEAR?
THERE'S ONLY ONE CHOICE THAT'S AVAILABLE TO YOU.
SNIFF SNIFF
EASY CHOICE...
...RIGHT ?
YOU'RE COMING WITH US.

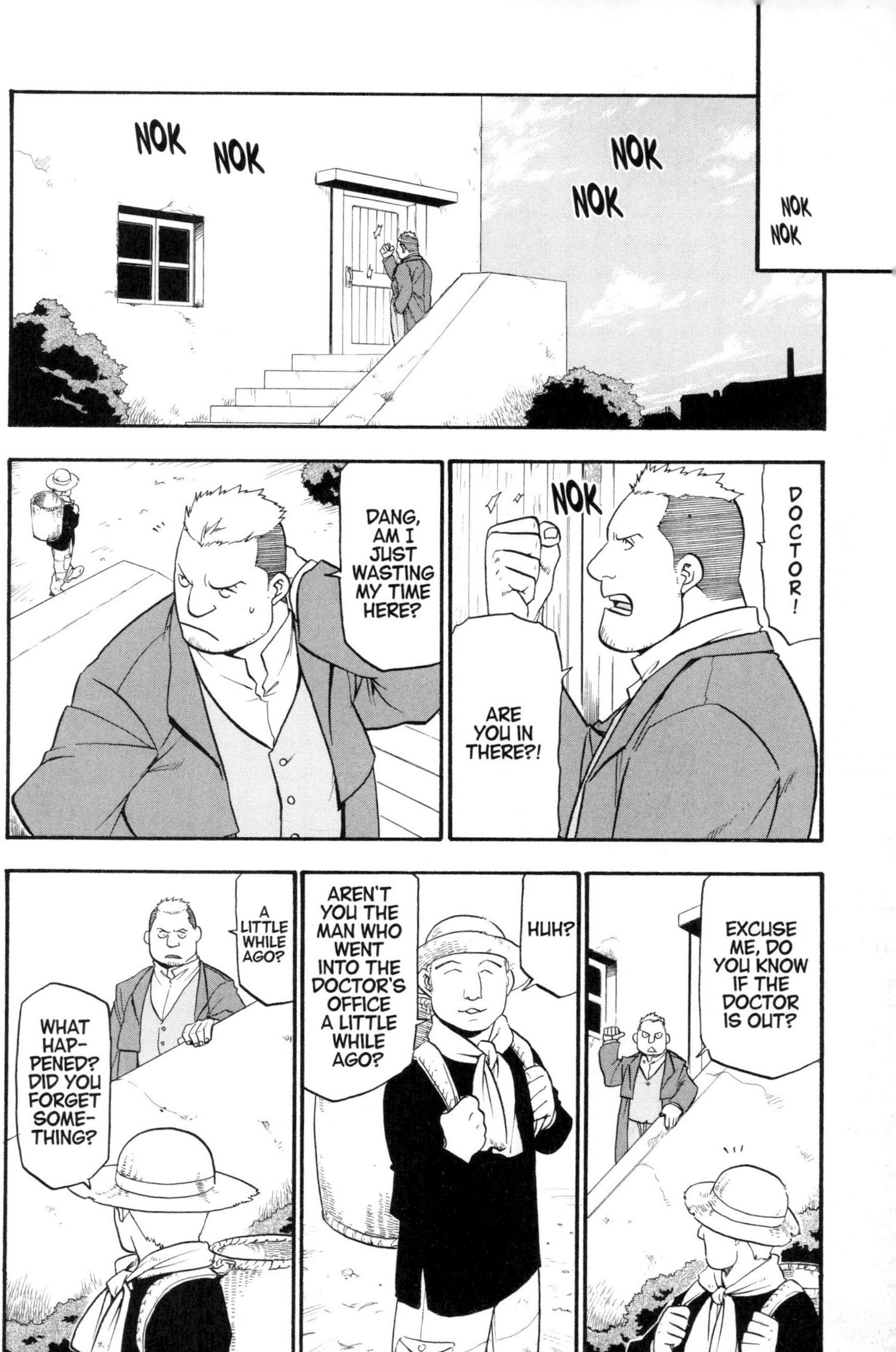
NOK
NOK
NOK
NOK
NOK
NOK
DOCTOR!
NOK
ARE YOU IN THERE?!
DANG, AM I JUST WASTING MY TIME HERE?
EXCUSE ME, DO YOU KNOW IF THE DOCTOR IS OUT?
HUH?
AREN'T YOU THE MAN WHO WENT INTO THE DOCTOR'S OFFICE A LITTLE WHILE AGO?
A LITTLE WHILE AGO?
WHAT HAP-PENED? DID YOU FORGET SOME-THING?

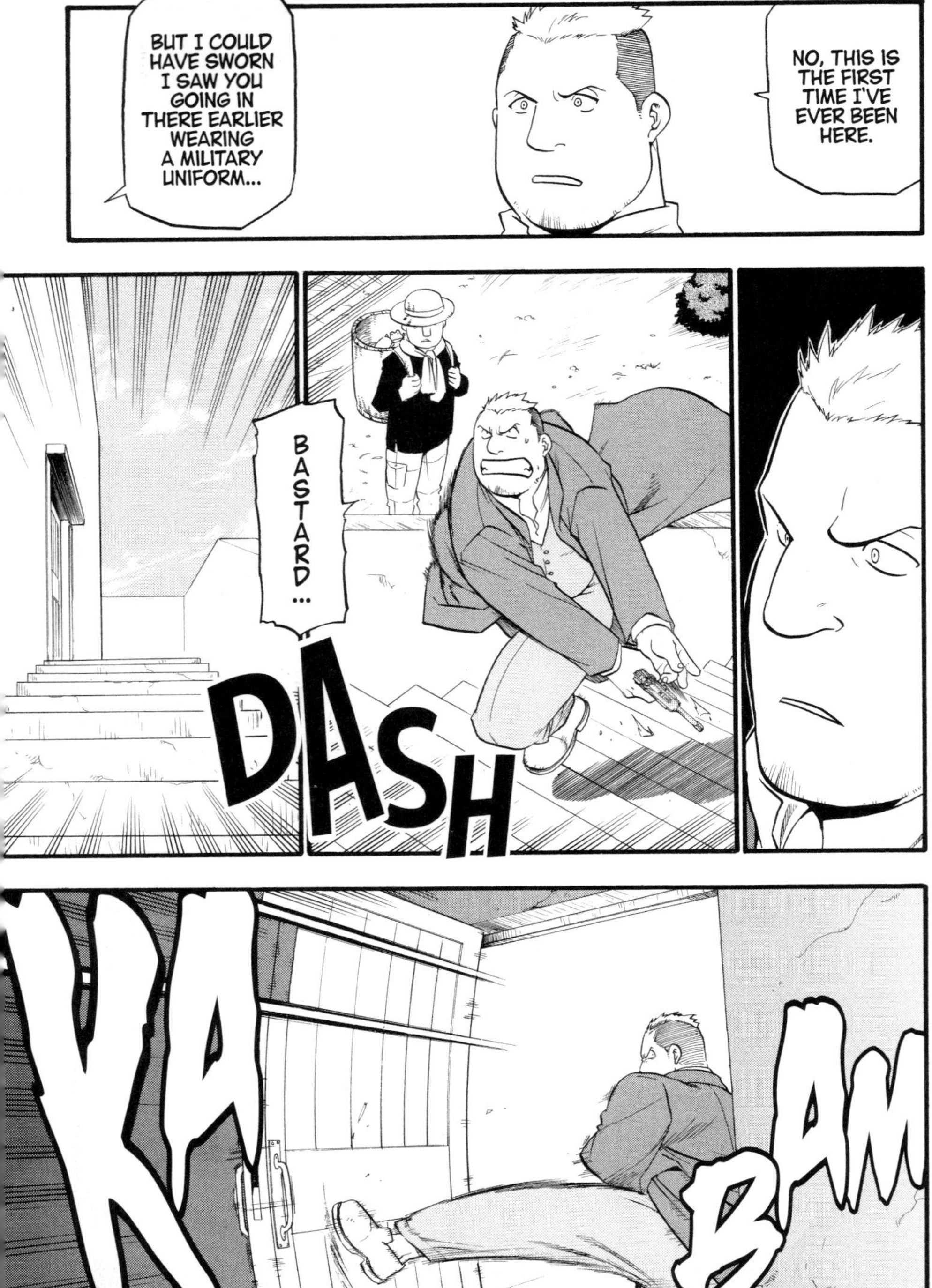
NO, THIS IS THE FIRST TIME I'VE EVER BEEN HERE.
BUT I COULD HAVE SWORN I SAW YOU GOING IN THERE EARLIER WEARING A MILITARY UNIFORM...
BASTARD...
DASH
KA BAM

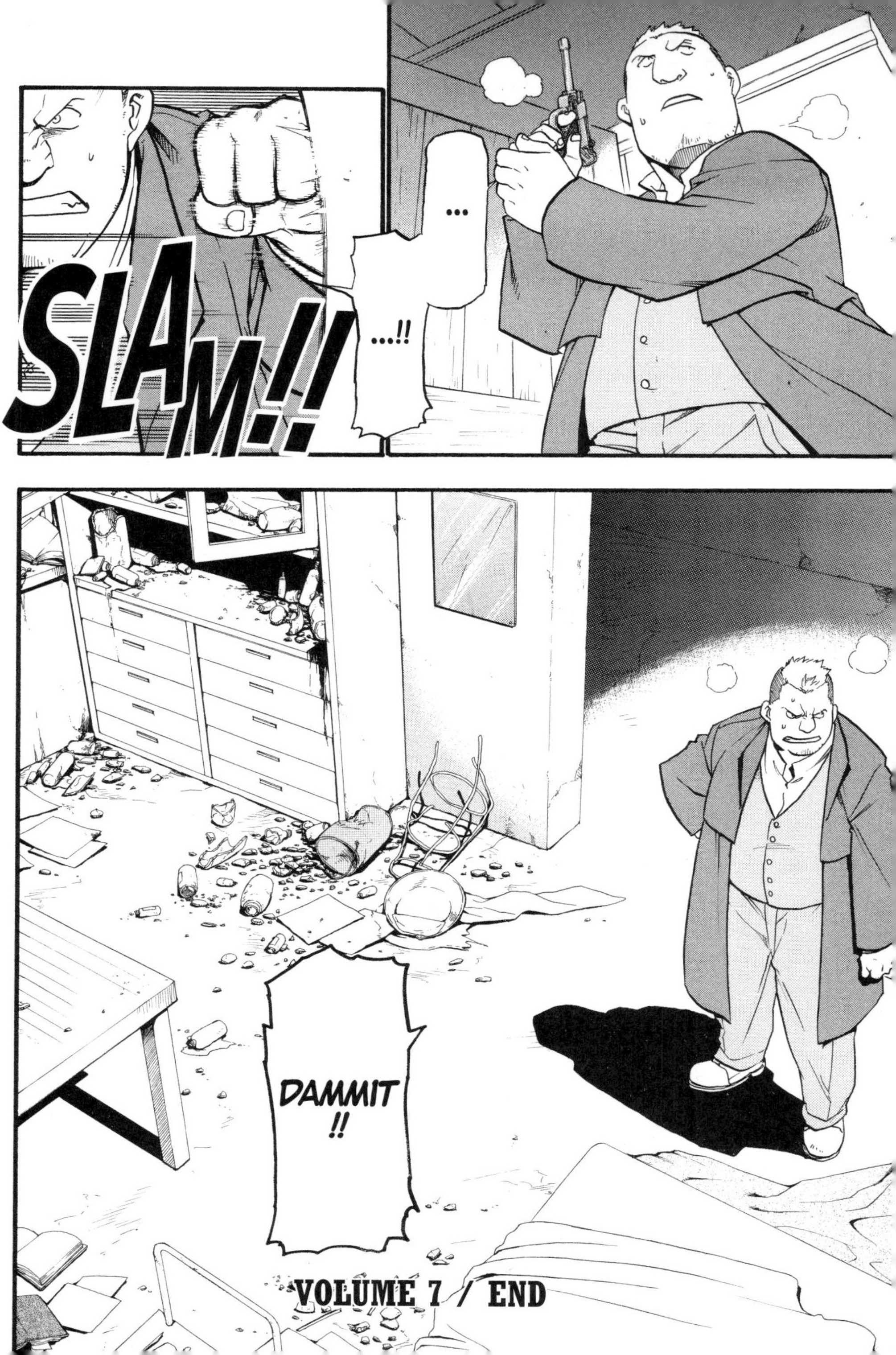
...
...!!
SLAM!!
DAMMIT!!
VOLUME 7 / END

FULLMETAL EDITION

FULLMETAL ALCHEMIST

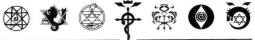

CONCEPT SKETCHES

07

This is a doodle from when I was trying to design the ruins of Xerxes. Should they be in a desert? On a craggy mountain...?

クセルクセス 周辺の
デザイン どうしようかなー、
砂漠か岩山か…… とか
考えてた時のらくがき。

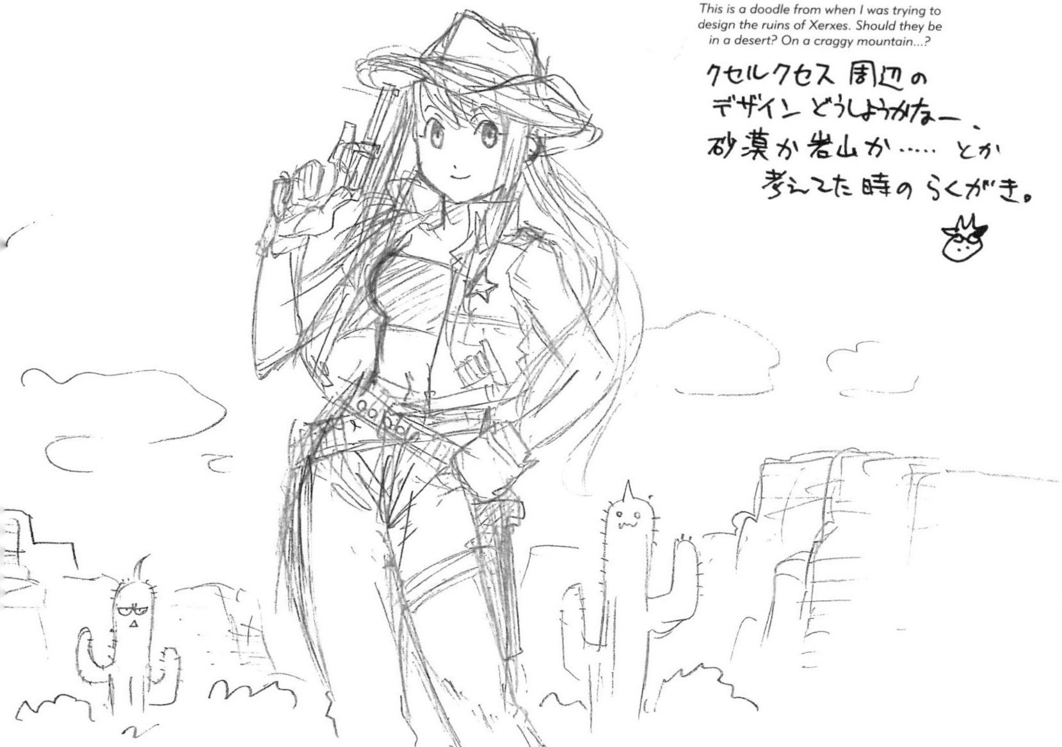

I can't for the life of me find any early drawings of May Chang! But while I was rummaging through my old sketches, I instead found a rejected manga page where I mixed up Ed's right and left hands. I didn't realize it even after I'd inked it. Gah…

メイ・チャンの初期 デザインが見当たらない!!
…で らくがき あさってたら、
素で 右手と左手 まちがった ボツ原稿が 出てきました。↓
ペン入れした後も 気付かないって どんだけ…

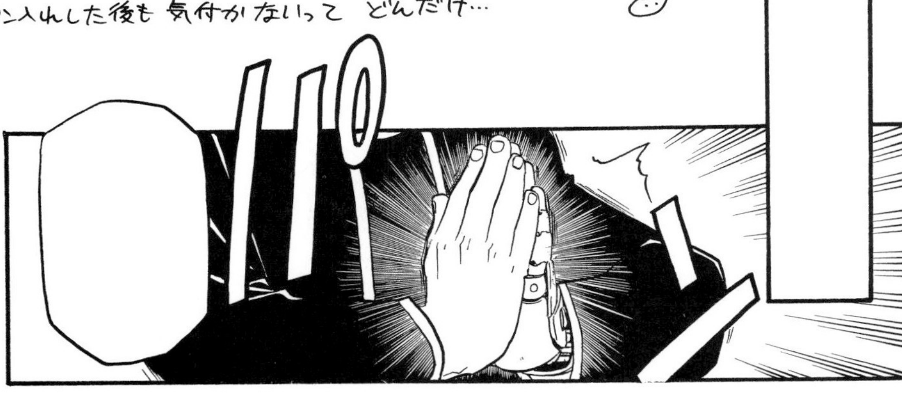

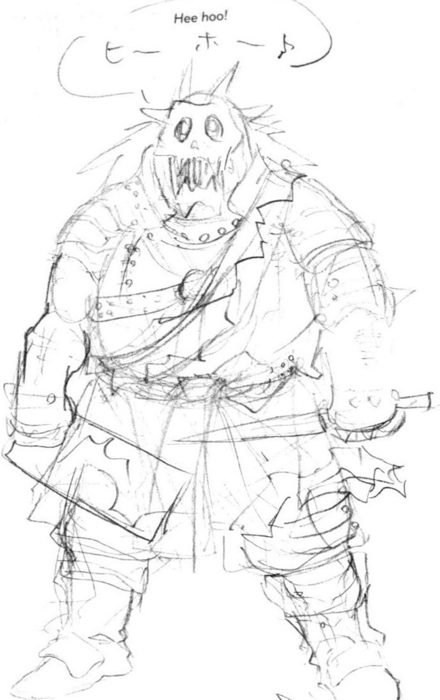
Hee hoo!
ヒ〜 ホ〜♪

Barry the Chopper Initial Design

バリー・ザ・チョッパー初期案

本体もそうですけど
割と最初からデザインが
かたまってたようです。

Both his body and soul designs were pretty settled right from the start.

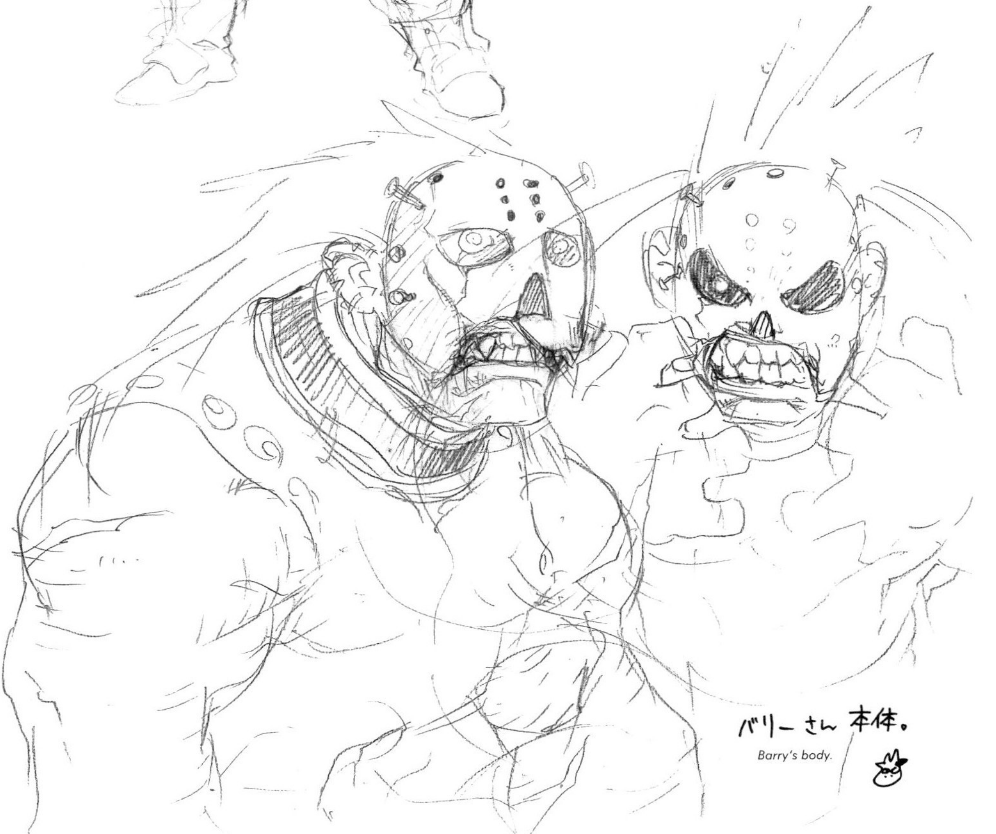

バリーさん本体。

Barry's body.

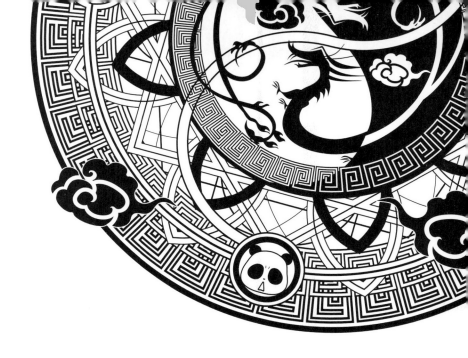

ABOUT THE AUTHOR

Born in Hokkaido, Japan, Hiromu Arakawa first attracted attention in 1999 with her award-winning manga *Stray Dog*. Her series *Fullmetal Alchemist* was serialized from 2001 to 2010 with a story that spanned 27 volumes and became an international critical and commercial success, receiving both the Shogakukan Manga Award and Seiun Award and selling over 70 million copies worldwide. *Fullmetal Alchemist* has been adapted into anime twice, first as *Fullmetal Alchemist* in 2003 and again as *Fullmetal Alchemist: Brotherhood* in 2009. The series has also inspired numerous films, video games and novels.

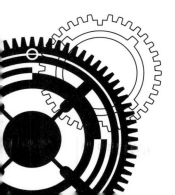

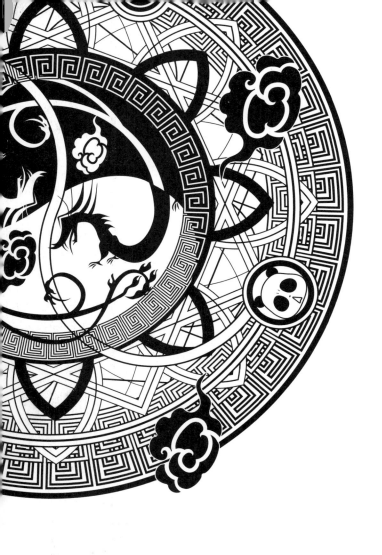

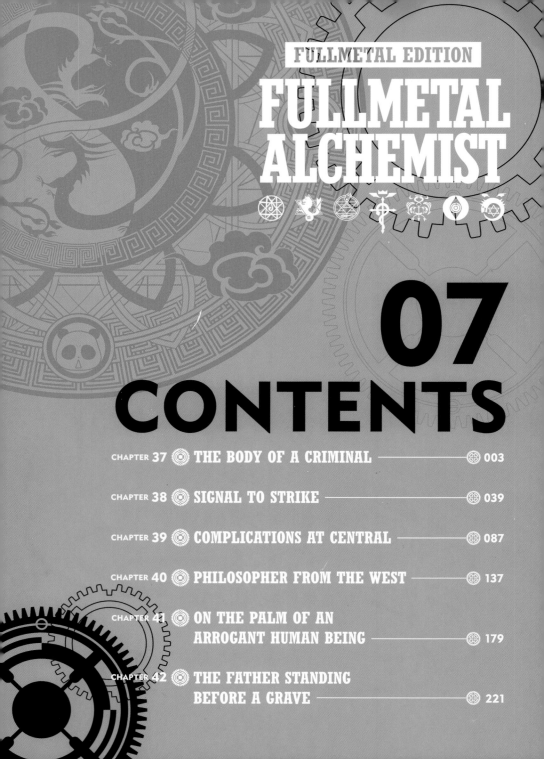

FULLMETAL EDITION

FULLMETAL ALCHEMIST

07

CONTENTS

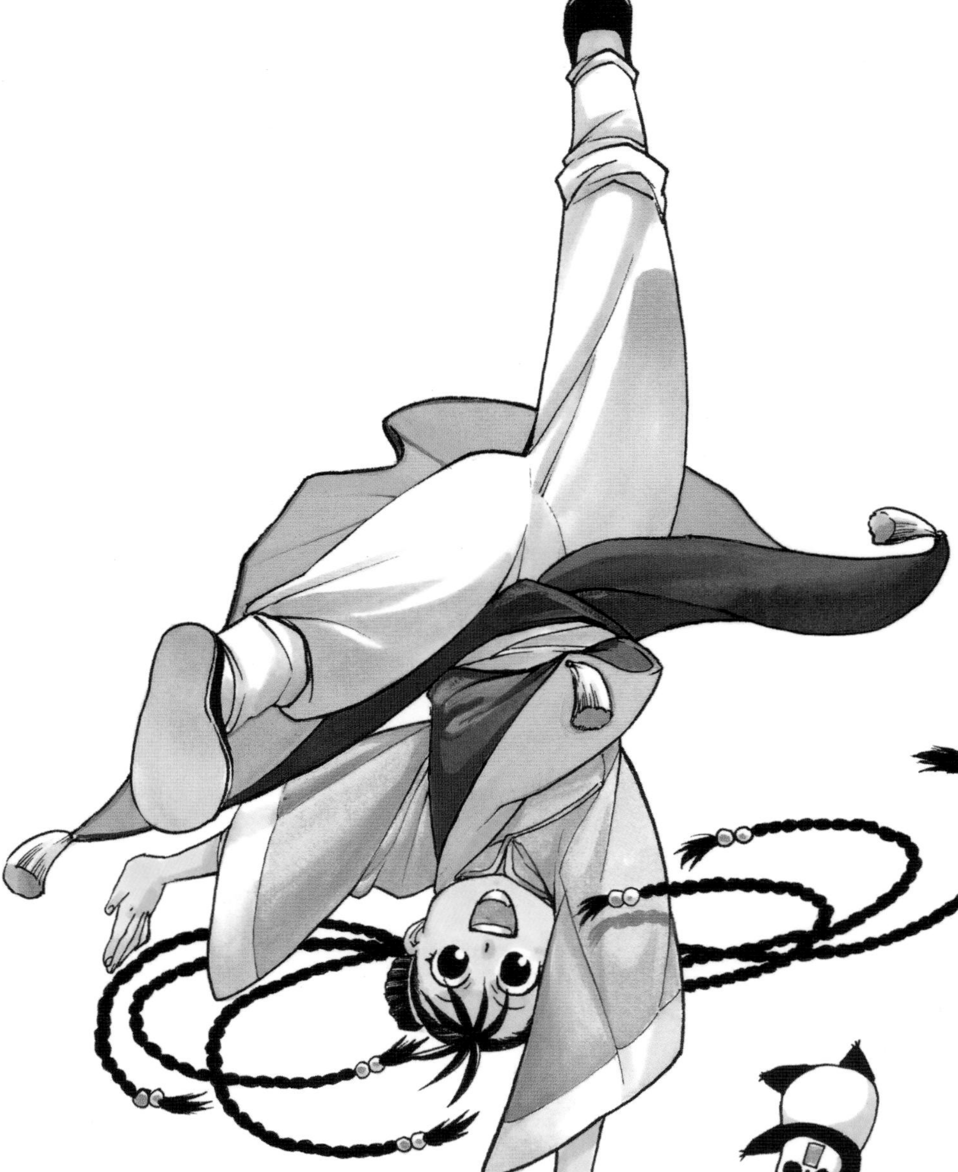

FULLMETAL EDITION

FULLMETAL
ALCHEMIST

by HIROMU ARAKAWA

07

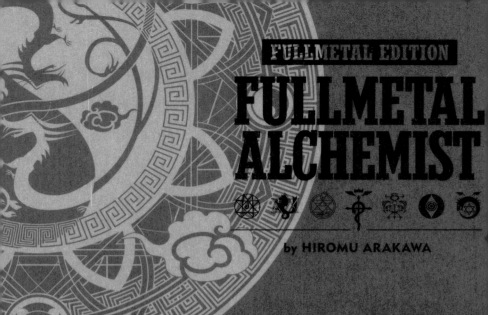

FULLMETAL EDITION
FULLMETAL ALCHEMIST

by HIROMU ARAKAWA

07